Axelrod & Cooper's

Concise Guide to Writing

Sixth Edition

Axelrod & Cooper's
Concise Guide to Writing

Rise B. Axelrod
University of California, Riverside

Charles R. Cooper
University of California, San Diego

Bedford / St. Martin's

Boston ● New York

For Bedford/St. Martin's

Executive Editor: Alexis P. Walker
Production Editor: Peter Jacoby
Senior Production Supervisor: Dennis J. Conroy
Senior Marketing Manager: Molly Parke
Associate Editor: Andrew Flynn
Copy Editor: Alice Vigliani
Indexer: Kirsten Kite
Photo Researcher: Naomi Kornhauser
Permissions Manager: Kalina Ingham Hintz
Art Director: Lucy Krikorian
Text Design: Linda M. Robertson
Cover Design: Donna Lee Dennison
Composition: Nesbitt Graphics, Inc.
Printing and Binding: RR Donnelley and Sons

President: Joan E. Feinberg
Editorial Director: Denise B. Wydra
Editor in Chief: Karen S. Henry
Director of Development: Erica T. Appel
Director of Marketing: Karen R. Soeltz
Director of Production: Susan W. Brown
Associate Director, Editorial Production: Elise S. Kaiser
Managing Editor: Shuli Traub

Library of Congress Control Number: 2011927767

Manufactured in the United States of America.
6 5 4 3
f e d

For information, write: Bedford/St. Martin's, 75 Arlington Street, Boston, MA 02116
(617-399-4000)

ISBN: 978–0–312–66890–7

Acknowledgments

Preface for Instructors

When we first wrote *The St. Martin's Guide to Writing,* we aimed to demystify writing and authorize students as writers. We wanted to help students learn to commit themselves to writing projects, communicate effectively with chosen readers, and question their own certainties. We also wanted them to understand that knowledge of writing comes both from analyzing writing and from working hard on their own writing. To achieve this aim, we took what we had learned from classical rhetoric and from contemporary composition theory and did our best to make it accessible to students.

The response from instructors and students was overwhelmingly positive: The first edition of *The Guide,* published in 1985, immediately became the most widely adopted text of its kind in the nation. In 1993, we published the first edition of *Axelrod & Cooper's Concise Guide to Writing* in response to requests from instructors who appreciated the pedagogy of *The St. Martin's Guide to Writing* but wanted a briefer text.

As with every new edition, we began work on this sixth edition with the goal of adapting the best of current composition research and practice to the needs of instructors and students. We listened closely to dozens of talented reviewers (students as well as instructors), and we were confirmed in our belief that the essential purpose and approach of the *Concise Guide* is more relevant than ever: Students need clear guidance and practical strategies to harness their potential as writers — an achievement that will be key to their success in their other college courses, in their jobs, and in the wider world.

An Overview of the Book

The *Concise Guide* offers everything you need for the writing course.

Part One: Writing Activities

Part One presents six different genres of writing, all reflecting actual writing assignments that students may encounter both in and out of college. While the chapters can be taught in any order, we have organized Part One to move from writing based on personal experience and reflection, through writing based on research and observation, to writing about controversial issues and problems.

Each chapter follows the same organizational plan:

- Three brief illustrated **scenarios** providing examples of how the genre is used in college courses, in the community, and in the workplace
- A brief **introduction** to the genre
- A **collaborative activity** helping students start working in the genre
- An orientation to the genre's **basic features** and to questions of **purpose and audience** specific to the genre, featuring examples drawn from real-world contexts
- A set of **readings** illustrating the genre, accompanied by **questions and prompts** designed to help students explore connections to their culture and experience and to analyze the basic features and writing strategies
- A **Guide to Writing,** tailored to the genre, that helps students refine their own writing processes, with activities for invention and research, easy-reference guides for drafting and revision, a Critical Reading Guide for peer review, strategies for integrating sources, and more
- **Editing and proofreading guidelines,** based on our nationwide study of errors in first-year college students' writing, to help students check for one or two sentence-level problems likely to occur in a given genre
- **Critical thinking activities** designed to help students reflect on what they learned and consider the social dimensions of the genre taught in the chapter

Part Two: Strategies for Critical Thinking, Reading, and Writing

Part Two offers seven chapters covering the following:

- Heuristics for invention and inquiry and for reading (Chapters 8 and 9)
- Strategies for cueing the reader (Chapter 10)
- Instruction on analyzing arguments and visuals and on synthesizing sources (Chapters 11 and 12)
- Strategies for arguing (Chapter 13)
- Advice on designing written and online documents (Chapter 14)

Part Three: Doing Research

Part Three discusses field as well as library and Internet research and includes thorough, up-to-date guidelines for using and documenting sources, with detailed examples of the 2009 Modern Language Association (MLA) and 2010 American Psychological Association (APA) documentation styles. An annotated sample student research paper models ways students can integrate citations into their own work in accordance with the rules for MLA documentation. The final chapter in Part Three, new to the sixth edition of the *Concise Guide*, offers detailed guidelines for creating annotated bibliographies.

Changes in the Sixth Edition

In this edition, we have taken instructors' advice and revised the text to make it an even more effective teaching tool.

- **Streamlined and redesigned Part One chapters** provide more visual cues for students who learn visually, more "easy-reference" features for students who need help navigating a lengthy text, and more "ways in" to each assignment for students whose writing processes don't conform to an imaginary norm.

  - **The Basic Features** of each chapter's genre of writing are now **introduced at the start of the chapter,** to lay the groundwork for students' understanding of the genre and to prepare them for their work with that chapter's readings.

  - A **new color-coding system** calls out the Basic Features in the annotated student essay, the post-reading apparatus, and throughout the Guide to Writing, helping students see the connections among the chapter's various parts and more easily grasp what makes a successful example of a given genre.

  - **New easy-reference charts** in each Guide to Writing — **"Starting Points"** and **"Troubleshooting Your Draft"** — help students self-assess and efficiently find the advice and models they need for overcoming individual writing challenges.

  - **Newly designed Invention activities** highlight different paths through the processes of generating and shaping material.

- **New material** brings the book up-to-date and teaches students what they'll need to succeed at academic writing.

  - To help students develop their abilities to analyze complex arguments and synthesize a variety of sources, we have included a **new Chapter 11, "Analyzing and Synthesizing Arguments."** The chapter features detailed instruction on these two skills, which are absolutely essential for writing compelling essays, and also includes a sample student essay on the morality of torture that models these skills.

  - To help students understand and evaluate the visual data that increasingly dominate our culture, we have added a **new Chapter 12, "Analyzing Visuals,"** which provides clear guidance on how to critically read and write about photos, ads, works of art, and other image-based texts. The chapter also offers a multi-stage model of a student's analysis of a photo by Gordon Parks, as well as exercises in visual analysis that students can do in class or on their own.

  - To help students cope with information overload while doing research, we have added a **new Chapter 18, "Annotated Bibliographies,"** which offers detailed guidance on this important element of the research process.

  - To help students make useful connections between their previous writing experiences and the writing they will do in college, **Chapter 1** now focuses on the **literacy narrative,** encouraging students to reflect on their own literacy experiences in preparation for the reading and writing challenges they'll encounter in the course.

- **New readings** introduce compelling topics, multicultural perspectives, and fresh voices, including **Trey Ellis** on his father's battle with AIDS and **Amy Goldwasser** on what kids learn online — and why it matters.

Additional Resources

The benefits of using the *Concise Guide* don't stop with the print text. Online, in print, and in digital format, you'll find both free and affordable premium resources to help students get even more out of the book and your course. You'll also find course management solutions and convenient instructor resources, such as sample syllabi, suggested classroom activities, and even a nationwide community of teachers. To learn more about or order any of the products below, contact your Bedford/St. Martin's sales representative, e-mail sales support (sales_support@bfwpub.com), or visit the Web site at bedfordstmartins.com/conciseguide/catalog.

Student Resources

The Concise Guide Book Companion Site (bedfordstmartins.com/conciseguide). Send students to free and open resources, allow them to choose an affordable e-book option, or upgrade to an expanding collection of innovative digital content — all in one place.

- **Free and open resources for the** *Concise Guide* provide students with easy-to-access **book-specific materials, exercises, and downloadable content,** including electronic versions of the Critical Reading Guides, "Starting Points" and "Troubleshooting Your Draft" charts, and tutorials for the sentence strategies in the Part One chapters. Additional free resources include ***Research and Documentation Online*** by Diana Hacker, with clear advice on how to integrate outside material into a paper, how to cite sources correctly, and how to format the paper in MLA, APA, *Chicago*, or CSE style; and ***Exercise Central***, a database of over 9,000 editing exercises designed to help identify students' strengths and weaknesses, recommend personalized study plans, and provide tutorials for common writing problems.

- The *Concise Guide* is available as an e-book from CourseSmart, offering page fidelity, highlighting, and notetaking. Students can choose whether to download the e-book to access it from one machine or purchase the online version to access it from many. The *Concise Guide* is also available in other popular e-book formats for computers, tablets, and e-readers. Visit bedfordstmartins.com/ebooks for more information.

- *Re:Writing Plus,* now with *VideoCentral,* gathers all of Bedford/St. Martin's premium digital content for composition into one online collection. It includes hundreds of model documents and *VideoCentral,* a growing collection of over 140 brief videos for the writing classroom. *Re:Writing Plus* can be purchased separately at the companion Web site or packaged with the print book at a significant discount. An activation code is required.

Sticks and Stones and Other Student Essays, Seventh Edition. Available for packaging **free** with new copies of the *Concise Guide, Sticks and Stones* is a collection of essays written by students across the nation using *The St. Martin's Guide to Writing*. Each essay is accompanied by a headnote that spotlights some of the ways the writer uses the genre successfully, invites students to notice other achievements, and supplies context where necessary.

Who Are We? Readings in Identity and Community and Work and Career. Available for packaging **free** with new copies of the *Concise Guide, Who Are We?* contains selections that expand on themes foregrounded in the *Concise Guide*. Full of ideas for classroom discussion and writing, the readings offer students additional perspectives and thought-provoking analysis.

i-series. **Free** when packaged with new copies of the *Concise Guide*, the *i-series* includes multimedia tutorials in flexible formats — because there are things you can't do in a book:

- *ix visualizing composition 2.0* (available online) helps students visualize and put into practice key rhetorical and visual concepts.
- *i-claim visualizing argument* (available on CD-ROM) offers a new way to see argument — with 6 tutorials, an illustrated glossary, and over seventy multimedia arguments.
- *i-cite visualizing sources* (available on CD-ROM and online as part of *Re: Writing Plus*) brings research to life through an animated introduction, four tutorials, and hands-on source practice.

Ordering Information (Package ISBNs)

To order any of the following items with the print text you order for your students, please use the ISBNs provided below. For different packages or a more complete listing of supplements, contact your Bedford/St. Martin's sales representative, e-mail sales support at sales_support@bfwpub.com, or visit the Web site at bedfordstmartins .com/conciseguide/catalog.

Re:Writing Plus	ISBN 978-1-4576-1052-3
Sticks and Stones and Other Student Essays, Seventh Edition	ISBN 978-1-4576-1051-6
Who Are We? Readings in Identity and Community and Work and Career	ISBN 978-1-4576-1090-5
VideoCentral: English	ISBN 978-1-4576-1050-9
ix Visualizing Composition 2.0	ISBN 978-1-4576-1275-6

Instructor Resources

You have a lot to do in your course. Bedford/St. Martin's wants to make it easy for you to find the support you need — and to get it quickly.

Instructor's Resource Manual (ISBN 978-1-4576-0607-6, print; also available for download at bedfordstmartins.com/conciseguide). The Instructor's Resource Manual includes helpful advice for new instructors, guidelines on common teaching practices such as assigning journals and setting up group activities, guidelines on responding to and evaluating student writing, course plans, detailed chapter plans, an annotated bibliography in composition and rhetoric, and a selection of background readings.

Bedford Coursepacks for the most common course management systems — Blackboard, WebCT, Angel, and Desire2Learn — make it simple to build a course around the *Concise Guide.* The downloadable content is drawn from the Web site and includes activities, models, reference materials, and the *ExerciseCentral* gradebook.

The Elements of Teaching Writing (A Resource for Instructors in All Disciplines) (ISBN 978-0-312-40683-7). Written by Katherine Gottschalk and Keith Hjortshoj, *The Elements of Teaching Writing* provides time-saving strategies and practical guidance in a brief reference form. Drawing on their extensive experience training instructors in all disciplines to incorporate writing into their courses, Gottschalk and Hjortshoj offer reliable advice, accommodating a wide range of teaching styles and class sizes, about how to design effective writing assignments and how to respond to and evaluate student writing in any course.

TeachingCentral (bedfordstmartins.com/teachingcentral). Designed for the convenience of instructors, this rich Web site lists and describes Bedford/St. Martin's acclaimed print series of free professional sourcebooks, background readings, and bibliographies for teachers. In addition, *TeachingCentral* offers a host of free online resources, including

- *Bits,* a blog that collects creative ideas for teaching composition from a community of teachers, scholars, authors, and editors. Instructors are free to take, use, adapt, and pass the ideas around, in addition to sharing new suggestions.
- *Take 20* — a sixty-minute film for teachers, by teachers, in which twenty-two writing teachers answer twenty questions on current practices and emerging ideas in composition.

Acknowledgments

We owe an enormous debt to all the rhetoricians and composition specialists whose theory, research, and pedagogy have informed *Axelrod & Cooper's Concise Guide to Writing.* We would be adding many pages to an already long book if we were to name everyone to whom we are indebted; suffice it to say that we have been eclectic in our borrowing. We extend our thanks to the following instructors, who reviewed the fifth edition of the *Concise Guide* and made myriad suggestions that we incorporated into this edition: Nicol Augusté, Savannah College of Art and Design; Diane Baker, Castleton State College; Amy Brust, North Carolina State University; Erin Campbell, Abraham Baldwin College; Sherry Cisler, Arizona State University; Christine Cucciarre, University of Delaware; Lauren Hornberger, University of Delaware; Cynthia Hubble, Bakersfield College; Courtney Huse-Wika, University of South Dakota; Raymond Janifer, Shippensburg University; Katherine Kapitan, Buena Vista University; Koren Kessler, North Carolina State University; Daniel King, Ohio University; Frederick Lord, Southern New Hampshire University; Elaine Mawhinney, Southern New Hampshire University; James McFadden, Buena Vista University; Alexis McMillan-Clifton, Tacoma Community College; Carolyn Mello, Lamar State College–Orange; LeRoy Miller, Northern Kentucky University; Lisa Muir, Wilkes Community College; Patricia Murphy, SUNY Institute of Technology; Derri Scarlett, Bismarck State College; Terry Sciabica, Modesto Junior College; Carrie Tippen, West Virginia Wesleyan College; Tish Twomey, SUNY Institute of Technology; Kristi Walker, Tacoma Community College; Rebecca Werland, Spoon River College; Cassundra White, Crafton Hills College; Mike Wilcomb, Northern Essex Community College; James Wilson, Victor Valley College; and Susan Youngs, Southern New Hampshire University.

We must also acknowledge immeasurable lessons learned from all the writers, professional and student alike, whose work we analyzed and whose writing we used in this and earlier editions.

So many instructors and students have contributed ideas and criticism over the years. The members of the advisory board for the ninth edition of *The St. Martin's Guide to Writing*, a group of dedicated composition instructors from across the country, have provided us with extensive insights and suggestions on the eighth edition and have given us the benefit of their advice on new readings and other new features for the ninth. For their many contributions, we would like to thank Samantha Andrus-Henry, Grand Rapids Community College; Melissa Batai, Triton College; Mary Bishop, Holmes Junior College–Ridgeland; Jo Ann Buck, Guilford Technical Community College; Kevin Cantwell, Macon State College; Anne Dvorak, Longview Community College; Leona Fisher, Chaffey College; Diana Grahn, Longview Community College; Dawn Hubbell-Staeble, Bowling Green State University; Amy Morris-Jones, Baker College of Muskegon; Gray Scott, University of California, Riverside; and Susan Sebok, South Suburban College.

For this new edition of the *Concise Guide*, we also gratefully acknowledge the special contributions of the following: Paul Tayyar, who drafted the new "Analyzing Visuals" chapter; Gray Scott, who drafted the new "Annotated Bibliographies" chapter; and Jill Markgraf, Judith Van Noate, Debbi Renfrow, Jaena Hollingsworth, and Beth Downs, who provided expert advice on the revised coverage of library and Internet research. We want especially to thank the many instructors at the University of California, Riverside, who offered advice and class tested new material, including Stephanie Kay, Leona Fisher, Gray Scott, Elizabeth Spies, Elissa Weeks, Rob d'Annibale, Kimberly Turner, Amanda Uvalle, Joshua Fenton, Benedict Jones, and Sandra Baringer.

Finally, we are especially grateful to the student authors for allowing us to use their work in *Sticks and Stones, Marriage 101*, and the *Concise Guide*.

We want to thank many people at Bedford/St. Martin's, especially editors Andrew Flynn and Alexis Walker, whose wisdom, skill, and tireless enthusiasm made this edition possible, and our production team of Peter Jacoby, Shuli Traub, and Dennis Conroy. Alice Vigliani made many valuable contributions to this revision with her careful copyediting, as did Diana Puglisi George with her meticulous proofreading. Andrew Flynn managed and edited the Instructor's Resource Manual, and the *Concise Guide* Web site. Without the help of Rebecca Merrill, the new media supplements to the *Concise Guide* would not have been possible.

Thanks also to the immensely talented design team — book designer Jerilyn Bockorick as well as Bedford/St. Martin's art directors Anna Palchik and Lucy Krikorian — for making the sixth edition so attractive and usable. Our gratitude also goes to Linda Winters for her hard work clearing permissions, and Martha Friedman and Naomi Kornhauser for imaginative photo research.

We wish finally to express our heartfelt appreciation to Nancy Perry for helping us to launch *The St. Martin's Guide* successfully so many years ago and continuing to stand by us. Over the years, Nancy has generously and wisely advised us on everything from planning new editions to copyediting manuscripts. We also want to thank Erica Appel, director of development, and Karen Henry, editor-in-chief, who offered valued advice at many critical stages in the process. Thanks as well to Joan Feinberg and Denise Wydra for their adroit leadership of Bedford/St. Martin's, and to marketing director Karen Soeltz and marketing manager Molly Parke — along with the extraordinarily talented and hardworking sales staff — for their tireless efforts on behalf of our texts.

Features of *Axelrod & Cooper's Concise Guide to Writing*, Sixth Edition, Correlated to the WPA Outcomes Statement

Desired Student Outcomes	Relevant Features of the *Concise Guide*
Rhetorical Knowledge	
Focus on a purpose	Each writing assignment chapter in Part One offers extensive discussion of the purpose(s) for the genre of writing covered in that chapter.
Respond to the needs of different audiences	Each chapter in Part One discusses the need to consider one's audience for the particular genre covered in that chapter. In Chapters 5–7, which cover argument, there is also extensive discussion of the need to anticipate opposing positions and readers' objections to the writer's thesis.
Respond appropriately to different kinds of rhetorical situations	Each chapter in Part One gives detailed advice on responding to a particular rhetorical situation, from remembering an event (Chapter 2) to justifying an evaluation (Chapter 7).
Use conventions of format and structure appropriate to the rhetorical situation	Each chapter in Part One points out features of effectively structured writing, and the Guides to Writing help students systematically develop their own effective structures. Document design is covered in a dedicated Chapter 14, "Designing Documents."
Adopt appropriate voice, tone, and level of formality	Many of the Sentence Strategies sections in each chapter in Part One deal with these issues. Also see purpose and audience coverage mentioned previously.
Understand how genres shape reading and writing	Each chapter in Part One offers student and professional readings accompanied by annotations, questions, and commentary that draw students' attention to the key features of the genre and stimulate ideas for writing. Each chapter's Guide to Writing offers detailed, step-by-step advice for writing in the genre and for offering constructive peer criticism. In addition, "In College Courses," "In the Community," and "In the Workplace" sections that open each Part One chapter show how the various genres are used outside the composition course.
Write in several genres	The Guides to Writing in each of the six chapters in Part One offer specific advice on writing to remember an event; to profile a person, activity, or place; to explain a concept; to argue a position; to propose a solution; and to justify an evaluation. In addition, Chapters 15–18 cover research strategies that many students will use while writing in the genres covered in Part One.

(*continued*)

Desired Student Outcomes	Relevant Features of the *Concise Guide*
Critical Thinking, Reading, and Writing	
Use writing and reading for inquiry, learning, thinking, and communicating	Each writing assignment chapter in Part One emphasizes the connection between reading and writing in a particular genre: Each chapter begins with a group of readings whose apparatus introduces students to thinking about the features of the genre; then a Guide to Writing leads them through the process of applying these features to an essay of their own. Chapter 8, "Strategies for Invention and Inquiry," and Chapter 9, "Strategies for Reading Critically," prompt students to engage actively in invention, inquiry, and reading. Other Part Two chapters include coverage of specific invention, inquiry, reading, and writing strategies useful in a variety of genres.
Understand a writing assignment as a series of tasks, including finding, evaluating, analyzing, and synthesizing appropriate primary and secondary sources	The Guides to Writing in each chapter in Part One break writing assignments down into doable, focused thinking and writing activities that engage students in the recursive process of invention and research to find, analyze, and synthesize information and ideas. "Working with Sources" sections teach specific strategies of evaluating and integrating source material. Chapter 9, "Strategies for Reading Critically," covers various strategies useful in working with sources, including annotating, summarizing, and synthesizing. Chapter 17, "Using Sources," offers detailed coverage of finding, evaluating, using, and acknowledging primary and secondary sources, while Chapter 18, "Annotated Bibliographies," helps students master this essential research-based task.
Integrate their own ideas with those of others	Chapter 17, "Using Sources," offers detailed advice on how to integrate and introduce quotations, how to cite paraphrases and summaries so as to distinguish them from the writer's own ideas, and how to avoid plagiarism. "Sentence Strategy" and "Working with Sources" in several Part One chapters offer additional support.
Understand the relationships among language, knowledge, and power	"Making Connections," a recurring section in the apparatus following the professional readings in Part One chapters, encourages students to put what they've read in the context of the world they live in. These preliminary reflections come into play in the Guides to Writing, where students are asked to draw on their experiences in college, community, and career in order to begin writing. "Thinking Critically about What You Have Learned" sections that conclude Part One chapters ask students to reconsider what they have learned, often in a social/political context.
Processes	
Be aware that it usually takes multiple drafts to create and complete a successful text	The need for a critical reading of a draft and for revision is emphasized in Chapter 1 as well as in the Guides to Writing in each chapter of Part One.

Desired Student Outcomes	Relevant Features of the *Concise Guide*
Processes (continued)	
Develop flexible strategies for generating ideas, revising, editing, and proofreading	The Guides to Writing in each Part One chapter offer genre-specific coverage of invention and research, getting a critical reading of a draft, revising, editing, and proofreading. Also in each Part One chapter, "Ways In" invention activities encourage students to start from their strengths, and "Starting Points" and "Troubleshooting Your Draft" charts offer specific, targeted advice for students with different challenges. A dedicated Chapter 8, "Strategies for Invention and Inquiry," offers numerous helpful suggestions for idea generation.
Understand writing as an open process that permits writers to use later invention and rethinking to revise their work	The Guides to Writing in each Part One chapter offer extensive, genre-specific advice on rethinking and revising at multiple stages. "Ways In" activities, "Starting Points" charts, and "Troubleshooting Your Draft" charts in Part One chapters encourage students to discover, review, and revise their own process(es) of writing.
Understand the collaborative and social aspects of writing processes	Each chapter in Part One includes several opportunities for and guides to collaboration: "Practice" activities at the beginning of the chapter, "Making Connections" activities after the readings, and, in the Guides to Writing, "Testing Your Choice" activities and the Critical Reading Guide.
Learn to critique their own and others' works	The Critical Reading Guide and Revising sections in the Guides to Writing in each Part One chapter offer students specific advice on constructively criticizing — and praising — their own work and the work of their classmates.
Learn to balance the advantages of relying on others with the responsibility of doing their part	This goal is implicit in several collaborative activities: "Practice" activities at the beginning of the chapter, "Making Connections" activities after the readings, and, in the Guides to Writing, "Testing Your Choice" activities and the Critical Reading Guide.
Use a variety of technologies to address a range of audiences	Each Guide to Writing in Part One chapters includes advice on using the Web for various stages of the writing process. See also Chapter 16, "Library and Internet Research," for extensive coverage of finding, evaluating, and using print and electronic resources and of responsibly using the Internet, e-mail, and online communities for research, and Chapter 14, "Designing Documents," which offers advice on creating visuals on a computer or downloading them from the Web. Finally, the *Concise Guide*'s electronic ancillaries include a robust companion Web site.
Knowledge of Conventions	
Learn common formats for different kinds of texts	Document design is covered in a dedicated Chapter 14. Examples of specific formats for a range of texts appear on pp. 518–25 (research paper); pp. 433–34 (memo); p. 434

(continued)

Desired Student Outcomes	Relevant Features of the *Concise Guide*
Knowledge of Conventions *(continued)*	
	(business letter); pp. 434–36 (e-mail); pp. 436–38 (résumé); p. 438 (job application letter); pp. 438–40 (lab report); and pp. 424–30 (table, diagrams, graphs, charts, map, and other figures).
Develop knowledge of genre conventions ranging from structure and paragraphing to tone and mechanics	Each chapter in Part One presents several basic features of a specific genre, which are introduced up front and then consistently reinforced throughout the chapter. Genre-specific issues of structure, paragraphing, tone, and mechanics are also addressed in the "Sentence Strategies" and "Editing and Proofreading" sections of each Guide to Writing.
Practice appropriate means of documenting their work	Chapter 17, "Using Sources," offers detailed advice on how to integrate and introduce quotations, how to cite paraphrases and summaries so as to distinguish them from the writer's own ideas, and how to avoid plagiarism. This chapter also offers coverage of MLA and APA documentation in addition to an annotated sample student research paper. Chapter 12, "Analyzing Visuals," also offers a complete student paper with MLA documentation. In addition, "Working with Sources" sections in each Guide to Writing in the Part One chapters help students with the details of using and appropriately documenting sources by providing genre-specific examples of what (and what not) to do.
Control such surface features as syntax, grammar, punctuation, and spelling	Genre-specific editing and proofreading advice is given in two sections in each Guide to Writing in the Part One chapters: "Sentence Strategies" and "Editing and Proofreading."

Preface for Students: How to Use the *Concise Guide*

We have written this book with you, the student reading and using it, always in the forefront of our minds. Although it is a long book that covers many different topics, at its heart is a simple message: The best way to become a good writer is to study examples of good writing, then to apply what you have learned from those examples to your own work. Accordingly, we have provided numerous carefully selected examples of the kinds of writing you are likely to do both in and out of college, and we have accompanied them with detailed advice on writing your own essays. In this preface, we explain how the various parts of the book work together to achieve this goal.

The Organization of the Book

Following Chapter 1 — an introduction to writing that gives general advice about how to approach different parts of a writing assignment — the *Concise Guide* is divided into three major parts:

Part One: Writing Activities (Chapters 2–7)
Part Two: Strategies for Critical Thinking, Reading, and Writing (Chapters 8–14)
Part Three: Doing Research (Chapters 15–18)

The Part One Chapters

For now, to understand how to use the book effectively to improve your writing, you first need to know that the most important part — the part that all of the rest depends on — is Part One, Chapters 2 through 7. Each of these chapters is organized to teach you about one important specific *genre*, or type of writing:

- autobiography
- profile of a person, activity, or place
- explanation of a concept
- argument supporting your position
- proposal to solve a problem
- evaluation

Each Part One chapter follows essentially the same structure, beginning with three scenarios that provide examples of how that kind of writing could be used in a college course, in a workplace, and in a community setting such as a volunteer program or civic organization.

Next come a brief introduction to the genre, a collaborative activity to get you thinking about the genre, and an introduction to the genre's basic features, each of which is assigned a specific color.

Reading Remembered Event Essays

Basic Features

Basic Features

As you read remembered event essays in this chapter, you will see how different authors incorporate the basic features of the genre.

● **A Well-Told Story**

Read first to enjoy the story. Remembered event essays are autobiographical stories that recount an important event in the writer's life; the best ones are first and foremost a pleasure to read. A well-told story

- arouses curiosity and suspense by structuring the narrative around conflict, building to a climax, and leading to a change or discovery of some kind;
- is set in a specific time and place, often using dialogue to heighten immediacy and

The genre's basic features are introduced toward the beginning of the chapter, so you know what to look for in the readings. Each basic feature is assigned a color, which is used whenever that basic feature is discussed later in the chapter.

Next, you'll find a series of readings that will help you see how writers deploy the basic features of the genre for different purposes and audiences. The first reading in each chapter is always written by a first-year college student. These readings include color coding that highlights the writer's use of the basic features of the genre, as well as marginal questions that ask you to analyze the essay and also call your attention to particular writing strategies — such as quoting sources, using humor, providing definitions, and giving examples — that the writer used.

Usually, the remaining readings in the chapter are by professional writers. Each of these additional essays is accompanied by the following groups of questions and activities to help you learn how essays in that genre work:

Making Connections invites you to explore an issue raised by the reading that is related to your own experience and often to broader social or cultural issues.

Analyzing Writing Strategies helps you examine closely some specific strategies the writer used. The questions in this section are organized according to the basic features of the genre, to help you keep track of different aspects of the essay's construction. Following essays that include visuals, an *Analyzing Visuals* section asks you to examine what graphics, photographs, and the like contribute to the written text.

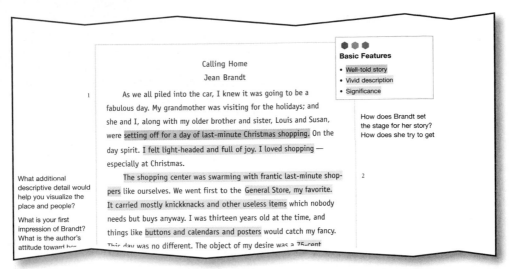

Color-coded highlighting in the chapter's first essay calls attention to the student writer's use of the basic features of the genre; questions in the margin ask you to analyze and reflect on the writer's use of various strategies.

Considering Topics for Your Own Essay suggests subjects that you might write about in your own essay.

Following the readings, each assignment chapter also includes the following sections:

- a Guide to Writing that will help you write an effective essay in the genre for your particular audience and purpose. The Guides to Writing, the most important parts of the entire book, will be explained fully in the next section.
- a concluding section titled Thinking Critically about What You Have Learned, which invites you to reflect on the work you did for that chapter and to consider some of its wider social and cultural implications.

The Guides to Writing

Just as the Part One assignment chapters are the heart of the book, the heart of each assignment chapter is the Guide to Writing.

Writing an essay does not usually proceed in a smooth, predictable sequence — often, for example, a writer working on a draft will go back to what is usually an earlier step, such as invention and research, or jump ahead to what is usually a later one, such as editing and proofreading. But to make the process more understandable and manageable, we have divided each Guide to Writing into the same elements that appear in the same order:

- the Writing Assignment;
- Invention and Research;

- Planning and Drafting;
- a Critical Reading Guide;
- Revising;
- and Editing and Proofreading.

The Writing Assignment. Each Guide to Writing begins with an assignment that defines the general purpose and basic features of the genre you have been studying in the chapter.

"Starting Points" chart. Each Guide to Writing opens with an easy-reference "Starting Points" chart, which is designed to help you efficiently find the advice you need for getting past writer's block and other early-stage difficulties.

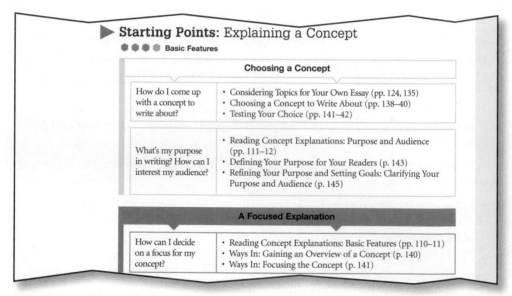

▶ **Starting Points:** Explaining a Concept

●●●● Basic Features

Choosing a Concept	
How do I come up with a concept to write about?	• Considering Topics for Your Own Essay (pp. 124, 135) • Choosing a Concept to Write About (pp. 138–40) • Testing Your Choice (pp. 141–42)
What's my purpose in writing? How can I interest my audience?	• Reading Concept Explanations: Purpose and Audience (pp. 111–12) • Defining Your Purpose for Your Readers (p. 143) • Refining Your Purpose and Setting Goals: Clarifying Your Purpose and Audience (p. 145)

A Focused Explanation	
How can I decide on a focus for my concept?	• Reading Concept Explanations: Basic Features (pp. 110–11) • Ways In: Gaining an Overview of a Concept (p. 140) • Ways In: Focusing the Concept (p. 141)

Each Guide to Writing opens with an easy-reference "Starting Points" chart, with advice for getting started.

Invention and Research. Every Guide to Writing includes invention activities designed to help you

- find a topic;
- discover what you already know about the topic;
- consider your purpose and audience;
- research the topic further — in the library, on the Internet, through observation and interviews, or some combination of these methods;
- explore and develop your ideas;
- and compose a tentative thesis statement to guide your planning and drafting.

Planning and Drafting. To get you started writing a draft of your essay, each Guide to Writing includes suggestions for planning your essay. The section is divided into three parts:

- *Refining Your Purpose and Setting Goals* involves reviewing what you have discovered about your subject, purpose, and audience and helps you think about your goals for the various parts of your essay.
- *Outlining Your Draft* suggests some of the ways you might organize your essay.
- *Drafting* launches you on the writing of your draft, providing both general advice and suggestions about one or two specific sentence strategies that you might find useful for the particular genre.

The Planning and Drafting section also includes a section called Working with Sources, which offers advice (using examples from one or more of the readings) on a particular issue related to incorporating materials from research sources into your essay.

Critical Reading Guide. Once you have finished a draft, you may want to have someone else read the draft and comment on how to improve it. Each Guide to Writing includes a Critical Reading Guide, color-coded to correspond to that genre's basic features, which will help you get good advice on improving your draft as well as help you make helpful suggestions to improve others' drafts. (These Guides break out suggestions for both praise and critique — because we all sometimes need reminding that pointing out what works well can be as helpful as pointing out what needs improvement in a piece of writing.)

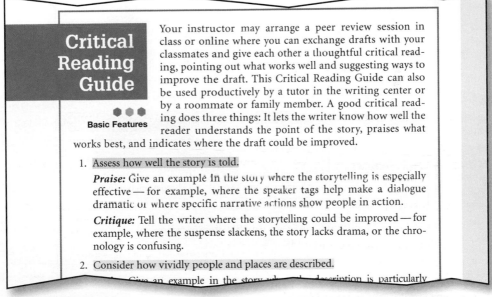

Critical Reading Guide

● ● ●
Basic Features

Your instructor may arrange a peer review session in class or online where you can exchange drafts with your classmates and give each other a thoughtful critical reading, pointing out what works well and suggesting ways to improve the draft. This Critical Reading Guide can also be used productively by a tutor in the writing center or by a roommate or family member. A good critical reading does three things: It lets the writer know how well the reader understands the point of the story, praises what works best, and indicates where the draft could be improved.

1. Assess how well the story is told.

    Praise: Give an example in the story where the storytelling is especially effective — for example, where the speaker tags help make a dialogue dramatic or where specific narrative actions show people in action.

    Critique: Tell the writer where the storytelling could be improved — for example, where the suspense slackens, the story lacks drama, or the chronology is confusing.

2. Consider how vividly people and places are described.

    Give an example in the story where the description is particularly

Critical Reading Guides suggest ways of giving constructive criticism, as well as praise, for your classmates' drafts.

Revising. Each Guide to Writing includes a Revising section to help you get an overview of your draft, consider readers' comments, chart a plan for revision, and carry out the revisions.

A new easy-reference chart in the Revising section called "Troubleshooting Your Draft" offers specific advice for problems many students encounter at this critical stage of the writing process.

✔ Troubleshooting Your Draft

● ● ● Basic Features

A Well-Told Story

The story starts too slowly.	☐ Shorten the exposition. ☐ Move a bit of dialogue or specific narrative action up front. ☐ Start with something surprising. ☐ Consider beginning with a flashback or flashforward.
The chronology is confusing.	☐ Add or change time transitions. ☐ Clarify verb tenses.
The suspense slackens or the story lacks drama.	☐ Add remembered feelings and thoughts to heighten anticipation. ☐ Add dialogue and specific narrative action. ☐ Build rising action in stages with multiple high points. ☐ Move or cut background information and description.
The conflict is vague or seems unconnected to the significance.	☐ Add dramatized dialogue or specific narrative actions. ☐ Clarify your remembered feelings or thoughts. ☐ Reflect on the conflict from your present perspective.

Vivid Description of People and Places

Places are hard to visualize.	☐ Name objects in the scene. ☐ Add sensory detail. ☐ Try out a comparison to evoke a particular mood. ☐ Consider adding a visual — a photograph or other memorabilia.
People do not come alive.	☐ Describe a physical feature or mannerism that gives each person individuality. ☐ Add speaker tags to characterize people and show their feelings. ☐ Liven up the dialogue with faster repartee.
	☐ Omit extr...

"Troubleshooting Your Draft" charts offer specific advice for revising your essay.

Editing and Proofreading. Each Guide to Writing ends with a section to help you recognize and fix specific kinds of problems in grammar, punctuation, and sentence structure that are common in essays in that genre of writing.

The Other Parts of the Book

Parts Two and Three provide more help and practice with specific strategies for reading critically, analyzing arguments and visuals, synthesizing sources, designing documents, and many other key aspects of writing and research.

would be easier to ignore). After noting these things, however, we are immediately struck by what is wrong with the picture: the fish is tiny — a far cry from the sort of catch any normal fisherman would be satisfied with — the lake in the background is almost entirely dried up, and the fisherman is covered in bloody sores from severe sun damage.

So what do we make of the disruption of the convention (the vacation photo) on which the PSA image is based? In trying to decide, most of us will look next to the text below the image: "Ignoring global warming won't make it go away." The disjunction between the fisherman's pleased expression and the barren lake and measly catch — not to mention his grotesquely sunburned skin — turns out to be the

Figure 12.2 "Fishing," from the WWF's 2007 "Beautiful Day U.S." Series

Chapter 12, "Analyzing Visuals," helps you approach visual texts critically and analytically.

Also included are up-to-date guidelines for choosing, using, and documenting different kinds of sources (library sources, the Internet, and your own field research); writing annotated bibliographies; taking essay exams; and assembling a portfolio of your writing.

Brief Contents

1 Introduction: Thinking about Writing   1

● ● ● ● **PART 1** Writing Activities

2 Remembering an Event   14

3 Writing Profiles   56

4 Explaining a Concept   106

5 Arguing a Position   158

6 Proposing a Solution   206

7 Justifying an Evaluation   260

● ● ● ● **PART 2** Strategies for Critical Thinking, Reading, and Writing

8 Strategies for Invention and Inquiry   316

9 Strategies for Reading Critically   329

10 Cueing the Reader   353

11 Analyzing and Synthesizing Arguments   368

12 Analyzing Visuals   387

13 Arguing   404

14 Designing Documents   417

●●●● PART 3 Doing Research
15 Field Research   444
16 Library and Internet Research   457
17 Using Sources   486
18 Annotated Bibliographies   526

Contents

Preface for Instructors v

Preface for Students xvii

1 INTRODUCTION: THINKING ABOUT WRITING 1

Why Writing Is Important 1

Writing Influences the Way You Think • Writing Helps You Learn • Writing Fosters Personal Development • Writing Connects You to Others • Writing Promotes Success in College and at Work

How Writing Is Learned 4

Learning to Write by Reading • Learning Writing Strategies • Using the Guides to Writing • Thinking Critically

•••• PART 1 Writing Activities

2 REMEMBERING AN EVENT 14

Remembering an Event 16

Reading and Writing about Remembered Events 16

A Collaborative Activity: Practice Remembering an Event 17

• Reading Remembered Event Essays 17

Basic Features 17

Purpose and Audience 18

● **Readings** 19

Jean Brandt, "Calling Home" (annotated student essay)   19
Annie Dillard, "An American Childhood"   23
Trey Ellis, "When the Walls Came Tumbling Down"   29

● **Guide to Writing** 36

The Writing Assignment 36
Starting Points: Remembering an Event   37

Invention and Research 38
Choosing an Event to Write About
Ways In: Constructing a Well-Told Story   40
Creating a Dominant Impression ● Testing Your Choice ●
A Collaborative Activity: Testing Your Choice ● Exploring
Memorabilia
Ways In: Reflecting on the Event's
Autobiographical Significance   43
Defining Your Purpose and Audience ● Considering Your Thesis

Planning and Drafting 45
Refining Your Purpose and Setting Goals ● Outlining Your Draft ●
Drafting ● Working with Sources: Quoting, Paraphrasing, and
Summarizing

Critical Reading Guide 49

Revising 50
Troubleshooting Your Draft   51

Editing and Proofreading 52
Missing Commas after Introductory Elements ● Using the Past
Perfect ● Fused Sentences

● **Thinking Critically about
What You Have Learned** 54

Reflecting on Your Writing 54

**Considering the Social Dimensions:
Autobiography and Self-Discovery** 54

3 WRITING PROFILES 56

Profiles 58

Reading and Writing Profiles 58
A Collaborative Activity: Practice Conducting an Interview   59

● Reading Profiles   60

   Basic Features   60

   Purpose and Audience   61

● Readings   62

   Brian Cable, "The Last Stop" (annotated student essay)   62
   John T. Edge, "I'm Not Leaving Until I Eat This Thing"   67
   Amanda Coyne, "The Long Good-Bye: Mother's Day
      in Federal Prison"   74

● Guide to Writing   82

   The Writing Assignment   82
      Starting Points: Writing a Profile   83

   Invention and Research   84
   Choosing a Subject to Profile
      Ways In: Finalizing Your Choice   86
   Testing Your Choice ● A Collaborative Activity: Testing Your
   Choice ● Setting Up a Tentative Schedule
      Ways In: Collecting Information from Field Research   89
      Ways In: Reflecting on Your Purpose and the
      Profile's Perspective   92
   Considering Your Thesis ● Designing Your Document

   Planning and Drafting   93
   Refining Your Purpose and Setting Goals ● Outlining Your Draft
   ● Drafting ● Working with Sources: Integrating Quotations from
   Your Interviews

   Critical Reading Guide   98

   Revising   99
      Troubleshooting Your Draft   100

   Editing and Proofreading   102
   Checking the Punctuation of Quotations ● A Common ESL
   Problem: Adjective Order

● **Thinking Critically about
   What You Have Learned**   104

   Reflecting on Your Writing   104

   **Considering the Social Dimensions: Entertaining
   Readers, or Showing the Whole Picture?**   105

4 EXPLAINING A CONCEPT 106

Explaining Concepts 108

Reading and Writing Concept Explanations 108
A Collaborative Activity: Practice Explaining a Concept 109

● Reading Concept Explanations 110

Basic Features 110

Purpose and Audience 111

● Readings 112

Linh Kieu Ngo, "Cannibalism: It Still Exists"
(annotated student essay) 112
Anastasia Toufexis, "Love: The Right Chemistry" 117
Jeffrey Kluger, "What Makes Us Moral" 124

● Guide to Writing 136

The Writing Assignment 136
Starting Points: Explaining a Concept 137

Invention and Research 138
Choosing a Concept to Write About
Ways In: Gaining an Overview of a Concept 140
Ways In: Focusing the Concept 141
Testing Your Choice ● A Collaborative Activity: Testing Your
Choice ● Designing Your Document ● Defining Your Purpose for
Your Readers ● Formulating a Tentative Thesis Statement

Planning and Drafting 144
Refining Your Purpose and Setting Goals ● Outlining Your Draft ●
Drafting ● Working with Sources: Using Descriptive Verbs to
Introduce Information

Critical Reading Guide 149

Revising 150
Troubleshooting Your Draft 151

Editing and Proofreading 153
Using Punctuation with Adjective Clauses ● Using Commas with
Interrupting Phrases

● **Thinking Critically about What You Have Learned** 155

Reflecting on Your Writing 155

Considering the Social Dimensions: Concept Explanations and the Nature of Knowledge 156

5 ARGUING A POSITION 158

Arguing a Position 161

Reading and Writing Arguments 161
A Collaborative Activity: Practice Arguing a Position 162

● **Reading Essays Arguing a Position** 163

Basic Features 163

Purpose and Audience 165

● **Readings** 165

Jessica Statsky, "Children Need to Play, Not Compete" (annotated student essay) 165
Amitai Etzioni, "Working at McDonald's" 171
Amy Goldwasser, "What's the Matter with Kids Today?" 177

● **Guide to Writing** 183

The Writing Assignment 183
Starting Points: Arguing a Position 184

Invention and Research 185
Choosing an Issue to Write About
Ways In: Bringing the Issue and Your Audience into Focus 187
Testing Your Choice ● A Collaborative Activity: Testing Your Choice
Ways In: Developing Your Argument and Counterargument 189
Researching Your Argument ● Defining Your Purpose for Your Readers ● Formulating a Tentative Thesis Statement

Planning and Drafting 193

Refining Your Purpose and Setting Goals • Outlining Your Draft • Drafting • Working with Sources: Fairly and Accurately Quoting Opposing Positions

Critical Reading Guide 199

Revising 200

Troubleshooting Your Draft 201

Editing and Proofreading 202

Using Commas before Coordinating Conjunctions • Using Punctuation with Conjunctive Adverbs • A Common ESL Problem: Subtle Differences in Meaning

• **Thinking Critically about What You Have Learned** 204

Reflecting on Your Writing 205

Considering the Social Dimensions: Suppressing Dissent 205

6 PROPOSING A SOLUTION 206

Proposing a Solution 209

Reading and Writing Essays Proposing a Solution 209

A Collaborative Activity: Practice Proposing a Solution to a Problem 210

• **Reading Essays Proposing a Solution** 211

Basic Features 211

Purpose and Audience 212

• **Readings** 213

Patrick O'Malley, "More Testing, More Learning" (annotated student essay) 213
Karen Kornbluh, "Win-Win Flexibility" 219
Robert Kuttner, "Good Jobs for Americans Who Help Americans" 227

• **Guide to Writing** 236

The Writing Assignment 236

Starting Points: Proposing a Solution 237

Invention and Research 238

Choosing a Problem to Write About

Ways In: Bringing the Problem and
Your Audience into Focus 240

Ways In: Exploring Your Tentative Solution 242

Testing Your Choice • A Collaborative Activity: Testing
Your Choice

Ways In: Counterarguing Alternative Solutions 244

Researching Your Proposal • Defining Your Purpose for Your
Readers • Formulating a Tentative Thesis Statement

Planning and Drafting 246

Refining Your Purpose and Setting Goals • Outlining Your Draft •
Drafting • A Sentence Strategy: Rhetorical Questions • Working
with Sources: Establishing the Problem's Existence and Seriousness

Critical Reading Guide 253

Revising 254

Troubleshooting Your Draft 255

Editing and Proofreading 256

Avoiding Ambiguous Use of *This* and *That* • Revising Sentences
That Lack an Agent

• **Thinking Critically about
What You Have Learned** 258

Reflecting on Your Writing 258

**Considering the Social Dimensions:
The Frustrations of Effecting Real Change** 259

7 JUSTIFYING AN EVALUATION 260

Justifying an Evaluation 262

Reading and Writing Evaluations 262

A Collaborative Activity: Practice Evaluating a Subject 263

• **Reading Essays Justifying Evaluations** 264

Basic Features 264

Purpose and Audience 265

● **Readings**   266

Wendy Kim, "Grading Professors" (annotated student essay)   266
Ann Hulbert, "*Juno* and the Culture Wars"   273
Christine Romano, "'Children Need to Play, Not Compete,' by
  Jessica Statsky: An Evaluation" (student essay)   280

● **Guide to Writing**   289

The Writing Assignment   289
  Starting Points: Justifying an Evaluation   290

Invention and Research   291
Choosing a Subject to Write About
  Ways In: Bringing the Subject and
  Your Audience into Focus   293
Making a Tentative Judgment ● Testing Your Choice ●
A Collaborative Activity: Testing Your Choice
  Ways In: Developing Your Argument and
  Counterargument   295
Researching Your Argument ● Defining Your Purpose for Your
Readers ● Formulating a Tentative Thesis Statement

Planning and Drafting   298
Refining Your Purpose and Setting Goals ● Outlining Your Draft ●
Drafting ● Working with Sources: Using Summary to Support Your
Evaluative Argument

Critical Reading Guide   306

Revising   307
  Troubleshooting Your Draft   308

Editing and Proofreading   310
Complete, Correct Comparisons ● Combining Sentences

● **Thinking Critically about
What You Have Learned**   312

Reflecting on Your Writing   312

**Considering the Social Dimensions:
Evaluators' Hidden Assumptions**   312

●●●● PART **2** Strategies for Critical Thinking, Reading, and Writing

8 STRATEGIES FOR INVENTION AND INQUIRY 316

Mapping 316
Clustering ● Listing ● Outlining

Writing 322
Cubing ● Dialoguing ● Dramatizing ● Keeping a Journal ● Looping ● Questioning ● Quick Drafting

9 STRATEGIES FOR READING CRITICALLY 329

Annotating 330
Martin Luther King Jr., An Annotated Sample from "Letter from Birmingham Jail" 330

Taking Inventory 337

Outlining 337

Paraphrasing 340

Summarizing 341

Synthesizing 342

Contextualizing 343

Exploring the Significance of Figurative Language 344

Looking for Patterns of Opposition 346

Reflecting on Challenges to Your Beliefs and Values 347

Evaluating the Logic of an Argument 348
Testing for Appropriateness ● Testing for Believability ● Testing for Consistency and Completeness

Recognizing Emotional Manipulation   350

Judging the Writer's Credibility   351
Testing for Knowledge • Testing for Common Ground • Testing for Fairness

10 CUEING THE READER   353

Orienting Statements   353
Thesis Statements • Forecasting Statements

Paragraphing   355
Paragraph Cues • Topic Sentence Strategies

Cohesive Devices   359
Pronoun Reference • Word Repetition • Synonyms • Sentence Structure Repetition • Collocation

Transitions   363
Logical Relationships • Temporal Relationships • Spatial Relationships

Headings and Subheadings   366
Heading Systems and Levels • Headings and Genres • Frequency and Placement of Headings

11 ANALYZING AND SYNTHESIZING ARGUMENTS   368

Analyzing Arguments   368
Applying the Criteria for Analyzing Arguments • Annotating a Text and Creating a Chart • Coming Up with a Focus for Your Analysis

A Sample Analysis   372
Mirko Bagaric and Julie Clarke, "A Case for Torture"   372
Melissa Mae's Annotations • Melissa Mae's Analysis

From Analysis to Synthesis   380

A Sample Synthesis   380
Melissa Mae's Process

12 ANALYZING VISUALS   387

Criteria for Analyzing Visuals   389

A Sample Analysis   391

13 ARGUING   404

Asserting a Thesis   404
Arguable Assertions ● Clear and Precise Wording ● Appropriate Qualification

Giving Reasons and Support   407
Examples ● Statistics ● Authorities ● Anecdotes ● Textual Evidence

Counterarguing   413
Acknowledging Readers' Concerns ● Accommodating Readers' Concerns ● Refuting Readers' Objections

Logical Fallacies   416

14 DESIGNING DOCUMENTS   417

The Impact of Document Design   417

Considering Context, Audience, and Purpose   418

Elements of Document Design   419
Font Style and Size ● Headings and Body Text ● Numbered and Bulleted Lists ● Colors ● White Space

Visuals   424
Choose Appropriate Visuals and Design Them with Their Final Use in Mind ● Number and Title Your Visuals ● Label the Parts of Your Visuals and Include Descriptive Captions ● Cite Your Visual Sources ● Integrate the Visuals into the Text ● Use Common Sense When Creating Visuals on a Computer

Sample Documents   432
Memos ● Letters ● E-mail ● Résumés ● Job-Application Letters ● Lab Reports ● Web Pages

●●●● **PART 3** Doing Research

15 FIELD RESEARCH   444

Observations   444
Planning the Visit ● Observing and Taking Notes ● Reflecting
on Your Observations ● Writing Up Your Notes ● Preparing for
Follow-Up Visits

Interviews   447
Planning and Setting Up the Interview ● Taking Notes during the
Interview ● Reflecting on the Interview ● Writing Up Your Notes

Questionnaires   451
Focusing Your Study ● Writing Questions ● Designing the
Questionnaire ● Testing the Questionnaire ● Administering the
Questionnaire ● Writing Up the Results

16 LIBRARY AND INTERNET RESEARCH   457

Orienting Yourself to the Library   457
Taking a Tour ● Consulting Librarians

Getting Started   459
Knowing Your Research Task ● Finding Out What Your Library
Offers ● Consulting Encyclopedias ● Consulting Bibliographies

Keeping Track of Your Research   462
Keeping a Working Bibliography ● Taking Notes

Finding Library Sources   465
General Search Strategies ● Finding Books: Using the Online
Library Catalog ● Finding Articles ● Finding Government and
Statistical Information ● Finding Other Library Sources

Determining the Most Promising Sources   476

Using the Web for Research   478
Finding the Best Information Online ● Using E-mail and Online
Communities for Research

Evaluating Sources   482
Selecting Relevant Sources ● Identifying Bias

17 USING SOURCES 486

Acknowledging Sources 486

Avoiding Plagiarism 487

Quoting, Paraphrasing, and Summarizing 487
Deciding Whether to Quote, Paraphrase, or Summarize •
Quoting • Integrating Quotations • Introducing Quotations •
Punctuating within Quotations • Avoiding Grammatical •
Tangles • Paraphrasing and Summarizing

Documenting Sources 495
The MLA System of Documentation • The APA System of
Documentation

Some Sample Research Papers 516

An Annotated Research Paper 517

18 ANNOTATED BIBLIOGRAPHIES 526

Basic Features 526

Purpose and Audience 527

Examples of Annotated Bibliographies 528
Different Types of Annotation • A Map for Writing an Annotated
Bibliography

Subject Index I-1

Axelrod & Cooper's

Concise Guide
to Writing

Introduction: Thinking about Writing

1

Philosopher Edmund Burke once said that "reading without reflecting is like eating without digesting." We believe that what Burke said about reading applies to writing as well, and that reflecting on writing is one of the best ways to become a better and more versatile writer. That is why quotes from writers are sprinkled throughout this chapter. That is also why in this chapter and throughout this book, we ask you to write brief reflections, ultimately constructing a **literacy narrative**, a multifaceted story about yourself as a writer.

Reflection 1. A Literacy Story

Take five to ten minutes to write a story of your experience with writing. Consider the following suggestions, but do not be limited by them:

- Recall an early experience of writing: What did you write? Did anyone read it? What kind of feedback did you get? How did you feel about yourself?
- Think of a turning point when your attitude toward writing changed or crystallized. What happened? What changed?
- Recall a person — a teacher, classmate, family member, published writer, or someone else — who influenced your writing, for good or ill. How was your writing affected?
- Cast yourself as the main character of a story about writing. How would you describe yourself — as a "natural" writer; as someone who struggles to write well; or somewhere in between? Consider your trajectory or "narrative arc": Over the years, would you say you have showed steady improvement; ups and downs; more downs than ups; a decline?

Why Writing Is Important

Writing helps you think and learn, enhances your chances of success, contributes to your personal development, and strengthens your relationships with other people.

Writing Influences the Way You Think

The very act of writing encourages you to be creative as well as organized and logical in your thinking. When you write sentences, paragraphs, and whole essays, you generate ideas and connect these ideas in systematic ways. By combining words into phrases and sentences with conjunctions, you create complex new ideas: For example, *and* brings out similarities, *but* emphasizes differences, and *because* supports general ideas with specific reasons, facts, and examples.

By writing essays for different purposes as you work through the *Concise Guide*, you will develop your thinking in different ways. For example, writing about a remembered event will inspire you to reflect on what happened and why it is memorable; proposing a solution to a problem will deepen your ability to analyze and synthesize different points of view; arguing for a position on a controversial issue will hone your reasoning skills; and making evaluations will help you examine underlying assumptions about what you value and why.

> The mere process of writing is one of the most powerful tools we have for clarifying our own thinking. I am never as clear about any matter as when I have just finished writing about it.   — JAMES VAN ALLEN

Writing Helps You Learn

Writing contributes to learning by helping you remember what you are studying, by leading you to analyze and connect information and ideas from different sources, and by inspiring new insights and understanding. Writing as you read — taking notes, annotating the text, and responding in writing to the text's assumptions and arguments — makes you a better reader. Reflecting in writing on what you are learning consolidates your understanding of and response to new material.

Different kinds of writing contribute to learning in different ways. Writing essays of various kinds, or **genres**, as you work through the *Concise Guide* will help you organize and present what you have learned and, in the process, clarify and extend your own ideas. Arguing a position teaches you not only to support your reasons but also to refute objections to your argument. Researching a profile, you learn to make precise observations and ask pertinent questions. Explaining a concept requires you to inform yourself about your subject and organize the information in a way that makes it clear to readers.

> Writing has been for a long time my major tool for self-instruction and self-development.   — TONI CADE BAMBARA

Writing Fosters Personal Development

In addition to influencing the ways you think and learn, writing can help you grow as an individual. Writing leads you to reflect on your experience, for example, when you write to understand the significance of a particular life event. Writing about a controversial issue can make you examine some of your most basic beliefs. Writing an evaluation requires that you think about what you value and how your values compare to those of others. Perhaps most important, becoming an author confers authority on you; it gives you confidence to assert your own ideas and feelings.

In a very real sense, the writer writes in order to teach himself, to understand himself, to satisfy himself. . . . — ALFRED KAZIN

Some of the things that happen to us in life seem to have no meaning, but when you write them down, you find the meanings for them. . . .
— MAXINE HONG KINGSTON

Writing Connects You to Others

Nearly all of us use writing in one form or another — whether via e-mail, text messaging, instant messaging, blogging, Twitter, or Facebook — to keep in touch with friends and family. Many of us also use writing to take part in academic discussions and participate in civic debate and decision making. By writing about our experiences, ideas, and observations, we reach out to readers, offering them our own points of view and inviting them to share theirs in return.

The writing you do for your composition class will likewise help you connect with others. In writing an argument, for example, as you clarify your perspective and reexamine your own reasoning, you may ultimately influence other people's opinions on your topic. Their responses to your writing may, in turn, cause you to reevaluate your own ideas. Collaborative writing — as, for example, if you are assigned to write a proposal with a group of classmates — enables you to work directly with others to invent new ways of solving complex problems.

Writing is the act of saying I, of imposing oneself upon other people, of saying listen to me, see it my way, change your mind. — JOAN DIDION

It's the sense of being in contact with people who are part of a particular audience that really makes a difference to me in writing.
— SHERLEY ANNE WILLIAMS

Writing Promotes Success in College and at Work

As a student, you are probably aware of the many ways writing can contribute to your success in school. Students who learn to write for different readers and purposes do well in courses throughout the curriculum. Eventually, you will need to use writing to advance your career by writing persuasive application letters for jobs or graduate school admission. At work, you will be expected to write effective e-mail messages, memos, and reports that present clear explanations, well-reasoned arguments, convincing evaluations, and constructive proposals.

People think it's sort of funny that I went to graduate school as a biologist and then became a writer. . . . What I learned [in science] is how to formulate or identify a new question that hasn't been asked before and then to set about solving it, to do original research to find the way to an answer. And that's what I do when I write a book. — BARBARA KINGSOLVER

Reflection 2.   Writing That Mattered

Write a page or two describing an occasion when writing helped you accomplish something. Here are some possibilities to consider:

- an occasion when you used writing to prepare for a test or otherwise help you remember critical material
- an occasion when writing helped you better understand a difficult subject or reading
- an occasion when you worked through a personal or an intellectual problem by writing
- an occasion when you used writing to influence someone else
- an occasion when writing enabled you to express your feelings or made you feel connected
- an occasion when your writing helped you get a better grade or succeed in some way
- an occasion when your writing made others take notice

How Writing Is Learned

There are many myths about writing and writers. For example, some people assume that people who are good at writing do not have to spend a lot of time learning to write — that they just naturally know how. Others assume that "real" writers write perfectly the first time, every time, dashing off an essay with minimal effort. Writers' testimonies, however, together with extensive research on how people write and learn to write, show that writing can — indeed, must — be learned. All writers work at their writing. Some writers may be more successful and influential than others. Some may find writing easier and more satisfying than others. But no one is born knowing how to write.

> Learning to write well takes time and much effort, but it can be done.
> — MARGARET MEAD

> It's none of their business that you have to learn to write. Let them think you were born that way.   — ERNEST HEMINGWAY

Reflection 3.   How You Became Literate

Write a page or two describing how and why you became literate and what happened as a result. You may choose to write about your early memories of learning to read and write either at home or at school. Or you could think of literacy more broadly, focusing, for example, on one or more of the following:

- computer literacy — learning how to program, how to "read" the Web efficiently, or how to communicate through text messaging, blogging, and so on
- workplace literacy, perhaps including ways of talking to customers, colleagues, and managers

- academic literacy, perhaps focusing on learning to think, talk, and write as a scientist, historian, literary critic, and so on
- sports literacy, as a player, coach, or fan
- music literacy, as a musician or as a fan of certain kinds of music
- community literacy — learning to communicate with people of different ages or with people who speak different languages or dialects

In reflecting on the results of your learning to be literate, you might want to consider the following:

- how your new literacy changed you or changed your relationships
- ways in which you may have had more power in certain contexts — and perhaps less power in others
- how you felt about being bilingual or multiliterate, and how you used your new literacy

The *Concise Guide to Writing* has helped many students become more thoughtful, effective, confident writers. From reading and analyzing an array of different kinds of essays, you will learn how other writers make their texts work. From writing for different audiences, you will learn to compose texts that readers want to read. To help you take full advantage of what you are learning, the *Concise Guide* will also help you reflect on your learning so that you will be able to remember, apply, and build on what you have learned.

> If you want to be a writer, you must do two things above all others: read a lot and write a lot. There's no way around these two things that I'm aware of, no shortcut. — STEPHEN KING

Learning to Write by Reading

Believe it: Reading will help you become a better writer. In fact, most professional writers are avid readers who read not only for enjoyment and information but also to refine their craft.

Reading to Understand How Texts Work

Readers will have specific expectations of a text as soon as they recognize it as a particular genre or type of writing. For example, readers of a story about a past event in the writer's life will likely recognize it as a form of autobiography, which leads them to expect a story that changes, challenges, or complicates the writer's sense of self or connection with others. If the event seems trivial or the story lacks interest, then readers' expectations will be disappointed, and the text will not succeed. Similarly, if the text takes a position on a controversial issue, readers will recognize it as an opinion piece and expect it to not only assert and support that position, but also refute possible objections. If the argument lacks credible support or ignores thoughtful objections or alternative points of view, readers are likely to decide that the essay is not convincing.

Although individual texts within the same genre vary a great deal — no two proposals, even those arguing for the same solution, will be identical — they nonetheless follow a general pattern that provides a certain amount of predictability without which communication would be difficult, if not impossible. But these language patterns, also called **conventions**, should not be thought of as rigid formulas. Conventions are broad frameworks within which writers are free to be creative. Most writers, in fact, find that working within a framework allows them to be more creative, not less so.

> You would learn very little in this world if you were not allowed to imitate. And to repeat your imitations until some solid grounding . . . was achieved and the slight but wonderful difference — that made you and no one else — could assert itself. — MARY OLIVER

Reading to Write Texts That Work

To learn the conventions of a particular genre, you need to read examples of that genre so that you begin to recognize its predictable patterns as well as the possibilities for innovation. At the same time, you should also practice writing in the genre.

> Read, read, read. . . . Just like a carpenter who works as an apprentice and studies the master. Read! — WILLIAM FAULKNER

The *Concise Guide* provides an array of sample essays in the genres you are learning to write and helps you analyze patterns in these essays. It also helps you practice using these patterns in your own writing to achieve your own purposes. Seeing, for example, how writers define key terms and integrate quotations from their sources in an essay explaining a concept introduces you to strategies you may use when you write in this genre.

> I practiced writing in every possible way that I could. I wrote a pastiche of other people. Just as a pianist runs his scales for ten years before he gives his concert: because when he gives that concert, he can't be thinking of his fingering or of his hands, he has to be thinking of his interpretation. He's thinking of what he's trying to communicate. — KATHERINE ANNE PORTER

> I went back to the good nature books that I had read. And I analyzed them. I wrote outlines of whole books — outlines of chapters — so that I could see their structure. And I copied down their transitional sentences or their main sentences or their closing sentences or their lead sentences. — ANNIE DILLARD

Reading to Design Texts That Work

Writers have long recognized that no matter how well organized, well reasoned, or compelling a piece of writing may be, the way it looks on the page influences to some extent how well it works for readers. Today, writers have more options for designing their documents than ever before. Digital photography, scanning, and integrated word processing and graphics programs make it relatively easy for writers to heighten the visual impact of the page. For example, they can change typefaces and add colors, charts, diagrams, and photographs to written documents. In constructing Web pages or DVDs, writers can add sound, video, and hyperlinks.

These multiple possibilities, however, do not guarantee a more effective document. In order to design effective texts, writers need to study documents that capture readers' attention and enhance understanding. As someone who has likely grown up watching television and movies, playing computer games, and surfing the Internet, you are already a sophisticated visual consumer who has learned many of the conventions of document design for different genres and writing situations. This book will help you become aware of what you already know and help you make new discoveries about document design that you may be able to use in your own writing.

> Design is a funny word. Some people think design means how it looks. But of course, if you dig deeper, it's really how it works. — STEVE JOBS

Reflection 4.   Your Experience with Different Genres of Writing

Make two lists: one of the genres you have *read* — for example, Tweets from your friends; music reviews on iTunes — and another of genres you have *written* — for example, e-mails to your parents; job applications; or a paper for your American history class. Try to come up with at least five entries for each list. Include reading and writing you have done in school, at work, at home, and at play.

Genres You Have Read	Genres You Have Written
1.	1.
2.	2.
3.	3.
4.	4.
5.	5.
6.	6.
7.	7.

Learning Writing Strategies

It might sound strange, but it's true: One of the best ways to become a better writer is by writing. Practice will make your writing more thoughtful and productive. By offering guidance and support as you practice, the *Concise Guide* will help you develop a richer and more flexible repertoire of writing strategies to meet the demands of different writing situations.

Strategies for Getting Started

We all know what it's like to stare at a blank computer screen or a stark white page of paper waiting for inspiration. As a student, however, you're in the position of all those who write under deadlines — you can't simply sit back and wait for inspiration. Instead, you need an array of reliable thinking and writing strategies that you can use not only to write the paper by the due date, but also to help you write it analytically, critically, and creatively.

Invention is the word used since the time of Plato and Aristotle to describe the process of thinking as we compose. Invention includes deciding on your purpose in writing to a particular audience and figuring out how best to achieve your purpose, analyzing and questioning other people's ideas as well as your own, assimilating information from different sources, and organizing your writing logically.

As writers we cannot choose *whether* to invent; we can only choose *how* to invent. The *Concise Guide* offers many invention strategies from which to choose, strategies that will help you meet the demands of each kind of writing you attempt.

> Inspiration usually comes during work, rather than before it.
>
> — MADELEINE L'ENGLE

Strategies for Discovering New Ideas

Few writers begin writing with a complete understanding of a subject. Most use writing as a means of **discovery** — that is, as a way to learn about the subject, trying out ideas and information they have collected, exploring connections and implications, and reviewing what they have written in order to expand and develop their ideas.

> When I start a project, the first thing I do is write down, in longhand, everything I know about the subject, every thought I've ever had on it. This may be twelve or fourteen pages. Then I read it through, for quite a few days . . . then I try to find out what are the salient points that I must make. And then it begins to take shape.   — MAYA ANGELOU

Writing, then, is not something you do after thinking, but in order to help you think. Writers often reflect on this so-called **generative** aspect of writing, echoing E. M. Forster's much-repeated adage: "How do I know what I think until I see what I say?" Here are some other versions of the same insight:

> Every book that I have written has been an education, a process of discovery.   — AMITAV GHOSH

> I don't see writing as a communication of something already discovered, as "truths" already known. Rather, I see writing as a job of experiment. It's like any discovery job; you don't know what's going to happen until you try it.
>
> — WILLIAM STAFFORD

> Don't tear up the page and start over again when you write a bad line — try to write your way out of it. Make mistakes and plunge on. . . . Writing is a means of discovery, always.   — GARRISON KEILLOR

Writers obviously do not give birth to a text as a whole, but must work cumulatively, focusing first on one thing, then on another. Writing therefore may seem to progress in a linear, step-by-step fashion. But in fact it almost always proceeds **recursively**, which means that writers return over and over again to ideas that they are trying to clarify or extend, or to gaps in their information or logic that they are trying to fill. Most writers plan and then revise their plans, draft and revise their drafts, write and read what they have written, and then write and revise some more. In this way, the experience of writing is less like marching in a straight line from first sentence to last and more like exploring an uphill trail with frequent switchbacks. It may appear that you are retracing old ground, but you are really rising to new levels as you learn the terrain.

> It's a matter of piling a little piece here and a little piece there, fitting them together, going on to the next part, then going back and gradually shaping the whole piece into something.   — DAVE BARRY

Strategies for Organizing Your Ideas

Writers need strategies that make writing systematic but do not stifle inventiveness. For this reason, most writers begin drafting with some type of plan — a list, a scratch outline, or a detailed storyboard like that used by filmmakers. Outlines can be very helpful, but they must be tentative and flexible if writers are to benefit from writing's natural recursiveness.

> I began [*Invisible Man*] with a chart of the three-part division. It was a conceptual frame with most of the ideas and some of the incidents indicated.
> — RALPH ELLISON

> You are always going back and forth between the outline and the writing, bringing them closer together, or just throwing out the outline and making a new one.   — ANNIE DILLARD

Strategies for Drafting and Revising

While composing a draft, writers benefit from frequent pauses to reread what they have written. Rereading often leads to further discovery — adding an example, choosing different words that unpack or separate ideas, filling in a gap in the logic of an argument. In addition, rereading frequently leads to substantial rethinking and revising: cutting, reorganizing, rewriting whole sections to make the writing more effective.

> You have to work problems out for yourself on paper. Put the stuff down and read it — to see if it works.   — JOYCE CARY

> As a writer, I would find out most clearly what I thought, and what I only thought I thought, when I saw it written down.   — ANNA QUINDLEN

Rereading your own writing in order to improve it can be difficult, though, because it is hard to see what the draft actually says, as opposed to what you were trying to say. For this reason, most writers also give their drafts to others to read. Students generally seek advice from their teachers and other students in the class because they understand the assignment. Published writers also share their work in progress with others. Poets, novelists, historians, scientists, newspaper reporters, magazine essayists, and even textbook writers actively seek constructive critical comments by joining writers' workshops or getting help from editors.

> I was lucky because I was always going to groups where the writers were at the same level or a little better than me. That really helped.
>
> — MANIL SURI

> [Ezra Pound] was a marvelous critic because he didn't try to turn you into an imitation of himself. He tried to see what you were trying to do.
>
> — T. S. ELIOT

Using the Guides to Writing

As you have seen, students learning to write need to be flexible and yet systematic. The Guides to Writing in Part One of this book are designed to meet this need. The first few times you write in a new genre, you can rely on these guides. They provide scaffolding to support your work until you become more familiar with the demands and possibilities of each genre. The Guides will help you develop a repertoire of strategies for creatively solving problems in your writing, such as deciding how to interest readers, how to refute opposing arguments, what to quote from a source, and how to integrate quotations into your writing.

When people engage in any new and complex activity — driving, playing an instrument, skiing, or writing — they may divide it into a series of manageable tasks. In learning to play tennis, for example, you might concentrate separately on lobbing, volleying, or serving, before putting your skills together in a game. Similarly, in writing an argument on a controversial issue, you can focus at first on separate tasks such as defining the issue, developing your reasons, and anticipating readers' objections. Dividing your writing in this way enables you to tackle a complex subject without either oversimplifying it or becoming overwhelmed.

Here is a writer's quotation that has been especially helpful for us as we have written and revised the *Concise Guide to Writing*:

You know when you think about writing a book, you think it is overwhelming. But, actually, you break it down into tiny little tasks any moron could do.

— ANNIE DILLARD

Reflection 5. Your Last Writing Project

Write a couple of pages describing how you went about writing the last time you wrote an essay (or something else) that took time and effort. Use the following questions to help you recall what you did, but feel free to write about any other aspects of your writing that you think are important.

- What did you write, and when?
- Who were you writing for, and why were you writing? What did you hope to accomplish?
- What technologies did you use (a computer? a pen?), and how do you think using these technologies affected the way you wrote?
- What kinds of planning did you do, if any, before you began writing the first draft?
- If you discussed your ideas and plans with someone, how did discussing them help you? If you had someone read your draft, how did getting a response help?
- If you rewrote, moved, added, or cut anything in your first draft, describe what you changed.
- Did you write pretty much the way you usually do, or did you do something differently? If you did it differently, why did you make the change?
- Were you satisfied with your writing process and with the final draft that resulted? What would you have changed if you had more time or knew what you know now?

Thinking Critically

As we said at the beginning, reflecting on your literacy experiences helps you become a better, more versatile writer. Reflecting makes you aware of what you already know and what you still need to learn. Reflecting enhances **metacognition**, which is a scholarly word for awareness of your own thinking processes.

As young children, we learn to use language primarily from hearing others talk and from being talked to. Learning language seems magical because we are not conscious of being taught. But we learn because others are modeling language use for us all the time, and sometimes they even correct our pronunciation, word choice, and grammar.

We learn the most common types of communicating such as storytelling in the same way. We listen to others tell stories and read to us; we watch stories portrayed on television, in film, and in video games; and eventually we read stories for ourselves. Being immersed in storytelling, we learn conventional ways of beginning and ending, strategies for building suspense, techniques for making time sequences clear, methods for using dialogue to develop character, and so on. As we get older, we can reinforce and increase our repertoire of storytelling strategies by analyzing stories and by consciously trying the strategies in our own oral and written stories. This is true of all literacy learning. We learn from a combination of modeling, immersion, and thinking critically about what we are learning.

In addition to modeling good writing and guiding you in writing on your own, the *Concise Guide to Writing* helps you think critically about your writing. Each writing assignment chapter in Part One of the *Concise Guide* includes many opportunities for you to think critically and reflect on your understanding of the **rhetorical situation** — the context, composed of genre, purpose, and audience — in which you are writing. In addition, a section titled Thinking Critically about What You Have Learned concludes each chapter, giving you an opportunity to look back and reflect on how you used your writing process creatively and how you expanded your understanding of the genre.

Reflection 6. Your Literacy Experience, through Metaphor and Simile

Write two or three **similes** (comparisons using *like* or *as*) or **metaphors** (implied comparisons, not using *like* or *as*) that express some aspect of your literacy experience. Then write a page or so explaining and expanding on the ideas and feelings you expressed in one or more of them. Here are some examples from professional writers:

> Writing is like exploring . . . as an explorer makes maps of the country he has explored, so a writer's works are maps of the country he has explored.
>
> — LAWRENCE OSGOOD

> The writer must soak up the subject completely, as a plant soaks up water, until the ideas are ready to sprout.
>
> — MARGUERITE YOURCENAR

> Writing is manual labor of the mind: a job, like laying pipe.
>
> — JOHN GREGORY DUNNE

> If we had to say what writing is, we would define it essentially as an act of courage.
>
> — CYNTHIA OZICK

To get at the meanings in your metaphors and similes, it may help also to write ones that express opposite ideas. For example, if you begin with "writing is like building a house," you could also try "writing is like taking things apart, brick by brick" to get at both the constructive and analytical aspects of the process. Or you could try "writing is like walking into a new house" to move from the work involved in composing to the discovery of something new.

Writing Activities

2

Remembering an Event

IN COLLEGE COURSES In a linguistics course, students are assigned a paper in which they are supposed to discuss published research in the context of their own experience. The class had recently read Deborah Tannen's *Gender and Discourse*, in which Tannen discusses differences in how men and women talk about problems: According to Tannen, women tend to spend a lot of time talking about the problem and their feelings about it, while men typically cut short the talk about feelings and focus on solutions.

One student decides to write about Tannen's findings in light of a conversation she recently had with her brother about their father's drinking. Before writing, she rereads a diary entry she had written shortly after the conversation, which she found frustrating. She begins her essay by reconstructing the conversation, quoting some dialogue from her diary and paraphrasing other parts from memory. Then she analyzes the conversation, using Tannen's categories. She discovers that what bothered her about the conversation was less its content than her brother's way of communicating.

IN THE COMMUNITY As part of a local history series in a newspaper serving a small western ranching community, an amateur historian volunteers to help an elderly rancher write about the winter of 1938, when a six-foot snowstorm isolated the rancher's family for nearly a month. The historian tapes the rancher talking about how he, his wife, and his infant son survived, including an account of how he snowshoed eight miles to a logging train track in order to get a message to relatives. On a second visit, the historian and the rancher listen to the tape recording and brainstorm on further details to make the event more complete and dramatic for readers.

The historian writes a rough outline, which he and the rancher discuss, and then a draft, which the rancher reads and elaborates on. The rancher also offers several photos for possible inclusion. The historian revises and edits the story and submits it, along with two photos, to the project's editor for publication.

IN THE WORKPLACE A respected longtime regional manager for a state's highway department has been asked to give the keynote speech at a meeting on workplace safety. The manager has long considered employee relations of paramount importance in keeping the workplace safe, so he decides to open his speech by recounting his recent dramatic confrontation with an unhappy employee who complained bitterly about the work schedule he had been given and threatened to harm the manager and his family if the manager did not give him a better schedule.

The manager reflects on his fear and on his frustration over not knowing how to handle the confrontation because the department's published procedures on workplace safety offered no specific advice on such a situation. Finally, the manager summarizes data he compiled on the nature and frequency of such workplace incidents nationwide and concludes by calling for new guidelines on how to handle them.

Remembering an Event

We remember events in many ways. Physical memorials such as statues, plaques, monuments, and buildings are traditional means of ensuring that important events remain in our collective memory: Relatively recent examples include the Vietnam Veterans Memorial in Washington, D.C., and the planned commemorative complex at the site of the 9/11 World Trade Center attack in New York City. Community gatherings, which often include speeches, music, and visual tributes, and community activities like the ongoing creation of the AIDS Memorial Quilt, are also means of remembering events. Films, books, plays, music, art exhibits, and Web sites are

still other means by which people in our culture retell the stories of important events, encouraging us to reexperience them and reflect on their significance.

In this chapter, we ask you to write an essay about an event in your life that will engage readers and that will, at the same time, help them understand its significance.

The Vietnam Veterans Memorial (left, foreground) and the Washington Monument (right, background).

Reading and Writing about Remembered Events

People write about their experiences in various contexts, for different purposes and audiences. The scenarios on p. 15, for example, show people in different rhetorical situations reflecting on an event that has significance not only for them, but also for their audience. The student turns an academic assignment into an opportunity to make sense of a family conflict. In collaborating on an article about his past, the rancher records the history of a community and reveals the challenges of living in an earlier era. The manager uses a report on a confrontation to convince colleagues that workplace safety procedures need to be revamped.

Not only can writing about your experience serve different purposes, but immersing yourself in the sights, sounds, and sensations of memory can also be pleasurable in itself. Even when the memories arouse mixed feelings, reflecting on the events and people important in your life can be deeply satisfying. Writing can help you understand and come to terms with the influences in your family and community that have helped shape your thinking and values.

Similarly, reading about other people's experiences can be both entertaining and challenging. As readers, we take pleasure in seeing reflections of our own experience in other people's stories. Encountering unfamiliar experiences can also be fascinating, however, and can lead us to question some of the ways we have learned to think about ourselves and others. For example, one of the writers whose work is reprinted in this chapter remembers that when she was arrested for shoplifting she felt excited, as if she were acting in a movie.

From readings like these in the first part of this chapter, you will see how others put their memories into words. The Guide to Writing that follows will support you as you compose your own remembered event essay; it will show you how to tell your story vividly and dramatically, entertaining readers but also giving them insight into the event's meaning and importance in your life.

A Collaborative Activity:
Practice Remembering an Event

Part 1. Take turns telling a story about an important event in your life. Each story should take just a few minutes to tell. Prepare by choosing an event you feel comfortable describing in this situation, and quickly plan how you will describe it. Then get together with two or three other students, and take turns telling your stories.

Part 2. Discuss what happened when you told about a remembered event:

- To think about your purpose and audience, see whether the students in your group understand why the event is important to you. What in your story, if anything, helped them identify with you?

- Compare your thoughts with the others in your group on what was easiest and hardest about telling the story: for example, making the story dramatic, balancing your account of what happened with your feelings and thoughts about it, deciding how much to tell about the people involved.

Reading Remembered Event Essays

Basic Features

Basic Features

As you read remembered event essays in this chapter, you will see how different authors incorporate the basic features of the genre.

● A Well-Told Story

Read first to enjoy the story. Remembered event essays are autobiographical stories that recount an important event in the writer's life; the best ones are first and foremost a pleasure to read. A well-told story

- arouses curiosity and suspense by structuring the narrative around conflict, building to a climax, and leading to a change or discovery of some kind;
- is set in a specific time and place, often using dialogue to heighten immediacy and drama;
- lets readers into the narrator's point of view (written in the first person *I*) and enables readers to empathize and possibly identify with the writer.

● Vivid Description of People and Places

Read for the author's description of people and places. In the essays in this chapter, notice

- the specific details describing what people look like, how they dress, gesture, and talk;
- the sensory images showing what the narrator saw, heard, smelled, touched, and tasted.

● Autobiographical Significance

Read also to understand the story's autobiographical significance. This is the point the writer is trying to make — the purpose for writing to a particular audience. Effective writers both tell and show

- by remembering feelings and thoughts from the time the event took place;
- by reflecting on the past from the present perspective;
- by choosing details and words that create a dominant impression.

Purpose and Audience

Whatever the writing situation, writers usually have various purposes in mind, including both self-discovery and self-presentation. Keep in mind, however, that the remembered event essay is a public genre meant to be read by others. Sometimes the audience is specific, as in a personal essay composed for a college or job application. Often, however, the audience is more general, as in an academic essay written in a college course to be read by the instructor and fellow students.

*As you read remembered event essays, ask yourself what seems to be the writer's **purpose** in writing about this particular experience.* For example, does the writer seem to be writing

- to understand what happened and why, perhaps to confront motives?
- to relive an intense experience, perhaps to work though complex and ambivalent feelings?
- to win over readers, perhaps to justify or rationalize choices made, actions taken, words used?

You should be aware that as an insightful reader, you may be able to see larger themes or deeper implications — what we call **significance** — beyond those the writer consciously intends or even acknowledges.

*As you read, also try to grasp the writer's assumptions about the **audience**.* For example, does the writer

- expect readers to be impressed by the writer's courage, honesty, ability, and so on?
- assume readers will have had similar experiences and therefore appreciate what the writer went through and not judge the writer too harshly?
- try to convince the reader that the writer was innocent, well intended, a victim, or something else?
- hope readers will laugh with and not at the writer, seeing the writer's failings as amusing foibles and not as serious shortcomings?

Readings

JEAN BRANDT wrote this essay as a first-year college student. In it, she tells about a memorable event that occurred when she was thirteen. Reflecting on how she felt at the time, Brandt writes, "I was afraid, embarrassed, worried, mad." In disclosing her tumultuous and contradictory remembered feelings, Brandt makes her story dramatic and resonant. Even if readers have not had a similar experience, they are likely to empathize with Brandt and grasp the significance of this event in her life.

As you read, look for places where Brandt lets us know how she felt at the time the event occurred. Also consider the questions in the margin. Your instructor may ask you to post your answers or bring them to class.

Basic Features

- Well told story
- Vivid description
- Significance

Calling Home

Jean Brandt

1   As we all piled into the car, I knew it was going to be a fabulous day. My grandmother was visiting for the holidays; and she and I, along with my older brother and sister, Louis and Susan, were setting off for a day of last-minute Christmas shopping. On the way to the mall, we sang Christmas carols, chattered, and laughed.

How does Brandt set the stage for her story? How does she try to get you to identify with her?

With Christmas only two days away, we were caught up with holiday spirit. I felt light-headed and full of joy. I loved shopping — especially at Christmas.

What additional descriptive detail would help you visualize the place and people?

What is your first impression of Brandt? What is the author's attitude toward her younger self?

The shopping center was swarming with frantic last-minute shoppers like ourselves. We went first to the General Store, my favorite. It carried mostly knickknacks and other useless items which nobody needs but buys anyway. I was thirteen years old at the time, and things like buttons and calendars and posters would catch my fancy. This day was no different. The object of my desire was a 75-cent Snoopy button. Snoopy was the latest. If you owned anything with the Peanuts on it, you were "in." But since I was supposed to be shopping for gifts for other people and not myself, I couldn't decide what to do. I went in search of my sister for her opinion. I pushed my way through throngs of people to the back of the store where I found Susan. I asked her if she thought I should buy the button. She said it was cute and if I wanted it to go ahead and buy it.

When I got back to the Snoopy section, I took one look at the lines at the cashiers and knew I didn't want to wait thirty minutes to buy an item worth less than one dollar. I walked back to the basket where I found the button and was about to drop it when suddenly, instead, I took a quick glance around, assured myself no one could see, and slipped the button into the pocket of my sweatshirt.

What is the effect of all these action verbs (highlighted) in pars. 3–5?

I hesitated for a moment, but once the item was in my pocket, there was no turning back. I had never before stolen anything; but what was done was done. A few seconds later, my sister appeared and asked, "So, did you decide to buy the button?" "No, I guess not." I hoped my voice didn't quaver. As we headed for the entrance, my heart began to race. I just had to get out of that store. Only a few more yards to go and I'd be safe. As we crossed the threshold, I heaved a sigh of relief. I was home free. I thought about how sly I had been and I felt proud of my accomplishment.

An unexpected tap on my shoulder startled me. I whirled around to find a middle-aged man, dressed in street clothes, flashing some type of badge and politely asking me to empty my pockets. Where did this man come from? How did he know? I was so sure that no one had seen me!

On the verge of panicking, I told myself that all I had to do was give this man his button back, say I was sorry, and go on my way. After all, it was only a 75-cent item.

6   Next thing I knew, he was talking about calling the police and having me arrested and thrown in jail, as if he had just nabbed a professional thief instead of a terrified kid. I couldn't believe what he was saying.

7   "Jean, what's going on?"

8   The sound of my sister's voice eased the pressure a bit. She always managed to get me out of trouble. She would come through this time too.

9   "Excuse me. Are you a relative of this young girl?"

10   "Yes, I'm her sister. What's the problem?"

11   "Well, I just caught her shoplifting and I'm afraid I'll have to call the police."

12   "What did she take?"

13   "This button."

14   "A button? You are having a thirteen-year-old arrested for stealing a button?"

15   "I'm sorry, but she broke the law."

16   The man led us through the store and into an office, where we waited for the police officers to arrive. Susan had found my grandmother and brother, who, still shocked, didn't say a word. The thought of going to jail terrified me, not because of jail itself, but because of the encounter with my parents afterward. Not more than ten minutes later, two officers arrived and placed me under arrest. They said that I was to be taken to the station alone. Then, they handcuffed me and led me out of the store. I felt alone and scared. I had counted on my sister being with me, but now I had to muster up the courage to face this ordeal all by myself.

17   As the officers led me through the mall, I sensed a hundred pairs of eyes staring at me. My face flushed and I broke out in a sweat. Now everyone knew I was a criminal. In their eyes I was a juvenile delinquent, and thank God the cops were getting me off the streets. The worst part was thinking my grandmother might be having the same thoughts. The humiliation at that moment was

What do you learn about Brandt from her remembered thoughts in pars. 5–8?

How does your understanding of Brandt deepen or change through what she writes in pars. 16–18?

overwhelming. I felt like Hester Prynne being put on public display for everyone to ridicule.

That short walk through the mall seemed to take hours. But once we reached the squad car, time raced by. I was read my rights and questioned. We were at the police station within minutes. Everything happened so fast I didn't have a chance to feel remorse for my crime. Instead, I viewed what was happening to me as if it were a movie. Being searched, although embarrassing, somehow seemed to be exciting. All the movies and television programs I had seen were actually coming to life. This is what it was really like. But why were criminals always portrayed as frightened and regretful? I was having fun. I thought I had nothing to fear — until I was allowed my one phone call. I was trembling as I dialed home. I didn't know what I was going to say to my parents, especially my mother. 18

"Hi, Dad, this is Jean." 19

"We've been waiting for you to call." 20

"Did Susie tell you what happened?" 21

"Yeah, but we haven't told your mother. I think you should tell her what you did and where you are." 22

"You mean she doesn't even know where I am?" 23

"No, I want you to explain it to her." 24

There was a pause as he called my mother to the phone. For the first time that night, I was close to tears. I wished I had never stolen that stupid pin. I wanted to give the phone to one of the officers because I was too ashamed to tell my mother the truth, but I had no choice. 25

"Jean, where are you?" 26

"I'm, umm, in jail." 27

"Why? What for?" 28

"Shoplifting." 29

"Oh no, Jean. Why? Why did you do it?" 30

"I don't know. No reason. I just did it." 31

"I don't understand. What did you take? Why did you do it? You had plenty of money with you." 32

"I know but I just did it. I can't explain why. Mom, I'm sorry." 33

How does the dialogue in pars. 21–24 add to the drama?

34   "I'm afraid sorry isn't enough. I'm horribly disappointed in you."

35   Long after we got off the phone, while I sat in an empty jail cell, waiting for my parents to pick me up, I could still distinctly hear the disappointment and hurt in my mother's voice. I cried. The tears weren't for me but for her and the pain I had put her through. I felt like a terrible human being. I would rather have stayed in jail than confront my mom right then. I dreaded each passing minute that brought our encounter closer. When the officer came to release me, I hesitated, actually not wanting to leave. We went to the front desk, where I had to sign a form to retrieve my belongings. I saw my parents a few yards away and my heart raced. A large knot formed in my stomach. I fought back the tears.

What is the effect of interweaving storytelling and describing with remembering thoughts and feelings in par. 35?

36   Not a word was spoken as we walked to the car. Slowly, I sank into the back seat anticipating the scolding. Expecting harsh tones, I was relieved to hear almost the opposite from my father.

What do you make of Brandt's account of her father's reaction? Her mother's?

37   "I'm not going to punish you and I'll tell you why. Although I think what you did was wrong, I think what the police did was more wrong. There's no excuse for locking a thirteen-year-old behind bars. That doesn't mean I condone what you did, but I think you've been punished enough already."

38   As I looked from my father's eyes to my mother's, I knew this ordeal was over. Although it would never be forgotten, the incident was not mentioned again.

How well does this ending work?

ANNIE DILLARD, professor emerita at Wesleyan University, won the Pulitzer Prize for nonfiction writing in 1975 with her first book, *Pilgrim at Tinker Creek* (1974). Since then, she has written eleven other books in a variety of genres. They include *Teaching a Stone to Talk* (1988), *The Writing Life* (1990), *The Living* (1993), *Mornings Like This* (1996), and *The Maytrees* (2007). Dillard also wrote an autobiography of her early years, *An American Childhood* (1987), from which the following selection comes.

This reading relates an event that occurred one winter morning when the seven-year-old Dillard and a friend were chased by an adult stranger. Dillard admits that she was terrified at the time, and yet she asserts that she has "seldom been happier since." As you read, think about how this paradox helps you grasp the autobiographical significance of this experience for Dillard.

AN AMERICAN CHILDHOOD
Annie Dillard

Some boys taught me to play football. This was fine sport. You thought up a new strategy for every play and whispered it to the others. You went out for a pass, fooling everyone. Best, you got to throw yourself mightily at someone's running legs. Either you brought him down or you hit the ground flat out on your chin, with your arms empty before you. It was all or nothing. If you hesitated in fear, you would miss and get hurt: you would take a hard fall while the kid got away, or you would get kicked in the face while the kid got away. But if you flung yourself wholeheartedly at the back of his knees — if you gathered and joined body and soul and pointed them diving fearlessly — then you likely wouldn't get hurt, and you'd stop the ball. Your fate, and your team's score, depended on your concentration and courage. Nothing girls did could compare with it.   1

Boys welcomed me at baseball, too, for I had, through enthusiastic practice, what was weirdly known as a boy's arm. In winter, in the snow, there was neither baseball nor football, so the boys and I threw snowballs at passing cars. I got in trouble throwing snowballs, and have seldom been happier since.   2

On one weekday morning after Christmas, six inches of new snow had just fallen. We were standing up to our boot tops in snow on a front yard on trafficked Reynolds Street, waiting for cars. The cars traveled Reynolds Street slowly and evenly; they were targets all but wrapped in red ribbons, cream puffs. We couldn't miss.   3

I was seven; the boys were eight, nine, and ten. The oldest two Fahey boys were there — Mikey and Peter — polite blond boys who lived near me on Lloyd Street, and who already had four brothers and sisters. My parents approved Mikey and Peter Fahey. Chickie McBride was there, a tough kid, and Billy Paul and Mackie Kean too, from across Reynolds, where the boys grew up dark and furious, grew up skinny, knowing, and skilled. We had all drifted from our houses that morning looking for action, and had found it here on Reynolds Street.   4

It was cloudy but cold. The cars' tires laid behind them on the snowy street a complex trail of beige chunks like crenellated castle walls. I had stepped on some earlier; they squeaked. We could not have wished for more traffic. When a car came, we all popped it one. In the intervals between cars we reverted to the natural solitude of children.   5

I started making an iceball — a perfect iceball, from perfectly white snow, perfectly spherical, and squeezed perfectly translucent so no snow remained all the way through. (The Fahey boys and I considered it unfair actually to throw an iceball at somebody, but it had been known to happen.)   6

I had just embarked on the iceball project when we heard tire chains come clanking from afar. A black Buick was moving toward us down the street. We all spread out,   7 banged together some regular snowballs, took aim, and, when the Buick drew nigh, fired.

8   A soft snowball hit the driver's windshield right before the driver's face. It made a smashed star with a hump in the middle.

9   Often, of course, we hit our target, but this time, the only time in all of life, the car pulled over and stopped. Its wide black door opened; a man got out of it, running. He didn't even close the car door.

10   He ran after us, and we ran away from him, up the snowy Reynolds sidewalk. At the corner, I looked back; incredibly, he was still after us. He was in city clothes: a suit and tie, street shoes. Any normal adult would have quit, having sprung us into flight and made his point. This man was gaining on us. He was a thin man, all action. All of a sudden, we were running for our lives.

11   Wordless, we split up. We were on our turf; we could lose ourselves in the neighborhood backyards, everyone for himself. I paused and considered. Everyone had vanished except Mikey Fahey, who was just rounding the corner of a yellow brick house. Poor Mikey, I trailed him. The driver of the Buick sensibly picked the two of us to follow. The man apparently had all day.

12   He chased Mikey and me around the yellow house and up a backyard path we knew by heart: under a low tree, up a bank, through a hedge, down some snowy steps, and across the grocery store's delivery driveway. We smashed through a gap in another hedge, entered a scruffy backyard, and ran around its back porch and tight between houses to Edgerton Avenue; we ran across Edgerton to an alley and up our own sliding woodpile to the Halls' front yard; he kept coming. We ran up Lloyd Street and wound through mazy backyards toward the steep hilltop at Willard and Lang.

13   He chased us silently, block after block. He chased us silently over picket fences, through thorny hedges, between houses, around garbage cans, and across streets. Every time I glanced back, choking for breath, I expected he would have quit. He must have been as breathless as we were. His jacket strained over his body. It was an immense discovery, pounding into my hot head with every sliding, joyous step, that this ordinary adult evidently knew what I thought only children who trained at football knew: that you have to fling yourself at what you're doing, you have to point yourself, forget yourself, aim, dive.

14   Mikey and I had nowhere to go, in our own neighborhood or out of it, but away from this man who was chasing us. He impelled us forward; we compelled him to follow our route. The air was cold; every breath tore my throat. We kept running, block after block; we kept improvising, backyard after backyard, running a frantic course and choosing it simultaneously, failing always to find small places or hard places to slow him down, and discovering always, exhilarated, dismayed, that only bare speed could save us — for he would never give up, this man — and we were losing speed.

15   He chased us through the backyard labyrinths of ten blocks before he caught us by our jackets. He caught us and we all stopped.

16   We three stood staggering, half blinded, coughing, in an obscure hilltop backyard: a man in his twenties, a boy, a girl. He had released our jackets, our pursuer, our captor,

our hero: he knew we weren't going anywhere. We all played by the rules. Mikey and I unzipped our jackets. I pulled off my sopping mittens. Our tracks multiplied in the backyard's new snow. We had been breaking new snow all morning. We didn't look at each other. I was cherishing my excitement. The man's lower pants legs were wet; his cuffs were full of snow, and there was a prow of snow beneath them on his shoes and socks. Some trees bordered the little flat backyard, some messy winter trees. There was no one around: a clearing in a grove, and we the only players.

It was a long time before he could speak. I had some difficulty at first recalling why we were there. My lips felt swollen; I couldn't see out of the sides of my eyes; I kept coughing.   17

"You stupid kids," he began perfunctorily.   18

We listened perfunctorily indeed, if we listened at all, for the chewing out was redundant, a mere formality, and beside the point. The point was that he had chased us passionately without giving up, and so he had caught us. Now he came down to earth. I wanted the glory to last forever.   19

But how could the glory have lasted forever? We could have run through every backyard in North America until we got to Panama. But when he trapped us at the lip of the Panama Canal, what precisely could he have done to prolong the drama of the chase and cap its glory? I brooded about this for the next few years. He could only have fried Mikey Fahey and me in boiling oil, say, or dismembered us piecemeal, or staked us to anthills. None of which I really wanted, and none of which any adult was likely to do, even in the spirit of fun. He could only chew us out there in the Panamanian jungle, after months or years of exalting pursuit. He could only begin, "You stupid kids," and continue in his ordinary Pittsburgh accent with his normal righteous anger and the usual common sense.   20

If in that snowy backyard the driver of the black Buick had cut off our heads, Mikey's and mine, I would have died happy, for nothing has required so much of me since as being chased all over Pittsburgh in the middle of winter — running terrified, exhausted — by this sainted, skinny, furious redheaded man who wished to have a word with us. I don't know how he found his way back to his car.   21

MAKING CONNECTIONS: ACTING FEARLESSLY

At the beginning of the essay, Dillard tells about being taught by the neighborhood boys the joy of playing football, particularly the "all or nothing" of flinging yourself "fearlessly" (par. 1).

With other students in your class, discuss an occasion when you had an opportunity to fling yourself fearlessly into an activity that posed some challenge or risk or required special effort. For example, like Dillard, you may have been challenged by your team members at a football game or by a group of volunteers helping during a natural disaster. Or you may have felt pressured by friends to do something that went against your better judgment, was illegal, or was dangerous.

Take turns briefly telling what happened. Then, together, consider the following questions as you discuss what now seems significant about this particular experience:

- What made you embrace the challenge or resist it? What do you think your choice tells about you at the time of the event?

- Dillard uses the value term *courage* to describe the fearless behavior she learned playing football. What value term would you use to describe your own experience? For example, were you being selfless or *self-serving; responsible* or *irresponsible;* a *follower, leader,* or *self-reliant individual*?

ANALYZING WRITING STRATEGIES

Basic Features

Your instructor may assign these activities in class or as homework, for you to do by yourself or with classmates.

● A Well-Told Story

To construct an action sequence in writing, Dillard combines two narrating strategies: *specific narrative actions* and *prepositional phrases.* **Specific narrative actions** show people moving and gesturing through the use of

- action verbs (for example, "He *ran* after us, and we *ran* away from him. . . . We *were running* for our lives" in par. 10), and

- modifying phrases that use the *-ing* form of the verb as a modifier (for example, "Every time I glanced back, *choking* for breath" in par. 13).

Prepositional phrases tell us where the action is taking place. When combined with specific narrative actions, prepositional phrases enable Dillard to create continuing movement through space. To see how she does this, look at the first sentence in paragraph 12 with the prepositional phrases highlighted:

> He chased Mikey and me around the yellow house and up a backyard path we knew by heart: under a low tree, up a bank, through a hedge, down some snowy steps, and across the grocery store's delivery driveway.

To analyze how Dillard uses specific narrative actions with prepositional phrases, do the following:

- Reread paragraphs 11–13, and find three other examples of specific narrative actions combined with prepositional phrases.

- Write a sentence about how well you think these narrating strategies work in the essay. What effect do they have?

● **Vivid Description of People and Places**

Describing — naming objects and detailing their colors, shape, size, textures, and other qualities — is an important writing strategy in remembered event essays. To see how writers use **naming** and **detailing** to create vivid images, look closely at Dillard's description of an iceball:

> I started making an iceball — a [perfect] iceball, from [perfectly white] snow, [perfectly spherical], and [squeezed perfectly translucent] so no snow remained all the way through. (par. 6)

Notice that she names two things (underlined): *iceball* and *snow*. She adds to these names descriptive details (in brackets) — *white* (color), *spherical* (shape), and *translucent* (appearance) — that help readers imagine more precisely what an iceball looks like. She also repeats the words *perfect* and *perfectly* (highlighted) to emphasize the color, shape, and appearance of this particular iceball.

To analyze Dillard's use of the describing strategies of naming and detailing to present places and people, do the following:

- Reread paragraphs 10 and 12, where she describes the man and the neighborhood through which he chases her and Mikey.
- Underline the names of people and objects (nouns).
- Put brackets around the words and phrases that modify the nouns they name.
- Write a couple of sentences explaining what you notice about the relative amount of naming and detailing Dillard uses in these paragraphs and the kinds of details she chooses to include.

● **Autobiographical Significance**

Writers convey significance by a combination of *showing* and *telling*. **Showing**, through the careful choice of words and details, creates an overall or *dominant impression*. **Telling** includes the narrator's *remembered feelings and thoughts* together with her *present perspective* on what happened and why it is significant.

To analyze Dillard's use of **showing** to convey significance, do the following:

- Reread paragraphs 7, 10, 13, 16, 18, 20–21, and highlight the details Dillard uses to describe the man, how he dresses, the car he drives, and especially the way he talks when he catches the kids.
- Write a couple of sentences characterizing the dominant impression you get of the man from these details and what they suggest about why he chases the kids.

To analyze Dillard's use of **telling** to convey significance, do the following:

- Reread paragraphs 15–21, and highlight the key words Dillard uses to tell readers what she thinks of the man and the chase.
- Write a couple of sentences explaining what these key words tell you about the significance of the experience for Dillard.

- Write another sentence discussing how the opening anecdote about learning to play football fearlessly and courageously helps you understand the significance of the event for Dillard.

CONSIDERING TOPICS FOR YOUR OWN ESSAY

Like Dillard, you could write about a time when an adult did something entirely unexpected during your childhood, an action that seemed dangerous or threatening to you, or something humorous, kind, or generous. List two or three of these occasions. Consider unpredictable actions of adults in your immediate or extended family, adults you had come to know outside your family, and strangers. As you consider these possible topics, think about your purpose and audience: What would you want your instructor and classmates to learn about you from reading about this particular event?

 TREY ELLIS is a film professor at Columbia University and a prolific writer. He has written novels including *Right Here, Right Now* (1999), winner of the American Book Award; plays and screenplays, including *The Tuskegee Airmen* (1995); and essays published in notable newspapers and magazines such as the *Washington Post, Newsweek*, and *Salon*. He also does commentary for NPR's *All Things Considered* and blogs for the *Huffington Post* and his own Web site, *treyellis.com*. His most recent publication is *Bedtime Stories: Adventures in the Land of Single-Fatherhood* (2008), from which this essay was adapted for publication in the *New York Times*.

The reading tells what happened when Ellis was twenty-two years old and visited his father in France. Ellis includes a photograph of his father. As you read, think about what the photograph adds to your reading of the essay.

When the Walls Came Tumbling Down

TREY ELLIS

1   A year before his death, my dad was forced to come out to me. I thought he was in Paris for a vacation. Instead, he was there for treatment with AZT, which in 1986 was experimental and not yet approved in the United States for people infected with the virus that causes AIDS.

■ The author's father, Dr. William Ellis, in 1983, a few years before he became ill.

After my mother died when I was 16, my dad fulfilled his life-long dream and moved us from Hamden, a suburb of New Haven, to Manhattan and there raised me alone. Moving from our modest three-bedroom in suburban Connecticut to a majestic pre-war on the corner of West 81st Street and Riverside Drive made me feel like George Jefferson in the television comedy series "The Jeffersons." During my first year there, I unconsciously found myself humming the show's theme song, "Movin' On Up," every time I passed our uniformed doormen.

I might have had my suspicions about my father's sexuality (finding an International Male catalog, with its all-male photo layouts, under his mattress probably should have tipped me off years earlier). But back then I couldn't reconcile my love for him with my own juvenile homophobia.

That August, I was 22, a year out of college and visiting my father in Paris, where he had found a sublet off Place d'Italie on the Boulevard de Port Royal. He said he was interviewing for a spot as a roving State Department psychiatrist based there. The job was a world away from his work at the time, as a child psychiatrist shepherding hundreds of troubled kids at a center run by Harlem Hospital.

It wasn't until my father opened the door that I realized something terrifyingly life-altering was about to be revealed. Always movie-star handsome, he looked older than I had remembered him, and his light green eyes had gone dull.

"Trey, I'm not here to work for the State Department," he said. "I wanted to, but then I got sick."

O.K. He's sick. He'll get better. I'll help him get better.

"Have you heard of ARC, AIDS-related complex?"

Did he just say he's got AIDS?

"It's not AIDS. They just don't want it to ever turn into AIDS so I came here to try this new drug called AZT."

"Rock Hudson came here, right? He took the same stuff and he died."

"Not everyone dies."

He told me he had been with some men, but that he thought he had always been careful.

I said I had to go for a walk.

This is impossible, I was thinking. My mom killed herself when I was still a teenager. After she died, I loved my dad so hard, for both of them. But remember it's not AIDS, I told myself, just some sort of pre-AIDS. The best scientists in the world are working on only this problem. They'll find some pill, I told myself. I'll help them find some pill. We'll get though this and say: "Phew! That was a close one!"

16   When I returned to his apartment, I was almost smiling. My bad luck would be cosmically counterbalanced by the miraculous good luck of having a father who would be the very first person in the world to recover from AIDS.

17   We never left each other's sight that week. Without his huge secret between us, we could now talk about anything. He told me about his boyfriends and girlfriends and his heartaches, and as long as he didn't give too much information I was happy to listen.

18   We became best friends. And when he returned home to New York, I was his live-in nurse for those last six months, supercharging his Cream of Wheat with heavy cream to try to keep his weight up, emptying his dialysis bag several times a day after his kidneys failed, and sharing his king-size bed.

19   By Christmas he seemed better and my plan was for the cure to arrive some time in the middle of the following year. So in mid-January, when he was admitted into St. Luke's Roosevelt Hospital Center with AIDS-related pneumonia, I refused to panic. The doctors said opportunistic infections were to be expected. Sitting up in his hospital bed, my dad displayed a calm nobility I still try to remember to emulate. He explained that if the pneumonia didn't surrender to the antibiotics, he very likely would die.

20   He said that at his memorial service he wanted a childhood friend turned opera singer to sing an old spiritual, "There's a Man Goin' Round Taking Names." I took notes just to humor him, but assured him that he was just being a drama queen. Five days later, my godfather, also a physician, called me at 3 a.m. and told me to hurry back to the hospital.

21   When I showed up, my father's eyes were Caribbean clear, yet huge and eerily calm, though it was hard to see the rest of his face through all the white tape and the plastic tubing. My fingers found his, and we stared at each other as I cried.

22   I wished he could still speak, because I was in no shape to say anything more than that I loved him. I wanted to tell him that I'd be fine. That he'd raised me just perfectly right. I went home to the apartment. A few hours later he was dead, four days short of 50.

23   In those days, no one spoke about AIDS. No one outside a small circle knew for sure why my father died. Even now, 22 years later, what's left of my family has pleaded with me not to tell the truth.

24   My dad never understood how he could have contracted AIDS. He swore that he was scrupulously hygienic. I subsequently learned from a family doctor, who had checked my dad's records, that my father's AIDS must have been passed along by a tainted blood transfusion.

25   The explanation was an odd blessing. If my dad had known what caused his AIDS, he probably never would have come out to me. He would have died with so many secrets still lodged in his heart. And I would have never known my father with the fullness every child craves. Embarrassment is always the price we pay for more intimacy. Perhaps there is no such thing as too much information.

MAKING CONNECTIONS: INTIMACY

Ellis concludes his essay by pointing out the irony that if his father had known that he got AIDS from a blood transfusion, "he probably never would have come out to me. . . . Embarrassment is always the price we pay for more intimacy. Perhaps there is no such thing as too much information." Ellis seems to be defining intimacy as the ability to be open with another person and share the most personal information. He describes how after his father came out to him, they became "best friends" because they could "talk about anything" (pars. 17–18).

With other students in your class, discuss your experience and understanding of intimacy by describing a relationship you have with a close friend or family member. Note that we're not talking about sexual intimacy, but about strictly emotional intimacy. You may choose to talk about a relationship that has *not* become intimate, perhaps because of embarrassment, lack of trust, fear of being rejected, or the need to control. Don't feel constrained to share details; just describe the kinds of things you feel comfortable sharing.

Discuss what you learned about intimacy from this relationship. To help keep your discussion focused, consider the following questions:

- What do you look for in an intimate relationship?

- Ellis generalizes that embarrassment is a barrier to intimacy. What else could have prevented the relationship between Ellis and his father from becoming intimate?

ANALYZING WRITING STRATEGIES

● ● ●
Basic Features

● **A Well-Told Story**

To keep readers' interest, even the most exciting stories, like Dillard's story of being chased through city streets and backyards, need to be organized in a way that builds suspense and tension. A common way to represent the dramatic organization of a narrative is with a pyramid:

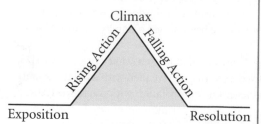

Climax

Rising Action Falling Action

Exposition Resolution

Exposition: Background information is presented, the scene set, and characters introduced.
Rising Action: The basic conflict is set off by an inciting incident, arousing curiosity and suspense, and possibly leading to other conflicts and complications.
Climax: The emotional high point, often a turning point marking a change for good or ill, is reached.
Falling Action: Tension subsides and conflicts unravel, but may include a final surprise.
Resolution: Conflicts come to an end, but may not be fully resolved.

You can use this pyramid to analyze the structure of a story you're reading or to out-line a story you're planning to write (see p. 45).

If you compare the dramatic structure of Dillard's story to Brandt's, you will see that the two writers give more space to different elements of the story. After several paragraphs of exposition, Dillard devotes most of the story to the rising action as the man chases Dillard and Mikey relentlessly through streets and backyards. The climax comes when he catches the kids, but the story ends without description of the falling action or resolution. Brandt has a more complicated rising action that includes the mini-climaxes of getting caught and getting arrested before the final confrontation with her parents, followed by falling action and a briefly stated resolution.

To analyze how Ellis organizes his story, do the following:

- Skim the essay and note in the margin where you find the exposition, rising action, climax, falling action, and resolution. Does Ellis's story have one climax or more than one?

- Write a few sentences indicating how useful it is for you to outline the story in this way. Describe another way of outlining the story if you think that it would be more useful.

● Vivid Description of People

Writers of remembered event essays typically describe people sparingly, using just a few choice details. For example, Brandt names her relatives but never describes them; although she does mention looking into her parents' eyes, she doesn't describe their expressions. The only person she describes is the store detective: a "middle-aged man, dressed in street clothes, flashing some type of badge" (par. 5). Dillard, in contrast, gives us brief descriptions of several neighborhood boys: "Mikey and Peter — polite blond boys," as well as the other boys "from across Reynolds, where the boys grew up dark and furious, grew up skinny, knowing, and skilled" (par. 4). As you've discovered in analyzing how she describes the man who chased her and Mikey, Dillard's descrip-tion is brief but vivid.

To analyze how Ellis describes his father, do the following:

- Reread the following two brief descriptions, underlining the objects being described and putting brackets around the words and phrases that describe them (detailing such things as the color, shape, size, and appearance of the objects):

It wasn't until my father opened the door that I realized something terrifyingly life-altering was about to be revealed. Always movie-star handsome, he looked older than I had remembered him, and his light green eyes had gone dull. (par. 5)

When I showed up, my father's eyes were Caribbean clear, yet huge and eerily calm, though it was hard to see the rest of his face through all the white tape and the plastic tubing. (par. 21)

- Write a couple of sentences reflecting on the **dominant impression** created by these two descriptions, pointing out the naming and detailing that stands out for you.

Autobiographical Significance

Writers convey the significance of events by telling how they felt and what they thought at the time the event occurred and by telling what they think now as they look back on the event. Here's an example from Brandt's essay where she presents her **remembered feelings and thoughts**:

> I felt like a terrible human being. I would rather have stayed in jail than confront my mom right then. I dreaded each passing minute that brought our encounter closer. (par. 35)

The following example from Dillard's essay shows the writer's reflections looking back on the event from her **present perspective**:

> . . . what precisely could he have done to prolong the drama of the chase and cap its glory? I brooded about this for the next few years. (par. 20)

Obviously, in writing about his father's illness and death, Ellis has chosen a subject that is inherently significant — both important in his life and deeply meaningful.

To analyze how Ellis presents his remembered feelings and thoughts as well as his present perspective, follow these suggestions:

- Reread paragraphs 6–10, where Ellis alternates dialogue with thoughts he had but didn't express at the time, and highlight the remembered thoughts.
- Reread paragraphs 22–24, and highlight in another color Ellis's present reflections from his perspective.
- Write a few sentences explaining what you learn about Ellis from his remembered thoughts and from his present perspective.

> ##### ANALYZING VISUALS
>
> ---
>
> #### PHOTOGRAPH OF TREY ELLIS'S FATHER
>
> Write a paragraph or two analyzing the photograph Ellis includes in his remembered event essay and explaining what it contributes to the essay.
>
> To analyze the visual, you can use the Criteria for Analyzing Visuals chart on pp. 390–91. The chart offers a series of questions you can ask yourself under two categories: Key Components and Rhetorical Context. You will see that there are a lot of questions, but don't feel you have to answer all of them. Focus on the questions that seem most productive in helping you write a short analysis. Try beginning with these questions that specifically refer to Ellis's photograph:
>
> **People**
>
> - Why do you think Ellis chose a photograph of his father alone rather than one with both of them in it?

Scene

- Why do you think Ellis chose a photograph of his father in his office rather than at home or elsewhere?
- What impression do you get of Ellis's dad from the way his office looks — for example, from the piles of files and books as well as the other objects on the desk?

Rhetorical Context

- How does the photograph's portrayal of Ellis's dad add to Ellis's description of him in paragraphs 5 and 21? Note that in the original *New York Times* article, the photo was black-and-white. What, if anything, is the effect of reproducing it in color, as we do here?
- How does seeing Ellis's father as a doctor help you understand the tone his dad adopts when he tells Ellis about his illness in paragraphs 6, 8, 10, and 12?

CONSIDERING TOPICS FOR YOUR OWN ESSAY

In one sense, the event Ellis writes about was tragic: The news his father broke to him was of an illness that led to his death a few short months later. Ellis tells us, however, that the event had an unexpectedly positive side effect: It gave him an opportunity to help his dad and get to know him in a new way. For your own essay, you, too, might consider writing about an event that had an unexpectedly positive outcome. Ellis's essay also suggests the possibility of writing about an event that challenged your preconceptions or prejudices. Ellis tells us that learning about his father's sexual orientation challenged his "own juvenile homophobia" (par. 3). As you consider these possible topics, think about your purpose and audience. What would you want your instructor and classmates to learn about you from reading about this particular event?

Guide to Writing

The Writing Assignment

Write an essay about an event in your life that will engage readers and that will, at the same time, help them understand the significance of the event. Tell your story dramatically and vividly.

This Guide to Writing will help you apply what you have learned about how writers invest their remembered event essays with drama, vividness, and significance. The Guide is divided into five sections with various activities in each section:

- **Invention and Research**
- **Planning and Drafting**
- **Critical Reading Guide**
- **Revising**
- **Editing and Proofreading**

The Guide is designed to escort you through the writing process, from finding an event to editing your finished essay. Your instructor may require you to follow the Guide to Writing from beginning to end. Working through the Guide to Writing in this way will help you — as it has helped many other college students — write a thoughtful, fully developed, polished essay.

If, however, your instructor gives you latitude to choose and if you have had experience writing a remembered event essay, then you can decide on the order in which you'll do the activities in the Guide to Writing. For example, the Invention and Research section includes activities to help you find an event, sketch the story, describe the people and places, and explore significance. Obviously, finding an event must precede the other activities, but you may come to the Guide with an event already in mind, and you may choose to explore its significance before sketching the story or begin by describing the place it happened because it is particularly vivid in your memory. In fact, you may find your response to one of the invention activities expanding into a draft before you've had a chance to do any of the other activities. That's a good thing — but you should later flesh out your draft by going back to the activities you skipped and layering the new material into your draft.

The following chart will help you find answers to many of the questions you might have about planning, drafting, and revising a remembered event essay. The page references in the right-hand column refer to examples from the readings and activities in the Guide to Writing.

Starting Points: Remembering an Event

●●● Basic Features

Choosing an Event	
How do I come up with an event to write about?	• Considering Topics for Your Own Essay (pp. 29, 35) • Choosing an Event to Write About (pp. 38–40) • Testing Your Choice (p. 42)
What's my purpose in writing? How can I interest my audience?	• Defining Your Purpose and Audience (p. 44) • Refining Your Purpose and Setting Goals (p. 45)

A Well-Told Story	
How can I make the story of my event dramatic?	• Add specific narrative actions (p. 27) • Construct a narrative outline (pp. 32–33) • Constructing a Well-Told Story: Explore a Revealing or Pivotal Moment (p. 40) • Refining Your Purpose and Setting Goals (p. 45)
How can I help readers keep track of what happened?	• Use prepositional phrases (p. 27) • A Sentence Strategy: Time Transitions and Verb Tenses (pp. 47–48)
How should I organize my story?	• Construct a narrative outline (pp. 32–33) • Outlining Your Draft (pp. 45–46)

Vivid Description of People and Places	
How can I make my description of the place where the event happened vivid and specific?	• Use concrete naming and specific detailing (p. 28) • Constructing a Well-Told Story: Describing the Place (p. 41) • Exploring Memorabilia (pp. 42–43)
How can I create a vivid impression of people?	• Use concrete naming and specific detailing (p. 28) • Constructing a Well-Told Story: Recalling Key People (p. 41) • Exploring Memorabilia (pp. 42–43)

	Autobiographical Significance
How can I help readers grasp the significance of my story?	• Use showing and telling (p. 28) • Constructing a Well-Told Story: Reflect on the Conflict and Its Significance (p. 40) • Reflecting on the Event's Autobiographical Significance (pp. 43–44) • Considering Your Thesis (p. 44) • Refining Your Purpose and Setting Goals (pp. 45–46)
How can I make a dominant impression?	• Constructing a Well-Told Story: Create a Dominant Impression (p. 41) • Considering Your Thesis (p. 44)

Invention and Research

The following invention activities are easy to complete and take only a few minutes. Spreading out the activities over several days will stimulate your memory, enabling you to recall details and to reflect deeply on the event's meaning. Remember to keep a written record of your invention work: You'll need it when you draft the essay and later when you revise it.

Choosing an Event to Write About

List several significant past events in your life, and choose one to explore. This will come more easily to some of us than to others. Bear in mind that you're looking for an event that meets the following criteria:

Criteria for Choosing an Event: A Checklist

The event should
- ☐ take place over a short period of time (preferably just a few hours);
- ☐ center on conflict (a personal struggle or an external confrontation);
- ☐ disclose something significant about your life;
- ☐ allow you to portray yourself in a way that you feel comfortable sharing with your instructor and classmates;
- ☐ reveal complex or ambivalent feelings (rather than superficial and sentimental ones);
- ☐ lead readers to think about their own experience and about the cultural forces that shape their lives.

If you're like most people, you'll need some help in coming up with a number of good options. To get your juices flowing, you might first try quickly rereading the Considering Topics for Your Own Essay activities following the readings, and recalling any events those suggestions brought to mind. Reread any notes you might have made in response to these suggestions.

For further ideas, consult the suggestions in the following sections:

Types of Events to Consider

- a difficult situation (for example, when you had to make a tough choice and face the consequences, or when you let someone down or someone you admired let you down)

- an occasion when things did not turn out as expected (for example, when you expected to be criticized but were praised or ignored instead, or when you were convinced you would succeed but failed)

- an incident that changed you in a particular way or revealed an aspect of your personality you had not seen before (for example, dependence, insecurity, ambition, jealousy, or heroism)

- an event in which an encounter with another person led you to consider seriously someone else's point of view or changed you (for example, the way you view yourself, your ideas about how you fit into a particular group or community)

- an incident in which you had a conflict with someone else or a serious misunderstanding that made you feel unjustly treated or in which you realize you mistreated someone else (for example, an incident of racial bias, sexual harassment, false accusation, or hurtful gossip)

- an incident that made you reexamine a basic value or belief (for example, when you were expected to do something that went against your values or make a decision about which you were deeply conflicted)

- an event that made you aware of your interest in or aptitude for a particular career or convinced you that you were not cut out for a particular career

- an event that revealed to you other people's surprising assumptions about you (as a student, friend, colleague, or worker)

Using the Web to Find and Explore an Event

Exploring Web sites where people write about their life experiences might inspire you by triggering memories of similar events in your own life. Moreover, the Internet provides a rich repository of cultural and historical information, including photographs and music, which you might be able to use to prime your memory and create a richly detailed, multimedia text for your readers.

Here are some suggestions:

- Investigate Web sites such as Citystories.com, StoryPreservation.com, and MemoryArchive.org where people post brief stories about their lives.

- Search sites like Facebook featuring people you are writing about, as well as sites of friends, family members, or others who have been important to you.

- Look for sites related to places or activities — such as neighborhoods, schools, workplaces, sports events, or films — that you associate with the event you are writing about.

- Take a look at narrative history sites such as Survivors' Stories, Katrina Stories, and Sixties Personal Narrative Project to see what people who experienced these events are writing about.

Make notes of any ideas, memories, or insights suggested by your online research, and download any visuals you might include in your essay, being sure to get the information necessary to cite any online sources. (See pp. 505–07 for the MLA citation format for electronic sources.)

Ways In: Constructing a Well-Told Story

Basic Features

Once you've made a preliminary choice of an event, the following activities will help you begin to construct a well-told story, with vivid descriptions of people and places. You can begin with whichever basic activity you want, but wherever you begin, be sure to return to the other activities to fill in the details.

Shaping the Story

Sketch the Story. *Write a quick sketch telling roughly what happened.* Don't worry about what you're leaving out; you can fill in the details later.

Explore a Revealing or Pivotal Moment. *Write for a few minutes developing a moment of surprise, confrontation, crisis, change, or discovery that may become the climax of your story.* To dramatize it, try using specific narrative actions and dialogue.

Reflect on the Conflict and Its Significance. *Identify the conflict, and do some exploratory writing about it.* If it was an internal conflict, a struggle within yourself, how does the event reflect what you were going through? If it was an external confrontation between you and someone else, how can you dramatize what occurred? Do exploratory writing of both kinds if the conflict was both internal and external, as it was for Brandt.

Describing the Place

Reimagine the Place. *Identify the place where the event occurred, and describe it.* What do you see, hear, or smell? Use details — shape, color, texture — to evoke the scene.

Research Visuals. *Try to locate visuals you could include in your essay:* Look through memorabilia such as family photographs, yearbooks, newspaper articles, concert programs, ticket stubs, or T-shirts — anything that might stimulate your memory and help you reflect on the place. If you submit your essay electronically or post it online, also consider adding music that you associate with the event. (You may need to cite where you found your sources, so keep a record.)

Recalling Key People

Describe People. *Write about people who played a role in the event.* For each person, name and detail a few distinctive physical features, mannerisms, dress, and so on.

Create a Dialogue. *Reconstruct one important conversation you had during the event.* You will probably not remember exactly what was said, but try to re-create the spirit of the interaction.

Research People. *Do some research, and add to your invention notes any thoughts or feelings suggested by what you find.* Look for photographs, e-mails, letters, or videos from the time of the event. Contact people involved in the event. Imagine having a conversation with someone who was there: What would you say about what happened? How might the person respond?

Creating a Dominant Impression

Reread what you have written for Shaping the Story, Describing the Place, and Recalling Key People, and consider the overall or dominant impression of your descriptions. Review your word choices and descriptive details, and add language to strengthen the impression you want to make. Imagine writing a song or making a film based on this event. If you were making a film, what mood or atmosphere would you try to create? If you were writing a song, what kind would you write — blues, hip-hop, country, rock? What kind of refrain would it have? Try not to oversimplify or sugarcoat the meanings; instead, note where your description points to complexities and contradictions that could deepen your story.

Testing Your Choice

After having made some attempts to construct the story, you should pause to decide whether you recall enough of the event and care enough about it to write about it. Test your choice using the following questions:

- *Will I be able to reconstruct enough of the story and describe the place and people with enough vivid detail to make my story dramatic and create a dominant impression?*
- *Do I feel drawn toward understanding what this event meant to me then and means to me now?* You need not yet understand the significance, but you should feel compelled to explore it — keeping in mind that you will decide what you want to disclose in your essay.
- *Do I feel comfortable writing about this event for my instructor and classmates?* You are not writing a diary entry. Rather, you are writing a public document — a fact that may give you pause, but may also inspire you.

If you lose confidence in your choice, return to the list of possible events you made, and choose another event.

A Collaborative Activity:

Testing Your Choice

Get together with two or three other students to try out your story. Your classmates' reactions will help you determine whether you have chosen an event you can present in an interesting way.

Storytellers: Take turns telling your story briefly, describing the place and key people. Try to pique your listeners' curiosity and build suspense.

Listeners: Briefly tell each storyteller what you found most intriguing about the story. For example, consider these questions:

- Were you eager to know how the story would turn out?
- Was there a clear conflict that seemed important enough to write about?
- Were you able to identify with the storyteller?
- Could you understand why the event was significant for the storyteller?

Exploring Memorabilia

Memorabilia are visual images, video clips, recordings, and objects that can help you remember details and explore the personal and cultural significance of an event. Examples include photographs, Facebook pages, e-mails, old telephone book entries, newspaper clippings, music, and ticket stubs. Memorabilia are not required for success with this assignment, but they may prove helpful in stimulating your memory.

Look for memorabilia relevant to the event, and add to your invention notes details about the time period, places, and people that the memorabilia suggest. In addition to personal memorabilia, you could do research on the historical period or the cultural context in which the event you are writing about took place, collecting images or other records of relevant material. Consider including memorabilia in your essay by photo-copying, scanning, or downloading images or other records into your electronic document. If your project will be submitted electronically, you should consider including sound, video, links, and other digital material that's relevant to your event.

Ways In: Reflecting on the Event's Autobiographical Significance

Basic Features

The following activities will help you to understand the meaning that the event holds in your life and to develop ways to convey this significance to your readers. It might help to move back and forth between your memory of the experience and how you see it now — examining changes in your attitude toward the event and your younger self. Also move between your past and present feelings and the dominant impression your description and narrative makes. Often, our word choices — what we focus on and how we describe it, especially the comparisons we draw — can tell us a lot about our feelings.

Recalling Your Remembered Feelings and Thoughts

Write for a few minutes, exploring what you can say or show that will let readers know how you felt and what you thought at the time the event occurred.

- What did you feel — angry or subdued, in control or vulnerable, proud or embarrassed, or a combination of contradictory feelings?
- How did you show or express your feelings?
- What did you want others to think of you at the time?
- What did you think of yourself? If at the time you thought the event was memorable, why? If not, what made you change your mind?
- How aware were you at the time of the cultural context in which the event took place? How do you think it affected you?

Exploring Your Present Perspective

Write for a few minutes, exploring what you can say or show that will let readers know what you now think and feel about the event as you look back.

- How have your feelings changed?
- What do your actions at the time of the event say about the person you were then? How would you respond to the same event today?

(continued)

(continued)

> • What do you understand now about the conflicts, internal and external, underlying the event? For example, did you struggle with contradictory desires? Were your needs in conflict with someone else's?
> • Try to recall what else was happening in your life at the time and how it may have affected your experience. What music, movies, sports, or books did you like? What concerns did you have at home, school, work, play? What do they suggest about who you were at the time?
> • How did the event relate to power — that is, to asserting yourself, pleasing someone, or being pressured by someone else?
> • How can looking at the event historically or culturally help explain it? How did your situation resemble what was happening to other people at the time? How did it relate to social norms and expectations?

Defining Your Purpose and Audience

Write for several minutes exploring what you want your readers to understand about the significance in your life of the event you have chosen to write about. Use these questions to help you clarify your thoughts:

- *Who are my readers, and what are they likely to think of me when they read about this event? What do I want them to think of me?*

- *What about this event is likely to be familiar to my readers and what might surprise them, perhaps encouraging them to think in new ways or to question some of their assumptions and stereotypes?*

- *What will writing about this event enable me to suggest about myself as an individual?*

- *What will it let me suggest about the social and cultural forces that helped shape me — for example, how people exercise power over one another, how family or community values and attitudes affect individuals, or how economic and social conditions impact our lives?*

Considering Your Thesis

Review what you wrote for Reflecting on the Event's Autobiographical Significance and Defining Your Purpose and Audience, and add another two or three sentences extending your insights. These sentences must necessarily be tentative because you may not yet fully understand the event's significance.

Keep in mind that readers do not expect you to begin your remembered event essay with the kind of explicit thesis statement typical of argumentative or explanatory writing. You are not obliged to announce the significance, but you must convey it through the way you tell the story and through the dominant impression you create.

Planning and Drafting

The following activities will help you refine your purpose, set goals for your draft, and outline it. In addition, this section will help you write a draft by writing opening sentences, trying out a useful sentence strategy, and learning how to work with sources.

Refining Your Purpose and Setting Goals

Here are some questions that may help you sharpen your purpose for your audience and set goals before you start to draft. Your instructor may ask you to write out your answers to some of these questions or simply to think about them as you plan and draft your essay.

Clarifying Your Purpose and Audience

- *What do I want my readers to think of me as I was then and as I am now?*
- *How can I avoid viewing the past with nostalgia, oversimplifying complicated feelings, or tacking on a moral?*
- *How can I help readers understand the event's meaning in my life — for example, how it tested or changed me, gave me insight, or made me question my assumptions?*
- *How can I lead readers to think in new ways or to question some of their own assumptions or stereotypes?*

Crafting Your Story

- *How can I present the conflict so that readers identify with me and can vicariously experience what I felt?*
- *How can I make my story dramatic — arousing curiosity and building suspense?*
- *How can I not only make the climax an emotional high point in the story but also explain it as a meaningful turning point in my life?*
- *How can I describe people and places vividly so that readers can imagine what it was like and also create a dominant impression that shows the event's significance?*
- *How can I tell readers what I thought and felt at the time, and feel now looking back, without self-justification or moralizing?*

Outlining Your Draft

With your purpose and goals in mind, reread what you wrote in response to the Shaping the Story activity (p. 40). Then make an outline to plan your story. You can make a simple scratch outline or create a chart like the one that follows, which shows the elements of the dramatic narrative pyramid (see p. 32) with examples from Jean Brandt's essay.

Example: "Calling Home" by Jean Brandt (pp. 19–23)

Exposition	I want to set the stage — the time, place, people, and mood — at the very beginning: Christmas, busy mall, good mood of family. Have to mention fact that Snoopy anything was really big at the time.
Rising Action	The "inciting incident" would be my stealing the button. The action will rise in 3 stages: (1) I'm caught shoplifting; (2) I'm taken to the station; (3) I'm waiting to see my parents.
Climax	I talk to my parents on the phone.
Falling Action	I cry.
Resolution	In the end, I realize it's finally all over.

Once you have the basic storyline, you can add notes about where you might put some of your invention writing — description of people and places, dialogue, remembered feelings and thoughts, and reflections on the event from your present perspective. You also may see where you still need to fill in details. Use this outline to guide your drafting, but do not feel tied to it because you are likely to make discoveries as you draft your essay. Your outline may also be helpful when you revise your draft, so be sure to hang on to it.

Drafting

If you have not already begun to draft your essay, this section will help by suggesting how to craft your opening sentences; how to use temporal transitions and verb tenses to draft a narrative that readers will be able to follow; and how to decide when to quote, paraphrase, or summarize. Drafting isn't always a smooth process, so don't be afraid to skip the hard parts or to write notes to yourself about what you could do next. If you get stuck while drafting, go back over your invention writing. You may be able to copy and paste some of it into your evolving draft. Or you may need to do some additional invention to fill in details in your draft.

Writing the Opening Sentences

You could try out one or two different ways of beginning your story — possibly from the list that follows — but do not agonize over the first sentences because you are likely to discover the best way to begin only after you have written a rough draft. Review your invention writing to see if you have already written something that would work to launch your story. To engage your readers' interest from the start, consider setting the stage with the following opening strategies:

- a compelling graphic description of the place or a person
- a startling specific narrative action you or someone else took that would surprise readers and arouse curiosity

- a telling bit of dialogue
- your present reflections on your past self or on the context of the event
- your feelings at the time

A Sentence Strategy: Time Transitions and Verb Tenses

As you draft a remembered event essay, you will be trying to help readers follow the sequence of actions in time. To prevent readers from becoming confused about the chronology, writers use a combination of time transitions and verb tenses to help readers understand when the event occurred and when particular actions occurred in relation to other actions.

Cite calendar or clock time to establish when the event took place and to help readers follow the action over time. Writers often situate the event in terms of the date or time. Brandt, for example, establishes in the opening paragraph that the event occurred when she went to the mall for "a day of last-minute Christmas shopping." Early in her essay, Dillard identifies when the event took place: "On one weekday morning after Christmas . . ." (par. 3). Ellis also uses calendar time to establish the time the event began, but because his narrative spans months instead of hours, he gives readers a series of time cues throughout the essay so we can easily follow the progression: "A year before his death" (par. 1); "That August, I was 22" (par. 4); and so on.

Use temporal transitions combined with appropriate verb tenses to help readers follow a sequence of actions. Writers can employ temporal transitions such as *after, before, in the meantime,* and *simultaneously* to help readers keep track of the sequence of actions:

> *When* I got back to the Snoopy section, I took one look at the lines. . . . (Brandt, par. 3)

In this example, *when* signals that one action followed another in time: Brandt did not take a look at the lines until she got back to the Snoopy section. Here's another example of a simple one-thing-and-then-another time progression:

> We all spread out, banged together some regular snowballs, took aim, and, *when* the Buick drew nigh, fired. (Dillard, par. 7)

In this example, the word *when* together with a series of simple past-tense verbs indicates that a sequence of actions took place in a straightforward chronological order: they took their positions, made snowballs, aimed, the Buick came near, they threw their snowballs.

Transitions can also signal a more complicated relationship between the actions:

> *As* we all piled into the car, I knew it was going to be a fabulous day. (Brandt, par. 1)

In this example, *as* indicates that the first action (piling into the car) occurred at the same time as the second action (I knew).

In many cases, the transition itself makes clear the order of the actions. But in some cases, readers have to pay attention to the verb tenses as well as the transitional word:

> *When I returned* to his apartment, *I was almost smiling.* (Ellis, par. 16)

In this example, Ellis uses *when* to indicate that both actions (returning and smiling) took place at the same time. Ellis's first verb — *returned* — is in simple past tense, indicating that the action began and ended in the past, but his second verb — *was . . . smiling* — is in the past progressive tense, indicating that the action began and continued. In other words, he began smiling before he returned and continued to do so after he returned.

For more on transitions, go to **bedfordstmartins.com/conciseguide** and click on Sentence Strategies; see also p. 363–65 in Chapter 10.

Working with Sources:
Quoting, Paraphrasing, and Summarizing

The primary source for remembered event essays is the writer's memory of what was said at the time the event occurred. Although writers may not remember exactly what was said, they often reconstruct dialogue in order to make their stories dramatic. Quoting tends to be more dramatic than either paraphrasing or summarizing, but you can use any of these strategies as you draft and revise your remembered event essay.

When you quote, you must enclose the words, phrases, or sentences within quotation marks. You may present a sequence of quotations, each in its own paragraph, as in this example of turn-taking:

"Excuse me. Are you a relative of this young girl?"

"Yes, I'm her sister. What's the problem?"

"Well, I just caught her shoplifting and I'm afraid I'll have to call the police."

"What did she take?"

"This button."

In this example from paragraphs 9–13, Brandt is careful to present the dialogue in a way that lets readers know who is speaking during each turn. Sometimes writers identify the speakers in the paragraphs that come before the turn-taking, as in this example:

There was a pause as he called my mother to the phone. For the first time that night, I was close to tears. I wished I had never stolen that stupid pin. I wanted to give the phone to one of the officers because I was too ashamed to tell my mother the truth, but I had no choice.

"Jean, where are you?"

"I'm, umm, in jail." (Brandt, pars. 25–27)

You can learn more about speaker tags in the Working with Sources section in Chapter 3, pp. 97–98.

Paraphrasing and summarizing are alternatives to quoting that you should consider in cases where your readers need only a sense of what was said. Whereas quoting presents the words as if they had been spoken, paraphrase and summary use the writer's own words without quotation marks. Here are several examples of paraphrasing:

> She said it was cute and if I wanted it to go ahead and buy it. (Brandt, par. 2)

> Next thing I knew, he was talking about calling the police and having me arrested and thrown in jail. . . . (Brandt, par. 6)

> He explained that if the pneumonia didn't surrender to the antibiotics, he very likely would die. (Ellis, par. 19)

> He said that at his memorial service he wanted a childhood friend turned opera singer to sing an old spiritual, "There's a Man Goin' Round Taking Names." (Ellis, par. 20)

Notice that these paraphrases essentially repeat the substance of what was said without representing it as the speaker's words. Now look at two examples of summarizing:

> He told me about his boyfriends and girlfriends and his heartaches. . . . (Ellis, par. 17)

> In those days, no one spoke about AIDS. (Ellis, par. 23)

Notice that these summaries identify the topics, giving the gist but none of the details of what was said.

To learn more about quoting, paraphrasing, and summarizing, see Chapter 17, pp. 487–95.

Critical Reading Guide

Basic Features

Your instructor may arrange a peer review session in class or online where you can exchange drafts with your classmates and give each other a thoughtful critical reading, pointing out what works well and suggesting ways to improve the draft. This Critical Reading Guide can also be used productively by a tutor in the writing center or by a roommate or family member. A good critical reading does three things: It lets the writer know how well the reader understands the point of the story, praises what works best, and indicates where the draft could be improved.

1. Assess how well the story is told.

   Praise: Give an example in the story where the storytelling is especially effective — for example, where the speaker tags help make a dialogue dramatic or where specific narrative actions show people in action.

   Critique: Tell the writer where the storytelling could be improved — for example, where the suspense slackens, the story lacks drama, or the chronology is confusing.

2. Consider how vividly people and places are described.

   Praise: Give an example in the story where the description is particularly vivid — for example, where sensory description is particularly powerful or an apt comparison makes an image come alive.

Critique: Tell the writer where the description could be improved — for example, where objects in the scene are not named or described with specific sensory detail, where the description is sparse or seems to contradict rather than reinforce the significance.

3. Evaluate how well the autobiographical significance is conveyed.

   Summarize: Tell the writer what you understand is the story's basic conflict and significance.

   Praise: Give an example where the significance comes across effectively — for example, where remembered feelings are poignant, the present perspective seems insightful, or the description creates a strong dominant impression that reinforces the significance.

   Critique: Tell the writer where the significance could be strengthened — for example, if the conflict is too easily resolved, if a moral seems tacked on at the end, or if a more interesting meaning could be drawn out of the experience.

4. If the writer has expressed concern about anything in the draft that you have not discussed, respond to that concern.

Making Comments Electronically Most word processing software offers features that allow you to insert comments directly into the text of someone else's document. Many readers prefer to make their comments this way because it tends to be faster than writing on hard copy and space is virtually unlimited; it also eliminates the process of deciphering handwritten comments. Where such features are not available, simply typing comments directly into a document in a contrasting color can provide the same advantages.

For a printable version of this Critical Reading Guide, go to **bedfordstmartins.com/conciseguide**.

Revising

Very likely you have already thought of ways to improve your draft, and you may even have begun to revise it. In this section is a Troubleshooting chart that may help. Before using the chart, however, it is a good idea to

- review critical reading comments from your classmates, instructor, or writing center tutor, and
- make an outline of your draft so that you can look at it analytically.

You may have made an outline before writing your draft, but after drafting you need to see what you actually wrote, not what you intended to write. You can outline the draft quickly by noting in the margin the elements of the dramatic narrative pyramid — exposition, rising action, climax, falling action, and resolution — and highlighting the basic features — storytelling, describing people and places, and indicating significance.

For an electronic version of the Troubleshooting chart, go to **bedfordstmartins.com/conciseguide**.

✓ Troubleshooting Your Draft

● ● ● **Basic Features**

A Well-Told Story	
The story starts too slowly.	☐ Shorten the exposition. ☐ Move a bit of dialogue or specific narrative action up front. ☐ Start with something surprising. ☐ Consider beginning with a flashback or flashforward.
The chronology is confusing.	☐ Add or change time transitions. ☐ Clarify verb tenses.
The suspense slackens or the story lacks drama.	☐ Add remembered feelings and thoughts to heighten anticipation. ☐ Add dialogue and specific narrative action. ☐ Build rising action in stages with multiple high points. ☐ Move or cut background information and description.
The conflict is vague or seems unconnected to the significance.	☐ Add dramatized dialogue or specific narrative actions. ☐ Clarify your remembered feelings or thoughts. ☐ Reflect on the conflict from your present perspective.

Vivid Description of People and Places	
Places are hard to visualize.	☐ Name objects in the scene. ☐ Add sensory detail. ☐ Try out a comparison to evoke a particular mood. ☐ Consider adding a visual — a photograph or other memorabilia.
People do not come alive.	☐ Describe a physical feature or mannerism that gives each person individuality. ☐ Add speaker tags to characterize people and show their feelings. ☐ Liven up the dialogue with faster repartee.
Some descriptions weaken the dominant impression.	☐ Omit extraneous details. ☐ Add a simile or metaphor to strengthen the dominant impression. ☐ Rethink the impression you want your writing to convey and the significance it suggests.

Autobiographical Significance	
Readers do not identify or empathize with the writer.	☐ Tell about your background or the particular context. ☐ Give readers a glimpse of the continuing significance of the event years later. ☐ Reveal the cultural influences acting on you, or emphasize the historical period in which the event occurred.
Readers do not understand the significance.	☐ Try explaining the significance directly by explaining your present perspective.
The significance seems too pat or simplistic.	☐ Develop contradictions, or show ambivalences. ☐ Stress the social or cultural dimensions of the event. ☐ Try to develop a more complex and interesting significance.

Editing and Proofreading

Several errors occur often in essays about remembered events: missing commas after introductory elements, fused sentences, and misused past-perfect verbs. The following guidelines will help you check your essay for these common errors.

Missing Commas after Introductory Elements

The Problem: Remembered event essays often include sentences with introductory elements, especially temporal transitions to indicate calendar or clock time and to show when one action occurred in relation to other actions. A comma after such an element tells readers that the main part of the sentence is about to begin. If the introductory element is lengthy or complex, leaving the comma out can make your sentence confusing.

How to Correct It: Add a comma for clarity.

▶ Through the nine-day run of the play, the acting just kept getting better and better.

▶ Knowing that the struggle was over, I felt through my jacket to find tea bags and cookies the robber had taken from the kitchen.

▶ As I stepped out of the car, I knew something was wrong.

For practice, go to **bedfordstmartins.com/conciseguide/exercisecentral** and click on Commas after Introductory Elements.

Using the Past Perfect

The Problem: One common problem in writing about a remembered event is the failure to use the past perfect when it is needed, which can sometimes make your meaning unclear (what happened when, exactly?).

How to Correct It: Check passages where you recount events to be sure you are using the past perfect to indicate an action that was completed at the time of another past action (she *had finished* her work when we saw her).

                                    had

▶ I had three people in the car, something my father told me not to do on several

   occasions.

         had run

▶ Coach Kernow told me I ~~ran~~ faster than ever before.

ESL Note: It is important to remember that the past perfect is formed with *had* followed by a past participle. Past participles usually end in *-ed, -d, -en, -n,* or *-t: worked, hoped, eaten, taken, bent.*

                                           spoken

▶ Before Tania went to Moscow last year, she had not really ~~speak~~ Russian.

For practice, go to **bedfordstmartins.com/conciseguide/exercisecentral** and click on The Past Perfect and/or A Common ESL Problem: Forming the Past Perfect.

Fused Sentences

The Problem: When you write about a remembered event, you try to re-create a scene. This sometimes results in fused sentences, where two independent clauses are joined with no punctuation or connecting word between them.

How to Correct It:

- Rewrite the sentence, subordinating one clause.
- Make the clauses separate sentences.
- Join the two clauses with a comma and *and, but, or, nor, for, so,* or *yet.*
- Join the two clauses with a semicolon.

                          The

▶ Sleet glazed the windshield. ~~the~~ wipers were frozen stuck.

                         , and

▶ Sleet glazed the windshield the wipers were frozen stuck.

▶ Sleet glazed the windshield; the wipers were frozen stuck.

   As sleet   *became*

▶ ~~Sleet~~ glazed the windshield the wipers ~~were~~ frozen stuck.

For practice, go to **bedfordstmartins.com/conciseguide/exercisecentral** and click on Fused Sentences.

Thinking Critically about What You Have Learned

In this chapter, you have learned a great deal about this genre from reading several autobiographical stories and writing one of your own. To consolidate your learning, it is helpful to think metacognitively; that is, to reflect not only on what you learned but on how you learned it. Following are two brief activities your instructor may ask you to do.

Reflecting on Your Writing

Your instructor may ask you to turn in with your essay and process materials a brief metacognitive essay or letter reflecting on what you have learned about writing your essay remembering an event. Choose from the following invention activities those that seem most productive for you:

- Explain how your purpose and audience — what you wanted your readers to learn about you from reading your story — influenced *one* of your decisions as a writer, such as what you put in the exposition section of your story, how you used dialogue to intensify the drama of the climax, or how you integrated your remembered thoughts and feelings into your storytelling.

- Discuss what you learned about yourself as a writer in the process of writing this particular essay. For example, what part of the process did you find most challenging, or did you try something new like getting a critical reading of your draft or outlining your draft in order to revise it?

- If you were to give advice to a friend who was about to write a remembered event essay, what would you say?

- Which of the readings in this chapter influenced your essay? Explain the influence, citing specific examples from your essay and the reading.

- If you got good advice from a critical reader, explain exactly how the person helped you — perhaps by questioning the conflict in a way that enabled you to refocus your story's significance or by pointing out passages that needed clearer time markers to better orient readers.

Considering the Social Dimensions: Autobiography and Self-Discovery

If writing a remembered event essay leads to self-discovery, what do we mean by the "self"? Should we think of the self as our "true" essence or as the different roles we play in different situations? If we accept the idea of an essential self, writing about significant events in our lives can help us in the search to discover who we truly are. Given this idea of the self, we might see Jean Brandt, for example, as searching to understand whether she is the kind of person who breaks the law and only cares when she is caught and has to face her parents' disapproval. If, however, we accept the idea that the various roles we play are what create the self, then writing about a remembered event allows us to reveal the many sides of our personalities. This view of the self assumes that we present different self-images to different people in different situations. Given this idea, we might see Brandt as presenting her sassy teenage side to the police but keeping her vulnerability hidden from them.

1. *Consider how your remembered event essay might be an exercise in self-discovery.* While planning and writing your essay, did you see yourself as discovering your true self or examining how you reacted in a particular situation? Do you think your essay reveals your single, essential, true self, or does it show only an aspect of the person you understand yourself to be?

2. *Write a page or so explaining your ideas about self-discovery and truth in remembered event essays.* Connect your ideas to your own essay and to the readings in this chapter.

3

Writing Profiles

IN COLLEGE COURSES To fulfill a requirement for an education course, a student who plans to teach sixth grade decides to study collaborative learning. The student arranges to visit a class that is beginning a project on immigration. On three visits, she observes a group of students working together and interviews them individually and as a group.

The student roughs out outlines for both narrative and topical organizations of her profile, and she decides that a narrative plan would be more likely to engage her readers. She then writes a draft. To keep the focus on students and their progress, she reports as a spectator, weaving her insights about collaborative learning into a detailed narrative of a typical half-hour meeting. From her profile emerges the central idea that sixth graders' collaborative work is unlikely to succeed unless the students frequently reflect on what they are learning and on how they can work together more productively. After completing her project, she decides to publish it online for classmates and others interested in collaborative learning.

IN THE COMMUNITY A newspaper reporter is assigned to write a profile of a mural project recently commissioned by the city.

The reporter visits the studio of the local artist in charge of the project. They discuss the specifics of the mural project and the artist's views of other civic art projects. The artist invites the reporter to spend the following day at the site.

The next day, the artist puts the reporter to work alongside two volunteers. The reports intends to use this firsthand experience, interviews with volunteers, and photos to describe the painting from a participant observer's point of view.

Later, writing copy for the Sunday paper, the reporter organizes the profile around different topics: the artist's goals for the project; the experience of the volunteers; and the mural's importance as civic art.

IN THE WORKPLACE For a company newsletter, a public-relations officer profiles the corporation's new chief executive officer (CEO). He follows the CEO from meeting to meeting, taking photographs and observing. Between meetings, he records interviews with her about her management philosophy and her five-year plan for the corporation. Immediately after the interviews he listens to the recordings, making notes and writing down questions to ask as follow-up.

A day later, the CEO invites the writer to visit her at home. He watches the CEO help her daughter with homework, converses with her husband, and takes more photographs.

The writer reviews his notes, the recordings of their interviews, and the photos he took. He decides to illustrate the profile with images of the CEO at a meeting and with her daughter. As he reports on some of the challenges she anticipates for the corporation, he tries to convey the confidence she shows both at work and at home.

Profiles

One meaning of the word *profile* is the outline or shape of a person's face when viewed from the side, and one traditional means of *profiling* a person, place, or activity is by creating a visual portrait. Visual portraits such as photographer Dorothea Lange's iconic photographs of destitute migrant workers in 1930s California can tell the viewer a great deal about the subject beyond what they look(ed) like: Clothing, attitude and posture,

setting, other people and objects in the frame, and artistic decisions convey abundant additional information about the subject, his or her world, and the attitude of the portraitist.

Many other forms of profile are common in our culture — films, books, plays, songs, and Web sites, among other modes of expression. Many of us are probably most familiar with profiles as the self-descriptions we create on Web sites like Facebook, LinkedIn, and the like. The various sections of such profiles — Information, Friends, Photos, the "Wall," and so on — provide a basic template of identity that many of us find recognizable and useful, both for presenting ourselves and for understanding others.

Dorothea Lange, "Migrant Mother" (1936)

In this chapter, we ask you to write a profile of an unfamiliar subject — a person, a place, or an activity — that will allow both you and your readers to understand it better or differently.

Reading and Writing Profiles

The writers in the scenarios on p. 57 profile a group of young students involved in a complex learning activity, an artist and neighborhood volunteers creating a public mural, and a high-ranking business executive going about her daily activities. Whatever their subject, profile writers strive most of all to enable readers to imagine a person, place, or activity by using specific and vivid details: how the person dresses, gestures, and talks; what the place looks, sounds, and smells like; what the activity requires of those who participate in it. At the same time, the writer strives to convey his or her perspective, offering some insight, idea, or interpretation of the subject's cultural significance.

Profiles share many features — including description, narration, and dialogue — with essays about remembered events. However, the differences are also important. To write about a remembered event, you look inside for memories in order to write about yourself and your experiences with other people. To write a profile, you look outside for fresh observations of an unfamiliar subject in order to understand it better.

The scope of your profile may be large or small. You could, for example, attend a single event such as a parade, a dress rehearsal for a play, or a city council meeting and write a profile based solely on your observations; or you might write a more complete profile based on several visits to a place and interviews with various people there.

Writing your own profile will make you a more insightful reader of the cultural practices of everyday life. Doing the research needed to write a profile will also give you confidence in your observational skills and your ability to ask probing questions. At the same time, you will learn how to write in an engaging way to interest readers and keep them reading.

From readings like those in the first part of this chapter, you will see how other writers have profiled people, places, and activities. The Guide to Writing that follows these readings will support you as you compose your own profile, showing how to describe your subject vividly and dramatically, entertaining readers but also giving them insight into your subject's significance.

A Collaborative Activity:
Practice Conducting an Interview

Part 1. Get together in a small group, and ask someone to volunteer to be the interviewee while the rest of the group acts as interviewers. The interviewers should spend a couple of minutes preparing questions and then, after choosing an interviewer to begin, take turns asking questions. When you act as interviewer, be sure to listen to what the interviewee says and ask follow-up questions. All interviewers should take notes quoting and summarizing what the interviewee says as well as describing the interviewee's tone of voice, facial expressions, and gestures.

Part 2. Discuss these questions as a group:

- What was the hardest part of interviewing: thinking of questions, following up, taking notes, or something else?

- If you were to write a brief profile based on this interview to present to the rest of the class, what information would you emphasize? What would you quote? How would you describe the interviewee? What would guide these choices?

Reading Profiles

Basic Features

As you read the profiles in this chapter, you will see how different authors incorporate the basic features of the genre.

● Detailed Information about the Subject

Read first to identify the subject of the profile. Profiles are about the following subjects:

- a place where something interesting happens (such as a hospital emergency room)
- an activity (such as the mural project in the second scenario)
- a person (such as the CEO profiled in the third scenario)
- a group of people (such as the students profiled in the first scenario)

Much of the pleasure of reading a profile comes from the way the writer presents *detailed information* about the subject. To make the information entertaining as well as readable and interesting, profile writers interweave bits of information into a tapestry that includes vivid descriptions, lively anecdotes, and arresting quotations.

Because profile writers get their information primarily from observing and interviewing, and because they try to give readers a vivid picture of the subject, *describing* is perhaps the most important writing strategy for presenting information. **Describing** includes the following activities:

- *detailing* what people look like and how they dress, gesture, and talk
- *showing* what the observer saw, heard, smelled, touched, and tasted
- *quoting, summarizing,* or *paraphrasing* the people interviewed

Look also for these other ways of presenting information about the subject: *classifying, defining new terms, comparing and contrasting, identifying causes or effects,* and *giving examples.*

● A Clear Organizational Plan

Profiles can be organized according to two different plans:

- a **narrative plan** that interweaves the information with elements of a story
- a **topical plan** that groups the information into topics and moves from one topic to another

Whereas a narrative plan may be more engaging, a topical plan may deliver information more efficiently. *As you read the profiles in this chapter, consider why the writer might have chosen one plan or the other.* What was gained? Was anything lost?

● A Role for the Writer

Look also at the role that the writer assumes in relation to his or her subject:

- As a **spectator** or **detached observer**, the writer's position is like that of the reader, an outsider looking in on the people and their activities (such as the college student in the first scenario).

- As a **participant observer**, the writer participates in the activity being profiled and acquires insider knowledge (such as the reporter in the second scenario profiling the mural project).

● A Perspective on the Subject

All of the basic features listed above — detailed information, the plan of the profile, and the writer's role — support the writer's **perspective on the subject**, the main idea or cultural significance that the writer wants readers to take away from reading the profile. Profiles, like remembered event essays, seldom state the thesis directly. Instead, they convey it by creating a *dominant impression* from the descriptive details and other kinds of information together with the writer's thoughts and comments.

Purpose and Audience

Profiles are a popular way to learn about interesting people, activities, and places. You can find profiles in many different venues — blogs, television, and radio, as well as traditional magazines, newspapers, and books. Academic disciplines such as cultural studies, anthropology, and literacy studies often use a type of profile called an *ethnography*. Ethnographies use the same field research methods and employ the same writing strategies as more traditional journalistic profiles. They differ in that ethnographers do their research over an extended period of time and usually study groups of people who identify themselves as members of a particular community (for example, a group of Twitter users, Facebook friends, or students who share a dorm room or belong to the same club). Depending on their academic interest, ethnographers may focus on the group's patterns of communication, how newcomers are initiated into the group, how conflicts are handled, how relationships form and dissolve, and so on. Though you will not have the time or resources to study your subject in as much depth as an ethnographer normally does, any of these topics could become the focus of the profile you write for this course.

*As you read profiles, ask yourself what seems to be the writer's **purpose** in writing about this particular subject.* For example, does the writer seem to be writing

- to inform readers about some aspect of everyday life — the places and activities that surround us but that we may not notice, let alone get to know intimately?

- to give readers an in-depth, behind-the-scenes look at an intriguing or unusual activity — for example, a fascinating hobby or challenging career?
- to surprise readers by presenting unusual subjects or familiar ones in new ways?
- to give readers a new way to look at and think about the cultural significance of the subject?
- to present vivid descriptions and engaging stories showing how people communicate and work together, construct their identities, and define their values?

As you read, also try to grasp the writer's assumptions about the **audience**. For example, does the writer

- assume readers will know nothing or very little about the subject?
- expect readers to be interested and possibly amused by a particular aspect of the subject?
- hope readers will be intrigued by the perspective the writer takes or fascinated by certain quotes or descriptive details?

Readings

BRIAN CABLE wrote this profile of a neighborhood mortuary when he was a first-year college student. "Death," as he explains in the opening sentence, "is a subject largely ignored by the living," so it is not surprising that he notices people averting their eyes as they walk past the mortuary on a busy commercial street. Cable, however, walks in and takes readers on a guided tour of the premises. As he presents information he learned from observing how the mortuary works — from the reception room up front to the embalming room in back — and from interviewing the people who work there, Cable lets us know his feelings and his thoughts on cultural attitudes about death.

■ A recent photo of Goodbody Mortuary, the subject of Cable's profile. Does this photo match Cable's description? How would the addition of such a photo, or other photos of the mortuary, have strengthened Cable's profile?

As you read, notice how Cable uses humor to defuse the inherent seriousness of the place. Also consider the questions in the margin. Your instructor may ask you to post your answers or bring them to class.

The Last Stop

Brian Cable

Let us endeavor so to live that when we come to die even the undertaker will be sorry.

— Mark Twain

● ● ● ●
Basic Features

- Detailed Information
- Organizational Plan
- Writer's Role
- Perspective on the Subject

1　Death is a subject largely ignored by the living. We don't discuss it much, not as children (when Grandpa dies, he is said to be "going away"), not as adults, not even as senior citizens. Throughout our lives, death remains intensely private. The death of a loved one can be very painful, partly because of the sense of loss, but also because someone else's mortality reminds us all too vividly of our own.

What expectations do the title and epigraph (opening quote) raise for you?

2　More than a few people avert their eyes as they walk past the dusty-pink building that houses the Goodbody Mortuaries. It looks a bit like a church — tall, with gothic arches and stained glass — and somewhat like an apartment complex — low, with many windows stamped out of red brick.

Cable begins by sharing his thoughts and observations. What impression does this opening create?

3　It wasn't at all what I had expected. I thought it would be more like Forest Lawn, serene with lush green lawns and meticulously groomed gardens, a place set apart from the hustle of day-to-day life. Here instead was an odd pink structure set in the middle of a business district. On top of the Goodbody Mortuaries sign was a large electric clock. What the hell, I thought. Mortuaries are concerned with time, too.

4　I was apprehensive as I climbed the stone steps to the entrance. I feared rejection or, worse, an invitation to come and stay. The door was massive, yet it swung open easily on well-oiled hinges. "Come in," said the sign. "We're always open." Inside was a cool and quiet reception room. Curtains were drawn against the outside glare, cutting the light down to a soft glow.

What organizational plan for the profile emerges in pars. 4 and 5?

5　I found the funeral director in the main lobby, adjacent to the reception room. Like most people, I had preconceptions about what an undertaker looked like. Mr. Deaver fulfilled my expectations entirely. Tall and thin, he even had beady eyes and a bony face. A low, slanted forehead gave way to a beaked nose. His skin, scrubbed of all color, contrasted sharply with his jet black hair. He was wearing a starched

What does the detailed description of Deaver in pars. 5 and 6 contribute to Cable's profile of the mortuary?

white shirt, gray pants, and black shoes. Indeed, he looked like death on two legs.

He proved an amiable sort, however, and was easy to talk to. As funeral director, Mr. Deaver ("Call me Howard") was responsible for a wide range of services. Goodbody Mortuaries, upon notification of someone's death, will remove the remains from the hospital or home. They then prepare the body for viewing, whereupon features distorted by illness or accident are restored to their natural condition. The body is embalmed and then placed in a casket selected by the family of the deceased. Services are held in one of three chapels at the mortuary, and afterward the casket is placed in a "visitation room," where family and friends can pay their last respects. Goodbody also makes arrangements for the purchase of a burial site and transports the body there for burial.

All this information Howard related in a well-practiced, professional manner. It was obvious he was used to explaining the specifics of his profession. We sat alone in the lobby. His desk was bone clean, no pencils or paper, nothing — just a telephone. He did all his paperwork at home; as it turned out, he and his wife lived right upstairs. The phone rang. As he listened, he bit his lips and squeezed his Adam's apple somewhat nervously.

"I think we'll be able to get him in by Friday. No, no, the family wants him cremated."

His tone was that of a broker conferring on the Dow Jones. Directly behind him was a sign announcing "Visa and Master Charge Welcome Here." It was tacked to the wall, right next to a crucifix.

"Some people have the idea that we are bereavement specialists, that we can handle emotional problems which follow a death: Only a trained therapist can do that. We provide services for the dead, not counseling for the living."

Physical comfort was the one thing they did provide for the living. The lobby was modestly but comfortably furnished. There were several couches, in colors ranging from earth brown to pastel blue, and a coffee table in front of each one. On one table lay some magazines and a vase of flowers. Another supported an aquarium. Paintings of pastoral scenes

Marginal notes:

What role has Cable adopted in writing the profile? When does it become clear?

Why do you think Cable summarizes the information in par. 6 instead of quoting Howard?

What does this observation reveal about Cable's perspective?

Why do you think he quotes Howard in par. 10, instead of paraphrasing or summarizing?

Paragraph numbers: 6, 7, 8, 9, 10, 11

hung on every wall. The lobby looked more or less like that of an old hotel. Nothing seemed to match, but it had a homey, lived-in look.

What does this observation contribute to the dominant impression?

12   "The last time the Goodbodies decorated was in '59, I believe. It still makes people feel welcome."

13   And so "Goodbody" was not a name made up to attract customers but the owner's family name. The Goodbody family started the business way back in 1915. Today, they do over five hundred services a year.

14   "We're in *Ripley's Believe It or Not*, along with another funeral home whose owners' names are Baggit and Sackit," Howard told me, without cracking a smile.

15   I followed him through an arched doorway into a chapel that smelled musty and old. The only illumination came from sunlight filtered through a stained glass ceiling. Ahead of us lay a casket. I could see that it contained a man dressed in a black suit. Wooden benches ran on either side of an aisle that led to the body. I got no closer. From the red roses across the dead man's chest, it was apparent that services had already been held.

How does Cable make the transition from topic to topic in pars. 15–18?

16   "It was a large service," remarked Howard. "Look at that casket — a beautiful work of craftsmanship."

17   I guess it was. Death may be the great leveler, but one's coffin quickly reestablishes one's status.

18   We passed into a bright, fluorescent-lit "display room." Inside were thirty coffins, lids open, patiently awaiting inspection. Like new cars on the showroom floor, they gleamed with high-gloss finishes.

19   "We have models for every price range."

20   Indeed, there was a wide variety. They came in all colors and various materials. Some were little more than cloth-covered cardboard boxes, others were made of wood, and a few were made of steel, copper, or bronze. Prices started at $400 and averaged about $1,800. Howard motioned toward the center of the room: "The top of the line."

How does the comparison to a new car showroom in pars. 18–21 reveal Cable's perspective?

21   This was a solid bronze casket, its seams electronically welded to resist corrosion. Moisture-proof and air-tight, it could be hermetically sealed off from all outside elements. Its handles were plated with 14-karat gold. The price: a cool $5,000.

Where does the information in pars. 22–23 come from?

A proper funeral remains a measure of respect for the deceased. But it is expensive. In the United States the amount spent annually on funerals is about $2 billion. Among ceremonial expenditures, funerals are second only to weddings. As a result, practices are changing. Howard has been in this business for forty years. He remembers a time when everyone was buried. Nowadays, with burials costing $2,000 a shot, people often opt instead for cremation — as Howard put it, "a cheap, quick, and easy means of disposal." In some areas of the country, the cremation rate is now over 60 percent. Observing this trend, one might wonder whether burials are becoming obsolete. Do burials serve an important role in society?

What is the function of this rhetorical question?

For Tim, Goodbody's licensed mortician, the answer is very definitely yes. Burials will remain in common practice, according to the slender embalmer with the disarming smile, because they allow family and friends to view the deceased. Painful as it may be, such an experience brings home the finality of death. "Something deep within us demands a confrontation with death," Tim explained. "A last look assures us that the person we loved is, indeed, gone forever."

Apparently, we also need to be assured that the body will be laid to rest in comfort and peace. The average casket, with its innerspring mattress and pleated satin lining, is surprisingly roomy and luxurious. Perhaps such an air of comfort makes it easier for the family to give up their loved one. In addition, the burial site fixes the deceased in the survivors' memory, like a new address. Cremation provides none of these comforts.

Whose perspective does this statement reflect? How do you know?

Tim started out as a clerk in a funeral home but then studied to become a mortician. "It was a profession I could live with," he told me with a sly grin. Mortuary science might be described as a cross between pre-med and cosmetology, with courses in anatomy and embalming as well as in restorative art.

Is Tim's definition of mortuary science helpful? Why or why not?

Tim let me see the preparation, or embalming, room, a whitewalled chamber about the size of an operating room. Against the wall was a large sink with elbow taps and a draining board. In the center of the room stood a table with equipment for preparing the arterial embalming fluid, which consists primarily of formaldehyde,

Which of the information in par. 26 comes from observation and which comes from interviewing Tim? How do you know?

22

23

24

25

26

a preservative, and phenol, a disinfectant. This mixture sanitizes and also gives better color to the skin. Facial features can then be "set" to achieve a restful expression. Missing eyes, ears, and even noses can be replaced.

27   I asked Tim if his job ever depressed him. He bridled at the question: "No, it doesn't depress me at all. I do what I can for people and take satisfaction in enabling relatives to see their loved ones as they were in life." He said that he felt people were becoming more aware of the public service his profession provides. Grade-school classes now visit funeral homes as often as they do police stations and museums. The mortician is no longer regarded as a minister of death.

28   Before leaving, I wanted to see a body up close. I thought I could be indifferent after all I had seen and heard, but I wasn't sure. Cautiously, I reached out and touched the skin. It felt cold and firm, not unlike clay. As I walked out, I felt glad to have satisfied my curiosity about dead bodies, but all too happy to let someone else handle them.

> How effective is this ending?

JOHN T. EDGE directs the Southern Foodways Symposium, which is part of the Center for the Study of Southern Culture at the University of Mississippi, and edits the *Encyclopedia of Southern Culture*. He has written *A Gracious Plenty: Recipes and Recollections from the American South* (1999); *Southern Belly* (2000), a portrait of southern food told through profiles of people and places; and a series of books on specific foods, including *Fried Chicken* and *Apple Pie* (2004) and *Hamburgers and Fries* (2005).

Edge also contributes to a number of magazines, newspapers, and radio and television programs, including NPR's *All Things Considered*, *Gourmet* magazine, the *Atlanta Journal-Constitution*, and the *Oxford American*, in which this profile originally appeared. In it, Edge profiles Farm Fresh Food Supplier, a small business located in Louisiana, and introduces readers to its pickled meat products. As you read, enjoy Edge's struggle to eat a pickled pig lip, but notice also how much you are learning about this bar snack as Edge details his discomfort in trying to eat it.

I'm Not Leaving Until I Eat This Thing

John T. Edge

t's just past 4:00 on a Thursday afternoon in June at Jesse's Place, a country juke 17 miles south of the Mississippi line and three miles west of Amite, Louisiana. The air conditioner hacks and spits forth torrents of Arctic air, but the heat of summer can't be kept at bay. It seeps around the splintered doorjambs and settles in, transforming the squat particleboard-plastered roadhouse into a sauna. Slowly, the dank barroom fills with grease-smeared mechanics from the truck stop up the road and farmers straight from the fields, the soles of their brogans thick with dirt clods. A few weary souls make their way over from the nearby sawmill. I sit alone at the bar, one empty bottle of Bud in front of me, a second in my hand. I drain the beer, order a third, and stare down at the pink juice spreading outward from a crumpled foil pouch and onto the bar. [1]

I'm not leaving until I eat this thing, I tell myself. [2]

Half a mile down the road, behind a fence coiled with razor wire, Lionel Dufour, proprietor of Farm Fresh Food Supplier, is loading up the last truck of the day, wheeling case after case of pickled pork offal out of his cinder-block processing plant and into a semitrailer bound for Hattiesburg, Mississippi. [3]

His crew packed lips today. Yesterday, it was pickled sausage; the day before that, pig feet. Tomorrow, it's pickled pig lips again. Lionel has been on the job since 2:45 in the morning, when he came in to light the boilers. Damon Landry, chief cook and maintenance man, came in at 4:30. By 7:30, the production line was at full tilt: [4]

six women in white smocks and blue bouffant caps, slicing ragged white fat from the lips, tossing the good parts in glass jars, the bad parts in barrels bound for the rendering plant. Across the aisle, filled jars clatter by on a conveyor belt as a worker tops them off with a Kool-Aid-red slurry of hot sauce, vinegar, salt, and food coloring. Around the corner, the jars are capped, affixed with a label, and stored in pasteboard boxes to await shipping.

Unlike most offal — euphemistically called "variety meats" — lips belie their provenance. Brains, milky white and globular, look like brains. Feet, the ghosts of their cloven hoofs protruding, look like feet. Testicles look like, well, testicles. [5]

> **"Lips are all meat," Lionel told me earlier in the day. "No gristle, no bone, no nothing. They're bar food, hot and vinegary, great with a beer."**

But lips are different. Loosed from the snout, trimmed of their fat, and dyed a preternatural pink, they look more like candy than like carrion.

At Farm Fresh, no swine root in an adjacent feedlot. No viscera-strewn killing floor lurks just out of sight, down a darkened hallway. These pigs died long ago at some Midwestern abattoir. By the time the lips arrive in Amite, they are, in essence, pig Popsicles, 50-pound blocks of offal and ice.

"Lips are all meat," Lionel told me earlier in the day. "No gristle, no bone, no nothing. They're bar food, hot and vinegary, great with a beer. Used to be the lips ended up in sausages, headcheese, those sorts of things. A lot of them still do."

Lionel, a 50-year-old father of three with quick, intelligent eyes set deep in a face the color of cordovan, is a veteran of nearly 40 years in the pickled pig lips business. "I started out with my daddy when I wasn't much more than 10," Lionel told me, his shy smile framed by a coarse black mustache flecked with whispers of gray. "The meatpacking business he owned had gone broke back when I was 6, and he was peddling out of the back of his car, selling dried shrimp, napkins, straws, tubes of plastic cups, pig feet, pig lips, whatever the bar owners needed. He sold to black bars, white bars, sweet shops, snowball stands, you name it. We made the rounds together after I got out of school, sometimes staying out till two or three in the morning. I remember bringing my toy cars to this one joint and racing them around the floor with the bar owner's son while my daddy and his father did business."

For years after the demise of that first meatpacking company, the Dufour family sold someone else's product. "We used to buy lips from Dennis Di Salvo's company down in Belle Chasse," recalled Lionel. "As far as I can tell, his mother was the one who came up with the idea to pickle and pack lips back in the '50s, back when she was working for a company called Three Little Pigs over in Houma. But pretty soon, we were selling so many lips that we had to almost beg Di Salvo's for product. That's when we started cooking up our own," he told me, gesturing toward the cast-iron kettle that hangs from the rafters by the front door of the plant. "My daddy started cooking lips in that very pot."

Lionel now cooks lips in 11 retrofitted milk tanks, dull stainless-steel cauldrons shaped like oversized cradles. But little else has changed. Though Lionel's father has passed away, Farm Fresh remains a family-focused company. His wife, Kathy, keeps the books. His daughter, Dana, a button-cute college student who has won numerous beauty titles, takes to the road in the summer, selling lips to convenience stores and wholesalers. Soon, after he graduates from business school, Lionel's younger son, Matt, will take over operations at the plant. And his older son, a veterinarian, lent his name to one of Farm Fresh's top sellers, Jason's Pickled Pig Lips.

"We do our best to corner the market on lips," Lionel told me, his voice tinged with bravado. "Sometimes they're hard to get from the packing houses. You gotta kill a lot of pigs to get enough lips to keep us going. I've got new customers calling every day; it's all I can do to keep up with demand, but I bust my ass to keep up. I do what I can for my family — and for my customers.

"When my customers tell me something," he continued, "just like when my daddy told me something, I listen. If my customers wanted me to dye the lips green, I'd ask, 'What shade?' As it is, every few years we'll do some red and some blue for the Fourth of July. This year we did jars full of Mardi Gras lips — half purple, half gold," Lionel recalled with a chuckle. "I guess we'd had a few beers when we came up with that one."   12

Meanwhile, back at Jesse's Place, I finish my third Bud, order my fourth. *Now,* I tell myself, my courage bolstered by booze, *I'm ready to eat a lip.*   13

They may have looked like candy in the plant, but in the barroom they're carrion once again. I poke and prod the six-inch arc of pink flesh, peering up from my reverie just in time to catch the barkeep's wife, Audrey, staring straight at me. She fixes me with a look just this side of pity and asks, "You gonna eat that thing or make love to it?"   14

Her nephew, Jerry, sidles up to a bar stool on my left. "A lot of people like 'em with chips," he says with a nod toward the pink juice pooling on the bar in front of me. I offer to buy him a lip, and Audrey fishes one from a jar behind the counter, wraps it in tinfoil, and places the whole affair on a paper towel in front of him.   15

I take stock of my own cowardice, and, following Jerry's lead, reach for a bag of potato chips, tear open the top with my teeth, and toss the quivering hunk of hog flesh into the shiny interior of the bag, slick with grease and dusted with salt. Vinegar vapors tickle my nostrils. I stifle a gag that rolls from the back of my throat, swallow hard, and pray that the urge to vomit passes.   16

With a smash of my hand, the potato chips are reduced to a pulp, and I feel the cold lump of the lip beneath my fist. I clasp the bag shut and shake it hard in an effort to ensure chip coverage in all the nooks and crannies of the lip. The technique that Jerry uses — and I mimic — is not unlike that employed by home cooks mixing up a mess of Shake 'n Bake chicken.   17

I pull from the bag a coral crescent of meat now crusted with blond bits of potato chips. When I chomp down, the soft flesh dissolves between my teeth. It tastes like a flaccid cracklin', unmistakably porcine, and not altogether bad. The chips help, providing texture where there was none. Slowly, my brow unfurrows, my stomach ceases its fluttering.   18

Sensing my relief, Jerry leans over and peers into my bag. "Kind of look like Frosted Flakes, don't they?" he says, by way of describing the chips rapidly turning to mush in the pickling juice. I offer the bag to Jerry, order yet another beer, and turn to eye the pig feet floating in a murky jar by the cash register, their blunt tips bobbing up through a pasty white film.   19

MAKING CONNECTIONS: AVERSION TO NEW FOODS

Edge uses the words *courage* (par. 13) and *cowardice* (par. 16) to describe his squeamishness about eating pickled pig lip. And when he finally eats a bite of pig lip, he feels queasy. Although his nausea is undoubtedly real, it may be caused more by anxiety than by anything sickening in the food itself.

With other students, discuss the kinds of food you feel uncomfortable eating — foods you have anxiety eating, foods that gross you out, or foods you stay away from for some other reason such as a religious dietary restriction or a moral conviction. Begin by briefly telling one another about the kinds of foods you avoid. Then, together consider the following questions as you discuss the reasons for your strong feelings about certain kinds of food:

- What role do factors such as family, ethnic, or religious traditions play in your food choices? If your food aversions are unusual in your family or community, consider how other family or community members regard your choice — for example, as a quirk or as a rejection of something they value. If you find it hard to try foods from different cultures, why do you think that is?

- Early in the essay, Edge makes clear that he is squeamish about eating a pickled pig lip even though he is a southerner and it is a popular southern delicacy. How does his difficulty eating the pig lip set him apart from the other people in the bar? What else separates him from them?

ANALYZING WRITING STRATEGIES

● ● ● ●
Basic Features

● Detailed Information about the Subject

Profiles present information primarily from the writer's direct observation of the subject, plus what was learned from interviews and from background Internet and library research. Because profile writers get much of their information from observation and because they try to give readers a vivid picture of the subject, *describing* is their most important writing strategy.

Edge probably assumes that most of his readers have never seen a pickled pig lip, much less eaten one. Therefore, he describes this product carefully. To describe an object like a pickled pig lip, writers use **naming**, **detailing**, and **comparing** to create vivid images. Consider, for example, Edge's description of the brine in which the pig lips swim as "Kool-Aid-red slurry" (par. 4). *Slurry*, which Edge uses to *name* the mixture of ingredients in the brine, is also descriptive, because the term *slurry* derives from mining and other industrial uses, where it denotes a slimy liquid or thin mud. The *detail* "Kool-Aid-red," with its implied *comparison* with the popular, artificially colored children's drink, creates a vivid visual image for anyone familiar with Kool-Aid.

Descriptive details such as these provide sensory information — color, shape, smell, taste, or texture — and may also identify qualities and make evaluations (for example, the "good" and "bad" parts of the pig lip in par. 4).

Writers use the following familiar figures of speech when they make comparisons:

- **Simile**, in which two things are *explicitly* compared using the words *like* or *as*.
- **Metaphor**, in which two things are *implicitly* compared by calling one thing something else.

For example, Edge uses simile (note the word <u>like</u>) when he writes that pig lips "look more like candy than like carrion" (par. 5), and he employs metaphor when he describes the temperature of the air conditioning at Jesse's Place as "Arctic" (par. 1).

To analyze Edge's use of the describing strategies of naming, detailing, and comparing, do the following:

- Reread paragraphs 5–7, 14, and 16–18. Underline two things Edge names, put brackets around four descriptive details, and circle any similes and metaphors that he uses to help readers imagine eating a pig lip.

- Write a few sentences about the overall or **dominant impression** Edge's description of pickled pig lips makes. If you have never seen a pickled pig lip, what more do you need to know to imagine what it looks, smells, feels, tastes, and sounds like when you chomp down on it? Which details make a lip seem appealing to you? Which ones make it seem unappealing?

● A Clear Organizational Plan

A profile may be presented **narratively**, as a sequence of events observed by the writer during an encounter with the place, person, or activity; or it may be presented **topically**, as a series of topics of information gathered by the writer about the person, place, or activity. Sometimes profile writers, like Edge, use both narrative and topical organization. Edge frames (begins and ends) his profile with a story about his attempt to eat a pig lip.

To analyze how Edge uses both a narrative and a topical organization, do the following:

- Reread paragraphs 16–18, and highlight places where the sequence of actions involved in eating a pig lip are narrated.

- Skim paragraphs 3–12, and note in the margin where Edge presents the following topics: the production process, the various products produced by Farm Fresh, the source of the products, and the history of the Farm Fresh business.

- Write a few sentences explaining what, if anything, you learn from Edge's narrative that you cannot find out from the topics he presents in paragraphs 3–12.

● A Role for the Writer

Profile writers can choose to adopt the role of a *spectator* or the role of a *participant*. For example, in the preceding essay, Cable takes the role of spectator when he talks to Howard and Tim and takes a tour of the Goodbody mortuary. To take on a participant role, Cable would have had to help the funeral director or embalmer in his daily activities.

To analyze how Edge uses both roles in this essay, do the following:

- Skim the essay, and note in the margin where Edge uses the spectator role and where he uses the participant role.
- Write a few sentences giving an example of each role and explaining how the examples show which role he is using. How does he keep the two roles separate?

● A Perspective on the Subject

Profile writers do not merely present information about the subject; they also offer their insights. They may convey a perspective on their subject by stating it explicitly or by implying it through the descriptive details and information they choose to include in the essay. Brian Cable, for example, by comparing the display of caskets to shiny new cars in a showroom, shares his realization about Americans' denial of death and our inclination to profit from it.

To analyze Edge's perspective in this essay, do the following:

- Reread paragraph 1, and highlight the descriptions of the patrons of Jesse's Place, noting particularly information suggesting the kinds of work they do and their socioeconomic class.
- Skim paragraph 15, where Jerry shows Edge how people like to eat pickled pig lips.
- Write a few sentences explaining Edge's perspective on this popular southern bar snack and how it may reflect his own class position.

❯ ANALYZING VISUALS

PHOTOGRAPH OF A PIG

Write a paragraph or two analyzing the photograph Edge includes in his essay, and explain what it contributes to the profile.

To analyze the visual, you can use the Criteria for Analyzing Visuals chart in Chapter 12 on pp. 390–91. The chart offers a series of questions you can ask yourself under two categories: Key Components and Rhetorical Context. You will see that there are a lot of questions, but don't feel you have to answer all of them. Focus on the questions that seem most productive in helping you write a short analysis. Try beginning with these questions:

Composition

- Edge could have used a full-body photograph of a pig, a photo of pigs at play, or some other composition. Why do you think he chose a close-up of a pig's face taken from one particular angle?

(continued)

(continued)

Rhetorical Context

- Given his purpose and audience, why do you think Edge chose a photograph of a pig instead of a photograph of pig lips in a jar or of people eating lips in a site like Jesse's Place? Why did he not choose a photograph of the Farm Fresh company or the Dufour family? What does the choice of visual suggest about the subject and the writer's perspective?

CONSIDERING TOPICS FOR YOUR OWN ESSAY

Consider writing about a place that serves, produces, or sells something unusual, perhaps something that, like Edge, you could try yourself for the purpose of further informing and engaging your readers. There are many possibilities: producer or packager of a special ethnic or regional food or a local café that serves it, licensed acupuncture clinic, caterer, novelty and toy balloon store, microbrewery, chain saw dealer, boat builder, talent agency, manufacturer of ornamental iron, bead store, nail salon, pet fish and aquarium supplier, detailing shop, tattoo parlor, scrap metal recycler, fly-fishing shop, handwriting analyst, dog or cat sitting service. If none of these appeal to you, try browsing the Yellow Pages in print or online at yellow.com. Remember that relating your experience with the service or product is a good idea but not a requirement for a successful profile.

 AMANDA COYNE, an award-winning staff writer for the *Anchorage Press*, earned an MFA in nonfiction writing from the University of Iowa. Coauthor of *Alaska Then and Now* (2008), a profile of Alaska across the decades, Coyne has written for the *New York Times Magazine* and *Newsweek*, among other national publications. Coyne also blogs on the *Huffington Post* and contributes to National Public Radio's *All Things Considered* and PRI's *This American Life*. "The Long Good-Bye," her first piece of published writing, originally appeared in *Harper's Magazine*.

Coyne's "Long Good-Bye" takes a more ethnographic turn than the other profiles in this chapter, in that she uses direct observation and interview over an extended period of time to study the behavior of a particular community. In this profile, Coyne examines women who have been incarcerated and separated from their children to see how the mothers and children negotiate their difficult relationships. As you read, think about what you learn about the stresses on these parent-child relationships. Which of these stresses seem particular to the situation Coyne describes? Are any of the factors present recognizable in the relationships of parents and children where prison is not a factor?

The Long Good-Bye: Mother's Day in Federal Prison

Amanda Coyne

1   You can spot the convict-moms here in the visiting room by the way they hold and touch their children and by the single flower that is perched in front of them — a rose, a tulip, a daffodil. Many of these mothers have untied the bow that attaches the flower to its silver-and-red cellophane wrapper and are using one of the many empty soda cans at hand as a vase. They sit proudly before their flower-in-a-Coke-can, amid Hershey bar wrappers, half-eaten Ding Dongs, and empty paper coffee cups. Occasionally, a mother will pick up her present and bring it to her nose when one of the bearers of the single flower — her child — asks if she likes it. And the mother will respond the way that mothers always have and always will respond when presented with a gift on this day. "Oh, I just love it. It's perfect. I'll put it in the middle of my Bible." Or, "I'll put it on my desk, right next to your school picture." And always: "It's the best one here."

2   But most of what is being smelled today is the children themselves. While the other adults are plunking coins into the vending machines, the mothers take deep whiffs from the backs of their children's necks, or kiss and smell the backs of their knees, or take off their shoes and tickle their feet and then pull them close to their noses. They hold them tight and take in their own second scent — the scent assuring them that these are still their children and that they still belong to them.

3   The visitors are allowed to bring in pockets full of coins, and today that Mother's Day flower, and I know from previous visits to my older sister here at the Federal Prison Camp for women in Pekin, Illinois, that there is always an aberrant urge to gather immediately around the vending machines. The sandwiches are stale, the coffee weak, the candy bars the ones we always pass up in a convenience store. But after we hand the children over to their mothers, we gravitate toward those machines. Like milling in the kitchen at a party. We all do it, and nobody knows why. Polite conversation ensues around the microwave while the popcorn is popping and the processed-chicken sandwiches are being heated. We ask one another where we are from, how long a drive we had. An occasional whistle through the teeth, a shake of the head. "My, my, long way from home, huh?"

> While the other adults are plunking coins into the vending machines, the mothers take deep whiffs from the backs of their children's necks, or kiss and smell the backs of their knees, or take off their shoes and tickle their feet and then pull them close to their noses.

"Staying at the Super 8 right up the road. Not a bad place." "Stayed at the Econo Lodge last time. Wasn't a good place at all." Never asking the questions we really want to ask: "What's she in for?" "How much time's she got left?" You never ask in the waiting room of a doctor's office either. Eventually, all of us — fathers, mothers, sisters, brothers, a few boyfriends, and very few husbands — return to the queen of the day, sitting at a fold-out table loaded with snacks, prepared for five or so hours of attempted normal conversation.

Most of the inmates are elaborately dressed, many in prison-crafted dresses and sweaters in bright blues and pinks. They wear meticulously applied makeup in corresponding hues, and their hair is replete with loops and curls — hair that only women with the time have the time for. Some of the better seamstresses have crocheted vests and purses to match their outfits. Although the world outside would never accuse these women of making haute-couture fashion statements, the fathers and the sons and the boyfriends and the very few husbands think they look beautiful, and they tell them so repeatedly. And I can imagine the hours spent preparing for this visit — hours of needles and hooks clicking over brightly colored yards of yarn. The hours of discussing, dissecting, and bragging about these visitors — especially the men. Hours spent in the other world behind the door where we're not allowed, sharing lipsticks and mascaras, and unraveling the occasional hair-tangled hot roller, and the brushing out and lifting and teasing . . . and the giggles that abruptly change into tears without warning — things that define any female-only world. Even, or especially, if that world is a female federal prison camp.   4

While my sister Jennifer is with her son in the playroom, an inmate's mother comes over to introduce herself to my younger sister, Charity, my brother, John, and me. She tells us about visiting her daughter in a higher-security prison before she was transferred here. The woman looks old and tired, and her shoulders sag under the weight of her recently acquired bitterness.   5

"Pit of fire," she says, shaking her head. "Like a pit of fire straight from hell. Never seen anything like it. Like something out of an old movie about prisons." Her voice is getting louder and she looks at each of us with pleading eyes. "My *daughter* was there. Don't even get me started on that place. Women die there."   6

John and Charity and I silently exchange glances.   7

"My daughter would come to the visiting room with a black eye and I'd think, 'All she did was sit in the car while her boyfriend ran into the house.' She didn't even touch the stuff. Never even handled it."   8

She continues to stare at us, each in turn. "Ten years. That boyfriend talked and he got three years. She didn't know anything. Had nothing to tell them. They gave her ten years. They called it conspiracy. Conspiracy? Aren't there real criminals out there?" She asks this with hands outstretched, waiting for an answer that none of us can give her.   9

The woman's daughter, the conspirator, is chasing her son through the maze of chairs and tables and through the other children. She's a twenty-four-year-old blonde, whom I'll call Stephanie, with Dorothy Hamill hair and matching dimples.   10

She looks like any girl you might see in any shopping mall in middle America. She catches her chocolate-brown son and tickles him, and they laugh and trip and fall together onto the floor and laugh harder.

11   Had it not been for that wait in the car, this scene would be taking place at home, in a duplex Stephanie would rent while trying to finish her two-year degree in dental hygiene or respiratory therapy at the local community college. The duplex would be spotless, with a blown-up picture of her and her son over the couch and ceramic unicorns and horses occupying the shelves of the entertainment center. She would make sure that her son went to school every day with stylishly floppy pants, scrubbed teeth, and a good breakfast in his belly. Because of their difference in skin color, there would be occasional tension — caused by the strange looks from strangers, teachers, other mothers, and the bullies on the playground, who would chant after they knocked him down, "Your Momma's white, your Momma's white." But if she were home, their weekends and evenings would be spent together transcending those looks and healing those bruises. Now, however, their time is spent eating visiting-room junk food and his school days are spent fighting the boys in the playground who chant, "Your Momma's in prison, your Momma's in prison."

12   He will be ten when his mother is released, the same age my nephew will be when his mother is let out. But Jennifer, my sister, was able to spend the first five years of Toby's life with him. Stephanie had Ellie after she was incarcerated. They let her hold him for eighteen hours, then sent her back to prison. She has done the "tour," and her son is a well-traveled six-year-old. He has spent weekends visiting his mother in prisons in Kentucky, Texas, Connecticut (the Pit of Fire), and now at last here, the camp — minimum security, Pekin, Illinois.

13   Ellie looks older than his age. But his shoulders do not droop like his grandmother's. On the contrary, his bitterness lifts them and his chin higher than a child's should be, and the childlike, wide-eyed curiosity has been replaced by defiance. You can see his emerging hostility as he and his mother play together. She tells him to pick up the toy that he threw, say, or to put the deck of cards away. His face turns sullen, but she persists. She takes him by the shoulders and looks him in the eye, and he uses one of his hands to swat at her. She grabs the hand and he swats with the other. Eventually, she pulls him toward her and smells the top of his head, and she picks up the cards or the toy herself. After all, it is Mother's Day and she sees him so rarely. But her acquiescence makes him angrier, and he stalks out of the playroom with his shoulders thrown back.

14   Toby, my brother and sister and I assure one another, will not have these resentments. He is better taken care of than most. He is living with relatives in Wisconsin. Good, solid, middle-class, churchgoing relatives. And when he visits us, his aunts and his uncle, we take him out for adventures where we walk down the alley of a city and pretend that we are being chased by the "bad guys." We buy him fast food, and his uncle, John, keeps him up well past his bedtime enthralling him with stories of the monkeys he met in India. A perfect mix, we try to convince one another. Until we take him to see his mother and on the drive back he asks the question that most confuses

him, and no doubt all the other children who spend much of their lives in prison visiting rooms: "Is my Mommy a bad guy?" It is the question that most seriously disorders his five-year-old need to clearly separate right from wrong. And because our own need is perhaps just as great, it is the question that haunts us as well.

Now, however, the answer is relatively simple. In a few years, it won't be. In a few years we will have to explain mandatory minimums, and the war on drugs, and the murky conspiracy laws, and the enormous amount of money and time that federal agents pump into imprisoning low-level drug dealers and those who happen to be their friends and their lovers. In a few years he might have the reasoning skills to ask why so many armed robbers and rapists and child-molesters and, indeed, murderers are punished less severely than his mother. When he is older, we will somehow have to explain to him the difference between federal crimes, which don't allow for parole, and state crimes, which do. We will have to explain that his mother was taken from him for five years not because she was a drug dealer but because she made four phone calls for someone she loved. **15**

But we also know it is vitally important that we explain all this without betraying our bitterness. We understand the danger of abstract anger, of being disillusioned with your country, and, most of all, we do not want him to inherit that legacy. We would still like him to be raised as we were, with the idea that we live in the best country in the world with the best legal system in the world — a legal system carefully designed to be immune to political mood swings and public hysteria; a system that promises to fit the punishment to the crime. We want him to be a good citizen. We want him to have absolute faith that he lives in a fair country, a country that watches over and protects its most vulnerable citizens: its women and children. **16**

So for now we simply say, "Toby, your mother isn't bad, she just did a bad thing. Like when you put rocks in the lawn mower's gas tank. You weren't bad then, you just did a bad thing." **17**

Once, after being given this weak explanation, he said, "I wish I could have done something really bad, like my Mommy. So I could go to prison too and be with her." **18**

It's now 3:00. Visiting ends at 3:30. The kids are getting cranky, and the adults are both exhausted and wired from too many hours of conversation, too much coffee and candy. The fathers, mothers, sisters, brothers, and the few boyfriends, and the very few husbands are beginning to show signs of gathering the trash. The mothers of the infants are giving their heads one last whiff before tucking them and their paraphernalia into their respective carrying cases. The visitors meander toward the door, leaving the older children with their mothers for one last word. But the mothers never say what they want to say to their children. They say things like, "Do well in school," "Be nice to your sister," "Be good for Aunt Berry, or Grandma." They don't say, "I'm sorry I'm sorry I'm sorry. I love you more than anything else in the world and I think about you every minute and I worry about you with a pain that shoots straight to my heart, a pain so great I think I will just burst when I think of you alone, without me. I'm sorry." **19**

20   We are standing in front of the double glass doors that lead to the outside world. My older sister holds her son, rocking him gently. They are both crying. We give her a look and she puts him down. Charity and I grasp each of his small hands, and the four of us walk through the doors. As we're walking out, my brother sings one of his banana songs to Toby.

21   "Take me out to the — " and Toby yells out, "Banana store!"

22   "Buy me some — "

23   "Bananas!!"

24   "I don't care if I ever come back. For it's root, root, root for the — "

25   "Monkey team!"

26   I turn back and see a line of women standing behind the glass wall. Some of them are crying, but many simply stare with dazed eyes. Stephanie is holding both of her son's hands in hers and speaking urgently to him. He is struggling, and his head is twisting violently back and forth. He frees one of his hands from her grasp, balls up his fist, and punches her in the face. Then he walks with purpose through the glass doors and out the exit. I look back at her. She is still in a crouched position. She stares, unblinking, through those doors. Her hands have left her face and are hanging on either side of her. I look away, but before I do, I see drops of blood drip from her nose, down her chin, and onto the shiny marble floor.

MAKING CONNECTIONS: UNFAIR PUNISHMENT

Coyne reflects near the end of the essay that she wishes her nephew Toby would "have absolute faith that he lives in a fair country" (par. 16). Yet she expects that, like Stephanie's son Ellie, Toby will become bitter and angry when he understands that "his mother was taken from him for five years not because she was a drug dealer but because she made four phone calls for someone she loved" (par. 15).

With other students in your class, discuss an occasion when you broke a rule or neglected to fulfill an obligation and believe your punishment did not fit the crime. Perhaps you broke a school regulation, violated a rule at work or on a team, or failed to meet a reasonable expectation of your parents or a friend. Perhaps you failed someone who trusted you and whose trust you valued. Although you willingly admit having done it, you may still feel the punishment was unjustified. Begin by briefly telling one another what you did and why you think the punishment was unfair. Then, together, consider the following questions as you discuss your ideas about what is fair and unfair:

- Why do you think the punishment was unfair? Were the rules or expectations that you broke clear and reasonable? Were they applied to everyone or only applied selectively or at the whim of those in power?

- Coyne uses the value term *fair* to describe what's wrong with the punishment her sister and some of the other women received. Why do you think Coyne believes her sister's punishment is unfair? Why does Stephanie's mother think her daughter's punishment is unfair? Do you agree or disagree?

ANALYZING WRITING STRATEGIES

Detailed Information about the Subject

Coyne conveys a lot of information about her sister and the other inmates. She focuses, however, on the effects of separation on mothers and children. The most powerful effects are revealed in Coyne's *anecdotes* portraying what happened between Stephanie and her son Ellie during this particular visit. **Anecdotes** are brief narratives about one-time events.

To analyze how Coyne uses anecdotes to present information about the effects of separation, do the following:

- Reread paragraphs 13 and 26, underlining the words that Coyne uses to present Ellie's hostile actions and putting brackets around the words Coyne uses to present his mother's reactions.

- Write a few sentences explaining what you learn from these anecdotes about the effects on Stephanie and Ellie of enforced separation.

A Clear Organizational Plan

Coyne's plan for her profile is narrative, spanning visiting hours at the Federal Prison Camp on one particular day, Mother's Day. The essay begins early in the visit and stops a few hours later, when the visiting period ends. But it does not follow a strict chronological order. Some events occur at the same time as other events. For example, paragraphs 1 to 3 present actions that occur at the same time: While mothers are getting reacquainted with their children (pars. 1 and 2), the family members are using the vending machines and chatting with one another.

To analyze Coyne's organizational plan, follow these suggestions:

- Reread the rest of the essay, noting in the margin when the events are happening in relation to the events in earlier paragraphs and highlighting any words, phrases, or sentences that let you know the time of the events.

- Write a few sentences analyzing and evaluating the effectiveness of this plan. Coyne could have chosen to organize her essay topically, by presenting a series of insights and impressions from the many visits she made instead of focusing on this particular Mother's Day. How does the focus Coyne chose help you understand the situation of the women and their families?

A Role for the Writer

Profile writers usually adopt either the role of a participant or the role of a spectator. Sometimes, they manage to use both roles, as Edge does. Because Coyne made her observations during a family visit to her sister, she has the opportunity to use both the spectator and the participant role in her essay.

To analyze the way Coyne uses the two roles, do the following:

- Skim the essay, looking for passages where Coyne shifts from the spectator to the participant role and back again to the spectator role. Note in the margin the role she is using, and highlight the words that let you know what her role is.

- Write a sentence or two describing how she uses the two roles and how she avoids confusing readers when she shifts from one role to the other.

● A Perspective on the Subject

Coyne seems concerned both about the difficult relationship between incarcerated mothers and their children and about the plight of women in the legal system. Coyne makes a judgment about the fairness of the laws that sent women like her sister Jennifer and Stephanie to prison, but she does not state it explicitly. Instead, she conveys her perspective indirectly through the dialogue, stories, and descriptive details she includes in the profile. Rather than *telling* readers what to think about this issue, she *shows* them what she used to reach her own conclusions, and hopes her readers will agree with her.

To analyze Coyne's perspective, do the following:

- Reread paragraphs 5–10 to see how Stephanie's mother explains her daughter's dilemma, paragraph 11 where Coyne presents a scene she imagines, and paragraph 15 to see what *Coyne speculates about.*

- Write a few sentences explaining how these three episodes convey Coyne's perspective. Give specific examples from the essay to help your readers understand why you think these episodes convey this particular perspective.

CONSIDERING TOPICS FOR YOUR OWN ESSAY

In researching her profile, Coyne spends the day in the visitor's room of a prison where she can observe and talk to prisoners and visitors, both adults and children. She has the advantage of having made many previous visits to this same prison's visitor's room, yet nearly all of the information presented in her profile comes from this one visit. You can replicate Coyne's method by profiling an activity occurring over a short period of time, in a relatively small space, and involving only a few people. You should visit the place several times beforehand, observing and talking to people on every visit, making notes in the process, and perhaps capturing a few digital images. Here are some manageable possibilities:

- the waiting room of the student health service's clinic on your campus, a day-care center, a hospital emergency room

- the practice sessions of a college sport or rehearsals of a small music ensemble

- the research lab where a small group of students is collaborating on the same project, or the campus learning or writing center where students come for help with their studies

- the broadcast room of a campus radio station or a production studio where film students are assembling a film

Guide to Writing

The Writing Assignment

Write an essay about an intriguing person, group of people, place, or activity in your community. Observe your subject closely, and then present what you have learned in a way that both informs and engages readers.

This Guide to Writing will help you apply what you have learned about how writers make their profile essays informative and entertaining. The Guide is divided into five sections with various activities in each section:

- **Invention and Research**
- **Planning and Drafting**
- **Critical Reading Guide**
- **Editing and Proofreading**
- **Revising**

The Guide is designed to escort you through the writing process, from finding an event to editing your finished essay. Your instructor may require you to follow the Guide to Writing from beginning to end. Working through the Guide to Writing in this way will help you — as it has helped many other college students — write a thoughtful, fully developed, polished essay.

If, however, your instructor gives you latitude to choose and if you have had experience writing a profile essay, then you can decide on the order in which you'll do the activities in the Guide to Writing. For example, the Invention and Research section includes activities to help you find a subject, choose a role, explore your preconceptions, research the subject, and develop a perspective you want your profile essay to take on the subject. Obviously, finding a subject must precede the other activities, but you may come to the Guide with a subject and a role already in mind, and you may do some preliminary research before you explore your preconceptions or choose to explore your preconceptions and develop a perspective as you are researching the subject. In fact, you may find your response to one of the invention activities expanding into a draft before you have had a chance to do any of the other activities. Writers sometimes find that, in writing up their observation and interview notes, they are in effect drafting parts of their essay. That is a good thing — but you should later flesh out your draft by going back to the activities you skipped and layering the new material into your draft.

The following chart will help you find answers to many of the questions you might have about planning, drafting, and revising a profile. The page references in the right-hand column refer to examples from the readings, activities in the Guide to Writing, and chapters later in the book.

Starting Points: Writing a Profile

●●●● Basic Features

Choosing a Subject	
How do I come up with an appropriate subject to profile?	• Considering Topics for Your Own Essay (pp. 74, 81) • Choosing a Subject to Profile (pp. 84–86) • Finalizing Your Choice (pp. 86–87) • Testing Your Choice (p. 88) • Setting Up a Tentative Schedule (pp. 88–89)
What's my purpose in writing? How can I convince my audience that the subject is worth profiling?	• Reading Profiles: Purpose and Audience (pp. 61–62) • Exploring Your Preconceptions (p. 87) • Reflecting on Your Purpose and the Profile's Perspective (p. 92) • Refining Your Purpose and Setting Goals (pp. 93–94)

Detailed Information about the Subject	
How can I gather information on my subject?	• Collecting Information from Field Research (pp. 89–91) • Chapter 15, "Field Research"
How can I make my subject come to life?	• Reading Profiles: Basic Features (pp. 60–61) • Use naming, detailing, and comparing (metaphor and simile) (pp. 71–72) • Use anecdotes (p. 80) • A Sentence Strategy: Absolute Phrases (p. 96) • Working with Sources: Integrating Quotations from Your Interviews (pp. 97–98)

A Clear Organizational Plan	
How should I organize my profile?	• Reading Profiles: Basic Features (pp. 60–61) • Using a narrative or topical plan (p. 72) • Refining Your Purpose and Setting Goals: Presenting the Information (p. 94) • Outlining Your Draft (p. 95)

A Role for the Writer	
What role should I adopt in researching and presenting my subject?	• Reading Profiles: Basic Features (pp. 60–61) • Choose a role: spectator or participant (p. 61) • Refining Your Purpose and Setting Goals: Using Your Role (p. 94)

	A Perspective on the Subject
How do I develop and express a clear perspective on the subject?	• Reading Profiles: Basic Features (pp. 60–61) • Exploring Your Preconceptions (p. 87) • Reflecting on Your Purpose and the Profile's Perspective (p. 92) • Considering Your Thesis (pp. 92–93) • Refining Your Purpose and Setting Goals: Clarifying the Dominant Impression (pp. 93–94)

Invention and Research

Some of the following invention activities will take only a few minutes each to complete, but the field research — making detailed observations and conducting interviews — will take more time to plan and carry out. There is much to learn about observing, interviewing, and writing about what you have discovered, and these activities will support your learning. Remember to keep a written record of your invention work: You will need it when you draft the essay and later when you revise it.

Choosing a Subject to Profile

List several possible subjects, and choose one to explore. You may already have a subject in mind, perhaps one suggested by the Considering Topics for Your Own Essay activities following the readings. Reread any notes you might have made in response to those suggestions. Below are criteria you should keep in mind as you make your choice. Also consider the kinds of subjects listed below and the advice on using the Web to find a subject.

Criteria for Choosing a Profile Subject: A Checklist

Your subject — whether it's a person, a group of people, a place, or an activity — should be

☐ a subject that you can gain access to in the time allowed for researching the essay, enabling you to make detailed observations;

☐ a subject about which (or with whom) you can conduct in-depth interviews;

☐ a subject about which/whom you can find background information (if required by your instructor);

☐ a subject about which/whom you have special insight, or at least strong ideas or curiosity;

☐ a subject your readers would find interesting and informative.

Kinds of Subjects to Consider

Community-Related Subjects

- an activity that takes a "broken windows" approach to community improvement (for example, helping people in a neighborhood fix broken windows, paint their homes, plant trees, or remove graffiti)

- a facility that provides a needed service at your college or in the community (for example, a legal advice bureau, child-care center, medical clinic, or homeless shelter)

- a place where people come together because they are of the same age, gender, or ethnic group (for example, a foreign language–speaking dorm or Lesbian Gay Bisexual Transgender club) or a place where people of different ages, genders, or ethnic groups have formed a community (for example, a Sunday morning pickup basketball game in the park, political action headquarters, or barber shop)

- a person who is a community leader, a volunteer, or an elected official with the ability to bring people together or solve local problems

Career- and Work-Related Subjects

- activities performed by researchers on your campus (for example, nanotechnology, forensics, entomology, indigenous languages, or religious studies)

- a place where people are trained for a certain kind of work (for example, a police academy, cosmetology program, or truck driving school) or a person preparing for a particular kind of work (for example, a boxer preparing for a fight, an attorney preparing for a trial, or an actor rehearsing a role)

- activities performed on your campus by a department, program, club, or center (for example, a center for crime and justice studies, medical and health career program, or center for sustainable development)

- a place where you could learn more about the kind of career you would like to pursue (for example, a law office, dental office, or television station) or where people do a kind of work you would like to know more about (for example, a clothing factory, dairy farm, or racetrack)

- a person working in the career you are thinking of pursuing or a college senior or graduate student in a major you are considering who could help you learn about the kind of preparation needed

- people working together for a particular purpose (for example, students and their teacher working together to prepare for the academic decathlon competition, employees working together to produce something, or scientists collaborating on a research project)

Using the Web to Find and Explore a Profile Subject

You could search the following Internet sites for possible subjects:

- your campus Web site for potentially intriguing places, activities, people, or programs (for example, campus freshman tours, disability services, student clubs, or the academic senate)
- a city or state Web site for interesting places or people (for example, the city council, EMS department, public records department, or a jury room)
- Google or YellowPages.com for unusual local restaurants or small businesses (like these near Riverside, California: Al Kauser Halal Meat, Association of Nigerian Physicians in the Americas, La Sierra Fire Equipment, or Scuba Bee Supplies)

Once you have found a subject, exploring the Web may help you find background information that could help you develop questions to ask in your interview:

- Google the subject to find possible sources of information. (For example, if you are planning on interviewing a local beekeeper, Googling "beekeeping" will give you a lot of information about the process and history as well as possible causes and effects of the die-off of honey bees.)
- If you are writing about a person, try searching Facebook or some other social networking site for background on him or her.

Make notes of any information or insights suggested by your online research, and download any visuals you might include in your essay, being sure to get the information necessary to cite any online sources. (See p. 505–07 for the MLA citation format for electronic sources.)

●●
Ways In: Finalizing Your Choice
Basic Features

To be certain that the subject you have chosen will work, you need to check that you can get access to the subject and also see whether the role you want to adopt will be possible. You may do these in either order or even at the same time.

Checking That You Can Do the Field Research

- Check to be sure that you can get access to the place or activity you want to observe and/or the people you want to interview. Observing some places and activities may not require special planning, but interviews will nearly always require advance scheduling.
- You may have to go to the place to find out who you need to get permission from, or you may be able to phone or e-mail your request. Either way, build in time for a response to your request.

- Explain that your project is for a class and why you are interested. Most people tend to be surprisingly generous with their time and eager to help students, but be prepared for occasional refusals, and always make an effort to be polite, dress properly, come on time, and conduct yourself professionally.

(See Chapter 15 for more advice on planning your observations and interviews.)

Getting Permission for Your Role

You may need to get permission to do your research from someone in authority and also from your instructor.

Participant Observer

- If you are new to the subject, ask permission to take part in a small way for a limited time (for example, by making a hamburger at a fast-food restaurant).
- If you are already an insider, ask your instructor whether you should assume your regular role; he or she may require you to find a new angle instead so that you learn something new. (For example, if you're on the football team, you might focus not on the players but on the cheerleaders or the people who maintain the field.)

Spectator Role. To use this role effectively, you need to get close enough to look over the shoulder of people who are centrally involved. Ask permission from those in charge to interview participants and observe them in action.

● Exploring Your Preconceptions

Write a paragraph or two describing what you already know and think about your subject and what you would like to learn about it. The following questions will get you started:

What I Already Know about This Subject

- *How can I define or describe it?*
- *What are its chief qualities or parts?*
- *Whom do I associate with it?*
- *What is its purpose or function?*
- *How does it compare with other subjects with which I am more familiar?*

My Expectations about This Subject

- *Why do I assume it will be interesting to me and to my readers?*
- *What do I hope to learn about it?*
- *How does this subject reflect cultural or community values and concerns?*

Testing Your Choice

Decide whether you should proceed with this particular subject. Giving up on a profile subject is bound to be frustrating, but if, after doing some work on it, the subject does not seem a strong possibility for you to research and write about, starting over may be the wisest course of action. The questions that follow may help you decide whether to go on with this subject or begin looking for an alternative.

- *After reviewing my possible subjects, do I still feel that I have made the best choice, or does another subject seem more promising?*
- *Do I still feel curious about the subject?*
- *Am I confident I will be able to make the subject interesting for my readers?*
- *Do I believe that I can research this subject sufficiently in the time I have?*

A Collaborative Activity: Testing Your Choice

Get together with two or three other students, and describe the subject you have chosen to profile.

Presenters: Take turns identifying your subjects. Explain your interest in the subject, and speculate about why you think it will interest readers.

Listeners: Briefly tell each presenter what you already know about his or her subject, if anything, and what might make it interesting to readers.

Setting Up a Tentative Schedule

Create a tentative schedule for your observations, interviews, and background research. You might use a chart like the one that follows, which you can update as you go along. Think about the order in which each activity should be completed. Sometimes it's best to start with observations; other times it's best to begin with an interview, a trip to the library, or an Internet search for background information. Notice that immediately after the observations and interviews, you need to give yourself five minutes or so to clarify and add to your notes. It is also a good idea to do write-ups for each observation and interview; your instructor may ask you to bring your write-ups to class, and you can use them when you draft your essay. (See the sections that follow for more information on making observations and conducting interviews, and refer to Chapter 15: Field Research for more detail.)

Date	Time Needed	Purpose	Preparation
10/22	30 minutes	Background Internet research	Print map, bookmark potentially useful sites
10/23	30 minutes	1st observation: Find out whom to interview, pick up any materials	Bring map, directions, paper & pen
10/23	30 minutes	Write up 1st observation (for class) & schedule interview	Review observation notes
10/24	45 minutes	1st interview. While there schedule 2nd interview	Prepare questions
10/24	20 minutes	Write up 1st interview (for class)	Review interview notes
10/25	1 hour	2nd observation and interview	Bring notes on needed details & prepare 2nd interview questions

Ways In: Collecting Information from Field Research

Basic Features

The following activities will help you make observations and conduct interviews. Many writers begin with observation to get the lay of the land and decide whom to interview, but you can start with either one. You may also be able to make observations and conduct interviews during the same visit.

Making Observations

Come Prepared. *Bring a notepad, pen, and any necessary devices (such as a phone with a camera and audio recorder) to each observational visit.*

Take Notes. *Use all of your senses — sight, hearing, smell, taste, and touch:*

- Describe the place from multiple vantage points, noting furnishings, décor, etc.
- Sketch the layout.
- Describe people's appearance, dress, gestures, and actions, but be careful not to invade people's privacy.

(continued)

(continued)

- Note what is happening, who does what, how people seem to feel.
- Make a record of interesting overheard conversation.
- Note your reactions, insights, and ideas, especially in relation to your preconceptions and the perspective you might take in your essay.

Collect Visuals. *Look for artifacts, and consider taking photographs you could include in your profile.*

- Collect any brochures or other written material you might be able to use either to prepare for interviews or to include in your essay.
- Consider taking photographs or videos (but be sure to ask permission of the people you are photographing).
- Take a 360-degree video of the place, a pan shot scanning the scene from side to side, or a tracking shot indicating what you see as you enter or walk through the place.

Reflect on Your Observations. *Take five minutes right after your visit to think about what you observed, and write a few sentences about your impressions of the subject:*

- What seems most interesting to you now?
- How did your visit confirm or change your preconceptions?
- What is your dominant impression of the subject?

Write Up Your Observations. *Compose a few paragraphs reporting on your visit.* Your instructor may ask you to bring these paragraphs to class, and writing up your observations may produce language you can use in your draft. It will certainly help you think about how to describe your subject, what impression you want to create, and the perspective your profile should take.

Do a Follow-up Observation. *Consider returning for a follow-up visit, which you could combine with a scheduled interview.* Examine other aspects of the place or activity, and try to answer questions you still have. Consider whether the impression you had on the first visit holds and what else you could note that would make your description vivid.

Conducting Interviews

Come Prepared. *Bring preliminary questions, a notepad, pen, and any necessary recording devices to each interview.*

Take Notes. *Write down potentially important information and anything quotable.* Describe the interviewee's tone, gestures, mannerisms — anything that would provide vivid description and add to the overall impression.

- To generate **anecdotes,** ask how the interviewee got involved in the first place; if there was a high or a low point, a breakthrough, or a key event worth noting; what most concerns the interviewee; what has been the biggest influence for good or ill.
- To elicit **process narratives,** ask how it works; what happens if it breaks down; whether it was always done the same way; how it has changed; how it could be improved.
- To **classify, compare,** or **contrast,** ask what kind of thing it is; how it is like and unlike others of its kind; how it compares to what it was like in the past.
- To help you think about your **perspective,** ask why the interviewee thinks it is important, needed, helpful, etc., and who would agree and disagree; what the purpose of it is or how it contributes to the community; what its shortcomings are or how it could be improved.

Reflect on the Interview. *Take five minutes right after your interview to review your notes.* Later, you can listen to or watch any recordings you made at the scene and add to your notes. Focus now on your first impressions. Mark the promising material — for example:

- anything new or surprising that calls into question your own or your readers' likely preconceptions;
- sensory details you could use to create a vivid portrait of the place, people, and activity;
- quotable words and phrases that could help you capture the tone or mood of the subject;
- questions you still need answered;
- insights and ideas you might research further; and
- anything that could help you clarify or develop your perspective on the subject.

Write Up Your Interview. *Write a few paragraphs, deciding what to quote, summarize, paraphrase, or leave out.* Be sure to describe the person's tone of voice, gestures, and appearance as well as any details you noticed about the place. You may decide not to include all of this material in your essay, but it will help you figure out what is important and interesting.

Do a Follow-up Interview. *If your interviewee said you could e-mail or phone to check your facts, follow up with questions or requests for clarification.* You might also arrange to talk to another person who has different kinds of information to share.

Ways In: Reflecting on Your Purpose and the Profile's Perspective

● **Basic Features**

The following activities, which can be done in any order, will help you deepen your analysis and think of ways to help your readers gain a better understanding of your subject's cultural significance.

Developing a Perspective

Write for five minutes exploring your perspective on the subject — what it is about the subject that seems important and meaningful.

- If you are focusing on a **place**, ask yourself what is interesting to you about its culture: What rituals are practiced there? Who visits it? What is its function in the community?
- If you are focusing on an **activity**, consider how it has changed over time, for good or for ill; how outsiders are initiated into the activity; who benefits from the activity; and what its value is for the community.
- If you are focusing on a **person** or **group**, ask yourself what sense of identity they have; what customs and ways of communicating they follow; what their values and attitudes are; what they think about social hierarchies or gender difference; and how they see their role in the community.

Defining Your Purpose for Your Readers

Write for five minutes exploring what you want your readers to learn about the subject. Use these questions to help you clarify your thinking:

- Who are your intended readers? What are they likely to know and think about your subject?
- What about your subject will be surprising to them?
- How can you make your perspective on this subject interesting to your readers?
- How can you help readers examine their own preconceptions or stereotypes about the subject?
- How can you lead readers to think about the subject's social and cultural significance — that is, what it implies about our shared or different values and concerns?

Considering Your Thesis

Review what you wrote under Developing a Perspective and Defining Your Purpose for Your Readers, and add a couple of sentences summarizing the main idea you want readers to take away from your essay.

Remember that readers do not expect a profile to have the kind of explicit thesis statement typical of argumentative essays, but they do need the descriptive details and other information to work together to create a dominant impression.

Designing Your Document

Think about whether visual or audio elements — photographs, postcards, menus, or snippets from films, television programs, or songs — would strengthen your profile. These are not a requirement for an effective profile, but they can be helpful. Consider also whether your readers might benefit from design features such as headings, bulleted or numbered lists, or other typographic elements that can make an essay easier to follow.

Think of the profiles you have seen in a magazine or on a Web page or television show. What visual or audio elements, if any, were used to create a strong sense of the subject being profiled? Photographs? Postcards? Menus? Signs? Song lyrics?

As you review the questions on the next few pages, especially those under "Refining Your Purpose and Setting Goals," think about the ways in which you might show as well as tell readers about your object of study. (Remember that you must cite the source of any visual or audio element you do not create yourself, and you should also request permission from the source if your essay is going to be posted on a Web site that is not password-protected.)

Planning and Drafting

The following activities will help you refine your purpose, set goals for your draft, and outline it. In addition, this section will help you write a draft by writing opening sentences, trying out a useful sentence strategy, and learning how to work with sources.

Refining Your Purpose and Setting Goals

Before starting to draft, here are some questions that may help you sharpen your purpose for your audience and set goals for your draft. Your instructor may ask you to write out your answers to some of these questions or simply to think about them as you plan and draft your essay.

Clarifying the Dominant Impression

Although you are trying to create a dominant impression with the description and information you include in your essay, you should be careful not to oversimplify or whitewash it. Readers appreciate profiles that reveal the richness and complexity of the subject. For example, even as Brian Cable shows that the Goodbody Mortuary is guided by crass commercialism, he also gets readers to think about cultural attitudes about death, perhaps exemplified in his own complex feelings.

- Review your observation and interview notes and write-ups, highlighting in one color the descriptive language that supports the dominant impression you want your essay to create.

- Highlight in a second color any descriptions that seem to create a different impression.

- Write for a few minutes exploring how these different impressions relate to one another. Consider whether they reveal complexity in the subject or ambivalence in your perspective that could be developed further in your essay.

Presenting the Information

Review your invention writing, noting in the margin which bits of information you should include in your draft and how you might present them. Consider the following:

- *What special terms will I need to define for my readers?*

- *What comparisons or contrasts might make the information clearer and more memorable?*

- *Which information could be listed or categorized?*

- *How can I present causes or effects in a vivid way?*

- *From my interview(s) and background research, what lively language should I quote (instead of summarizing or paraphrasing)?*

Using Your Role

Whether you chose to adopt a participant-observer or spectator role, you need to think about how you can use your role to engage readers and present the information you have chosen to include. Either role can be used to help readers identify with you. For example, if you are entering a place most of us avoid (as Cable does when he enters the mortuary), you can take us with you as you learn about the place and look over other people's shoulders to see what they are doing. Or if you act as a participant trying to learn how to do what others routinely do (as Edge does when he tries to eat a pickled pig lip), readers can imagine themselves in your shoes.

Regardless of your role, also consider how to refer to yourself in your draft. Here are some possibilities:

- Use the first-person pronoun. (For example, "*I'm not leaving until I eat this thing, I tell myself*" [Edge, par. 2].)

- Place yourself at the scene. (For example, "I followed him through an arched doorway into a chapel that smelled musty and old" [Cable, par. 15].)

- Refer to your own actions. (For example, "John and Charity and I silently exchange glances" [Coyne, par. 7].)

- Share your thoughts and feelings. (For example, "Death may be the great leveler, but one's coffin quickly reestablishes one's status" [Cable, par. 17].)

Outlining Your Draft

It may already be clear to you whether you should organize your information topically or narratively — or try to combine the two as Edge does when he uses his story about eating a pig lip as a frame for the topical presentation of the information he learned from observing and interviewing at the Farm Fresh Food Supplier plant.

If you plan to arrange your material *narratively*, plot the key events on a timeline. The following suggests one possible way to organize a narrative profile of a place:

I. Begin by describing the place from the outside.

II. Present background information.

III. Describe what you see as you enter.

IV. Introduce the people and activities.

V. Tour the place, describing what you see as you move from one part to the next.

VI. Fill in information wherever you can, and comment about the place or the people.

VII. Conclude with reflections on what you have learned about the place.

If you plan to arrange your material *topically*, use clustering or outlining to help you divide and group related information. Here is a suggested outline for a topical profile about a person:

I. Begin with a vivid image of the person in action.

II. Present the first topic. (A topic could be a characteristic of the person or one aspect of his or her work.) Use dialogue, description, narration, process description, evaluation, or interpretation to illustrate this topic.

III. Present the second topic. Use dialogue, description, narration, process description, evaluation, or interpretation to illustrate this topic.

IV. Present the third topic (and continue as above until you have presented all topics).

V. Conclude with a bit of action or dialogue.

The tentative plan you choose should reflect the possibilities in your material as well as your purpose and readers. As you begin drafting, you will almost certainly discover new ways of organizing parts of your material.

For more on clustering and outlining, see Chapter 8, pp. 317–22.

Drafting

If you have not already begun to draft your essay, this section will help by suggesting how to write your opening sentences, how to use temporal transitions and verb tense to draft a narrative that readers will be able to follow, and how to integrate quotations from your interviews. Drafting isn't always a smooth process, so don't be afraid to leave spaces where you don't know what to put in or to write notes to yourself about what you still need to do. If you get stuck while drafting, go back over your invention writing: You may be able to copy and paste some of it into your evolving draft, or you may need to do some additional invention to fill in details in your draft.

Writing the Opening Sentences

You could try out one or two different ways of beginning your essay — possibly from the list that follows — but do not agonize over the first sentences because you are likely to discover the best way to begin only as you draft your essay. Review your invention writing to see if you have already written something that would work to launch your essay. To engage your readers' interest from the start, consider the following opening strategies:

- a remarkable thought or occasion that triggers your observational visit (like Cable)
- a vivid description (like Coyne)
- a compelling description of the time and place (like Edge)
- a surprising statement
- an arresting quotation
- a fascinating bit of information
- an amusing anecdote

A Sentence Strategy: Absolute Phrases

As you draft your profile, you will need to help your readers imagine your subject. A grammatical structure called an **absolute phrase** is useful for this purpose. Here is an example, with the absolute phrase in italics:

> I offer the bag to Jerry, order yet another beer, and turn to eye the pig feet floating in a murky jar by the cash register, *their blunt tips bobbing up through a pasty white film.* (Edge, par. 19)

Edge could have presented his observation of the pickled pig feet in a separate sentence, but the sentence he wrote brings together his turning and looking and what he actually saw, emphasizing the at-a-glance instant of another possible stomach flutter.

Absolute phrases modify a whole sentence or a clause, rather than a single word. They are nearly always attached to the end of a main clause, adding various kinds of details to it to create a more complex, informative sentence. They are usually introduced by a noun (like *tips*) or a possessive pronoun (like *his, its,* or *their*), followed by participial phrases (like *bobbing up . . .*). Here are two further examples of absolute phrases from this chapter's readings:

> This was a solid bronze casket, *its seams electronically welded to resist corrosion.* (Cable, par. 21)

> Slowly, the dank barroom fills with grease-smeared mechanics from the truck stop up the road and farmers straight from the fields, *the soles of their brogans thick with dirt clods.* (Edge, par. 1)

Absolute phrases are certainly not required for a successful profile — experienced writers use them only occasionally — yet they do offer writers an effective sentence option. Try them out in your own writing.

For more on using absolute phrases, go to **bedfordstmartins.com/conciseguide** and click on Sentence Strategies.

Working with Sources:
Integrating Quotations from Your Interviews

One of the ways profiles present information from interviews is by quoting. These quotations can be especially revealing because they let readers hear different people speaking for themselves. Nevertheless, it is the writer who decides which quotations to use and how. Therefore, one major task you face in drafting and revising your essay is to choose quotations from your notes, present them in a timely way to reveal the style and character of people you interviewed, and integrate these quotations smoothly into your sentences.

When you directly quote (rather than paraphrase or summarize) what someone has said, you will usually need to identify the speaker. The principal way to do so is to create what is called a **speaker tag**. You may rely on a general or all-purpose speaker tag, such as *said*:

> Once, after being given this weak explanation, he *said,* "I wish I could have done something really bad, like my Mommy. So I could go to prison too and be with her." (Coyne, par. 18)

Other speaker tags are more specific:

> "It was a large service," *remarked* Howard. (Cable, par. 16)

> "Something deep within us demands a confrontation with death," Tim *explained.* (Cable, par. 23)

> "Take me out to the" — and Toby *yells out,* "Banana store!" (Coyne, par. 21)

As you draft your profile, consider using specific speaker tags. They give readers more help with imagining speakers' attitudes and personal styles. You may also add a word or phrase to any speaker tag to identify or describe the speaker or to reveal more about *how, where, when,* or *why* the speaker speaks:

> "We're in *Ripley's Believe It or Not,* along with another funeral home whose owners' names are Baggit and Sackit," Howard told me, *without cracking a smile.* (Cable, par. 14)

> "I started out with my daddy when I wasn't much more than 10," Lionel told me, *his shy smile framed by a coarse black mustache flecked with whispers of gray.* (Edge, par. 8)

> "Kind of look like Frosted Flakes, don't they?" he says, *by way of describing the chips rapidly turning to mush in the pickling juice.* (Edge, par. 19)

In addition to being carefully introduced, quotations must be precisely punctuated, and fortunately there are only two general rules:

1. Enclose all quotations in quotation marks. These always come in pairs: one at the beginning, one at the end of the quotation. Be especially careful not to forget to include the one at the end.

2. Separate the quotation from its speaker tag with appropriate punctuation, usually a comma. But if you have more than one sentence be careful to punctuate the separate sentences properly.

For more on integrating quotations, go to **bedfordstmartins.com/conciseguide** and click on Bedford Research Room; see also Chapter 17, pp. 490–91.

Critical Reading Guide

Basic Features

Your instructor may arrange a peer review session in class or online where you can exchange drafts with your classmates and give one another a thoughtful critical reading, pointing out what works well and suggesting ways to improve the draft. This Critical Reading Guide can also be used productively by a tutor in the writing center or by a roommate or family member. A good critical reading does three things: It lets the writer know how the reader understands the point of the profile, praises what works best, and indicates where the draft could be improved.

1. Assess the quality and presentation of information about the subject.

    Summarize: Tell the writer one thing you learned about the subject from reading the essay.

    Praise: Point out one passage where the description seems especially vivid, a quotation stands out, or another writing strategy — defining, comparing or contrasting, classifying, explaining causes or effects, narrating anecdotes or processes, giving examples or lists — works particularly well to present information.

    Critique: Point out one passage where description could be added or where the description could be made more vivid, where a quotation falls flat and should be paraphrased or summarized, or where another writing strategy — defining, comparing or contrasting, classifying, explaining causes or effects, narrating anecdotes or processes, giving examples or lists — could be added or improved.

2. Analyze the organizational plan.

    Summarize: Identify the kind of plan — narrative, topical, or both — the draft uses.

    Praise: Comment on the plan's effectiveness. For example, point to a place where one topic leads logically to the next or where temporal transitions help you follow the narrative organization. Also, indicate what in the opening paragraphs grabs your attention or why you think the ending works well.

    Critique: Point to information that seems out of place or where the chronology is confusing. If you think the opening or ending could be improved, suggest an alternative passage in the essay that could work as an opening or an ending.

3. Evaluate the writer's role.

    Summarize: Identify the role — spectator or participant observer — the writer adopts.

Praise: Point to a passage where the spectator or participant-observer role enables you to identify with the writer, enhancing the essay's immediacy or interest.

Critique: Point out any problems with the role — for example, if the participant-observer role becomes tiresome or distracting, or if the spectator role seems too mechanical and distant.

4. Evaluate how well the author's perspective on the subject and the dominant impression are conveyed.

Summarize: State briefly what you believe to be the writer's perspective on the subject and the dominant impression you get from the essay.

Praise: Give an example where you have a strong sense of the writer's perspective through a comment, description, quotation, or bit of information.

Critique: Tell the writer if the essay does not have a clear perspective or convey a dominant impression. To help him or her find one, explain what interests you about the subject and what you think is important. If you see contradictions in the draft that could be developed to make the profile more complex and illuminating, briefly explain.

5. If the writer has expressed concern about anything in the draft that you have not discussed, respond to that concern.

Making Comments Electronically Most word processing software offers features that allow you to insert comments directly into the text of someone else's document. Many readers prefer to make their comments this way because it tends to be faster than writing on hard copy and space is virtually unlimited; it also eliminates the process of deciphering handwritten comments. Where such features are not available, simply typing comments directly into a document in a contrasting color can provide the same advantages.

For a printable version of this Critical Reading Guide, go to **bedfordstmartins.com/conciseguide**.

Revising

Very likely you have already thought of ways to improve your draft, and you may even have begun to revise it. In this section is a Troubleshooting chart that may help. Before using the chart, however, it is a good idea to

- review critical reading comments from your classmates, instructor, or writing center tutor, and
- make an outline of your draft so that you can look at it analytically.

Making an outline of the draft, even if you made an outline before drafting, can help you see what you actually wrote as opposed to what you intended to write. Your aim should not be to make your draft conform to your original draft, but to make your draft as good as it can be.

For an electronic version of the Troubleshooting chart, go to **bedfordstmartins.com/conciseguide**.

✔ Troubleshooting Your Draft

● ● ● ● **Basic Features**

Detailed Information about the Subject	
People do not come alive.	☐ Describe a physical feature or mannerism that gives each person individuality. ☐ Add speaker tags to characterize how people talk. ☐ Liven up the dialogue with faster repartee. ☐ Add details to help readers see the person. ☐ Consider adding a comparison. ☐ Use anecdotes or specific narrative action to show the person in action.
The place is hard to visualize.	☐ Name objects in the scene. ☐ Add sensory detail — sight, sound, smell, taste, touch. ☐ Say what the place is like or unlike. ☐ Consider adding a visual — a photograph or sketch, for example.
There is too much information — it is not clear what is important.	☐ Cut extraneous information, or make clearer why the information is important. ☐ Break up long blocks of informational text with description of scenes or people, narration of events, or examples. ☐ Vary the writing strategies used to present the information: For example, add a comparison or discuss known causes or effects. ☐ Consider which parts of the information would be more engaging if presented through dialogue or summarized more succinctly.
Visuals could be added or improved.	☐ Use a photo, map, drawing, cartoon, or other visual that might make the place and people easier to imagine or the information more understandable. ☐ Consider adding textual references to any images in your essay or positioning images more effectively.

A Clear Organizational Plan

The narrative plan drags or rambles.	☐ Try adding drama through dialogue or specific narrative action. ☐ Summarize or paraphrase instead if dialogue seems pointless or uninteresting. ☐ Give the narrative shape — for example, by building suspense or tension. ☐ Make sure the narrative unfolds or develops and has a direction that is clear.
Topically arranged essay is disorganized or out of balance.	☐ Try rearranging topics to see whether another order makes more sense. ☐ Add clearer, more explicit transitions or topic sentences. ☐ Move or condense information to restore balance.
The opening fails to engage readers' attention.	☐ Consider alternatives. Think of questions, an engaging image, or dialogue you could open with. ☐ Go back to your notes for other ideas. ☐ Recall how the writers in this chapter open their profiles: Cable stands on the street in front of the mortuary, Edge sits at a bar staring at a pig lip.
Transitions are missing or are confusing.	☐ Add appropriate transitional words or phrases. ☐ Revise sentences to make transitions clearer or smoother.
The ending seems weak.	☐ Consider ending earlier or moving a striking insight to the end. ☐ Review your invention and research notes to see if you overlooked something that would make for a strong ending. ☐ Recall how the writers in this chapter end their profiles: Cable touches the cold flesh of a cadaver, Edge stares at pig feet.
Visual features are not effective.	☐ Use an image, as Edge does. Consider adding textual references to any images in your essay or positioning images more effectively. ☐ Think of other possible design features — drawings, lists, tables, graphs, cartoons, headings — that might make the place and people easier to imagine or the information more understandable.

A Role for the Writer	
The spectator role is too distant.	☐ Consider placing yourself in the scene as you describe it. ☐ Add your thoughts and reactions to one of the interviews.
Participation is distracting.	☐ Bring other people forward by adding material about them. ☐ Reduce the material about yourself.

A Perspective on the Subject	
The perspective or dominant impression is unclear.	☐ Try stating it more directly by adding your thoughts or someone else's. ☐ Be sure that the descriptive and narrative details reinforce the dominant impression you want your essay to convey. ☐ If your perspective is complex, you may need to discuss more directly the contradictions or complications you see in the subject.
Readers don't find the perspective interesting.	☐ Consider how you can appeal to readers' interests. ☐ Reconsider what you think is important about the subject in light of readers' ideas, and consider expanding your ideas. ☐ Elaborate on your perspective, helping readers understand why you think it is culturally significant.

Editing and Proofreading

Now is the time to check your revised draft for errors in grammar, punctuation, and mechanics. Our research has identified several errors that occur often in profiles, including problems with the punctuation of quotations and the order of adjectives. The following guidelines will help you check your essay for these common errors.

Checking the Punctuation of Quotations

Because most profiles are based in part on interviews, you probably have quoted one or more people in your essay. When you quote someone's exact words, you must enclose these words in quotation marks and observe strict conventions for punctuating them.

What to Check For:

- All quotations should have quotation marks at the beginning and the end.

  ▶ "What exactly is civil litigation?" I asked.

- Commas and periods go *inside* quotation marks.

  ▶ "I'm here to see Anna Post ," I replied nervously.

  ▶ Tony explained, "Fraternity boys just wouldn't feel comfortable at the Chez Moi Café."

- Question marks and exclamation points go *inside* closing quotation marks if they are a part of the quotation, *outside* if they are not.

  ▶ After a pause, the patient asked, "Where do I sign ?"

  ▶ Willie insisted, "You can *too* learn to play Super Mario !"

  ▶ When was the last time someone you just ticketed said to you, "Thank you, Officer, for doing a great job ?"

- Use commas with speaker tags (*he said, she asked*, etc.) that accompany direct quotations.

  ▶ "This sound system costs only four thousand dollars ," Jorge said.

  ▶ I asked ,"So where were these clothes from originally?"

For practice, go to **bedfordstmartins.com/conciseguide/exercisecentral** and click on Punctuation of Quotations.

A Common ESL Problem: Adjective Order

The Problem: In trying to present the subject of your profile vividly and in detail, you probably have included many descriptive adjectives. When you include more than one adjective in front of a noun, you may have difficulty sequencing them. For example, do you write *a large old ceramic pot* or *an old large ceramic pot?*

How to Correct It: The following list shows the order in which adjectives are ordinarily arranged in front of a noun:

1. *Amount* (a/an, the, six)
2. *Evaluation* (good, beautiful, ugly, serious)

3. *Size* (large, small, tremendous)

4. *Shape, length* (round, long, short)

5. *Age* (young, new, old)

6. *Color* (red, black, green)

7. *Origin* (Asian, Brazilian, German)

8. *Material* (wood, cotton, gold)

9. Noun used as an adjective (computer [as in *computer program*], cake [as in *cake pan*])

       1.   *3.*   *6.*
▶ Seventeen small green buds appeared on my birch sapling.

               1. *2.* *5.* *6.*   *9.*
▶ He tossed his daughter a nice new yellow tennis ball.

      1.   *4.*   *7.*   *8.*
▶ The slender German-made gold watch cost a great deal of money.

For practice, go to **bedfordstmartins.com/conciseguide/exercisecentral** and click on A Common ESL Problem: Adjective Order.

Thinking Critically about What You Have Learned

In this chapter, you have learned a great deal about this genre from reading several profiles and writing one of your own. To consolidate your learning, it is helpful to think metacognitively — that is, to reflect not only on what you learned but on how you learned it. Following are two brief activities your instructor may ask you to do.

Reflecting on Your Writing

Your instructor may ask you to turn in with your essay and process materials a brief metacognitive essay or letter reflecting on what you have learned about writing your profile. Choose from the following invention activities those that seem most productive for you:

- Explain how your purpose and audience — what you wanted your readers to learn about your subject from reading your profile — influenced *one* of your decisions as a writer, such as what kinds of descriptive detail you included, what method of organization you used, or the role you adopted in writing about your subject.

- Discuss what you learned about yourself as a writer in the process of writing this profile. For example, what part of the process did you find most challenging? Did you try anything new, like getting a critical reading of your draft or outlining your draft in order to revise it? If so, how well did it work?

- If you were to give advice to a friend who was about to write a profile, what would you say?

- Which of the readings in this chapter influenced your essay? Explain the influence, citing specific examples from your profile and the reading.

- If you got good advice from a critical reader, explain exactly how the person helped you — perhaps by questioning your perspective in a way that enabled you to refocus your profile's dominant impression or by pointing out passages that needed more information or clearer chronology to better orient readers.

Considering the Social Dimensions: Entertaining Readers, or Showing the Whole Picture?

Profiles broaden our view of the world by entertaining and informing us with portraits of people, places, or things. It is important to recognize, however, that profiles — even effective ones — sometimes offer a limited view of their subjects. For example, the impulse to entertain readers may lead a profile writer to focus exclusively on the dramatic, colorful, or humorous aspects of a person, a place, or an activity, ignoring the equally important humdrum, routine, or otherwise less appealing aspects. Imagine a profile that focuses on the dramatic moments in an emergency-room doctor's shift but ignores the routine cases and the slow periods when nothing much is happening. Such a profile would provide a limited and distorted picture of an emergency-room doctor's work.

In addition, by focusing on the dramatic or glamorous aspects of a subject, profile writers tend to ignore economic or social consequences and to slight supporting players. Profiling the highly praised chef in a trendy new restaurant, a writer might not ask whether the chef participates in the city's leftover-food-collection program for the homeless or find out who the kitchen workers and wait staff are, how the chef treats them, or how much they are paid. Profiling the campus bookstore, a writer might become so caught up in the details of ordering books for hundreds of courses and selling them efficiently to hordes of students during the first week of a semester that he or she could forget to ask about textbook costs, pricing policies, profit margins, and payback on used textbooks.

1. *Consider whether any of the profiles you have read glamorize or sensationalize their subjects.* Do they ignore less colorful but centrally important everyday activities? Is this a problem with your own profile?

2. *Write a page or so explaining what the omissions signify.* What do they suggest about the readers' desires to be entertained and the profile writer's reluctance to present the subject in a more complete way?

4

Explaining a Concept

IN COLLEGE COURSES For a linguistics course, a student is assigned a paper explaining the development in children's control of sentences, or *syntax*. She reviews the relevant sections in her linguistics textbook and then goes to the library and finds a few sources recommended by the textbook. She then goes to her professor's office hours and asks for advice on other articles or books.

From these sources, she learns about stages that children go through as they gain control of syntax, beginning with the one-word, or holophrastic, stage (*mommy*) and progressing through the two-word stage (*baby sleep* or *want toy*) and the multiword stages (*no sit there*). After presenting this initial research to her peer group in class, she takes their advice and decides to organize her essay around these stages. Even though she is writing for her professor, an expert in child language development, she carefully defines key terms to show she understands them.

IN THE COMMUNITY A manager at a marketing research firm has been tutoring fifth-grade students in math for a few hours each month. Aware of the manager's market research expertise, the teacher asks her to do a presentation on *surveying*, an important research method in the social sciences.

The manager begins by having students fill out a brief survey on their television-watching habits. When they are done, she asks them to speculate on what they expect their answers to show, and how this data might be used by advertisers and television programmers. Then, with the students' help, she begins to analyze the data by selecting the variables that seem significant: the respondents' gender and place in the family structure, the number of hours spent watching television, and the types of shows watched.

At home, using PowerPoint, the manager prepares charts and graphs from the data. At the next class meeting, she distributes the data and asks the students to see whether it matches their initial assumptions.

She concludes by giving examples of questions from other surveys and explaining who does them, what they hope to learn, and how they report and use the results. Finally, she passes out a quiz so that she and each student can find out how much has been learned about surveys.

IN THE WORKPLACE At a seminar on the national security implications of satellite photography, the CEO of a space-imaging company takes part in the debate about *symmetrical transparency*, which involves using satellite photography to make everything on the planet visible at one-meter resolution — enough detail to reveal individual cars in parking lots.

Aware of the financial implications for his company, the executive drafts a presentation that will explain the relevant issues to his employees. He provides an overview of the impact of changing technologies and the politics of global terrorism; he then gives a brief overview of key issues in the debate on symmetrical transparency. He accompanies his remarks with PowerPoint slides that highlight statistics and lend emphasis to his key points.

Explaining Concepts

Concepts are ideas. They can range from the very general, like *space* and *time*, to the very specific, like *supersymmetry* and *metanarrative*. We share a common understanding of many basic concepts (like *outside* or *pain*), but many human activities involve specialized concepts that so-called "insiders" must explain to "outsiders." You probably have "insider" knowledge of various kinds. This chapter asks you to demonstrate such knowledge by explaining a concept of your choosing. For example, if you know a lot about music, you might be able to explain a concept such as *meter, rhythm, counterpoint*, or *harmonics*. If you are an avid video game player, you could explain *game mechanics* or *real-time strategy*. If you are a sports fan, you could clarify a concept such as the *curve ball* or the *Wing-T offense*.

These days, visuals — especially graphs, charts, diagrams, and tables — are increasingly common components of concept explanations. For example, most of us

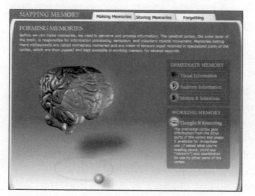

have taken Web tutorials that use video, audio, illustrations, and text to explain concepts like *metadata* or *macros*. So-called "infographics" like the "Mapping Memory" interactive feature reproduced here from *National Geographic* online are often employed by news media to help explain complex concepts.

As you compose your concept explanation while working through this chapter, you should consider whether the use of visuals or multimedia would help your readers more immediately or more fully grasp your concept.

"Mapping Memory," interactive graphic from *National Geographic* online.

Reading and Writing Concept Explanations

The scenarios about the linguistics student, the classroom volunteer, and the CEO on p. 107 demonstrate the important role that concept explanations play in various situations. The student demonstrates that she understands the concepts she is learning, like *syntax*, by using them correctly. The tutor explains concepts such as *surveying* to teach students about marketing research. Finally, the CEO teaches his employees about the concept of *symmetrical transparency* in order to prepare for impending business challenges.

Learning to explain a concept is especially important for you as a college student. It will prepare you to write a common type of exam and paper assignment; it will help you read critically; and it will acquaint you with the basic strategies common to all types of expository writing — defining, classifying, comparing and contrasting, and describing and narrating processes. Moreover, it will sharpen your skill in researching and using sources, abilities that are essential for success in college no matter what your major might be.

In trying to decide on a concept you would like to write about, you should focus on something that matters to you, whether it comes from a hobby, a job, or an academic course. Tackling a concept from a course you are taking now can be particularly useful. Every field of study has suitable concepts — for example, philosophy has *ethics, metaphysics,* and *epistemology*; physics has *string theory, entropy,* and *quantum mechanics*; economics has *Keynesian theory, macroeconomics,* and *monetary policy*; social psychology has *altruism, aggression, prejudice,* and so on — and explaining these concepts in close detail will help you truly understand them.

In the following section, you will read essays explaining *cannibalism* (an anthropological concept), *romantic love* (a cultural concept), and *morality* (a philosophical concept). These readings illustrate the strategies writers typically use when composing concept explanations. The Guide to Writing that follows will support you as you compose your own concept explanation, showing you ways to use the basic features of the genre to focus your concept, to explain it both readably and effectively, and to smoothly integrate sources supporting your explanation.

A Collaborative Activity:
Practice Explaining a Concept

Part 1. Choose one concept to explain to two or three other students. When you have chosen a concept, think about what others in the group are likely to know about it. Consider how you will define the concept and what other strategies you might use — description, comparison, and so on — to explain it in an interesting, memorable way.

Get together with two or three other students, and explain your concepts to one another.

Part 2. Discuss what happened when you explained your concept:

- To think about your purpose and audience, take turns asking the students in your group whether they were interested in and understood your explanation. In particular, find out whether your explanation would have been clearer with examples, definitions, comparisons with more familiar concepts, or something else.

- Compare your thoughts with the others in your group on what was easiest and hardest about explaining a concept: for example, focusing the concept, appealing to your listeners' interests, or organizing the explanation.

Reading Concept Explanations

Basic Features

As you read the essays in this chapter, you will see how different authors incorporate the basic features of concept explanations.

● A Focused Explanation

Read first to identify the concept. A concept may be any of the following:

- a principle, an ideal, or a value (such as the American dream or equal justice)
- a theory (such as theory of mind, relativity, or evolution)
- an idea (such as utilitarianism, panopticism, or realism)
- a condition (such as the state of flow, paranoia, or neurosis)
- a specialized or technical term (such as *markedness* in linguistics, *path dependence* in economics, or *high intensity interval training (HIIT)* in sports medicine)

Concepts are typically general notions that mean different things to different people (such as friendship, happiness, or family). Effective writers narrow the general concept, providing an explanation that is focused on an aspect of the concept likely to be of interest to readers. Some concepts, for example, benefit from being examined in terms of their cultural context (such as the Asian concept of face) or their historical context (such as the changing customs of calling, dating, and hooking up).

● A Readable Plan

Effective concept explanations have to be readable. *As you read the essays in this chapter, notice how each writer develops a plan that does the following:*

- divides the information into clearly distinguishable topics
- forecasts the topics
- presents the topics in a logical order
- gives readers cues or road signs to guide them, such as topic sentences, transitions, and summaries

● Appropriate Explanatory Strategies

Writers of essays explaining a concept typically present information by using a number of different strategies, such as the following:

- defining key terms
- classifying or grouping together related material
- comparing and contrasting

- narrating anecdotes or processes
- illustrating with examples, visuals, or lists of facts and details
- reporting established causes and effects

As you read the essays in this chapter, notice how they make use of these strategies. Note that essays explaining concepts depend especially on clear definitions; any key terms that are likely to be unfamiliar or misunderstood must be explicitly defined. Illustrations usually also play a key role because examples, visuals, and other details can help make abstract concepts understandable.

● Smooth Integration of Sources

Finally, as you read, think about how the writer establishes authority by smoothly integrating sources into the explanation. Although writers often draw on their own experiences and observations, they almost always do additional research into what others have to say about their subject.

How writers treat sources depends on the writing situation. Certain formal situations, such as college assignments or scholarly publications, have rules for citing and documenting sources. Students and scholars are expected to cite their sources formally because readers judge their work in part by what the writers have read and how they have used their reading. For more informal writing — magazine articles, for example — readers do not expect or want page references or publication information, but they do expect sources to be identified and their expertise established in some way.

Purpose and Audience

*As you read concept explanations, ask yourself what seems to be the writer's **purpose** in explaining this concept.* For example, does the writer seem to be writing

- to teach readers about an unfamiliar concept?
- to engage readers' interest in the concept?
- to better understand the concept by explaining it to others?
- to demonstrate knowledge of the concept and the ability to apply it?

*As you read, also try to determine what the writer assumes about the **audience**.* For example, does the writer

- expect the readers to be generally well informed but not knowledgeable about this particular concept?
- assume the readers may not be especially interested in the concept?
- know that the only or primary reader is an instructor who knows more about the concept than the writer does and who is evaluating the writer's knowledge?

- anticipate that readers will be unfamiliar with the concept, so that the essay will serve as an introduction?
- anticipate that readers will know something about the concept, so that the essay may add to their prior knowledge or provide a new perspective?

Readings

LINH KIEU NGO wrote this essay as a first-year college student. In it, he explains the concept of cannibalism, the eating of human flesh by other humans. Most Americans know about survival cannibalism — eating human flesh to avoid starvation — but Ngo also explains the historical importance of dietary and ritual cannibalism.

As you read, notice how he uses examples to illustrate the three types of cannibalism. Also consider the questions in the margin. Your instructor may ask you to post your answers or bring them to class.

Basic Features

- A Focused Explanation
- A Readable Plan
- Appropriate Explanatory Strategies
- Smooth Integration of Sources

Cannibalism: It Still Exists

Linh Kieu Ngo

Fifty-five Vietnamese refugees fled to Malaysia on a small fishing boat to escape communist rule in their country following the Vietnam War. During their escape attempt, the captain was shot by the coast guard. The boat and its passengers managed to outrun the coast guard to the open sea, but they had lost the only person who knew the way to Malaysia, the captain.

The men onboard tried to navigate the boat, but after a week fuel ran out, and they drifted farther out to sea. Their supply of food and water was gone; people were starving, and some of the elderly were near death. The men managed to produce a small amount of drinking water by boiling salt water, using dispensable wood from the boat to create a small fire near the stern. They also tried to fish but had little success.

A month went by, and the old and weak died. At first, the crew threw the dead overboard, but later, out of desperation, they turned to human flesh as a source of food. Some people vomited as they

How effectively does this anecdote about a one-time event introduce the concept to readers?

1

2

3

attempted to eat it, while others refused to resort to cannibalism and see the bodies of their loved ones sacrificed for food. Those who did not eat died of starvation, and their bodies in turn became food for others. Human flesh was cut out, washed in salt water, and hung to dry for preservation. The liquids inside the cranium were drunk to quench thirst. The livers, kidneys, hearts, stomachs, and intestines were boiled and eaten.

4   Five months passed before a whaling vessel discovered the drifting boat, looking like a graveyard of bones. There was only one survivor.

5   Cannibalism, the act of human beings eating human flesh (Sagan 2), has a long history and continues to hold interest and create controversy. Many books and research reports offer examples of cannibalism, but a few scholars have questioned whether it actually was ever practiced anywhere, except in cases of ensuring survival in times of famine or isolation (Askenasy 43–54). Recently, some scholars have tried to understand why people in the West have been so eager to attribute cannibalism to non-Westerners (Barker, Hulme, and Iversen). Cannibalism has long been a part of American popular culture. For example, Mark Twain's "Cannibalism in the Cars" tells a humorous story about cannibalism by well-to-do travelers on a train stranded in a snowstorm, and cannibalism is still a popular subject for jokes ("Cannibal Jokes").

> Ngo shifts from narrating to presenting research in this paragraph. How does he introduce his sources?

6   If we assume there is some reality to the reports about cannibalism, how can we best understand this concept? Cannibalism can be broken down into two main categories: exocannibalism, the eating of outsiders or foreigners, and endocannibalism, the eating of members of one's own social group (Shipman 70). Within these categories are several functional types of cannibalism, three of the most common being survival cannibalism, dietary cannibalism, and religious and ritual cannibalism.

> How effectively does Ngo introduce the thesis and forecast the topics of the essay?

7   Survival cannibalism occurs when people trapped without food have to decide "whether to starve or to eat fellow humans" (Shipman 70). In the case of the Vietnamese refugees, the crew and passengers on the boat ate human flesh to stay alive. They did not kill people to get human flesh for nourishment but instead waited until the people had died. Even after human carcasses were sacrificed as food, the boat

How do Ngo's anec-
dotes and examples
here and later in the
essay help you under-
stand the concept?

people ate only enough to survive. Another case of survival cannibalism occurred in 1945, when General Douglas MacArthur's forces cut
supply lines to Japanese troops stationed in the Pacific Islands. In
one incident, Japanese troops were reported to have sacrificed the
Arapesh people of northeastern New Guinea for food in order to avoid
death by starvation (Tuzin 63). The most famous example of survival
cannibalism in American history comes from the diaries, letters, and
interviews of survivors of the California-bound Donner Party, who in
the winter of 1846 were snowbound in the Sierra Nevada Mountains
for five months. Thirty-five of eighty-seven adults and children died,
and some of them were eaten (Hart 116–117; Johnson).

How do Ngo's topic
sentences fulfill the
promise of the forecast
in par. 6 and help you
follow the explanation?

Unlike survival cannibalism, in which human flesh is eaten as a
last resort after a person has died, in dietary cannibalism humans are
purchased or trapped for food and then eaten as a part of a culture's
traditions. In addition, survival cannibalism often involves people
eating other people of the same origins, whereas dietary cannibalism
usually involves people eating foreigners.

8

What writing strategy
is Ngo using in pars.
9–10?

In the Miyanmin society of the west Sepik interior of Papua,
New Guinea, villagers do not value human life over that of pigs or
marsupials because human flesh is part of their normal diet (Poole 7).
The Miyanmin people observe no differences in "gender, kinship,
ritual status, and bodily substance"; they eat anyone, even their own
dead. In this respect, then, they practice both endocannibalism and
exocannibalism; and to ensure a constant supply of human flesh for
food, they raid neighboring tribes and drag their victims back to their
village to be eaten (Poole 11). Perhaps, in the history of this society,
there was at one time a shortage of wild game to be hunted for food,
and because people were more plentiful than fish, deer, rabbits, pigs,
or cows, survival cannibalism was adopted as a last resort. Then, as
their culture developed, the Miyanmin may have retained the practice
of dietary cannibalism, which has endured as a part of their culture.

9

How does Ngo's use
of the terms *endo-* and
exocannibalism here
help orient the reader?

Similar to the Miyanmin, the people of the Leopard and Alligator
societies in South America eat human flesh as part of their cultural
tradition. Practicing dietary exocannibalism, the Leopard people hunt
in groups, with one member wearing the skin of a leopard to conceal

10

the face. They ambush their victims in the forest and carry their victims back to their village to be eaten. The Alligator people also hunt in groups, but they hide themselves under a canoelike submarine that resembles an alligator, then swim close to a fisherman's or trader's canoe to overturn it and catch their victims (MacCormack 54).

11   Religious or ritual cannibalism is different from survival and dietary cannibalism in that it has a ceremonial purpose rather than one of nourishment. Sometimes only a single victim is sacrificed in a ritual, while at other times many are sacrificed. For example, the Bangala tribe of the Congo River in central Africa honors a deceased chief or leader by purchasing, sacrificing, and feasting on slaves (Sagan 53). The number of slaves sacrificed is determined by how highly the tribe members revered the deceased leader.

12   Ritual cannibalism among South American Indians often serves as revenge for the dead. Like the Bangalas, some South American tribes kill their victims to be served as part of funeral rituals, with human sacrifices denoting that the deceased was held in high honor. Also like the Bangalas, these tribes use outsiders as victims. Unlike the Bangalas, however, the Indians sacrifice only one victim instead of many in a single ritual. For example, when a warrior of a tribe is killed in battle, the family of the warrior forces a victim to take the identity of the warrior. The family adorns the victim with the deceased warrior's belongings and may even force him to marry the deceased warrior's wives. But once the family believes the victim has assumed the spiritual identity of the deceased warrior, the family kills him. The children in the tribe soak their hands in the victim's blood to symbolize their revenge of the warrior's death. Elderly women from the tribe drink the victim's blood and then cut up his body for roasting and eating (Sagan 53–54). The people of the tribe believe that by sacrificing a victim, they have avenged the death of the warrior and the soul of the deceased can rest in peace.

13   In the villages of certain African tribes, only a small part of a dead body is used in ritual cannibalism. In these tribes, where the childbearing capacity of women is highly valued, women are obligated to eat small, raw fragments of genital parts during fertility rites. Elders of the

How does this topic sentence help you understand how the information in pars. 11–13 fits into Ngo's plan? What other words or phrases help you follow his comparisons and contrasts?

tribe supervise this ritual to ensure that the women will be fertile. In the Bimin-Kuskusmin tribe, for instance, a widow eats a small, raw fragment of flesh from the penis of her deceased husband in order to enhance her future fertility and reproductive capacity. Similarly, a widower may eat a raw fragment of flesh from his deceased wife's vagina along with a piece of her bone marrow; by eating her flesh, he hopes to strengthen the fertility of his daughters borne by his dead wife, and by eating her bone marrow, he honors her reproductive capacity. Also, when an elder woman of the village who has shown great reproductive capacity dies, her uterus and the interior parts of her vagina are eaten by other women who hope to benefit from her reproductive power (Poole 16–17).

What does Ngo hope to achieve in this conclusion? How well does it work for you?

Members of developed societies in general practice none of these forms of cannibalism, with the occasional exception of survival cannibalism when the only alternative is starvation. It is possible, however, that our distant-past ancestors were cannibals who through the eons turned away from the practice. We are, after all, descended from the same ancestors as the Miyanmin, the Alligator, and the Leopard people, and survival cannibalism shows that people are capable of eating human flesh when they have no other choice.

14

Works Cited

Askenasy, Hans. *Cannibalism: From Sacrifice to Survival*. Amherst, NY: Prometheus, 1994. Print.

Barker, Francis, Peter Hulme, and Margaret Iversen, eds. *Cannibalism and the New World*. Cambridge: Cambridge UP, 1998. Print.

Brown, Paula, and Donald Tuzin, eds. *The Ethnography of Cannibalism*. Washington: Society of Psychological Anthropology, 1983. Print.

What makes Ngo's sources seem authoritative (or not)?

"Cannibal Jokes." *Bored.com*. N.p., n.d. Web. 22 Sept. 2008.

Hart, James D. *A Companion to California*. Berkeley: U of California P, 1987. Print.

Johnson, Kristin. *New Light on the Donner Party*. Kristin Johnson, 5 Nov. 2006. Web. 28 Sept. 2008.

MacCormack, Carol. "Human Leopard and Crocodile." Brown and Tuzin 54–55.

Poole, Fitz John Porter. "Cannibals, Tricksters, and Witches." Brown and
    Tuzin 16–17.

Sagan, Eli. *Cannibalism*. New York: Harper, 1976. Print.

Shipman, Pat. "The Myths and Perturbing Realities of Cannibalism."
    Discover Mar. 1987: 70+. Print.

Tuzin, Donald. "Cannibalism and Arapesh Cosmology." Brown and Tuzin
    61–63.

Twain, Mark. "Cannibalism in the Cars." *The Complete Short Stories of
    Mark Twain*. Ed. Charles Neider. New York: Doubleday, 1957. 9–16.
    Print.

What can you learn
about creating a
works-cited list from
this example?

ANASTASIA TOUFEXIS has been an associate editor of *Time*, senior editor of *Discover*, and editor in chief of *Psychology Today*. She has written
on subjects as diverse as medicine, health and fitness, law, environment,
education, science, and national and world news. Toufexis has won a number of awards for her writing, including a Knight-Wallace Fellowship at the
University of Michigan and an Ocean Science Journalism Fellowship at
Woods Hole Oceanographic Institution. She has also lectured on science
writing at Columbia University, the University of North Carolina, and the School of Visual
Arts in New York.

The following essay was originally published in 1993 in *Time* magazine. As you read,
notice how Toufexis brings together a variety of sources of information to present a neuro-
chemical perspective on love.

Love: The Right Chemistry

Anastasia Toufexis

> Love is a romantic designation for a most ordinary biological — or, shall we say,
> chemical? — process. A lot of nonsense is talked and written about it.
> — Greta Garbo to Melvyn Douglas in *Ninotchka*

1   O.K., let's cut out all this nonsense about romantic love. Let's bring some scientific precision to the party. Let's put love under a microscope.

2   When rigorous people with Ph.D.s after their names do that, what they
see is not some silly, senseless thing. No, their probe reveals that love rests firmly

on the foundations of evolution, biology and chemistry. What seems on the surface to be irrational, intoxicated behavior is in fact part of nature's master strategy — a vital force that has helped humans survive, thrive and multiply through thousands of years. Says Michael Mills, a psychology professor at Loyola Marymount University in Los Angeles: "Love is our ancestors whispering in our ears."

It was on the plains of Africa about 4 million years ago, in the early days of the human species, that the notion of romantic love probably first began to blossom or at least that the first cascades of neurochemicals began flowing from the brain to the bloodstream to produce goofy grins and sweaty palms as men and women gazed deeply into each other's eyes. When mankind graduated from scuttling around on all fours to walking on two legs, this change made the whole person visible to fellow human beings for the first time. Sexual organs were in full display, as were other characteristics, from the color of eyes to the span of shoulders. As never before, each individual had a unique allure. 3

When the sparks flew, new ways of making love enabled sex to become a romantic encounter, not just a reproductive act. Although mounting mates from the rear was, and still is, the method favored among most animals, humans began to enjoy face-to-face couplings; both looks and personal attraction became a much greater part of the equation. 4

> While Western culture holds fast to the idea that true love flames forever . . . nature apparently meant passions to sputter out in something like four years.

Romance served the evolutionary purpose of pulling males and females into long-term partnership, which was essential to child rearing. On open grasslands, one parent would have a hard — and dangerous — time handling a child while foraging for food. "If a woman was carrying the equivalent of a 20-lb. bowling ball in one arm and a pile of sticks in the other, it was ecologically critical to pair up with a mate to rear the young," explains anthropologist Helen Fisher, author of *Anatomy of Love*. 5

While Western culture holds fast to the idea that true love flames forever (the movie *Bram Stoker's Dracula* has the Count carrying the torch beyond the grave), nature apparently meant passions to sputter out in something like four years. Primitive pairs stayed together just "long enough to rear one child through infancy," says Fisher. Then each would find a new partner and start all over again. 6

What Fisher calls the "four-year itch" shows up unmistakably in today's divorce statistics. In most of the 62 cultures she has studied, divorce rates peak around the fourth year of marriage. Additional youngsters help keep pairs together longer. If, say, a couple have another child three years after the first, as often occurs, then their union can be expected to last about four more years. That makes them ripe for the more familiar phenomenon portrayed in the Marilyn Monroe classic *The Seven-Year Itch*. 7

If, in nature's design, romantic love is not eternal, neither is it exclusive. Less than 5% of mammals form rigorously faithful pairs. From the earliest days, contends Fisher, the human pattern has been "monogamy with clandestine adultery." Occasional flings upped the chances that new combinations of genes would be passed on to 8 the next generation. Men who sought new partners had more children. Contrary to common assumptions, women were just as likely to stray. "As long as prehistoric females were secretive about their extramarital affairs," argues Fisher, "they could garner extra resources, life insurance, better genes and more varied DNA for their biological futures. . . ."

9   Lovers often claim that they feel as if they are being swept away. They're not mistaken; they are literally flooded by chemicals, research suggests. A meeting of eyes, a touch of hands or a whiff of scent sets off a flood that starts in the brain and races along the nerves and through the blood. The results are familiar: flushed skin, sweaty palms, heavy breathing. If love looks suspiciously like stress, the reason is simple: the chemical pathways are identical.

10   Above all, there is the sheer euphoria of falling in love — a not-so-surprising reaction, considering that many of the substances swamping the newly smitten are chemical cousins of amphetamines. They include dopamine, norepinephrine and especially phenylethylamine (PEA). Cole Porter knew what he was talking about when he wrote, "I get a kick out of you." "Love is a natural high," observes Anthony Walsh, author of *The Science of Love: Understanding Love and Its Effects on Mind and Body*. "PEA gives you that silly smile that you flash at strangers. When we meet someone who is attractive to us, the whistle blows at the PEA factory."

11   But phenylethylamine highs don't last forever, a fact that lends support to arguments that passionate romantic love is short-lived. As with any amphetamine, the body builds up a tolerance to PEA; thus it takes more and more of the substance to produce love's special kick. After two to three years, the body simply can't crank up the needed amount of PEA. And chewing on chocolate doesn't help, despite popular belief. The candy is high in PEA, but it fails to boost the body's supply.

12   Fizzling chemicals spell the end of delirious passion; for many people that marks the end of the liaison as well. It is particularly true for those whom Dr. Michael Liebowitz of the New York State Psychiatric Institute terms "attraction junkies." They crave the intoxication of falling in love so much that they move frantically from affair to affair just as soon as the first rush of infatuation fades.

13   Still, many romances clearly endure beyond the first years. What accounts for that? Another set of chemicals, of course. The continued presence of a partner gradually steps up production in the brain of endorphins. Unlike the fizzy amphetamines, these are soothing substances. Natural pain-killers, they give lovers a sense of security, peace and calm. "That is one reason why it feels so horrible when we're abandoned or a lover dies," notes Fisher. "We don't have our daily hit of narcotics."

14   Researchers see a contrast between the heated infatuation induced by PEA, along with other amphetamine-like chemicals, and the more intimate attachment fostered and prolonged by endorphins. "Early love is when you love the way the other person makes you feel," explains psychiatrist Mark Goulston of the University of California, Los Angeles. "Mature love is when you love the person as he or she is." It is the difference between passionate and compassionate love,

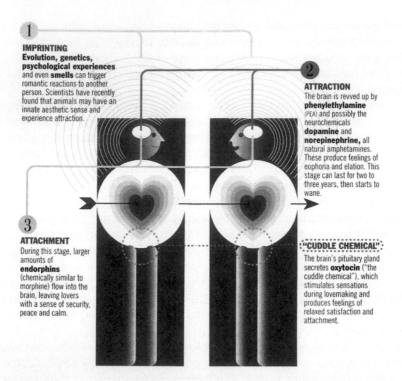

1

IMPRINTING
Evolution, genetics,
psychological experiences
and even **smells** can trigger
romantic reactions to another
person. Scientists have recently
found that animals may have an
innate aesthetic sense and
experience attraction.

2

ATTRACTION
The brain is revved up by
phenylethylamine
(PEA) and possibly the
neurochemicals
dopamine and
norepinephrine, all
natural amphetamines.
These produce feelings of
euphoria and elation. This
stage can last for two to
three years, then starts to
wane.

3

ATTACHMENT
During this stage, larger
amounts of
endorphins
(chemically similar to
morphine) flow into the
brain, leaving lovers
with a sense of security,
peace and calm.

"CUDDLE CHEMICAL"
The brain's pituitary gland
secretes **oxytocin** ("the
cuddle chemical"), which
stimulates sensations
during lovemaking and
produces feelings of
relaxed satisfaction and
attachment.

observes Walsh, a psychobiologist at Boise State University in Idaho. "It's Bon
Jovi vs. Beethoven."

Oxytocin is another chemical that has recently been implicated in love. 15
Produced by the brain, it sensitizes nerves and stimulates muscle contraction.
In women it helps uterine contractions during childbirth as well as production
of breast milk, and seems to inspire mothers to nuzzle their infants. Scientists
speculate that oxytocin might encourage similar cuddling between adult women
and men. The versatile chemical may also enhance orgasms. In one study of men,
oxytocin increased to three to five times its normal level during climax, and it may
soar even higher in women.

Chemicals may help explain (at least to scientists) the feelings of passion and 16
compassion, but why do people tend to fall in love with one partner rather than a
myriad of others? Once again, it's partly a function of evolution and biology. "Men
are looking for maximal fertility in a mate," says Loyola Marymount's Mills. "That is
in large part why females in the prime childbearing ages of 17 to 28 are so desirable." Men can size up youth and vitality in a glance, and studies indeed show that
men fall in love quite rapidly. Women tumble more slowly, to a large degree because
their requirements are more complex; they need more time to check the guy out.
"Age is not vital," notes Mills, "but the ability to provide security, father children,
share resources and hold a high status in society are all key factors."

17   Still, that does not explain why the way Mary walks and laughs makes Bill dizzy with desire while Marcia's gait and giggle leave him cold. "Nature has wired us for one special person," suggests Walsh, romantically. He rejects the idea that a woman or a man can be in love with two people at the same time. Each person carries in his or her mind a unique subliminal guide to the ideal partner, a "love map," to borrow a term coined by sexologist John Money of Johns Hopkins University.

18   Drawn from the people and experiences of childhood, the map is a record of whatever we found enticing and exciting — or disturbing and disgusting. Small feet, curly hair. The way our mothers patted our head or how our fathers told a joke. A fireman's uniform, a doctor's stethoscope. All the information gathered while growing up is imprinted in the brain's circuitry by adolescence. Partners never meet each and every requirement, but a sufficient number of matches can light up the wires and signal, "It's love." Not every partner will be like the last one, since lovers may have different combinations of the characteristics favored by the map.

19   O.K., that's the scientific point of view. Satisfied? Probably not. To most people — with or without Ph.D.s — love will always be more than the sum of its natural parts. It's a commingling of body and soul, reality and imagination, poetry and phenylethylamine. In our deepest hearts, most of us harbor the hope that love will never fully yield up its secrets, that it will always elude our grasp.

❯

MAKING CONNECTIONS: LOVE MAPS

The chemistry of love is easily summarized: Amphetamines fuel romance; endorphins and oxytocin sustain lasting heterosexual relationships. As Toufexis makes clear, however, these chemical reactions do not explain why specific people are initially attracted to each other. Toufexis observes that an initial attraction occurs because each of us carries a "unique subliminal guide" or "love map" (par. 17) that leads us unerringly to a partner.

With two or three other students, discuss these explanations for attraction between the sexes. Begin by briefly taking turns describing the qualities you are attracted to in a partner. Then consider together the following questions as you discuss your love map:

- What role do factors such as family, friends, community, the media, and advertising play in constructing your love map?

- Do you think an individual's love map can change over time? If so, what might contribute to such changes?

- According to Toufexis, men typically look for "maximal fertility," whereas women look for security, resources, status, and a willingness to father children (par. 16). Does this explanation seem convincing to you? Why or why not?

ANALYZING WRITING STRATEGIES

● A Focused Explanation of the Concept

Obviously, essays explaining concepts cannot communicate everything that is known about a concept. Writers must limit the scope of their explanation. They choose a focus in part by considering the rhetorical situation — the purpose and audience — in which they are writing. Linh Kieu Ngo, for example, is writing for a college composition course, where he can expect his readers not to know very much about anthropology or research on cannibalism. For this reason, Ngo chose to give readers a rather simple overview of the research by explaining the three "most common" types of cannibalism (par. 6). To set up his explanation, Ngo uses an anecdote about survival cannibalism, the type his readers are most likely to have heard about. Beginning his essay by describing a familiar type of cannibalism confirms for readers what they already know and at the same time arouses curiosity and makes them want to learn more.

To analyze how Toufexis focuses her explanation and engages her readers, do the following:

- Write a sentence or two describing how she focuses her explanation.
- Add another couple of sentences explaining how she tries to capture her readers' interest and assessing how effective her strategy is for you as a reader.

● A Readable Plan

Experienced writers know that readers often have a hard time making their way through new and difficult material and sometimes give up in frustration. To avoid this problem, effective writers construct a reader-friendly plan by dividing the information into clearly distinguishable topics. They also give readers cues or road signs to guide them through the explanation.

Early in the essay, the **thesis statement** announces the concept. It also may **forecast** the topics, giving readers a preview so that they know where they are headed. For example, in paragraphs 5–6 of his essay, Ngo announces that he is writing about the much-written-about concept of cannibalism and forecasts the topics he uses to organize his essay, the three types of cannibalism: survival, dietary, and ritual cannibalism.

To analyze how Toufexis constructs a readable plan, try the following:

- Skim the essay, and note in the margin where she announces her concept and forecasts the topics she uses to organize her essay. Highlight the point at which she begins discussing each topic.
- Write a sentence or two assessing how well her forecast works to make her essay readable.

▪ Add another sentence explaining how Toufexis connects the topic of "love maps" (pars. 17–18) to the topics she discussed earlier in the essay.

For more on constructing a readable plan, see Chapter 10.

● Appropriate Explanatory Strategies

When writers organize and present information, they rely on writing strategies that are the building blocks of explanatory essays: **defining**, **classifying** or **dividing**, **comparing and contrasting**, **narrating** anecdotes or processes, **illustrating** with examples or lists of facts and details, and reporting known **causes and effects**. Toufexis uses classification along with comparison and contrast when she explains the roles played by two types of chemicals: amphetamine-like chemicals, especially phenylethylamine (PEA), and endorphins, such as oxytocin. But her primary writing strategy is reporting causes and effects.

To analyze how Toufexis reports causes and effects, do the following:

▪ Reread paragraph 9 where she explains the causes and effects of the rush of amphetamine-like chemicals, and highlight the causes in one color and the effects in another color (or underline one and put brackets around the other).

▪ Reread paragraphs 13 and 15, and highlight the effects of chemicals produced in the brain.

▪ Write a sentence or two assessing how well Toufexis explains causes and effects.

● Smooth Integration of Sources

Writers of explanatory essays have to convince readers that the information they have used to explain the concept is trustworthy. They do this by acknowledging their expert sources. Academic writers provide detailed information about their sources so that scholars can consult the original sources. For example, the essay by Linh Kieu Ngo written for a college composition course demonstrates the MLA style of citing sources. Writing for college courses, you will be expected to cite your sources in a conventional academic way — with parenthetical citations in the body of your essay keyed to a works-cited list at the end.

Writing for a nonacademic publication, Toufexis does not need to cite sources using the MLA or another academic style sheet. But she does need to reassure readers that her sources are authoritative.

To analyze how Toufexis cites sources, follow these steps:

▪ Skim the essay, and underline the name of each source she mentions.

▪ Write a few sentences describing the kinds of information she gives readers about her sources and assessing how well she establishes their authority.

For more on integrating sources, see pp. 490–95. For more on MLA documentation, see pp. 497–500.

ANALYZING VISUALS

USING A FLOWCHART

Analyze the visual Toufexis includes in her essay, and write a few sentences explaining how you read the visual and assessing how well it helps you understand her explanation of the concept.

Toufexis's visual is a flowchart, a diagram that shows the steps in a process. To determine how effective this visual is, consider the following questions:

- When you initially read the essay, did you stop to study the visual, just glance at it in passing, go back to it after finishing the essay, or not look at it at all?

- How does the flowchart clarify the role played by each element of the diagram? Are there any seemingly extraneous elements?

- Is the flowchart easy to read or too complicated, attractive or dull, eye-candy or actually useful? Explain your answer.

- If the flowchart repeats information already presented in the text of the essay, what does it contribute to the explanation?

- If the flowchart adds new information not presented in the text of the essay, how effective is it?

CONSIDERING TOPICS FOR YOUR OWN ESSAY

Like Toufexis, you could write an essay about love or romance, but you could choose a different focus: its history (how and when did romantic love develop as an idea in the West?), its cultural characteristics (how is love regarded currently among different American ethnic groups or world cultures?), its excesses or extremes, or the phases of falling in and out of love. Also consider writing about other concepts involving personal relationships, such as jealousy, codependency, idealization, stereotyping, or homophobia.

 JEFFREY KLUGER has written several books, including *Splendid Solution: Jonas Salk and the Conquest of Polio* and *Lost Moon: The Perilous Voyage of Apollo 13*, upon which the 1995 film *Apollo 13* was based. He has written for *Discover, Science Digest,* and the *New York Times' Business World Magazine.* A staff writer for *Time* magazine, Kluger wrote this essay in November 2007.

As you read, notice how the visuals contribute to the essay.

What Makes Us Moral

Jeffrey Kluger

1   If the entire human species were a single individual, that person would long ago have been declared mad. The insanity would not lie in the anger and darkness of the human mind — though it can be a black and raging place indeed. And it certainly wouldn't lie in the transcendent goodness of that mind — one so sublime, we fold it into a larger "soul." The madness would lie instead in the fact that both of those qualities, the savage and the splendid, can exist in one creature, one person, often in one instant.

2   We're a species that is capable of almost dumbfounding kindness. We nurse one another, romance one another, weep for one another. Ever since science taught us how, we willingly tear the very organs from our bodies and give them to one another. And at the same time, we slaughter one another. The past 15 years of human history are the temporal equivalent of those subatomic particles that are created in accelerators and vanish in a trillionth of a second, but in that fleeting instant, we've visited untold horrors on ourselves — in Mogadishu, Rwanda, Chechnya, Darfur, Beslan, Baghdad, Pakistan, London, Madrid, Lebanon, Israel, New York City, Abu Ghraib, Oklahoma City, an Amish schoolhouse in Pennsylvania — all of the crimes committed by the highest, wisest, most principled species the planet has produced. That we're also the lowest, cruelest, most blood-drenched species is our shame — and our paradox.

> The deeper that science drills into the substrata of behavior, the harder it becomes to preserve the vanity that we are unique among Earth's creatures.

3   The deeper that science drills into the substrata of behavior, the harder it becomes to preserve the vanity that we are unique among Earth's creatures. We're the only species with language, we told ourselves — until gorillas and chimps mastered sign language. We're the only one that uses tools — but that's if you don't count otters smashing mollusks with rocks or apes stripping leaves from twigs and using them to fish for termites.

4   What does, or ought to, separate us then is our highly developed sense of morality, a primal understanding of good and bad, of right and wrong, of what it means to suffer not only our own pain — something anything with a rudimentary nervous system can do — but also the pain of others. That quality is the distilled essence of what it means to be human. Why it's an essence that so often spoils, no one can say.

5   Morality may be a hard concept to grasp, but we acquire it fast. A preschooler will learn that it's not all right to eat in the classroom, because the teacher says it's not. If the rule is lifted and eating is approved, the child will happily comply. But if the same teacher says it's also O.K. to push another student off a chair, the child hesitates. "He'll respond, 'No, the teacher shouldn't say that,'" says psychologist

Michael Schulman, coauthor of *Bringing Up a Moral Child*. In both cases, somebody taught the child a rule, but the rule against pushing has a stickiness about it, one that resists coming unstuck even if someone in authority countenances it. That's the difference between a matter of morality and one of mere social convention, and Schulman and others believe kids feel it innately.

Of course, the fact is, that child will sometimes hit and won't feel particularly bad about it either — unless he's caught. The same is true for people who steal or despots who slaughter. "Moral judgment is pretty consistent from person to person," says Marc Hauser, professor of psychology at Harvard University and author of *Moral Minds*. "Moral behavior, however, is scattered all over the chart." The rules we know, even the ones we intuitively feel, are by no means the rules we always follow. 6

Where do those intuitions come from? And why are we so inconsistent about following where they lead us? Scientists can't yet answer those questions, but that hasn't stopped them from looking. Brain scans are providing clues. Animal studies are providing more. Investigations of tribal behavior are providing still more. None of this research may make us behave better, not right away at least. But all of it can help us understand ourselves — a small step up from savagery perhaps, but an important one. 7

The Moral Ape

The deepest foundation on which morality is built is the phenomenon of empathy, the understanding that what hurts me would feel the same way to you. And human ego notwithstanding, it's a quality other species share. 8

It's not surprising that animals far less complex than we are would display a trait that's as generous of spirit as empathy, particularly if you decide there's no spirit involved in it at all. Behaviorists often reduce what we call empathy to a mercantile business known as reciprocal altruism. A favor done today — food offered, shelter given — brings a return favor tomorrow. If a colony of animals practices that give-and-take well, the group thrives. 9

But even in animals, there's something richer going on. One of the first and most poignant observations of empathy in nonhumans was made by Russian primatologist Nadia Kohts, who studied nonhuman cognition in the first half of the 20th century and raised a young chimpanzee in her home. When the chimp would make his way to the roof of the house, ordinary strategies for bringing him down — calling, scolding, offers of food — would rarely work. But if Kohts sat down and pretended to cry, the chimp would go to her immediately. "He runs around me as if looking for the offender," she wrote. "He tenderly takes my chin in his palm . . . as if trying to understand what is happening." 10

You hardly have to go back to the early part of the past century to find such accounts. Even cynics went soft at the story of Binti Jua, the gorilla who in 1996 rescued a 3-year-old boy who had tumbled into her zoo enclosure, rocking him gently in her arms and carrying him to a door where trainers could enter and collect him. "The capacity of empathy is multilayered," says primatologist Frans de Waal of Emory University, author of *Our Inner Ape*. "We share a core with lots of animals." 11

While it's impossible to directly measure empathy in animals, in humans it's another matter. Hauser cites a study in which spouses or unmarried couples underwent 12

MORAL DILEMMA
The Sinking Lifeboat

You are adrift in a life raft after your cruise ship has sunk. There are too many survivors for the life rafts, and yours is dangerously overloaded. The raft is certain to sink, and even with life vests on, all the passengers are sure to die because of the frigid temperature of the water. One person on the boat is awake and alert but gravely ill and will not survive the journey no matter what. Throwing that person overboard would prevent the raft from sinking. Could you be the one who tosses the person out?

I COULD THROW A SURVIVOR OVERBOARD

❏ Yes
❏ No

functional magnetic resonance imaging (fMRI) as they were subjected to mild pain. They were warned before each time the painful stimulus was administered, and their brains lit up in a characteristic way signaling mild dread. They were then told that they were not going to feel the discomfort but that their partner was. Even when they couldn't see their partner, the brains of the subjects lit up precisely as if they were about to experience the pain themselves. "This is very much an 'I feel your pain' experience," says Hauser.

13   The brain works harder when the threat gets more complicated. A favorite scenario that morality researchers study is the trolley dilemma. You're standing near a track as an out-of-control train hurtles toward five unsuspecting people. There's a switch nearby that would let you divert the train onto a siding. Would you do it? Of course. You save five lives at no cost. Suppose a single unsuspecting man was on the siding? Now the mortality score is 5 to 1. Could you kill him to save the others? What if the innocent man was on a bridge over the trolley and you had to push him onto the track to stop the train?

14   Pose these dilemmas to people while they're in an fMRI, and the brain scans get messy. Using a switch to divert the train toward one person instead of five increases

activity in the dorsolateral prefrontal cortex — the place where cool, utilitarian choices are made. Complicate things with the idea of pushing the innocent victim, and the medial frontal cortex — an area associated with emotion — lights up. As these two regions do battle, we may make irrational decisions. In a recent survey, 85% of subjects who were asked about the trolley scenarios said they would not push the innocent man onto the tracks — even though they knew they had just sent five people to their hypothetical death. "What's going on in our heads?" asks Joshua Greene, an assistant professor of psychology at Harvard University. "Why do we say it's O.K. to trade one life for five in one case and not others?"

How We Stay Good

Merely being equipped with moral programming does not mean we practice moral behavior. Something still has to boot up that software and configure it properly, and that something is the community. Hauser believes that all of us carry what he calls a sense of moral grammar — the ethical equivalent of the basic grasp of speech that most linguists believe is with us from birth. But just as syntax is nothing until words are built upon it, so too is a sense of right and wrong useless until someone teaches you how to apply it.   15

It's the people around us who do that teaching — often quite well. Once again, however, humans aren't the ones who dreamed up such a mentoring system. At the Arnhem Zoo in the Netherlands, de Waal was struck by how vigorously apes enforced group norms one evening when the zookeepers were calling their chimpanzees in for dinner. The keepers' rule at Arnhem was that no chimps would eat until the entire community was present, but two adolescents grew willful, staying outside the building. The hours it took to coax them inside caused the mood in the hungry colony to turn surly. That night the keepers put the delinquents to bed in a separate area — a sort of protective custody to shield them from reprisals. But the next day the adolescents were on their own, and the troop made its feelings plain, administering a sound beating. The chastened chimps were the first to come in that evening. Animals have what de Waal calls "oughts" — rules that the group must follow — and the community enforces them.   16

Human communities impose their own oughts, but they can vary radically from culture to culture. Take the phenomenon of Good Samaritan laws that require passersby to assist someone in peril. Our species has a very conflicted sense of when we ought to help someone else and when we ought not, and the general rule is, Help those close to home and ignore those far away. That's in part because the plight of a person you can see will always feel more real than the problems of someone whose suffering is merely described to you. But part of it is also rooted in you from a time when the welfare of your tribe was essential for your survival but the welfare of an opposing tribe was not — and might even be a threat.   17

In the 21st century, we retain a powerful remnant of that primal dichotomy, which is what impels us to step in and help a mugging victim — or, in the astonishing case of Wesley Autrey, New York City's so-called Subway Samaritan, jump onto the tracks in front of an oncoming train to rescue a sick stranger — but allows us to decline to send a small contribution to help the people of Darfur. "The idea that you can save the life of a stranger on the other side of the world by making a modest material sacrifice is not the kind of situation our social brains are prepared for," says Greene.   18

MORAL DILEMMA
The Runaway Trolley

A runaway trolley is heading down the tracks toward five workmen who can't be warned in time. You are standing near a switch that would divert the trolley onto a siding, but there is a single unsuspecting workman there. Would you throw the switch, killing one to save five? Suppose the workman was on a bridge with you and you could save the men only by pushing him onto the tracks? (He's large enough to stop the train; you're not.) Suppose you could throw a switch dropping him through a trapdoor — thus not physically pushing him?

DIVERT TRAIN	PUSH MAN	USE TRAPDOOR
❏ Yes	❏ Yes	❏ Yes
❏ No	❏ No	❏ No

19   Throughout most of the world, you're still not required to aid a stranger, but in France and elsewhere, laws now make it a crime for passersby not to provide at least the up-close-and-personal aid we're good at giving. In most of the U.S., we make a distinction between an action and an omission to act. Says Hauser: "In France they've done away with that difference."

20   But you don't need a state to create a moral code. The group does it too. One of the most powerful tools for enforcing group morals is the practice of shunning. If membership in a tribe is the way you ensure yourself food, family and protection from predators, being blackballed can be a terrifying thing. Religious believers as diverse as Roman Catholics, Mennonites and Jehovah's Witnesses have practiced their own forms of shunning — though the banishments may go by names like *excommunication* or *disfellowshipping*. Clubs, social groups and fraternities expel undesirable members, and the U.S. military retains the threat of discharge as a disciplinary tool, even grading the punishment as "other than honorable" or "dishonorable," darkening the mark a former service person must carry for life.

21   Sometimes shunning emerges spontaneously when a society of millions recoils at a single member's acts. O.J. Simpson's 1995 acquittal may have outraged people, but

it did make the morality tale surrounding him much richer, as the culture as a whole turned its back on him, denying him work, expelling him from his country club, refusing him service in a restaurant. In November his erstwhile publisher, who was fired in the wake of her and Simpson's disastrous attempt to publish a book about the killings, sued her ex-employer, alleging that she had been "shunned" and "humiliated." That, her former bosses might well respond, was precisely the point.

"Human beings were small, defenseless and vulnerable to predators," says 22 Barbara J. King, biological anthropologist at the College of William and Mary and author of *Evolving God*. "Avoiding banishment would be important to us."

Why We Turn Bad

With so many redundant moral systems to keep us in line, why do we so often fall 23 out of ranks? Sometimes we can't help it, as when we're suffering from clinical insanity and behavior slips the grip of reason. Criminal courts are stingy about finding such exculpatory madness, requiring a disability so severe, the defendant didn't even know the crime was wrong. That's a very high bar that prevents all but a few from proving the necessary moral numbness.

Things are different in the case of the cool and deliberate serial killer, who knows 24 the criminality of his deeds yet continues to commit them. For neuroscientists, the iciness of the acts calls to mind the case of Phineas Gage, the Vermont railway worker who in 1848 was injured when an explosion caused a tamping iron to be driven through his prefrontal cortex. Improbably, he survived, but he exhibited stark behavioral changes — becoming detached and irreverent, though never criminal. Ever since, scientists have looked for the roots of serial murder in the brain's physical state.

A study published last year in the journal *NeuroImage* may have helped provide 25 some answers. Researchers working through the National Institute of Mental Health scanned the brains of 20 healthy volunteers, watching their reactions as they were presented with various legal and illegal scenarios. The brain activity that most closely tracked the hypothetical crimes — rising and falling with the severity of the scenarios — occurred in the amygdala, a deep structure that helps us make the connection between bad acts and punishments. As in the trolley studies, there was also activity in the frontal cortex. The fact that the subjects themselves had no sociopathic tendencies limits the value of the findings. But knowing how the brain functions when things work well is one good way of knowing where to look when things break down.

Fortunately, the overwhelming majority of us never run off the moral rails in 26 remotely as awful a way as serial killers do, but we do come untracked in smaller ways. We face our biggest challenges not when we're called on to behave ourselves within our family, community or workplace but when we have to apply the same moral care to people outside our tribe.

The notion of the "other" is a tough one for *Homo sapiens*. Sociobiology has 27 been criticized as one of the most reductive of sciences, ascribing the behavior of all living things — humans included — as nothing more than an effort to get as many genes as possible into the next generation. The idea makes sense, and all creatures can be forgiven for favoring their troop over others. But such bias turns dark fast.

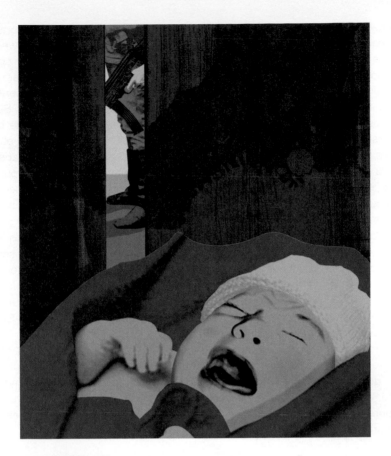

MORAL DILEMMA

The Crying Baby

It's wartime, and you're hiding in a basement with your baby and a group of other people. Enemy soldiers are outside and will be drawn to any sound. If you're found, you will all be killed immediately. Your baby starts to cry loudly and cannot be stopped. Smothering him to death is the only way to silence him and save the lives of everyone in the room. Could you do so? Assume the baby is not yours, the parents are unknown and there will be no penalty for killing him. Could you be the one who smothers this baby if no one else would?

YOUR BABY	SOMEONE ELSE'S BABY
☐ Yes	☐ Yes
☐ No	☐ No

28   Schulman, the psychologist and author, works with delinquent adolescents at a residential treatment center in Yonkers, New York, and was struck one day by the outrage that swept through the place when the residents learned that three of the boys

had mugged an elderly woman. "I wouldn't mug an old lady. That could be my grand-mother," one said. Schulman asked whom it would be O.K. to mug. The boy answered, "A Chinese delivery guy." Explains Schulman: "The old lady is someone they could empathize with. The Chinese delivery guy is alien, literally and figuratively, to them."

This kind of brutal line between insiders and outsiders is evident everywhere — mobsters, say, who kill promiscuously yet go on rhapsodically about "family." But it has its most terrible expression in wars, in which the dehumanization of the out-sider is essential for wholesale slaughter to occur. Volumes have been written about what goes on in the collective mind of a place like Nazi Germany or the collapsing Yugoslavia. While killers like Adolf Hitler or Slobodan Milosevic can never be put on the couch, it's possible to understand the xenophobic strings they play in their people. 29

"Yugoslavia is the great modern example of manipulating tribal sentiments to create mass murder," says Jonathan Haidt, associate professor of psychology at the University of Virginia. "You saw it in Rwanda and Nazi Germany too. In most cases of genocide, you have a moral entrepreneur who exploits tribalism for evil purposes." 30

That, of course, does not take the stain of responsibility off the people who follow those leaders — a case that war-crimes prosecutors famously argued at the Nuremberg trials and a point courageous people have made throughout his-tory as they sheltered Jews during World War II or refuse to murder their Sunni neighbor even if a militia leader tells them to. 31

For grossly imperfect creatures like us, morality may be the steepest of all developmental mountains. Our opposable thumbs and big brains gave us the tools to dominate the planet, but wisdom comes more slowly than physical hardware. We surely have a lot of killing and savagery ahead of us before we fully civilize ourselves. The hope — a realistic one, perhaps — is that the struggles still to come are fewer than those left behind. 32

MAKING CONNECTIONS: COMMUNITY MORALITY

Kluger explains that the community plays a central role in disciplining us so that we practice moral behavior. Most of us, however, belong to more than one com-munity, which may each have different and possibly contradictory standards and expectations — for example, parents versus friends, or college friends versus neigh-borhood or high school friends.

With two or three other students, discuss how community enforces morality. Begin by briefly taking turns telling one another about a conflict you encountered in the moral codes of different groups or a case where someone was disciplined by other members of a particular community. Then consider together the following questions:

- If you have experienced a conflict between different community expectations, how did you deal with it?

- If someone was disciplined by a community, what kind of discipline was it and how effective was it?

- To explain the power of *shunning*, Kluger quotes Barbara J. King, who makes the point that avoiding banishment from the group was especially important when we were "small, defenseless and vulnerable to predators" (par. 22). Do you fear shunning? If so, what makes shunning powerful for you and your friends today?

ANALYZING WRITING STRATEGIES

Basic Features

● A Focused Explanation of the Concept

To focus his essay and interest readers, Kluger introduces his explanation by establishing what he calls at the end of paragraph 2 "our *paradox*." A **paradox** is a statement that contradicts itself. For example, the statement "I always lie" is a paradox because if the statement is true, it also must be false. Paradoxes work by setting up an apparent opposition (such as telling the truth and lying) that upon closer examination may not be contradictory after all.

To analyze how Kluger introduces the concept and focuses his explanation, do the following:

- Reread paragraphs 1–7, and note in the margin the oppositions Kluger uses to set up his explanation.
- Write a few sentences identifying the oppositions and summarizing the paradox Kluger presents in this introductory section of the essay.
- Add another sentence or two explaining how he focuses his explanation and how well this focus helps you understand what Kluger acknowledges is "a hard concept to grasp" (par. 5).

● A Readable Plan

Writers of essays explaining concepts seek to make the information easy for readers to follow. To do so, they employ various cues, such as a *thesis statement, topic sentences, headings,* and various *transitional words and phrases*. Writers also use an array of cohesive devices including *word repetition* and *synonyms*.

To analyze how Kluger uses some of these cues, do the following activities:

Topic Sentences and Headings

- Reread the second section (pars. 8–14). Highlight the sentence or sentences that announce the topic of these paragraphs.
- Write a few sentences explaining why you think the text you highlighted serves as this section's topic sentence(s).
- Add a sentence speculating about why Kluger uses the heading "The Moral Ape" for this section.

Word Repetition and Synonyms

- Skim paragraphs 15 and 16 to see how Kluger uses word repetition and synonyms as cohesive devices to help readers follow the movement from topic to topic. For example, the last sentence in paragraph 15 uses the word *teaches* and the first two sentences of paragraph 16 use repetition (*teaching*) and a synonym (*mentoring system*).

- Reread paragraphs 20–22, and underline the word repetitions and synonyms Kluger uses.

- Write a sentence or two describing the word repetitions and synonyms Kluger uses in paragraphs 20–22.

To learn more about cueing strategies, see Chapter 10.

● Appropriate Explanatory Strategies

Kluger uses many of the explanatory strategies we've seen in the other essays explaining a concept, but he relies primarily on *examples* from research studies. To present these examples, he has to summarize the study succinctly so that readers can see how the example illustrates the topic he's discussing. For example, in paragraph 10, Kluger relates the anecdote that summarizes Nadia Kohts's research finding about the ability of chimpanzees to experience and act on empathy. (Interestingly, Kluger ends his brief summary with a quotation that could raise questions about the subjectivity of Kohts's interpretation of the chimp's behavior.)

To analyze Kluger's use of examples, do the following:

- Reread the examples in paragraphs 11–14.
- Write a sentence or two explaining how each example relates to Kluger's explanation.

● Smooth Integration of Sources

When writers integrate source material into their concept explanations, they have choices to make about what to quote and what to summarize or paraphrase. Because he is relating several research reports, Kluger quotes and summarizes a lot. Let's look at an example:

> While it's impossible to directly measure empathy in animals, in humans it's another matter. Hauser cites a study in which spouses or unmarried couples underwent functional magnetic resonance imaging (fMRI) as they were subjected to mild pain. They were warned before each time the painful stimulus was administered, and their brains lit up in a characteristic way signaling mild dread. They were then told that they were not going to feel the discomfort but that their partner was. Even when they couldn't see their partner, the brains of the subjects lit up precisely as if they were about to experience the pain themselves. "This is very much an 'I feel your pain' experience," says Hauser. (par. 12)

The first sentence (highlighted) is the topic sentence announcing what the paragraph is about. The next four sentences summarize Hauser's research study, beginning with a brief process narrative explaining how the study was conducted and concluding with a sentence (underlined) summarizing the results of the experiment. The final sentence of the paragraph, a quotation from the researcher, comments on the results using down-to-earth language to discuss what the experiment reveals about empathy, the topic of the paragraph. This is a clear, efficient, and interesting way to present information.

To analyze how Kluger integrates sources into his essay, do the following:

 Choose one of the following paragraphs to read, and analyze it using the method presented in the sample analysis above: paragraph 5, 10, 14, or 16.

 Write a few sentences describing the results of your analysis.

For more on summary, paraphrase, and quotation, see Chapter 17, pp. 487–95.

> ❯

ANALYZING VISUALS

"MORAL DILEMMAS"

The visuals included in this essay accompany brief scenarios called "Moral Dilemmas." Examine each "Moral Dilemma" carefully, and then write a few sentences describing them and explaining what they contribute to Kluger's explanation of the concept. In performing your analysis, consider the following questions:

- When you initially read the essay, did you stop to study any of the scenarios, just glance at them in passing, go back to them after finishing the essay, or not look at them at all?

- What purpose do the scenarios serve?

- The scenarios use words as well as illustrations. What do the illustrations contribute to the scenarios?

- Do the scenarios repeat information already presented in the text of the essay, or do they add new information?

- Each "Moral Dilemma" invites readers to answer questions. Online, this was an interactive feature of the essay, and the original print publication directed readers to the online activity. How effective is this type of visual in a print publication compared to an online one?

> ❯

CONSIDERING TOPICS FOR YOUR OWN ESSAY

Kluger mentions several concepts you might think about exploring further for your own essay: empathy, reciprocal altruism, nonhuman cognition, tribalism, shunning, clinical insanity, sociobiology, and xenophobia. Alternatively, you could focus on one of the many research studies Kluger refers to, explaining in depth one of the key concepts the study investigates; or you could focus on relevant research Kluger does not mention, such as the famous experiment on obedience to authority conducted by psychologist Stanley Milgram in the early 1960s, or the recent re-staging of this experiment done by Jerry Burger at Santa Clara University. You could also consider writing about a different concept from Western philosophy such as metaphysics, truth, epistemology, idealism, pragmatism, logical positivism, or existentialism; or you could examine a concept related to an Eastern philosophy such as Confucianism, Taoism, karma, nirvana, or Zoroastrianism.

Guide to Writing

The Writing Assignment

Write an essay about a concept that interests you and that you want to study further. When you have a good understanding of the concept, explain it to your readers, considering carefully what they already know about it and how your essay might add to what they know.

This Guide to Writing will help you apply what you have learned about how writers create concept explanations that are focused, readable, well explained, and supported by credible sources. The Guide is divided into five sections with various activities in each section:

- **Invention and Research**
- **Planning and Drafting**
- **Critical Reading Guide**
- **Editing and Proofreading**
- **Revising**

The guide is designed to escort you through the writing process, from finding a concept to editing your finished essay. Your instructor may require you to follow the Guide to Writing from beginning to end. Working through the Guide to Writing in this way will help you — as it has helped many other college students — write a thoughtful, fully developed, polished essay.

If, however, your instructor gives you latitude to choose and if you have had experience writing a concept explanation, then you can decide on the order in which you'll do the activities in the Guide to Writing. For example, the Invention and Research section includes activities to help you find a concept, get an overview of it, focus it, research your focus, and consider explanatory strategies. Obviously, finding a concept must precede the other activities, but you may come to the Guide with a concept already in mind, and you may choose to do research on it before you focus your explanation. In fact, you may find your response to one of the invention activities expanding into a draft before you've had a chance to do any of the other activities. That's a good thing — but you should later flesh out your draft by going back to the activities you skipped and layering the new material into your draft.

The following chart will help you find answers to many of the questions you might have about planning, drafting, and revising a concept explanation. The page references in the right-hand column refer to examples from the readings, activities in the Guide to Writing, and chapters later in the book.

▶ Starting Points: Explaining a Concept

● ● ● ● Basic Features

Choosing a Concept	
How do I come up with a concept to write about?	• Considering Topics for Your Own Essay (pp. 124, 135) • Choosing a Concept to Write About (pp. 138–40) • Testing Your Choice (pp. 141–42)
What's my purpose in writing? How can I interest my audience?	• Reading Concept Explanations: Purpose and Audience (pp. 111–12) • Defining Your Purpose for Your Readers (p. 143) • Refining Your Purpose and Setting Goals: Clarifying Your Purpose and Audience (p. 145)

A Focused Explanation	
How can I decide on a focus for my concept?	• Reading Concept Explanations: Basic Features (pp. 110–11) • Ways In: Gaining an Overview of a Concept (p. 140) • Ways In: Focusing the Concept (p. 141)

A Readable Plan	
How should I arrange my explanation so that it's logical and easy to read? What kinds of cues should I provide?	• Reading Concept Explanations: Basic Features (pp. 110–11) • Use forecasting (p. 122) • Use cues and cohesive devices (pp. 133–34) • Formulating a Tentative Thesis Statement (p. 144) • Refining Your Purpose and Setting Goals: Presenting the Information and the Ending (p. 145) • Outlining Your Draft (pp. 145–46)

Appropriate Explanatory Strategies	
What's the best way to explain my concept? What kinds of writing strategies should I use?	• Reading Concept Explanations: Basic Features (pp. 110–11) • Use explanatory writing strategies (p. 123) • Use examples (p. 134) • Doing In-Depth Research on Your Focused Concept (p. 142) • Considering Explanatory Strategies (pp. 142–43) • Designing Your Document (p. 143)
How do I write clear definitions?	• A Sentence Strategy: Appositives (p. 147)

(continued)

(continued)

Smooth Integration of Sources	
How should I integrate sources so that they support my argument?	• Reading Concept Explanations: Basic Features (pp. 110–11) • Use summary and paraphrase (pp. 134–35) • Working with Sources: Using Descriptive Verbs to Introduce Information (pp. 148–49)

Invention and Research

The following invention activities are easy to complete and take only a few minutes. Spreading out the activities over several days will stimulate your creativity, enabling you to find a concept and an approach to explaining it that works for both you and your readers. Remember to keep a written record of your invention work: You will need it when you draft the essay and later when you revise it.

Choosing a Concept to Write About

List several concepts that you might like to explore. Include concepts you already know something about as well as some you know only slightly and would like to research further — the longer your list, the more likely you are to find the right concept, and should your first choice not work out, you will have a ready list of alternatives. Bear in mind that you are looking for a concept that meets the following criteria.

Criteria for Choosing a Concept: A Checklist
The concept should be: ☐ a concept that you feel eager to learn more about; ☐ a concept that will interest your readers; ☐ a concept that you can research sufficiently in the allotted time; ☐ a concept that you can explain fully and clearly in the length prescribed by your instructor.

If you're like most people, you'll need some help in coming up with a number of good options. To get your juices flowing, you might first try quickly rereading the Considering Topics for Your Own Essay activities following the readings, and thinking about any concepts those suggestions brought to mind. Reread any notes you might have made in response to the suggestions. Consider also any concepts related to your hobbies or special interests.

For further ideas, consult the suggestions in the following sections.

Possible Concepts to Consider. Your work in this or your other courses can provide concepts you might be interested in exploring. Try skimming through your class notes and your textbooks. Here are a few possibilities, by discipline:

- **Literature:** irony, semiotics, hero, dystopia, picaresque, the absurd, canon, modernism, identity politics, queering
- **Philosophy:** nihilism, logical positivism, determinism, metaphysics, ethics, natural law, Zeno's paradox, epistemology, ideology
- **Business management:** quality circle, cybernetic control system, management by objectives, zero-based budgeting, liquidity gap
- **Psychology:** assimilation/accommodation, social cognition, moratorium, intelligence, operant conditioning, the Stroop effect
- **Government:** majority rule, minority rights, federalism, popular consent, exclusionary rule, hegemony
- **Biology:** photosynthesis, mitosis, karyotype analysis, morphogenesis, electron transport, plasmolysis, phagocytosis, homozygosity, diffusion
- **Art:** cubism, Dadaism, surrealism, expressionism, perspective, collage
- **Math:** polynomials, boundedness, null space, permutations and combinations, factoring, Rolle's theorem, continuity, derivative, indefinite integral
- **Physical sciences:** matter, mass, weight, energy, gravity, atomic theory, law of definite proportions, osmotic pressure, first law of thermodynamics, entropy
- **Public health:** addiction, seasonal affective disorder, contraception, prenatal care, toxicology, glycemic index
- **Environmental studies:** acid rain, recycling, ozone depletion, toxic waste, endangered species, sustainability
- **Sports:** squeeze play (baseball), power play (hockey), wishbone offense (football), serve and volley (tennis), inside game (basketball)
- **Personal finance:** reverse mortgage, budget, insurance, deduction, revolving credit, interest rates, dividend, bankruptcy, socially conscious investing
- **Law:** tort, contract, garnishment, double indemnity, reasonable doubt, class action suits, product liability, lemon law
- **Sociology:** norm, deviance, role conflict, ethnocentrism, class, social stratification, acculturation, Whorf-Sapir hypothesis, machismo

Also consider exploring concepts that relate to issues of identity and community, such as self-esteem, character, autonomy, narcissism, multiculturalism, ethnicity, race, racism, social contract, community policing, social Darwinism, identity politics, special-interest groups, colonialism, public space, the other, or agency.

Finally, consider exploring concepts that relate to your work experiences and career aspirations, such as free enterprise, minimum wage, affirmative action, stock option, glass ceiling, downsizing, collective bargaining, service sector, entrepreneur, bourgeoisie, underclass, working class, middle class, monopoly, automation, robotics, management style, deregulation, or multinational corporation.

Ways In: Gaining an Overview of a Concept

Basic Features

Your research efforts for a concept essay can be divided into three stages. First, you must gain an overview of the concept; next, you will identify an aspect of it to focus on; finally, you will do in-depth research in order to gather information. The activities below will help you gain an overview of your concept. You can begin with whichever activity you want, but wherever you begin, be sure to return to the other activities to gather sufficient information.

Discovering What You Already Know

Take a few minutes to write about what you already know about the concept. Consider, too, why you have chosen the concept and why you find it interesting. Write quickly, without planning or organizing. Note questions you have about the concept. Also, check any materials you have at hand that explain your concept. (If you are considering a concept from one of your other courses, for example, check your textbook or your lecture notes first.)

Doing Research

To find comprehensive, up-to-date information on your concept, locate relevant articles, books, and encyclopedias through your library. Chapter 16, Library and Internet Research, has general information that will help you do research productively. When you find potentially useful information, take accurate notes, make a photocopy, or save the information electronically, always being sure to record exact source information for your works-cited list. Depending on your topic, you might also consider consulting experts on campus or in the community, and visiting other potential sources of information such as museums or research centers.

Doing a General Internet Search

Do an Internet search to help you find a focus for your essay. Try entering the word "overview" or "definition" together with the name of your concept, in order to confine your results to introductions and overviews. Bookmark Web sites you find that invite more than a quick glance, and copy or save any potentially useful information — making sure to include the URL, the title of the site, the date the information was posted (if available), and the date you accessed the site. As always, if your first searches do not turn up much of use, be sure to try variations on the search terms you use.

Ways In: Focusing the Concept

The following activities will help you determine a focus for your concept. Concepts can be approached from many perspectives (for example, history, definition, known causes or effects), and you cannot realistically explain every aspect of any concept, so you must limit your explanation to reflect both your special interest in the concept and your readers' likely knowledge and interest.

Exploring Your Own Interests

Make a list of two or three aspects of the concept that could become a focus for your essay, and evaluate what you know about each aspect. Under each possible focus in your list, make notes about why it interests you, what you know about it already, and what questions you want to answer about it.

Analyzing Your Readers

Take a few minutes to write about your readers. Ask the following questions to help clarify your thinking:

- Who are your readers likely to be?
- What do they already know about the concept or about related concepts?
- Are they likely to be interested in the concept or related concepts? If not, how could you interest them?
- What would be useful for them to know about this concept — perhaps something that could relate to their life or work?

Even if you are writing only for your instructor, you should give some thought to what he or she knows and thinks about the concept.

After doing the activities above, choose an aspect of your concept on which to focus, and write a sentence justifying its appropriateness.

Testing Your Choice

After you have chosen a concept and attempted to focus it, you should pause to decide whether you should write about it. As painful as it may be to consider, starting over with a new concept is better than continuing with an unworkable one. Test your choice using the questions that follow.

- *Can I learn what I need to know in the time I have available to write a concept explanation with this focus?*
- *Am I likely to understand the concept well enough to make it clear to my readers?*

- *Do I feel a personal interest in the concept and the particular focus I have chosen? If so, what is the basis for this interest? Is the concept so interesting to me that I am willing to spend the next two or three weeks on an essay explaining it?*
- *Do I think I can make the concept and the focus I have chosen interesting to readers? Can I relate the concept to something readers already know? Can I think of any anecdotes or examples that will make the concept more meaningful to them?*

If you lose confidence in your choice, return to the list of possible concepts you made, and choose another one.

A Collaborative Activity:

Testing Your Choice

Get together with two or three other students to find out what your readers are likely to know about your subject and what might interest them about it.

Presenters: Take turns briefly explaining your concept, describing your intended readers, and identifying the aspect of the concept that you will focus on.

Listeners: Briefly tell the presenter whether the focus sounds appropriate and interesting for the intended readers. Share what you think readers are likely to know about the concept and what information might be especially interesting to them.

● Doing In-Depth Research on Your Focused Concept

Having chosen a concept and a focus for your explanation of it, begin your in-depth search of the library, Internet, and other relevant sources for information on your concept. You will want to keep careful records of all sources you believe will contribute in any way to your essay. If possible, scan or make photocopies of print sources, and save other sources electronically. If you must rely on notes, be sure to copy any quotations exactly and enclose them in quotation marks. Since you do not know which sources you will ultimately use, keep careful records of the author, title, publication information, page numbers, and other required information for each source you gather so that you can acknowledge your sources. Check with your instructor about whether you should follow the documentation style of the Modern Language Association (MLA), the American Psychological Association (APA), or a different style.

● Considering Explanatory Strategies

Before you move on to plan and draft your essay, consider some possible ways of presenting the concept. Try to answer each of the following questions in a sentence or two. Questions that you can answer readily may identify the best strategies for presenting your focused concept.

- What term is typically used to name the concept, and what does it mean? (*definition*)

- How is this concept like or unlike related concepts with which your readers may be more familiar? (*comparison and contrast*)

- How can an explanation of this concept be divided into parts to make it easier for readers to understand? (*classification*)

- How does this concept happen, or how does one go about doing it? (*process narration*)

- What are this concept's known causes or effects? (*cause and effect*)

- What examples or anecdotes can make the concept less abstract and more memorable? (*example* or *anecdote*)

Designing Your Document

Think about whether visual elements — tables, graphs, drawings, photographs — would make your explanation clearer. These are not a requirement, but they could be helpful. Consider also whether your readers might benefit from design features such as headings, bulleted or numbered lists, or other elements that would present information efficiently or make your explanation easier to follow. You could construct your own graphic elements (using word processing software to create bar graphs or pie charts, for example), download materials from the Internet, copy images from television or DVDs, or scan visuals from books and magazines. Remember that you must cite the source of any visual you do not create yourself, and you should also request permission from the source of the visual if your paper is going to be posted on a Web site that is not password-protected.

Defining Your Purpose for Your Readers

Write a few sentences that define your purpose in writing about this particular concept for your readers. Remember that you have already identified and analyzed your readers and that you have begun to research and develop your explanation with these readers in mind. Try now to define your purpose in explaining the concept to them. Use these questions to focus your thoughts:

- *Are my readers familiar with the concept? If not, how can I relate it to what they already know? If so, will my focus allow my readers to see the familiar concept in a new light?*

- *If I suspect that my readers have misconceptions about the concept, how can I correct the misconceptions without offending my readers?*

- *Will I need to arouse readers' interest in information that may seem at first to be less than engaging?*

- *Do I want readers to see that the information I have to report is relevant to their lives, families, communities, work, or studies?*

Formulating a Tentative Thesis Statement

Write one or more sentences, stating your focused concept, that could serve as a thesis statement. You might also want to forecast the topics you will use to explain the concept.

Anastasia Toufexis begins her essay with this thesis statement:

> O.K., let's cut out all this nonsense about romantic love. Let's bring some scientific precision to the party. Let's put love under a microscope.
>
> When rigorous people with Ph.D.s after their names do that, what they see is not some silly, senseless thing. No, their probe reveals that love rests firmly on the foundations of evolution, biology and chemistry.

Toufexis's concept is *love,* and her focus is the scientific explanation of love — specifically the evolution, biology, and chemistry of love. In announcing her focus, she forecasts the order in which she will present information from the three most relevant academic disciplines — anthropology (which includes the study of human evolution), biology, and chemistry. These discipline names become her topics.

In his essay on cannibalism, Linh Kieu Ngo offers his thesis statement in paragraph 6:

> Cannibalism can be broken down into two main categories: exocannibalism, the eating of outsiders or foreigners, and endocannibalism, the eating of members of one's own social group (Shipman 70). Within these categories are several functional types of cannibalism, three of the most common being survival cannibalism, dietary cannibalism, and religious and ritual cannibalism.

Ngo's concept is *cannibalism,* and his focus is on three common types of cannibalism. He carefully forecasts how he will divide the information to create topics and the order in which he will explain each of the topics.

As you draft your own tentative thesis statement, take care to make the language clear. Although you may want to revise your thesis statement as you draft your essay, trying to state it now will give your planning and drafting more focus and direction. Keep in mind that the thesis in an explanatory essay merely announces the subject; it never asserts a position that requires an argument to defend it.

Planning and Drafting

The following guidelines will help you get the most out of your invention notes, determine specific goals for your essay, and write a first draft. In addition, this section will help you write a draft by writing opening sentences, trying out a useful sentence strategy, and learning how to work with sources.

Refining Your Purpose and Setting Goals

Successful writers are always looking beyond the next sentence to larger goals. Indeed, the next sentence is easier to write if you keep larger goals in mind. The following questions can help you set these goals. Consider each one now, and then return to them as necessary while you write.

Clarifying Your Purpose and Audience

- *How can I build on my readers' knowledge?*
- *What new information can I present to them?*
- *How can I organize my essay so that my readers can follow it easily?*
- *What tone would be most appropriate? Would an informal tone like Toufexis's or a formal one like Ngo's be more appropriate to my purpose?*

Presenting the Information

- *Should I name and define my concept early in the essay, as Ngo and Toufexis do? Or should I lead up to it gradually by providing illustrations, as Kluger does?*
- *Could I develop my explanation by dividing my concept into different categories, as Ngo does?*
- *How can I establish the authority of my sources? Should I refer to specific publications or research, as Ngo, Toufexis, and Kluger do? Will my instructor require me to use APA style, MLA style — as Ngo's instructor did — or some other documentation style?*
- *How can I make it easy for readers to follow my explanation? Should I simply use clear and explicit transitions when I move from one topic to another, as Ngo does, or also include rhetorical questions, as Toufexis and Kluger do?*
- *Should I use visuals, as Toufexis and Kluger do?*

The Ending

- *Should I end with speculation, as Ngo does?*
- *Should I frame the essay by relating the ending to the beginning, as Toufexis and Kluger do?*

Outlining Your Draft

The goals that you have set should help you draft your essay, but first you might want to make a quick scratch outline. In your outline, list the main topics into which you have divided the information about your concept. Use this outline to guide your drafting, but do not feel tied to it. As you draft, you may find a better way to sequence the action and integrate these features.

An essay explaining a concept is made up of four basic parts:

- an attempt to engage readers' interest
- the thesis statement, announcing the concept, its focus, and its topics
- an orientation to the concept, which may include a description or definition of the concept
- information about the concept

Here is a possible outline for an essay explaining a concept:

I. Introduction (attempt to gain readers' interest in the concept)
II. Thesis statement
III. Definition of the concept
IV. Topic 1 with illustration
V. Topic 2 with illustration
 (Topic 3, etc.)
VI. Conclusion

An attempt to gain readers' interest could take as little as two or three sentences or as many as four or five paragraphs. The thesis statement and definition are usually quite brief — sometimes only a few sentences. A topic illustration may occupy one or several paragraphs, and there can be few or many topics, depending on how the information has been divided up. A conclusion might summarize the information presented, give advice about how to use or apply the information, or speculate about the future of the concept.

Drafting

If you have not already begun to draft your essay, this section will help by suggesting how to choose an opening sentence strategy, how to use appositive phrases, and how to use descriptive verbs to introduce information from sources. Drafting isn't always a smooth process, so don't be afraid to leave spaces where you don't know what to put in or write notes to yourself about what you could do next. If you get stuck while drafting, go back over your invention writing: You may be able to copy and paste some of it into your evolving draft, or you may need to do some additional invention to fill in details in your draft.

Writing the Opening Sentences

You could try out one or two different ways of beginning your essay — possibly from the list that follows — but do not agonize over the first sentences because you are likely to discover the best way to begin only after you have written a rough draft. Review your invention writing to see if you have already written something that would work to launch your essay. To engage your readers' interest from the start, consider the following opening strategies:

- a surprising or provocative quotation (like Toufexis)
- an anecdote illustrating the concept (like Ngo)
- a paradox or surprising aspect of the concept (like Kluger)
- a fascinating bit of information
- a comparison or contrast
- a concrete example
- an announcement of the concept
- a forecast of the topics

A Sentence Strategy: Appositives

As you draft an essay explaining a concept, you have a lot of information to present, such as definitions of terms and credentials of experts. Appositives provide an efficient, clear way to integrate these kinds of information into your sentences. An appositive is a noun or pronoun that, along with modifiers, gives more information about another noun or pronoun. Here is an example from Ngo's concept essay (the appositive is in italics and the noun it refers to is underlined):

> Cannibalism, *the act of human beings eating human flesh* (Sagan 2), has a long history and continues to hold interest and create controversy. (par. 5)

By placing the definition in an appositive phrase right after the word it defines, this sentence locates the definition exactly where readers need it.

Writers explaining concepts rely on appositives because they serve many different purposes needed in concept essays, as the following examples demonstrate. (Again, the appositive is in italics and the noun it refers to is underlined.)

Defining a New Term

> The deepest foundation on which morality is built is the phenomenon of empathy, *the understanding that what hurts me would feel the same way to you.* (Kluger, par. 8)

Introducing a New Term

> Each person carries in his or her mind a unique subliminal guide to the ideal partner, a "*love map.*" (Toufexis, par. 17)

> Behaviorists often reduce what we call empathy to a mercantile business known as *reciprocal altruism.* (Kluger, par. 9)

Giving Credentials of Experts

> "Love is a natural high," observes Anthony Walsh, *author of The Science of Love: Understanding Love and Its Effects on Mind and Body.* (Toufexis, par. 10)

> "He'll respond, 'No, the teacher shouldn't say that,'" says psychologist Michael Schulman, *coauthor of Bringing Up a Moral Child.* (Kluger, par. 5)

Identifying People and Things

> Even cynics went soft at the story of Binti Jua, *the gorilla who in 1996 rescued a 3-year-old boy who had tumbled into her zoo enclosure.* . . . (Kluger, par. 11)

Giving Examples or Specifics

> The madness would lie instead in the fact that both of those qualities, *the savage and the splendid,* can exist in one creature, one person, often in one instant.

For more on appositives, go to **bedfordstmartins.com/conciseguide** and click on Appositives.

Working with Sources:

Using Descriptive Verbs to Introduce Information

When explaining concepts, writers usually need to present information from different sources. There are many verbs writers can choose to introduce the information they quote or summarize. Here are a few examples from the concept essays in this chapter (the verbs are in italics):

> "That is one reason why it feels so horrible when we're abandoned or a lover dies," *notes* Fisher. (Toufexis, par. 13)

> In one incident, Japanese troops *were reported* to have sacrificed the Arapesh people of northeastern New Guinea for food in order to avoid death by starvation (Tuzin 63). (Ngo, par. 7)

> "This is very much an 'I feel your pain' experience," *says* Hauser. (Kluger, par. 12)

Toufexis's verb *notes*, Ngo's *were reported*, and Kluger's *says* indicate that they are not characterizing or judging their sources, but simply reporting them. Often, however, writers are more descriptive — even evaluative — when they introduce information from sources, as these examples demonstrate:

> "As long as prehistoric females were secretive about their extramarital affairs," *argues* Fisher, "they could garner extra resources, life insurance, better genes and more varied DNA for their biological futures. . . ." (Toufexis, par. 8)

> In both cases, somebody taught the child a rule, but the rule against pushing has a stickiness about it, one that resists coming unstuck even if someone in authority countenances it. That's the difference between a matter of morality and one of mere social convention, and Schulman and others *believe* kids feel it innately. (Kluger, par. 5)

The verbs in these examples — *argues* and *believe* — describe the particular role played by the source in explaining the concept. Verbs like *argues* emphasize that what is being reported is an interpretation that others may disagree with. Kluger chooses *believe* to designate a conclusion or speculation made by researchers.

As you refer to sources in your concept explanation, you will want to choose carefully from a wide variety of precise verbs. You may find this list of verbs helpful in selecting the right verbs to introduce your sources when you are explaining a concept: *suggests, reveals, questions, brings into focus, finds, notices, observes, emphasizes.*

Notice that Ngo tends not to introduce his sources in the body of his essay; instead, he simply integrates the information from them into his sentences, and readers can see from the parenthetical citation and the works-cited list where the information came from. Here is an example from paragraph 9 in which Ngo includes a quotation together with information he paraphrases from his source:

> The Miyanmin people observe no differences in "gender, kinship, ritual status, and bodily substance"; they eat anyone, even their own dead. In this respect, then, they practice both endo-cannibalism and exocannibalism; and to ensure a constant supply of human flesh for food, they raid neighboring tribes and drag their victims back to their village to be eaten (Poole 11).

This strategy of integrating source material allows Ngo to emphasize the information and downplay the source.

You can find more information about integrating sources into your sentences and constructing signal phrases in Chapter 17.

Critical Reading Guide

Basic Features

Your instructor may arrange a peer review session in class or online where you can exchange drafts with your classmates and give one another a thoughtful critical reading, pointing out what works well and suggesting ways to improve the draft. This Critical Reading Guide can also be used productively by a tutor in the writing center or by a roommate or family member. A good critical reading does three things: It lets the writer know how well the reader understands the concept explanation, praises what works best, and indicates where the draft could be improved.

1. Evaluate how effectively the concept is focused.

   Summarize: Tell the writer, in one sentence, what you understand the concept to mean.

   Praise: Give an example of something in the draft that you think will especially interest the intended readers.

   Critique: Tell the writer about any confusion or uncertainty you have about the concept's meaning. Does the focus seem too broad or too narrow for the intended readers? Can you think of a more interesting way to focus the explanation?

2. Assess how readable the explanation is.

   Look at the way the essay is organized by making a scratch outline.

   - Does the information seem to be logically divided?
   - Does the *beginning* pull readers into the essay and make them want to continue? Does it adequately forecast the direction of the essay?
   - Do *transitions* helpfully guide the reader from part to part?
   - Is the *ending* effective?

   Praise: Give an example of where the essay succeeds in being readable — for instance, in its overall organization, its use of transitions, its beginning, or its ending.

   Critique: Tell the writer where the readability could be improved. Can you suggest a better way of sequencing the information, for example? Can the use of transitions be improved, or transitions added where they are lacking? Can you suggest a better beginning or a more effective ending?

3. Consider how effectively explanatory strategies are used.

   Praise: Give an example of the effective use of writing strategies such as defining, classifying or dividing, comparing and contrasting, narrating anecdotes or processes, illustrating with examples or lists of facts and details, and reporting causes and effects. Point out places where definitions succeed in conveying information clearly, and places where visuals (if visuals are present) aid in helping readers understand important concepts.

Critique: Tell the writer where a different writing strategy might help in conveying information effectively. Point out places where definitions might be needed or existing definitions need clarification or expansion. Suggest places where additional information is needed. Note places in the essay where the addition of visuals such as charts, graphics, or tables could help in making the concept clearer.

4. Evaluate how smoothly sources are integrated.

   Praise: Give an example of the effective use of sources — a particularly well-integrated quotation, paraphrase, or summary that supports the writer's claims. Note any especially descriptive verbs used to introduce information.

   Critique: Tell the writer where a quote, paraphrase, or summary could be more smoothly integrated. Suggest places where it would be better to summarize or paraphrase than to quote, or vice versa. If the list of sources used is less balanced than it should be, suggest types of sources that would strengthen it, or suggest sources that would be better left out.

5. If the writer has expressed concern about anything in the draft that you have not discussed, respond to that concern.

Making Comments Electronically Most word processing software offers features that allow you to insert comments directly into the text of someone else's document. Many readers prefer to make their comments this way because it tends to be faster than writing on hard copy and space is virtually unlimited; it also eliminates the process of deciphering handwritten comments. Where such features are not available, simply typing comments directly into a document in a contrasting color can provide the same advantages.

For a printable version of this Critical Reading Guide, go to **bedfordstmartins.com/conciseguide**.

Revising

Very likely you have already thought of ways to improve your draft, and you may even have begun to revise it. In this section is a Troubleshooting chart that may help. Before using the chart, however, it is a good idea to

- review critical reading comments from your classmates, instructor, or writing center tutor, and

- make an outline of your draft so that you can look at it analytically.

You may have made an outline before writing your draft, but after drafting you need to see what you actually wrote, not what you intended to write. You can outline the draft quickly by highlighting the basic features — focus, readability, use of explanatory strategies, and integration of sources.

For an electronic version of this Troubleshooting chart, go to **bedfordstmartins.com/conciseguide**.

☑ Troubleshooting Your Draft

■ ■ ■ ◈ **Basic Features**

A Focused Explanation	
I have too much to cover. (The focus is too broad.)	☐ Narrow your concept to a specific cultural or historical context — for example, instead of "dating," try "U.S. dating conventions in the mid-twentieth century." ☐ Consider what aspects of your concept would be of particular interest to your audience. Refocus accordingly. ☐ If your concept comes from another course you are taking, check your textbook or lecture notes for a way to focus it.
I don't have enough to write about. (The focus is too narrow.)	☐ Broaden your concept by adding cultural or historical comparisons and contrasts. ☐ Look up your concept in your library catalog or online, and browse for larger concepts that include it. ☐ If your concept comes from another course you are taking, check your textbook or lecture notes for broader, related topics.

A Readable Plan	
The organization is not logical.	☐ Reread your thesis statement to be sure that it clearly announces the concept and forecasts the topics in the order they appear in the essay. ☐ Look for topic sentences in each paragraph. (If you find them difficult to locate, your reader will, too.) Clarify where necessary.
The beginning does not draw readers in.	☐ Try starting with an anecdote, interesting quotation, surprising aspect of the concept, concrete example, or a similar lead-in. ☐ Consider stating explicitly what makes the concept worth thinking about and how it relates to your readers' interests.
The essay does not flow smoothly from one part to the next.	☐ Outline your essay, noting where transitions between paragraphs or sections could be added or made clearer. ☐ Consider adding headings to make the connections among parts clearer.

(continued)

(continued)

The ending falls flat.	☐ Consider ending by speculating on what the future will bring — how the concept might be redefined, for example. ☐ Consider relating the ending to the beginning — for example, by recalling an example or a comparison.

Appropriate Explanatory Strategies

The information is not getting through to readers as clearly as it should.	☐ Consider whether you have used the best writing strategies — defining, classifying, comparing and contrasting, narrating, illustrating, describing, and explaining cause and effect — for your topic. ☐ Recheck your definitions for clarity. Be sure that you have explicitly defined any key terms your readers might not know.
Readers want more information about certain aspects of the concept.	☐ Reread existing definitions and illustrations, and expand or clarify where necessary. ☐ Do additional research on your topic, and cite it in your essay.
Definitions need work.	☐ Consider providing synonyms or antonyms for terms you are defining. ☐ Consider supplementing definitions with illustrations or examples. ☐ Consider using appositives to define terms efficiently and clearly.
Readers want visuals to help them understand certain concepts.	☐ Check whether your sources use visuals (tables, graphs, drawings, photographs, and the like) that might be appropriate for your explanation. ☐ Consider drafting your own charts, tables, or graphs or adding your own photographs or illustrations.

Smooth Integration of Sources

Summaries lack oomph; paraphrases are too long or too close to original source; quotations are too long or uninteresting.	☐ If a summary is too long-winded, try providing only the necessary source information and the single key idea that illuminates your topic. ☐ If a paraphrase is too long or too close to the original, try to restate it more succinctly. If you feel you are losing essential information by paraphrasing, consider using a quotation instead. ☐ If a quotation is too long, locate the essential information in it and consider excerpting that information only, using ellipses to make it flow naturally with your prose. ☐ If a quotation is uninteresting, paraphrase or summarize the information instead.
Quotes, summary, and/or paraphrase do not flow smoothly with the rest of the essay.	☐ Check to be sure that you have appropriately commented on all cited material, making its relation to your own ideas clear. ☐ Consider using descriptive verbs to give your readers more information about what your source is saying and why you are referring to it.

Editing and Proofreading

Two kinds of errors occur often in concept explanations: punctuation around adjective clauses, and commas around interrupting phrases. The following guidelines will help you check your essay for these common errors.

Using Punctuation with Adjective Clauses

What Is an Adjective Clause? Adjective clauses include both a subject and a verb. They give information about a noun or a pronoun. They often begin with *who*, *which*, or *that*. Here is an example from a student essay explaining the concept of *schizophrenia*, a type of mental illness:

> It is common for schizophrenics to have delusions *that they are being persecuted.*

Because adjective clauses add information about the nouns they follow — defining, illustrating, or explaining — they can be useful in writing that explains a concept.

The Problem: Adjective clauses may or may not need to be set off with a comma or commas. To decide, first you have to determine whether the clause is essential to the meaning of the sentence. Clauses that are essential to the meaning of a sentence should not be set off with a comma; clauses that are not essential to the meaning must be set off with a comma.

How to Correct It: Mentally delete the clause. If taking out the clause does not change the basic meaning of the sentence or make it unclear, add a comma or commas.

▶ Postpartum neurosis, which can last for two weeks or longer, can adversely affect a mother's ability to care for her infant.

▶ The early stage starts with memory loss, which usually causes the patient to forget recent life events.

If the clause follows a proper noun, add a comma/commas.

▶ Nanotechnologists defer to K. Eric Drexler, who speculates imaginatively about the use of nonmachines.

If taking out the clause changes the basic meaning of the sentence or makes it unclear, do *not* add a comma or commas.

▶ Seasonal affective disorders are mood disturbances, that occur with a change of season.

▶ The coaches, who do the recruiting should be disciplined.

For practice, go to **bedfordstmartins.com/conciseguide/exercisecentral** and click on Adjective Clauses.

Using Commas with Interrupting Phrases

What Is an Interrupting Phrase? When writers are explaining a concept, they need to supply a great deal of information. They add much of this information in phrases that interrupt the flow of a sentence, as in the following example:

People on the West Coast, especially in Los Angeles, have always been receptive to new ideas.

Interrupting phrases are typically set off with commas.

The Problem: Forgetting to set off an interrupting phrase with commas can make sentences difficult to read or unclear.

How to Correct It: Add a comma on either side of an interrupting phrase.

▶ People on the West Cost ˏ especially in Los Angeles ˏ have always been receptive to new ideas.

▶ Alzheimer's disease ˏ named after the German neuropathologist Alois Alzheimer ˏ is a chronic degenerative illness.

▶ These examples ˏ though simple ˏ present equations in terms of tangible objects.

For practice, go to **bedfordstmartins.com/conciseguide/exercisecentral** and click on Interrupting Phrases.

Thinking Critically about What You Have Learned

In this chapter, you have learned a great deal about this genre from reading several concept explanations and writing one of your own. To consolidate your learning, it is helpful to think **metacognitively** — that is, to reflect not only on what you learned but on how you learned it. Following are two brief activities your instructor may ask you to do.

Reflecting on Your Writing

Your instructor may ask you to turn in with your essay and process materials a brief metacognitive essay or letter reflecting on what you have learned about writing your concept explanation. Choose from the following invention activities those that seem most productive for you:

- Explain how your purpose and audience — what you wanted your readers to learn from reading your concept explanation — influenced *one* of your decisions as a writer, such as how you focused the concept, how you organized your explanation, how you used writing strategies to convey information, or how you integrated sources into your essay.

- Discuss what you learned about yourself as a writer in the process of writing this particular essay. For example, what part of the process did you find most challenging, or did you try something new like getting a critical reading of your draft or outlining your draft in order to revise it?
- If you were to give advice to a friend who was about to write a concept explanation, what would you say?
- Which of the readings in this chapter influenced your essay? Explain the influence, citing specific examples from your essay and the reading.
- If you got good advice from a critical reader, explain exactly how the person helped you — perhaps by questioning your definitions, your use of visuals, the way you began or ended your essay, or the kinds of sources you used.

Considering the Social Dimensions: Concept Explanations and the Nature of Knowledge

Concepts are the building blocks of knowledge, essential to its creation and acquisition. We use concepts to name and organize ideas and information in areas as diverse as snowboarding and psychiatry. Academic disciplines and most professions are heavily concept-based, enabling newcomers to be introduced efficiently, if abstractly, to the basic knowledge they need to begin learning. As you have learned from your reading, research, and writing for this chapter, writers explaining concepts present knowledge as established and uncontested. They presume to be unbiased and objective, and they assume that readers will not doubt or challenge the truth or the value of the knowledge they present. This stance encourages readers to feel confident about the validity of the explanation. However, explanatory writing should not always be accepted at face value.

Textbooks and reference materials, in particular, sometimes present a limited view of knowledge in an academic discipline. Because introductory textbooks must be highly selective, they necessarily leave out certain sources of information and types of knowledge.

1. *Consider the claim that concept explanations attempt to present their information as uncontested truths.* Identify a reading in this chapter that particularly seems to support this claim, and then think about how it does so. Do the same for a chapter or section in a textbook you are reading for another course.

2. *Reflect on how concept explanations present established knowledge.* How do you think knowledge gets established in academic disciplines such as biology, psychology, and history? How might the prominent researchers and professors in a discipline go about deciding what is to be considered established knowledge for now? How might they decide when that established knowledge needs to be revised? If possible, ask these questions of a professor in a subject you are studying.

3. *Write a page or two explaining your initial assumptions about the knowledge or information you presented about a concept in your essay.* When you were doing research on the concept, did you discover that some of the information was being challenged by experts? Or did the body of knowledge seem settled and established? Did you at any point think that your readers might question any of the information you were presenting? How did you decide what information might seem new or even surprising to readers? Did you feel comfortable in your roles as the selector and giver of knowledge?

5

Arguing a Position

IN COLLEGE COURSES For a political science course, a student writes an essay arguing in favor of the controversial Employee Free Choice Act (EFCA). She begins by explaining that the EFCA would reform current labor law by allowing workers to unionize if a majority simply signed a card requesting it; under current law, their employer can require a secret ballot. Those who oppose the new law claim that without a secret ballot, workers could be intimidated into voting for the union.

The student's essay argues that under existing law employers routinely make use of the time required to set up a secret ballot to dissuade workers from voting to unionize. To support her argument, she cites statistics from the National Labor Relations Board and other sources showing, among other things, that 88 percent of the unfair labor practice citations in 2006 and 2007 were against employers, not unions.

IN THE COMMUNITY   In a letter to the school board, a group of parents writes a petition in favor of a proposal to institute a Peacemakers program at the local middle school. They begin with anecdotal reports of bullying at the school to underscore the need for action. They emphasize that the program's primary goal — teaching children not to avoid conflict but to manage conflict constructively — is one all parents could endorse, and they argue that those who oppose the program misunderstand it. They demonstrate parents' misunderstanding of the program's methods — for example, the ideas that students must keep their hands clasped behind their backs when walking down the halls and that students cannot play contact sports like basketball and football. To clarify the Peacemakers' actual methods, they briefly describe the negotiation procedure children are taught that involves articulating what they want, listening to what others want, and cooperatively inventing ways of resolving the conflict. They conclude by claiming that learning negotiation skills like these will help children throughout their lives.

IN THE WORKPLACE   An executive in the financial industry defends American International Group (AIG) on a blog for paying out $165 million in bonuses after the company was saved from bankruptcy by taxpayers. The executive begins by acknowledging the justifiable public indignation. Nevertheless, he argues that AIG had no choice but to honor the bonus contracts. He claims that efforts by the government to void the contracts would set a dangerous precedent. He concludes by reminding his readers of what he assumes is a shared value: Not getting paid for work already performed is un-American.

To his surprise, his blog entry provokes nearly two hundred responses, most of which disagree with his defense of the bonuses, arguing that incompetence and greed should not be federally subsidized.

The "It's Only Another Beer"
Black and Tan

8 oz. pilsner lager
8 oz. stout lager
1 frosty mug
1 icy road
1 pick-up truck
1 10-hour day
1 tired worker
A few rounds with the guys

Mix ingredients.
Add 1 totalled vehicle.

Never underestimate 'just a few.'
Buzzed driving is drunk driving.

U.S. Department of Transportation

Arguing a Position

You may associate argument with quarreling or with the in-your-face exchanges we hear so often on radio and television talk shows. Although this kind of "argument" lets people vent strong feelings, it seldom leads them to consider seriously other points of view or to reflect on their own thinking. This chapter presents a more deliberative kind of argument that depends on giving reasons rather than raising voices.

Our culture is not entirely devoid of reasoned argument, however. In fact, you are probably quite familiar with at least some of its many forms, from newspaper editorials to formal debates to courtroom summations. Other examples of argument can be found in brochures, Web sites, documentaries, and advertisements.

While such arguments typically rely on written or spoken language, visuals can also play a significant role. As an example, consider the public service announcement (PSA) reproduced here. Using a single image and relatively few words, the PSA makes a surprisingly effective argument: Even a couple of beers can be a recipe for disaster, given the right conditions — so don't drink and drive. The serene visual, the familiar recipe format, and the use of realistic language expressing a seemingly moderate perspective ("It's only another a beer"; "just a few") reach out to average adults, who likely do not think of themselves as reckless or irresponsible, and remind them that it can be a short step from an ordinary evening relaxing with coworkers to a catastrophic accident.

In this chapter, we ask you to compose an argument on a topic of your choosing. As you compose your argument, you should consider whether the use of visuals or multimedia would help your readers more immediately or more fully grasp your position.

Reading and Writing Arguments

Like the writers in the chapter-opening scenarios — the college student supporting the Employee Free Choice Act, the parents arguing in favor of the Peacemakers program, and the financial industry executive defending AIG bonuses — writers who advocate controversial positions know that they will have a better chance of convincing others if they present the issue and their positions clearly, offer plausible reasons and support for their positions, and acknowledge other points of view.

Controversial issues often provoke strong feelings. Perhaps criticisms are being leveled against a widely accepted practice, like allowing college athletes to register for courses before all other students to accommodate practice and travel schedules, or maybe someone is proposing a radical divergence from established policy, like the U.S. government's use of torture to get information from prisoners. People may agree about goals but disagree about the best way to achieve them, as in the perennial debate over how to make a public college education affordable to all qualified students, or they may disagree about fundamental values and beliefs, as in the debate over granting citizenship to immigrants who have entered the United States illegally.

As you can see from these examples, many controversial issues have no obviously right answer, so simply gathering information — finding the facts or learning from experts — will not settle disagreements about them. However, it is possible through reasoned argument to convince others to accept or reject a particular position.

Improving our research and argument strategies has practical advantages in college, where we often are judged by our ability to argue convincingly, and in the workplace, where we may want to take a stand on issues concerning working conditions, environmental impact, or pay and promotional policies. Furthermore, as citizens in a democracy, we have a special duty to inform ourselves about pressing issues and to participate constructively in the public debate. Therefore, learning to make reasoned arguments is not a luxury; it is a necessity if our form of government is to survive and flourish.

In the following section, you will read essays arguing about children's sports, fast-food jobs, and the habits of the rising generation (yourself and your peers). These readings illustrate the strategies writers typically use when composing arguments. The Guide to Writing that follows will support you as you compose your own argument, showing ways to use the basic features of the genre to present your issue, state your position, offer plausible reasons and support, and make counterarguments.

A Collaborative Activity:
Practice Arguing a Position

To get a sense of the complexities and possibilities involved in arguing a position, get together with two or three other students, and discuss an issue you have strong feelings about. Here are some guidelines to follow:

Part 1.

- As a group, choose one issue from the following list, or think of a different college issue you all know about:

    - Should admission to college be based solely on high school grade-point average?
    - Should there be a community service requirement for graduation from college?
    - Should college students be required to take courses outside their major?
    - Should the federal government subsidize everyone's college education?
    - Should sororities and fraternities be banned from college campuses?
    - Should drinking alcohol on college campuses be permitted?
    - Should college students living in residence halls be allowed to have pets?
    - Should college athletes be paid?

- Decide which audience you are trying to convince of your position on this particular issue — college administrators, your parents, or your fellow students.

- Divide into two teams — pro (those in favor) and con (those opposed) — and take a few minutes to think of reasons why your audience should accept your position.

- Take turns presenting your argument. You may have only a few minutes each, so set a phone alarm or countdown timer.

Part 2. Discuss what you learned about making an argument for your position on a controversial issue.

- How did knowing whether you were addressing administrators, parents, or students affect which reasons you used and how you presented them? Why did you expect your audience to accept your reasons?

- To set up a debate, we asked you to think in pro/con terms, but there are usually more than two points of view on most controversial issues. What values, priorities, or interests do you think are most important to your audience when they think about this issue? What is most important to you?

Reading Essays Arguing a Position

Basic Features

Basic Features

As you read essays in this chapter arguing a position, you will see how different authors incorporate the basic features of the genre.

● A Well-Presented Issue

Read first to see how the writer presents the issue. Is the issue controversial and clearly arguable — a matter on which people can reasonably disagree — or is the issue not arguable because opinions are based on belief, faith, or personal taste?

Writers may also use a variety of strategies to present the issue. Their choice of strategies depends in part on what they assume readers already know and what they want readers to think about the issue. For current, hotly debated issues, the title may be enough to identify the issue, but for less well-known issues, the writer may need to establish that the issue exists and is serious enough to deserve readers' attention. To inform readers about the issue's seriousness and to arouse readers' concern, writers may

- give examples or statistics that show how many people are affected by the issue and how they are affected;
- use scenarios or anecdotes that resonate with readers' own experiences and raise their concern; or
- quote authorities or research studies to show that the issue deserves attention.

Do not assume that the writer's presentation of the issue is objective. Writers almost always try to define or *frame* the issue in a way that promotes their position, usually by emphasizing values, priorities, and interests that are important to the reader. So as you read essays in this chapter, be attentive to how the writers frame the issues, and consider how this framing affects your response to the essays.

● A Well-Supported Position

Find where the essay states and supports the writer's position on the issue. Very often, writers declare their position in a thesis statement early in the essay. If you cannot at first find a direct statement of the writer's position, consider the title and the first and last paragraphs, and then read the entire essay through. Once you have decided what position the author is arguing, determine whether the argument is plausible by assessing whether the supporting reasons and evidence clearly back up the writer's claims and come from trustworthy sources. For example, consider the following questions:

- Are statements asserted to be *facts* widely accepted as true and complete?
- Are *examples* and *anecdotes* representative or idiosyncratic, and are they illustrative or manipulative?
- Are cited *authorities* credible and trustworthy?
- Are *statistics* taken from reliable sources and representative population samples?

● An Effective Counterargument

Read also to see how the writer responds to possible objections readers might raise as well as to opposing positions. Writers may counterargue in one or more of the following ways:

- by acknowledging readers' concerns and points of view
- by conceding an objection and modifying the argument to accommodate it
- by refuting readers' objections or by arguing against opposing positions

● A Readable Plan

Finally, examine the essay to see whether the writer provides a readable plan. Essays arguing a position need to explain the issue, provide a reasoned argument for the position, and counterargue objections and alternative positions, backing everything up with solid support and clear citations. Therefore, it is especially important to have a readable plan that helps readers follow the twists and turns of the argument.

To make their essays easy to read, writers usually include some or all of the following:

- a forecast of the argument
- key words introduced in the thesis and forecasting statement
- topic sentences introducing paragraphs or groups of paragraphs
- repeated use of key words and synonyms throughout the essay, particularly in topic sentences
- clear transitional words and phrases

Purpose and Audience

People sometimes write position essays to clarify their own reasons for taking a particular position, but most position essays are written to influence readers' thinking on the issue. *As you read essays arguing a position, ask yourself what seems to be the writer's **purpose** in writing.* For example, does the writer seem to be writing

- to change readers' minds?
- to confirm readers' opinions?
- to supply readers with reasons and evidence to support the writer's position?
- to convince readers to look at the issue in a new way?
- to move readers to take action?
- to establish common ground on which people might be able to agree?
- to win readers' respect for a different point of view?

*As you read, also try to guess what the writer assumes about the **audience**.* For example, does the writer assume readers will

- be only mildly interested or know little about the issue?
- care deeply about the issue and have strong convictions?
- oppose or be skeptical of the writer's position?
- have their own position on the issue?
- have serious objections to the writer's argument?

Readings

JESSICA STATSKY wrote the following essay about children's competitive sports for her college composition course. Before reading, recall your own experiences as an elementary student playing competitive sports, either in or out of school. If you were not actively involved yourself, did you know anyone who was? Looking back, do you think that winning was unduly emphasized? What value was placed on having a good time? On learning to get along with others? On developing athletic skills and confidence?

As you read, consider the questions in the margin. Your instructor may ask you to post your answers or bring them to class.

Basic Features

- A Well-Presented Issue
- A Well-Supported Position
- An Effective Counterargument
- A Readable Plan

Children Need to Play, Not Compete

Jessica Statsky

How does Statsky present the issue in a way that prepares readers for her argument?

Over the past three decades, organized sports for children have increased dramatically in the United States. And though many adults regard Little League Baseball and Peewee Football as a basic part of childhood, the games are not always joyous ones. When overzealous parents and coaches impose adult standards on children's sports, the result can be activities that are neither satisfying nor beneficial to children.

1

How does she qualify her position in par. 2?

I am concerned about all organized sports activities for children between the ages of six and twelve. The damage I see results from noncontact as well as contact sports, from sports organized locally as well as those organized nationally. Highly organized competitive sports such as Peewee Football and Little League Baseball are too often played to adult standards, which are developmentally inappropriate for children and can be both physically and psychologically harmful. Furthermore, because they eliminate many children from organized sports before they are ready to compete, they are actually counterproductive for developing either future players or fans. Finally, because they emphasize competition and winning, they unfortunately provide occasions for some parents and coaches to place their own fantasies and needs ahead of children's welfare.

2

What reasons does she forecast here, and in which paragraphs does she discuss each reason?

How does Statsky try to establish the credibility of her sources in pars. 3–5?

One readily understandable danger of overly competitive sports is that they entice children into physical actions that are bad for growing bodies. Although the official Little League Web site acknowledges that children do risk injury playing baseball, it insists that "severe injuries . . . are infrequent," the risk "far less than the risk of riding a skateboard, a bicycle, or even the school bus" ("What about My Child?"). Nevertheless, Leonard Koppett in *Sports Illusion, Sports Reality* claims that a twelve-year-old trying to throw a curve ball, for example, may put abnormal strain on developing arm and shoulder muscles, sometimes resulting in lifelong injuries (294). Contact sports like football can be even more hazardous. Thomas Tutko, a psychology

3

professor at San Jose State University and coauthor of the book *Winning Is Everything and Other American Myths,* writes:

> I am strongly opposed to young kids playing tackle football. It is not the right stage of development for them to be taught to crash into other kids. Kids under the age of fourteen are not by nature physical. Their main concern is self-preservation. They don't want to meet head on and slam into each other. But tackle football absolutely requires that they try to hit each other as hard as they can. And it is too traumatic for young kids. (qtd. in Tosches A1)

4 As Tutko indicates, even when children are not injured, fear of being hurt detracts from their enjoyment of the sport. The Little League Web site ranks fear of injury as the seventh of seven reasons children quit ("What about My Child?"). One mother of an eight-year-old Peewee Football player explained, "The kids get so scared. They get hit once and they don't want anything to do with football anymore. They'll sit on the bench and pretend their leg hurts . . ." (qtd. in Tosches A1). Some children are driven to even more desperate measures. For example, in one Peewee Football game, a reporter watched the following scene as a player took himself out of the game:

> "Coach, my tummy hurts. I can't play," he said. The coach told the player to get back onto the field. "There's nothing wrong with your stomach," he said. When the coach turned his head the seven-year-old stuck a finger down his throat and made himself vomit. When the coach turned back, the boy pointed to the ground and told him, "Yes there is, coach. See?" (Tosches A33)

5 Besides physical hazards and anxieties, competitive sports pose psychological dangers for children. Martin Rablovsky, a former sports editor for the *New York Times,* says that in all his years of watching young children play organized sports, he has noticed very few of them smiling. "I've seen children enjoying a spontaneous pre-practice scrimmage become somber and serious when the coach's whistle blows," Rablovsky says. "The spirit of play suddenly disappears, and sport becomes joblike" (qtd. in Coakley 94). The primary goal of a professional athlete — winning — is not appropriate for

Why do you think she uses block quotations instead of integrating these quotes into her own sentences?

children. Their goals should be having fun, learning, and being with friends. Although winning does add to the fun, too many adults lose sight of what matters and make winning the most important goal. Several studies have shown that when children are asked whether they would rather be warming the bench on a winning team or playing regularly on a losing team, about 90 percent choose the latter (Smith, Smith, and Smoll 11).

How does Statsky try to refute this objection?

Winning and losing may be an inevitable part of adult life, but they should not be part of childhood. Too much competition too early in life can affect a child's development. Children are easily influenced, and when they sense that their competence and worth are based on their ability to live up to their parents' and coaches' high expectations — and on their ability to win — they can become discouraged and depressed. Little League advises parents to "keep winning in perspective" ("Your Role"), noting that the most common reasons children give for quitting, aside from change in interest, are lack of playing time, failure and fear of failure, disapproval by significant others, and psychological stress ("What about My Child?"). According to Dr. Glyn C. Roberts, a professor of kinesiology at the Institute of Child Behavior and Development at the University of Illinois, 80 to 90 percent of children who play competitive sports at a young age drop out by sixteen (Kutner).

6

How effective do you think Statsky's argument in par. 7 is? Why?

This statistic illustrates another reason I oppose competitive sports for children: because they are so highly selective, very few children get to participate. Far too soon, a few children are singled out for their athletic promise, while many others, who may be on the verge of developing the necessary strength and ability, are screened out and discouraged from trying out again. Like adults, children fear failure, and so even those with good physical skills may stay away because they lack self-confidence. Consequently, teams lose many promising players who with some encouragement and experience might have become stars. The problem is that many parent-sponsored, out-of-school programs give more importance to having a winning team than to developing children's physical skills and self-esteem.

7

Indeed, it is no secret that too often scorekeeping, league standings, and the drive to win bring out the worst in adults who are more

8

absorbed in living out their own fantasies than in enhancing the quality of the experience for children (Smith, Smith, and Smoll 9). Recent newspaper articles on children's sports contain plenty of horror stories. *Los Angeles Times* reporter Rich Tosches, for example, tells the story of a brawl among seventy-five parents following a Peewee Football game (A33). As a result of the brawl, which began when a parent from one team confronted a player from the other team, the teams are now thinking of hiring security guards for future games. Another example is provided by a *Los Angeles Times* editorial about a Little League manager who intimidated the opposing team by setting fire to one of their team's jerseys on the pitcher's mound before the game began. As the editorial writer commented, the manager showed his young team that "intimidation could substitute for playing well" ("The Bad News").

9   Although not all parents or coaches behave so inappropriately, the seriousness of the problem is illustrated by the fact that Adelphi University in Garden City, New York, offers a sports psychology workshop for Little League coaches, designed to balance their "animal instincts" with "educational theory" in hopes of reducing the "screaming and hollering," in the words of Harold Weisman, manager of sixteen Little Leagues in New York City (Schmitt). In a three-and-one-half-hour Sunday morning workshop, coaches learn how to make practices more fun, treat injuries, deal with irate parents, and be "more sensitive to their young players' fears, emotional frailties, and need for recognition." Little League is to be credited with recognizing the need for such workshops.

10   Some parents would no doubt argue that children cannot start too soon preparing to live in a competitive free-market economy. After all, secondary schools and colleges require students to compete for grades, and college admission is extremely competitive. And it is perfectly obvious how important competitive skills are in finding a job. Yet the ability to cooperate is also important for success in life. Before children are psychologically ready for competition, maybe we should emphasize cooperation and individual performance in team sports rather than winning.

In criticizing some parents' behavior in pars. 8–9, Statsky risks alienating her readers. How effective is this part of her argument?

How effective is Statsky's use of concession and refutation here?

Many people are ready for such an emphasis. In 1988, one New York Little League official who had attended the Adelphi workshop tried to ban scoring from six- to eight-year-olds' games — but parents wouldn't support him (Schmitt). An innovative children's sports program in New York City, City Sports for Kids, emphasizes fitness, self-esteem, and sportsmanship. In this program's basketball games, every member on a team plays at least two of six eight-minute periods. The basket is seven feet from the floor, rather than ten feet, and a player can score a point just by hitting the rim (Bloch). I believe this kind of local program should replace overly competitive programs like Peewee Football and Little League Baseball. As one coach explains, significant improvements can result from a few simple rule changes, such as including every player in the batting order and giving every player, regardless of age or ability, the opportunity to play at least four innings a game (Frank).

11

How effectively does Statsky conclude her argument?

Authorities have clearly documented the excesses and dangers of many competitive sports programs for children. It would seem that few children benefit from these programs and that those who do would benefit even more from programs emphasizing fitness, cooperation, sportsmanship, and individual performance. Thirteen- and fourteen-year-olds may be eager for competition, but few younger children are. These younger children deserve sports programs designed specifically for their needs and abilities.

12

Works Cited

"The Bad News Pyromaniacs?" Editorial. *Los Angeles Times* 16 June 1990: B6. *LexisNexis*. Web. 16 May 2011.

Bloch, Gordon B. "Thrill of Victory Is Secondary to Fun." *New York Times* 2 Apr. 1990, late ed.: C12. *LexisNexis*. Web. 14 May 2011.

Coakley, Jay J. *Sport in Society: Issues and Controversies*. St. Louis: Mosby, 1982. Print.

Frank, L. "Contributions from Parents and Coaches." *CYB Message Board*. AOL, 8 July 1997. Web. 14 May 2011.

Koppett, Leonard. *Sports Illusion, Sports Reality*. Boston: Houghton, 1981. Print.

Are Statsky's sources adequate to support her position, in number and kind? Has she documented them clearly and accurately?

Kutner, Lawrence. "Athletics, through a Child's Eyes." *New York Times* 23 Mar. 1989, late ed.: C8. *LexisNexis*. Web. 15 May 2011.

Schmitt, Eric. "Psychologists Take Seat on Little League Bench." *New York Times* 14 Mar. 1988, late ed.: B2. *LexisNexis*. Web. 14 May 2011.

Smith, Nathan, Ronald Smith, and Frank Smoll. *Kidsports: A Survival Guide for Parents*. Reading: Addison, 1983. Print.

Tosches, Rich. "Peewee Football: Is It Time to Blow the Whistle?" *Los Angeles Times* 3 Dec. 1988: A1+. *LexisNexis*. Web. 22 May 2011.

"What about My Child?" *Little League Online*. Little League Baseball, Incorporated, 1999. Web. 30 May 2011.

"Your Role as a Little League Parent." *Little League Online*. Little League Baseball, Incorporated, 1999. Web. 30 May 2011.

CONSIDERING TOPICS FOR YOUR OWN ESSAY

List some issues that involve what you believe to be unfair treatment of any group. For example, should a law be passed to make English the official language in this country, requiring that election ballots and drivers' tests be printed only in English? Should teenagers be required to get their parents' permission to obtain birth-control information and contraception? What is affirmative action, and should it be used in college admissions for underrepresented groups? Should schools create and enforce guidelines to protect individuals from bullying and discrimination? Should everyone, regardless of their sexual orientation, be allowed to marry?

AMITAI ETZIONI is a sociologist who has taught at Columbia, Harvard, and George Washington universities, where he currently directs the Institute for Communitarian Policy Studies. He has written numerous articles and more than two dozen books reflecting his commitment to peace in a nuclear age (for example, *Winning without War* [1964]); overcoming excessive individualism through communitarianism (for example, *The Spirit of Community: The Reinvention of American Society* [1983]); limiting the erosion of privacy in an age of technological surveillance (for example, *The Limits of Privacy* [2004]); and most recently, rethinking foreign policy in an age of terrorism (for example, *Security First: For a Muscular, Moral Foreign Policy* [2007]).

The following essay was originally published in the *Miami Herald*. The original headnote identifies Etzioni as the father of five sons, including three teenagers, and points out that his son Dari helped Etzioni write this essay — although it does not say what Dari contributed.

As you read, think about what you learned from the various summer and school-year jobs you have held.

Working at McDonald's

AMITAI ETZIONI

McDonald's is bad for your kids. I do not mean the flat patties and the white-flour buns; I refer to the jobs teen-agers undertake, mass-producing these choice items.

As many as two-thirds of America's high school juniors and seniors now hold down part-time paying jobs, according to studies. Many of these are in fast-food chains, of which McDonald's is the pioneer, trend-setter and symbol.

At first, such jobs may seem right out of the Founding Fathers' educational manual for how to bring up self-reliant, work-ethic-driven, productive youngsters. But in fact, these jobs undermine school attendance and involvement, impart few skills that will be useful in later life, and simultaneously skew the values of teen-agers — especially their ideas about the worth of a dollar.

It has been a longstanding American tradition that youngsters ought to get paying jobs. In folklore, few pursuits are more deeply revered than the newspaper route and the sidewalk lemonade stand. Here the youngsters are to learn how sweet are the fruits of labor and self-discipline (papers are delivered early in the morning, rain or shine), and the ways of trade (if you price your lemonade too high or too low . . .).

Roy Rogers, Baskin Robbins, Kentucky Fried Chicken, *et al.* may at first seem nothing but a vast extension of the lemonade stand. They provide very large numbers of teen jobs, provide regular employment, pay quite well compared to many other teen jobs and, in the modern equivalent of toiling over a hot stove, test one's stamina.

Closer examination, however, finds the McDonald's kind of job highly uneducational in several ways. Far from providing opportunities for entrepreneurship (the lemonade stand) or self-discipline, self-supervision and self-scheduling (the paper route), most teen jobs these days are highly structured — what social scientists call "highly routinized."

True, you still have to have the gumption to get yourself over to the hamburger stand, but once you don the prescribed uniform, your task is spelled out in minute detail. The franchise prescribes the shape of the coffee cups; the weight, size, shape and color of the patties; and the texture of the napkins (if any). Fresh coffee is to be made every eight minutes. And so on. There is no room for initiative, creativity, or even elementary rearrangements. These are breeding grounds for robots working for yesterday's assembly lines, not tomorrow's high-tech posts.

There are very few studies on the matter. One of the few is a 1984 study by Ivan Charper and Bryan Shore Fraser. The study relies mainly on what teen-agers write in response to questionnaires rather than actual observations of fast-food jobs. The authors argue that the employees develop many skills such as how to operate a food-preparation machine and a cash register. However, little attention is paid to how long it takes to acquire such a skill, or what its significance is.

9   What does it matter if you spend 20 minutes to learn to use a cash register, and then —
"operate" it? What "skill" have you acquired? It is a long way from learning to work with a lathe
or carpenter tools in the olden days or to program computers in the modern age.

10   A 1980 study by A. V. Harrell and P. W. Wirtz found that, among those students who
worked at least 25 hours per week while in school, their unemployment rate four years
later was half of that of seniors who did not work. This is an impressive statistic. It must
be seen, though, together with the finding that many who begin as part-time employees in
fast-food chains drop out of high school and are gobbled up in the world of low-skill jobs.

11   Some say that while these jobs are rather unsuited for college-bound, white, middle-
class youngsters, they are "ideal" for lower-class, "non-academic," minority youngsters.
Indeed, minorities are "over-represented" in these jobs (21 percent of fast-food employees). While it is true that these places provide income, work and even some training to
such youngsters, they also tend to perpetuate their disadvantaged status. They provide no
career ladders, few marketable skills, and undermine school attendance and involvement.

12   The hours are often long. Among those 14 to 17, a third of fast-food employees (including some school dropouts) labor more than 30 hours per week, according to the Charper-
Fraser study. Only 20 percent work 15 hours or less. The rest: between 15 and 30 hours.

13   Often the stores close late, and after closing one must clean up and tally up. In
affluent Montgomery County, Md., where child labor would not seem to be a widespread
economic necessity, 24 percent of the seniors at one high school in 1985 worked as much
as five to seven days a week; 27 percent, three to five. There is just no way such amounts
of work will not interfere with school work, especially homework. In an informal survey
published in the most recent yearbook of the high school, 58 percent of seniors acknowledged that their jobs interfere with their school work.

14   The Charper-Fraser study sees merit in learning teamwork and working under
supervision. The authors have a point here. However, it must be noted that such learning
is not automatically educational or wholesome. For example, much of the supervision in
fast-food places leans toward teaching one the wrong kinds of compliance: blind obedience, or shared alienation with the "boss."

15   Supervision is often both tight and woefully inappropriate. Today, fast-food chains
and other such places of work (record shops, bowling alleys) keep costs down by having
teens supervise teens with often no adult on the premises.

16   There is no father or mother figure with which to identify, to emulate, to provide a role
model and guidance. The work-culture varies from one place to another: Sometimes it is a
tightly run shop (must keep the cash registers ringing); sometimes a rather loose pot party
interrupted by customers. However, only rarely is there a master to learn from, or much
worth learning. Indeed, far from being places where solid adult work values are being transmitted, these are places where all too often delinquent teen values dominate. Typically, when
my son Oren was dishing out ice cream for Baskin Robbins in upper Manhattan, his fellow
teen-workers considered him a sucker for not helping himself to the till. Most youngsters
felt they were entitled to $50 severance "pay" on their last day on the job.

17   The pay, oddly, is the part of the teen work-world that is most difficult to evaluate. The lemonade stand or paper route money was for your allowance. In the old days,

apprentices learning a trade from a master contributed most, if not all, of their income to their parents' household. Today, the teen pay may be low by adult standards, but it is often, especially in the middle class, spent largely or wholly by the teens. That is, the youngsters live free at home ("after all, they are high school kids") and are left with very substantial sums of money.

Where this money goes is not quite clear. Some use it to support themselves, especially among the poor. More middle-class kids set some money aside to help pay for college, or save it for a major purchase — often a car. But large amounts seem to flow to pay for an early introduction into the most trite aspects of American consumerism: flimsy punk clothes, trinkets and whatever else is the last fast-moving teen craze.

18

One may say that this is only fair and square; they are being good American consumers and spend their money on what turns them on. At least, a cynic might add, these funds do not go into illicit drugs and booze. On the other hand, an educator might bemoan that these young, yet unformed individuals, so early in life driven to buy objects of no intrinsic educational, cultural or social merit, learn so quickly the dubious merit of keeping up with the Joneses in ever-changing fads, promoted by mass merchandising.

19

Many teens find the instant reward of money, and the youth status symbols it buys, much more alluring than credits in calculus courses, European history or foreign languages. No wonder quite a few would rather skip school — and certainly homework — and instead work longer at a Burger King. Thus, most teen work these days is not providing early lessons in the work ethic; it fosters escape from school and responsibilities, quick gratification and a short cut to the consumeristic aspects of adult life.

20

Thus, parents should look at teen employment not as automatically educational. It is an activity — like sports — that can be turned into an educational opportunity. But it can also easily be abused. Youngsters must learn to balance the quest for income with the needs to keep growing and pursue other endeavors that do not pay off instantly — above all education.

21

Go back to school.

22

MAKING CONNECTIONS: JOB SKILLS

Etzioni argues that fast-food jobs do not qualify as meaningful work experience because they do not teach young people the skills and habits they will need for fulfilling careers: "entrepreneurship . . . self-discipline, self-supervision and self-scheduling" (par. 6).

With two or three other students, discuss what you have learned from your summer and after-school jobs. Begin by taking turns briefly describing the various jobs you have held. If you have never held a job, describe other significant activities you have participated in that required time and effort. Then, together consider the following questions:

- Which, if any, of the skills and habits Etzioni lists as important did you practice at your job or through the activities in which you participated?
- Why do you think these skills and habits are worth learning? If you think other skills and habits are as important or even more important, explain what they are and why you think so.

ANALYZING WRITING STRATEGIES

● ● ● ●
Basic Features

● A Well-Presented Issue

From the first sentence, it is clear that Etzioni's primary audience is parents of teenagers, rather than the teenagers themselves. Given his readers, it may seem fitting that Etzioni refers to "a longstanding American tradition that youngsters ought to get paying jobs" and what he calls the "folklore" associated with "the newspaper route and the sidewalk lemonade stand" (par. 4). In other words, Etzioni begins his essay by assuming the issue has already been *framed* for his audience through their associations and experience.

Writers frame issues (and reframe issues that have already been framed) to influence how readers think about the issue. **Framing** an issue is like putting a frame around a picture, or in digital terms, using an editing program to crop and resize a photograph to focus the viewer's eye on the part of the picture you think is most important. Framing, like cropping, cuts some parts out altogether or moves them to the margins. Framing an issue essentially does the same thing by focusing attention on a certain way of seeing the issue.

To get his readers to listen to his argument, Etzioni has to *reframe* the issue — to show that today's McDonald's-type jobs are not the same as the newspaper route and lemonade stand of yesteryear.

To analyze how Etzioni tries to reframe the issue, try the following:

▪ Reread paragraphs 1–7, highlighting the qualities — values and skills — associated with traditional jobs and with McDonald's-type jobs, at least according to Etzioni.

▪ Write a couple of sentences explaining how Etzioni tries to reframe the issue and whether you think the story he tells about McDonald's-type jobs compared to traditional jobs is likely to make his readers reconsider their assumption that McDonald's-type jobs are good for kids.

● A Well-Supported Position

Writers may use various kinds of support for their arguments. Like Statsky, Etzioni cites authorities. For example, Statsky quotes the official Little League Web site, professors, journalists, and parents. She carefully identifies her sources by supplying their credentials — for example, "Thomas Tutko, a psychology professor at San Jose State University and coauthor of the book *Winning Is Everything and Other American Myths*" (par. 3).

While Statsky cites credible authorities and tends to present their evidence confidently, she also *qualifies* it where appropriate — that is, she presents it tentatively when there can be reasonable debate about whether it qualifies as fact. For example, she reports that "Leonard Koppett in *Sports Illusion, Sports Reality* claims that a twelve-year-old trying to throw a curve ball . . . may put abnormal strain on developing arm and shoulder muscles, sometimes resulting in lifelong injuries" (par. 3). Notice that Statsky uses the word *claims* to indicate that the statement's status as fact is not certain, and she also uses the words *may* and *sometimes* to emphasize that throwing a curve ball is not necessarily injurious. This is the kind of careful qualification of sources that readers deserve and academic audiences typically require.

To analyze how Etzioni uses **statistics**, numerical data about a given population sample, to support his position, try the following:

- Reread paragraphs 8–15, where Etzioni reports on two research studies. Both studies provide Etzioni with statistics. Underline the statistics, and note what each statistic is being used to illustrate or prove. Why do you think Etzioni relies on statistics?

- Write a few sentences reporting what you have learned about Etzioni's use of statistics to argue for his position on a controversial issue.

● An Effective Counterargument

At key points throughout his essay, Etzioni acknowledges readers' likely objections and then counterargues them. In paragraph 3, he acknowledges that some readers will believe that McDonald's-type jobs are good because they teach teenagers to become "self-reliant, work-ethic-driven, productive youngsters." Although he agrees with his readers that these are valuable objectives, Etzioni makes clear that he disagrees about how well fast-food jobs fulfill these goals.

To analyze how Etzioni counterargues, try the following activity:

- Examine how Etzioni refutes findings of the Charper-Fraser study — specifically, the claims that employees in McDonald's-type jobs develop many skills (pars. 8 and 9) and that they learn how to work under supervision (pars. 14–16). Highlight places where he presents the claims, and note how he asserts and supports his refutation.

- Write a couple of sentences explaining how Etzioni refutes the findings of this particular research study. Add another sentence assessing the effectiveness of Etzioni's counterargument.

● A Readable Plan

The *thesis statement* in a position essay is particularly important because it asserts the writer's position on the issue. Most writers also use the thesis statement to forecast the reasons they will develop and support in the essay. Jessica Statsky, for example, asserts her position in paragraph 1 and uses paragraph 2 to qualify and clarify the position and to forecast her three reasons for it.

To analyze how Etzioni forecasts his argument, try the following:

- Etzioni states his thesis in the opening sentence of paragraph 1. But he does not preview his reasons until paragraph 3. Find and underline the forecasting statement in which he does so.

- Skim the essay, and note in the margin where Etzioni supports his reasons.
- Write a couple of sentences indicating whether Etzioni's method of forecasting his reasons makes his argument easy to follow.

CONSIDERING TOPICS FOR YOUR OWN ESSAY

Etzioni focuses on a single kind of part-time work, takes a position on how worth-while it is, and recommends against it. You could write a similar kind of essay. For example, you could take a position for or against students' participating in other kinds of part-time work or recreation during the high school or college academic year — for example, playing on an interscholastic or collegiate sports team, doing volunteer work, or taking an elective class. You might pursue a different argument, taking a position on students' doing a certain kind of work or recreation during the summer months — say, working or volunteering in a job related to a career they would like to pursue; focusing on learning something important to them, such as another language or a musical instrument; or participating in an exercise program. If you work to support yourself and pay for college, you could focus on why the job either strengthens or weakens you as a person, given your life and career goals. Writing for other students, you would either recommend the job or activity to them or discourage them from pursuing it, giving reasons and support for your position. Like Etzioni, you might enrich your argument by citing studies or by interviewing students who participate in the activity.

AMY GOLDWASSER is a writer and editor. Her writing has appeared in a wide array of journals and Web sites including the *New Yorker*, *Vogue*, and *Salon*, where this essay first appeared. She has served as the executive editor of *Elle* and *Seventeen*, features editor of *New York Magazine*, and staff editor at *Outside*. A volunteer at the Lower Eastside Girls Club in New York, Goldwasser founded a writing and blogging program that led to her editing a collection of essays called *Red: The Next Generation of American Writers — Teenage Girls — on What Fires Up Their Lives Today* (2007). "I came to realize," Goldwasser observed in an interview, "how much more excited I was about the writing I was getting from the girls than the writing I was getting from professional writers in my day job." You can learn about the book and the authors at www.redthebook.com.

   This position essay was occasioned by the publication of a 2008 survey called "Still at Risk: What Students Don't Know, Even Now," which is easily accessible at aei.org. As Goldwasser indicates, the report is the latest in a series of critiques of the Millennial or Google generation, as it is sometimes called. As you read, think about why Goldwasser uses the pronouns *we* and *they* repeatedly throughout the essay.

What's the Matter with Kids Today?

AMY GOLDWASSER ▼

The other week was only the latest takedown of what has become a fashionable segment of the population to bash: the American teenager. A phone (land line!) survey of 1,200 17-year-olds, conducted by the research organization Common Core and released Feb. 26, found our young people to be living in "stunning ignorance" of history and literature.

This furthered the report that the National Endowment for the Arts came out with at the end of 2007, lamenting "the diminished role of voluntary reading in American life," particularly among 13-to-17-year-olds, and Doris Lessing's condemnation, in her acceptance speech for the Nobel Prize in literature, of "a fragmenting culture" in which "young men and women . . . have read nothing, knowing only some specialty or other, for instance, computers."

Kids today — we're telling you! — don't read, don't write, don't care about anything farther in front of them than their iPods. The Internet, according to 88-year-old Lessing (whose specialty is sturdy typewriters, or perhaps pens), has "seduced a whole generation into its inanities."

Or is it the older generation that the Internet has seduced — into the inanities of leveling charges based on fear, ignorance and old-media, multiple-choice testing? So much so that we can't see that the Internet is only a means of communication, and one that has created a generation, perhaps the first, of writers, activists, storytellers? When the world worked in hard copy, no parent or teacher ever begrudged teenagers who disappeared into their rooms to write letters to friends — or a movie review, or an editorial for the school paper on the first president they'll vote for. Even 15-year-old boys are sharing some part of their feelings with someone out there.

We're talking about 33 million Americans who are fluent in texting, e-mailing, blogging, IM'ing and constantly amending their profiles on social network sites — which, on average, 30 of their friends will visit every day, hanging out and writing for 20 minutes or so each. They're connected, they're collaborative, they're used to writing about themselves. In fact, they choose to write about themselves, on their own time, rather than its being a forced labor when a paper's due in school. Regularly, often late at night, they're generating a body of intimate written work. They appreciate the value of a good story and the power of a speech that moves: Ninety-seven percent of the teenagers in the Common Core survey connected "I have a dream" with its speaker — they can watch Dr. King deliver it on demand — and eight in 10 knew what "To Kill a Mockingbird" is about.

This is, of course, the kind of knowledge we should be encouraging. The Internet has turned teenagers into honest documentarians of their own lives — reporters embedded in their homes. their schools. their own heads.

7   But this is also why it's dangerous, why we can't seem to recognize that it's just a medium. We're afraid. Our kids know things we don't. They drove the presidential debates onto YouTube and very well may determine the outcome of this election. They're texting at the dinner table and responsible for pretty much every enduring consumer cultural phenomenon: iPod, iTunes, iPhone; Harry Potter, "High School Musical"; large hot drinks with gingerbread flavoring. They can sell ads on their social network pages, and they essentially made MySpace worth $580 million and "Juno" an Oscar winner.

8   Besides, we're tired of having to ask them every time we need to find Season 2 of "Heroes," calculate a carbon footprint or upload photos to Facebook (now that we're allowed on).

9   Plus, they're blogging about us.

10   So we've made the Internet one more thing unknowable about the American teenager, when, really, it's one of the few revelations. We conduct these surveys and overgeneralize — labeling like the mean girls, driven by the same jealousy and insecurity.

11   Common Core drew its multiple-choice questions for teens from a test administered by the federal government in 1986. Twenty-plus years ago, high school students didn't have the Internet to store their trivia. Now they know that the specific dates and what-was-that-prince's-name will always be there; they can free their brains to go a little deeper into the concepts instead of the copyrights, step back and consider what Scout and Atticus were really fighting for. To criticize teenagers' author-to-book title matching on the spot, over the phone, is similar to cold-calling over-40s and claiming their long-division skills or date of "Jaws" recall is rusty. This is what we all rely on the Internet for.

12   That's not to say some of the survey findings aren't disturbing. It's crushing to hear that one in four teens could not identify Adolf Hitler's role in world history, for instance. But it's not because teenagers were online that they missed this. Had a parent introduced 20 minutes of researching the Holocaust to one month of their teen's Internet life, or a teacher assigned "The Diary of Anne Frank" (arguably a 13-year-old girl's blog) — if we worked with, rather than against, the way this generation voluntarily takes in information — we might not be able to pick up the phone and expose tragic pockets of ignorance.

13   The average teen chooses to spend an average of 16.7 hours a week reading and writing online. Yet the NEA report did not consider this to be "voluntary" reading and writing. Its findings also concluded that "literary reading declined significantly in a period of rising Internet use." The corollary is weak — this has as well been a period of rising franchises of frozen yogurt that doesn't taste like frozen yogurt, of global warming, of declining rates of pregnancy and illicit drug use among teenagers, and of girls sweeping the country's most prestigious high school science competition for the first time.

14   Teenagers today read and write for fun; it's part of their social lives. We need to start celebrating this unprecedented surge, incorporating it as an educational tool instead of meeting it with punishing pop quizzes and suspicion.

We need to start trusting our kids to communicate as they will online — even when that comes with the risk that they'll spill the family secrets or campaign for a candidate who's not ours.   15

Once we stop regarding the Internet as a villain, stop presenting it as the enemy of history and literature and worldly knowledge, then our teenagers have the potential to become the next great voices of America. One of them, 70 years from now, might even get up there to accept the very award Lessing did — and thank the Internet for making him or her a writer and a thinker.   16

MAKING CONNECTIONS: THE INFORMATION AGE

It is often said that we live in an Age of Information. But, as Goldwasser suggests, there may now be a generational shift in the way information is thought of and accessed.

With two or three other students, discuss your own experience. Begin by taking turns listing the ways you use technology to transmit and retrieve information on a typical day. Then, together consider the following questions:

- Goldwasser reports that the National Endowment for the Arts laments "the diminished role of voluntary reading in American life" (par. 2). How much time do you spend reading in a typical day? What kinds of things do you read?

- What kinds of information do you typically look up in the course of a day? How do you most commonly look it up? Would your answers to these questions be different if you did not have easy access to the Internet?

- Goldwasser distinguishes between "concepts" (for example, "Adolf Hitler's role in world history" [par. 12] and "what 'To Kill a Mockingbird' is about" [par. 5]) and "copyrights" or "trivia" (for example, dates and author-to-book title matching [par. 11]). Why do you think she distinguishes between what you should know and what you could just as easily look up when you need it? What do you think about Goldwasser's distinction?

ANALYZING WRITING STRATEGIES

● ● ● ●
Basic Features

● A Well-Presented Issue

Like the other writers in this chapter, Goldwasser tries to reframe the issue for her readers. Her title, "What's the Matter with Kids Today?," is the title of a song from *Bye Bye Birdie*, a late-1950s musical. The lyrics tell the story of how the issue has traditionally been framed:

> Why can't they be like we were,
> Perfect in every way?
> What's the matter with kids today?

To analyze how Goldwasser tries to reframe the issue, try the following:

- Reread paragraph 7 to determine what story Goldwasser is telling about the generational divide. How does this story reframe the issue?
- Who are the *we* and the *they* in this paragraph? Assuming Goldwasser is addressing the *we*, how effective do you think this way of reframing the issue is likely to be for these particular readers?

● A Well-Supported Position

In arguing for a position, writers may provide various kinds of supporting evidence, including facts, statistics, examples, anecdotes, and quotes from authorities.

- **Facts** are statements that can be proven to be true. However, a statement that is not true or only partially true may be asserted as fact. Therefore, readers may need to be reassured that an asserted fact is reliable and comes from a trustworthy source.
- **Statistics** are sometimes mistaken for facts, but they are only interpretations or correlations of numerical data. Their reliability depends on how and by whom the information was collected and interpreted.
- **Examples** and **anecdotes** illustrate what may be true in certain situations; effective writers do not usually offer them as hard-and-fast evidence of the universal truth of their positions. Using them can, however, make an argument less abstract and enable readers to identify with those affected by the issue.
- **Quotes from authorities** can carry weight if readers see them as knowledgeable and trustworthy.

To analyze how Goldwasser supports her position, try the following:

- Reread the essay, and highlight at least two places where Goldwasser presents different kinds of supporting evidence. Examine each instance to determine how she uses the evidence to support her argument, and consider how effective the evidence is likely to be in convincing her readers.
- Write a few sentences explaining what you discovered about Goldwasser's use of supporting evidence in this essay.

● An Effective Counterargument

Some position essays are essentially organized as a defense or refutation. This is the case with Goldwasser's essay. As she explains in the opening paragraph, it has become "fashionable" to "bash" teenagers, and her essay attempts to defend against this "latest takedown." One object of her counterargument is the Common Core phone survey, but she also counterargues the claims made by the National Endowment for the Arts (NEA) and Doris Lessing in her Nobel Prize acceptance speech.

Before examining how Goldwasser tries to refute these authorities, however, look at one passage where she makes a concession. In paragraph 12, she begins by acknowledging that "some of the survey findings" are "disturbing." In fact, she calls it "crushing" that "one in four teens could not identify Adolf Hitler's role in world history." Not only does this concession allow her to express her strong feelings, but it is also a smart rhetorical strategy in that it shows readers that she shares their values about the kinds of knowledge that really are important for everyone to learn.

To analyze Goldwasser's counterargument, try the following:

- Reread paragraphs 4–5, where she tries to defend teenagers' use of the Internet against Doris Lessing's criticism.

- Notice that one of her strategies is to support her counterargument with the same Common Core survey that was used to attack teenagers' use of the Internet. How effective is this strategy likely to be for her readers? Ask yourself what these statistics allow Goldwasser to demonstrate.

- Write a few sentences describing what you have learned about Goldwasser's use of counterargument.

● A Readable Plan

Writers of position essays sometimes repeat in the conclusion language or ideas introduced in the opening paragraphs of the essay. For example, Statsky comes back in the last paragraph to her concerns about "the excesses and dangers" of competitive sports, ideas she introduced in her first two paragraphs.

To analyze how Goldwasser uses this strategy, try the following:

- Reread the opening and closing paragraphs of Goldwasser's essay, and highlight any language or ideas that are repeated.

- Write a few sentences describing what you found and discussing whether you think this strategy of repeating material makes her essay more readable.

CONSIDERING TOPICS FOR YOUR OWN ESSAY

You could consider writing a position essay on some other aspect of contemporary culture and its effects on relationships, education, work, or recreation. For example, social networking sites cost businesses a lot of money in lost productivity: Should they be banned at workplaces? Social networking sites are increasingly being used by school administrations, law enforcement officials, and human resources departments to check up on students, parolees and suspects, and job applicants: Should the information on these sites be protected from such uses? Should music lyrics be censored for violence and exploitation? Should the legal drinking age be lowered? Should community service be required of all high school or college students? Is video gaming a harmless hobby or a health hazard?

Guide to Writing

The Writing Assignment

Write an essay on a controversial issue. Learn more about the issue, and take a position on it. Present the issue to readers, and develop a well-supported argument for the purpose of confirming, challenging, or changing your readers' views on the issue.

This Guide to Writing will help you apply what you have learned about how writers clearly present an issue, argue effectively for their position on it, present counter-arguments to opposing positions, and deliver their argument in a readable manner. The Guide is divided into five sections with various activities in each section:

- Invention and Research
- Planning and Drafting
- Critical Reading Guide
- Revising
- Editing and Proofreading

The Guide is designed to escort you through the writing process, from finding an issue to editing your finished essay. Your instructor may require you to follow the Guide to Writing from beginning to end. Working through the Guide to Writing in this way will help you — as it has helped many other college students — write a thoughtful, fully developed, polished essay.

If, however, your instructor gives you latitude to choose and if you have had experience writing an essay in which you argue a position, then you can decide on the order in which you will do the activities in the Guide to Writing. For example, the Invention and Research section includes activities to help you find an issue to write about, explore it, analyze and define your audience and purpose, and formulate a tentative position on it, among other things.

Obviously, finding an issue must precede the other activities, but you may come to the Guide with an issue already in mind, and you may choose to define your audience and purpose before turning to a fuller exploration of the issue itself. In fact, you may find your response to one of the invention activities expanding into a draft before you have had a chance to do any of the other activities. That is a good thing — but you should later flesh out your draft by going back to the activities you skipped and layering the new material into your draft.

The chart on pp. 184–85 will help you find answers to many of the questions you might have about planning, drafting, and revising an essay arguing a position. Because we know different students will start at different places, we designed the chart so you could find the information you need, when you need it. The page references in the right-hand column refer to examples from the readings and activities in the Guide to Writing.

183

Starting Points: Arguing a Position

●●●● Basic Features

A Well-Presented Issue	
How do I come up with an issue to write about?	• Considering Topics for Your Own Essay (pp. 171, 177, 182) • Choosing an Issue to Write About (pp. 185–87) • Testing Your Choice (pp. 188–89)
What is my purpose in writing? How can I convince my audience that the issue is real and serious?	• Reading Essays Arguing a Position (pp. 163–65) • Ways In: Bringing the Issue and Your Audience into Focus (pp. 187–88) • Framing the Issue for Your Readers (p. 188) • Defining Your Purpose for Your Readers (p. 192) • Refining Your Purpose and Setting Goals (pp. 193–94)
How can I effectively frame the issue for my readers?	• Framing (concept) (pp. 163, 175, 180–81) • Framing the Issue for Your Readers (p. 188)

A Well-Supported Position	
How do I come up with a plausible position?	• Ways In: Bringing the Issue and Your Audience into Focus (pp. 187–88) • Ways In: Developing Your Argument and Counterargument (pp. 189–91)
How do I construct an argument supporting my position?	• Ways In: Developing Your Argument and Counterargument (pp. 189–91) • Researching Your Argument (p. 192) • Formulating a Tentative Thesis Statement (p. 193)

An Effective Counterargument	
How do I counter possible objections to my position?	• Counterarguing Readers' Objections (pp. 190–91) • A Sentence Strategy: Concession Followed by Refutation (pp. 196–98)
How do I respond to possible alternative positions?	• Counterarguing Opposing Positions (p. 191) • Working with Sources: Fairly and Accurately Quoting Opposing Positions (pp. 198–99)

A Readable Plan	
How can I help my readers follow my argument?	• Outlining Your Draft (pp. 195–96) • Drafting: Writing the Opening Sentences (p. 196) • Revising (pp. 200–2) • Editing and Proofreading (pp. 202–4)

Invention and Research

The following activities should take only a few minutes to complete. Spreading them out over several days will stimulate your creativity, enabling you to consider many more potential issues to address and possible ways in which to address them. Remember to keep a record of your invention work: You will need it when you draft and revise your essay.

Choosing an Issue to Write About

List several issues that you might like to write about. You may already have an issue in mind, possibly one suggested by the topics you considered following the readings. If you want to try writing about that issue, make sure it meets the criteria below; if so, go on to the next section. If you are not ready to make a choice, the suggestions below may help you think of issues to consider.

Criteria for Choosing an Issue: A Checklist

The issue should be

☐ controversial — an issue that people disagree about, sometimes passionately;

☐ arguable — a matter of opinion on which there is no absolute proof or authority;

☐ one about which you already know something, or about which you want to know more;

☐ one that you can research, if necessary, in the time you have; and

☐ one that you care about.

Listing Issues

Make a list of issues you might consider writing about. Begin your list now, and add to it over the next few days. It might help you generate ideas if, at first, you focus on three categories: school, community, and work. Put the issues you come up with in the form of questions, as in the following examples.

School

- Should boys and girls be educated in single-sex schools or classrooms?
- Should local school boards be allowed to ban books from school libraries or block access to selected Internet sites?
- Should students attending public colleges be required to pay higher tuition fees if they have been full-time students but have not graduated within four years?

Community

- Should businesses remain loyal to their communities, or should they move wherever labor costs, taxes, or other conditions are most favorable?
- Should materials related to voting, driving, and income-tax reporting be written only in English or also in other languages read by members of the community?
- Should the racial, ethnic, or gender makeup of a police force resemble the makeup of the community it serves?

Work

- When people choose careers, should they look primarily for jobs that are well paid or for jobs that are personally fulfilling, morally acceptable, or socially responsible?
- Should the state or federal government provide job training or temporary employment to people who are unemployed but willing to work?
- Should drug testing be mandatory for people such as bus drivers, heavy-equipment operators, and airplane pilots?

Going Local

Proposing to write on an issue directly related to a community to which you belong gives you an important advantage: You know something about the history of the issue, and you might already have taken a position on it. Equally important, you will know your readers, and you can interview them to get their views of the issue and your position on it. From such knowledge and authority comes confident, convincing writing.

If you want to argue your position on an issue of national scope, try to concentrate on one with which you have some direct experience. Even better, focus on unique local aspects of the issue. For example, instead of writing generally about school boards that block access to Internet sites, write about efforts to do so at your former high school. If you are concerned about the effect of megachains like Walmart and Home Depot on small businesses nationwide, you could write your argument about whether a new big-box store should be allowed in your area.

Using the Web to Find or Explore an Issue

Exploring Web sites can provide you with an idea of what to write about, if you have not already chosen an issue, and it can enrich your understanding of an issue you have already chosen. Moreover, the Web provides a rich repository of cultural and historical information, including photographs and music, which you might be able to use to create a richly detailed, multimedia text for your readers.

Here are some suggestions:

- Look for sites related to the community, workplace, or group you are writing about. See what issues are of concern to members of those groups and whether you might write about one of them.

- Consider getting in touch with others who are concerned about the issue that concerns you. If your conversation is fruitful, ask their permission to include their insights in your project.

- Do a Google search on a particular issue, and try to get a sense of how common it might be — or, in contrast, of how specific it might be to your local community, campus, or workplace.

Make notes of any ideas or insights suggested by your online research, and download any visuals you might include in your essay, being sure to get the information necessary to cite any online sources.

(See pp. 505–7 for MLA citation format for electronic sources.)

Ways In: Bringing the Issue and Your Audience into Focus

Basic Features

Once you have made a preliminary choice of an issue, the following activities will help you explore what you know now about it, determine what else you need to find out, and discover ways of presenting the issue to your readers. You can begin with whichever activity you want, but wherever you begin, be sure to return to the other activities to bring the issue and your readers fully into focus.

Exploring the Issue

Define the Issue. *Write for a few minutes explaining how you think people currently understand the issue.* Focus on clarifying the issue by considering questions like these:

- *Who has taken a position on this issue, and what positions have they taken? What position am I inclined to take?*
- *What typically causes people to disagree about this issue? On what about the issue, if anything, do people agree?*
- *What is the issue's history? How long has it been an issue? Has it changed over time? What makes it important now?*

(continued)

(continued)

> **Learn More about the Issue.** *If you do not know very much about the issue, do some preliminary research to help you decide whether you want to write about it.* You might start by talking to other people about the issue and their opinions; doing a search online; or searching your school's library for information. If you find that you are not interested in an issue, do not have the time to research it fully, or do not have a strong opinion yourself, you should switch to another issue. Return to your list of possible issues, and make another choice.

Identifying Your Possible Readers

> *Write several sentences describing the readers to whom you will be addressing your argument.* Begin by briefly identifying your readers; then use the following questions to help you describe them:
>
> • *What do my readers know about the issue? In what contexts are they likely to have encountered it? In what ways might the issue affect them personally or professionally?*
> • *What positions will my readers likely take on this issue? How strongly do they hold these positions? Which of my readers' values, priorities, and interests might influence their views?*
> • *How far apart on the issue are my readers and I? What fundamental differences in worldview or experience might keep us from agreeing? What shared values and concerns might enable us to find common ground?*
> • *What could I realistically hope to achieve with these particular readers — convincing them to adopt my point of view, getting them to reconsider their own position, confirming or challenging some of their underlying beliefs and values?*

● Framing the Issue for Your Readers

Write several sentences exploring ways you might frame or reframe the issue for your readers. If the issue has already been framed for your readers in a particular way, you may want to reframe it. Specifically, ask yourself what the argument over this issue has tended to be about and what you think it *should* be about. What values, priorities, and interests are at stake? For example, Statsky assumed her readers would be uncritically in favor of Little League–type sports for children because they are healthy and fun, so she tried to reframe the issue in terms of the potential physical and psychological damage they can have for young children.

Testing Your Choice

Test your choice by asking yourself the following questions:

■ *Do I now know enough about the issue, or can I learn what I need to know in the time I have remaining?*

- *Have I begun to understand the issue well enough to present it to readers — to frame or reframe it in a way that might make readers open to my point of view?*

- *Do I feel a personal need to reach a deeper understanding of the issue? Do I want to learn about other people's points of view on the issue and to develop an argument that addresses our shared concerns as well as our different perspectives?*

- *Does the issue matter to other people? If the issue is not currently one of widespread concern, would I be able to argue convincingly at the beginning of my essay that it ought to be of concern?*

As you plan and draft your argument, you will probably want to consider these questions again. If at any point you cannot answer them with a confident *yes,* you may want to consider taking a different position on the issue or choose a different issue to write about. If you have serious doubts, consider discussing them with your instructor.

A Collaborative Activity:
Testing Your Choice

Get together with two or three other students, and take turns discussing the issues you have tentatively chosen.

> **Presenters:** Begin by identifying your issue and briefly explaining the values, priorities, and interests you think are at stake.

> **Listeners:** Tell the presenter how you understand the issue — the values, priorities, or interests that are at stake for you.

Ways in: Developing Your Argument
and Counterargument

 Basic Features

The following activities will help you develop your argument and counterargument by finding plausible reasons and evidence for your position and by anticipating readers' objections to your argument. You can begin with whichever activity you want, but wherever you begin, be sure to return to the other activities to explore all possibilities.

You may need more information to fully develop your argument. If so, you could start with these activities to develop the outlines of an argument and then do research, using the suggestions on p. 192, to fill in the details. Alternatively, you could start with research and return to these activities afterward. Wherever you start, keeping careful notes will make it easy to fill in details and ideas as you develop your essay.

Developing Your Argument

State Your Tentative Position. *Briefly state your current position on the issue.* As you develop your argument and counterargument, you will refine this claim and decide how to formulate it effectively for your readers. For now, say as directly as you can where you stand on the issue.

List Possible Reasons. *List the reasons for your position.* Try to come up with as many reasons as you can. Later, you may add reasons or modify the ones you have listed.

Collect Evidence. *Make notes of the evidence — such as authorities, facts, anecdotes, and statistics — you might be able to use to support your reasons.* You may already have some evidence you could use. If you need to do research, make notes of sources you could consult.

Choose the Most Plausible Reasons. *Write several sentences explaining why you think each reason would be likely to convince your particular readers to take your argument seriously.* Then identify your most plausible reasons. If you decide that none of your reasons seems very plausible, you might need to reconsider your position, do some more research, or choose another issue.

Counterarguing Readers' Objections

List Possible Objections. *Look for places where your argument is vulnerable.* For example, think of an assumption that you are making that others might not accept or a value others might not share. Imagine how people in different situations — different neighborhoods, occupations, age groups, living arrangements — might react to each of your reasons.

Accommodate a Legitimate Objection. *Choose one objection that makes sense to you, and write for a few minutes on how you could accommodate it in your argument.* You may be able simply to acknowledge an objection and explain why you think it does not negatively affect your argument. If the criticism is more serious, consider conceding the point and qualifying your position or changing the way you argue for it. If the criticism seems so damaging that you cannot accommodate it in your argument, however, you may need to rethink your position.

Refute an Illegitimate Objection. *Choose one objection that seems to challenge or weaken your argument, and write for a few minutes on how you could refute it.* Do not choose to refute only the weakest objection while ignoring the strongest one. Consider whether you can show that the objection is based on a misunderstanding or that it does not really damage your argument. You may also need to modify your position to make sure the objection is not valid.

Counterarguing Opposing Positions

Consider Other Positions. *Identify one or more widely held opposing positions, and consider the one you think most likely to be attractive to your particular readers.* Try to represent the argument accurately and fairly. Decide whether you need to do research to find out more about this opposing position.

List Reasons for the Opposing Position. *List as many reasons as you can think of that your readers are likely to give in support of this position.*

Accommodate a Plausible Reason. *Choose one reason that makes sense to you, and write for a few minutes on how you could accommodate it in your argument.* Consider whether you can concede the point and yet put it aside as not really damaging to your central argument. You may also have to consider qualifying your position or changing the way you argue for it.

Refute an Implausible Reason. *Choose one reason that you do not accept, and write for a few minutes on how you could refute it.* Consider trying one of these strategies: Argue that readers' values are better served by your position; point out where the reasoning is flawed (for instance, that it commits a straw-man fallacy by refuting your weakest reason and ignoring stronger ones); show that the argument lacks convincing support (for instance, that an example applies only to certain people in certain situations or that alternative authorities disagree). If you do not have all the information you need, make a note of what you need and where you might find it. (Note: Do not choose to refute a position no one takes seriously. Also, be careful not to misrepresent other people's positions or to criticize people personally.)

Researching Your Argument

Do some library and Internet research to find out how others have framed the issue and what positions they have taken. If you are writing on an issue relating to your school, community, or workplace, you may also want to conduct interviews to see how people view the issue, what they know about its history, what positions they take, and how they react to your position.

Searching the Web can be a productive way of learning more about arguments other people have made on your issue and gathering additional information. Here are some suggestions for conducting an efficient search:

- Enter keywords — words or brief phrases related to the issue or your position — into a search tool such as Google. For example, Statsky could have tried keywords such as *children's competitive sports*, or she could have tried the question *Should children participate in competitive sports?* You could also try Googling your keywords plus *statistics, anecdotes,* or *facts.*

- If you think your issue has been dealt with by a government agency, you could try entering your keywords on FirstGov.gov, the U.S. government's official Web portal. If you want to see whether the issue has been addressed in your state or by local government, you can go to the Library of Congress Internet Resource Page on State and Local Governments (www.loc.gov/global/state/) and follow the links.

Bookmark or keep a record of the URLs of promising sites. You may want to download or copy information you could use in your essay, including visuals; if so, remember to record source information.

For more information on library and Internet research, see Chapter 16.

Defining Your Purpose for Your Readers

Write a few sentences defining your purpose. Remember that you have already identified your readers and developed a tentative argument with these readers in mind. Try now to define your purpose by considering the following questions:

- *If my readers are likely to be sympathetic to my point of view, what is my aim in writing — to give them reasons to commit to my position, to suggest arguments they can use, and/or to win their respect and admiration?*

- *If my readers are likely to be hostile to my point of view, what is my aim in writing — to get them to take my point of view seriously, to make them defend their reasons, to show them how knowledgeable and committed I am to my position, or to show them how well I can argue?*

- *If my readers are likely to take an opposing position but are not staunchly committed to it, what should I try to do — make them question or doubt the reasons and the kinds of support they have for their position, show them how my position serves their interests better, appeal to their values and sense of responsibility, or make them reconsider their preconceptions and prejudices against my position?*

Formulating a Tentative Thesis Statement

Write a few sentences that could serve as a thesis—that is, a statement that tells your readers simply and directly what you want them to think about the issue and why. You might also forecast your reasons, mentioning them in the order in which you will take them up in your argument.

Etzioni states his thesis in paragraph 6: "Closer examination, however, finds the McDonald's kind of job highly uneducational in several ways." Perhaps the most explicit and fully developed thesis statement in this chapter's readings is Jessica Statsky's. She asserts her thesis at the end of paragraph 1 and then qualifies it and forecasts her reasons in paragraph 2:

> When overzealous parents and coaches impose adult standards on children's sports, the result can be activities that are neither satisfying nor beneficial to children.
>
> I am concerned about all organized sports activities for children between the ages of six and twelve. The damage I see results from noncontact as well as contact sports, from sports organized locally as well as those organized nationally. Highly organized competitive sports such as Peewee Football and Little League Baseball are too often played to adult standards, which are developmentally inappropriate for children and can be both physically and psychologically harmful. Furthermore, because they eliminate many children from organized sports before they are ready to compete, they are actually counterproductive for developing either future players or fans. Finally, because they emphasize competition and winning, they unfortunately provide occasions for some parents and coaches to place their own fantasies and needs ahead of children's welfare.

As you draft your own thesis, pay attention to the language you use. It should be clear and unambiguous, emphatic but appropriately qualified. Although you will probably refine your thesis as you draft and revise your essay, trying now to articulate it will help give your planning and drafting direction and impetus.

For more on thesis and forecasting statements, see Chapter 13.

Planning and Drafting

The following activities will help you refine your purpose, set goals for your draft, and outline it. In addition, this section will help you write a draft with advice on writing opening sentences, using effective sentence strategies, and working with sources.

Refining Your Purpose and Setting Goals

Before starting to draft, here are some questions that may help you sharpen your purpose for your audience and set goals for your draft. Your instructor may ask you to write out your answers to some of these questions or simply to think about them as you plan and draft your essay.

Clarifying Your Purpose and Audience

- *Who are my readers, and what can I realistically hope to accomplish by addressing them?*
- *Should I write primarily to change readers' minds, to get them to consider my arguments seriously, to confirm their opinions, to urge them to do something about the issue, or to accomplish some other purpose?*
- *How can I present myself so that my readers will consider me informed, knowledgeable, and fair?*

Presenting the Issue

- *Should I place the issue in a personal, political, or historical context, as Etzioni does?*
- *Should I use examples — real or hypothetical — to make the issue concrete for readers, as Statsky does?*
- *Should I try to demonstrate that the issue is important by citing statistics, quoting authorities, or describing its negative effects, as Statsky and Goldwasser do?*
- *Should I try to reframe the issue by showing how first impressions are wrong, as Etzioni does?*

Making Your Argument and Counterargument

- *How can I present my reasons so that readers will see them as plausible, logically supporting my position?*
- *If I have more than one reason, how should I sequence them?*
- *Should I forecast my reasons or counterarguments early in the essay, as Statsky does?*
- *Which objections should I anticipate? Can I concede any objections without undermining my argument, as Goldwasser does?*
- *Should I refute any objections, as Etzioni and Goldwasser do?*
- *Which opposing positions should I anticipate?*
- *Can I counterargue by showing that the statistics offered by others are not relevant, as Etzioni does?*
- *Can I support my reasoning by pointing out benefits (Goldwasser), stressing benefits and losses (Etzioni, Statsky), or quoting research (Etzioni, Statsky)?*

The Ending

- *How can I conclude my argument effectively? Should I reiterate my position, as Etzioni does?*
- *Could I conclude by looking to the future or by urging readers to take action or make changes, as Statsky and Goldwasser do?*
- *Should I conclude with a challenge, as Etzioni does?*

Outlining Your Draft

With your purpose and goals in mind, you might want to make a quick scratch outline that includes the following:

   I. Presentation of the issue
  II. A clear position
 III. Reasons and support
  IV. Anticipation of opposing positions and objections

This simple plan is nearly always complicated by other factors, however. In outlining your material, you must take into consideration whether your readers are likely to agree or disagree with your position, which will determine how you will present the issue and how much attention you should give to readers' likely objections and to alternative solutions.

If most or all of your readers are likely to disagree with you, for example, you might try to redefine the issue so that these readers can see the possibility that they may share some common values with you after all. To reinforce your connection to readers, you could go on to concede the wisdom of an aspect of their position before presenting the reasons and support for your position. You would conclude by reiterating the shared values on which you hope to build agreement. In this case, an outline might look like this:

   I. Presentation of the issue
  II. Accommodation of some aspect of an opposing position
 III. Thesis statement
  IV. First reason with support
   V. Second reason with support (etc.)
  VI. Conclusion

If you have decided to write primarily for readers who agree rather than disagree with you, then you might choose to strengthen your readers' convictions by organizing your argument as a refutation of opposing arguments, and you might conclude by calling your supporters to arms. Here is an outline showing what this kind of essay might look like:

   I. Presentation of the issue
  II. Thesis statement
 III. Your most plausible reasons
  IV. First opposing argument with refutation
   V. Second opposing argument with refutation (etc.)
  VI. Conclusion

Your outline will, of course, reflect your own writing situation. Once you have a working outline, you should not hesitate to change it as necessary while drafting and revising. For instance, you might find it more effective to hold back on presenting your own position until you have discussed alternative but unacceptable positions. Or you might find a better way to order the reasons for supporting your position. The purpose of an outline is to identify the basic components of your argument and to help you organize them effectively, not to lock you into a particular structure.

For more on outlining, see Chapter 8.

Drafting

If you have not already begun to draft your essay, this section will help by suggesting how to write your opening sentences; how to use the sentence strategy of concession followed by refutation; and how to cite opposing arguments. Drafting is not always a smooth process, so do not be afraid to leave spaces where you do not know what to put in or to write notes to yourself about what you could do next. If you get stuck while drafting, go back over your invention writing: You may be able to copy and paste some of it into your evolving draft, or you may find that you need to do some additional invention to fill in details in your draft.

Writing the Opening Sentences

You could try out one or two different ways of beginning your essay — possibly from the list that follows — but do not agonize over the first sentences because you are likely to discover the best way to begin only after you have written a rough draft. Again, you might want to review your invention writing to see if you have already written something that would work to launch your essay.

To engage your readers' interest from the start, consider the following opening strategies:

- a surprising statement (like Etzioni)
- an assertion of an issue's increasing significance (like Statsky)
- statistics (like Etzioni)
- a research study (like Goldwasser)
- an anecdote or personal reminiscence
- a scenario
- a historical analogy
- criticism of an alternative position

A Sentence Strategy: Concession Followed by Refutation

As you draft, you will need to move back and forth smoothly between arguments for your position and counterarguments against your readers' likely objections and preferred positions. One useful strategy for making this move is to *concede* the value of a likely criticism and then to *refute* it immediately, either in the same sentence or in the next one.

The following sentences from Jessica Statsky's essay illustrate several ways to make this move (the concessions are in italics, the refutations in bold):

> The primary goal of a professional athlete — winning — is not appropriate for children. Their goals should be having fun, learning, and being with friends. *Although winning does add to the fun,* **too many adults lose sight of what matters and make winning the most important goal.** (par. 5)

> *And it is perfectly obvious how important competitive skills are in finding a job.* **Yet the ability to cooperate is also important for success in life.** (par. 10)

In both these examples from different stages in her argument, Statsky concedes the importance or value of some of her readers' likely objections, but then firmly refutes them. (Because these illustrations are woven into an extended argument, you may be better able to appreciate them if you look at them in context by turning to the paragraphs where they appear.) The following examples come from other readings in the chapter:

> *The authors argue that the employees develop many skills such as how to operate a food-preparation machine and a cash register.* **However, little attention is paid to how long it takes to acquire such a skill, or what its significance is.** (Etzioni, par. 8)

> *That's not to say some of the survey findings aren't disturbing. It's crushing to hear that one in four teens could not identify Adolf Hitler's role in world history, for instance.* **But it's not because teenagers were online that they missed this. Had a parent introduced 20 minutes of researching the Holocaust to one month of their teen's Internet life, or a teacher assigned "The Diary of Anne Frank" (arguably a 13-year-old girl's blog) . . . we might not be able to pick up the phone and expose tragic pockets of ignorance.** (Goldwasser, par. 12)

The concession-refutation move, sometimes called the "yes-but" strategy, is important in most arguments. Following is an outline of some other kinds of language authors rely on to introduce their concession-refutation moves:

Introducing the Concession	*Introducing the Refutation That Follows*
I understand that _____.	What I think is _____.
I cannot prove _____.	But I think _____.
X claims that _____.	As it happens _____.
It is true that _____.	But my point is _____.
Another argument _____.	But _____.
It has been argued that _____.	Nevertheless, _____.
We are told that _____.	My own belief is _____.
Proponents argue that _____.	This argument, however, _____.
This argument seems plausible _____.	But experience and evidence show _____.
One common complaint is _____.	In recent years, however, _____.
I am not saying _____, nor am I saying _____.	But I am saying _____.

Activists insist _____.

A reader might ask _____.

Still, in spite of their good intentions _____.

But the real issue _____.

For more on concession followed by refutation, go to **bedfordstmartins.com/conciseguide** and click on Sentence Strategies.

Working with Sources:

Fairly and Accurately Quoting Opposing Positions

How you represent the views of those who disagree with your position is especially important because it affects your credibility with readers. If you do not represent your opponents' views fairly and accurately, readers very likely will — and probably should — question your honesty. One useful strategy is to quote your sources.

Compare the sentence from paragraph 3 of Statsky's essay to the passage from her source, the Little League Web site. The words Statsky quotes are highlighted.

Quote: Although the official Little League Web site acknowledges that children do risk injury playing baseball, it insists that "severe injuries . . . are infrequent," the risk "far less than the risk of riding a skateboard, a bicycle, or even the school bus" ("What about My Child?").

Source: (1) We know that injuries constitute one of parents' foremost concerns, and rightly so. (2) Injuries seem to be inevitable in any rigorous activity, especially if players are new to the sport and unfamiliar with its demands. (3) But because of the safety precautions taken in Little League, severe injuries such as bone fractures are infrequent. (4) Most injuries are sprains and strains, abrasions and cuts and bruises. (5) The risk of serious injury in Little League Baseball is far less than the risk of riding a skateboard, a bicycle, or even the school bus.

Statsky accurately condenses her source's second sentence ("Injuries seem to be inevitable in any rigorous activity, especially if players are new to the sport and unfamiliar with its demands") into one clause ("children do risk injury playing baseball"). She makes clear in the second part of her sentence that although the Little League agrees with her on the risk of injury, it disagrees about the seriousness of that risk. By quoting ("it insists that 'severe injuries . . . are infrequent,' 'far less than the risk of riding a skateboard, a bicycle, or even the school bus'"), she assures readers she has not distorted the Little League's position.

Quoting Appropriately to Avoid Plagiarism

In an earlier, rough draft, Statsky omitted the quotation marks in her sentence. Below is part of her draft sentence, followed by the source with the quoted words highlighted.

. . . it insists that severe injuries are infrequent, the risk far less than the risk of riding a skateboard, a bicycle, or even the school bus ("What about My Child?").

. . . severe injuries such as bone fractures are infrequent. Most injuries are sprains and strains, abrasions and cuts and bruises. The risk of serious injury in Little League Baseball is far less than the risk of riding a skateboard, a bicycle, or even the school bus.

Even though Statsky cites the source, this failure to use quotation marks around language that is borrowed amounts to plagiarism. Use quotation marks whenever you use phrases from your source *and* indicate your source. Doing one or the other is not enough; you must do both.

For more information on integrating language from sources into your own sentences, see pp. 490–91 in Chapter 17. For more help avoiding plagiarism, go to **bedfordstmartins.com/conciseguide** and click on Videos and Tutorials.

Critical Reading Guide

Your instructor may arrange a peer review session in class or online where you can exchange drafts with your classmates and give one another a thoughtful critical reading — pointing out what works well and suggesting ways to improve the draft. This Critical Reading Guide can also be used productively by a tutor in the writing center or by a roommate or family member.

●●●●
Basic Features

A good critical reading does three things: It lets the writer know how the reader understands the point of the story, praises what works best, and indicates where the draft could be improved.

1. Evaluate how well the issue is presented.

   Summarize: Tell the writer what you understand the issue to be about. If you were already familiar with it and understand it differently, briefly explain.

   Praise: Give an example from the essay where the issue and its significance come across effectively.

   Critique: Tell the writer where more information about the issue is needed, where more might be done to establish its seriousness, or how the issue could be reframed in a way that would better prepare readers for the argument.

2. Assess how well the position is supported.

   Summarize: Underline the thesis statement and the main reasons.

   Praise: Give an example in the essay where the argument is especially effective — for example, indicate which reason is especially convincing or which supporting evidence is particularly compelling.

   Critique: Tell the writer where the argument could be strengthened — for example, indicate how the thesis statement could be made clearer or more appropriately qualified, how the argument could be developed, or where additional support is needed.

3. Consider how effectively objections and alternative positions are counterargued.

   Praise: Give an example in the essay where a concession seems particularly well done or a refutation is convincing.

   Critique: Tell the writer how a concession or refutation could be made more convincing, what objection or alternative position should be counterargued, or where common ground could be sought.

4. Assess how readable the argument is.

   Praise: Give an example of where the essay succeeds in being especially easy to read, either in its overall organization, clear presentation of the thesis, clear transitions, effective opening or closing, or by other means.

   Critique: Tell the writer where the readability could be improved. Can you, for example, suggest better forecasting, clearer transitions, or a more effective ending? If the overall organization of the essay needs work, make suggestions for rearranging parts or strengthening connections.

5. If the writer has expressed concern about anything in the draft that you have not discussed, respond to that concern.

Making Comments Electronically Most word processing software offers features that allow you to insert comments directly into the text of someone else's document. Many readers prefer to make their comments this way because it tends to be faster than writing on hard copy and space is virtually unlimited; it also eliminates the process of deciphering handwritten comments. Where such features are not available, simply typing comments directly into a document in a contrasting color can provide the same advantages.

For a printable version of this Critical Reading Guide, go to **bedfordstmartins.com/conciseguide**.

Revising

Very likely you have already thought of ways to improve your draft, and you may even have begun to revise it. In this section is a Troubleshooting chart that may help. Before using the chart, however, it is a good idea to

- review critical reading comments from your classmates, instructor, or writing center tutor, and
- make an outline of your draft so that you can look at it analytically.

You may have made an outline before writing your draft, but after drafting you need to see what you actually wrote, not what you intended to write. You can outline the draft quickly by highlighting the basic features — presenting the issue, supporting a position, effectively anticipating counterarguments and alternative positions, and making the argument readable.

For an electronic version of this Troubleshooting chart, go to **bedfordstmartins.com/conciseguide**.

✔ Troubleshooting Your Draft

● ● ● ● **Basic Features**

A Well-Presented Issue

The issue is not clear to readers.	☐ Add information — statistics, examples, anecdotes, and so on. ☐ Consider adding visuals — graphs, tables, or charts.
Readers understand the issue differently than I do.	☐ Show the limitations of how the issue has traditionally been understood. ☐ Reframe the issue by showing how it relates to values, concerns, needs, and priorities you share with readers. ☐ Give concrete examples or anecdotes, facts, and details that could help readers see the issue as you see it.

A Well-Supported Position

My readers are not convinced that my position is reasonable and/or persuasive.	☐ Explain your reasons. ☐ Add additional supporting evidence. ☐ Ask yourself whether you have inadvertently offended or alienated readers. If so, change the way you have presented your position. ☐ Consider whether your position is in fact arguable. If you cannot provide reasons and support for it, consider modifying your position or writing about a different issue.
My readers do not understand my position.	☐ Go over the way you present your position; if necessary, explain it and your supporting reasons more clearly. ☐ Try outlining your argument; if the organization or coherence is weak, try reorganizing it.

An Effective Counterargument

My readers continue to raise objections to my position.	☐ Address the objections directly in your argument. If possible, refute them, using clear reasons and support. ☐ If objections cannot be completely refuted, acknowledge them but demonstrate that they do not make your position invalid. Try using sentence openers like *It is true that* ____ , *but my point is* ____ . ☐ If you can neither refute nor accommodate objections, rethink your position or add qualifications.

(continued)

(continued)

My readers have proposed opposing positions that I do not discuss in my argument.	☐ Address opposing positions directly. Establish common ground with opponents, if possible, but use clear reasons and support to show why their positions are not as reasonable as yours. ☐ If you cannot show that your position is preferable, show why it is likely to garner more support or have fewer negative side effects.

A Readable Plan

My readers are confused by my essay or find it difficult to read.	☐ Outline your essay. If necessary, move, add, or delete sections to strengthen coherence. ☐ Consider adding a forecasting statement with key terms that are repeated in topic sentences throughout the essay. ☐ Check for appropriate transitions between sentences, paragraphs, and major sections of your essay. ☐ Review your opening and closing paragraphs. Be sure that your thesis is clearly expressed and that you review your main points in your closing.

Editing and Proofreading

Our research indicates that particular errors occur often in essays that argue a position: incorrect comma usage in sentences with coordinating conjunctions, and punctuation errors in sentences that use conjunctive adverbs. The following guidelines will help you check your essay for these common errors.

Using Commas before Coordinating Conjunctions

The Problem. In essays that argue a position, writers often link related ideas by joining independent clauses — groups of words that can stand alone as complete sentences — with coordinating conjunctions (*and, but, for, or, nor, so, yet*). Consider this example from Jessica Statsky's essay:

> Winning and losing may be an inevitable part of adult life, but they should not be part of childhood. (par. 6)

In this sentence, Statsky links two complete ideas: (1) that winning and losing may be part of adult life, and (2) that they should not be part of childhood. She links these ideas using a comma and the coordinating conjunction *but.*

A common error in sentences like these is the omission of the comma, which makes it difficult for the reader to see where one idea stops and the next one starts.

How to Correct It. Add a comma before coordinating conjunctions that join two independent clauses, as in the examples below:

▶ The new immigration laws will bring in more skilled people, but their presence will take jobs away from other Americans.

▶ Sexually transmitted diseases are widespread, and many students are sexually active.

Note: Do *not* use a comma when coordinating conjunctions join phrases that are not independent clauses, as in the following examples:

▶ Newspaper reporters have visited pharmacies, and observed pharmacists selling steroids illegally.

▶ We need people with special talents, and diverse skills to make the United States a stronger nation.

For practice, go to **bedfordstmartins.com/conciseguide/exercisecentral** and click on Commas before Coordinating Conjunctions.

Using Punctuation with Conjunctive Adverbs

The Problem. When writers take a position, the reasoning they need to employ invites the use of conjunctive adverbs (*consequently, furthermore, however, moreover, therefore, thus*) to connect sentences and clauses. Sentences that use conjunctive adverbs require different punctuation, depending on how the conjunctive adverbs are used. Incorrect use of punctuation can make the sentences grammatically incorrect and/or difficult to understand.

How to Correct It. Conjunctive adverbs that open a sentence should be followed by a comma:

▶ Consequently, many local governments have banned smoking.

▶ Therefore, talented teachers will leave the profession because of poor working conditions and low salaries.

If a conjunctive adverb joins two independent clauses, it must be preceded by a semicolon and followed by a comma:

▶ The recent vote on increasing student fees produced a disappointing turnout↓; moreover↑ the presence of campaign literature on ballot tables violated voting procedures.

▶ Children watching television recognize violence but not its intention↑ thus↑ they become desensitized to violence.

For practice, go to **bedfordstmartins.com/conciseguide/exercisecentral** and click on Punctuation with Conjunctive Adverbs.

Conjunctive adverbs that fall in the middle of an independent clause should be set off with commas:

▶ Due to trade restrictions↑ however↑ sales of Japanese cars did not surpass sales of domestic cars.

A Common ESL Problem: Subtle Differences in Meaning

Because the distinctions in meaning among some common conjunctive adverbs are subtle, nonnative speakers often have difficulty using them accurately. For example, the difference between *however* and *nevertheless* is small; each is used to introduce a statement that contrasts with what precedes it. But *nevertheless* emphasizes the contrast, whereas *however* softens it. Check usage of such terms in an English dictionary rather than a bilingual one. *The American Heritage Dictionary of the English Language* has special usage notes to help distinguish frequently confused words.

For practice, go to **bedfordstmartins.com/conciseguide/exercisecentral** and click on A Common ESL Problem: Subtle Differences in Meaning.

Thinking Critically about What You Have Learned

To consolidate what you have learned in this chapter, it is helpful to think metacognitively — that is, to reflect not only on what you learned but also on how you learned it.

Reflecting on Your Writing

Your instructor may ask you to turn in with your essay and process materials a metacognitive essay or letter. Choose from the following invention activities those that seem most productive for you.

- Explain how your purpose and audience influenced *one* of your decisions as a writer, such as the strategies you used in arguing your position, or the ways in which you attempted to counter possible objections.

- Discuss what you learned about yourself as a writer. For example, what part of the process did you find most challenging? Did you try anything new, like getting a critical reading of your draft or outlining it?

- Which of the readings in this chapter influenced your essay? Explain the influence, citing specific examples from your essay and the reading.

- If you got good advice from a reader, explain how the person helped you — perhaps by questioning the way you addressed your audience or the evidence you offered.

Considering the Social Dimensions: Suppressing Dissent

Some critics argue that society privileges reasoned argument over other ways of arguing in order to control dissent. Instead of expressing concern through passionate language, dissenters are urged to be dispassionate and reasonable. They may even be encouraged to try to build their arguments on shared values even though they are arguing with people whose views they find repugnant. While it may help prevent violent confrontation, this emphasis may also prevent an honest and open exchange of differences.

1. *In your own experience of writing an essay arguing a position, did having to give reasons and support discourage you from choosing any particular issue or from expressing strong feelings?* Reflect on the issues you listed as possible subjects for your essay and how you made your choice. Did you reject any issues because you could not come up with reasons and support for your position? When you made your choice, did you think about whether you could be dispassionate and reasonable about it?

2. *Consider the readings in this chapter and the essays you read by other students in the class.* Do you think any of these writers felt limited by the need to give reasons and support for their position? Which of the essays you read, if any, seemed to you to express strong feelings about the issue? Which, if any, seemed dispassionate?

3. *Consider the kind of arguing you typically witness in the media — radio, television, newspapers, magazines, the Internet.* Some would say that in the media, giving reasons and support and anticipating readers' objections is less common than a more contentious, in-your-face style of arguing. Think of media examples of these different ways of arguing. What would you conclude about the claim that reasoned argument can stifle dissent?

4. *Write a page or two explaining your ideas about whether reasoned argument suppresses dissent.* Connect your ideas to your own essay and to the readings in this chapter.

6

Proposing a Solution

IN COLLEGE COURSES In an early childhood education class, a student becomes interested in the potential of television for educational purposes. Online, he learns about laws that require publicly owned airwaves to serve the public interest and encourage commercial stations to provide educational children's programming. The student discovers that commercial networks actually offer little educational programming for children.

He decides to develop a proposal that would require networks to provide programming to help preschool children learn English. After consulting his professor and the college reference librarian, the student finds statistics that establish the need for such programming. In addition, he interviews both an educational researcher who specializes in the impact of media on children's language acquisition and the programming coordinator for a national network. In writing his proposal, he counters possible objections of impracticality by citing two model programs, public television's *Sesame Street* and cable's *Mi Casita (My Little House)*.

IN THE COMMUNITY A social services administrator in a large city becomes concerned about a rise in the number of adolescents in jail. He visits a university library and locates recent studies, from which he concludes that the problem is national. He comes to the conclusion that a partial solution to the problem would be to intervene at the first sign of delinquent behavior in eight- to twelve-year-olds.

In developing a proposal to circulate locally, the administrator begins by describing the consequences of jailing young criminals, focusing on the costs of incarceration and the high rate of return to criminal activity. He provides the case histories of several offenders he has worked with. He then discusses the major components of his program, which include finding mentors for struggling adolescents and placing social workers with troubled families. The administrator acknowledges the costs of the program but points to lowered costs for incarceration if it is successful.

IN THE WORKPLACE A truck driver has an idea for a solution to the shortage of well-qualified drivers at her company. She convinces two coworkers to help her write a proposal suggesting that the company recruit more women. The driver talks to the owner and to the few other women drivers she knows and concludes that women tend to be turned off by truck-driving schools, which are male dominated. In industry magazines, one of her coauthors finds statistics they can use to argue for a new training program that would exceed the Professional Truck Driver Institute standard. Recruits would be assigned to experienced drivers serving as paid mentors. The students would not have to attend a truck-driving school, but they would be required to drive for the company at a reduced salary for a number of months.

In the final draft of the proposal, the coauthors argue that everyone benefits. The company gets a skilled workforce. The experienced drivers get additional income. The recruits get experience without the cost of tuition. The three coauthors give the proposal to the company president, and it is published in an online industry newsletter.

That 9 dollar lunch is worth more than you think. Like 19,000 dollars more.

Pack your own lunch instead of going out. $6 saved a day x 5 days a week x 10 years x 6% interest = $19,592. That could be money in your pocket. Small changes today. Big bucks tomorrow. Go to feedthepig.org for free savings tips.

Proposing a Solution

Proposals for solving problems take many forms in our culture. Formal written proposals are used often in business, government, and the academic world to present possible solutions to particular problems, like spiraling costs or lower-than-expected revenue. Effectively composed formal proposals exhibit all of the basic features of the proposal essay discussed in this chapter: a well-defined problem, a well-argued solution, an effective counterargument, and a readable plan.

Other forms of cultural expression propose solutions as well, and many of them exhibit some if not all of the basic features of the proposal essay. Open, or publicly addressed, proposals to problems of concern to a community or a nation have a long tradition in our culture; they are perhaps most famously embodied in Jonathan Swift's "Modest Proposal," which satirically recommends cannibalism as a remedy for the desperate poverty of eighteenth-century Irish peasants. Self-help literature, such as *The Secret* or *The Seven Habits of Highly Effective People*, is an immensely popular (and profitable) contemporary genre that proposes solutions to common problems.

Many advertisements also propose solutions. While ads do not generally exhibit all of the basic features present in formal proposals, the best ones use images and text efficiently in order to define a problem (poor money management, for example, in the ad reproduced on the opposite page) and suggest a solution (in this case, packing a lunch rather than buying it).

In this chapter, we ask you to write a proposal for a solution to a problem that concerns you. As you compose your proposal, you should consider whether the use of visuals or multimedia would help your readers more immediately or more fully grasp your proposed solution.

Reading and Writing Essays
Proposing a Solution

In the chapter-opening scenarios, you read examples of how proposals are used in college, in the community, and in the workplace. The college student, for example, writes a proposal to support the creation of educational television programming for children learning English. The school counselor proposes an early intervention program for at-risk children in the city where he works. Finally, in order to redress a shortage of qualified drivers, three employees of a trucking company draft a proposal for a recruitment program aimed at women.

As a special form of argument, proposals have much in common with position papers, described in Chapter 5. Both take a stand on a subject about which there is disagreement, and both make a reasoned argument acknowledging readers' likely objections. Proposals, however, go further: They urge readers to take specific action. They argue for a proposed solution to a problem, and they succeed or fail by the strength of that argument.

Good proposals are creative as well as convincing. After all, problem-solving depends on a questioning attitude — wondering about alternative approaches to bringing about change and posing challenges to the status quo. Because a proposal tries to convince readers that its way of defining and solving the problem makes sense, proposal writers must also be sensitive to readers' needs and expectations. Readers may be wary of costs and demands on their time. Consequently, they need to know details of the solution and to be convinced that it is the best solution to the problem and that it can be implemented.

While many proposals, like the one to train women as truck drivers, are relatively narrow in scope, proposals are also vital to a democracy. By reading proposals, citizens learn about problems that affect their well-being and explore possible actions to solve those problems. By writing proposals, citizens can significantly affect the ways in which individuals, families, and communities function. In the chapter-opening scenarios, for example, the proposals for more educational television programming and for early childhood intervention programs address problems of broad social import.

In this chapter, you will read proposals designed to change the ways in which students are evaluated in college courses, to address the problems of child care faced by families with multiple wage earners, and to expand and improve the pool of applicants for teaching jobs. The Guide to Writing that follows the readings will support you as you compose your own proposal, showing you ways to use the basic features of the genre to write a creative and convincing argument for change.

A Collaborative Activity:
Practice Proposing a Solution to a Problem

To get a sense of the complexities and possibilities involved in proposing solutions, think through a specific problem with two or three other students, and try to come up with a *feasible* proposal — one that could actually help solve the problem and be implemented:

Part 1. Select a problem in your college community that you know something about — for example, overly complicated registration procedures or noisy residence halls.

- Discuss possible solutions, and identify one solution that seems feasible. (You need not all be equally enthusiastic about this solution.)

- Determine who can act on your proposed solution and how to convince them that it could be implemented and would indeed help solve the problem.

Part 2. As a group, discuss your efforts.

- How did you think of possible solutions — for example, did you consider comparable problems and borrow their solutions, try to figure out what caused the problem and how to eliminate it, or use some other strategies?

- What seemed most challenging about constructing an argument to convince people to take action on your proposed solution — for example, showing how your solution could be implemented, proving it would help solve the problem, or something else?

Reading Essays Proposing a Solution

Basic Features

As you read essays proposing a solution in this chapter, you will see how different authors incorporate the basic features of the genre.

● A Well-Defined Problem

Read first to see how the writer presents the problem. Writers try to define the problem in a way that establishes the need to find a solution. Notice which strategies, such as the following, the writer uses to present the problem as real and serious:

- giving examples to make the problem specific
- using scenarios or anecdotes to dramatize the problem
- quoting testimony from those affected by the problem
- citing statistics to show the severity of the problem
- vividly describing the problem's negative consequences

● A Well-Argued Solution

To find where the essay advocates a solution, look for the thesis statement. A good thesis statement in an essay proposing a solution makes clear exactly what is being proposed and may also forecast the reasons for it that will be developed and supported in the essay. Check to see that the argument for the proposed solution offers concrete reasons and support showing that the solution is feasible — meaning it meets the following criteria:

- it will help solve the problem;
- it can be implemented; and
- it is worth the expense, time, and effort.

For example, a writer might demonstrate that

- the proposed solution would reduce or eliminate a major cause of the problem;
- a similar solution has worked elsewhere;
- the necessary steps to put the solution into practice can be taken without excessive cost or inconvenience; or
- stakeholders could come together behind the proposal.

● An Effective Counterargument

Read also to see how the writer responds to possible objections and alternative solutions. Writers may counterargue in one or more of the following ways:

- by acknowledging an objection
- by conceding the point and modifying the proposal to accommodate it

211

- by refuting criticism — for example, by arguing that an alternative solution would be more costly or less likely to solve the problem than the proposed solution.

● A Readable Plan

Finally, read to see how clearly the writer presents the proposal. Essays proposing a solution tend to be rather complicated because the writer has to establish the problem, argue for the proposed solution, and counterargue against objections and alternative solutions — all of which must be backed with solid support and clear citations. Therefore, it is especially important to have a readable plan that helps readers follow the twists and turns of the argument.

To make their essays easy to read, writers usually include some or all of the following:

- a forecast of the argument
- key words introduced in the thesis and forecasting statement
- topic sentences introducing paragraphs or groups of paragraphs
- repeated use of key words and synonyms throughout the essay, particularly in topic sentences
- clear transitional words and phrases
- headings that explicitly identify different sections of the essay
- visuals, including charts that present information in an easy-to-read format

Purpose and Audience

An effective proposal is one that readers take seriously and that stands a chance of convincing them to support or act on the proposed solution. To be effective, a writer must establish credibility by anticipating readers' needs and concerns and by representing readers' views fairly.

*As you read essays proposing solutions, ask yourself what seems to be the writer's **purpose** in writing.* For example, does the writer seem to be writing primarily

- to convince readers that the problem truly exists and needs immediate action?
- to assure readers that the problem can indeed be solved?
- to persuade readers that the writer's proposed solution is better than alternative solutions?
- to inspire readers to take action?
- to rekindle readers' interest in a long-standing problem?

*As you read, also try to determine what the writer assumes about the **audience.*** For example, does the writer assume most readers will

- be unaware of the problem?
- recognize the existence of the problem but fail to take it seriously?
- think the problem has already been solved?
- feel it is someone else's problem and not of concern to them?
- be skeptical about the cost and possibility of implementing the proposed solution?
- prefer an alternative solution?

Readings

PATRICK O'MALLEY wrote the following proposal while he was a first-year college student frustrated by what he calls "high-stakes exams." O'Malley interviewed two professors (his writing instructor and the writing program director), talked with several students, and read published research on the subject of testing. Notice how he anticipates professors' likely objections to his proposed solution and argues against their preferred solutions to the problem. Where do you think his argument is strongest? Weakest?

As you read the essay, which follows APA style, consider the questions in the margin. Your instructor may ask you to post your answers or bring them to class.

Basic Features

- A Well-Defined Problem
- A Well-Argued Solution
- An Effective Counterargument
- A Readable Plan

More Testing, More Learning
Patrick O'Malley

1   It's late at night. The final's tomorrow. You got a C on the midterm, so this one will make or break you. Will it be like the midterm? Did you study enough? Did you study the right things? It's too late to drop the course. So what happens if you fail? No time to worry about that now — you've got a ton of notes to go over.

What is the function of this opening paragraph?

2   Although this last-minute anxiety about midterm and final exams is only too familiar to most college students, many professors may not realize how such major, infrequent, high-stakes exams work against the best interests of students both psychologically and intellectually. They cause unnecessary amounts

How does defining the problem this way set up the solution?

of stress, placing too much importance on one or two days in the students' entire term, judging ability on a single or dual performance. They don't encourage frequent study, and they fail to inspire students' best performance. If professors gave additional brief exams at frequent intervals, students would be spurred to study more regularly, learn more, worry less, and perform better on midterms, finals, and other papers and projects.

How does O'Malley use the key terms introduced here throughout the essay?

What does par. 3 contribute to the argument?

Ideally, a professor would give an in-class test or quiz after each unit, chapter, or focus of study, depending on the type of class and course material. A physics class might require a test on concepts after every chapter covered, while a history class could necessitate quizzes covering certain time periods or major events. These exams should be given weekly or at least twice monthly. Whenever possible, they should consist of two or three essay questions rather than many multiple-choice or short-answer questions. To preserve class time for lecture and discussion, exams should take no more than 15 or 20 minutes.   3

How does O'Malley introduce this reason? What kinds of support does he offer?

The main reason professors should give frequent exams is that when they do and when they provide feedback to students on how well they are doing, students learn more in the course and perform better on major exams, projects, and papers. It makes sense that in a challenging course containing a great deal of material, students will learn more of it and put it to better use if they have to apply or "practice" it frequently on exams, which also helps them find out how much they are learning and what they need to go over again. A 2006 study reported in *Psychological Science* journal concluded that "taking repeated tests on material leads to better long-term retention than repeated studying," according to the study's coauthors, Henry L. Roediger and Jeff Karpicke. When asked what the impact of this breakthrough research would be, they responded: "We hope that this research may be picked up in educational circles as a way to improve educational practices, both for students in the classroom and as a study strategy outside of class" (ScienceWatch.com, 2008). "Incorporating more frequent classroom testing into a course," the study concludes, "may improve students' learning and promote retention of material long after a course has ended" (qtd. in Science Blog,   4

How does O'Malley integrate sources into his text and cite them?

2006). Many students already recognize the value of frequent testing, but their reason is that they need the professor's feedback. A Harvard study notes students' "strong preference for frequent evaluation in a course." Harvard students feel they learn least in courses that have "only a midterm and a final exam, with no other personal evaluation." They believe they learn most in courses with "many opportunities to see how they are doing" (Light, 1990, p. 32). In a review of a number of studies of student learning, Frederiksen (1984) reports that students who take weekly quizzes achieve higher scores on final exams than students who take only a midterm exam and that testing increases retention of material tested.

5   Another, closely related argument in favor of multiple exams is that they encourage students to improve their study habits. Greater frequency in test taking means greater frequency in studying for tests. Students prone to cramming will be required — or at least strongly motivated — to open their textbooks and notebooks more often, making them less likely to resort to long, kamikaze nights of studying for major exams. Since there is so much to be learned in the typical course, it makes sense that frequent, careful study and review are highly beneficial. But students need motivation to study regularly, and nothing works like an exam. If students had frequent exams in all their courses, they would have to schedule study time each week and gradually would develop a habit of frequent study. It might be argued that students are adults who have to learn how to manage their own lives, but learning history or physics is more complicated than learning to drive a car or balance a checkbook. Students need coaching and practice in learning. The right way to learn new material needs to become a habit, and I believe that frequent exams are key to developing good habits of study and learning. The Harvard study concludes that "tying regular evaluation to good course organization enables students to plan their work more than a few days in advance. If quizzes and homework are scheduled on specific days, students plan their work to capitalize on them" (Light, 1990, p. 33).

6   By encouraging regular study habits, frequent exams would also decrease anxiety by reducing the procrastination that produces anxiety.

How does O'Malley support this reason? Why does he include it?

How does O'Malley introduce and respond to this possible objection?

Students would benefit psychologically if they were not subjected to the emotional ups and downs caused by major exams, when after being virtually worry-free for weeks they are suddenly ready to check into the psychiatric ward. Researchers at the University of Vermont found a strong relationship among procrastination, anxiety, and achievement. Students who regularly put off studying for exams had continuing high anxiety and lower grades than students who procrastinated less. The researchers found that even "low" procrastinators did not study regularly and recommended that professors give frequent assignments and exams to reduce procrastination and increase achievement (Rothblum, Solomon, & Murakami, 1986, pp. 393–394).

How effectively does O'Malley use this source?

Research supports my proposed solution to the problems I have described. Common sense as well as my experience and that of many of my friends support it. Why, then, do so few professors give frequent brief exams?

What is the purpose of this question?

7

Some believe that such exams take up too much of the limited class time available to cover the material in the course. Most courses meet 150 minutes a week — three times a week for 50 minutes each time. A 20-minute weekly exam might take 30 minutes to administer, and that is one-fifth of each week's class time. From the student's perspective, however, this time is well spent. Better learning and greater confidence about the course seem a good trade-off for another 30 minutes of lecture. Moreover, time lost to lecturing or discussion could easily be made up in students' learning on their own through careful regular study for the weekly exams. If weekly exams still seem too time-consuming to some professors, their frequency could be reduced to every other week or their length to 5 or 10 minutes. In courses where multiple-choice exams are appropriate, several questions could be designed to take only a few minutes to answer.

8

How does O'Malley argue against possible objections in pars. 8 and 9?

Another objection professors have to frequent exams is that they take too much time to read and grade. In a 20-minute essay exam, a well-prepared student can easily write two pages. A relatively small class of 30 students might then produce 60 pages, no small amount of material to read each week. A large class of 100 or more students would produce an insurmountable pile of material. There are

9

a number of responses to this objection. Again, professors could give exams every other week or make them very short. Instead of reading them closely they could skim them quickly to see whether students understand an idea or can apply it to an unfamiliar problem; and instead of numerical or letter grades they could give a plus, check, or minus. Exams could be collected and responded to only every third or fourth week. Professors who have readers or teaching assistants could rely on them to grade or check exams. And the Scantron machine is always available for instant grading of multiple-choice exams. Finally, frequent exams could be given *in place of* a midterm exam or out-of-class essay assignment.

10   Since frequent exams seem to some professors to create too many problems, however, it is reasonable to consider alternative ways to achieve the same goals. One alternative solution is to implement a program that would improve study skills. While such a program might teach students how to study for exams, it cannot prevent procrastination or reduce "large test anxiety" by a substantial amount. One research team studying anxiety and test performance found that study skills training was not effective in reducing anxiety or improving performance (Dendato & Diener, 1986, p. 134). This team, which also reviewed other research that reached the same conclusion, did find that a combination of "cognitive/relaxation therapy" and study skills training was effective. This possible solution seems complicated, however, not to mention time-consuming and expensive. It seems much easier and more effective to change the cause of the bad habit rather than treat the habit itself. That is, it would make more sense to solve the problem at its root: the method of learning and evaluation.

11   Still another solution might be to provide frequent study questions for students to answer. These would no doubt be helpful in focusing students' time studying, but students would probably not actually write out the answers unless they were required to. To get students to complete the questions in a timely way, professors would have to collect and check the answers. In that case, however, they might as well devote the time to grading an exam. Even if it asks the same questions, a scheduled exam is preferable to a set of study

How effectively does O'Malley present alternative solutions in pars. 10–12?

How do the highlighted words and phrases make the argument easy to follow?

questions because it takes far less time to write in class, compared to the time students would devote to responding to questions at home. In-class exams also ensure that each student produces his or her own work.

Another possible solution would be to help students prepare for midterm and final exams by providing sets of questions from which the exam questions will be selected or announcing possible exam topics at the beginning of the course. This solution would have the advantage of reducing students' anxiety about learning every fact in the text-book, and it would clarify the course goals, but it would not motivate students to study carefully each new unit, concept, or text chapter in the course. I see this as a way of complementing frequent exams, not as substituting for them.

12

How effective is this conclusion?

From the evidence and from my talks with professors and students, I see frequent, brief in-class exams as the only way to improve students' study habits and learning, reduce their anxiety and procrastination, and increase their satisfaction with college. These exams are not a panacea, but only more parking spaces and a winning football team would do as much to improve college life. Professors can't do much about parking or football, but they can give more frequent exams. Campus administrators should get behind this effort, and professors should get together to consider giving exams more frequently. It would make a difference.

13

References

Dendato, K. M., & Diener, D. (1986). Effectiveness of cognitive/relaxation therapy and study skills training in reducing self-reported anxiety and improving the academic performance of test-anxious students. *Journal of Counseling Psychology, 33,* 131–135.

Frederiksen, N. (1984). The real test bias: Influences of testing on teaching and learning. *American Psychologist, 39,* 193–202.

Light, R. J. (1990). *Explorations with students and faculty about teaching, learning, and student life.* Cambridge, MA: Harvard

Why do you think O'Malley assumes these sources would carry weight with his readers?

University Graduate School of Education and Kennedy School of Government.

Rothblum, E. D., Solomon, L., & Murakami, J. (1986). Affective, cognitive, and behavioral differences between high and low procrastinators. *Journal of Counseling Psychology, 33,* 387–394.

ScienceBlog. (2006, March 7). To learn something, testing beats studying [Blog posting]. Retrieved from http://www.scienceblog .com/cms/to_learn_something_testing_beats_studying_10161 .html

ScienceWatch.com. (2008, February). Fast Breaking Papers - 2008 [Interview with authors Henry L. Roediger & Jeff Karpicke about journal article Test-enhanced learning: Taking memory tests improves long-term retention]. Retrieved from http://sciencewatch .com/dr/fbp/2008/08febfbp/08febfbpRoedigerETAL/

KAREN KORNBLUH earned a B.A. in economics and English and an M.A. from Harvard University's Kennedy School of Government. She worked in the private sector as an economist and management consultant and in the public sector as director of the office of legislative and inter-governmental affairs at the Federal Communications Commission before becoming the deputy chief of staff at the Treasury Department in the Clinton administration. Kornbluh is ambassador to the Organization for Economic Co-operation and Development in the Obama administration.

As director of the Work and Family Program of the New America Foundation, a non-profit, nonpartisan institute that sponsors research and conferences on public policy issues, Kornbluh led an effort to change the American workplace to accommodate what she calls the new "juggler family," in which parents have to juggle their time for parenting and work. Her book *Running Harder to Stay in Place: The Growth of Family Work Hours and Incomes* was published in 2005 by the New America Foundation, and Kornbluh's articles have appeared in such distinguished venues as the *New York Times,* the *Washington Post,* and the *Atlantic Monthly.* The following proposal was published in 2005 by the Work and Family Program.

As you read, think about your own experiences as a child, a parent, or both and how they affect your response to Kornbluh's proposal. Have you or your parents had to juggle time for parenting and work — and if so, how did you or they manage it?

WIN-WIN FLEXIBILITY
Karen Kornbluh

Introduction

Today fully 70 percent of families with children are headed by two working parents or by an unmarried working parent. The "traditional family" of the breadwinner and home-maker has been replaced by the "juggler family," in which no one is home full-time. Two-parent families are working 10 more hours a week than in 1979 (Bernstein and Kornbluh). [1]

To be decent parents, caregivers, and members of their communities, workers now need greater flexibility than they once did. Yet good part-time or flex-time jobs remain rare. Whereas companies have embraced flexibility in virtually every other aspect of their businesses (inventory control, production schedules, financing), full-time workers' schedules remain largely inflexible. Employers often demand workers be available around the clock. Moreover, many employees have no right to a minimum number of sick or vacation days; almost two thirds of all workers — and an even larger percentage of low-income parents — lack the ability to take a day off to care for a family member (Lovell). The Family and Medical Leave Act (FMLA) of 1993 finally guaranteed that workers at large companies could take a leave of absence for the birth or adoption of a baby, or for the illness of a family member. Yet that guaranteed leave is unpaid. [2]

Many businesses are finding ways to give their most valued employees flexibility but, all too often, workers who need flexibility find themselves shunted into part-time, tem-porary, on-call, or contract jobs with reduced wages and career opportunities — and, often, no benefits. A full quarter of American workers are in these jobs. Only 15 percent of women and 12 percent of men in such jobs receive health insurance from their employers (Wenger). A number of European countries provide workers the right to a part-time schedule and all have enacted legislation to implement a European Union di-rective to prohibit discrimination against part-time workers. [3]

In America, employers are required to accommodate the needs of employees with disabilities — even if that means providing a part-time or flexible schedule. Employers may also provide religious accommodations for employees by offering a part-time or flexible schedule. At the same time, employers have no obligation to allow parents or employees caring for sick relatives to work part-time or flexible schedules, even if the cost to the employer would be inconsequential. [4]

In the 21st Century global economy, America needs a new approach that allows busi-nesses to gain flexibility in staffing without sacrificing their competitiveness and enables workers to gain control over their work-lives without sacrificing their economic security. This win-win flexibility arrangement will not be the same in every company, nor even for each employee working within the same organization. Each case will be different. But flexibility will not come for all employees without some education, prodding, and leader-ship. So, employers and employees must be required to come to the table to work out a solution that benefits everyone. American businesses must be educated on strategies for [5] giving employees flexibility without sacrificing productivity or morale. And businesses should be recognized and rewarded when they do so.

6   America is a nation that continually rises to the occasion. At the dawn of a new century, we face many challenges. One of these is helping families to raise our next generation in an increasingly demanding global economy. This is a challenge America must meet with imagination and determination.

Background: The Need for Workplace Flexibility

7   Between 1970 and 2000, the percentage of mothers in the workforce rose from 38 to 67 percent (Smolensky and Gootman). Moreover, the number of hours worked by dual-income families has increased dramatically. Couples with children worked a full 60 hours a week in 1979. By 2000 they were working 70 hours a week (Bernstein and Kornbluh). And more parents than ever are working long hours. In 2000, nearly 1 out of every 8 couples with children was putting in 100 hours a week or more on the job, compared to only 1 out of 12 families in 1970 (Jacobs and Gerson).

8   In addition to working parents, there are over 44.4 million Americans who provide care to another adult, often an older relative. Fifty-nine percent of these caregivers either work or have worked while providing care ("Caregiving").

9   In a 2002 report by the Families and Work Institute, 45 percent of employees reported that work and family responsibilities interfered with each other "a lot" or "some" and 67 percent of employed parents report that they do not have enough time with their children (Galinksy, Bond, and Hill).

10   Over half of workers today have no control over scheduling alternative start and end times at work (Galinksy, Bond, and Hill). According to a recent study by the Institute for Women's Policy Research, 49 percent of workers — over 59 million Americans — lack basic paid sick days for themselves. And almost two-thirds of all workers — and an even larger percentage of low-income parents — lack the ability to take a day off to care for a family member (Lovell). Thirteen percent of non-poor workers with caregiving responsibilities lack paid vacation leave, while 28 percent of poor caregivers lack any paid vacation time (Heymann). Research has shown that flexible arrangements and benefits tend to be more accessible in larger and more profitable firms, and then to the most valued professional and managerial workers in those firms (Golden). Parents with young children and working welfare recipients — the workers who need access to paid leave the most — are the least likely to have these benefits, according to research from the Urban Institute (Ross Phillips).

11   In the US, only 5 percent of workers have access to a job that provides paid parental leave. The Family and Medical Leave Act grants the right to 12 weeks of unpaid leave for the birth or adoption of a child or for the serious illness of the worker or a worker's family member. But the law does not apply to employees who work in companies with fewer than 50 people, employees who have worked for less than a year at their place of employment, or employees who work fewer than 1,250 hours a year. Consequently, only 45 percent of parents working in the private sector are eligible to take even this unpaid time off (Smolensky and Gootman).

Workers often buy flexibility by sacrificing job security, benefits, and pay. Part-time workers are less likely to have employer-provided health insurance or pensions and their hourly wages are lower. One study in 2002 found that 43 percent of employed parents said that using flexibility would jeopardize their advancement (Galinksy, Bond, and Hill). | 12

Children, in particular, pay a heavy price for workplace inflexibility (Waters Boots 2004). Almost 60 percent of child care arrangements are of poor or mediocre quality (Smolensky and Gootman). Children in low-income families are even less likely to be in good or excellent care settings. Full-day child care easily costs $4,000 to $10,000 per year — approaching the price of college tuition at a public university. As a result of the unaffordable and low quality nature of child care in this country, a disturbing number of today's children are left home alone: Over 3.3 million children age 6–12 are home alone after school each day (Vandivere et al). | 13

Many enlightened businesses are showing the way forward to a 21st century flexible workplace. Currently, however, businesses have little incentive to provide families with the flexibility they need. We need to level the playing field and remove the competitive disadvantages for all businesses that do provide workplace flexibility. | 14

This should be a popular priority. A recent poll found that 77 percent of likely voters feel that it is difficult for families to earn enough and still have time to be with their families. Eighty-four percent of voters agree that children are being shortchanged when their parents have to work long hours. . . . | 15

Proposal: Win-Win Flexibility

A win-win approach in the US to flexibility . . . might function as follows. It would be "soft touch" at first — requiring a process and giving business an out if it would be costly to implement — with a high-profile public education campaign on the importance of workplace flexibility to American business, American families, and American society. A survey at the end of the second year would determine whether a stricter approach is needed. | 16

Employees would have the right to make a formal request to their employers for flexibility in the number of hours worked, the times worked, and/or the ability to work from home. Examples of such flexibility would include part-time, annualized hours,[1] compressed hours,[2] flex-time,[3] job-sharing, shift working, staggered hours, and telecommuting. | 17

The employee would be required to make a written application providing details on the change in work, the effect on the employer, and solutions to any problems caused to the employer. The employer would be required to meet with the employee and give the employee a decision on the request within two weeks, as well as provide an opportunity for an internal appeal within one month from the initial request. | 18

The employee request would be granted unless the employer demonstrated it would require significant difficulty or expense entailing more than ordinary costs, decreased | 19

---

[1]*Annualized hours* means working different numbers of hours a week but a fixed annual total.

[2]*Compressed hours* means working more hours a day in exchange for working fewer days a week.

[3]*Flex-time* means working on an adjustable daily schedule.

job efficiency, impairment of worker safety, infringement of other employees' rights, or conflict with another law or regulation.

20 The employer would be required to provide an employee working a flexible schedule with the same hourly pay and proportionate health, pension, vacation, holiday, and FMLA benefits that the employee received before working flexibly and would be required thereafter to advance the employee at the same rate as full-time employees.

21 *Who would be covered:* Parents (including parents, legal guardians, foster parents) and other caregivers at first. Eventually all workers should be eligible in our flexible, 24×7 economy. During the initial period, it will be necessary to define non-parental "caregivers." One proposal is to define them as immediate relatives or other caregivers of "certified care recipients" (defined as those whom a doctor certifies as having three or more limitations that impede daily functioning — using diagnostic criteria such as Activities of Daily Living [ADL]/Instrumental Activities of Daily Living [IADL] — for at least 180 consecutive days). . . .

22 *Public Education:* Critical to the success of the proposal will be public education along the lines of the education that the government and business schools conducted in the 1980s about the need for American business to adopt higher quality standards to compete against Japanese business. A Malcolm Baldridge–like award[4] should be created for companies that make flexibility win-win. A public education campaign conducted by the Department of Labor should encourage small businesses to adopt best practices of win-win flexibility. Tax credits could be used in the first year to reward early adopters.

Works Cited

Bernstein, Jared, and Karen Kornbluh. *Running Faster to Stay in Place: The Growth of Family Work Hours and Incomes.* Washington: New America Foundation, 2005. *New America Foundation.* Web. 22 May 2008.

Galinsky, Ellen, James Bond, and Jeffrey E. Hill. *Workplace Flexibility: What Is It? Who Has It? Who Wants It? Does It Make a Difference?* New York: Families and Work Institute, 2004. Print.

Golden, Lonnie. *The Time Bandit: What U.S. Workers Surrender to Get Greater Flexibility in Work Schedules.* Washington: Economic Policy Institute, 2000. *Economic Policy Institute.* Web. 18 May 2008.

Heymann, Jody. *The Widening Gap: Why America's Working Families Are in Jeopardy — and What Can Be Done About It.* New York: Basic, 2000. Print.

Jacobs, Jerry, and Kathleen Gerson. *The Time Divide: Work, Family and Gender Inequality.* Cambridge: Harvard UP, 2004. Print.

Lovell, Vickey. *No Time to Be Sick: Why Everyone Suffers When Workers Don't Have Paid Sick Leave.* Washington: Institute for Women's Policy Research, 2004. *Institute for Women's Policy Research.* Web. 20 May 2008.

National Alliance for Caregiving and AARP. *Caregiving in the U.S.* Bethesda: NAC, 2004. *National Alliance for Caregiving.* Web. 20 May 2008.

---

[4]The Malcolm Baldridge National Quality Award is given by the U.S. President to outstanding businesses.

Ross Phillips, Katherine. *Getting Time Off: Access to Leave among Working Parents.* Washington: Urban Institute, 2004. *Urban Institute.* Web. 21 May 2008. New Federalism: National Survey of America's Families B-57.

Smolensky, Eugene, and Jennifer A. Gootman, eds. *Working Families and Growing Kids: Caring for Children and Adolescents.* Washington: The National Academies P, 2004. Print.

Vandivere, Sharon, et al. *Unsupervised Time: Family and Child Factors Associated with Self-Care.* Washington: Urban Institute, 2003. *Urban Institute.* Web. 21 May 2008. Assessing the New Federalism 71.

Waters Boots, Shelley. *The Way We Work: How Children and Their Families Fare in a 21st Century Workplace.* Washington: New America Foundation, 2004. *New America Foundation.* Web. 22 May 2008.

Wenger, Jeffrey. *Share of Workers in "Nonstandard" Jobs Declines.* Briefing Paper. Washington: Economic Policy Institute, 2003. *Economic Policy Institute.* Web. 18 May 2008.

MAKING CONNECTIONS: THE PROBLEM OF CHILD CARE

Many of you have probably grown up during the period Kornbluh is describing, and your family may have been configured more as a "juggler" than as a "traditional family" (par. 1). Kornbluh asserts in paragraph 13 that it is the children in juggler families who "pay a heavy price." She is particularly critical of child care, which she says is very expensive and of low quality, especially for low-income families. She cites Vandivere et al. to argue that more than "3.3 million children age 6–12 are home alone after school each day" (par. 13).

With two or three other students, discuss how well Kornbluh's argument compares with your experiences as a child. Begin by taking turns telling whether you attended after-school programs, were a "latchkey child," or had some other arrangement. Then, together consider the following questions:

- Kornbluh cites research claiming that "60 percent of child care arrangements are of poor or mediocre quality" (par. 13). Looking back, how would you rate your child-care arrangements?

- Based on your experience, what kinds of child-care arrangements do you think would serve children and their parents best today?

ANALYZING WRITING STRATEGIES

● ● ● ●
Basic Features

Your instructor may assign these activities in class or as homework for you to do by yourself or with classmates.

● A Well-Defined Problem

Every proposal begins with a problem. What writers say about the problem and how much space they devote to it depend on what they assume their readers already know and think about the problem.

Some problems require more explanation than others. For problems that are new to readers, writers not only need to explain the problem but also need to convince readers that it exists and is serious enough to justify taking the actions the writer thinks are necessary to solve it. Kornbluh assumes readers will not be familiar with key aspects of the problem she is writing about, so she spends the first part of her essay introducing the problem and the second part establishing the problem's existence and seriousness.

To analyze how Kornbluh defines the problem, do the following:

- Skim the first two sections, highlighting each time she uses some form of the word *flexibility.*

- Write a few sentences explaining how Kornbluh establishes that there is a lack of workplace flexibility for the "juggler family" and why it is a serious problem that needs to be solved.

● A Well-Argued Solution

You have seen that O'Malley gives three reasons why he thinks a greater number of brief exams will solve the problem he addresses and how he supports each reason with published research studies as well as his own experience. Kornbluh does not have to prove that her proposed solution would help solve the problem because it is obvious that a flexible work schedule would help juggler families juggle their responsibilities. But she does have to argue that her solution is feasible (possible). Readers of essays proposing a solution to a problem need to be told precisely what the solution is that the writer is advocating. Therefore, writers describe the proposed solution simply and directly in a way that readers cannot miss.

O'Malley presents his solution in his title, as does Kornbluh. But they both go on to describe the solution and to argue for it by trying to convince readers that the proposed solution would help solve the problem, is feasible, and could be implemented within a reasonable time and budget.

To analyze how Kornbluh argues that her solution can be implemented, try the following:

- Reread paragraph 5, where she sets out some general principles, and paragraphs 16–22, where she details what is needed to implement her solution. As you read, highlight the guidelines for what employees as well as what employers should do, and also underline the *would, should,* and *could* verb forms.

- Write a few sentences explaining how well you think the procedure she outlines satisfies the goals Kornbluh sets out in paragraph 5. What, if anything, do you think is missing?

▪ Add a sentence speculating about why Kornbluh uses *would, should,* and *could* verb forms, as O'Malley does in paragraph 3 of his essay.

● An Effective Counterargument

Writers of essays proposing solutions need to anticipate other solutions their readers may prefer. O'Malley, for example, brings up several alternative solutions his readers might prefer: implementing programs to improve students' study skills, giving students frequent study questions, and handing out possible exam topics to help students prepare. He acknowledges the benefits of some of these solutions but also points out their shortcomings, arguing that his solution is preferable to the alternatives.

To analyze how Kornbluh anticipates alternative solutions and counterargues, do the following:

▪ Reread paragraphs 10–12.

▪ Write a sentence or two for each alternative solution she brings up in paragraphs 16–22, explaining what the solution is and how effectively she handles it.

● A Readable Plan

Writers sometimes use headings to make it easy for readers to follow the argument. In long proposals, headings can be especially helpful. But what do you think they add to a short essay like this one?

To analyze how Kornbluh uses headings, follow these suggestions:

▪ Skim the essay, noting how each heading functions.

▪ Write a few sentences describing the function of the headings and indicating whether you think they are helpful.

▪ Add another sentence or two comparing Kornbluh's headings to the headings in Robert Kuttner's essay (pp. 227–32), if you have read that essay as well.

CONSIDERING TOPICS FOR YOUR OWN ESSAY

Consider making a proposal to improve the operation of an organization, a business, or a club to which you belong. For example, you might propose that your college keep administrative offices open in the evenings or on weekends to accommodate working students or that a child-care center be opened for students who are parents of young children. For a business, you might propose a system to handle customer complaints or a fairer way for employees to arrange their schedules. If you belong to a club that has a problem with the collection of dues, you might propose a new collection system or suggest alternative ways of raising money.

ROBERT KUTTNER is a journalist and economist who cofounded the Economic Policy Institute as well as the journal the *American Prospect,* of which he is also a coeditor. A regular columnist for *Business Week* and the *Boston Globe,* his essays have appeared in such distinguished publications as the *New York Times Magazine,* the *Atlantic,* the *New Yorker, Harvard Business Review,* and the *New England Journal of Medicine.* His most recent books include *The Squandering of America: How the Failure of Our Politics Undermines Our Prosperity* (2007) and *Obama's Challenge: America's Economic Crisis and the Power of a Transformative Presidency* (2008). He has taught at various colleges including Harvard's Institute of Politics and the University of California at Berkeley.

This proposal originally appeared in the *American Prospect* in May 2008, months before the "severe recession" he predicts was in full swing. As you read Kuttner's essay, consider whether any of his ideas have been implemented since he wrote it, and if so, how effective they have been.

Good Jobs for Americans Who Help Americans

Robert Kuttner

For three decades, the supply of good jobs has been dwindling. The causes include globalization, deregulation, and weaker worker protections, such as minimum-wage laws and government defense of the right to unionize. Now, after three decades of stagnant incomes, we are heading for a severe recession. Higher unemployment will reduce worker bargaining power even further. The cure will require a much more active government role in the economy — both as a regulator and as a source of funds.

Let's have a national policy to make every human-service job a good job.

In the same 30 years, the service sector has exploded as a source of jobs. The American work force has gone from 28 percent factory workers and 72 percent service workers in 1978 to 16 percent factory workers and 84 percent service workers today. But the service sector encompasses tens of millions of bad jobs — in routine clerical work, retail sales, fast food, low-end human services — and a relatively small number of very well compensated professional positions, among them doctor, lawyer, scientist, and investment banker.

Here is a very straightforward proposal. Let's have a national policy to make every human-service job a good job — one that pays a living wage with good benefits, and includes adequate training, professional status, and the prospect of advancement — a career rather than casual labor.

Don't Mourn — Professionalize

These, after all, are jobs caring for our parents, our children, and ourselves. Transforming all human-service work into good jobs would not merely replenish the supply of decent work. It would vastly improve the quality of care delivered to the elderly at home or in institutions; to young children in pre-kindergartens or day-care facilities; and to sick people whether in hospitals, hospices, outpatient settings, or their homes.

These are also the jobs that cannot be outsourced. Even if we succeed in reviving American manufacturing, the process of automation means that America is almost certain to become even more of a service economy over time. Good service-sector jobs can help replace good factory jobs.

Many economists once thought that widening income inequality was caused in part by the shift to a service economy. Factory jobs, the argument went, tended to pay above the median wage because each job added a lot of value. The more productive and capital-intensive the machinery became over time, the more value each job added. So by the mid-20th century, industrial workers could command middle-class wages and good fringe benefits. By contrast, human-service jobs were hands-on and labor intensive. A nursing-home worker or a pre-k teacher was low-tech. So the pay was low, too.

We now know that this picture was highly misleading. How do we know? Just look at the global economy. Autoworkers in Mexico use the same production technology as workers in Michigan, but their pay is about $2 an hour. In China, autoworkers may earn 50 cents a day. American autoworkers were paid middle-class wages not because of something inherent about making cars but because the United Auto Workers had the power to negotiate good wages. Conversely, Scandinavia has no low-wage human-service workers because it has made a decision that everyone who takes care of the sick, the old, or the young is a professional or at least a paraprofessional and is compensated as such.

Since most human-service costs are paid socially, choices about how to compensate workers are social decisions. In the United States, with our meager social outlay, we define these human-service positions as low-wage, casual jobs. In the Nordic countries, the people who work in pre-kindergartens or child-care centers are either teachers or apprentice teachers. In France, to work in a *crèche maternelle*,[1] you need more qualifications than a public school teacher — additional courses in child development and public health. When I recently

3

4

5

6

7

8

---

[1] A French communal nursery or child-care facility for children from birth to three years old.

interviewed Michel Rocard, who served as French prime minister from 1988–1991, he told me that his proudest success in resisting austerity demands was preventing the budget-cutters from reducing the qualifications and pay of pre-kindergarten teachers.

9   But in America, how can we possibly make all human-service jobs into good jobs? And aren't some of these jobs inherently low-skill? How much training, after all, does it take to empty a bedpan or change linen?

All It Takes Is Money

10   Start with the fact that at least 60 percent of the funding for these jobs is ultimately public money. Government pays upward of half of all health-care costs through Medicare, Medicaid, the State Children's Health Insurance Program, the Veterans Administration, and the health insurance of public employees. Forty-five percent of nursing-home care is paid by Medicaid. Home care is heavily subsidized by public agencies. And in early childhood education and day care, while the affluent may have nannies or private day-care arrangements, Head Start is a public program, and state, local, and federal agencies subsidize day care through a variety of social-service programs.

11   Clearly, the government has the leverage to set standards. The federal Davis-Bacon Act is a rough model. It was enacted in 1931 to assure that nonunion construction contractors would not undercut prevailing wage scales. Davis-Bacon requires that all federally funded construction pay prevailing wages, which in practice turns out to mean union-scale wages.

12   Davis-Bacon, of course, has its critics. There was a time when union bargaining power was accused of stimulating inflation by driving contract settlements that increased wages and benefits in excess of the rate of productivity growth. But whatever the reality of that long-ago charge, that time is long gone. Today, the problem is the opposite — wages lag far behind productivity increases, and the gains go instead to the top.

13   America needs a good-jobs strategy. And human-service jobs are a good place to begin.

14   How would such a transformation happen? Congress could require that any job in the human services supported in whole or in part by federal funds would have to pay a professional wage and be part of a career track. A minimum starting annual salary might be $24,000 a year, or about $12 an hour, an increase from the current common wage of around $9 an hour for nurse's-aide and home-care workers, and a sharp jump from the median wage of $7.69 for direct child-care providers. Opportunities for genuine advancement with pay increases would have to be part of the plan. For example, instead of defining a nurse's aide as a high-turnover, low-qualification, low-pay occupation, the job would require substantially more training, much of which could be done on the job. Such jobs would also be entry points to higher-level positions, such as licensed practical nurse. With more training and qualifications, these workers could be entrusted with more responsibilities, and nursing-home residents would get better care.

In the area of pre-kindergarten and day care, all such jobs would be teaching jobs   15
rather than the high-turnover, largely custodial jobs of the current system. Raising the
qualifications and pay of pre-k teachers, at least to the level of public school teachers,
would be part of a national strategy of universal pre-kindergarten.

What of the argument that you don't need much training to baby-sit kids   16
or provide basic care to senescent old folks? In fact, the development of young
children and the quality of life of the elderly are profoundly affected by the quality of their caregivers. One of the best established findings of recent research on
child development is that a dollar invested in early childhood education is one of
the most cost-effective investments we can make. (See the *Prospect*'s December
2007 special report, "Life Chances: The Case for Early Investment in Our Kids.")
The difference between child-development and baby-sitting, of course, is the availability of well-trained professionals who work with young children. Likewise, in the
care of the elderly, having well-trained people improves not just seniors' comfort
but seniors' physical health, cognitive stimulation, and capacity to live fulfilling lives.

We have seen a rough model of this kind of upgrading and professionalization   17
in the strategies of unions that represent home-care workers. Home-care workers
are often classified as independent contractors. As a result, they have no bargaining
power, and public and nonprofit agencies often try to solve their own budget problems by paying home-care workers as little as possible. This creates a vicious circle
of burnout and high turnover, even though the vast majority of these workers are conscientious and eager to perform well. Recently, in several states led by California,
the Service Employees International Union (SEIU) and the American Federation of
State, County and Municipal Employees succeeded in persuading legislatures and
governors to approve laws or executive orders establishing public agencies with
which home-care workers could bargain collectively. In California, the typical wage
went from minimum wage to $10 an hour.

Another pressing need is public subsidy to help low-wage human-service work-   18
ers ascend career ladders. In some occupations, these ladders exist in principle, and
there are heartening individual stories of the nurse's aide who graduated to licensed
practical nurse, or the classroom aide who went to night school and earned a teaching credential. Despite a few model programs, our society seems determined to
make this path as arduous as possible. Almost by definition, someone working for
$6 or $7 an hour, often with family responsibilities, has an extreme shortage of time
as well as money. Though some rare individuals do succeed, it takes uncommon
tenacity and self-sacrifice, and sometimes the sacrifice of one's own children. Why
should we make this so hard? Other societies provide subsidies for living expenses
during training.

This effort would be part of two broader labor-policy shifts that America sorely   19
needs. First, we need to reverse the trend toward casualization of labor that has
been occurring for three decades. One of the great advances of the 20th century was
regularization of the employment relationship. Through successful social struggle,
growth of unions, and enactment of legislation, most jobs came to provide decent
wages and fringe benefits. Workers could not be fired without cause. Loyalty to the

firm was reciprocated. Grievance systems were created and respected. Economists termed these jobs primary labor-market jobs. Casual, secondary labor-market jobs, which paid less and offered no such guarantees, continued to exist, but they were the exception. In recent years, however, the shift to casual jobs has become the norm, and in low-paid human-service work, casual, high-turnover jobs are the industry standard.

20   Second, the upgrading of human-service work would reverse another insidious trend — the employer's habit of trying to increase the efficiency of labor by fragmenting jobs into separate tasks and paying the lowest possible wage for each task — a strategy known as Taylorism, after the early 20th-century "efficiency expert," Fredrick Winslow Taylor, who first recommended it.

21   However, when it comes to human services, many of the supposed gains of Taylorism are false economies. Studies of nursing homes have shown that better trained and paid workers can head off expensive conditions such as bedsores. Whereas registered nurses once performed a multiplicity of tasks and became very familiar with each patient, many hospitals have created a plethora of lower-wage occupations — phlebotomists to draw blood, technicians to perform tests, nurse's aides to take blood pressures — leaving the RN to cover more patients and do a far narrower range of tasks. But when the Massachusetts General Hospital ran an experiment, putting all care on one floor directly in the hands of RNs, the results were better patient outcomes and a more efficient use of human resources. The upgrading of human-service work would be part of an overdue process of reversing Taylorism. More workers would use a broader range of human skills to care for whole human beings.

But How Much Money?

22   A rough estimate of the cost of upgrading all low-wage human-service work into decent professional career paths is about $150 billion a year. A generally accepted figure of the cost of providing universal, high-quality pre-kindergarten and child care is about $50 billion a year. Upgrading existing jobs in day care for older children, care of seniors, and low-wage hospital-based work would cost roughly another $100 billion.

23   Isn't that a lot of money? It certainly is, if you're invoking conventional budget assumptions that predate the current recession and financial collapse — though it's not a lot of money compared to the cost of military operations in Iraq and Afghanistan, which is now budgeted at $188 billion annually. To put this in perspective, $150 billion a year is approximately 1 percent of gross domestic product.

24   But for the rest of this decade, and perhaps well beyond, the American economy faces two huge challenges. The first is to dig out of the most serious financial collapse since the Great Depression and its spillover effects into the rest of the economy. The second is to restore the income of American workers.

25   A strategy that increases Americans' purchasing power can take a variety of forms. Besides good human-service jobs, it could include massive public spending on deferred public infrastructure needs, as well as a green recovery path, creating new alternative-energy industries and jobs retrofitting homes and offices. Both

strategies would also create decent job opportunities. Enacting the Employee Free Choice Act, protecting collective bargaining rights, would also increase the ability of workers to bargain for a decent share of the pie.

Voters are only going to embrace serious public spending if we think big. The promise of millions of good service-sector jobs that can't be exported — providing superior care to our children, our parents, and ourselves — is an example of the kind of idea that could capture the national imagination and rekindle the necessary political support for serious public outlay. This is the kind of idea that could be embraced by a broad coalition of experts, opinion leaders, editorial writers, grass-roots groups — and the next administration. It touches a national nerve of anxiety about where the good jobs will be for our children — and who will take care of us as we age.

26

I don't mean to suggest that we should ignore the upgrading of other service jobs. As our friends at the SEIU have shown, collective bargaining can improve janitor jobs as well as jobs of home-care workers, just as unions once upgraded factory jobs. The labor union UNITE-HERE has turned low-wage hotel jobs into middle-class jobs. We need a decent-work strategy for the whole economy. But human services are one place where the federal government has direct leverage.

27

Before this recession is over, we will need to find several hundred billion dollars a year for a recovery strategy — and what better place to begin than by restoring workers' paychecks? We can find that money by reclaiming progressive taxation, by defending deficit spending in a deep recession, by shifting federal dollars from a pointless war to a domestic recovery, and reviving trade unionism. The political situation is comparable to the one that Franklin Roosevelt faced in 1933. Policies that were unthinkable yesterday are just the bare beginning of an adequate response today.

28

MAKING CONNECTIONS: PROFESSIONALIZING SERVICE JOBS

Although Kuttner focuses on human service jobs, he starts out by talking more generally about the explosion of jobs in the "service sector." These include jobs in fast-food restaurants and in stores like Walmart, jobs with which you may have experience. You may also have experience babysitting or doing other human service jobs.

With two or three other students, discuss Kuttner's argument that such jobs should be professionalized, with jobholders given "adequate training" and "the prospect of advancement" as well as being paid a "living wage" (par. 3). Begin by taking turns briefly telling about your experience in the service sector, or any other work experience that you think is relevant — for example, as a camp counselor or tutor. Then, together consider the following questions:

- Were you given adequate training, possibilities for advancement, and/or a living wage? If you were not given any of them, why not? Should you have been given them?

- How does the practice of Taylorism that Kuttner explains in paragraphs 20–21 apply to the work you have done? Do you agree with Kuttner that Taylorism ought to be eliminated?

ANALYZING WRITING STRATEGIES

Basic Features

● A Well-Defined Problem

One of the most persuasive strategies for writing a proposal is to define the problem in terms of its causes and then to propose a solution that eliminates those causes. Kornbluh employs this strategy when she cites a lack of flexibility in the workplace as a principal cause of the "juggler family" problem and then, logically, argues that the problem can be fixed by adding flexibility to the workplace.

To analyze how Kuttner defines the problem in terms of its possible causes, try the following:

- Reread the first three paragraphs, noting where he talks about the causes of the problem and forecasts his proposed "cure."

- Write a couple of sentences explaining the connection between one or more of the causes he lists and the cure or solution he proposes.

● A Well-Argued Solution

Like the other writers in this chapter, Kuttner argues for his solution, in part, by demonstrating that it is feasible because it can be implemented. For example, in paragraph 14, he explicitly raises the question likely to be on readers' minds: "How would such a transformation happen?" He then offers specific details and examples to show how his proposed solution could be put into effect. Similarly, in paragraph 17, Kuttner argues that his proposal is workable by pointing out that it has already been done for "home-care workers."

In addition to arguing that the solution is feasible, proposal writers also usually offer reasons claiming that the proposed solution is a good idea because it has this or that particular benefit. For example, O'Malley's main reason for frequent exams is that students learn more and do better on subsequent assignments (par. 4). He assumes that, like him, his readers place a high value on learning. This value is the common ground on which he tries to build a logical argument. If he can convince readers that frequent exams do indeed foster better learning, then he is likely also to convince them to accept his solution.

To analyze how Kuttner argues for his solution, follow these suggestions:

- Reread paragraphs 4–5, and write a sentence or two summarizing the two reasons Kuttner offers for his proposed solution.

- Choose one of these reasons, and add a few sentences explaining the value that underlies Kuttner's argument and why he assumes the argument based on it will be likely to convince his readers.

● An Effective Counterargument

Writers often announce objections and questions they are counterarguing. Kuttner, for example, introduces an objection in paragraph 6 this way: "Many economists once thought. . . ." In the next paragraph, he begins his counterargument with "We now know. . . ." He then uses the rhetorical question "How do we know?" to anticipate the question readers are likely to be thinking themselves.

To answer the question and support his argument, Kuttner compares American wages for factory and human service workers to those of other countries, showing that there is no universal agreement about the value of one kind of work over another and that "choices about how to compensate workers are social decisions" (par. 8). Convincing readers of this point is crucial because if wages are based on "choices," then we can do what he proposes in paragraph 3 — set a new "national policy to make every human-service job a good job."

To analyze how Kuttner responds to possible objections, follow these suggestions:

- Reread paragraphs 11–12 and 16, and write a few sentences briefly summarizing the objections Kuttner anticipates in these paragraphs and assessing how he refutes them.

- Alternatively, reread paragraphs 20–21, and write a couple of sentences explaining Taylorism and how Kuttner argues against it. What is the implicit objection that he is counterarguing?

● A Readable Plan

Because proposals present a complex, multipart argument — to establish the seriousness of the problem, to convince readers that the proposed solution is feasible, and to refute objections and persuade readers that the proposed solution is better than alternatives — writers try to make it easy for readers to navigate the essay. Among the cueing strategies writers use to orient readers are the use of transitional words and phrases, and rhetorical questions.

Transitions or connectives help readers understand the logical connection between one paragraph or sentence and the one that follows. Here is a brief chart showing several transitions and the logical relationships they signal:

Function	Transitional Words and Phrases
To introduce another item in a series	first . . . second; in addition; moreover; furthermore
To introduce an example or illustration	for example; that is; in particular; specifically
To counterargue	but; however; nevertheless; in contrast; neither
To concede an objection	granted; of course; to be sure; certainly
To resume the argument after acknowledging an objection or alternative solution	nonetheless; even though; still; all the same

In addition to logical transitions, writers may also use rhetorical questions to orient readers. **Rhetorical questions** are questions writers pose but then go on to answer themselves. For example, Patrick O'Malley uses this rhetorical question to make a transition from arguing for his proposed solution to counterarguing possible objections: "Why, then, do so few professors give frequent brief exams?" (par. 7).

To analyze how Kuttner uses logical transitions and/or rhetorical questions to make his argument easy to follow, consider these suggestions:

- Find two examples in Kuttner's essay of logical transitions or rhetorical questions (or one example of each), and determine how each example functions.
- Write a couple of sentences describing how they work.

For a more complete discussion of transitions, see Chapter 10, Cueing the Reader.

For additional uses of rhetorical questions in essays proposing solutions, see A Sentence Strategy: Rhetorical Questions on pp. 249–51.

CONSIDERING TOPICS FOR YOUR OWN ESSAY

Kuttner's topic suggests a type of proposal you might want to consider for your essay — a proposal to improve the living or working conditions of a group of people. You could focus on a particular category of people and a problem they face. For example, think of ways to help elderly and infirm people in your community who need transportation or elementary-school kids who have no after-school programs. Think, too, about solutions to problems that affect students — for example, the creation of job-training or referral programs to help college students find work on or near campus, or recycling and "green" energy solutions that will help students living in dorms limit their impact on the environment.

Guide to Writing

The Writing Assignment

Write an essay proposing a solution to a problem. Choose a problem faced by a community or group to which you belong, and address your proposal to one or more members of the group or to outsiders who might help solve the problem.

This Guide to Writing will help you apply what you have learned about how proposal writers clearly define a problem, argue effectively for a particular solution, and present counterarguments to possible objections and alternative solutions. The Guide is divided into five sections with various activities in each section:

- **Invention and Research**
- **Planning and Drafting**
- **Critical Reading Guide**
- **Revising**
- **Editing and Proofreading**

The Guide is designed to escort you through the writing process, from deciding which problem to address to editing your finished essay. Your instructor may require you to follow the Guide to Writing from beginning to end. Working through the Guide in this way will help you — as it has helped many other college students — write a thoughtful, fully developed, polished essay.

If, however, your instructor gives you latitude to choose and if you have had experience writing a proposal, then you can decide on the order in which you'll do the activities in the Guide to Writing. For example, the Invention and Research section includes activities to help you find a problem to write about, analyze and define it, identify your readers, and find a tentative solution, among other things. Obviously, choosing a problem to write about must precede the other activities, but you may come to the Guide with a problem already in mind and want to focus first on exploring how you would solve it before deciding how to establish that the problem exists and is serious. In fact, you may find your response to one of the invention activities expanding into a draft before you have had a chance to do any of the other activities. That is a good thing — but you should later flesh out your draft by going back to the activities you skipped and layering the new material into your draft.

The following chart will help you find answers to many of the questions you might have about planning, drafting, and revising an essay proposing a solution to a problem. The page references in the right-hand column refer to examples from the readings and activities in the Guide to Writing.

Starting Points: Proposing a Solution

● ● ● ● **Basic Features**

Choosing a Problem to Write About

How do I come up with a problem to write about?	• Considering Topics for Your Own Essay (pp. 226, 235) • Choosing a Problem to Write About (pp. 238–40) • Testing Your Choice (p. 243)

A Well-Defined Problem

How can I best define the problem for my readers?	• Ways In: Bringing the Problem and Your Audience into Focus (pp. 240–41) • Refining Your Purpose and Setting Goals: Defining the Problem (pp. 246–47) • Working with Sources: Establishing the Problem's Existence and Seriousness (pp. 251–53)

A Well-Argued Solution

How do I come up with a plausible solution?	• Listing Possible Solutions (pp. 241–42) • Refining Your Purpose and Setting Goals: Describing the Proposed Solution (p. 247)
How do I construct an argument supporting my solution?	• Ways In: Exploring Your Tentative Solution: Constructing an Argument (p. 242) • Researching Your Proposal (p. 245)

An Effective Counterargument

How do I counter possible objections to my solution?	• Ways In: Exploring Your Tentative Solution: Planning a Counterargument (p. 243) • Refining Your Purpose and Setting Goals: Counterarguing Readers' Objections (p. 247)
How do I respond to possible alternative solutions?	• Ways In: Counterarguing Alternative Solutions (p. 244) • Researching Your Proposal (p. 245) • Refining Your Purpose and Setting Goals: Counterarguing Alternative Solutions (p. 247)

(continued)

(continued)

A Readable Plan	
How can I help my readers follow my argument?	• Formulating a Tentative Thesis Statement (pp. 245–46) • Outlining Your Draft (p. 248) • A Sentence Strategy: Rhetorical Questions (pp. 249–51)

Invention and Research

The following invention activities are easy to complete and take only a few minutes. Spreading out the activities over several days will stimulate your creativity, enabling you to consider many more potential problems to address and possible ways in which to address them.

Remember to keep a written record of your invention work: You will need it when you draft the essay and later when you revise it.

Choosing a Problem to Write About

List several problems that you might like to explore. This will come more easily to some of us than to others. As you explore possibilities, bear in mind that you are looking for a problem that meets the following criteria:

Criteria for Choosing a Problem: A Checklist

The problem should be

☐ important to you and of concern to others;

☐ solvable, at least in part;

☐ one that you can research in the time you have;

☐ one that you can explore in detail and are willing to discuss in writing.

If you're like most people, you'll need some help in coming up with a number of good options. To get your juices flowing, you might first try rereading the Considering Topics for Your Own Essay activities following the readings and recalling any problems those suggestions brought to mind. Reread any notes you might have made in response to these suggestions. For further ideas, consult the suggestions in the following sections.

Making a Chart

Divide a piece of paper or a new file on your computer screen into two columns. In the left-hand column, list communities you are part of (for example, your residence hall, gym, or hometown), groups you have joined (for example, a sports team, multiplayer online game site, or garage band), organizations to which you belong (for example, your high school, church, or a local photography museum), and places you have worked (for example, a coffee shop, community pool, or college radio station). In the right-hand column, list any problems that exist within each context. Here is how such a chart might look:

Community/Group/Work	Problem
School	lousy food noisy residence halls lack of enough sections of required courses no school spirit too few computers in library
My Neighborhood	need for traffic signal at dangerous intersection run down lack of safe places for children to play terrible zoning laws (factory next to housing development)
Work (radio station)	inadequate training conflicts with supervisor unfair shift assignments unsatisfactory facilities
Still Alive (band)	too little time to practice no good place to practice too few venues for performance crazy expenses for equipment
Volunteer Work (tutoring)	disorganized schedules no money for materials no training apathetic students

Proposing to solve a problem in a group or community to which you belong or a workplace with which you are familiar gives you an important advantage: You can write as an expert. You know the history of the problem, have felt the urgency to solve it, and perhaps have already thought of possible solutions. Equally important, you will know to whom to address the proposal, and you can interview others in the group to get their views of the problem and your solution. From such a position of knowledge and authority comes confident, convincing writing.

Should you want to propose a solution for a problem of national scope, concentrate on one with which you have direct experience and for which you can suggest a detailed plan of action. Even better, focus on unique local aspects of the problem. For example, if you are concerned about the rise of smoking among young people, you can offer a solution for a particular location or organization — for example, you could organize an information campaign on campus.

Using the Web to Find or Explore a Problem

While we encourage you to "go local" with the problem you treat in this essay, exploring Web sites where people write about similar problems and about potential solutions might inspire you. Moreover, the Web provides a rich repository of cultural and historical information, including photographs and music, which you might be able to use to create a richly detailed, multimedia text for your readers.

Here are some suggestions:

- Look for sites related to the community, workplace, or group you are writing about. See if others have noted problems that are the same as or similar to those you have noted. Do they offer solutions? Do these solutions seem viable, or at least worth exploring?

- Consider getting in touch with others who are concerned about the problem that concerns you. If your conversation is fruitful, ask their permission to include their insights in your project.

- Do a Google search on a particular problem, and try to get a sense of how common it might be — or, in contrast, of how specific it might be to your local group or workplace.

Make notes of any ideas, memories, or insights suggested by your online research, and download any visuals you might include in your essay, being sure to get the information necessary to cite any online sources. (See pp. 505–7 for the MLA citation format for electronic sources.)

Ways in: Bringing the Problem and Your Audience into Focus

Basic Features

Once you have made a preliminary choice of a problem, try the following activities to help you understand the problem, determine what else you need to find out about it, and discover ways of defining the problem for your readers. You can begin with whichever activity you want, but wherever you begin, be sure to return to the other activities to fill in the details.

Identifying Your Possible Readers

In a few sentences, explore your readers. In addition to your instructor and classmates, think about writing to people who are affected by the problem or those in a position to take action to solve it. The following questions will help you develop an understanding of your readers:

- *How informed are my readers likely to be about the problem? Have they shown any awareness of it?*
- *Why would my readers care about solving this problem?*
- *Have my readers supported any other proposals to solve this problem? If so, what do those proposals have in common with mine?*
- *What values and concerns do my readers and I share that could bring us together to solve the problem?*

Analyzing the Problem

Explore What You Know. *Figure out what you know now about the problem and what you still need to find out by jotting down answers to the questions below:*

- *How do I know the problem exists and that it is serious?*
- *What could cause a problem like this?*
- *Who suffers from the problem? What evidence of it have I seen or experienced myself?*
- *Who, if anyone, would benefit from* not *changing the way things work now?*

Identify Research Questions.

- *Where can I find a history of the problem, details describing its negative consequences, statistics, or expert analyses?*
- *Are there people I could interview to get additional information?*
- *If an institution or organization is part of the problem, can I find public information about its funding or budget and about the way it operates? Can I interview its leadership, employees, and customers or clients?*

● Defining the Problem

Write a paragraph or two describing the problem for your readers. Be as specific and vivid in your explanation as possible given the information you currently have. Writing a very rough draft of this part of your essay should help clarify what additional information you will need.

● Listing Possible Solutions

It usually helps to consider several possible solutions before focusing on one solution, so problem solving requires creativity. *Use the following questions to help you make a list of creative solutions you could consider for your essay:*

- Can you adapt a solution that has already been tried or proposed for related problems?
- What smaller, more manageable aspect of the larger problem could you solve?
- Could re-imagining the goal help you make fundamental changes?
- Could the problem be solved from the bottom up instead of from the top down?
- Could an ongoing process help solve the problem?

● Making a Tentative Choice

In a sentence or two, describe the solution you want to explore further. You cannot know for certain whether you will be able to construct a convincing argument to support this solution, but you should choose a solution that you feel motivated to pursue.

Ways in: Exploring Your Tentative Solution

●● Basic Features

These activities will help you decide whether you can support your tentative solution and respond to your readers' likely objections. You can begin with whichever activity you want, but wherever you begin, be sure to return to the other activities to fill in the details.

Constructing an Argument

Explain Why It Would Solve the Problem. *Write for a few minutes explaining why you think this solution could solve the problem.* For example, would it

- eliminate one or more causes?
- change people's attitudes?
- re-imagine the objective?
- reduce anxiety and tension?

Show Why It Is Possible. *Write for a few minutes explaining why people could agree to put the solution into effect.* For example, what would it cost them in time or money?

Explain How It Could Be Implemented. *Write down the major stages or steps necessary to carry out your solution.* This list of steps will provide an early test of whether your solution can, in fact, be implemented.

Plan Follow-Up Research. Add notes about the kinds of information you think would help make your argument convincing for your readers and where you think you can find this information.

Planning a Counterargument

Anticipate Objections. *Write a few sentences responding to the following objections you think are most likely:*

- We can't afford it.
- It would take too long.
- People would not do it.
- Too few would benefit.
- You would benefit personally.
- We already tried that, with unsatisfactory results.

Plan Follow-Up Research. Add notes about the kinds of information you think would help make your counterargument convincing for your readers and where you think you can find this information.

Testing Your Choice

Now test your choice by asking yourself the following questions:

- *Do I understand the problem well enough to convince my readers that it really exists and is serious?*
- *Do I have some idea of how to argue that my solution is feasible — that it really can solve the problem and that it can be implemented?*
- *Will I be able to answer objections readers are likely to raise?*
- *Do I know enough about the problem, or can I learn what I need to know in the time remaining?*

As you plan and draft your proposal, you will probably want to consider these questions again. If at any point you cannot answer them with a confident yes, you may want to consider proposing a different solution to the problem or choose a different problem to write about. If you have serious doubts, consider discussing them with your instructor.

A Collaborative Activity:
Testing Your Choice

Get together with two or three other students, and present your proposal to one another.

Presenters: Take turns briefly defining the problem you hope to solve, identifying your intended readers, and describing your proposed solution.

Listeners: Tell the presenter whether the proposed solution seems feasible for the situation and intended readers. Suggest objections you have or the intended readers are likely to have. Tell the writer if you know of any alternative solutions to the problem.

Ways in: Counterarguing Alternative Solutions

Basic Features

These activities will help you counterargue your readers' alternative solutions. You can begin with whichever activity you want, but wherever you begin, be sure to return to the other activities to fill in the details.

Using the Web to Research Alternative Solutions

Do online research to identify at least two alternative solutions to your problem and gather information to evaluate them. To search, try the following:

- entering various keywords into a search engine such as Google.
- adding the word *government* to a Google search.
- entering your keywords on FirstGov.gov.
- going to the Library of Congress Internet Resource Page on State and Local Governments (www.loc.gov/global/state/).

Bookmark promising sites. If you download or copy information, record source information.

Considering Alternative Solutions

List two or three alternative solutions that others have proposed or tried. You may have discovered these alternatives during interviews or in your library research. You do not have to list every solution that has been mentioned, but you should include the most popular or serious alternatives. If you include only obviously weak solutions in your argument, your credibility will be harmed and you could be accused of committing the *straw man fallacy*, which involves directing your counterargument against an alternative that nobody takes seriously anyway.

Developing Your Counterargument

Write a paragraph for each alternative solution you think you should include in your argument. Describe the alternative solution fairly, quoting supporters if possible. Then work out the reasons you believe the alternative solution

- would not be feasible,
- would not solve the problem,
- would not be approved,
- would be hard to implement, or
- would be too costly, disruptive, or time-consuming to put into effect.

Researching Your Proposal

You may have already identified research questions about the problem and made notes about the kinds of information you need to support your argument and counterargument. Doing research with your questions and notes in mind will help you work efficiently. But researching sometimes is most productive when you have the time to go into unexplored territory. You may find support for your argument, but you also may find contradictory evidence and decide to change your plans as a result.

If you are proposing a solution to a problem about which others have written, you will want to do library and Internet research to find out how they have defined the problem and what solutions they have proposed or tried. If you are proposing a solution to a problem in a group or workplace, you may want to conduct interviews to see how people are affected by the problem, what they know about its history, what solutions they prefer, and how they react to your solution.

Defining Your Purpose for Your Readers

Write a few sentences defining your purpose. Remember that you have already identified your readers and developed your proposal with these readers in mind. Try now to define your purpose by considering the following questions:

- *Do I seek incremental, moderate, or radical change? Am I being realistic about what my readers are prepared to support? How can I overcome their likely resistance to change?*

- *How can I ensure that my readers will not remain indifferent to the problem?*

- *Whom can I count on for support, and what can I do to secure that support? Who will oppose my solution? Shall I write them off or seek common ground with them?*

- *What exactly do I want my readers to do — take my proposed solution as a starting point for further discussion? Take action immediately? Take preliminary steps, like seeking funding or testing the feasibility of the solution?*

Formulating a Tentative Thesis Statement

Write one or more sentences to serve as your tentative thesis statement. In most essays proposing solutions to problems, the thesis statement is a concise announcement of the solution. Think about how emphatic you should make the thesis and whether you should forecast your reasons.

Review the readings in this chapter to see how other writers construct their thesis statements. For example, recall that Patrick O'Malley states his thesis in paragraph 2:

> If professors gave additional brief exams at frequent intervals, students would be spurred to study more regularly, learn more, worry less, and perform better on midterms, finals, and other papers and projects.

O'Malley's thesis announces his solution — brief, frequent exams — and lists the reasons students would benefit from the solution. (A forecast of reasons is not a requirement in a thesis, but it does enable readers to predict the stages of the argument, thereby increasing their understanding.)

As you draft your own thesis, pay attention to the language you use. It should be clear and unambiguous, emphatic but appropriately qualified. Although you will probably refine your thesis as you draft and revise your essay, trying now to articulate it will help give your planning and drafting direction and impetus.

For more on thesis and forecasting statements, see Chapter 10.

Planning and Drafting

The following activities will help you refine your purpose, set goals for your draft, and outline it. In addition, this section will help you write a draft by writing opening sentences, trying out a useful sentence strategy, and learning how to work with sources.

Refining Your Purpose and Setting Goals

Before starting to draft, here are some questions that may help you sharpen your purpose for your audience and set goals for your draft. Your instructor may ask you to write out your answers to some of these questions or simply to think about them as you plan and draft your essay.

Clarifying Your Purpose and Audience

- *What do my readers already know about this problem? Should I assume, as O'Malley does, that my readers are unfamiliar with the problem? Or should I assume, as Kornbluh does, that my readers know about the problem but do not realize how serious it is?*

- *How can I gain readers' enthusiastic support? Can I convince them that solving the problem is in everyone's interest, as Kornbluh and Kuttner try to do?*

- *How can I present myself so that I seem both reasonable and authoritative?*

- *Should I aim to show that I am not dictating a one-size-fits-all solution but trying to get those involved to find solutions that work for them, as O'Malley and Kornbluh try to do?*

Defining the Problem

- *How can I demonstrate that the problem really exists? Can I present statistics, as Kornbluh and Kuttner do?*

- *How can I show the seriousness and urgency of the problem? Should I stress negative consequences, as all the writers do? Can I use quotations or cite research to stress the problem's importance, as Kornbluh and Kuttner do?*

- *Will reporting or speculating about the problem's causes or history help readers understand why it needs attention? Can I use comparison and contrast, as Kornbluh does?*
- *How much space should I devote to defining the problem? Only a little space (like O'Malley) or a lot of space (like Kornbluh)?*

Describing the Proposed Solution

- *How can I describe my solution so that it will look like the best way to proceed?*
- *Should I give examples to show how solutions like mine have worked, as Kuttner does? Or should I focus on my reasons to support my solution, as O'Malley does?*
- *Should I make the solution seem easy to implement, as O'Malley does, or should I acknowledge that the solution will require effort and compromise, as Kornbluh does?*

Counterarguing Readers' Objections

- *How do I decide which objections to include?*
- *Should I accommodate or concede certain objections by modifying my proposal, as O'Malley does?*
- *How can I support my refutation? Should I cite statistics or research studies, as Kuttner does?*

Counterarguing Alternative Solutions

- *How do I decide which alternative solutions to mention?*
- *How can I support my refutation of alternative solutions? Can I argue that they are too expensive and time-consuming, as O'Malley does, or that they will not really solve the problem, as Kornbluh does?*
- *How can I reject these other solutions without seeming to criticize their proponents? Can I provide reasons, as O'Malley does, or marshal statistics, as Kornbluh does?*

The Ending

- *How should I conclude? Should I end by summarizing my solution and its advantages, as O'Malley and Kuttner do? Should I end with a scenario suggesting the consequences of a failure to solve the problem? Can I end with an inspiring call to action? Might a shift to humor or satire provide an effective ending?*
- *Is there something special about the problem that I should remind readers of at the end, as Kornbluh does when she urges that an award be given to the companies that lead the way?*

Outlining Your Draft

With your purpose and goals in mind, you might want to make a quick scratch outline that includes the following:

- a clear statement of the problem
- your thesis statement, announcing the proposed solution and forecasting your reasons for it
- your argument for the solution, giving reasons and support
- anticipation of counterarguments and a response to objections readers might have about the proposed solution

This simple plan is nearly always complicated by other factors, however. In outlining your material, you must take into consideration whether readers already recognize the problem, how much agreement exists on the need to solve the problem, and how much attention must be given to readers' likely objections and to alternative solutions.

Here is a possible outline for a proposal where readers may not understand the problem fully:

I. Presentation of the problem

   A. Its existence

   B. Its seriousness

   C. Its causes

II. Consequences of failing to solve the problem

III. Description of the proposed solution

IV. List of steps for implementing the solution

V. Reasons and support for the solution

   A. Acknowledgment of objections

   B. Accommodation or refutation of objections

VI. Consideration of alternative solutions and their disadvantages

VII. Restatement of the proposed solution and its advantages

Your outline will of course reflect your own writing situation. Once you have a working outline, you should not hesitate to change it as necessary while drafting and revising. For instance, you might find it more effective to hold back on presenting your own solution until you have discussed alternative but unacceptable solutions. Or you might find a better way to order the reasons for adopting your proposal. The purpose of an outline is to identify the basic features of your proposal and to help you organize them effectively, not to lock you into a particular structure.

For more on outlining, see Chapter 8.

Drafting

If you have not already begun to draft your essay, this section will help by suggesting how to write your opening sentences, how to use rhetorical questions, and how to cite sources to define the problem. Drafting isn't always a smooth process, so don't be afraid to leave spaces where you don't know what to put in or write notes to yourself about what you could do next. If you get stuck while drafting, go back over your invention writing: You may be able to copy and paste some of it into your evolving draft, or you may find that you need to do some additional invention to fill in details in your draft.

Writing the Opening Sentences

You could try out one or two different ways of beginning your essay — possibly from the list below — but do not agonize over the first sentences because you are likely to discover the best way to begin only after you have written a rough draft. Again, you might want to review your invention writing to see if you have already written something that would work to launch your essay.

To engage your readers' interest from the start, consider the following opening strategies:

- a scenario (like O'Malley)
- statistics (like Kornbluh)
- a historical analogy (like Kuttner)
- a research study
- a comparison to other places where the solution has been tried successfully
- a preview of the negative consequences if the problem goes unsolved
- criticism of an alternative solution

A Sentence Strategy: Rhetorical Questions

As you draft an essay proposing a solution to a problem, you will want to connect with your readers. You will also want readers to become concerned with the seriousness of the problem and thoughtful about the challenge of solving it. Sentences that take the form of *rhetorical questions* can help you achieve these goals.

A **rhetorical question** is conventionally defined as a sentence posing a question to which the writer expects no answer from the reader. In proposals, however, rhetorical questions do important rhetorical work — that is, they assist a writer in realizing a particular purpose, and they influence readers in certain ways. Rhetorical questions are especially helpful for anticipating questions or confusions readers may have. (You might even read rhetorical questions as though they were coming from an essay's intended audience rather than from the writer.) Then the writer can address these questions directly, helping readers to better understand the argument and (the writer hopes) find it plausible.

In "Good Jobs for Americans Who Help Americans," Robert Kuttner uses rhetorical questions to anticipate his readers' questions in a number of ways, two of which are especially notable. Early on in the essay, Kuttner asks:

> How do we know? (par. 7)

This question aims to help readers better understand his proposal. To give readers background to his proposal, Kuttner lays out some arguments for why service jobs in the United States must pay low wages and then asserts that these arguments are mistaken. At this point, readers who are not economics whizzes are likely to be a little bit confused. How exactly are the arguments that Kuttner is critiquing supposed to work? What would count as evidence against them? Why does Kuttner think they are wrong? Kuttner alleviates these readers' worries by identifying with them: "How do we know?" This reassures readers that they are not lost and enables Kuttner to transition into a very clear discussion of the reasons why service jobs are arbitrarily low-paying. Once readers have grasped this argument, they will better understand what motivates Kuttner's proposal to create desirable service jobs in the United States.

At the end of the first section of Kuttner's proposal, before he gets into the policy details, he includes an entire paragraph made up of rhetorical questions:

> But in America, how can we possibly make all human-service jobs into good jobs?
> And aren't some of these jobs inherently low-skill? How much training, after all, does
> it take to empty a bedpan or change linen? (Kuttner, par. 9)

Here Kuttner is also anticipating readers' questions, but he does it ahead of time, before unpacking the details of how his proposal will work. Anticipating questions enables Kuttner to transition to the next topic, and lets him alert readers to which questions are most important and assure readers that he will answer those questions.

The writers in this chapter also use rhetorical questions for these and similar purposes:

- *Engaging readers' attention to or interest in the problem or the proposed solution.*

  > Will it be like the midterm? Did you study enough? Did you study the right things?
  > It's too late to drop the course. So what happens if you fail? (O'Malley, par. 1)

O'Malley uses his rhetorical questions to dramatize the plight of students studying for a high-stakes exam in order to engage his primary readers — professors capable of implementing his solution — and put them in a receptive frame of mind.

- *Orienting readers to a proposal and forecasting the plan of the argument or parts of it.*

  > Why, then, do so few professors give frequent brief exams? (O'Malley, par. 7)

O'Malley uses his rhetorical question as a transition to anticipating professors' likely objections to his proposed solution.

- *Acting as a topic sentence.*

  > How would such a transformation happen? (Kuttner, par. 14)

Isn't that a lot of money? (Kuttner, par. 23)

Kuttner uses each of these rhetorical questions not only as a topic sentence to introduce a paragraph or group of paragraphs, but also to anticipate readers' likely questions. By writing these simple and direct questions, Kuttner seeks to reassure readers that he knows what concerns them and will answer their questions in a straightforward manner.

While Kornbluh avoids rhetorical questions altogether, both Kuttner and O'Malley make significant use of them. Kuttner spreads them throughout the essay, while O'Malley bunches most of his questions in the opening paragraph. Clearly, then, rhetorical questions are useful, but they are not a requirement for a successful proposal. They should serve a specific purpose, and they should not be overused, because readers may begin to find them annoying. Who can blame them?

In addition to using rhetorical questions, you can strengthen your proposal with other kinds of sentences, such as those that introduce concession and refutation (pp. 196–98) and that signal explicitly the logical relationship to a previous sentence.

Working with Sources:
Establishing the Problem's Existence and Seriousness

Statistics can be helpful in establishing that the problem exists and is serious. For example, Patrick O'Malley cites research to support his assertion that students prefer frequent exams to fewer high-stakes exams: "A Harvard study notes students' 'strong preference for frequent evaluation in a course'" (par. 4). But his argument would have been stronger and possibly more convincing if he had cited statistics to support the study's conclusion. All of the other writers in this chapter cite statistics in their proposals. Let us look at some of the ways Karen Kornbluh uses statistics to define the problem.

> Today fully 70 percent of families with children are headed by two working parents or by an unmarried working parent. The "traditional family" of the breadwinner and homemaker has been replaced by the "juggler family," in which no one is home full-time. (par. 1)

Kornbluh begins with an impressive statistic, "fully 70 percent." But what does it mean? Seventy percent of how many? She does not answer this question with a number, but she does make clear that she is talking about nearly three-quarters of all "families with children," a number that we can infer is very large. At other points in the essay, Kornbluh does provide the raw numbers along with statistics such as percentages. Here are a couple of examples:

> In addition to working parents, there are over 44.4 million Americans who provide care to another adult, often an older relative. Fifty-nine percent of these caregivers either work or have worked while providing care ("Caregiving"). (par. 8)

> Over half of workers today have no control over scheduling alternative start and end times at work (Galinksy, Bond, and Hill). According to a recent study by the Institute for Women's Policy Research, 49 percent of workers — over 59 million Americans — lack basic paid sick days for themselves. (par. 10)

Because of the raw numbers, readers can see at a glance that the percentages Kornbluh cites are truly significant: 59 percent of 44.4 million people (who have worked while providing care to another adult) and 59 million people (who lack sick leave). Note that Kornbluh spells out some of the numbers she provides and uses numerals for others, depending on whether the number begins a sentence.

Kornbluh also compares different time periods to show that the problem has worsened over the last thirty years. Here are several examples from paragraph 7. Note that Kornbluh presents statistics in three different ways: percentages, numbers, and proportion.

> Between 1970 and 2000, the percentage of mothers in the workforce rose from 38 to 67 percent (Smolensky and Gootman). Moreover, the number of hours worked by dual-income families has increased dramatically. Couples with children worked a full 60 hours a week in 1979. By 2000 they were working 70 hours a week (Bernstein and Kornbluh). And more parents than ever are working long hours. In 2000, nearly 1 out of every 8 couples with children was putting in 100 hours a week or more on the job, compared to only 1 out of 12 families in 1970 (Jacobs and Gerson).

To establish that there is a widespread perception among working parents that the problem is serious, Kornbluh cites survey results:

> In a 2002 report by the Families and Work Institute, 45 percent of employees reported that work and family responsibilities interfered with each other "a lot" or "some" and 67 percent of employed parents report that they do not have enough time with their children (Galinksy, Bond, and Hill).

This example, from paragraph 9, shows that a large percentage, nearly half of all employees surveyed, are aware of interference between work and family responsibilities. The readers Kornbluh is addressing — employers — are likely to find this statistic important because it suggests that their employees are spending time worrying about or attending to family responsibilities instead of focusing on work.

For statistics to be persuasive, they must be from sources that readers consider reliable. Researchers' trustworthiness, in turn, depends on their credentials as experts in the field they are investigating and also on the degree to which they are disinterested, or free from bias.

Kornbluh provides a Works Cited list of sources that readers can follow up on to check whether the sources are indeed reliable. The fact that some of her sources are books published by major publishers (Harvard University Press and Basic Books, for example) helps establish their credibility. Other sources she cites are research institutes (such as New America Foundation, Economic Policy Institute, and Families and Work Institute) that readers can easily check out. Another factor that adds to the appearance of reliability is that Kornbluh cites statistics from a range of sources instead of relying on only one or two. Moreover, the statistics are current and clearly relevant to her argument.

Critical Reading Guide

Your instructor may arrange a peer review session in class or online where you can exchange drafts with your classmates and give one another a thoughtful critical reading, pointing out what works well and suggesting ways to improve the draft. This critical reading guide can also be used productively by a tutor in the writing center or by a roommate or family member.

Basic Features

A good critical reading does three things: It lets the writer know how the reader understands the point of the draft, praises what works best, and indicates where the draft could be improved.

1. Evaluate how well the problem is defined.

   Summarize: Tell the writer what you understand the problem to be.

   Praise: Give an example where the nature of the problem and its significance to readers comes across effectively.

   Critique: Tell the writer where the readers might need more information about the problem's causes and consequences, or where more might be done to establish its seriousness.

2. Assess how well the solution is argued.

   Summarize: Tell the writer what you understand the proposed solution to be.

   Praise: Give an example in the essay where support for the solution is presented especially effectively — for example, note particularly strong reasons, writing strategies that engage readers, or design or visual elements that make the solution clear and accessible.

   Critique: Tell the writer where the argument for the solution could be strengthened — for example, where steps for implementation could be laid out more clearly, where the practicality of the solution could be established more convincingly, or where additional support for reasons should be added.

3. Consider how effectively counterarguments are addressed and alternative solutions are offered.

   Praise: Give an example in the essay where the writer effectively responds to a likely objection to the argument, and where reasons against accepting other solutions are most effectively presented.

Critique: Tell the writer where concessions and refutations could be more convincing, where possible objections or reservations should be taken into account or alternative solutions discussed, where reasons against accepting other solutions need to be strengthened, or where common ground should be sought with advocates of other positions.

4. Assess how readable the proposal is.

   Praise: Give an example of where the essay succeeds in being readable — for example, in its overall organization, its use of forecasting statements or key terms introduced in its thesis and strategically repeated elsewhere, its use of topic sentences or transitions, an especially effective opening or closing, or by other means.

   Critique: Tell the writer where the readability could be improved. Can you point to places where key terms would help or where a topic sentence could be made clearer, for example? Can the use of transitions be improved, or transitions added where they are lacking? Can you suggest a better beginning or more effective ending?

5. If the writer has expressed concern about anything in the draft that you have not discussed, respond to that concern.

Making Comments Electronically Most word processing software offers features that allow you to insert comments directly into the text of someone else's document. Many readers prefer to make their comments this way because it tends to be faster than writing on hard copy and space is virtually unlimited; it also eliminates the process of deciphering handwritten comments. Where such features are not available, simply typing comments directly into a document in a contrasting color can provide the same advantages.

For a printable version of this Critical Reading Guide, go to **bedfordstmartins.com/conciseguide**.

Revising

Very likely you have already thought of ways to improve your draft, and you may even have begun to revise it. In this section is a Troubleshooting chart that may help. Before using the chart, however, it is a good idea to

- review critical reading comments from your classmates, instructor, or writing center tutor, and
- make an outline of your draft so that you can look at it analytically.

You may have made an outline before writing your draft, but after drafting you need to see what you actually wrote, not what you intended to write. You can outline your draft by highlighting the basic features — a well-defined problem, a clearly argued solution, a response to counterarguments, and a readable plan.

For an electronic version of this Troubleshooting chart, go to **bedfordstmartins.com/conciseguide**.

☑ Troubleshooting Your Draft

● ● ● ● **Basic Features**

A Well-Defined Problem

My readers are not convinced of the seriousness and/or the existence of the problem.	☐ Consider changing the way you present the problem to more directly address your audience's concerns. ☐ Add additional information — statistics, examples, description, etc. — likely to be of interest to your audience. ☐ Consider adding visuals — graphs, tables, or charts — if these would help clarify the nature of the problem for your audience.

A Well-Argued Solution

My readers are not convinced that my solution is a good one.	☐ Try to explain the solution more convincingly, perhaps by discussing similar solutions used elsewhere or by more clearly demonstrating how it will solve the problem. ☐ Add additional support for your reasons. ☐ Go over the way you present the steps needed to put your solution into place; if necessary, lay them out more clearly.

An Effective Counterargument

My readers continue to raise objections to my solution.	☐ Address the objections directly in your proposal. If possible, refute them, using solid reasons and support or citing authorities. ☐ If objections cannot be completely refuted, modify your solution to accommodate valid criticism. ☐ If you can neither refute nor accommodate objections, rethink your solution.
My readers have proposed alternative solutions that I do not discuss in my proposal.	☐ Address the alternative solutions directly. Establish common ground with those who propose alternatives, if possible, but show why their solutions will not work as well as yours. ☐ If you cannot demonstrate that your solution is preferable, consider arguing that both solutions deserve serious consideration.

	A Readable Plan
My readers are confused by my proposal or find it difficult to read.	☐ Try outlining your proposal to be sure that the overall organization is strong; if not, try rearranging parts by moving, adding, or deleting sections to strengthen coherence.
	☐ Consider adding a forecasting statement and using key terms in your thesis and repeating them when you introduce and later when you discuss main points.
	☐ Check to see that your main points are introduced clearly through the use of topic sentences and that you provide appropriate transitions, particularly in places where readers indicate the greatest trouble in following your argument.

Editing and Proofreading

Several errors occur often in essays that propose solutions: ambiguous use of *this* and *that*, and sentences that lack an agent. The following guidelines will help you check your essay for these common errors.

Avoiding Ambiguous Use of *This* and *That*

The Problem. Because you must frequently refer to the problem and the solution in a proposal, you will often use pronouns to avoid the monotony or wordiness of repeatedly referring to them by name. Using *this* and *that* vaguely to refer to other words or ideas, however, can confuse readers.

How to Correct It. Add a specific noun after *this* or *that*. For example, in his essay in this chapter, Patrick O'Malley writes:

> Another possible solution would be to help students prepare for midterm and final exams by providing sets of questions from which the exam questions will be selected.... *This solution* would have the advantage of reducing students' anxiety about learning every fact in the textbook.... (par. 12)

O'Malley avoids an ambiguous *this* in the second sentence by repeating the noun *solution*. (He might just as well have used *preparation* or *action* or *approach*.)

▶ Students would not resist a reasonable fee increase of about $40 a year.

       increase
This would pay for the needed dormitory remodeling.

▶ Compared with other large California cities, San Diego

has the weakest programs for conserving water.

neglect
This ‸ and our decreasing access to Colorado River water

give us reason to worry.

alternative
▶ Compared with other proposed solutions to this problem, that ‸ is clearly

the most feasible.

For practice, go to **bedfordstmartins.com/conciseguide/exercise central** and click on Ambiguous Use of *This* and *That*.

Revising Sentences That Lack an Agent

The Problem. A writer proposing a solution to a problem usually needs to indicate who exactly should take action to solve it. Such actors — those who are in a position to take action — are called "agents." Look, for example, at this sentence from O'Malley's proposal:

> To get students to complete the questions in a timely way, professors would have to collect and check the answers. (par. 11)

In this sentence, *professors* are the agents. They have the authority to assign and collect study questions, and they would need to take this action in order for this solution to be successfully implemented.

Had O'Malley instead written "the answers would have to be collected and checked," the sentence would lack an agent. Failing to name an agent would have made his argument less convincing, because it would have left unclear one of the key parts of any proposal: Who is going to take action.

How to Correct It. When you revise your work, ask yourself *who* or *what* performed the action in any given sentence. If there is no clear answer, rewrite the sentence to give it an agent. Watch in particular for forms of the verb *to be* (the balls *were* dropped, exams should *be* given, etc.), which often signal agentless sentences.

Your staff should plan a survey
▶ ‸A survey could be planned to find out more about students' problems in

scheduling the courses they need.

The registrar should extend
▶ ‸Extending the deadline to mid-quarter‸ would make sense.

Note: Sometimes, however, it is appropriate to write agentless sentences, as in the following examples from O'Malley's essay:

These exams should be given weekly or at least twice monthly. (par. 3)

Exams could be collected and responded to only every third or fourth week. (par. 9)

Still another solution might be to provide frequent study questions for students to answer. (par. 11)

Even though these sentences do not name explicit agents, they are all fine because it is clear from the larger context who will perform the action: a professor.

For practice, go to **bedfordstmartins.com/conciseguide/exercisecentral** and click on Sentences That Lack an Agent.

Thinking Critically about What You Have Learned

In this chapter, you have learned a great deal about this genre from reading several proposals and writing one of your own. To consolidate your learning, it is helpful to think metacognitively — that is, to reflect not only on what you learned but also on how you learned it. Following are two brief activities your instructor may ask you to do.

Reflecting on Your Writing

Your instructor may ask you to turn in with your essay and process materials a brief metacognitive essay or letter reflecting on what you have learned about writing your essay proposing a solution. Choose from the following invention activities those that seem most productive for you.

- Explain how your purpose and audience influenced *one* of your decisions as a writer, such as how you defined the problem, the strategies you used in presenting your solution, or the ways in which you attempted to counter possible objections.

- Discuss what you learned about yourself as a writer in the process of writing this particular essay. For example, what part of the process did you find most challenging? Did you try anything new, like getting a critical reading of your draft or outlining your draft in order to revise it?

- If you were to give advice to a friend who was about to write an essay proposing a solution to a problem, what would you say?

- Which of the readings in this chapter influenced your essay? Explain the influence, citing specific examples from your essay and the reading.

- If you got good advice from a critical reader, explain exactly how the person helped you — perhaps by questioning the way you addressed your audience or the kinds of support you offered in support of your proposed solution.

Considering the Social Dimensions: The Frustrations of Effecting Real Change

No matter how well researched and well argued, many proposals are simply never carried out. The head of a personnel department might spend weeks drawing up a persuasive and feasible proposal for establishing a company day-care center, only to have upper management decide not to commit the necessary resources. A team of educators and social scientists might spend several years researching and writing a comprehensive, book-length proposal for dealing with the nation's drastic illiteracy rate but never see their solutions carried out because of a lack of coordination among the country's various educational institutions and governing bodies. In fact, it might be argued that the most successful proposals often operate on the smallest scale. For example, a proposal suggesting ways for a single community to increase literacy rates would probably have a better chance of implementation and ultimate success than the more far-reaching national proposal. (Yet this observation does not rule out the value of the national proposal, on which the local proposal might, in fact, be based.)

Further, in choosing among competing alternative proposals, decision makers — who usually hold the power of the purse strings and necessarily represent a fairly conservative position — often go for the one that is cheapest, most expedient, and least disruptive. They may also choose small, incremental changes over more fundamental, radical solutions. While these may sometimes be the most pragmatic choice, such immediately feasible solutions may also merely patch over a problem, failing to solve it structurally. They may even inadvertently maintain the status quo. Worse, they can cause people to give up all attempts to resolve a problem after superficial treatments fail.

1. *Consider how proposals invite writers to select problems that are solvable and how they might inadvertently attempt to solve a minor problem that is actually only a small part of a major problem.* Do any of the proposals you have read and written reveal this misdirection? If so, which ones are they, and what do you think is the major problem in each case? Do you think the minor problem is worth solving as a first step toward solving the major problem, or is it perhaps an unfortunate diversion?

2. *Consider how the proposals you have read and written challenge the status quo.* What existing situation do they challenge, and just how do they challenge it? What roadblocks might deter these challenges? Might the proposals be more successfully carried out on a local scale?

3. *Reflect on commentators' arguments that we should not try to solve fundamental social problems by "throwing money at them."* Do you think this objection is a legitimate criticism of most proposals to solve social problems, or is it a manipulative justification for allowing the rich and powerful to maintain the status quo? What else, besides money, is required to solve serious social problems? Where are these other resources to come from?

4. *Write a page or two explaining your ideas about the frustrations of effecting real change.* Connect your ideas to your own essay and to the readings in this chapter.

Justifying an Evaluation

IN COLLEGE COURSES For a literature research paper, a student sets out to evaluate the 1995 film *Clueless*, a modern-day adaptation of Jane Austen's novel *Emma*. He had seen the film but decides to watch it before reading the novel. Then, while he is reading the novel, he reviews key scenes in the film to see how they have been translated to the screen.

While considering how to approach his evaluation, he does an Internet search for reviews of *Clueless* and discovers that there is a 1996 film called *Emma* set in early nineteenth-century England like the novel. He decides that his paper would be more interesting if he could write about both films. His professor responds enthusiastically to this idea.

The student then drafts his essay and selects stills from the films to illustrate his argument that *Clueless* is a more effective adaptation than *Emma*. *Emma*, he contends, while beautifully filmed, looks like a museum piece, and viewers cannot identify with the main characters. In contrast, he argues, the familiar setting and characters in *Clueless* engage viewers, allowing them to better appreciate Austen's social commentary.

IN THE COMMUNITY A motorcycle enthusiast rides to York, Pennsylvania, to tour the Harley-Davidson factory. He takes notes and photographs for a review on his blog. Before the tour begins, he and other visitors wander through the tour center, marveling at the vintage motorcycles on display. He watches a short film about the history of the company, and then he explores exhibits describing the plant and the manufacturing process.

Before entering the plant, he is given safety glasses and a headset so he can hear the tour guide on the noisy factory floor. The factory is housed in an immense building with over a thousand workers on each shift. He takes pictures and makes notes describing the manufacturing process.

At home, he spends a couple of days writing the review, enthusiastically recommending the tour. He illustrates his review with his photographs and supplements it with links to additional information online.

IN THE WORKPLACE For a conference panel on innovations in education, an elementary school teacher decides to give a talk on *Schoolhouse Rock!*, an animated television series. She had enjoyed the series when she was a child, so she bought the DVD and started showing segments to her students, who enjoyed them as much as she had.

To prepare for her talk, she plays four songs for her class. Following each, she gives her students a quiz to see how well they have learned the lesson. Finally, she conducts a poll to see whether the kids find this kind of learning enjoyable.

In her presentation, she describes her research and gives two reasons why the series is an effective tool: The witty lyrics and catchy tunes make the information memorable, and the animation makes the lessons vivid and enjoyable. She ends by expressing her hope that teachers will learn from the example of *Schoolhouse Rock!*

Justifying an Evaluation

Evaluation involves forming opinions and making judgments. Most of us have opinions on things that interest us — food, music, fashion, TV, sports, politicians, and so on. And in everyday interactions most of us express judgments of these things casually, saying "I like it" or "I don't like it," or silently awarding the subject an eye roll or a frown.

Slightly less casual are the kinds of judgments we express in reviews, which seem to appear everywhere these days in print and online. Some reviews, like the example here from *Consumer Reports*, are written by experts; increasingly, however, especially online at sites like Trip Advisor and Yelp, non-experts offer reviews of a wide range of products and services. Most online shopping sites allow consumers to post product reviews for the benefit of those who have not yet hit "buy." Typically, such sites have a numerical rating system (for example, users can give a book between one and five stars on amazon.com) and also allow for comments.

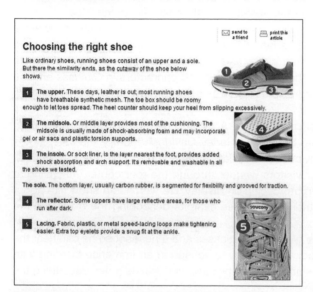

Screenshot of advice on choosing a shoe, from *Consumer Reports*. Used with permission from Consumers Union of United States, Inc.

In an interesting acknowledgment that not all evaluations are created equal, however, many sites that allow reviews encourage other visitors to rate the reviews as, for example, "helpful" or "not helpful." Evaluations must meet certain criteria in order to be considered effective. Reasoned, *justified* evaluations — the kind we discuss in this chapter — must include a well-presented subject, a clear and well-supported overall judgment, anticipation of counterarguments, and a readable plan.

In this chapter, we ask you to write an evaluation of a subject that interests you. As you write your evaluation, consider whether the use of visuals or multimedia would help your readers more immediately or more fully grasp your perspective on the subject.

Reading and Writing Evaluations

As we note above, written evaluations require reasons and support in order to be effective. In the chapter-opening scenario, the student evaluating film versions of Jane Austen's novel gives two reasons for arguing that *Clueless* is a more effective adaptation than *Emma* and supports his argument with examples, including still images from both films and passages from the novel. Similarly, evaluating the Harley-Davidson factory tour, the writer gives three reasons for recommending the tour (it is free, fun, and educational), supporting them with details and photographs. The teacher who gives a presentation on *Schoolhouse Rock!* uses examples of the songs as well as her quiz grades and survey results to support her reasons for praising the classic educational series.

Readers also need to agree that the criteria you use are appropriate for evaluating the subject. For example, in an evaluation of a film like *Die Hard*, you would want to show that you are judging the film according to standards most people would use in evaluating action films, such as special effects, action sequences, and, most important, the film's ability to generate excitement. Judging such a film for the realism of its dialogue (which we might expect from dramatic film) or the depth of its analysis of current events (which we might look for in a contemporary documentary) would simply be inappropriate.

In this chapter, you will read evaluations of a Web site (RateMyProfessors.com), the film *Juno*, and a student's argument about children's participation in competitive sports. The Guide to Writing that follows the readings will support you as you compose your own evaluation, showing you ways to use the basic features of the genre to write a well-reasoned judgment of your subject.

A Collaborative Activity:
Practice Evaluating a Subject

To get a sense of the complexities and possibilities involved in writing an evaluation, get together with two or three other students, and discuss your judgments of a subject with which you are all familiar. Here are some guidelines to follow:

Part 1.

- Select a subject you all know well — for example, a film, Web site, recent performance, or sports event.
- Discuss what you consider the pluses and minuses, what is good and what is bad about your subject. You do not have to agree; take notes on what you agree and disagree about.

Part 2. Talk about one or two occasions when your group disagreed, and try to determine what caused the disagreement:

- the standards or criteria used in evaluating a subject of this particular kind (for example, in evaluating a Web site, the relative importance of the information provided, ease of navigation, or credibility); or
- differing judgments on how the subject measured up to the standards (for example, whether the site was in fact easy to navigate, and why).

Reading Essays Justifying Evaluations

Basic Features

● ● ● ●
Basic Features

● A Well–Presented Subject

*Read first to see how the writer presents the **subject**.* For familiar subjects, writers may need only to identify the subject by name. Most often, however, writers provide some details to describe the subject — for example, identifying what kind of film is being reviewed, who is in it, and what it is about. Identifying the kind of subject being evaluated is especially important because the criteria or standards writers use to judge a subject depend on how people normally judge subjects of that kind. If a writer chooses to apply a standard readers consider unusual, it may be harder to convince readers that the writer's judgment can be relied upon.

● A Well-Supported Judgment

*Look for the overall **judgment** and the argument supporting it.* The judgment usually appears in a thesis statement early in the essay, and it may be repeated at other points in the essay. A good thesis statement in an evaluative essay makes a clear and unambiguous assertion about how the writer values the subject — whether it is good or bad, or better or worse than something else of the same kind. But writers also know that readers of evaluative essays appreciate measured or balanced judgments that are not exaggerated but carefully qualified, acknowledging the subject's strengths as well as its flaws.

Examine the argument, noting how each reason is explained and the kinds of evidence offered as backing, such as the following:

- examples
- facts
- statistics
- textual evidence in the form of quotations, summaries, or paraphrases
- expert testimony
- research studies

Determine whether the support is relevant and comes from reliable sources. Note also any comparisons and how well they demonstrate the appropriateness of the criteria being applied or substantiate the writer's judgment of the relative value of the subject compared to other similar subjects.

● An Effective Counterargument

*Read also to see how the writer responds to possible objections to the argument or alternative judgments with **an effective counterargument**.* Writers of evaluation often counterargue by simply acknowledging other judgments. More substantial counterargument could

264

include making concessions — for example, conceding an objection and modifying the judgment to accommodate it — or refuting readers' possible objections or alternative judgments.

● A Readable Plan

*Finally, examine the essay to see how the writer provides **a readable plan**.* Evaluative essays tend to analyze the subject in detail, so it is helpful to have a readable plan that gives readers a clear overview of the argument. To make their essays easy to read, writers usually include some or all of the following:

- a forecast of the argument
- key words introduced in the thesis and forecasting statement and repeated in topic sentences
- clear transitional words and phrases
- headings that explicitly identify different sections of the essay

Purpose and Audience

Although many evaluative essays seek to influence readers' judgments, their primary purpose is usually to explain and justify the writer's judgment. Readers may or may not find the argument convincing, but a well-written evaluation will be interesting and informative. It may also lead thoughtful readers to examine the values or criteria they think are important and to wonder why these particular values have become so important.

*As you read evaluation essays, ask yourself what seems to be the writer's **purpose** in writing.* The following purposes are common in evaluative essays:

- to convince readers that the writer's judgment is correct or preferable to other people's judgments
- to influence readers' judgments and possibly their actions
- to encourage readers to examine the values they use as criteria for judging subjects of this kind
- to get readers to look at the subject in a new way
- to stimulate readers' interest in the subject

*As you read, also try to guess what the writer assumes about the **audience**.* Which of the following assumptions about audience might apply?

- The audience will accept the writer's judgment.
- The audience will use the review to make their own independent, informed judgments of the subject.
- The audience will already have an independent judgment of the subject.
- The audience will have serious objections to the writer's argument.

Readings

Basic Features

- A Well-Presented Subject
- A Well-Supported Judgment
- An Effective Counterargument
- A Readable Plan

Is this opening effective? Why or why not?

How does this information help readers?

How well does Kim forecast her reasons here? Find where each reason is developed in the essay.

Why does Kim mention the class she took?

Grading Professors

Wendy Kim

"Where the Students Do the Grading" is the tagline for the Web site RateMyProfessors.com (RMP). Users just choose their state and find their school among the more than 6,000 campuses listed, and they're ready to start grading their professors. The home page proudly displays the numbers: last I looked, there were more than 6,200,000 ratings, covering more than 770,000 professors in the United States and Canada. In fact, RMP has been so successful that it has expanded to Australia, Ireland, and the United Kingdom, and its sister-site for high school students, RateMyTeachers.com, already has a user base of 3 million students (RateMyProfessors). While not everyone agrees that these ratings provide an entirely accurate assessment, many students, like me, routinely consult RMP at the beginning of every term to decide which classes to take. Overall, the Web site is well designed, extremely helpful, and amusing. 1

The design of RateMyProfessors.com makes the site attractive and easy to browse (see Fig. 1). In my senior year of high school, I took a class that taught me how to make a good Web site and learned that Web site design requires care in picking colors and in organizing the layout. The layout of RMP's home page is smart, with information grouped in clearly defined rectangular boxes. Across the top is a banner with the name in easy-to-read letters. Below the banner, the page is divided into 2

266

boxes, three across and two down, with plenty of white space along the left and right borders and bottom so that the page looks neatly organized and uncluttered. The top box on the left has the main menu in blue lettering against a white background with links to "Hot or Not," "Funny Ratings," "Signup Now," "Recent Press," and "Forum," five areas likely to be of most use to users. The placement of the menu is smart because readers of English are used to reading from left to right as well as top to bottom. Below the menu a box titled "Statistics" (which I cited in the first paragraph) reveals how many students use the ratings.

What purpose does her detailed description of the site in pars. 2 and 3 and the addition of Fig. 1 serve?

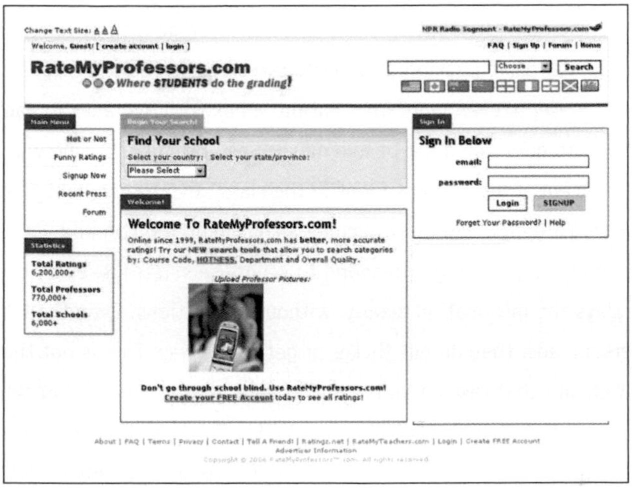

Fig. 1. *RateMyProfessors.com* home page; RateMyProfessors.com, 2006; Web; 13 May 2006.

3   The viewer's eye is drawn to the center box, which is twice as wide as the boxes on the sides and includes the all-important search function (set off against a distinctive yellow background). The box below this, which includes eye-catching graphics, serves as a portal to the Welcome page. The box in the top right-hand portion of the screen allows users to sign in conveniently. Ads fill the space in the lower right-hand portion of the screen; however, they coordinate in color with the rest of the elements on the page, so they're not too distracting. The placement of information seems just right.

How does Kim support her judgments about the site's design?

4   The navigation system is smooth and fast. When you log in, you get the main member page; from there, you easily link to your

school's page. On the member page, you can edit your ratings, go to the message board, or manage your account. Your school's page is the destination for checking out professors whose classes you are considering, entering your own rating of a professor, or adding a professor not already listed. Finding a particular professor is quick and easy because professors' names are listed in alphabetical order. The list is easy to skim and contains lots of valuable information. To the left of each name is a face icon (which I will explain in a minute) followed by a check icon that you can click on to add your own rating. To the right of the name is the professor's department, the date he or she was last rated, the number of ratings, and the vital average ratings for overall quality and ease. Clicking on a name takes you to the professor's page, which presents even more information: a box with averages in each rating category and a list of individual users' ratings, starting with the most recent. These ratings identify the class, give the student's rating in each category, and often include a comment. You can add your own rating of the professor or respond to other users' ratings. Every page displays the information clearly, without distractions. Even though there are ads, they do not flicker or get in the way. This is not the kind of Web site that takes minutes just to find what you need. Not only is it easy to browse, but it also doesn't lag because there are no large files or images to slow it down. For me, the longest it took to get to another page was two seconds using a cable modem.

Why do you think Kim introduces the next reason with this transition?

Most important, RateMyProfessors.com is full of useful information that can help students make informed decisions when it comes to choosing teachers and preparing for a class they are about to take. A student debating whether to take a history or a sociology class, for example, can go to the Web site, first look at the overall ratings of each professor, and then find user ratings for the classes being considered. Assuming the professor has been graded by other students, a great deal can be learned about the professor and possibly also about the specific class.

Professors are rated in several categories on a scale of 1 (worst) to 5 (best). The scores on clarity and helpfulness are averaged for the "Overall Quality rating," the overall rating that determines which icon

5

6

is placed next to the professor's name: A yellow smiley face indicates "good quality," a bluish-gray sad face "poor quality," and an indifferent-looking green face "average quality." The numerical rating in each category is displayed along with the face so that students and professors can see the breakdown. In addition to evaluating the professor's clarity and helpfulness, students also rate the difficulty of the course. This rating, however, has no effect on assigning the face icon because, as the site explains, "an Easiness rating of 5 may actually mean the teacher is TOO easy." Although RMP acknowledges that easiness is "definitely the most controversial" reason for judging a class, they still present it because "many students decide what class to take based on the difficulty of the teacher." Another category that is not included in the overall rating is "Rater Interest." To explain this category the Web site quotes from a study that found student "motivation correlated with the overall evaluation," meaning that the more motivated a student was to succeed in a course, the higher the professor's overall quality score. "Instructors," however, as RMP acknowledges, "usually have little control over student motivation" (RateMyProfessors).

7   The faces and numbers are informative, but I think the comments help the most because they are so detailed. Not surprisingly, the comments on RateMyProfessors.com tend to address many of the same issues that my college's course evaluation forms do. For example, one question on my campus evaluation form asks if the instructor presented the material in "an organized, understandable manner." Many of the RMP comments answer this question: from high praise ("lectures are interesting, and he's happy to answer whatever questions you could ask") to severe criticism ("lectures are BORING and POINTLESS" or "totally disorganized!! boring and reads off the power point!!"). Another question on my campus form asks if the instructor was "concerned about students learning and understanding the course material." This issue also draws many comments on RMP, from highly positive ("he wrote a personal whole-page to each of my papers. So I knew exactly what he liked and how to improve on my writing") to slams ("Kinda scary and intimidating" or "He does not care if the students are learning the basic concepts. He teaches as if he were teaching a

How do transitions like these help readers follow her argument?

How effectively does she refute these objections?

Why do you think Kim refers to her college's student evaluation forms?

How well does putting examples in parentheses work?

What purpose does this observation serve?

Graduate level class. This is an INTRO class, let us learn the basics 1st"). In addition to these kinds of comments, RMP also posts information that course evaluations do not include — advice on how to pass the course ("If you keep up w/ your notes and the reading, you should be fine. Pop quizzes every week." or "Has notes available online. Tests are extremely difficult and require a lot of reading from the book to be successful as well as attending class. Gives surprise quizzes"). The site also gives students warnings ("He's ****in' hard. Fails half his class." or "OMG, one of the worst teachers I've ever had . . . Does not know how to teach and wears the tightest pants ever . . . gross.")

Why do you think Kim presents this reason last?

And as this last comment suggests, we can't forget the last rating category: Is your professor hot or not? The answer to this question makes the Web site amusing. "Hot" professors are marked with a red chili pepper beside their names. Some students also include comments in this area: "good lookin guy, nice body" and "this chick [the professor] totally blew my mind. She was sooo hot. I'm serious take this class just to check her out. SEXY!!!!" In fact, this issue may not be just a sideline to ones that supposedly are more serious. Students give professors higher overall ratings if they are hot, according to a *New York Times* article, "The Hunk Differential," which the RMP site provides as the answer to its FAQ question "Why do you have the 'hot' category?" The article, written by a professor of business, economics, and information management, reports a study that found "good-looking professors got significantly higher teaching scores" than those who did not rate as high on a beauty scale (Varian). So it may be that a professor who is considered "hot" on the site may be judged on a more lenient scale of teaching effectiveness.

What objection does Kim anticipate here? How well does she counter it?

8

This question about the possible effect of the teacher's appearance on student response and learning leads to a more basic question about the credibility of the evaluations on RateMyProfessors.com: Are the ratings statistically valid? The simple answer, the Web site itself admits, is "Not really. They are a listing of opinions and should be judged as such" (RateMyProfessors). The results are statistically invalid, as one psychology professor explained, because the users are self-selected and not selected randomly (Harmon). And the fewer student ratings an instructor has been given, the less reliable the overall evaluation.

9

Nevertheless, RMP claims "we often receive emails stating that the ratings are uncannily accurate, especially for schools with over 1000 ratings" (RateMyProfessors). RMP also refers readers to an article reporting a study at the University of Waterloo, Canada (UW), that found fifteen of the sixteen Distinguished Teacher Award winners at UW also had yellow smiley faces on RateMyProfessors.com (ratemyprofessors). While this correlation is reassuring, students should not approach the ratings uncritically. And evidence suggests most don't. As one college newspaper reporter put it, "students claim they do not blindly follow the comments" (Espach). A recent study of RMP published in the *Journal of Computer-Mediated Communication* found that students "are aware that ratings and comments on the site could reflect students exacting revenge or venting" (Kindred and Mohammed). As one student explained: "If half the ratings are bad, I will ask around about the professor. If every rating is poor I won't take the teacher" (Espach).

10   There are other Internet professor evaluation sites, but none is as widely used or as easy to use as RateMyProfessors.com. I compared RMP with three competitors: ProfessorPerformance.com, Reviewum.com, and RatingsOnline. The user base of the first two sites looks too small to provide reliable information. Professor Performance has 73,040 evaluations at 1,742 colleges and universities, and Reviewum.com claims to have 20,098 records for 137 campuses. In addition, for the limited number of professors who are listed, there are only a small number of evaluations, not enough to enable students to make informed judgments.

11   Although RatingsOnline does not appear to display its statistics, it claims to have ratings for "thousands of professors." However, there are only 19 professors from my campus among the 1,252 listed on RMP. Still, RatingsOnline is better designed and includes more helpful information than the other two competitors, and it may even be better than RMP in terms of helpfulness. Students not only identify the class and term it was taken, but also are asked to list the grade they received. Of course, this information about the grade is no more reliable than any other information a user gives, but it could help students judge the user's credibility.

> How effectively does Kim use sources to support her counterargument here?

> Why do you think Kim compares RMP to other sites?

The ratings categories on RatingsOnline also seem more specific than on RMP: prepared, enthusiastic, focused, available, material, exam prep, quality. In addition, students are prompted to indicate the percentage given to homework, quizzes, and exams in determining the final grade. This information could be useful in helping students decide which classes to take, but only if there are enough reviews posted. In its design and potential helpfulness, RatingsOnline is a very good site but not likely to be as good as RMP because its user base appears to be smaller.

How effective are these final sentences?

When you have the option of choosing a teacher, wouldn't you really like some information? RateMyProfessors.com allows you to see what other students have to say about professors and courses you may be considering as well as to voice your opinion. As a Web site, it is not only helpful and easy to use, but it is also amusing to read.

12

Works Cited

Espach, Alison. "RateMyProfessors.com — Blessing or Bluffing?" *Cowl*. Providence College, 27 Apr. 2006. Web. 15 May 2011.

Harmon, Christine. "Professors Rate Reliability of RateMyProfessors.com." *Daily Forty-Niner*. California State U., Long Beach, 2 May 2011. Web. 15 May 2006.

Kindred, Jeannette, and Shaheed N. Mohammed. "'He Will Crush You Like an Academic Ninja!': Exploring Teacher Ratings on RateMyProfessors.com." *Journal of Computer-Mediated Communication* 10.3 (2005): n. pag. Web. 15 May 2011.

Professor Performance. Professorperformance.com, n.d. Web. 19 May 2011.

"ratemyprofessors.ca." *Teaching Matters Newsletter*. U. of Waterloo Teaching Resources Office, Sept. 2001. Web. 13 May 2011.

RateMyProfessors.com. Ratemyprofessors.com, 2006. Web. 13 May 2011.

RatingsOnline. Ratingsonline.com, n.d. Web. 19 May 2011.

Reviewum.com. Reviewum.com, 2006. Web. 19 May 2011.

Varian, Hal R. "The Hunk Differential." *New York Times*. New York Times, 28 Aug. 2003. Web. 14 May 2011.

Do Kim's sources seem credible and appropriate for the kind of argument she's making and the situation in which she is writing?

ANN HULBERT writes often about cultural issues. Her latest book, *Raising America: Experts, Parents, and a Century of Advice about Children* (2003), examines the political and social history of child-rearing advice books. She also writes regularly for newspapers and magazines, online and in print, including the *New Yorker*, the *New York Times*, and the *New York Times Magazine*. She was a senior editor and writer for the *New Republic* and is now a contributing editor for *Slate*, where this film review originally appeared. If you have seen *Juno*, consider how well Hulbert's evaluation of the film corresponds to your own evaluation. If you have not seen the film, consider whether or not Hulbert's review makes you want to see *Juno*.

Juno and the Culture Wars

ANN HULBERT ▼

1   I braced for a skirmish in the culture wars when reviews of *Juno* appeared the very same week that newspaper headlines announced a rise in the teenage birth rate — the first uptick in a decade and a half. "Not many [movies] are so daring in their treatment of teenage pregnancy, which this film flirts with presenting not just as bearable but attractive," wrote the *New York Times'* A. O. Scott, who added a wry homily: "Kids, please! Heed the cautionary whale." If the critic at liberal-media headquarters was mildly clucking, it was only a matter of time before anti-Hollywood moralizers would be up in arms about the corruption of youth (at the hands of a former-stripper-turned-screenwriter, Diablo Cody, no less). But among *Juno*'s distinctive charms is that it seems to have disarmed both

sides of the family values debate. And the feat gets pulled off in the wry style of the eponymous hero: The film doesn't offer up a formulaic or fervent call for family harmony. Instead, it takes idiosyncratic aim at everybody's pieties.

One by one, polarized positions on the hot-button issues get defused by a 16-year-old girl who has evidently never considered marching with any crowd — an approach hard enough to manage in life, never mind in high school. Let's start with Juno MacGuff's own profile. She has a blue-collar background, complete with parents who've never heard of Pilates and hoard kitsch in their house. But there isn't much sign of the red-America attitudes that either radio talk-show hosts, or snooty liberals, assume go with the pedigree. A heartland family, hers is not an intact one. An off-beat girl, she's a very good daughter whose dad adores her.

Supersmart but neither a teacher's pet nor a pariah, Juno eludes hip vs. square student stereotypes, too. Early on, she jokes about herself as the kind of freaky girl — "with horn-rimmed glasses and vegan footwear and Goth makeup" or Converse All-Stars and cello skills — whom jocks secretly want. But in fact she and her friend Bleeker, in his dweebily short running shorts, confound their peers' social categories altogether — and adults' preconceptions, too. Subverting age and gender expectations, Juno seems at once peculiarly mature and oddly childlike as she fearlessly figures things out for herself; she's neither the suave teen whom liberal types invoke nor the old-fashioned innocent whom the Christian right celebrates. And with her funky get-ups and wit, Juno is in no way sexualized, but she isn't de-sexed either, as her ever-bigger belly shows us.

Her take on the roster of family values issues is as heterodox as her image. Consider her sendup of the term *sexually active*, a trope of the sex-ed wars. Liberal advocates of honest, open sexual communication with teens embrace the epithet as though it were part and parcel of puberty. Abstinence promoters invoke it as the plague to be avoided at all costs. For Juno, it's ridiculous, an Orwellian phrase that in no way speaks to her actual experience (sex, once, in a chair) — as is surely true, when you stop and think about it, for the majority of high-school juniors who aren't virgins.

The real flashpoint issue in the film, of course, could have been abortion. Here Cody's politics (presumably pro-choice) are at odds with her plot needs (a birth) and, who knows, maybe commercial dictates, too, if studios worry about antagonizing the evangelical audience. It's a tension the screenplay finesses deftly, undercutting both pro-life and pro-choice purism. Pregnant Juno at first reflexively embraces abortion as the obvious option, and her best friend is at the ready with phone numbers; she's helped other classmates through this. But just when pro-lifers might be about to denounce this display of secular humanist decadence, Juno stomps out of the clinic, unable to go through with it.

She isn't moved by thoughts of the embryo's hallowed rights, however, but by a sense of her own autonomy. And for her, that doesn't mean a right to privacy, or to protect her body ("a fat suit I can't take off," she calls it at one point). Juno is driven by the chance to make her own unconventional choice. Parental notification doesn't quite follow the liberal or conservative scripts, either: Juno confides in her father and stepmother, initially portrayed as stock down-home folks who are completely surprised, not least to find themselves asking her if she's "considered, you know, the alternative" — not that they'd presume to pressure her. These are neither old-style authoritarians nor enlightened empathizers. They emerge as people who respect, and would do anything to support, their independent-minded kid.

7   Here *Juno* moves into the realm of marriage and childrearing, by way of the vexed terrain of assisted reproduction in its most traditional form, adoption. When Juno finds the perfect yuppie adoptive couple for her unborn baby — fussy Vanessa and mellow Mark — the film gets to address a bundle of politically charged questions: class mores, parenting styles, gender relations, and family structure. On every count, Juno skewers the assumptions of ideologues on both sides. She refuses to be either an exploited female at the service of the affluent, or a sacrificial vessel of life. She counters Vanessa's materialist and hyper-maternalist solicitude with her own hard-boiled attitude; appalled by the notion of open adoption (or compensation), she tells the couple she'd love to give over the kid immediately, but figures it needs more "cooking" until it gets cuter. And she quickly starts bonding with the laid-back husband, who is still nursing rock band dreams, where the uptight wife, worrying over the color palette for the nursery, turns her off.

8   Juno has a fun-loving adolescent's enthusiasm for the prospect of what sounds like a permissive family with a cool dad — until Mark suddenly upsets that ideal vision of the future. He — spoiler alert — stages a display of just the kind of egotistical guy regression that regularly induces female groans on the right and left, and that *Slate*'s Meghan O'Rourke recently examined in this piece about *Knocked Up*. (Suffice it to say, Vanessa finds herself stranded.) Stunned, Juno is suddenly furious at the infantile male and frantic that what she calls "the big-ass bump" end up in a family "not shitty and broken like everyone else's."

9   But *Juno* doesn't end there. Another twist, and the film closes with a celebration of single parenthood — anathema to family traditionalists. Yet Juno, in deciding to hand her baby over to a now-solo Vanessa, doesn't endorse the dour, who-needs-men-when-we-can-go-it-alone ethos of progressives who defend "permeable" arrangements, either. A great comic scene in a bustling mall has convinced Juno — and us in the audience — that Vanessa isn't actually a vain control freak whose life plan won't be complete without a perfect little appurtenance. Juno has stumbled on a woman who actually finds kids, of all things, fun and lovable. That is a figure whom both liberals and conservatives often seem to have forgotten, or lost faith in, as they endlessly lament the embattled family. If sharp-eyed girls can spot her in the fraught landscape, though, there's reason to hope the culture wars will wane and the American family, in its many forms, won't.

MAKING CONNECTIONS: DEFUSING "HOT-BUTTON ISSUES"

Ann Hulbert writes that when *Juno* first appeared, she "braced for a skirmish in the culture wars. . . . But among *Juno*'s distinctive charms is that it seems to have disarmed both sides of the family values debate" (par. 1). What fascinates her is the way *Juno* defuses such polarized issues as abortion by taking "idiosyncratic aim at everybody's pieties" (par. 1).

With two or three other students, discuss the "culture wars" and the possibility of finding common ground. Begin by taking turns telling about a time people were arguing about a polarized issue and someone (perhaps you) tried to defuse the argument. What did the person do, and what was the result? Then, together consider the following questions:

- Hulbert assumes undercutting stereotypes and breaking down polarized thinking is a good thing. Do you agree or disagree? Why?
- What strategies do you think work best in helping people find common ground on highly controversial issues?

ANALYZING WRITING STRATEGIES

● ● ● ●
Basic Features

● A Well-Presented Subject

Film reviews are one of the most familiar types of evaluation. Like other kinds of evaluation essays, film reviews begin by presenting the subject. If it is a well-publicized new film, readers may only need the name to identify it. But writers often provide additional information such as the director and main actors. They may also include one or more still photographs showing the main characters, as Hulbert does in this essay. (For more on the photograph, see Analyzing Visuals on p. 279.)

Reviewers usually begin by telling what the film is about and indicating the kind of film it is. Hulbert, for example, names the film in the title and opening sentence. She uses the phrase "culture wars" (also repeated in the title and opening sentence) to categorize *Juno* as a film about social problems. She also lets readers know that although the film treats a serious subject, it does so with humor or "wry style" (par. 1).

In describing a film, reviewers are guided by the *rhetorical situation* in which they are writing. In other words, they have to balance the needs and expectations of their readers against their own purposes in writing. Because reviewers know that most people read reviews primarily to decide whether or not to see the movie, they tend to be careful not to give away too much of the plot for fear of spoiling the surprise.

But not all film reviews share the same rhetorical situation. When you write for a course, you may be able to assume your readers are already familiar with the film or that they will not be concerned if you reveal the plot. Similarly, although Hulbert is writing for a Web site that features reviews of current films, she does not write a typical film review.

To analyze how Hulbert presents the film, try the following:

- Reread the opening paragraph, and write a few sentences suggesting how Hulbert conveys to readers that her essay is not a typical film review.

- Skim the essay, highlighting some of the plot details she chooses to reveal. (Note, for example, paragraphs 8 and 9, where she reveals plot twists and uses the phrase *spoiler alert.*)

- Write a few sentences identifying any plot details that you would not expect in a typical film review and speculating on why Hulbert chooses to reveal this information in her essay.

● A Well-Supported Judgment

The center of an evaluation is the argument supporting the writer's judgment. Writers usually assert their overall judgment in a thesis statement early in the essay. Wendy Kim, for example, presents her judgment of RateMyProfessors.com at the end of the opening paragraph: "While not everyone agrees that these ratings provide an entirely accurate assessment[,] . . . [o]verall, the Web site is well designed, extremely helpful, and amusing." By acknowledging that the Web site's ratings cannot be relied on as "accurate," Kim shows readers her judgment is thoughtful and measured. She also shows readers that her judgment is based on criteria or standards of judgment that readers would be likely to consider appropriate for judging the kind of subject being evaluated. As she develops her argument, Kim takes up each criterion in the order she introduced it. For example, her first reason is articulated in the opening sentence of paragraph 2: "The design of RateMyProfessors.com makes the site attractive and easy to browse." This sentence serves as the topic sentence for paragraphs 2–4. Paragraphs 5–7 address her second reason, and paragraph 8 develops her third reason.

An important way writers establish criteria is through comparison. In paragraphs 10–11, for example, Kim compares RateMyProfessor.com to three other professor evaluation Web sites. Whereas Kim makes an in-depth comparison, Hulbert makes only a passing reference to *Knocked Up*, another social problem film about unplanned pregnancy (par. 8). She uses the comparison to support her argument about the complexity of *Juno's* plot and its thoughtful representation of marriage and child-rearing.

Hulbert's argument is built on a single criterion, which she asserts in her opening paragraph: "But among *Juno's* distinctive charms is that it seems to have disarmed both sides of the family values debate." She goes on in the beginning of the next paragraph to claim that the film defuses "polarized positions on the hot-button issues" related to this debate. For readers to take her argument seriously, they need first to regard the standard she is using as appropriate to evaluating a film about a vexing social issue. Then they have to determine if the film succeeds according to the standard being applied.

To analyze how Hulbert supports her judgment of *Juno*, try the following:

- Consider whether it is appropriate that a film like *Juno*, which is about a heated cultural issue, should be judged by how effectively it undermines stereotypes and assumptions on all sides of the issue, "undercutting" what Hulbert calls "pro-life and pro-choice purism" (par. 5).

- Write a few sentences explaining why you think Hulbert's criterion is or is not appropriate for judging a film like *Juno*.

● An Effective Counterargument

Most film reviews appear when the film is initially released. Consequently, they seldom refer to other reviews. Hulbert's review, however, appeared some time after *Juno's* release, so she is able to acknowledge other reviews (the original *Slate* Web page included a link) and to quote one of them, A. O. Scott's *New York Times* review. Moreover, when she refers to the "newspaper headlines" (another link) that "announced a rise in the teenage birth rate," Hulbert describes the special context for her evaluation — what she calls "the family values debate."

To see how Hulbert acknowledges alternative judgments of *Juno*, try the following:

- Reread paragraph 1, where Hulbert sets up an opposition between what she labels the "liberal-media headquarters" (the *New York Times*) and "anti-Hollywood moralizers."

- Reread paragraphs 2–5, underlining the other labels Hulbert uses to categorize opposing points of view.

- Write a few sentences describing how Hulbert represents the cultural division in American society regarding the family values debate. Add another sentence or two giving an example of how, according to Hulbert, *Juno* attempts to break down these oppositional categories.

● A Readable Plan

Writing for *Slate*, Hulbert can expect readers to be fairly well educated and knowledgeable about current political and cultural issues. Consequently, she can assume her readers will know what she is talking about when she titles her essay "*Juno* and the Culture Wars" and refers to "the family values debate." She can also assume that if they do not know some of her vocabulary (such as *wry*, *eponymous*, and *pieties* in par. 1), they will look up the words with which they are unfamiliar. Hulbert cannot assume, however, that her readers will be able to follow her argument if she does not provide signposts along the way to signal when she is shifting from one topic to another.

To analyze how Hulbert uses transitions to help readers follow her argument, try these suggestions:

- Reread the first sentence of paragraph 4, where Hulbert provides a transition that identifies the topic she is about to discuss ("the roster of family values issues") as well as the topic she has just addressed (Juno's "image").

- Look back at the preceding paragraphs, and note in the margin where Hulbert discusses the topic of Juno's image.

- Skim paragraphs 4–6, and note in the margin where Hulbert brings up several different family values issues.
- Write a few sentences describing how effectively Hulbert guides the reader through the argument.

ANALYZING VISUALS

STILL PHOTOGRAPH OF *JUNO*'S MAIN CHARACTERS

Write a paragraph or two in which you analyze the photograph Hulbert includes in her evaluation essay and explain what it contributes to the essay.

To analyze the photo, start with the questions below (adapted from the Criteria for Analyzing Visuals in Chapter 12 on pp. 390–91):

People

- Why do you think Hulbert chose a still photograph that shows the two main characters, Juno and Bleeker?
- If you have not seen the film, what would you infer about Juno and Bleeker and their relationship from this picture?
- How would you describe their age, gender, subculture, ethnicity, and socioeconomic class?
- What do the facial expressions and body language tell you about power relationships and attitudes?

Composition

- What is the focal point of the photograph — the place your eyes are drawn to?
- What does this focal point bring to your attention? What does it suggest about the characters or their relationship?
- How is color used — for example, to draw your attention, to connect images, or something else?

Rhetorical Context

- How does the photograph's portrayal of Juno and Bleeker correspond to Hulbert's descriptions of them in paragraphs 2 and 3?
- If you have seen the film, what is happening in the scene depicted in this photograph? What ideas and feelings do you think readers familiar with the film are likely to experience as they look at the photograph and read Hulbert's essay?

CONSIDERING TOPICS FOR YOUR OWN ESSAY

List several movies that you have seen recently, and choose one from your list that you recall especially well and about which you already have a strong overall judgment. Then consider how you would argue for your judgment. Specifically, what reasons do you think you would give your readers? Why do you assume that your readers would accept these reasons as appropriate for evaluating this particular kind of film? (Note that if you were actually to write about this movie, you would need to see it at least twice to develop your reasons and find supporting examples. For this activity, however, you do not have to view your film again.)

CHRISTINE ROMANO wrote the following essay when she was a first-year college student. In it she evaluates another student's argument essay, Jessica Statsky's "Children Need to Play, Not Compete," which appears in Chapter 5 of this book (pp. 165–71). Romano focuses not on the writing strategies or basic features of an essay arguing a position but rather on its logic — on whether the argument is likely to convince its intended readers — according to the standards presented in Chapter 9. You might want to review these standards on pp. 348–50 before you read Romano's evaluation. Also, if you have not already read Statsky's essay, you might want to do so now, thinking about what seems most and least convincing to you about her argument that competitive sports can be harmful to young children.

"Children Need to Play, Not Compete," by Jessica Statsky:

An Evaluation

Christine Romano

Parents of young children have a lot to worry about and to hope   1
for. In "Children Need to Play, Not Compete," Jessica Statsky appeals to
their worries and hopes in order to convince them that organized competitive sports may harm their children physically and psychologically.
Statsky states her thesis clearly and fully forecasts the reasons she will
offer to justify her position: Besides causing physical and psychological
harm, competitive sports discourage young people from becoming players and fans when they are older and inevitably put parents' needs and
fantasies ahead of children's welfare. Statsky also carefully defines her
key terms. By *sports*, for example, she means to include both contact
and noncontact sports that emphasize competition. The sports may be

organized locally at schools or summer sports camps or nationally, as in the examples of Peewee Football and Little League Baseball. She is concerned only with children six to twelve years of age.

2   In this essay, I will evaluate the logic of Statsky's argument, considering whether the support for her thesis is appropriate, believable, consistent, and complete. While her logic *is* appropriate, believable, and consistent, her argument also has weaknesses. I will focus on two: Her argument seems incomplete because she neglects to anticipate parents' predictable questions and objections and because she fails to support certain parts of it fully.

3   Statsky provides appropriate support for her thesis. Throughout her essay, she relies for support on different kinds of information (she cites eleven separate sources, including books, newspapers, and Web sites). Her quotations, examples, and statistics all support the reasons she believes competitive sports are bad for children. For example, in paragraph 3, Statsky offers the reason that "overly competitive sports" may damage children's fragile bodies and that contact sports, in particular, may be especially hazardous. She supports this reason by paraphrasing Koppett's claim that muscle strain or even lifelong injury may result when a twelve-year-old throws curve balls. She then quotes Tutko on the dangers of tackle football. The opinions of both experts are obviously appropriate. They are relevant to her reason, and we can easily imagine that they would worry many parents.

4   Not only is Statsky's support appropriate, but it is also believable. Statsky quotes or summarizes authorities to support her argument in paragraphs 3–6, 8, 9, and 11. The question is whether readers would find these authorities credible. Since Statsky relies almost entirely on authorities to support her argument, readers must believe these authorities for her argument to succeed. I have not read Statsky's sources, but I think there are good reasons to consider them authoritative. First of all, the newspaper authors she quotes write for two of America's most respected newspapers, the *New York Times* and the *Los Angeles Times*. These newspapers are read across the country by political leaders and financial experts and by people interested in the arts and popular culture. Both have sports reporters who not only report on

sports events but also take a critical look at sports issues. In addition, both newspapers have reporters who specialize in children's health and education. Second, Statsky gives background information about the authorities she quotes, which is intended to increase the person's believability in the eyes of parents of young children. In paragraph 3, she tells readers that Thomas Tutko is "a psychology professor at San Jose State University and coauthor of the book *Winning Is Everything and Other American Myths*." In paragraph 5, she announces that Martin Rablovsky is "a former sports editor for the *New York Times*," and she notes that he has watched children play organized sports for many years. Third, she quotes from two Web sites — the official Little League site and a message board. Parents are likely to accept the authority of the Little League site and be interested in what other parents and coaches (most of whom are also parents) have to say.

In addition to quoting authorities, Statsky relies on examples and anecdotes to support the reasons for her position. If examples and anecdotes are to be believable, they must seem representative to readers, not bizarre or highly unusual or completely unpredictable. Readers can imagine a similar event happening elsewhere. For anecdotes to be believable, they should, in addition, be specific and true to life. All of Statsky's examples and anecdotes fulfill these requirements, and her readers would find them believable. For example, early in her argument, in paragraph 4, Statsky reasons that fear of being hurt greatly reduces children's enjoyment of contact sports. The anecdote comes from Tosches's investigative report on Peewee Football, as does the quotation by the mother of an eight-year-old player who says that the children become frightened and pretend to be injured in order to stay out of the game. In the anecdote, a seven-year-old makes himself vomit to avoid playing. Because these echo the familiar "I feel bad" or "I'm sick" excuse children give when they do not want to go somewhere (especially school) or do something, most parents would find them believable. They could easily imagine their own children pretending to be hurt or ill if they were fearful or depressed. The anecdote is also specific. Tosches reports what the boy said and did and what the coach said and did.

5

6   Other examples provide support for all the major reasons Statsky gives for her position:

- That competitive sports pose psychological dangers — children becoming serious and unplayful when the game starts (par. 5)

- That adults' desire to win puts children at risk — parents fighting each other at a Peewee Football game and a coach setting fire to an opposing team's jersey (par. 8)

- That organized sports should emphasize cooperation and individual performance instead of winning — a coach banning scoring but finding that parents would not support him and a New York City basketball league in which all children play an equal amount of time and scoring is easier (par. 11)

All of these examples are appropriate to the reason they support. They are also believable. Together, they help Statsky achieve her purpose of convincing parents that organized, competitive sports may be bad for their children and that there are alternatives.

7   If readers are to find an argument logical and convincing, it must be consistent and complete. While there are no inconsistencies or contradictions in Statsky's argument, it is seriously incomplete because it neglects to support fully one of its reasons, it fails to anticipate many predictable questions parents would have, and it pays too little attention to noncontact competitive team sports. The most obvious example of this support comes in paragraph 11, where Statsky asserts that many parents are ready for children's team sports that emphasize cooperation and individual performance. Yet the example of a Little League official who failed to win parents' approval to ban scores raises serious questions about just how many parents are ready to embrace noncompetitive sports teams. The other support, a brief description of City Sports for Kids in New York City, is very convincing but will only be logically compelling to those parents who are already inclined to agree with Statsky's position. Parents inclined to disagree with Statsky would need additional evidence. Most parents know that big cities receive special federal funding for evening, weekend, and summer recreation. Brief descriptions of six or eight noncompetitive

teams in a variety of sports in cities, rural areas, suburban neighbor-hoods — some funded publicly, some funded privately — would be more likely to convince skeptics. Statsky is guilty here of failing to accept the burden of proof, a logical fallacy.

Statsky's argument is also incomplete in that it fails to antici-pate certain objections and questions that some parents, especially those she most wants to convince, are almost sure to raise. In the first sentences of paragraphs 6, 9, and 10, Statsky does show that she is thinking about her readers' questions. She does not go nearly far enough, however, to have a chance of influencing two types of readers: those who themselves are or were fans of and participants in competitive sports and those who want their six- to twelve-year-old children involved in mainstream sports programs despite the risks, especially the national programs that have a certain prestige. Such parents might feel that competitive team sports for young children create a sense of community with a shared purpose, build character through self-sacrifice and commitment to the group, teach children to face their fears early and learn how to deal with them through the support of coaches and team members, and introduce children to the principles of social cooperation and collaboration. Some parents are likely to believe and to know from personal experience that coaches who burn opposing teams' jerseys on the pitching mound before the game starts are the exception, not the rule. Some young children idolize teachers and coaches, and team practice and games are the brightest moments in their lives. Statsky seems not to have consid-ered these reasonable possibilities, and as a result her argument lacks a compelling logic it might have had. By acknowledging that she was aware of many of these objections — and perhaps even accommodat-ing more of them in her own argument, as she does in paragraph 10, while refuting other objections — she would have strengthened her argument.

Finally, Statsky's argument is incomplete because she overlooks examples of noncontact team sports. Track, swimming, and tennis are good examples that some readers would certainly think of. Some elementary schools compete in track meets. Public and private clubs and recreational programs organize competitive swimming and tennis competitions. In these sports, individual performance is the focus. No one gets trampled. Children exert themselves only as much as they are able to. Yet individual performances are scored, and a team score is derived. Because Statsky fails to mention any of these obvious possibilities, her argument is weakened.

10   The logic of Statsky's argument, then, has both strengths and weaknesses. The support she offers is appropriate, believable, and consistent. The major weakness is incompleteness — she fails to anticipate more fully the likely objections of a wide range of readers. Her logic would prevent parents who enjoy and advocate competitive sports from taking her argument seriously. Such parents and their children have probably had positive experiences with team sports, and these experiences would lead them to believe that the gains are worth whatever risks may be involved. Many probably think that the risks Statsky points out can be avoided by careful monitoring. For those parents inclined to agree with her, Statsky's logic is likely to seem sound and complete. An argument that successfully confirms readers' beliefs is certainly valid, and Statsky succeeds admirably at this kind of argument. Because she does not offer compelling counterarguments to the legitimate objections of those inclined not to agree with her, however, her success is limited.

MAKING CONNECTIONS: COMPETITIVE TEAM SPORTS AND SOCIAL COOPERATION

Romano reasons in paragraph 8 that some parents "feel that competitive team sports for young children create a sense of community with a shared purpose, build character through self-sacrifice and commitment to the group, teach children to face their fears early and learn how to deal with them through the support of coaches and team members, and introduce children to the principles of social cooperation and collaboration."

With two or three other students, discuss this view of the role that sports plays in developing a child's sense of social cooperation.

- Begin by telling one another about your own, your siblings', or your children's experiences with team sports between the ages of six and twelve.

- Explain how participating in sports at this young age did or did not teach social cooperation. If you think team sports failed to teach cooperation or had some other effect, explain the effect it did have.

ANALYZING WRITING STRATEGIES

Basic Features

● A Well-Presented Subject

Christine Romano is writing for a uniquely academic rhetorical situation in that she has to assume that her readers — primarily her instructor, but also possibly other students — will have read the essay she is writing about and may even reread it with her evaluation in mind. Because she is responding to a specific assignment to evaluate a reading in the textbook, Romano can simply name the reading by title and author. Following her teacher's instructions, she refers to paragraphs rather than page numbers, and she does not include a formal works-cited page. If your instructor gives you the option of evaluating a reading — such as an essay, a story, or a poem — you may be required to cite the text using MLA style. For example, your list of works cited would cite Romano's essay this way:

> Romano, Christine. "'Children Need to Play, Not Compete,' by Jessica Statsky: An
> Evaluation." *Axelrod & Cooper's Concise*
> *Guide to Writing*. 6th ed. Ed. Rise B. Axelrod and Charles R. Cooper. Boston:
> Bedford, 2012. 166–71. Print.

In addition to identifying her subject, Romano begins her essay by summarizing Statsky's argument. To analyze how Romano represents the essay she is evaluating, try the following:

- Reread paragraph 1, and note in the margin the kinds of information about Statsky's essay that Romano includes.
- Write a couple of sentences indicating the kinds of information that Romano uses in her introductory paragraph. Add a sentence or two explaining why you think Romano chose to begin with this information.

For more information on citing sources, see Chapter 17.

● A Well-Supported Judgment

Writers who use textual evidence choose summarizing over quoting when they want to emphasize a text's ideas rather than its language. They choose summarizing over paraphrasing when they want to stress the source's main ideas or information and skip the details.

Kim and Romano are both writing about texts, and they therefore rely primarily on textual evidence in the form of quotation, paraphrase, and summary. Kim, for example, opens her essay by quoting the tagline for the RateMyProfessors.com Web site: "Where the students do the grading." She also quotes extensively from comments posted on the Web site in paragraph 7 to support her assertion that they may be the most informative parts of the site. To acknowledge readers' concerns, she quotes from several external sources in paragraphs 8 and 9.

In contrast, Romano quotes minimally and refers to no outside sources (following her teacher's instructions to focus solely on the text being evaluated): She chooses instead to summarize or paraphrase passages from the text she is evaluating. Here is an example where Romano uses summary:

> In the anecdote, a seven-year-old makes himself vomit to avoid playing. (par. 5)

The original passage (Statsky, par. 4) includes dialogue and detail that Romano decided was not needed to make her point. Her summary is concise, significantly shorter than Statsky's original (ten instead of sixty-nine words, a reduction of more than 85 percent). Here is an example of Romano's use of paraphrase:

> Besides causing physical and psychological harm, competitive sports discourage
> young people from becoming players and fans when they are older and inevitably put
> parents' needs and fantasies ahead of children's welfare. (par. 1)

Romano's paraphrase does not leave out very much detail or drastically condense Statsky's original passage from paragraph 2 (thirty-one words in the paraphrase compared to fifty-nine in the original, slightly less than a 50 percent reduction).

More important than whether the writer quotes, summarizes, or paraphrases is the way the writer explains how the textual evidence supports the point being made. To analyze Romano's use of summary to support her evaluation, try the following:

- Reread paragraph 5, where the summary quoted above is presented, and examine Romano's explanation of what the summary demonstrates. Notice how many sentences Romano uses before and after the summary to introduce and explain it.

- Write a couple of sentences about how Romano introduces the summary and explains what it demonstrates. Why do you think she devotes so much space to explaining the summary rather than letting it speak for itself?

For additional information on using these strategies for presenting textual evidence, see Chapter 5, Working with Sources, pp. 198–99; Chapter 13, p. 412; and Chapter 17, pp. 490–95.

● An Effective Counterargument

Writers of evaluation sometimes need to respond to readers' possible objections to the argument, which they may either concede or refute. Wendy Kim, for example, anticipates several concerns readers are likely to raise about RateMyProfessors.com. In paragraphs 6 and 8, she concedes criticism of the Easiness and Hot categories, both of which she acknowledges are controversial, but she refutes the implicit claim that these categories really affect what students learn from the site. Similarly, she concedes that the ratings are not statistically valid, and while quoting the Web site's claim that they are nevertheless "uncannily accurate" (par. 9), she concludes that "students should not approach the ratings uncritically."

To analyze how Romano attempts to anticipate readers' possible objections and develop an effective counterargument, write a few sentences describing her counterargument strategy and why you think it is or is not effective.

● A Readable Plan

Writers of evaluative essays usually try to make their argument clear and direct. To do so, they typically state their essay's thesis and forecast their reasons early on. Romano, for example, states her plan explicitly in paragraph 2: "In this essay, I will evaluate the logic of Statsky's argument, considering whether the support for her thesis is appropriate, believable, consistent, and complete." Although Romano could have skipped this sentence, it does help readers understand the criteria she intends to apply.

The next sentence states her judgment that Statsky's argument meets the first three criteria but falls short in the fourth criterion of completeness. This forecast of the reasons she will develop in the essay serves as a helpful map readers can use as they read her argument. Notice that Romano is careful to introduce these reasons in the order she first listed them — examining the appropriateness of Statsky's support in paragraph 3, believability in paragraphs 4–6, and consistency and completeness in paragraphs 7–9.

Romano also uses topic sentences and transitional words and phrases to make the organizational plan of her essay visible to readers.

To analyze how Romano helps her readers follow her argument, try the following:

- Reread paragraphs 3–9, and highlight the words *appropriate, believable, consistent,* and *complete.* (Highlight the words in any form they appear, for example, *incomplete*).

- Notice where these words appear in each paragraph, and whether they are used in topic sentences, transitions, or summaries.

- Write a couple of sentences assessing how well these key words help to keep readers oriented. Add a sentence or two describing where Romano tends to place them in a paragraph and why.

Guide to Writing

The Writing Assignment

Write an essay evaluating a specific subject. Examine your subject closely, and make a judgment about it. Give reasons for your judgment that are based on widely recognized criteria or standards for evaluating a subject like yours. Support your reasons with examples and other details primarily from your subject.

This Guide to Writing will help you apply what you have learned about how writers clearly present a subject, make a clear and well-supported judgment about it, present an effective counterargument to objections and alternative judgments, and make the whole thing readable. The Guide is divided into five sections with various activities in each section:

- **Invention and Research**
- **Planning and Drafting**
- **Critical Reading Guide**
- **Revising**
- **Editing and Proofreading**

The Guide is designed to escort you through the writing process, from finding a subject to editing your finished essay. Your instructor may require you to follow the Guide to Writing from beginning to end. Working through the Guide to Writing in this way will help you — as it has helped many other college students — write a thoughtful, fully developed, polished essay.

If, however, your instructor gives you latitude to choose, and if you have had experience writing an essay in which you justify an evaluation, then you can decide on the order in which you will do the activities in the Guide to Writing. For example, the Invention and Research section includes activities to help you find a subject to write about, explore it, analyze and define your audience and purpose, and formulate a tentative judgment of it, among other things. Obviously, finding a subject must precede the other activities, but you may come to the Guide with a subject already in mind, and you may choose to make a tentative judgment before considering your own and your readers' likely criteria. In fact, you may find your response to one of the invention activities expanding into a draft before you have had a chance to do any of the other activities. That is a good thing — but you should later flesh out your draft by going back to the activities you skipped and layering the new material into your draft.

The following chart will help you find answers to many of the questions you might have about planning, drafting, and revising an essay justifying an evaluation. The page references in the right-hand column refer to examples from the readings and activities in the Guide to Writing.

Starting Points: Justifying an Evaluation

●●●● **Basic Features**

A Well-Presented Subject

How do I come up with a subject to write about?	• Considering Topics for Your Own Essay (p. 280) • Choosing a Subject to Write About (pp. 291–93) • Testing Your Choice (p. 295) • Clarifying Your Purpose and Audience (p. 299)
What is my purpose in writing? How can I present my subject clearly and convincingly?	• Reading Essays Justifying Evaluations: Purpose and Audience (p. 265) • Defining Your Purpose for Your Readers (p. 297) • Presenting the Subject (p. 299)

A Well-Supported Judgment

How do I come up with a reasonable evaluation?	• Ways In: Bringing the Subject and Your Audience into Focus (pp. 293–94) • Making a Tentative Judgment (p. 295) • Researching Your Argument (p. 297)
How do I construct an argument supporting my judgment?	• Ways In: Developing Your Argument and Counterargument (pp. 295–96) • Your Reasons and Support (p. 300) • Working with Sources: Using Summary to Support Your Evaluative Argument (pp. 304–5)

An Effective Counterargument

How do I respond to possible objections and to alternative judgments?	• Ways In: Developing Your Argument and Counterargument (pp. 295–96) • Your Counterargument of Objections or Alternative Judgments (p. 300) • Two Sentence Strategies (pp. 302–3)

A Readable Plan

How can I help my readers follow my argument?	• Formulating a Tentative Thesis Statement (p. 298) • Outlining Your Draft (pp. 300–1) • Writing the Opening Sentences (p. 302)

Invention and Research

The following invention activities are easy to complete and take only a few minutes. Spreading out the activities over several days will stimulate your creativity, enabling you to consider many more potential issues to address and possible ways in which to address them. Remember to keep a written record of your invention work: You will need it when you draft the essay and later when you revise it.

Choosing a Subject to Write About

List several subjects that you might like to explore. This will come more easily to some of us than to others. As you explore possibilities, bear in mind that you are looking for a subject that meets the following criteria:

Criteria for Choosing a Subject: A Checklist

The subject should be
- ☐ one that has strengths and/or weaknesses you could write about;
- ☐ one that you can examine closely, that you can view and review;
- ☐ one that is typically evaluated according to criteria or standards of judgment that you understand.

If you are like most people, you will need some help in coming up with a number of good options. Review the Considering Topics for Your Own Essay activities following the readings, and recall any subjects those suggestions brought to mind. For further ideas, consult the suggestions in the following sections.

Listing Subjects

Make a list of subjects you might consider writing about. Because you will need to spend considerable time analyzing your subject, consider subjects that you can examine and reexamine, such as Web sites, DVDs, written texts, software programs, and the like. To get started, consider the suggestions below, organized by broad category:

- *Culture:* Film or television series, computer game, recorded performance, artist, individual work of art, museum, amusement park
- *Written work:* Essay, poem, short story, Web site, magazine, textbook, campus publication
- *Education:* Your high school, a particular program or major you are considering, a science lab, a teacher
- *Government:* Elected official or candidate for public office, proposed or existing law, agency, or program

- *A Particular Community:*
  - Evaluate how well one of the following meets the needs of residents of your town or city: the public library, health clinic, neighborhood watch or block parent program, meals-on-wheels program, theater or symphony.
  - Evaluate how well one of the following serves the members of your religious community: a religious school, youth or senior group, choir, building.
- *A Particular Career/Workplace:*
  - Evaluate a job you have had or currently have, or evaluate someone else you have observed closely, such as a coworker or supervisor.
  - Evaluate a local job-training program, either one in which you have participated or one where you can observe and interview trainees.

Using the Web to Find or Explore a Subject

Exploring Web sites can provide you with an idea of what to write about, if you have not already chosen a subject, and it can enrich your understanding of a subject you have already chosen. Moreover, the Web provides a rich repository of cultural and historical information, including photographs and music, which you might be able to use to create a richly detailed, multimedia text for your readers.

Here are some suggestions:

- If you do not yet have a subject but have an idea of what broad category interests you — films, music, books, computer games, software, technology, and so on — look for sites that evaluate such things, and get a sense of what criteria people usually use when evaluating them.
- If you have already chosen a subject to evaluate, find out how others have judged it and the criteria they have used in their evaluation. You may find points on which you agree as well as disagree that you can use in your essay to support your judgment or to counterargue.

Make notes of any ideas suggested by your online research, and download any visuals you might include in your essay, being sure to get the information necessary to cite any online sources. (See pp. 505–7 for the MLA citation guidelines for electronic sources.)

Familiarizing Yourself with the Subject

Before making a choice, take some time to study your subject, and take notes on what seem to be its strengths and weaknesses. The best subject is one you can view and review — for example, a DVD, Web site, printed text, software program, or piece of equipment. If you plan to evaluate a film or recorded performance, for example, you will want to have it on DVD or in digital form so that you can reexamine parts and possibly capture stills or a video clip.

Be aware that some subjects will require special planning. Evaluating a one-time performance or sports event that cannot be recorded is especially challenging because it requires advance planning (such as considering the criteria you expect to apply as you judge the performance), careful note-taking during the performance, and time devoted right after the performance to adding to and clarifying your notes. If you are evaluating something like a government agency or a campus program or lab, you will need to get permission to do field research, making observations and interviewing people.

Ways In: Bringing the Subject and Your Audience into Focus

Basic Features

Once you have made a preliminary choice of a subject, the following activities will help you explore what you already know about your subject, determine what else you need to find out, and discover ways of presenting the subject to your readers. You can begin with whichever activity you want, but wherever you begin, be sure to return to the other activities to fill in the details.

Exploring What You Know about the Subject

Examine Your First Impressions of the Subject. *Write for a few minutes about what you currently know and think about your subject.* Focus your writing by trying to answer one or both of these questions:

- What do I like and dislike about this subject?
- What are the subject's strengths and weaknesses?

Try to identify specific aspects of the subject and explain what it is about them that you think is good or bad, or strong or weak.

What is important is not just your judgment (which may change as you think about the subject), but also the kinds of things you choose to focus on. For example, if you were evaluating a particular sports event such as the Super Bowl, you might focus on the drama of the game, the quality of the defense, the performance of particular players, and so on.

Consider Your Criteria. Write for a few minutes considering your subject in light of the criteria or standards of judgment you typically apply to such subjects. The following questions may help you develop your thinking:

- *What kind of subject is it?* For example, if it is a film, what kind of film is it? Sometimes, subjects fit into more than one category — *Juno*, for instance, is a social problem film, but it is also an unconventional romantic comedy. Your judgment may depend on how you classify the subject and whether you appreciate that it pushes against conventional boundaries or stays within them.

(continued)

(continued)

> • *What criteria or standards of judgment do you usually apply in evaluating a subject of this kind?* For example, you might evaluate a film like *Juno* in terms of its plot, humor, acting, its realistic representation of "real" life situations and people, or, like Hulbert, on the way it handles controversial subject matter.
> • *What other subjects of this kind does this particular subject make you think of, and how do they compare to the subject you are evaluating now?*

Exploring What Your Readers Know about the Subject

Identify Your Readers. *Write several sentences describing your readers by answering the following questions:*

• For what particular readers am I writing this evaluation?
• What are these readers likely to know about my subject? Will I be introducing the subject to them (as in a typical film or book review), or will they already be familiar with it?
• If my readers are already familiar with the subject, what do I expect them to like and dislike about it?
• How might such factors as my readers' age, gender, education, socioeconomic status, work experience, and religious or political affiliation affect their judgment of the subject?

Consider Your Readers' Likely Criteria. Write for a few minutes considering the criteria or standards of judgment your readers are likely to apply to subjects like yours. The following questions may help you develop your analysis:

• *How have your readers judged similar subjects in the past?* For example, if you are evaluating a film like *Juno*, consider whether your readers tend to like films about social issues, films with a strong female character, films with a quirky sense of humor, and so on.
• *Can you predict your readers' reaction to a subject like yours?* For example, given your readers' age, are they likely to appreciate films about teenagers? Given their religious or political affiliations, are they likely to appreciate films that challenge their point of view?
• *Can you predict the criteria your readers are likely to apply to your subject?* For example, if your readers live in the suburbs, a small town, or the inner city, how might they judge a pregnant teenager with an attitude like Juno's?
• *Which of your readers' criteria do you share?* Can you build an argument for your judgment based on these criteria?
• *If your readers are not likely to share your criteria, how will you be able to explain and defend your judgment?*

Making a Tentative Judgment

Write a few sentences stating your current judgment of the subject. Try answering these two basic questions:

- In what ways is it a good example of this kind of subject?
- In what ways does it fall short?

Testing Your Choice

Now test your choice by asking yourself the following questions:

- *Do I know enough about the subject, or can I learn enough in the time I have, to write an argument supporting my judgment?*
- *Are my readers likely to share my criteria, or will I be able to justify my criteria in a way that will assure my readers that my judgment makes sense even if they do not agree with me?*

As you plan and draft your argument, you will probably want to consider these questions again. If at any point you cannot answer them with a confident *yes*, you may want to consider revising your evaluation or choosing a different subject to evaluate. If you have serious doubts, consider discussing them with your instructor.

A Collaborative Activity:

Testing Your Choice

Get together with two or three other students, and discuss the subjects you have tentatively chosen.

Presenters: Take turns briefly describing your subject and the judgment you plan to argue for.

Listeners: Explain to each presenter what criteria or standards of judgment you would use to evaluate a subject of this kind and how you think you would judge it. For example, would you judge a science-fiction film by the acting, ideas, special effects, or something else? Would you judge a lecture course by how organized the lectures are, whether images are shown, whether the tests reflect the lectures, or something else? In other words, tell the presenter what criteria you would apply to his or her particular subject.

Ways In: Developing Your Argument and Counterargument

Basic Features

The following activities will help you develop your argument by collecting reasons and evidence for your judgment and will also help you develop your counterargument by anticipating readers' objections and alternative judgments. You can begin with whichever activity you want, but wherever you begin, be sure to return to the other activities to explore the possibilities.

Depending on what you already know about your subject, you could use the activities to develop an outline of your argument and then do research to fill in the details, or you could start with research (see p. 297).

Developing Your Argument

List Possible Reasons. *Write down at least two or three reasons for your judgment, but try for as many as five.* Some of these reasons will turn out to be more promising than others. Try listing your reasons as *because* statements — for example,

RateMyProfessors.com is good *because* it is well designed

or *because* it has useful information.

Collect Evidence. *Make notes of the evidence — such as examples, authorities, textual evidence, images, statistics, and comparisons — you might be able to use to support each reason.* You may already have some evidence you could use. If you lack evidence for any of your reasons, you may need to collect additional material. (Make notes of your sources, perhaps in a working bibliography.)

Choose Your Strongest Reasons. *Write several sentences on each reason, trying out the evidence you have that supports it.* Then identify the reasons you think are compelling. These may be the ones most likely to be convincing to your particular readers, but some of your best reasons may be based on criteria your readers have not thought of or may not value as highly as you do.

Counterarguing Readers' Likely Objections or Alternative Judgments

Anticipate a Likely Objection or Alternative Judgment. *Write a few sentences describing an objection or an alternative judgment you expect some readers to raise.* Consider whether readers base their criticism on different criteria or analyze the subject differently than you do.

Consider Whether to Concede or Refute the Objection. *Write a few sentences trying out a possible counterargument.* You may be able simply to acknowledge an objection or alternative judgment. If the criticism is serious, consider conceding the point and qualifying your judgment. You might also try to refute it by arguing that the standards you are using are appropriate and important. (For example, Hulbert could have expected some readers to argue that *Juno* is a conventional romantic film, based primarily on Juno's quirky character and the seemingly happy ending. If you were to counterargue, you might concede the point about Juno's character but refute the idea that the film has a happy, romantic ending.)

Researching Your Argument

You may have identified questions you have about your subject and made notes about the kinds of information you need to support your argument and counterargument. Doing research with your questions and notes in mind will help you work efficiently. But researching sometimes is most productive when you have the time to go into unexplored territory. You may find support for the judgment you have made, but you also may find convincing opposing opinions and decide to modify your argument as a result.

If you are evaluating a subject that others have evaluated, you will want to do library and Internet research to find out what judgments they have made. If you are writing on an issue related to your school, community, or workplace, you may want to conduct interviews to see how people in those venues view the subject and how they react to your judgment.

If you do not know the criteria usually used to evaluate your subject, do some research. For example, if you are reviewing a particular kind of film, read a few recent reviews of the same kind of film you are reviewing, noting the standards that reviewers typically use and the reasons that they assert for liking or disliking that kind of film. If you are evaluating a soccer team, you could read about coaching or playing soccer or talk to an experienced soccer coach or player to learn about what makes an excellent team. If you are evaluating a civic, governmental, or religious program, look for information online or in the library about what makes a good program of its type. If you are evaluating an essay in this book, consult the standards suggested in the Purpose and Audience and the Basic Features sections of the chapter where the essay appears. If you are evaluating an argument essay from Chapters 5–7, you will find additional standards in Evaluating the Logic of an Argument, Recognizing Emotional Manipulation, and Judging the Writer's Credibility in Chapter 9 (pp. 348–52).

Defining Your Purpose for Your Readers

Write a few sentences defining your purpose. Remember that you have already identified your readers and developed a tentative argument with these readers in mind. Try now to define your purpose by considering the following questions:

- *If my readers are likely to agree with my overall judgment, what is my aim in writing — to confirm them in their judgment by giving them well-supported reasons for it, to help them refute others' judgments, or to suggest how they might respond to questions and objections?*

- *If my readers and I share criteria for making judgments of this kind but differ in the judgment we make about the subject, what is my aim in writing — to convince them to adopt my judgment, or just to compel them to admit that my judgment is a legitimate one?*

- *If my readers have different standards of judgment, should I try to convince them to consider seriously the criteria I am using?*

Formulating a Tentative Thesis Statement

Write several sentences that could serve as your thesis statement. Think about how you should state your overall judgment — how emphatic you should make it, whether you should qualify it, and whether you should include in the thesis a forecast of your reasons and support. Remember that a strong thesis statement should be clear, arguable, and appropriately qualified. As you consider your overall judgment, keep in mind that readers of evaluative essays expect writers to present a balanced evaluation of a subject by pointing out strengths as well as weaknesses. At the same time, however, readers expect to encounter a definitive judgment, not a vague, wishy-washy, or undecided judgment.

Review the readings in this chapter to see how other writers construct thesis statements. For example, Romano uses the thesis statement to forecast her reasons as well as to express her overall judgment. She begins by indicating the standards she thinks are appropriate for evaluating her subject. Her thesis statement shows that she bases her reasons on these standards. In addition, it lets readers know in advance what she likes about the subject she is evaluating as well as what she does not like: "While [Statsky's] logic *is* appropriate, believable, and consistent, her argument also has weaknesses" (par. 2). Romano makes her thesis statement seem thoughtful and balanced, but there is no ambivalence or confusion about her judgment. She is clear and emphatic, not vague or wishy-washy.

As you draft your own tentative thesis statement, think carefully about the language you use. It should be clear and unambiguous, emphatic but appropriately qualified. Although you will most likely refine your thesis statement as you draft and revise your essay, trying now to articulate it will help give direction and impetus to your planning and drafting.

For more on thesis and forecasting statements, see Chapter 13.

Planning and Drafting

The following activities will help you review what you have accomplished so far, refine your purpose, set goals for your draft, and outline it. In addition, this section will help you draft, with advice on writing opening sentences, using effective sentence strategies, and working with sources.

Refining Your Purpose and Setting Goals

Before starting to draft, review the questions below, which are designed to help you sharpen your purpose for your audience and set goals for your draft. Your instructor may ask you to write out your answers to some of these questions or simply to think about them as you plan and draft your essay.

Clarifying Your Purpose and Audience

- *What do I want my readers to think about the subject after reading my evaluation? Do I want them to appreciate the subject's strengths and weaknesses, as Kim and Romano do? Or do I want them to see why it succeeds (as Hulbert does) or fails?*

- *Should I assume, like Hulbert, that my readers may have read other evaluations of my subject? Or should I assume that I am introducing readers to the subject, as Kim and Romano seem to do?*

- *How should I present myself to my readers — as someone who is an expert on the subject (perhaps like Hulbert) or as someone who has examined the subject closely (like Kim)? Should I convey enthusiasm (as Kim and Hulbert do) or strike a more balanced, distanced tone (as Romano does)?*

The Beginning

- *How can I capture readers' attention from the start? Should I begin by naming and describing the subject, as Kim and Romano do? Should I open with a reference to current events, like Hulbert?*

- *When should I state my judgment — at the beginning of the opening paragraph; in the middle, like Romano; at the end, like Kim and Hulbert; or should I wait until later in the essay?*

- *Should I forecast the reasons for my judgment in the first couple of paragraphs, as Kim, Romano, and Hulbert do?*

Presenting the Subject

- *How should I identify the subject? In addition to naming it, as all the writers in this chapter do, should I place it in a recognizable category or genre, as Kim does when she talks about "Internet professor evaluation sites" (par. 10) or Hulbert does when she talks about "the culture wars" (title and par. 1)?*

- *What about the subject should I describe? Can I use visuals to illustrate, as Kim and Hulbert do? Should I place the subject politically, as Hulbert does?*

- *If the subject has a story, how much of it should I tell? Should I simply set the scene and identify the characters, or should I give details of the plot, even at the risk of spoiling the surprise, as Hulbert does?*

Your Overall Judgment

- *How should I state my thesis? Should I forecast my reasons early in the essay, as Kim, Romano, and Hulbert do? Should I place my thesis at the beginning or wait until after I have provided a context?*

- *How can I convince readers to consider my overall judgment seriously even if they disagree with it? Should I try to present a balanced judgment by praising some things and criticizing others, as all the writers but Hulbert do?*

Your Reasons and Support

- *How can I present my reasons and the criteria on which they are based? Should I try to justify my criteria, as Romano does by asserting the authority of her textbook, or as Kim does by telling readers she took a class in Web site design? Can I assume that my readers will share my criteria, as Hulbert does when she praises the film for taking "aim at everybody's pieties"?*

- *If I have more than one reason, how should I order them? Should I begin with my strongest reason or with the one I think is most likely to appeal to my readers, as Kim does when she begins with the Web site's design and navigability? In an evaluation that is generally positive, should I begin with the strengths of my subject and end with its weaknesses, as Romano does?*

- *How can I support my reasons — with example, paraphrase, and summary, as all the writers do? Should I quote the text, as Kim, Romano, and Hulbert do? Can I call on authorities and cite statistics, as Kim does?*

Your Counterargument of Objections or Alternative Judgments

- *What objections or alternative judgments should I anticipate? Should I assume that my readers will favor a subject I am criticizing?*

- *Should I concede legitimate objections and qualify my judgment, as Romano and Kim do? Or should I devote my essay to refuting the alternative judgment?*

The Ending

- *How should I conclude? Should I try to frame the essay by echoing something from the opening or from another part of the essay, as Hulbert does?*

- *Should I conclude by restating my overall judgment, as all the writers do?*

- *Should I include a rhetorical question at the end, as Kim does?*

Outlining Your Draft

An evaluative essay contains as many as four basic parts:

1. Presentation of the subject
2. Judgment of the subject
3. Presentation of reasons and support
4. Consideration of readers' objections and alternative judgments

These parts can be organized in various ways. If, for example, you expect readers to disagree with your judgment, you could show them what you think they have overlooked or misjudged about the subject. You could begin by presenting the subject; then you could assert your thesis, present your reasons and support, and anticipate and refute readers' likely objections, as illustrated in the following rough outline:

    I. Presentation of the subject

    II. Thesis statement (judgment)

    III. First reason and support

    IV. Anticipation and refutation of objection

    V. Second reason and support

    VI. Anticipation and accommodation of objection

    VII. Conclusion

If you expect some of your readers to disagree with your negative judgment even though they base their judgment on the same standards on which you base yours, you could try to show them that the subject really does not satisfy your shared standards. You could begin by restating these standards and then demonstrating how the subject fails to meet them:

    I. Establish shared standards

    II. Acknowledge alternative judgment

    III. State thesis (judgment) that subject fails to meet shared criteria

    IV. First reason and support showing how subject falls short

    V. Second reason and support

       (etc.)

    VI. Conclusion

There are, of course, many other possible ways to organize an evaluative essay, but these outlines should help you start planning your own essay.

Consider any outlining you do before you begin drafting to be tentative. Never be a slave to an outline. As you draft, you will usually see ways to improve your original plan. Be ready to revise your outline, shift parts around, or drop or add parts as you draft. If you use the outlining function of your word processing program, changing your outline will be simple, and you may be able to write the essay simply by expanding the outline.

For more on outlining, see Chapter 8.

Drafting

If you have not already begun to draft your essay, this section will help by suggesting how to write your opening sentences, how to use the sentence strategies of comparison and contrast and balance, and how to summarize your subject. Drafting is not always a smooth process, so do not be afraid to leave spaces where you do not know what to put in or to write notes to yourself about what you could do next. If you get stuck while drafting, go back over your invention writing. You may be able to copy and paste some of it into your evolving draft, or you may find that you need to do some additional invention to fill in details in your draft.

Writing the Opening Sentences

You could try out one or two different ways of beginning your essay — possibly from the list below — but do not agonize over the first sentences because you are likely to discover the best way to begin only after you have written a rough draft. Again, you might want to review your invention writing to see if you have already written something that would work to launch your essay.

To engage your readers' interest from the start, consider the following opening strategies:

- a surprising or provocative statement (like Romano)
- an assertion of an issue's increasing or immediate significance (like Hulbert)
- statistics (like Kim)
- an anecdote, quote, or personal reminiscence
- a research study
- a scenario
- a historical analogy
- criticism of an alternative position

Two Sentence Strategies

Comparing and Contrasting Your Subject with Similar Ones. As you draft an essay evaluating a subject, you may want to compare or contrast your subject with similar subjects to provide a frame of reference for them and to establish for readers your authority to evaluate the subject. To do so, you will need to use sentences that clearly and efficiently express comparisons or contrasts. These sentences often make use of key comparative terms like *more, less, most, least, as, than, like, unlike, similar,* or *dissimilar.*

Let us begin with three examples from Wendy Kim's essay "Grading Professors":

Still, RatingsOnline is *better* designed and includes *more helpful* information than the other two competitors, and it may even be *better* than RMP in terms of helpfulness. (par. 11)

The ratings categories on RatingsOnline also seem *more specific* than on RMP. (11)

In its design and potential helpfulness, RatingsOnline is a very good site but *not* likely to be *as good as* RMP because its user base appears to be *smaller.* (11)

In these sentences Kim compares Web sites that allow students to evaluate their instructors. The first sentence compares RatingsOnline and three other sites, including RateMyProfessors.com (RMP). In the second and third examples, she narrows the matchup to what she considers the two best Web sites, pointing out their relative strengths and weaknesses.

In the following example, Hulbert describes an event in *Juno* by referring to a similar event in the film *Knocked Up*:

> He — spoiler alert — stages a display of *just the kind of* egotistical guy regression that regularly induces female groans on the right and left, and that *Slate's* Meghan O'Rourke recently examined in this piece about *Knocked Up*. (par. 8)

Note that Hulbert leaves the task of making the full comparison to the reader, which in the original version she facilitates by inserting a hyperlink (underlined) to another online review.

For more on using sentences of comparison and contrast in evaluations, go to **bedfordstmartins.com/ conciseguide** and click on Sentence Strategies.

Balance Criticism and Praise. You should in most cases try to present a balanced evaluation of your subject, by criticizing one or more aspects of it if you generally praise it or by praising one or more aspects of it if you generally criticize it. To do so, you will need to use sentences that clearly and efficiently express comparisons or contrasts. In general, sentences that do this rely on words expressing contrast — *but, although, however, while,* and so on — to set up the shift between the two responses.

Praise followed by criticism:

> This information could be useful in helping students decide which classes to take, *but* only if there are enough reviews posted. (Kim, par. 11)

> . . . Statsky does show that she is thinking about her readers' questions. She does not go nearly far enough, *however,* to have a chance of influencing two types of readers. (Romano, par. 8)

Criticism followed by praise:

> Here Cody's politics (presumably pro-choice) are at odds with her plot needs (a birth) and, who knows, maybe commercial dictates, too, if studios worry about antagonizing the evangelical audience. It's a tension the screenplay finesses deftly, undercutting both pro-life and pro-choice purism. (Hulbert, par. 5)

Notice that the last example does not use an explicitly comparative term to set up the contrast. In her first sentence, Hulbert implies that there is a contradiction in the film that some would consider a flaw; in her second sentence, however, Hulbert states that the screenplay resolves the seeming contradiction in a way that makes it, in her view, more successful.

In addition to using sentences that make comparisons or contrasts with other subjects and sentences that balance criticism and praise, you can strengthen your evaluation with other kinds of sentences. You may want to review the information about using appositives (p. 147) and writing sentences introducing concession and refutation (pp. 196–98).

For more on using sentences that balance criticism and praise in evaluations, go to **bedfordstmartins .com/conciseguide** and click on Sentence Strategies.

Working with Sources:
Using Summary to Support Your Evaluative Argument

Writers of evaluation often use summary to support their argument. As the following examples show, evaluations may summarize an expert source (as Kim does in her Web site evaluation), the plot of a film or video game (as Hulbert does in her film review), or an aspect of an essay or story (as Romano does in her evaluation of another essay in this book), to name just a few of the more common uses of summary.

> The results are statistically invalid, as one psychology professor explained, because the users are self-selected and not selected randomly (Harmon). (Kim, par. 9)

> In the anecdote, a seven-year-old makes himself vomit to avoid playing. (Romano, par. 5)

> Pregnant Juno at first reflexively embraces abortion as the obvious option, and her best friend is at the ready with phone numbers. . . . But just when pro-lifers might be about to denounce this display of secular humanist decadence, Juno stomps out of the clinic, unable to go through with it. (Hulbert, par. 5)

To get a better understanding of how summaries can support an evaluative argument, let us look closely at another example of summarizing, from paragraph 3 of Christine Romano's essay. This summary, highlighted below, supports Romano's argument that Statsky provides "appropriate" support:

> Her quotations, examples, and statistics all support the reasons she believes competitive sports are bad for children. For example, in paragraph 3, Statsky offers the reason that "overly competitive sports" may damage children's fragile bodies and that contact sports, in particular, may be especially hazardous. She supports this reason by paraphrasing Koppett's claim that muscle strain or even lifelong injury may result when a twelve-year-old throws curve balls. She then quotes Tutko on the dangers of tackle football. The opinions of both experts are obviously appropriate. They are relevant to her reason, and we can easily imagine that they would worry many parents.

To understand how this summary works, compare it to the original:

Statsky's Original (par. 3)

> One readily understandable danger of overly competitive sports is that they entice children into physical actions that are bad for growing bodies. Although the official Little League Web site acknowledges that children do risk injury playing baseball, they insist that "severe injuries . . . are infrequent," the risk "far less than the risk of riding a skateboard, a bicycle, or even the school bus" ("What about My Child?"). Nevertheless, Leonard Koppett in *Sports Illusion, Sports Reality* claims that a twelve-year-old trying to

throw a curve ball, for example, may put abnormal strain on developing arm and shoulder muscles, sometimes resulting in lifelong injuries (294). Contact sports like football can be even more hazardous. Thomas Tutko, a psychology professor at San Jose State University and coauthor of the book *Winning Is Everything and Other American Myths,* writes:

> I am strongly opposed to young kids playing tackle football. It is not the right stage of development for them to be taught to crash into other kids. Kids under the age of fourteen are not by nature physical. Their main concern is self-preservation. They don't want to meet head on and slam into each other. But tackle football absolutely requires that they try to hit each other as hard as they can. And it is too traumatic for young kids. (qtd. in Tosches A1)

Romano not only repeats Statsky's main ideas in a condensed form (reducing 220 words to 105), but she also describes Statsky's moves as a writer:

Statsky offers the reason . . .

She supports this reason by paraphrasing Koppett's claim . . .

She then quotes Tutko . . .

Romano's description of each step in Statsky's argument shows readers exactly how Statsky uses her sources in constructing her argument.

Notice that in her summary, Romano puts quotation marks around only one of the phrases she borrows from Statsky ("overly competitive sports"). The most likely reason for this is that Romano considers the designation "overly competitive sports" debatable. She may have decided not to use quotation marks around other borrowed phrases such as *contact sports* and *tackle football* because they are common expressions and not specific to Statsky.

Because Romano makes it perfectly clear when she is re-presenting her source's language and ideas, and also includes careful citations to indicate where in the original text the material comes from, she could not be accused of plagiarism. Remember, though, that putting quotation marks around quoted words and phrases will eliminate any possible misunderstanding. If you are unsure about whether you need quotation marks, consult your instructor.

For additional information on summary, quotation, and paraphrase, see Chapter 17, Using Sources, pp. 487–95.

Critical Reading Guide

Your instructor may arrange a peer review session in class or online where you can exchange drafts with your classmates and give one another a thoughtful critical reading, pointing out what works well and suggesting ways to improve the draft. This Critical Reading Guide can also be used productively by a tutor in the writing center or by a roommate or family member.

Basic Features

A good critical reading does three things: It lets the writer know how the reader understands the point of the essay, praises what works best, and indicates where the draft could be improved.

1. Evaluate how well the subject is presented.

   Summarize: Tell the writer what you understand the specific subject of the evaluation to be and the kind of subject it is.

   Praise: Point to a place where the subject is presented effectively — for example, where it is described vividly and accurately, where it is named, or where it is clearly placed in a recognizable genre or category.

   Critique: Tell the writer where readers might need more information about the subject, and whether any information about it seems inaccurate or possibly only partly true. Suggest how the writer could clarify the kind of subject it is, either by identifying the category by name or by giving examples of familiar subjects of the same type.

2. Assess how well the judgment is supported.

   Summarize: Tell the writer what you understand the overall judgment to be and the criteria on which it is based.

   Praise: Identify a passage in the essay where support for the judgment is presented effectively — for example, note particularly strong supporting reasons, appeals to criteria readers are likely to share, or especially compelling evidence.

   Critique: Let the writer know if you cannot find a thesis statement or think it is vague or overstated. Tell the writer where the argument could be improved — for example, suggest another reason that could be added, propose a way to justify one of the criteria on which the argument is based, or recommend a source or an example that could be used to bolster the support for the argument.

3. Consider how effectively objections and alternative judgments are counterargued.

   Praise: Identify a passage in the essay where the writer counterargues an objection or alternative judgment effectively. An effective counterargument may include making a concession — for example, agreeing that a subject the writer is primarily criticizing has some good points, or that the subject has weaknesses as well as strengths.

Critique: Tell the writer where counterargument is needed or could be made more effective — for example, suggesting a likely objection or alternative judgment that should be taken into account, helping the writer understand the criteria behind an alternative judgment, or pointing to an example that could be used to refute an objection.

4. Assess how readable the argument is.

Praise: Give an example of where the essay succeeds in being readable — in its overall organization, clear presentation of the thesis, effective opening or closing, or by other means.

Critique: Tell the writer where the readability could be improved. Can you, for example, suggest a better beginning or more effective ending? If the overall organization of the essay needs work, make suggestions for rearranging parts or strengthening connections.

5. If the writer has expressed concern about anything in the draft that you have not discussed, respond to that concern.

Making Comments Electronically Most word processing software offers features that allow you to insert comments directly into the text of someone else's document. Many readers prefer to make their comments this way because it tends to be faster than writing on hard copy and space is virtually unlimited; it also eliminates the process of deciphering handwritten comments. Where such features are not available, simply typing comments directly into a document in a contrasting color can provide the same advantages.

For a printable version of this Critical Reading Guide, go to **bedfordstmartins.com/conciseguide**.

Revising

Very likely you have already thought of ways to improve your draft, and you may even have begun to revise it. In this section is a Troubleshooting chart that may help. Before using the chart, however, it is a good idea to do the following:

- Review critical reading comments from your classmates, instructor, or writing center tutor.
- Make an outline of your draft so that you can look at it analytically.

You may have made an outline before writing your draft, but after drafting you need to see what you actually wrote, not what you intended to write. You can outline the draft quickly by highlighting the basic features — presenting the subject, making and supporting an evaluation, effectively anticipating objections and alternative judgments, and making the argument readable.

For an electronic version of this Troubleshooting chart, go to **bedfordstmartins.com/conciseguide**.

✓ Troubleshooting Your Draft

● ● ● ● Basic Features

A Well-Presented Subject	
The subject is not identified or is vague.	☐ Identify the subject by name — such as the title and author, or director and main characters. ☐ Describe the subject — summarize what it is about, cite statistics that establish its importance, or give examples to make it concrete. ☐ Consider adding visuals — photographs, graphs, tables, or charts — if these would help clarify the subject.
It is not clear what kind of subject it is.	☐ Classify the subject by naming the genre or category a subject of this kind fits into. ☐ Refer to other reviews or reviewers of subjects of this kind. ☐ Compare your subject to other, better known subjects of the same kind.

A Well-Supported Evaluation	
My thesis or overall judgment is not clear.	☐ State your thesis early in the essay. ☐ Clarify the language in your thesis statement to indicate what your judgment is overall. ☐ Qualify your thesis if it seems overstated or does not correspond to your argument. ☐ Consider whether your judgment is in fact arguable. If you cannot provide reasons and support, then your judgment probably is not arguable. Consult your instructor about modifying your judgment or writing about a different subject.
My readers are not convinced that my evaluation is reasonable and/or persuasive.	☐ Clarify the criteria on which you base your argument and try to justify them — by citing authorities or other reviews of similar subjects, by making comparisons, or by explaining why your criteria are appropriate and perhaps preferable to other criteria readers may be more familiar with. ☐ Add additional support for your reasons — quoting respected experts or research studies, providing facts or statistics, giving specific examples, or citing textual evidence in the form of quotation, summary, or paraphrase.
My readers do not understand my evaluation.	☐ Go over the way you present your evaluation; if necessary, explain it and your supporting reasons more clearly. ☐ Try outlining your argument to be sure that the overall organization and coherence are strong; if they are not, try rearranging parts or strengthening connections.

An Effective Counterargument

My readers raise objections I haven't considered or find fault with my counterargument.	☐ Consider whether new objections need to be answered. Not every objection requires a response, so think about whether you can ignore it or dismiss it as only a minor concern. ☐ Take seriously important objections that undermine your argument. Try to refute them — showing they are not based on widely held or appropriate criteria, or that they misunderstand your argument or the subject. ☐ If objections cannot be refuted, acknowledge them but demonstrate that they do not make your evaluation invalid. Try using sentence openers like *I understand that . . . , but what I think is,* and *It is true that . . . , but my point is. . . .*
My readers have proposed alternative judgments or find fault with my handling of alternatives.	☐ Address the alternative judgments directly in your essay. Concede good or bad qualities of the subject others emphasize, even if you disagree on the overall value of the subject. ☐ Point out where you and your readers agree on criteria but perhaps disagree on how well the subject meets the criteria. ☐ Where you and your readers disagree on criteria, try to justify the standards you are applying by citing authorities or establishing your own authority.

A Readable Plan

My readers are confused by my essay or find it difficult to read.	☐ Review the overall organization of your essay by outlining it. If necessary, move, add, or delete sections to strengthen coherence. ☐ Consider adding a forecasting statement early in your essay. ☐ Repeat your key terms to keep readers oriented. ☐ Check to see that your reasons are introduced clearly through the use of topic sentences. ☐ Check to be sure that you provide appropriate transitions between sentences, paragraphs, and sections of your essay. Pay particular attention to these transitions at points where your readers indicate the greatest trouble in following your argument. ☐ Review your opening and closing paragraphs. Be sure that your overall judgment is clear and appropriately qualified.

Editing and Proofreading

Our research indicates that particular errors occur often in essays that justify an evaluation: incomplete and illogical comparisons, and short, choppy sentences. The following guidelines will help you check your essay for these common errors.

Complete, Correct Comparisons

The Problem. In essays that justify an evaluation, writers often engage in comparison — showing, for example, that one film is stronger than another, a new recording is inferior to an earlier one, or one restaurant is better than another. When comparisons are expressed incompletely, illogically, or incorrectly, however, the point of the comparison can be dulled or lost completely.

How to Correct It. Reread your comparisons, checking for completeness, logic, and correctness.

A comparison is complete if two terms are introduced and the relationship between them is clearly expressed:

▶ *Jazz* is as good, if not better than, Morrison's other novels.
   as

▶ I liked the Lispector story because it's so different.
   from anything else I've ever read.

A comparison is **logical** if the terms compared are parallel (and therefore comparable):

▶ Will Smith's Muhammad Ali is more serious than any role he's played.
   other

▶ Ohio State's offense played much better than ~~Michigan.~~
   Michigan's did.

Note that *different from* is correct; *different than*, while commonly used, is incorrect:

▶ Carrying herself with a confident and brisk stride, Katherine Parker seems
   different ~~than~~ the other women in the office.
   from

▶ Films like *Pulp Fiction* that glorify violence for its own sake are different ~~than~~ films
   like *Apocalypse Now* that use violence to make a moral point.
   from

For practice, go to **bedfordstmartins.com/conciseguide/exercisecentral** and click on Comparisons.

Combining Sentences

The Problem. When writers justify an evaluation, they generally present their subject in some detail — defining it, describing it, placing it in some context. Inexperienced writers often present such details one after another, in short, choppy sentences. These sentences can be difficult or irritating to read, and they provide the reader with no help in determining how the different details relate to each other.

How to Correct It. Combine sentences to make your writing more readable and to clarify the relationships among ideas. Two common strategies for sentence combining involve converting full sentences into **appositive phrases** (a noun phrase that renames the noun or pronoun that immediately precedes it) or **verbal phrases** (phrases using words derived from verbs that function as adjectives, adverbs, or nouns). Consider the following example:

▶ In paragraph 5, the details provide a different impression,↻ ~~It is~~ a comic or

perhaps even pathetic impression,↻ ~~The impression comes from~~ *based on* the boy's

attempts to dress up like a real westerner.

From three separate sentences, this writer smoothly combines details about the "different impression" into a single sentence, using an appositive phrase ("a comic or perhaps even pathetic impression") and a verbal phrase ("based on the boy's attempts to dress up like a real westerner").

Here are two additional examples of the first strategy (conversion into an appositive phrase):

▶ "Something Pacific" was created by Nam June Paik,↻ ~~He is~~ a Korean artist who is considered a founder of video art.

↻ *"Talkin' John Birch Paranoid Blues↻ "*
▶ One of Dylan's songs ridiculed the John Birch Society. ~~This song was called "Talkin' John Birch Paranoid Blues."~~

Finally, here are two additional examples of the second strategy (conversion into a verbal phrase):

carrying
▶ Spider-Man's lifesaving webbing sprung from his wristbands,↻ ~~They carried~~ Mary Jane Watson and him out of peril.

enticing
▶ The coffee bar flanks the bookshelves,↻ ~~It entices~~ readers to relax with a book.

For practice, go to **bedfordstmartins.com/conciseguide/exercisecentral** and click on Combining Sentences.

Thinking Critically about What You Have Learned

In this chapter, you have learned a great deal about this genre from reading several essays that justify an evaluation and from writing one of your own. To consolidate your learning, it is helpful to think metacognitively; that is, to reflect not only on what you learned but on how you learned it. Following are two brief activities your instructor may ask you to do.

Reflecting on Your Writing

Your instructor may ask you to turn in with your essay and process materials a brief metacognitive essay or letter reflecting on what you have learned about writing your essay justifying an evaluation. Choose from the following invention activities those that seem most productive for you.

- Explain how your purpose and audience influenced *one* of your decisions as a writer, such as how you presented the subject, the strategies you used in justifying your evaluation, or the ways in which you attempted to counter possible objections.

- Discuss what you learned about yourself as a writer in the process of writing this particular essay. For example, what part of the process did you find most challenging? Did you try anything new, like getting a critical reading of your draft or outlining your draft in order to revise it?

- If you were to give advice to a friend who was about to write an essay justifying an evaluation, what would you say?

- Which of the readings in this chapter influenced your essay? Explain the influence, citing specific examples from your essay and from the reading.

- If you got good advice from a critical reader, explain exactly how the person helped you — perhaps by questioning the way you addressed your audience or the kinds of support you offered in support of your position.

Considering the Social Dimensions: Evaluators' Hidden Assumptions

Good evaluative writing provides readers with reasons and support for the writer's judgment. However, the writer's personal experiences, cultural background, and political ideology are also reflected in written evaluations. Even the most fair-minded evaluators write from the perspective of their particular ethnicity, religion, gender, age, social class, sexual orientation, academic discipline, and so on. Writers seldom make their assumptions explicit, however. Consequently, while the reasons for an evaluation may make it seem fair and objective, the writer's judgment may result from hidden assumptions that even the writer has not examined critically.

1. ***Choose one reading from this chapter, and try to identify one of the hidden assumptions of its writer.*** Think of a personal or cultural factor that may have influenced the writer's judgment of the subject. For example, how do you imagine that Romano's gender may have influenced her judgment of Statsky's essay on competitive sports for children?

2. ***Reflect on your own experience of writing an evaluation essay.*** How do you think factors such as gender, age, social class, ethnicity, religion, geographical region, or political perspective may have influenced your own evaluation? Recall the subjects that you listed as possibilities for your essay and how you chose one to evaluate. Also recall how you arrived at your overall judgment and how you decided which reasons to use and which not to use in your essay.

3. ***Write a page or two explaining your ideas about how hidden assumptions play a role in evaluation essays.*** Connect your ideas to the readings in this chapter and to your own essay.

Strategies for Critical Thinking, Reading, and Writing

8 Strategies for Invention and Inquiry

Writers are like scientists: They ask questions, systematically inquiring about how things work, what they are, where they occur, and how more information can be learned about them. Writers are also like artists in that they use what they know and learn to create something new and imaginative.

The invention and inquiry strategies — also known as **heuristics** — described in this chapter are not mysterious or magical. They are available to all writers, and one or more of them may appeal to your common sense and experience. These techniques represent ways creative writers, engineers, scientists, composers — in fact, all of us — solve problems. Once you have mastered these strategies, you can use them to tackle many of the writing situations you will encounter in college, on the job, and in the community.

The strategies for invention and inquiry in this chapter are grouped into two categories:

Mapping: A brief visual representation of your thinking or planning

Writing: The composition of phrases or sentences to discover information and ideas and to make connections among them

These invention and inquiry strategies will help you explore and research a topic fully before you begin drafting and then help you creatively solve problems as you draft and revise. In this chapter, strategies are arranged alphabetically within each of the two categories.

Mapping

Mapping strategies involve making a visual record of invention and inquiry. In making maps, writers usually use key words and phrases to record material they want to remember, questions they need to answer, and new sources of information they want to check. The maps show the ideas, details, and facts as well as possible ways to connect and focus them. Mapping can be especially useful for working in collaborative writing situations, for preparing oral presentations, and for creating visual aids for written or oral reports. Mapping strategies include clustering, listing, and outlining.

Clustering

Clustering is a strategy for revealing possible relationships among facts and ideas. Unlike listing (the next mapping strategy), clustering requires a brief period of initial preparation when you divide your topic into parts or main ideas. Clustering works as follows:

1. In a word or phrase, write your topic in the center of a piece of paper. Circle it.
2. Also in words or phrases, write down the main parts or ideas of your topic. Circle these, and connect them with lines to the topic in the center.
3. Next, write down facts, details, examples, or ideas related to these main parts. Connect them with lines to the relevant main parts or ideas.

Clustering can be useful in the early stages of planning an essay to find subtopics and organize information. You may try out and discard several clusters before finding one that is promising. Many writers also use clustering to plan brief sections of an essay as they are drafting or revising. (A model of clustering is shown in Figure 8.1 below.)

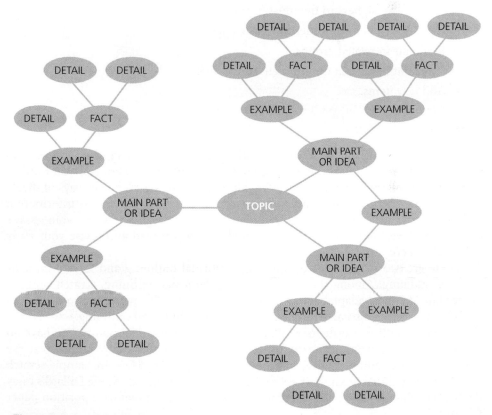

Figure 8.1 A model of clustering

Listing

Listing is a familiar activity. You make shopping lists and lists of errands to do or people to call. Listing can also be a great help in planning an essay. It enables you to recall what you already know about a topic and suggests what else you may need to find out.

A basic activity for all writers, listing is especially useful to those who have little time for planning — for example, reporters facing deadlines and college students taking essay exams. Listing lets you order your ideas quickly. It can also serve as a first step in discovering possible writing topics. Here is how listing works best for invention work:

1. Give your list a title that indicates your main idea or topic.
2. Write as fast as you can, relying on short phrases.
3. Include anything that seems at all useful. Try not to be judgmental at this point.
4. After you have finished or even as you write, reflect on the list, and organize it in the following way:
   - Put an asterisk next to the most promising items.
   - Number key items in order of importance.
   - Put items in related groups.
   - Cross out items that do not seem promising.
   - Add new items.

Outlining

Like listing and clustering, **outlining** is both a means of inventing what you want to say in an essay and a way of organizing your ideas and information. As you outline, you nearly always see new possibilities in your subject, discovering new ways of dividing or grouping information and noticing where you need additional information to develop your ideas. Because outlining lets you see at a glance where your essay's strengths and weaknesses lie, outlining can also help you read and revise your essay with a critical eye.

There are two main forms of outlining: informal outlining and formal topic or sentence outlining. Among the several types of informal outlining, scratch outlines are perhaps the most adaptable to a variety of situations. Chunking is another useful method. (Clustering also may be considered a type of informal outlining.)

A **scratch outline** is little more than a list of the essay's main points. You have no doubt made scratch outlines many times — to plan essays or essay exams, to revise your own writing, and to analyze a difficult reading passage. Here are sample scratch outlines for two different kinds of essays. The first is an outline of Annie Dillard's essay in Chapter 2 (pp. 24–26), and the second shows one way to organize a position paper (Chapter 5):

Scratch Outline: Essay about a Remembered Event

1. explains what she learned from playing football
2. identifies other sports she learned from boys in the neighborhood
3. sets the scene by describing the time and place of the event
4. describes the boys who were playing with her
5. describes what typically happened: a car would come down the street, they would throw snowballs, and then they would wait for another car
6. describes the iceball-making project she had begun while waiting
7. describes the Buick's approach and how they followed the routine
8. describes the impact of the snowball on the Buick's windshield
9. describes the man's surprising reaction: getting out of the car and running after them
10. narrates the chase and describes the man
11. explains how the kids split up and the man followed her and Mikey
12. narrates the chase and describes how the neighborhood looked as they ran through it
13. continues the narration, describing the way the man threw himself into the chase
14. continues the narration, commenting on her thoughts and feelings
15. narrates the ending or climax of the chase, when the man caught the kids
16. describes the runners trying to catch their breath
17. describes her own physical state
18. relates the man's words
19. explains her reactions to his words and actions
20. explains her later thoughts and feelings
21. explains her present perspective on this remembered event

Scratch Outline: Essay Arguing a Position

Presentation of the issue

Accommodation conceding some aspect of an opposing position

Thesis statement

First reason with support

Second reason with support

(etc.)

Conclusion

Remember that the items in a scratch outline do not necessarily coincide with paragraphs. Sometimes two or more items may be developed in the same paragraph or one item may be covered in two or more paragraphs.

Chunking, a type of scratch outline commonly used by professional writers in business and industry and especially well suited to writing in the electronic age, consists of a set of headings describing the major points to be covered in the final document. What makes chunking distinctive is that the blocks of text — or "chunks" — under each heading are intended to be roughly the same length and scope. These headings can be discussed and passed around among several writers and editors before writing begins, and different chunks may be written by different authors, simply by typing notes or text on a word processor into the space under each heading. The list of headings is subject to change during the writing, and new headings may be added or old ones subdivided or discarded as part of the drafting and editing process.

The advantage of chunking in your own writing is that it breaks the large task of drafting into smaller tasks in a simple, evenly balanced way; once you have determined the headings, the writing becomes just a matter of filling in the specifics that go in each chunk. Organization tends to improve as you get a sense of the weight of different parts of the document while filling in the blanks. Places where the essay needs more information or there is a problem with pacing tend to stand out because of the chunking structure, and you can either take the headings out of the finished essay or leave them in as devices to help guide readers. If you leave them in, they should be edited into parallel grammatical form like the items in a formal topic or sentence outline, as discussed below.

Topic outlines and **sentence outlines** are considered more formal than scratch outlines because they follow a conventional format of numbered and lettered headings and subheadings:

I. (Main topic)
   A. (Subtopic of I)
   B.
      1. (Subtopic of I.B)
      2.
         a. (Subtopic of I.B.2)
         b.
            (1) (Subtopic of I.B.2.b)
            (2)
   C.
      1. (Subtopic of I.C)
      2.

The difference between a topic and sentence outline is obvious: Topic outlines simply name the topics and subtopics, whereas sentence outlines use complete or abbreviated sentences. To illustrate, here are two partial formal outlines of an essay arguing a position, Jessica Statsky's "Children Need to Play, Not Compete," from Chapter 5 (pp. 166–71).

Formal Topic Outline

I. Organized sports harmful to children
   A. Harmful physically
      1. Curve ball (Koppett)
      2. Tackle football (Tutko)
   B. Harmful psychologically
      1. Fear of being hurt
         a. Little League Online
         b. Mother
         c. Reporter
      2. Competition
         a. Rablovsky
         b. Studies

Formal Sentence Outline

I. Highly organized competitive sports such as Peewee Football and Little League Baseball can be physically and psychologically harmful to children, as well as counterproductive for developing future players.
   A. Physically harmful because sports entice children into physical actions that are bad for growing bodies.
      1. Koppett claims throwing a curve ball may put abnormal strain on developing arm and shoulder muscles.
      2. Tutko argues that tackle football is too traumatic for young kids.
   B. Psychologically harmful to children for a number of reasons.
      1. Fear of being hurt detracts from their enjoyment of the sport.
         a. Little League Online ranks fear of injury seventh among the seven top reasons children quit.
         b. One mother says, "kids get so scared. . . . They'll sit on the bench and pretend their leg hurts."
         c. A reporter tells about a child who made himself vomit to get out of playing Peewee Football.
      2. Too much competition poses psychological dangers for children.
         a. Rablovsky reports: "The spirit of play suddenly disappears, and sport becomes joblike."
         b. Studies show that children prefer playing on a losing team to "warming the bench on a winning team."

In contrast to an informal outline in which anything goes, a formal outline must follow many conventions. The roman numerals and capital letters are followed by periods. In both topic and sentence outlines, the first word of each item is capitalized, but items in topic outlines do not end with a period as items in sentence outlines do. Every level of a formal outline except the top level (identified by the roman numeral *I*) must include at least two items. Items at the same level of indentation in a topic outline should be grammatically parallel — all beginning with the same part of speech. For example, *I.A.* and *I.B.* are parallel when they both begin with an adverb (*Physically harmful* and *Psychologically harmful*) or with an adjective (*Harmful physically* and *Harmful psychologically*); they would not be parallel if one began with an adverb (*Physically harmful*) and the other with an adjective (*Harmful psychologically*).

Writing

Unlike most mapping strategies, **writing strategies** invite you to produce complete sentences. Sentences provide considerable generative power. Because they are complete statements, they take you further than listing or clustering. They enable you to explore ideas and define relationships, bring ideas together or show how they differ, and identify causes and effects. Sentences can also help you develop a logical chain of thought.

Some of these invention and inquiry strategies are systematic, while others are more flexible. Even though they call for complete sentences that are related to one another, they do not require preparation or revision. You can use them to develop oral as well as written presentations.

These writing strategies include *cubing, dialoguing, dramatizing, keeping a journal, looping, questioning,* and *quick drafting.*

Cubing

Cubing is useful for quickly exploring a writing topic, probing it from six different perspectives. It is known as *cubing* because a cube has six sides. These are the six perspectives in cubing:

Describing: What does your subject look like? What size is it? What is its color? Its shape? Its texture? Name its parts.

Comparing: What is your subject similar to? Different from?

Associating: What does your subject make you think of? What connections does it have to anything else in your experience?

Analyzing: What are the origins of your subject? What are the functions or significance of its parts? How are its parts related?

Applying: What can you do with your subject? What uses does it have?

Arguing: What arguments can you make for your subject? Against it?

Here are some guidelines to help you use cubing productively.

1. Select a topic, subject, or part of a subject. This can be a person, a scene, an event, an object, a problem, an idea, or an issue. Hold it in focus.

2. Limit your writing to three to five minutes for each perspective. The whole activity should take no more than half an hour.

3. Keep going until you have written about your subject from all six perspectives. Remember that cubing offers the special advantage of enabling you to generate multiple perspectives quickly.

4. As you write from each perspective, begin with what you know about your subject. However, do not limit yourself to your present knowledge. Indicate what else you would like to know about your subject, and suggest where you might find that information.

5. Reread what you have written. Look for bright spots, surprises. Recall the part that was easiest for you to write. Recall the part where you felt a special momentum and pleasure in writing. Look for an angle or an unexpected insight. These special parts may suggest a focus or topic within a larger subject, or they may provide specific details to include in a draft.

Dialoguing

A *dialogue* is a conversation between two or more people. You can use **dialoguing** to search for topics, find a focus, explore ideas, or consider opposing viewpoints. When you write a dialogue as an invention strategy, you need to make up all parts of the conversation (unless, of course, you are writing collaboratively). To construct a dialogue independently or collaboratively, follow these steps:

1. Write a conversation between two speakers. Label the participants *Speaker A* and *Speaker B*, or make up names for them.

2. If you get stuck, you might have one of the speakers ask the other a question.

3. Write brief responses to keep the conversation moving fast. Do not spend much time planning or rehearsing responses. Write what first occurs to you, just as in a real conversation, where people take quick turns to prevent any awkward silences.

Dialogues can be especially useful with personal experience and persuasive essays because they help you remember conversations and anticipate objections.

Dramatizing

Dramatizing is an invention activity developed by the philosopher Kenneth Burke as a way of thinking about how people interact and as a way of analyzing stories and films.

Thinking about human behavior in dramatic terms can be very productive for writers. Drama has action, actors, setting, motives, and methods. Since stars and acting go

Figure 8.2 Dramatizing

together, you can use a five-pointed star to remember these five points of dramatizing: Each point on the star provides a different perspective on human behavior (see Figure 8.2).

Action. An action is anything that happens, has happened, will happen, or could happen. Action includes events that are physical (running a marathon), mental (thinking about a book you have read), and emotional (falling in love).

Actor. The actor is involved in the action — either responsible for it or simply affected by it. (The actor does not have to be a person. It can be a force, something that causes an action. For example, if the action is a rise in the price of gasoline, the actor could be increased demand or short supply.) Dramatizing may also include a number of coactors working together or at odds.

Setting. The setting is the situation or background of the action. We usually think of setting as the place and time of an event, but it may also be the historical background of an event or the childhood of a person.

Motive. The motive is the purpose or reason for an action — the actor's intention. Actions may have multiple, even conflicting, motives.

Method. The method explains how an action occurs, including the techniques an actor uses. It refers to whatever makes things happen.

Each of these points suggests a simple invention question:

Action: What?

Actor: Who?

Setting: When and where?

Motive: Why?

Method: How?

This list looks like the questions reporters typically ask. But dramatizing goes further: It enables us to consider relations between and among these five elements. We can think about actors' motives, the effect of the setting on the actors, the relations between actors, and so on.

You can use this invention strategy to learn more about yourself or about other significant people in your life. You can use it as well to explore, interpret, or evaluate characters in stories or movies. Moreover, dramatizing is especially useful in understanding the readers you want to inform or convince.

To use dramatizing, imagine the person you want to understand better in a particular situation. Holding this image in mind, write answers to any questions in the following list that apply. You may draw a blank on some questions, have little to say to some, and find a lot to say to others. Be exploratory and playful with the questions. Write responses quickly, relying on words and phrases, even drawings.

- What is the actor doing?
- How did the actor come to be involved in this situation?
- Why does the actor do what he or she does?
- What else might the actor do?
- What is the actor trying to accomplish?
- How do other actors influence — help or hinder — the main actor?
- What do the actor's actions reveal about him or her?
- What does the actor's language reveal about him or her?
- How does the event's setting influence the actor's actions?
- How does the time of the event influence what the actor does?
- Where does this actor come from?
- How is this actor different now from what he or she used to be?
- What might this actor become?
- How is this actor like or unlike the other actors?

Keeping a Journal

Professional writers often use **journals** to keep notes. Starting one is easy. Buy a special notebook, or open a new file on your computer, and start writing. Here are some possibilities:

- Keep a list of new words and concepts you learn in your courses. You could also write about the progress and direction of your learning in particular courses — the experience of being in the course, your feelings about what is happening, and what you are learning.
- Respond to your reading, both assigned and personal. As you read, write about your personal associations, reflections, reactions, and evaluations. Summarize or copy memorable or especially important passages, and comment on them. (Copying and commenting have been practiced by students and writers for centuries in special journals called *commonplace books.*)
- Write to prepare for particular class meetings. Write about the main ideas you have learned from assigned readings and about the relationship of these new ideas to other ideas in the course. After class, write to summarize what you have learned. List questions you have about the ideas or information discussed in class. Journal writing of this kind involves reflecting, evaluating, interpreting, synthesizing, summarizing, and questioning.

- Record observations and overheard conversations.
- Write for ten or fifteen minutes every day about whatever is on your mind. Focus these meditations on your new experiences as you try to understand, interpret, and reflect on them.
- Write sketches of people who catch your attention.
- Organize your time. Write about your goals and priorities, or list specific things to accomplish and what you plan to do.
- Keep a log over several days or weeks about a particular event unfolding in the news — a sensational trial, an environmental disaster, a political campaign, a campus controversy, or the fortunes of a sports team.

You can use a journal in many ways. All of the writing in your journal has value for learning. You may also be able to use parts of your journal for writing in your other courses.

Looping

Looping is especially useful for the first stages of exploring a topic. As its name suggests, **looping** involves writing quickly to explore some aspect of a topic and then looping back to your original starting point or to a new starting point to explore another aspect. Beginning with almost any starting point, looping enables you to find a center of interest and eventually a thesis for your essay. The steps are simple:

1. Write down your area of interest. You may know only that you have to write about another person or a movie or a cultural trend that has caught your attention. Or you may want to search for a topic in a broad historical period or for one related to a major political event. Although you may wander from this topic as you write, you will want to keep coming back to it. Your purpose is to find a focus for writing.

2. Write nonstop for ten minutes. Start with the first thing that comes to mind. Write rapidly, without looking back to reread or to correct anything. *Do not stop writing. Keep your pencil moving or keystrokes clacking.* Continuous writing is the key to looping. If you get stuck for a moment, rewrite the last sentence. Follow diversions and digressions, but keep returning to your topic.

3. After ten minutes, pause to reread what you have written. Decide what is most important — a single insight, a pattern of ideas, an emerging theme, a visual detail, anything at all that stands out. Some writers call this a "center of gravity" or a "hot spot." To complete the first loop, restate this center in a single sentence.

4. Beginning with this sentence, write nonstop for another ten minutes.

5. Summarize in one sentence again to complete the second loop.

6. Keep looping until one of your summary sentences produces a focus or thesis. You may need only two or three loops; you may need more.

Questioning

Questioning is a way to learn about a subject and decide what to write. When you first encounter a subject, your questions may be scattered. Also, you are not likely to think right away of the most important questions you ought to ask. The advantage of having a basic list of questions for invention, like the ones for cubing and for dramatizing discussed earlier in this chapter, is that it provides a systematic approach to exploring a subject.

The questions that follow come from classical rhetoric (what the Greek philosopher Aristotle called *topics*) and a modern approach to invention called *tagmemics*. Based on the work of linguist Kenneth Pike, tagmemics provides questions about different ways we make sense of the world, the ways we sort and classify experience in order to understand it.

Here are the steps in using questions for invention:

1. In a sentence or two, identify your subject. A subject could be any event, person, problem, project, idea, or issue — in other words, anything you might write about.

2. Start by writing a response to the first question in the following list, and move right through the list. Try to answer each question at least briefly with a word or a phrase. Some questions may invite several sentences or even a page or more of writing. You may draw a blank on a few questions. Skip them. Later, when you have more experience with questions for invention, you can start anywhere in the list.

3. Write your responses quickly, without much planning. Follow digressions or associations. Do not screen anything out. Be playful.

What Is Your Subject?

- What is your subject's name? What other names does it have? What names did it have in the past?
- What aspects of the subject do these different names emphasize?
- Imagine a still photograph or a moving picture of your subject. What would it look like?
- What would you put into a time capsule to stand for your subject?
- What are its causes and effects?
- How would it look from different vantage points or perspectives?
- What particular experiences have you had with the subject? What have you learned?

What Parts or Features Does Your Subject Have, and How Are They Related?

- Name the parts or features of your subject.
- Describe each one, using the questions in the preceding subject list.
- How is each part or feature related to the others?

How Is Your Subject Similar to and Different from Other Subjects?

- What is your subject similar to? In what ways?
- What is your subject different from? In what ways?
- What seems to you most unlike your subject? In what ways? Now, just for fun, note how they are alike.

How Much Can Your Subject Change and Still Remain the Same?

- How has your subject changed from what it once was?
- How is it changing now — moment to moment, day to day, year to year?
- How does each change alter your way of thinking about your subject?
- What are some different forms your subject takes?
- What does it become when it is no longer itself?

Where Does Your Subject Fit in the World?

- When and where did your subject originate?
- What would happen if at some future time your subject ceased to exist?
- When and where do you usually experience the subject?
- What is this subject a part of, and what are the other parts?
- What do other people think of your subject?

Quick Drafting

Sometimes you know what you want to say or have little time for invention. In these situations, **quick drafting** may be a good strategy. There are no special rules for quick drafting, but you should rely on it only if you know your subject well, have had experience with the kind of writing you are doing, and will have a chance to revise your draft. Quick drafting can help you discover what you already know about the subject and what you need to find out. It can also help you develop and organize your thoughts.

Strategies for Reading Critically

9

This chapter presents strategies to help you become a thoughtful reader. A thoughtful reader is above all a patient *re*reader, concerned not only with comprehending and remembering but also with interpreting and evaluating — on the one hand, striving to understand the text on its own terms; on the other hand, taking care to question its ideas.

The reading strategies in this chapter can help you enrich your thinking as a reader and participate in conversations as a writer. These strategies include the following:

- *Annotating:* Recording your reactions to, interpretations of, and questions about a text as you read it
- *Taking inventory:* Listing and grouping your annotations and other notes to find meaningful patterns
- *Outlining:* Listing the text's main ideas to reveal how it is organized
- *Paraphrasing:* Restating what you have read to clarify or refer to it
- *Summarizing:* Distilling the main ideas or gist of a text
- *Synthesizing:* Integrating into your own writing ideas and information gleaned from different sources
- *Contextualizing:* Placing a text in its historical and cultural contexts
- *Exploring the significance of figurative language:* Examining how metaphors, similes, and symbols are used in a text to convey meaning and evoke feelings
- *Looking for patterns of opposition:* Inferring the values and assumptions embodied in the language of a text
- *Reflecting on challenges to your beliefs and values:* Examining the bases of your personal responses to a text
- *Evaluating the logic of an argument:* Determining whether an argument is well reasoned and adequately supported
- *Recognizing emotional manipulation:* Identifying texts that unfairly and inappropriately use emotional appeals based on false or exaggerated claims
- *Judging the writer's credibility:* Considering whether writers represent different points of view fairly and know what they are writing about

Although mastering these strategies will not make critical reading easy, it can make your reading much more satisfying and productive and thus help you handle even difficult material with confidence. These reading strategies will, in addition, often be useful in your reading outside of school — for instance, these strategies can help you understand, evaluate, and comment on what political figures, advertisers, and other writers are saying.

Annotating

Annotations are the marks — underlines, highlights, and comments — you make directly on the page as you read. Annotating can be used to record immediate reactions and questions, outline and summarize main points, and evaluate and relate the reading to other ideas and points of view. Your annotations can take many forms, such as the following:

- Writing comments, questions, or definitions in the margins
- Underlining or circling words, phrases, or sentences
- Connecting ideas with lines or arrows
- Numbering related points
- Bracketing sections of the text
- Noting anything that strikes you as interesting, important, or questionable

Most readers annotate in layers, adding further annotations on second and third readings. Annotations can be light or heavy, depending on the reader's purpose and the difficulty of the material. Your purpose for reading also determines how you use your annotations.

The following selection, excerpted from Martin Luther King Jr.'s "Letter from Birmingham Jail," illustrates some of the ways you can annotate as you read. Add your own annotations, if you like.

> MARTIN LUTHER KING JR. (1929–1968) first came to national notice in 1955, when he led a successful boycott against the policy of restricting African American passengers to rear seats on city buses in Montgomery, Alabama, where he was minister of a Baptist church. He subsequently formed the Southern Christian Leadership Conference, which brought people of all races from all over the country to the South to fight nonviolently for racial integration. In 1963, King led demonstrations in Birmingham, Alabama, that were met with violence; a bomb was detonated in a black church, killing four young girls. King was arrested for his role in organizing the protests, and while in prison he wrote his "Letter from Birmingham Jail" to justify his strategy of civil disobedience, which he called "nonviolent direct action."

King begins his letter by discussing his disappointment with the lack of support he has received from white moderates, such as the group of clergy who published criticism of his organization in the local newspaper. As you read the following excerpt, try to infer what the clergy's specific criticisms might have been. Also, notice the tone King uses. Would you characterize the writing as apologetic, conciliatory, accusatory, or something else?

An Annotated Sample from "Letter from Birmingham Jail"

Martin Luther King Jr.

1 I must confess that over the past few years I have been gravely disappointed with the white moderate. I have almost reached the regrettable conclusion that the Negro's [great stumbling block in his stride toward freedom] is not the White Citizen's Counciler or the Ku Klux Klanner, but the white moderate, who is more devoted to "order" than to justice; who prefers a negative peace which is the absence of tension to a positive peace which is the presence of justice; who constantly says: "I agree with you in the goal you seek, but I cannot agree with your methods of direct action"; who paternalistically believes he can set the timetable for another man's freedom; who lives by a mythical concept of time and who constantly advises the Negro to wait for a "more convenient season." Shallow understanding from people of good will is more frustrating than absolute misunderstanding from people of ill will. Lukewarm acceptance is much more bewildering than outright rejection.

2 I had hoped that the white moderate would understand that law and order exist for the purpose of establishing justice and that when they fail in this purpose they become the [dangerously structured dams that block the flow of social progress.] I had hoped that the white moderate would understand that the present tension in the

¶1. White moderates block progress.

metaphor: white moderate = obstacle

Contrasts: order vs. justice, negative vs. positive peace, absence vs. presence, ends vs. means

(treating others like children)

more contrasts

¶2. What the moderates don't understand

metaphor: law and order = dams (faulty?)

South is a <u>necessary phase of the transition</u> from an [obnoxious

negative peace,] in which the Negro passively accepted his unjust

plight, to a [substantive and <u>positive peace,</u>] in which all men

will respect the dignity and worth of human personality. Actually,

we <u>who engage in nonviolent direct action are not the creators</u>

<u>of tension.</u> We merely bring to the surface the hidden tension

that is already alive. We bring it out in the open, where it can be seen

and dealt with. [<u>Like a boil</u> that can never be cured so long as it is

covered up but must be opened with all its ugliness to the natural

medicines of air and light, injustice must be exposed, with all the

tension its exposure creates, to the <u>light of human conscience and</u>

<u>the air of national opinion before it can be cured.</u>]

    In your statement you assert that <u>our actions,</u> even though 3

peaceful, must be <u>condemned</u> because they precipitate violence.

But is this a logical assertion? <u>Isn't this like condemning</u> (a robbed

man) because his possession of money precipitated the evil act

of robbery? <u>Isn't this like condemning</u> (Socrates) because his

unswerving commitment to truth and his philosophical inquiries

precipitated the act by the misguided populace in which they

made him drink hemlock? <u>Isn't this like condemning</u> (Jesus) because

his unique God-consciousness and never-ceasing devotion to

God's will precipitated the evil act of crucifixion? We must come

to see that, as the federal courts have consistently affirmed, it is

wrong to urge an individual to cease his efforts to gain his <u>basic</u>

<u>constitutional rights</u> because the question may precipitate violence.

[<u>Society must protect the robbed and punish the robber.</u>]

    I had also hoped that the white moderate would reject the <u>myth</u> 4

<u>concerning time</u> in relation to the struggle for freedom. I have just

received a letter from a white brother in Texas. He writes: "All Christians

know that the colored people will receive equal rights eventually, but

---

Margin annotations:

repeats contrast (negative/positive)

Tension already exists: We help dispel it. (True?)

simile: hidden tension is "like a boil"

¶3. Questions clergymen's logic: condemning his actions = condemning robbery victim, Socrates, Jesus.

repetition ("Isn't this like . . .")

(Yes!)

example of a white moderate's view

it is possible that you are in too great a religious hurry. It has taken Christianity almost two thousand years to accomplish what it has. The teachings of Christ take time to come to earth." Such an attitude stems from a tragic misconception of time, from the strangely irrational notion that there is something in the very flow of time that will inevitably cure all ills. (Actually, time itself is neutral; it can be used either destructively or constructively.) More and more I feel that the people of ill will have used time much more effectively than have the people of good will. We will have to repent in this generation not merely for the [hateful words and actions of the bad people] but for the [appalling silence of the good people.] Human progress never rolls in on [wheels of inevitability;] it comes through the tireless efforts of men willing to be co-workers with God, and without this hard work, time itself becomes an ally of the forces of social (stagnation.) [We must use time creatively, in the knowledge that the time is always ripe to do right.] Now is the time to make real the promise of democracy and transform our pending [national elegy] into a creative [psalm of brotherhood.] Now is the time to lift our national policy from the [quicksand of racial injustice] to the [solid rock of human dignity.]

¶4. *Time must be used to do right.*

Silence/passivity is as bad as hateful words and actions.

metaphor (mechanical?)

(decay)

metaphors (song, natural world)

5   You speak of our activity in Birmingham as extreme. At first I was rather disappointed that fellow clergymen would see my nonviolent efforts as those of an extremist. I began thinking about the fact that I stand in the middle of two opposing forces in the Negro community. One is a [force of complacency,] made up in part of Negroes who, as a result of long years of oppression, are so drained of self-respect and a sense of "somebodiness" that they have adjusted to segregation; and in part of a few middle-class Negroes, who because of a degree of academic and economic security and because in some ways they profit by segregation, have become insensitive to the problems of the

King accused of being an extremist.

¶5. *Puts self in middle of two extremes: complacency and bitterness.*

masses. The other [force is one of bitterness and hatred,] and it comes perilously close to advocating violence. It is expressed in the various black nationalist [groups that are springing up] across the nation, the largest and best-known being Elijah Muhammad's Muslim movement. Nourished by the Negro's frustration over the continued existence of racial discrimination, this movement is made up of people who have lost faith in America, who have absolutely repudiated Christianity, and who have concluded that the white man is an incorrigible "devil."

Malcolm X?

I have tried to stand between these two forces, saying that we need emulate neither the "do-nothingism" of the complacent nor the hatred and despair of the black nationalist. For there is the more excellent way of love and nonviolent protest. I am grateful to God that, through the influence of the Negro church, the way of nonviolence became an integral part of our struggle.

6 *¶6. Offers better choice: nonviolent protest.*

(How did nonviolence become part of King's movement?)

If this philosophy had not emerged, by now many streets of the South would, I am convinced, be flowing with blood. And I am further convinced that if our white brothers dismiss as "rabble-rousers" and "outside agitators" those of us who employ nonviolent direct action, and if they refuse to support our nonviolent efforts, millions of Negroes will, out of frustration and despair, seek solace and security in black-nationalist ideologies — a development that would inevitably lead to a frightening racial nightmare.

7 *¶7. Says movement prevents racial violence. (Threat?)*

(comfort)

Oppressed people cannot remain oppressed forever. The yearning for freedom eventually manifests itself, and that is what has happened to the American Negro. Something within has reminded him of his birthright of freedom, and something without has reminded him that it can be gained. Consciously or unconsciously, he has been caught up by the Zeitgeist, and with his black brothers of Africa and his brown and yellow brothers of

8

(spirit of the times)

Asia, South America and the Caribbean, the United States Negro is moving with a sense of great urgency toward the [promised land of racial justice.] If one recognizes this [vital urge that has engulfed the Negro community,] one should readily understand why public demonstrations are taking place. The Negro has many [pent-up resentments] and latent frustrations, and he must release them. So let him march; let him make prayer pilgrimages to the city hall; let him go on freedom rides — and try to understand why he must do so. If his repressed emotions are not released in nonviolent ways, they will seek expression through violence; this is not a threat but a fact of history. So I have not said to my people: "Get rid of your discontent." Rather, I have tried to say that this normal and healthy discontent can be [channeled into the creative outlet of nonviolent direct action.] And now this approach is being termed extremist.

Not a threat, but a fact —?

¶8. Discontent is normal, healthy, and historically inevitable, but it must be channeled.

9   But though I was initially disappointed at being categorized as an extremist, as I continued to think about the matter I gradually gained a measure of satisfaction from the label. Was not Jesus an extremist for love: "Love your enemies, bless them that curse you, do good to them that hate you, and pray for them which despitefully use you, and persecute you." Was not Amos an extremist for justice: "Let justice roll down like waters and righteousness like an everflowing stream." Was not Paul an extremist for the Christian gospel: "I bear in my body the marks of the Lord Jesus." Was not Martin Luther an extremist: "Here I stand; I cannot do otherwise, so help me God." And John Bunyan: "I will stay in jail to the end of my days before I make a butchery of my conscience." And Abraham Lincoln: "This nation cannot survive half slave and half free." And Thomas Jefferson: "We hold these truths to be self-evident, that all men are created equal. . . ." So the question is not whether

¶9. Redefines "extremism."

(Hebrew prophet)

(Christian apostle)

(Founder of Protestantism)

(English preacher)

we will be extremists, but what kind of extremists we will be. Will we be extremists for hate or for love? Will we be extremists for the preservation of injustice or for the extension of justice? In that dramatic scene on Calvary's hill three men were crucified. We must never forget that all three were crucified for the same crime — the crime of extremism. Two were extremists for immorality, and thus fell below their environment. The other, Jesus Christ, was an extremist for love, truth and goodness, and thereby rose above his environment. Perhaps the South, the nation and the world are in dire need of creative extremists.

Compares self to great "extremists"— including Jesus

I had hoped that the white moderate would see this need. Perhaps I was too optimistic; perhaps I expected too much. I suppose I should have realized that few members of the oppressor race can understand the deep groans and passionate yearnings of the oppressed race, and still fewer have the vision to see that [injustice must be rooted out] by strong, persistent and determined action. I am thankful, however, that some of our white brothers in the South have grasped the meaning of this social revolution and committed themselves to it. They are still all too few in quantity, but they are big in quality. Some — such as Ralph McGill, Lillian Smith, Harry Golden, James McBride Dabbs, Ann Braden and Sarah Patton Boyle — have written about our struggle in eloquent and prophetic terms. Others have marched with us down nameless streets of the South. They have languished in filthy, roach-infested jails, suffering the abuse and brutality of policemen who view them as "dirty nigger-lovers." Unlike so many of their moderate brothers and sisters, they have recognized the urgency of the moment and sensed the need for [powerful "action" antidotes] to combat the [disease of segregation.]

10 *Disappointed in the white moderate*

¶10. Praises whites who have supported movement.

(Who are they?)

(been left unaided)

Metaphor: segregation is a disease.

Checklist: Annotating

☐ Mark the text using notations like these:
  - Circle words to be defined in the margin.
  - Underline key words and phrases.
  - Bracket important sentences and passages.
  - Use lines or arrows to connect ideas or words.

☐ Write marginal comments like these:
  - Number and summarize each paragraph.
  - Define unfamiliar words.
  - Note responses and questions.
  - Identify interesting writing strategies.
  - Point out patterns.

☐ Layer additional markings on the text and comments in the margins as you reread for different purposes.

Taking Inventory

Taking inventory helps you analyze your annotations for different purposes. When you take inventory, you make various kinds of lists to explore patterns of meaning you find in the text. For instance, in reading the annotated passage by Martin Luther King Jr., you might have noticed that certain similes and metaphors are used or that many famous people are named. By listing the names (Socrates, Jesus, Luther, Lincoln, and so on) and then grouping them into categories (people who died for their beliefs, leaders, teachers, and religious figures), you could better understand why the writer refers to these particular people. Taking inventory of your annotations can be helpful if you plan to write about a text you are reading.

Checklist: Taking Inventory

☐ Examine your annotations for patterns or repetitions such as recurring images, stylistic features, repeated words and phrases, repeated examples or illustrations, and reliance on particular writing strategies.

☐ List the items in a pattern.

☐ Decide what the pattern might reveal about the reading.

Outlining

Outlining is an especially helpful reading strategy for understanding the content and structure of a reading. **Outlining,** which identifies the text's main ideas, may be part of the annotating process, or it may be done separately. Writing an outline in the margins of the text as you read and annotate makes it easier to find information later. Writing an outline on a separate piece of paper gives you more space to work with, and therefore such an outline usually includes more detail.

The key to outlining is distinguishing between the main ideas and the supporting material such as examples, quotations, comparisons, and reasons. The main ideas form the backbone, which holds the various parts of the text together. Outlining the main ideas helps you uncover this structure.

Making an outline, however, is not simple. The reader must exercise judgment in deciding which are the most important ideas. The words used in an outline reflect the reader's interpretation and emphasis. Readers also must decide when to use the writer's words, their own words, or a combination of the two.

You may make either a formal, multileveled outline or an informal scratch outline. A *formal outline* is harder to make and much more time-consuming than a scratch outline. You might choose to make a formal outline of a reading about which you are writing an in-depth analysis or evaluation. For example, here is a formal outline a student wrote for an essay evaluating the logic of the King excerpt.

For more on the conventions of formal outlines, see pp. 320–22.

Formal Outline of "Letter from Birmingham Jail"

I. "[T]he Negro's great stumbling block in his stride toward freedom is...the white moderate..." (par. 1).

    A. White moderates are more devoted to "order" than to justice; however,

        1. law and order exist only to establish justice (par. 2).

        2. law and order *without* justice actually threaten social order ("dangerously structured dams" metaphor, par. 2).

    B. White moderates prefer "negative peace" (absence of tension) to "positive peace" (justice); however,

        1. tension already exists; it is not created by movement (par. 2).

        2. tension is a necessary phase in progress to just society (par. 2).

        3. tension must be allowed outlet if society is to be healthy ("boil" simile, par. 2).

    C. White moderates disagree with methods of movement; however,

        1. nonviolent direct action can't be condemned for violent response to it (analogies: robbed man; Socrates; Jesus, par. 3).

        2. federal courts affirm that those who seek constitutional rights can't be held responsible for violent response (par. 3).

    D. White moderates paternalistically counsel patience, saying time will bring change; however,

        1. time is "neutral"--we are obligated to use it *actively* to achieve justice (par. 4).

        2. the time for action is now (par. 4).

II. Contrary to white moderates' claims, the movement is not "extremist," in the usual sense (par. 5 ff.).

   A. It stands between extremes in black community: passivity, seen in the oppressed and the self-interested middle-class; and violent radicalism, seen in Elijah Muhammad's followers (pars. 5-6).

   B. In its advocacy of love and nonviolent protest, the movement has forestalled bloodshed and kept more blacks from joining radicals (pars. 5-7).

   C. The movement helps blacks channel urge for freedom that's part of historical trend and the prevailing *Zeitgeist* (par. 8).

III. The movement can be defined as extremist if the term is redefined: "Creative extremism" is extremism in the service of love, truth, and goodness (examples of Amos, Paul, Luther, Bunyan, Lincoln, Jefferson, Jesus, par. 9).

IV. Some whites--"few in quantity, but...big in quality"--have recognized the truth of the arguments above and, unlike the white moderates, have committed themselves to the movement (par. 10).

A *scratch outline* will not record as much information as a formal outline, but it is sufficient for most reading purposes. To make a scratch outline, you first need to locate the topic of each paragraph in the reading. The topic is usually stated in a word or phrase, and it may be repeated or referred to throughout the paragraph. For example, the opening paragraph of the King excerpt (p. 331) makes clear that its topic is the white moderate.

After you have found the topic of the paragraph, figure out what is being said about it. To return to our example: King immediately establishes the white moderate as the topic of the opening paragraph and at the beginning of the second sentence announces the conclusion he has come to — namely, that the white moderate is "the Negro's great stumbling block in his stride toward freedom." The rest of the paragraph specifies the ways the white moderate blocks progress.

The annotations include a summary of each paragraph's topic. Here is a scratch outline that lists the topics:

Scratch Outline of "Letter from Birmingham Jail"

¶1. White moderates block progress

¶2. What the moderates don't understand

¶3. Questions clergymen's logic

¶4. Time must be used to do right

¶5. Puts self in the middle of two extremes: complacency and bitterness

¶6. Offers better choice: nonviolent protest

¶7. Says movement prevents racial violence

¶8. Discontent normal, healthy, and historically inevitable, but it must be channeled

¶9. Redefines "extremism," embraces "extremist" label

¶10. Praises whites who have supported movement

> ## Checklist: Outlining
>
> ☐ Reread each paragraph, identifying the topic and the comments made about the topic. Do not include examples, specific details, quotations, or other explanatory and supporting material.
>
> ☐ List the author's main ideas in the margin of the text or on a separate piece of paper.

Paraphrasing

Paraphrasing is restating a text you have read by using mostly your own words. It can help you clarify the meaning of an obscure or ambiguous passage. It is one of the three ways of integrating other people's ideas and information into your own writing, along with **quoting** (reproducing exactly the language of the source text) and **summarizing** (distilling the main ideas or gist of the source text). You might choose to paraphrase rather than quote when the source's language is not especially arresting or memorable. You might paraphrase short passages but summarize longer ones.

Following are two passages. The first is from paragraph 2 of the excerpt from King's "Letter." The second passage is a paraphrase of the first:

Original

I had hoped that the white moderate would understand that law and order exist for the purpose of establishing justice and that when they fail in this purpose they become the dangerously structured dams that block the flow of social progress. I had hoped that the white moderate would understand that the present tension in the South is a necessary phase of the transition from an obnoxious negative peace, in which the Negro passively accepted his unjust plight, to a substantive and positive peace, in which all men will respect the dignity and worth of human personality.

Paraphrase

King writes that he had hoped for more understanding from white moderates-- specifically that they would recognize that law and order are not ends in themselves but means to the greater end of establishing justice. When law and order do not serve this greater end, they stand in the way of progress. King expected the white moderate to recognize that the current tense situation in the South is part of a transition process that is necessary for progress. The current situation is bad because although there is peace, it is an "obnoxious" and "negative" kind of peace based on blacks passively accepting the injustice of the status quo. A better kind of peace--one that is "substan- tive," real and not imaginary, as well as "positive"--requires that all people, regardless of race, be valued.

When you compare the paraphrase to the original, you can see that the paraphrase contains all the important information and ideas of the original. Notice also that the paraphrase is somewhat longer than the original, refers to the writer by name, and encloses King's original words in quotation marks. The paraphrase tries to be *neutral*, to avoid inserting the reader's opinions or distorting the original writer's ideas.

Checklist: Paraphrasing

☐ Reread the passage to be paraphrased, looking up unfamiliar words in a college dictionary.

☐ Translate the passage into your own words, putting quotation marks around any words or phrases you quote from the original.

☐ Revise to ensure coherence.

Summarizing

Summarizing is important because it helps you understand and remember what is most significant in a reading. Another advantage of summarizing is that it creates a condensed version of the reading's ideas and information, which you can refer to later or insert into your own writing. Along with quoting and paraphrasing, summarizing enables you to integrate other writers' ideas into your own writing.

A **summary** is a relatively brief restatement, primarily in the reader's own words, of the reading's main ideas. Summaries vary in length, depending on the reader's purpose. Some summaries are very brief — a sentence or even a subordinate clause. For example, if you were referring to the excerpt from "Letter from Birmingham Jail" and simply needed to indicate how it relates to your other sources, your summary might look something like this: "There have always been advocates of extremism in politics. Martin Luther King Jr., in 'Letter from Birmingham Jail,' for instance, defends nonviolent civil disobedience as an extreme but necessary means of bringing about racial justice." If, however, you were surveying the important texts of the civil rights movement, you might write a longer, more detailed summary that not only identifies the reading's main ideas but also shows how the ideas relate to one another.

Many writers find it useful to outline the reading as a preliminary step to writing a summary. A paragraph-by-paragraph scratch outline (like the one on p. 339) lists the reading's main ideas in the sequence in which they appear in the original. But summarizing requires more than merely stringing together the entries in an outline. It fills in the logical connections between the author's ideas. Notice also in the following example that the reader repeats selected words and phrases and refers to the author by name, indicating, with verbs like *expresses, acknowledges,* and *explains,* the writer's purpose and strategy at each point in the argument.

Summary

King expresses his disappointment with white moderates who, by opposing his program of nonviolent direct action, have become a barrier to progress toward racial justice. He acknowledges that his program has raised tension in the South, but he explains that tension is necessary to bring about change. Furthermore, he argues that tension already exists, but because it has been unexpressed, it is unhealthy and potentially dangerous.

He defends his actions against the clergy's criticisms, particularly their argument that he is in too much of a hurry. Responding to charges of extremism, King claims that he has actually prevented racial violence by channeling the natural frustrations of oppressed blacks into nonviolent protest. He asserts that extremism is precisely what is needed now--but it must be creative, rather than destructive, extremism. He concludes by again expressing disappointment with white moderates for not joining his effort as some other whites have.

A summary presents only ideas. While it may use certain key terms from the source, it does not otherwise attempt to reflect the source's language, imagery, or tone; and it avoids even a hint of agreement or disagreement with the ideas it summarizes. Of course, however, a writer might summarize ideas in a source like "Letter from Birmingham Jail" to show readers that he or she has read it carefully and then proceed to use the summary to praise, question, or challenge King's argument. In doing so, the writer might quote specific language that reveals word choice, imagery, or tone.

Checklist: Summarizing

☐ Make a scratch outline of the reading.

☐ Write a paragraph or more that presents the author's main ideas largely in your own words. Use the outline as a guide, but reread parts of the original text as necessary.

☐ To make the summary coherent, fill in connections between the ideas you present.

Synthesizing

Synthesizing involves presenting ideas and information gleaned from different sources. It can help you see how different sources relate to one another. For example, one reading may provide information that fills out the information in another reading, or a reading could present arguments that challenge arguments in another reading.

When you synthesize material from different sources, you construct a conversation among your sources, a conversation in which you also participate. Synthesizing contributes most when writers use sources not only to support their ideas, but to challenge and extend them as well.

In the following example, the reader uses a variety of sources related to the King passage (pp. 331–36) and brings them together around a central idea. Notice how quotation, paraphrase, and summary are all used.

Synthesis

When King defends his campaign of nonviolent direct action against the clergymen's criticism that "our actions, even though peaceful, must be condemned because they precipitate violence" (King excerpt, par. 3), he is using what Vinit Haksar calls Mohandas Gandhi's "safety-valve argument" ("Civil Disobedience and Non-Cooperation" 117). According to Haksar, Gandhi gave a "non-threatening warning of worse things to come" if his demands were not met. King similarly makes clear that advocates of actions more extreme than those he advocates are waiting in the wings: "The other force is one of bitterness and hatred, and it comes perilously close to advocating violence" (King excerpt, par. 5). King identifies this force with Elijah Muhammad, and although he does not name him, King's contemporary readers would have known that he was referring also to Muhammad's disciple Malcolm X, who, according to Herbert J. Storing, "urged that Negroes take seriously the idea of revolution" ("The Case against Civil Disobedience" 90). In fact, Malcolm X accused King of being a modern-day Uncle Tom, trying "to keep us under control, to keep us passive and peaceful and nonviolent" (*Malcolm X Speaks* 12).

Checklist: Synthesizing

- ☐ Find and read a variety of sources on your topic, annotating the passages that give you ideas about the topic.

- ☐ Look for patterns among your sources, possibly supporting or challenging your ideas or those of other sources.

- ☐ Write a paragraph or more synthesizing your sources, using quotation, paraphrase, and summary to present what they say on the topic.

Contextualizing

All texts reflect historical and cultural assumptions, values, and attitudes that may differ from your own. To read thoughtfully, you need to become aware of these differences. **Contextualizing** is a critical reading strategy that enables you to make inferences about a reading's historical and cultural context and to examine the differences between its context and your own.

The excerpt from King's "Letter from Birmingham Jail" is a good example of a text that benefits from being read contextually. If you knew little about the history of slavery and segregation in the United States, it would be difficult to understand the passion expressed in this passage. To understand the historical and cultural context in which King wrote his "Letter from Birmingham Jail," you could do some library or Internet research. Comparing the situation at the time King wrote the "Letter" to situations with which you are familiar would help you understand some of your own attitudes toward King and the civil rights movement.

Here is what one reader wrote to contextualize King's writing:

Notes from a Contextualized Reading

1. I am not old enough to know what it was like in the early 1960s when Dr. King was leading marches and sit-ins, but I have seen television documentaries showing demonstrators being attacked by dogs, doused by fire hoses, beaten and dragged by helmeted police. Such images give me a sense of the violence, fear, and hatred that King was responding to.

    The tension King writes about comes across in his writing. He uses his anger and frustration creatively to inspire his critics. He also threatens them, although he denies it. I saw a film on Malcolm X, so I could see that King was giving white people a choice between his own nonviolent way and Malcolm's more confrontational way.

2. Things have certainly changed since the sixties. Legal segregation has ended, but there are still racists like the detective in the O. J. Simpson trial. African Americans like Condoleezza Rice and Barack Obama are highly respected and powerful. The civil rights movement is over. So when I'm reading King today, I feel like I'm reading history. But then again, every once in a while there are reports of police brutality because of race (think of Amadou Diallo) and of what we now call hate crimes.

Checklist: Contextualizing

☐ Describe the historical and cultural situation as it is represented in the reading and in other sources with which you are familiar. Your knowledge may come from other reading, television or film, school, or elsewhere. (If you know nothing about the historical and cultural context, you could do some library or Internet research.)

☐ Compare the historical and cultural situation in which the text was written with your own historical and cultural situation. Consider how your understanding and judgment of the reading are affected by your own context.

Exploring the Significance of Figurative Language

Figurative language — metaphor, simile, and symbolism — enhances literal meaning by implying abstract ideas through vivid images and by evoking feelings and associations.

Metaphor implicitly compares two different things by identifying them with each other. For instance, when King calls the white moderate "the Negro's great stumbling block in his stride toward freedom" (par. 1), he does not mean that the white moderate literally trips the Negro who is attempting to walk toward freedom. The sentence makes sense only if understood figuratively: The white moderate trips up the Negro by frustrating every effort to achieve justice.

Simile, a more explicit form of comparison, uses the word *like* or *as* to signal the relationship of two seemingly unrelated things. King uses simile when he says that injustice is "like a boil that can never be cured so long as it is covered up" (par. 2). This simile makes several points of comparison between injustice and a boil. It suggests that injustice is a disease of society as a boil is a disease of the skin and that injustice, like a boil, must be exposed or it will fester and infect the entire body.

Symbolism compares two things by making one stand for the other. King uses the white moderate as a symbol for supposed liberals and would-be supporters of civil rights who are actually frustrating the cause.

How these figures of speech are used in a text reveals something of the writer's feelings about the subject. Exploring possible meanings in a text's figurative language involves (1) annotating and then listing the metaphors, similes, and symbols you find in a reading; (2) grouping and labeling the figures of speech that appear to express related feelings or attitudes; and (3) writing to explore the meaning of the patterns you have found.

The following example shows the process of exploring figures of speech in the King excerpt.

Listing Figures of Speech

"stumbling block in his stride toward freedom" (par. 1)
"law and order...become the dangerously structured dams" (2)
"the flow of social progress" (2)
"Like a boil that can never be cured" (2)
"the light of human conscience and the air of national opinion" (2)
"the quicksand of racial injustice" (4)

Grouping and Labeling Figures of Speech

Sickness: "like a boil" (2); "the disease of segregation" (10)
Underground: "hidden tension" (2); "injustice must be exposed" (2); "injustice must be rooted out" (10)
Blockage: "dams," "block the flow" (2); "Human progress never rolls in on wheels of inevitability" (4); "pent-up resentments" (8); "repressed emotions" (8)

Writing to Explore Meaning

The patterns labeled underground and blockage suggest a feeling of frustration. Inertia is a problem; movement forward toward progress or upward toward the promised land is stalled. The strong need to break through the resistance may represent King's feelings about both his attempt to lead purposeful, effective demonstrations and his effort to write a convincing argument.

The simile of injustice being "like a boil" links the two patterns of underground and sickness, suggesting that something bad, a disease, is inside the people or the society. The cure is to expose or to root out the blocked hatred and injustice as well as to release the tension or emotion that has long been repressed. This implies that repression itself is the evil, not simply what is repressed. Therefore, writing and speaking out through political action may have curative power for individuals and society alike.

Checklist: Exploring the Significance of Figurative Language

☐ Annotate all the figures of speech you find in the reading — metaphors, similes, and symbols — and then list them.

☐ Group the figures of speech that appear to express related feelings and attitudes, and label each group.

☐ Write one or two paragraphs exploring the meaning of these patterns. What do they tell you about the text?

Looking for Patterns of Opposition

All texts carry within themselves voices of opposition. These voices may echo the views and values of readers the writer anticipates or predecessors to whom the writer is responding in some way; they may even reflect the writer's own conflicting values. Careful readers look closely for such a dialogue of opposing voices within the text.

When we think of oppositions, we ordinarily think of polarities: *yes* and *no, up* and *down, black* and *white, new* and *old*. Some oppositions, however, may be more subtle. The excerpt from King's "Letter from Birmingham Jail" is rich in such oppositions: *moderate* versus *extremist, order* versus *justice, direct action* versus *passive acceptance, expression* versus *repression*. These oppositions are not accidental; they form a significant pattern that gives a reader important information about the essay.

A careful reading will show that King always values one of the two terms in an opposition over the other. In the passage, for example, *extremist* is valued over *moderate* (par. 9). This preference for extremism is surprising. The reader should ask why, when white extremists like members of the Ku Klux Klan have committed so many outrages against African Americans, King would prefer extremism. If King is trying to convince his readers to accept his point of view, why would he represent himself as an extremist? Moreover, why would a clergyman advocate extremism instead of moderation?

Studying the **patterns of opposition** in the text enables you to answer these questions. You will see that King sets up this opposition to force his readers to examine their own values and realize that they are in fact misplaced. Instead of working toward justice, he says, those who support law and order maintain the unjust status quo. By getting his readers to think of white moderates as blocking rather than facilitating peaceful change, King brings readers to align themselves with him and perhaps even embrace his strategy of nonviolent resistance.

Looking for patterns of opposition involves annotating words or phrases in the reading that indicate oppositions, listing the opposing terms in pairs, deciding which term in each pair is preferred by the writer, and reflecting on the meaning of the patterns. Here is a partial list of oppositions from the King excerpt, with the preferred terms marked by an asterisk:

Listing Patterns of Opposition

moderate	*extremist
order	*justice
negative peace	*positive peace
absence of tension	*presence of justice
goals	*methods
*direct action	passive acceptance
*exposed tension	hidden tension

Checklist: Looking for Patterns of Opposition

- ☐ Annotate the selection for words or phrases indicating oppositions.
- ☐ List the pairs of oppositions. (You may have to paraphrase or even supply the opposite word or phrase if it is not stated directly in the text.)
- ☐ For each pair of oppositions, put an asterisk next to the term that the writer seems to value or prefer over the other.
- ☐ Study the patterns of opposition. How do they contribute to your understanding of the essay? What do they tell you about what the author wants you to believe?

Reflecting on Challenges to Your Beliefs and Values

To read thoughtfully, you need to scrutinize your own assumptions and attitudes as well as those expressed in the text you are reading. If you are like most readers, however, you will find that your assumptions and attitudes are so ingrained that you are not always fully aware of them. A good strategy for getting at these underlying beliefs and values is to identify and reflect on the ways the text challenges you, how it makes you feel — disturbed, threatened, ashamed, combative, pleased, exuberant, or some other way.

For example, here is what one student wrote about the King passage:

Reflections

In paragraph 1, Dr. King criticizes people who are "more devoted to 'order' than to justice." This criticism upsets me because today I think I would choose order over justice. When I reflect on my feelings and try to figure out where they come from, I realize that what I feel most is fear. I am terrified by the violence in society today. I'm afraid of sociopaths who don't respect the rule of law, much less the value of human life.

I know Dr. King was writing in a time when the law itself was unjust, when order was apparently used to keep people from protesting and changing the law. But things are different now. Today, justice seems to serve criminals more than it serves law-abiding citizens. That's why I'm for order over justice.

Checklist: Reflecting on Challenges to Your Beliefs and Values

☐ Identify challenges by marking the text where you feel your beliefs and values are being opposed, criticized, or unfairly characterized.

☐ Write a few paragraphs reflecting on why you feel challenged. Do not defend your feelings; instead, search your memory to discover where they come from.

Evaluating the Logic of an Argument

An argument includes a thesis backed by reasons and support. The **thesis** asserts a position on a controversial issue or a solution to a problem that the writer wants readers to accept. The **reasons** tell readers why they should accept the thesis, and the **support** (such as examples, statistics, authorities, and textual evidence) gives readers grounds for accepting it. For an argument to be considered logically acceptable, it must meet the three conditions of what we call the ABC test:

The ABC Test

A. The reasons and support must be *appropriate* to the thesis.

B. The reasons and support must be *believable*.

C. The reasons and support must be *consistent* with one another as well as *complete*.

For more on argument, see Chapter 13. For an example of the ABC test, see Christine Romano's essay in Chapter 7, pp. 280–85.

Testing for Appropriateness

To evaluate the logic of an argument, you first decide whether the argument's reasons and support are appropriate. To test for appropriateness, ask these questions: How does each reason or piece of support relate to the thesis? Is the connection between reasons and support and the thesis clear and compelling?

Readers most often question the appropriateness of reasons and support when the writer argues by analogy or by invoking authority. For example, in paragraph 2, King argues that when law and order fail to establish justice, "they become the dangerously structured dams that block the flow of social progress." The analogy asserts the following logical relationship: Law and order are to progress toward justice what a dam is to water. If you do not accept this analogy, the argument fails the test of appropriateness.

King uses both analogy and authority in paragraph 3: "Isn't this like condemning Socrates because his unswerving commitment to truth and his philosophical inquiries precipitated the act by the misguided populace in which they made him drink hemlock?" Not only must you judge the appropriateness of the analogy comparing the Greeks' condemnation of Socrates to the white moderates' condemnation of King, but you must also judge whether it is appropriate to accept Socrates as an authority. Since Socrates is generally respected for his teaching on justice, his words and actions are likely to be considered appropriate to King's situation in Birmingham.

For invoking authorities, see Chapter 13, pp. 409–10.

Testing for Believability

Believability is a measure of your willingness to accept as true the reasons and support the writer gives in defense of a thesis.

To test for believability, ask: On what basis am I being asked to believe this reason or support is true? If it cannot be proved true or false, how much weight does it carry?

In judging facts, examples, statistics, and authorities, consider the following points.

Facts are statements that can be proved objectively to be true. The believability of facts depends on their *accuracy* (they should not distort or misrepresent reality), their *completeness* (they should not omit important details), and the *trustworthiness* of their sources (sources should be qualified and unbiased). King, for instance, asserts as fact that the African American will not wait much longer for racial justice (par. 8). His critics might question the factuality of this assertion by asking, is it true of all African Americans? How does King know what African Americans will and will not do?

Examples and **anecdotes** are particular instances that may or may not make you believe a general statement. The believability of examples depends on their *representativeness* (whether they are truly typical and thus generalizable) and their *specificity* (whether particular details make them seem true to life). Even if a vivid example or gripping anecdote does not convince readers, it usually strengthens argumentative writing by clarifying the meaning and dramatizing the point. In paragraph 5 of the King excerpt, for example, King supports his generalization that some African American extremists are motivated by bitterness and hatred by citing the specific example of Elijah Muhammad's Black Muslim movement. Conversely, in paragraph 9 he refers to Jesus, Paul, Luther, and others as examples of extremists motivated by love and Christianity. These examples support his assertion that extremism is not in itself wrong and that any judgment of extremism must be based on its motivation and cause.

Statistics are numerical data. The believability of statistics depends on the *comparability* of the data (the price of apples in 1985 cannot be compared with the price of apples in 2010 unless the figures are adjusted to account for inflation), the *precision* of the methods employed to gather and analyze data (representative samples should be used and variables accounted for), and the *trustworthiness* of the sources.

Authorities are people to whom the writer attributes expertise on a given subject. Not only must such authorities be appropriate, as mentioned earlier, but they must be credible as well — that is, the reader must accept them as experts on the topic at hand. King cites authorities repeatedly throughout his essay. He refers to religious leaders (Jesus and Luther) as well as to American political leaders (Lincoln and Jefferson). These figures are likely to have a high degree of credibility among King's readers.

Testing for Consistency and Completeness

In looking for consistency, you should be concerned that all the parts of the argument work together and that they are sufficient to convince readers to accept the thesis or at least take it seriously. To test for consistency and completeness, ask: Are any of the reasons and support contradictory? Do they provide sufficient grounds for accepting the thesis? Does the writer fail to counterargue (to acknowledge, accommodate, or refute any opposing arguments or important objections)?

A thoughtful reader might regard as contradictory King's characterizing himself first as a moderate and later as an extremist opposed to the forces of violence. (King attempts to reconcile this apparent contradiction by explicitly redefining extremism in paragraph 9.) Similarly, the fact that King fails to examine and refute every legal recourse available to his cause might allow a critical reader to question the sufficiency of his argument.

For more on counterarguing, see Chapter 13, pp. 413–15.

⌐ **Checklist:** Evaluating the Logic of an Argument

Use the ABC test:

A. *Test for appropriateness* by checking that the reasons and support are clearly and directly related to the thesis.

B. *Test for believability* by deciding whether you can accept the reasons and support as likely to be true.

C. *Test for consistency and completeness* by deciding whether the argument has any contradictions and whether any important objections or opposing arguments have ⌐ been ignored.

Recognizing Emotional Manipulation

Writers often try to arouse emotions in readers to excite their interest, make them care, or move them to take action. There is nothing wrong with appealing to readers' emotions. What is wrong is manipulating readers with false or exaggerated appeals. Therefore, you should be suspicious of writing that is overly sentimental, that cites alarming statistics and frightening anecdotes, that demonizes others and identifies itself with revered authorities, or that uses potent symbols (for example, the American flag) or emotionally loaded words (such as *racist*).

King, for example, uses the emotionally loaded word *paternalistically* to refer to the white moderate's belief that "he can set the timetable for another man's freedom" (par. 1). In the same paragraph, King uses symbolism to get an emotional reaction from readers when he compares the white moderate to the "Ku Klux Klanner." To get readers to accept his ideas, he also relies on authorities whose names evoke the greatest respect, such as Jesus and Lincoln. But some readers might object that comparing his own crusade to that of Jesus is pretentious and manipulative. A critical reader might also consider King's discussion of African American extremists in paragraph 7 to be a veiled threat designed to frighten readers into agreement

> ### Checklist: Recognizing Emotional Manipulation
>
> ☐ Annotate places in the text where you sense emotional appeals are being used.
>
> ☐ Assess whether any of the emotional appeals are unfairly manipulative.

Judging the Writer's Credibility

Writers try to persuade readers by presenting an image of themselves in their writing that will gain their readers' confidence. This image must be created indirectly, through the arguments, language, and system of values and beliefs expressed or implied in the writing. Writers establish credibility in their writing in three ways:

- By showing their knowledge of the subject
- By building common ground with readers
- By responding fairly to objections and opposing arguments

Testing for Knowledge

Writers demonstrate their knowledge through the facts and statistics they marshal, the sources they rely on for information, and the scope and depth of their understanding. You may not be sufficiently expert on the subject yourself to know whether the facts are accurate, the sources are reliable, and the understanding is sufficient. You may need to do some research to see what others say about the subject. You can also check credentials — the writer's educational and professional qualifications, the respectability of the publication in which the selection first appeared, and reviews of the writer's work — to determine whether the writer is a respected authority in the field. For example, King brings with him the authority that comes from being a member of the clergy and a respected leader of the Southern Christian Leadership Conference.

Testing for Common Ground

One way writers can establish common ground with their readers is by basing their reasoning on shared values, beliefs, and attitudes. They use language that includes their readers (*we*) and qualify their assertions to keep them from being too extreme. Above all, they acknowledge differences of opinion. You want to notice such appeals.

King creates common ground with readers by using the inclusive pronoun *we*, suggesting shared concerns between himself and his audience. Notice, however, his use of masculine pronouns and other references ("the Negro . . . he," "our brothers"). Although King addressed his letter to male clergy, he intended it to be published in the local newspaper, where it would be read by an audience of both men and women. By using language that excludes women, a common practice at the time the selection was written, King may have missed the opportunity to build common ground with more than half of his readers.

Testing for Fairness

Writers reveal their character by the way they handle opposing arguments and objections to their argument. As a critical reader, pay particular attention to how writers treat possible differences of opinion. Be suspicious of those who ignore differences and pretend that everyone agrees with their viewpoints. When objections or opposing views are represented, consider whether they have been distorted in any way; if they are refuted, be sure they are challenged fairly — with sound reasoning and solid support.

One way to gauge the author's credibility is to identify the tone of the argument, for it conveys the writer's attitude toward the subject and toward the reader. Is the text angry? Sarcastic? Evenhanded? Shrill? Condescending? Bullying? Do you feel as if the writer is treating the subject — and you, as a reader — with fairness? King's tone might be characterized in different passages as patient (he doesn't lose his temper), respectful (he refers to white moderates as "people of good will"), or pompous (comparing himself to Jesus and Socrates).

> ## Checklist: Judging the Writer's Credibility
>
> ☐ Annotate for the writer's knowledge of the subject, how well the writer establishes common ground, and whether the writer deals fairly with objections and opposing arguments.
>
> ☐ Decide what in the essay you find credible and what you question.

Cueing the Reader

10

Readers need guidance. To guide readers through a piece of writing, a writer can provide five basic kinds of **cues**, or signals:

1. Thesis and forecasting statements, to orient readers to ideas and organization
2. Paragraphing, to group related ideas and details
3. Cohesive devices, to connect ideas to one another and bring about clarity
4. Transitions, to signal relationships or shifts in meaning
5. Headings and subheadings, to group related paragraphs and help readers locate specific information quickly

This chapter illustrates how each of these cueing strategies works.

Orienting Statements

To help readers find their way, especially in difficult and lengthy texts, you can provide two kinds of **orienting statements**: a thesis statement, which declares the main point, and a forecasting statement, which previews subordinate points, showing the order in which they will be discussed in the essay.

Thesis Statements

To help readers understand what is being said about a subject, writers often provide a thesis statement early in the essay. The **thesis statement**, which can comprise one or more sentences, operates as a cue by letting readers know which is the most important general idea among the writer's many ideas and observations. In "Love: The Right Chemistry" in Chapter 1, Anastasia Toufexis expresses her thesis in the second paragraph:

> O.K., let's cut out all this nonsense about romantic love. Let's bring some scientific precision to the party. Let's put love under a microscope.
>
> When rigorous people with Ph.D.s after their names do that, what they see is not some silly, senseless thing. No, their probe reveals that love rests firmly on the foundations of evolution, biology and chemistry.

353

Readers naturally look for something that will tell them the point of an essay, a focus for the many diverse details and ideas they encounter as they read. They expect to find some information early on that will give them a context for understanding the essay, particularly if they are reading about a new and difficult subject. Therefore, a thesis statement, like Toufexis's, placed at the beginning of an essay enables readers to anticipate the content of the essay and helps them understand the relationships among its various ideas and details.

Occasionally, however, particularly in fairly short, informal essays and in some autobiographical and argumentative essays, a writer may save a direct statement of the thesis until the conclusion. The Trey Ellis autobiographical essay "When the Walls Came Tumbling Down," for example, from Chapter 2, closes with a two-sentence thesis:

> Embarrassment is always the price we pay for more intimacy. Perhaps there is no such thing as too much information.

Ending with the thesis brings together the various strands of information or supporting details introduced over the course of the essay and makes clear the essay's main idea.

Some essays, particularly autobiographical essays, offer no direct thesis statement. While this can make the point of the essay more difficult to determine, it can be appropriate when the essay is more expressive and personal than it is informative. In all cases, careful writers keep readers' needs and expectations in mind when deciding how — and whether — to state the thesis.

Exercise 10.1

In the essay by Jessica Statsky in Chapter 5, underline the thesis statement, the last sentence in paragraph 1. Notice the key terms: "overzealous parents and coaches," "impose adult standards," "children's sports," "activities . . . neither satisfying nor beneficial." Then skim the essay, stopping to read the sentence at the beginning of each paragraph. Also read the last paragraph.

Consider whether the idea in every paragraph's first sentence is anticipated by the thesis's key terms. Consider also the connection between the ideas in the last paragraph and the thesis's key terms. What can you conclude about how a thesis might assert the point of an essay, anticipate the ideas that follow, and help readers relate the ideas to one another?

Forecasting Statements

Some thesis statements include a **forecast**, which overviews the way a thesis will be developed, as in the following example.

> In the three years from 1348 through 1350 the pandemic of plague known as the Black Death, or, as the Germans called it, the Great Dying, killed at least a fourth of the population of Europe. It was undoubtedly the worst disaster that has ever befallen mankind. Today we can have no real conception of the terror under which

people lived in the shadow of the plague. For more than two centuries plague has not been a serious threat to mankind in the large, although it is still a grisly presence in parts of the Far East and Africa. Scholars continue to study the Great Dying, however, as a historical example of human behavior under the stress of universal catastrophe. In these days when the threat of plague has been replaced by the threat of mass human extermination by even more rapid means, there has been a sharp renewal of interest in the history of the fourteenth-century calamity. With new perspective, students are investigating its manifold effects: demographic, economic, psychological, moral and religious.

— WILLIAM LANGER, "The Black Death"

As a reader would expect, Langer divides his essay into explanations of the research of these five effects of the Black Death, addressing them in the order in which they appear in the forecasting statement.

Exercise 10.2

Turn to Linh Kieu Ngo's essay in Chapter 4, and underline the forecasting statement in paragraph 6. Then skim the essay. Notice whether Ngo takes up every point he mentions in the forecasting statement and whether he sticks to the order he promises readers. How well does his forecasting statement help you follow his essay? What suggestions for improvement, if any, would you offer him?

Paragraphing

Paragraph cues as obvious as indentation keep readers on track. You can also arrange material in a paragraph to help readers see what is important or significant. For example, you can begin with a topic sentence, help readers see the relationship between the previous paragraph and the present one with an explicit transition, and place the most important information toward the end.

Paragraph Cues

One paragraph cue — the indentation that signals the beginning of a new paragraph — is a relatively modern printing convention. Old manuscripts show that paragraph divisions were not always marked. To make reading easier, scribes and printers began to use the symbol ¶ to mark paragraph breaks, and later, indenting became common practice. Even that relatively modern custom, however, has been abandoned by most business writers, who now distinguish one paragraph from another by leaving a line of space above and below each paragraph. Writing on the Internet is also usually paragraphed in this way.

Paragraphing helps readers by signaling when a sequence of related ideas begins and ends. Paragraphing also helps readers judge what is most important in what they are reading. Writers typically emphasize important information by placing it at the two points in the paragraph where readers are most attentive — the beginning and the end.

You can give special emphasis to information by placing it in its own paragraph.

For additional visual cues for readers, see Headings and Subheadings on pp. 366–67.

Exercise 10.3

Turn to Patrick O'Malley's essay in Chapter 6, and read paragraphs 4–6 with the following questions in mind: Does all the material in each paragraph seem to be related? Do you feel a sense of closure at the end of each paragraph? Does the last sentence offer the most important or significant or weighty information in the paragraph?

Topic Sentence Strategies

A **topic sentence** lets readers know the focus of a paragraph in simple and direct terms. It is a cueing strategy for the paragraph, much as a thesis or forecasting statement is for the whole essay. Because paragraphing usually signals a shift in focus, readers expect some kind of reorientation in the opening sentence. They need to know whether the new paragraph will introduce another aspect of the topic or develop one already introduced.

Announcing the Topic. Some topic sentences simply announce the topic. Here are some examples taken from Barry Lopez's book *Arctic Dreams:*

> A polar bear walks in a way all its own.

> What is so consistently striking about the way Eskimos used parts of an animal is the breadth of their understanding about what would work.

> The Mediterranean view of the Arctic, down to the time of the Elizabethan mariners, was shaped by two somewhat contradictory thoughts.

The following paragraph shows how one of Lopez's topic sentences (highlighted) is developed:

> What is so consistently striking about the way Eskimos used parts of an animal is the breadth of their understanding about what would work. Knowing that muskox horn is more flexible than caribou antler, they preferred it for making the side prongs of a fish spear. For a waterproof bag in which to carry sinews for clothing repair, they chose salmon skin. They selected the strong, translucent intestine of a bearded seal to make a window for a snowhouse — it would fold up for easy traveling and it would not frost over in cold weather. To make small snares for sea ducks, they needed a springy material that would not rot in salt water — baleen fibers. The down feather

of a common eider, tethered at the end of a stick in the snow at an angle, would reveal the exhalation of a quietly surfacing seal. Polar bear bone was used anywhere a stout, sharp point was required, because it is the hardest bone.

— BARRY LOPEZ, *Arctic Dreams*

Exercise 10.4

Turn to Jessica Statsky's essay in Chapter 5. Underline the topic sentence (the first sentence) in paragraphs 3 and 5. Consider how these sentences help you anticipate the paragraph's topic and method of development.

Making a Transition. Not all topic sentences simply point to what will follow. Some also refer to earlier sentences. Such sentences work both as topic sentences, stating the main point of the paragraph, and as transitions, linking that paragraph to the previous one. Here are a few topic sentences from "Quilts and Women's Culture," by Elaine Hedges, with transitions highlighted:

Within its broad traditionalism and anonymity, however, variations and distinctions developed.

Regionally, too, distinctions were introduced into quilt making through the interesting process of renaming.

Finally, out of such regional and other variations come individual, signed achievements.

Quilts, then, were an outlet for creative energy, a source and emblem of sisterhood and solidarity, and a graphic response to historical and political change.

Sometimes the first sentence of a paragraph serves as a transition, and a subsequent sentence states the topic, as in the following example:

... What a convenience, what a relief it will be, they say, never to worry about how to dress for a job interview, a romantic tryst, or a funeral!
Convenient, perhaps, but not exactly a relief. Such a utopia would give most of us the same kind of chill we feel when a stadium full of Communist-bloc athletes in identical sports outfits, shouting slogans in unison, appears on TV. Most people do not want to be told what to wear any more than they want to be told what to say. In Belfast recently four hundred Irish Republican prisoners "refused to wear any clothes at all, draping themselves day and night in blankets," rather than put on prison uniforms. Even the offer of civilian-style dress did not satisfy them; they insisted on wearing their own clothes brought from home, or nothing. Fashion is free speech, and one of the privileges, if not always one of the pleasures, of a free world.

— ALISON LURIE, *The Language of Clothes*

Occasionally, whole paragraphs serve as transitions, linking one sequence of paragraphs with those that follow. The transition paragraph below summarizes the contrasts between U.S. Civil War generals Grant and Lee and sets up an analysis of the similarities of the two men:

> Yet it was not all contrast, after all. Different as they were — in background, in personality, in underlying aspiration — these two great soldiers had much in common. Under everything else, they were marvelous fighters. Furthermore, their fighting qualities were really very much alike.
>
> — BRUCE CATTON, "Grant and Lee: A Study in Contrasts"

Exercise 10.5

Turn to Jeffrey Kluger's essay in Chapter 4, and read paragraphs 1–7. As you read, underline the part of the first sentence in paragraphs 2–7 that refers to the previous paragraph, creating a transition from one to the next. Notice the different ways Kluger creates these transitions. Consider whether they are all equally effective.

Positioning the Topic Sentence.   Although topic sentences may occur anywhere in a paragraph, stating the topic in the first sentence has the advantage of giving readers a sense of how the paragraph is likely to be developed. The beginning of the paragraph is therefore the most common position.

A topic sentence that does not open a paragraph is most likely to appear at the end. When a topic sentence concludes a paragraph, it usually summarizes or generalizes preceding information:

> Even black Americans sometimes need to be reminded about the deceptiveness of television. Blacks retain their fascination with black characters on TV: Many of us buy *Jet* magazine primarily to read its weekly television feature, which lists every black character (major or minor) to be seen on the screen that week. Yet our fixation with the presence of black characters on TV has blinded us to an important fact that *Cosby*, which began in 1984, and its offshoots over the years demonstrate convincingly: There is very little connection between the social status of black Americans and the fabricated images of black people that Americans consume each day. The representation of blacks on TV is a very poor index to our social advancement or political progress.
>
> — HENRY LOUIS GATES JR., "TV's Black World Turns — but Stays Unreal"

When a topic sentence is used in a narrative, it often appears as the last sentence as a way to evaluate or reflect on events:

> A cold sun was sliding down a gray fall sky. Some older boys had been playing tackle football in the field we took charge of every weekend. In a few years, they'd be called to Southeast Asia, some of them. Their locations would be tracked with pushpins in red, white, and blue on maps on nearly every kitchen wall. But that afternoon, they were quick as young deer. They leapt and dodged, dove from each other and collided in midair. Bulletlike passes flew to connect them. Or the ball spiraled in a high arc

across the frosty sky one to another. In short, they were mindlessly agile in a way that captured as audience every little kid within running distance of the yellow goalposts.

— MARY KARR, *Cherry*

It is possible for a single topic sentence to introduce two or more paragraphs. Subsequent paragraphs in such a sequence have no separate topic sentences of their own:

Anthropologists Daniel Maltz and Ruth Borker point out that boys and girls socialize differently. Little girls tend to play in small groups or, even more common, in pairs. Their social life usually centers around a best friend, and friendships are made, maintained, and broken by talk — especially "secrets." If a little girl tells her friend's secret to another little girl, she may find herself with a new best friend. The secrets themselves may or may not be important, but the fact of telling them is all-important. It's hard for newcomers to get into these tight groups, but anyone who is admitted is treated as an equal. Girls like to play cooperatively; if they can't cooperate, the group breaks up.

Little boys tend to play in larger groups, often outdoors, and they spend more time doing things than talking. It's easy for boys to get into the group, but not everyone is accepted as an equal. Once in the group, boys must jockey for their status in it. One of the most important ways they do this is through talk: verbal display such as telling stories and jokes, challenging and sidetracking the verbal displays of other boys, and withstanding other boys' challenges in order to maintain their own story — and status. Their talk is often competitive talk about who is best at what.

— DEBORAH TANNEN, *That's Not What I Meant!*

Exercise 10.6

Consider the variety and effectiveness of the topic sentences in your most recent essay. Begin by underlining the topic sentence in each paragraph after the first one. The topic sentence may not be the first sentence in a paragraph, though often it will be.

Then double-underline the part of the topic sentence that provides an explicit transition from one paragraph to the next. You may find a transition that is separate from the topic sentence. You may not always find a topic sentence.

Reflect on your topic sentences, and evaluate how well they serve to orient your readers to the sequence of topics or ideas in your essay.

Cohesive Devices

Cohesive devices guide readers, helping them follow your train of thought by connecting key words and phrases throughout a passage. Among such devices are pronoun reference, word repetition, synonyms, repetition of sentence structure, and collocation.

Pronoun Reference

One common cohesive device is **pronoun reference.** As noun substitutes, pronouns refer to nouns that either precede or follow them and thus serve to connect phrases or sentences. The nouns that come before the pronouns are called *antecedents.*

> In New York from dawn to dusk to dawn, day after day, you can hear the steady rumble of tires against the concrete span of the George Washington Bridge. The bridge is never completely still. It trembles with traffic. It moves in the wind. Its great veins of steel swell when hot and contract when cold; its span often is ten feet closer to the Hudson River in summer than in winter.
>
> — GAY TALESE, "New York"

This example has only one pronoun-antecedent chain, and the antecedent comes first, so all the pronouns refer back to it. When there are multiple pronoun-antecedent chains with references forward as well as back, writers have to make sure that readers will not mistake one pronoun's antecedent for another's.

Word Repetition

To avoid confusion, writers often use **word repetition.** The device of repeating words and phrases is especially helpful if a pronoun might confuse readers:

> Some odd optical property of our highly polarized and unequal society makes the poor almost invisible to their economic superiors. The poor can see the affluent easily enough — on television, for example, or on the covers of magazines. But the affluent rarely see the poor or, if they do catch sight of them in some public space, rarely know what they're seeing, since — thanks to consignment stores and, yes, Wal-Mart — the poor are usually able to disguise themselves as members of the more comfortable classes.
>
> — BARBARA EHRENREICH, *Nickel and Dimed*

In the next example, several overlapping chains of word repetition prevent confusion and help the reader follow the ideas:

> Natural selection is the central concept of Darwinian theory — the fittest survive and spread their favored traits through populations. Natural selection is defined by Spencer's phrase "survival of the fittest," but what does this famous bit of jargon really mean? Who are the fittest? And how is "fitness" defined? We often read that fitness involves no more than "differential reproductive success" — the production of more surviving offspring than other competing members of the population. Whoa! cries Bethell, as many others have before him. This formulation defines fitness in terms of survival only. The crucial phrase of natural selection means no more than "the survival of those who survive" — a vacuous tautology. (A tautology is a phrase — like "my father is a man" — containing no information in the predicate ["a man"] not inherent in the subject ["my father"]. Tautologies are fine as definitions, but not as testable scientific statements — there can be nothing to test in a statement true by definition.)
>
> — STEPHEN JAY GOULD, *Ever Since Darwin*

Synonyms

In addition to word repetition, you can use **synonyms**, words with identical or very similar meanings, to connect important ideas. In the following example, the author develops a careful chain of synonyms and word repetitions:

> Over time, small bits of knowledge about a region accumulate among local residents in the form of stories. These are remembered in the community; even what is unusual does not become lost and therefore irrelevant. These narratives comprise for a native an intricate, long-term view of a particular landscape. . . . Outside the region this complex but easily shared "reality" is hard to get across without reducing it to generalities, to misleading or imprecise abstraction.
>
> —BARRY LOPEZ, *Arctic Dreams*

Note the variety of synonym sequences:

"region," "particular landscape"

"local residents," "native"

"stories," "narratives"

"accumulate," "are remembered," "does not become lost"

"intricate, long-term view," "complex . . . (reality)"

The result is a coherent paragraph that constantly reinforces the author's point.

Sentence Structure Repetition

Writers occasionally use **sentence structure repetition** to emphasize the connections among their ideas, as in this example where Isaac Asimov repeats the same if/then sentence structure to show the relationship between his ideas:

> But the life forms are as much part of the structure of the Earth as any inanimate portion is. It is all an inseparable part of a whole. If any animal is isolated totally from other forms of life, then death by starvation will surely follow. If isolated from water, death by dehydration will follow even faster. If isolated from air, whether free or dissolved in water, death by asphyxiation will follow still faster. If isolated from the Sun, animals will survive for a time, but plants would die, and if all plants died, all animals would starve.
>
> —ISAAC ASIMOV, "The Case against Man"

Collocation

Collocation — the positioning of words together in expected ways around a particular topic — occurs quite naturally to writers and usually forms recognizable networks of meaning for readers. For example, in a paragraph on a high school graduation, a reader might expect to encounter such words as *valedictorian, diploma,* *commencement, honors, cap* and *gown,* and *senior class.* The paragraph that follows uses five collocation chains:

> housewife, cooking, neighbor, home
>
> clocks, calculated, progression, precise
>
> obstinacy, vagaries, problem
>
> sun, clear days, cloudy ones, sundial, cast its light, angle, seasons, sun, weather
>
> cooking, fire, matches, hot coals, smoldering, ashes, go out, bed-warming pan

The seventeenth-century housewife not only had to make do without thermometers, she also had to make do without clocks, which were scarce and dear throughout the sixteen hundreds. She calculated cooking times by the progression of the sun; her cooking must have been more precise on clear days than on cloudy ones. Marks were sometimes painted on the floor, providing her with a rough sundial, but she still had to make allowance for the obstinacy of the sun in refusing to cast its light at the same angle as the seasons changed; but she was used to allowing for the vagaries of sun and weather. She also had a problem starting her fire in the morning; there were no matches. If she had allowed the hot coals smoldering under the ashes to go out, she had to borrow some from a neighbor, carrying them home with care, perhaps in a bed-warming pan.

— WAVERLY ROOT AND RICHARD DE ROUCHEMENT, *Eating in America*

Exercise 10.7

Now that you know more about pronoun reference, word repetition, synonyms, sentence structure repetition, and collocation, turn to Brian Cable's essay in Chapter 3 and identify the cohesive devices you find in paragraphs 1–4. Underline each cohesive device you can find; there will be many. You might also want to connect with lines the various pronoun, related-word, and synonym chains you find. You could also try listing the separate collocation chains. Consider how these cohesive devices help you read and make sense of the passage.

Exercise 10.8

Choose one of your recent essays, and select any three contiguous paragraphs. Underline every cohesive device you can find; there will be many. Try to connect with lines the various pronoun, related-word, and synonym chains you find. Also try listing the separate collocation chains.

You will be surprised and pleased at how extensively you rely on cohesive ties. Indeed, you could not produce readable text without them. Consider these questions relevant to your development as a writer: Are all of your pronoun references clear? Are you straining for synonyms when repeated words would do? Do you ever repeat sentence structures to emphasize connections? Do you trust yourself to put collocation to work?

Transitions

A **transition** serves as a bridge to connect one paragraph, sentence, clause, or word with another. It also identifies the kind of connection by indicating to readers how the item preceding the transition relates to the one that follows it. Transitions help readers anticipate how the next paragraph or sentence will affect the meaning of what they have just read. There are three basic groups of transitions, based on the relationships they indicate: logical, temporal, and spatial.

Logical Relationships

Transitions help readers follow the **logical relationships** within an argument. How such transitions work is illustrated in this tightly and passionately reasoned paragraph by James Baldwin:

> The black man insists, by whatever means he finds at his disposal, that the white man cease to regard him as an exotic rarity and recognize him as a human being. This is a very charged and difficult moment, for there is a great deal of will power involved in the white man's naïveté. Most people are not naturally malicious, and the white man prefers to keep the black man at a certain human remove because it is easier for him thus to preserve his simplicity and to avoid being called to account for crimes committed by his forefathers, or his neighbors. He is inescapably aware, nevertheless, that he is in a better position in the world than black men are, nor can he quite put to death the suspicion that he is hated by black men therefore. He does not wish to be hated, neither does he wish to change places, and at this point in his uneasiness he can scarcely avoid having recourse to those legends which white men have created about black men, the most unusual effect of which is that the white man finds himself enmeshed, so to speak, in his own language which describes hell, as well as the attributes which lead one to hell, as being black as night.
> — JAMES BALDWIN, "Stranger in the Village"

Transitions Showing Logical Relationships

- *To introduce another item in a series:* first . . . , second; in the second place; for one thing . . . , for another; next; then; furthermore; moreover; in addition; finally; last; also; similarly; besides; and; as well as
- *To introduce an illustration or other specification:* in particular; specifically; for instance; for example; that is; namely
- *To introduce a result or a cause:* consequently; as a result; hence; accordingly; thus; so; therefore; then; because; since; for
- *To introduce a restatement:* that is; in other words; in simpler terms; to put it differently
- *To introduce a conclusion or summary:* in conclusion; finally; all in all; evidently; clearly; actually; to sum up; altogether; of course

- *To introduce an opposing point:* but; however; yet; nevertheless; on the contrary; on the other hand; in contrast; still; neither; nor
- *To introduce a concession to an opposing view:* certainly; naturally; of course; it is true; to be sure; granted
- *To resume the original line of reasoning after a concession:* nonetheless; all the same; even though; still; nevertheless

Temporal Relationships

In addition to showing logical connections, transitions may indicate **temporal relationships** — a sequence or progression in time — as this example illustrates:

> That night, we drank tea and then vodka with lemon peel steeped in it. The four of us talked in Russian and English about mutual friends and American railroads and the Rolling Stones. Seryozha loves the Stones, and his face grew wistful as we spoke about their recent album, *Some Girls.* He played a tape of "Let It Bleed" over and over, until we could translate some difficult phrases for him; after that, he came out with the phrases at intervals during the evening, in a pretty decent imitation of Jagger's Cockney snarl. He was an adroit and oddly formal host, inconspicuously filling our teacups and politely urging us to eat bread and cheese and chocolate. While he talked to us, he teased Anya, calling her "Piglet," and she shook back her bangs and glowered at him. It was clear that theirs was a fiery relationship. After a while, we talked about ourselves. Anya told us about painting and printmaking and about how hard it was to buy supplies in Moscow. There had been something angry in her dark face since the beginning of the evening; I thought at first that it meant she didn't like Americans; but now I realized that it was a constant, barely suppressed rage at her own situation.
>
> —ANDREA LEE, *Russian Journal*

Transitions Showing Temporal Relationships

- *To indicate frequency:* frequently; hourly; often; occasionally; now and then; day after day; every so often; again and again
- *To indicate duration:* during; briefly; for a long time; minute by minute; while
- *To indicate a particular time:* now; then; at that time; in those days; last Sunday; next Christmas; in 2003; at the beginning of August; at six o'clock; first thing in the morning; two months ago; when
- *To indicate the beginning:* at first; in the beginning; since; before then
- *To indicate the middle:* in the meantime; meanwhile; as it was happening; at that moment; at the same time; simultaneously; next; then
- *To indicate the end and beyond:* eventually; finally; at last; in the end; subsequently; later; afterward

Spatial Relationships

Transitions showing **spatial relationships** orient readers to the objects in a scene, as illustrated in these paragraphs:

> On Georgia 155, I crossed Troublesome Creek, then went through groves of pecan trees aligned one with the next like fenceposts. The pastures grew a green almost blue, and syrupy water the color of a dusty sunset filled the ponds. Around the farmhouses, from wires strung high above the ground, swayed gourds hollowed out for purple martins.
>
> The land rose again on the other side of the Chattahoochee River, and Highway 34 went to the ridgetops where long views over the hills opened in all directions. Here was the tail of the Appalachian backbone, its gradual descent to the Gulf. Near the Alabama stateline stood a couple of LAST CHANCE! bars. . . .
>
> — WILLIAM LEAST HEAT MOON, *Blue Highways*

Transitions Showing Spatial Relationships

- *To indicate closeness:* close to; near; next to; alongside; adjacent to; facing
- *To indicate distance:* in the distance; far; beyond; away; there
- *To indicate direction:* up/down; sideways; along; across; to the right/left; in front of/behind; above/below; inside/outside; toward/away from

Exercise 10.9

Turn to Trey Ellis's essay in Chapter 2. Relying on the lists of transitions just given, underline the *temporal* transitions in paragraphs 1–5. Consider how the transitions relate the ideas and events from sentence to sentence. Suggest any further transitions that could be added to make the relationships even clearer.

Exercise 10.10

Select a recent essay of your own. Choose at least three paragraphs, and underline the logical, temporal, and spatial transitions. Depending on the kind of writing you were doing, you may find few, if any, transitions in one category or another. For example, an essay speculating about causes may not include any spatial transitions; writing about a remembered event might not contain transitions showing logical relationships.

Consider how your transitions relate the ideas from sentence to sentence. Compare your transitions with those in the lists in this text. Do you find that you are making full use of the repertoire? Do you find gaps between any of your sentences that a well-chosen transition would close?

Headings and Subheadings

Headings and **subheadings** — brief phrases set off from the text in various ways — can provide visible cues to readers about the content and organization of a text. Headings can be distinguished from text in numerous ways, including the selective use of capital letters, bold or italic type, or different sizes of type. To be most helpful to readers, headings should be phrased similarly and follow a predictable system.

Heading Systems and Levels

In this chapter, the headings in the section Paragraphing, beginning on p. 355, provide a good example of a system of headings that can readily be outlined:

Paragraphing

Paragraph Cues

Topic Sentence Strategies

Announcing the Topic.

Making a Transition.

Positioning the Topic Sentence.

Notice that in this example, the heading system has three levels. The first-level heading sits on its own line and is set in a large, colored (blue) font; this heading stands out most visibly among the others. (It is one of five such headings in this chapter.) The second-level heading also sits on its own line, but is set in a smaller font (also blue). The first of these second-level headings has no subheadings beneath it, while the second has three. These third-level headings, in black, do not sit on their own lines — they run into the paragraph they introduce, as you can see if you turn back to pp. 356–58.

All of these headings follow a parallel grammatical structure: nouns at the first level; nouns at the second level ("cues" and "strategies"); and "-ing" nouns at the third level.

To learn more about distinguishing headings from surrounding text and about setting up systems of headings, see p. 421 in Chapter 14, Designing Documents.

Headings and Genres

Headings may not be necessary in short essays: Thesis statements, forecasting statements, well-positioned topic sentences, and transition sentences may be all the cues the reader needs. Headings are rare in some genres, such as essays about remembered events (Chapter 2) and essays profiling people and places (Chapter 3). Headings appear more frequently in genres such as concept explanations, position papers, public policy proposals, and evaluations (Chapters 4–7).

Frequency and Placement of Headings

Before dividing their essays into sections with headings and subheadings, writers need to make sure their discussion is detailed enough to support at least two headings at each level. The frequency and placement of headings depend entirely on the content and how it is divided and organized. Keep in mind that headings do not reduce the need for other cues to keep readers on track.

Exercise 10.11

Turn either to Jeffrey Kluger's "What Makes Us Moral" in Chapter 4 or to Robert Kuttner's "Good Jobs for Americans Who Help Americans" in Chapter 6, and survey that essay's system of headings. If you have not read the essay, read or skim it now. Consider how the headings help readers anticipate what is coming and how the argument is organized. Decide whether the headings substitute for or complement other cues for keeping readers on track. Consider whether the headings are grammatically parallel.

Exercise 10.12

Select one of your essays that might benefit from headings. Develop a system of headings, and insert them where appropriate. Be prepared to justify your headings in light of the discussion about headings in this section.

11 Analyzing and Synthesizing Arguments

Analyzing and synthesizing are complementary strategies: Whereas analyzing involves taking something apart, synthesizing involves bringing different things together. Anytime you use multiple sources, you need to begin by analyzing each source so that you can then synthesize the various sources' ideas, information, and arguments.

While any text — or anything, for that matter — can be analyzed, the skills involved are particularly critical in the realm of argument. For this reason, this chapter provides a set of strategies for analyzing and synthesizing arguments.

Analysis and synthesis do not have to be exhaustive. In fact, cataloging everything indiscriminately as if every detail were equally important is counterproductive. To be effective, analysis and synthesis must be selective and focus on what is significant in a text or group of texts.

Because arguments serve to express writers' views and aim to convince readers of the validity of those views, their most significant features are the ways in which they convey the writers' thoughts and attempt to influence readers. An **analysis** of an individual argument essay, then, examines how the writer's presentation of particular reasons or kinds of evidence reflects his or her views and how this presentation would likely appeal to the intended readers. If you examine multiple essays arguing about a controversial issue, their significant features for the purpose of a **synthesis** are the points of agreement and disagreement in the arguments.

Analyzing Arguments

To analyze an argument, you need to read it closely and critically, asking questions about how it is put together and what its underlying assumptions are. (Note that you will almost certainly need to read the text several times to get all you can out of it.) The Criteria for Analyzing Arguments chart on pp. 369–70 will help you do a probing critical analysis of any argument.

Applying the Criteria for Analyzing Arguments

The Criteria for Analyzing Arguments include two categories: basic features and motivating factors. The basic features include the issue, the position, the argument, and the counterargument. The motivating factors include values, ideology, concerns, and priorities.

Analyzing motivating factors is important because it helps you better understand the argument's basic features. You accomplish this analysis by considering the writer's reasons for choosing particular way(s) of framing the issue, establishing a position, constructing the argument, and anticipating and responding to counterarguments. For example, an analysis of the motivating factors behind the writer's way of framing the issue can lead to a more probing and critical understanding of the argument in its rhetorical context.

Let's take as an example the issue of whether the government should be allowed to torture suspected terrorists. Those in favor of torture often frame this issue in either/or terms: Either we use torture, or terrorists will destroy us. These proponents usually illustrate this way of framing by invoking the so-called "ticking time-bomb" scenario, which assumes that there is limited time to avert a disaster and that the government can only do so by forcing a wrongdoer to disclose the plans for it. Framing the issue in this way involves certain underlying assumptions: namely, that no action other than torture will elicit the needed information, and that the information gained through torture is reliable. It also implies a set of specific underlying values, including the following two judgments: that the terrorist's life and/or well-being is less important than the lives of those potentially harmed in a disaster, and that the torturer has the moral right to make this distinction. Throughout the rest of this chapter, we will show you how one student built an analysis and synthesis of this argument by applying the Criteria for Analyzing Arguments.

CRITERIA FOR ANALYZING ARGUMENTS

Features of the Argument

- **Issue.** What issue does the writer address? How does the writer define or frame the issue?

- **Position.** What is the writer's position on the issue (thesis statement)?

- **Argument.** What are the main reasons and kinds of evidence (facts, statistics, examples, authorities, etc.) the writer uses to support his or her position?

- **Counterargument.** What opposing arguments does the writer anticipate? Does the writer **concede** (agree with) or **refute** (disagree with) these arguments? How does the writer attempt to refute opposing arguments?

Motivating Factors

Factors such as the following may be stated explicitly or implied. If you find any other factor that you consider important but that is not on the list, give it a name and include it in your annotations.

(continued)

(continued)

- **Values — Moral, Ethical, or Religious Principles** (for example, justice, equality, the public good, "do unto others," social responsibility, stewardship of the natural environment)
- **Ideology and Ideals** (for example, democratic ideals — everyone is created equal and has the right to life, liberty, and the pursuit of happiness; capitalist ideals; socialist ideals; feminist ideals)
- **Needs and Interests** (for example, food, shelter, work, respect, privacy, choice)
- **Fears and Concerns** (for example, regarding safety, socioeconomic status, power, consequences of actions taken or not taken)
- **Priorities and Agendas** about what is most important or urgent (for example, whether law and order is more important than securing justice and equality, whether the right to life trumps all other concerns, whether combating global warming ought to be a principal concern of government)
- **Binary Thinking** (the assumption that things are "either/or" — for example, that only one of two outcomes is possible, that there can only be winners or losers in a situation, that only two positions are possible, that the world is divided into "us" against "them")

Annotating a Text and Creating a Chart

Annotating a given text and creating a chart like the one on p. 371 will make it easy for you to locate the argument's key features.

1. Begin by carefully reading and annotating the text, marking key passages, and adding questions, comments, and notes to the margins where you identify basic features and motivating factors.
2. Record the argument's basic features in a chart like the one on p. 371. Add paragraph numbers to the chart directing yourself to the places where the feature is evident. Add brief notes to the chart, or jot down key phrases to jog your memory.
3. Chart the argument's motivating factors, adding paragraph numbers and notes (if appropriate and helpful).
4. Chart any additional significant factors you might find, naming them appropriately.

Remember that you will not necessarily find evidence of *every* basic feature or motivating factor in each essay.

Analyzing [title of text]		
Features of the Text	*Issue*	
	Position (Thesis)	
	Argument (Main supporting reasons and evidence)	
	Counterargument (Refutation, concession)	
Motivating Factors	*Values (Moral, ethical, religious)*	
	Ideology and Ideals (Cultural, legal, political)	
	Needs and Interests	
	Fears and Concerns	
	Priorities and Agendas	
	Binary Thinking?	
Other Factors		

Coming Up with a Focus for Your Analysis

Simply re-presenting the notes you have recorded in your chart would constitute a summary of the argument, not an analysis. To write an effective analysis of an argument, you need to explain the significance of what you have found.

To do so, reread the notes you recorded on your chart, and try to identify something — either a basic feature or a motivating factor, or some combination — that strikes you as interesting, unusual, perplexing, or otherwise worth examining further. Try to express this insight in the form of an assertion about the text that will help your reader see it as you do. This insight will provide the focus for your analysis.

A Sample Analysis

In this section, you will see how student Melissa Mae used the Criteria for Analyzing Arguments to plan and write an analysis of "A Case for Torture," an essay that originally appeared in 2005 in the *Age*, a newspaper published in Melbourne, Australia. "A Case for Torture" was co-written by Mirko Bagaric, professor and coordinator of the Graduate Law Program at the Deakin Law School in Melbourne, Australia, and Julie Clarke, lecturer in the same program. Bagaric and Clarke also coauthored a book, *Torture: When the Unthinkable Is Morally Permissible* (2006).

A Case for Torture

MIRKO BAGARIC AND JULIE CLARKE

Recent events stemming from the "war on terrorism" have highlighted the prevalence of torture. This is despite the fact that torture is almost universally deplored. The formal prohibition against torture is absolute — there are no exceptions to it. 1

The belief that torture is always wrong is, however, misguided and symptomatic of the alarmist and reflexive responses typically emanating from social commentators. It is this type of absolutist and short-sighted rhetoric that lies at the core of many distorted moral judgements that we as a community continue to make, resulting in an enormous amount of injustice and suffering in our society and far beyond our borders. 2

Torture is permissible where the evidence suggests that this is the only means, due to the immediacy of the situation, to save the life of an innocent person. The reason that torture in such a case is defensible and necessary is because the justification manifests 3 from the closest thing we have to an inviolable right: the right to self-defence, which of course extends to the defence of another. Given the choice between inflicting a relatively small level of harm on a wrongdoer and saving an innocent person, it is verging on moral indecency to prefer the interests of the wrongdoer.

4   The analogy with self-defence is sharpened by considering the hostage-taking scenario, where a wrongdoer takes a hostage and points a gun to the hostage's head, threatening to kill the hostage unless a certain (unreasonable) demand is met. In such a case it is not only permissible, but desirable for police to shoot (and kill) the wrongdoer if they get a "clear shot." This is especially true if it's known that the wrongdoer has a history of serious violence, and hence is more likely to carry out the threat.

5   There is no logical or moral difference between this scenario and one where there is overwhelming evidence that a wrongdoer has kidnapped an innocent person and informs police that the victim will be killed by a co-offender if certain demands are not met.

6   In the hostage scenario, it is universally accepted that it is permissible to violate the right to life of the aggressor to save an innocent person. How can it be wrong to violate an even less important right (the right to physical integrity) by torturing the aggressor in order to save a life in the second scenario?

7   There are three main [objections] to even the above limited approval of torture. The first is the slippery slope argument: if you start allowing torture in a limited context, the situations in which it will be used will increase.

8   This argument is not sound in the context of torture. First, the floodgates are already open — torture is used widely, despite the absolute legal prohibition against it. Amnesty International has recently reported that it had received, during 2003, reports of torture and ill-treatment from 132 countries, including the United States, Japan and France. It is, in fact, arguable that it is the existence of an unrealistic absolute ban that has driven torture beneath the radar of accountability, and that legalisation in very rare circumstances would in fact reduce instances of it.

9   The second main argument is that torture will dehumanise society. This is no more true in relation to torture than it is with self-defence, and in fact the contrary is true. A society that elects to favour the interests of wrongdoers over those of the innocent, when a choice must be made between the two, is in need of serious ethical rewiring.

10   A third [objection] is that we can never be totally sure that torturing a person will in fact result in us saving an innocent life. This, however, is the same situation as in all cases of self-defence. To revisit the hostage example, the hostage taker's gun might in fact be empty, yet it is still permissible to shoot. As with any decision, we must decide on the best evidence at the time.

11   Torture in order to save an innocent person is the only situation where it is clearly justifiable. This means that the recent high-profile incidents of torture, apparently undertaken as punitive measures or in a bid to acquire information where there was no evidence of an immediate risk to the life of an innocent person, were reprehensible.

Will a real-life situation actually occur where the only option is between tor-   12
turing a wrongdoer or saving an innocent person? Perhaps not. However, a minor
alteration to the Douglas Wood situation illustrates that the issue is far from moot.
If Western forces in Iraq arrested one of Mr. Wood's captors, it would be a perverse
ethic that required us to respect the physical integrity of the captor, and not torture
him to ascertain Mr. Wood's whereabouts, in preference to taking all possible steps
to save Mr. Wood.*

Even if a real-life situation where torture is justifiable does not eventuate, the   13
above argument in favour of torture in limited circumstances needs to be made
because it will encourage the community to think more carefully about moral judgements we collectively hold that are the cause of an enormous amount of suffering in
the world.

First, no right or interest is absolute. Secondly, rights must always yield to con-   14
sequences, which are the ultimate criteria upon which the soundness of a decision is
gauged. Lost lives hurt a lot more than bent principles.

Thirdly, we must take responsibility not only for the things that we do, but also for   15
the things that we can — but fail to — prevent. The retort that we are not responsible for
the lives lost through a decision not to torture a wrongdoer because we did not create the
situation is code for moral indifference.

Equally vacuous is the claim that we in the affluent West have no responsibility for   16
more than 13,000 people dying daily due to starvation. Hopefully, the debate on torture
will prompt us to correct some of these fundamental failings.

_____

*Douglas Wood was taken hostage in Iraq in 2005. — Ed.

Melissa Mae's Annotations

Mae used the Criteria for Analyzing Arguments to guide her close reading of Bagaric
and Clarke's argument. When she first read the essay, she used a highlighter to mark
important passages, and she made a few annotations about the argument's basic
features. When she began to record her observations in a chart, she realized that her
annotations were too scanty to help her (or her reader) understand the essay deeply.
She therefore returned to the essay and reread it, this time using the Criteria more
systematically.

When she was done, Mae was surprised by how much she had written in the
margins. She found herself not only marking where each of the basic features
appears in the text, but also going deeper in her analysis by identifying the moral
values and ideological principles that energize the argument. Mae also added several questions to her annotations that reflect her uncertainty about the argument's
validity.

Below is an excerpt from Mae's annotations. Following this excerpt is the annotation chart she completed for the entire essay.

3   Torture is permissible where the evidence suggests that this is the only means, due to the immediacy of the situation, to save the life of an innocent person. The reason that torture in such a case is defensible and necessary is because the justification manifests from the closest thing we have to an inviolable right: the right to self-defence, which of course extends to the defence of another. Given the choice between inflicting a relatively small level of harm on a wrongdoer and saving an innocent person, it is verging on moral indecency to prefer the interests of the wrongdoer.

Thesis: Torture justified, even required to save innocent victim

Ideology (legal rights) True?

Saving victim outweighs harming wrongdoer

4   The analogy with self-defence is sharpened by considering the hostage-taking scenario, where a wrongdoer takes a hostage and points a gun to the hostage's head, threatening to kill the hostage unless a certain (unreasonable) demand is met. In such a case it is not only permissible, but desirable for police to shoot (and kill) the wrongdoer if they get a "clear shot." This is especially true if it's known that the wrongdoer has a history of serious violence, and hence is more likely to carry out the threat.

Does self-defense analogy hold up?

5   There is no logical or moral difference between this scenario and one where there is overwhelming evidence that a wrongdoer has kidnapped an innocent person and informs police that the victim will be killed by a co-offender if certain demands are not met.

Closer to terrorist situation?

6   In the hostage scenario, it is universally accepted that it is permissible to violate the right to life of the aggressor to save an innocent person. How can it be wrong to violate an even less important right (the right to physical integrity) by torturing the aggressor in order to save a life in the second scenario?

True?

Logic: If killing to save life OK, then torturing to save life also OK.

Melissa Mae's Analysis

In reviewing her annotations of "A Case for Torture," Mae decided that Bagaric and Clarke's essay fell short in three areas: its assumptions about moral "truths," its use of a faulty analogy, and its confusion of moral and legal imperatives. Mae decided that her challenge to the argument's validity on these three grounds was strong enough to provide the focus of her analysis, which she envisioned as inviting further discussion on the issue of government-sponsored torture.

Melissa Mae's Annotation Chart: Analyzing "A Case for Torture"		
Features of the Text	**Issue**	1 (war on terrorism)
	Position (Thesis)	3 ("Torture permissible . . . only means . . . to save the life of an innocent person.")
	Argument (Main supporting reasons and evidence)	Torture sometimes OK 3 (analogy: self-defense) 4-6 (analogy: hostage-talking scenario ⟶ b/c If it's right to kill to save innocent life, then it's right to torture) 13 (b/c it's necessary in real life — Wood example) 14 (b/c "no right or interest is absolute")
	Counterargument (Refutation, concession)	1-2 (Refutes "absolute" prohibition against torture argument) 7-10 (Refutes slippery slope, dehumanizes society, & info untrustworthy arguments) 11 (Concedes cases torture is wrong ⟶ therefore qualifies thesis: not when punitive, only in immediate risk)
Motivating Factors	**Values (Moral, ethical, religious)**	2-3 (save innocent life) 13-16 (need "to think more carefully about moral judgments")
	Ideology and Ideals (Cultural, legal, political)	3 (right to self-defense) 6 ("universally accepted . . . to violate the right to life of the aggressor to save an innocent person") 14 ("Lost lives hurt a lot more than bent principles.")
	Fears and Concerns	1 (post 9/11 fear of terrorism)
	Priorities and Agendas	3 (save innocent life)
	Binary Thinking?	12 ("only option [is] between torturing a wrong-doer or saving an innocent person? Perhaps not. However . . .")

"A Case for Torture": A Questionable Argument
Melissa Mae

1   In 2004, when the abuse of detainees at Abu Ghraib was
revealed, many people here and around the world became concerned
that the United States was breaking with long-established tradition
and the Geneva Conventions by using torture to interrogate war-on-
terror detainees. Although the government denied a torture program
existed, we now know that the Bush administration did order what it
called "enhanced interrogation techniques" such as waterboarding and
sleep deprivation, which clearly fell under the common understanding
of torture.

2   The central question of whether torture should be used has
been the subject of much heated debate. In a 2005 article, "A Case
for Torture," Mirko Bagaric and Julie Clarke, law faculty at Australia's
Deakin University, argue that torture is justifiable, morally as well
as legally. In fact, they claim that torture is not only "defensible"
but "necessary" under certain circumstances (par. 3). The authors
raise some interesting points, but their argument has several fundamental problems: They present debatable moral claims as obvious
truths, they make use of a faulty analogy, and they do not consider
the crucial distinction between what is morally justified and what is
legally prudent.

3   In their opening paragraphs, Bagaric and Clarke make clear
that they are arguing against the position that torture is always
wrong and should never be used. They call this view "absolutist"
and therefore "misguided" (par. 2). Although they claim that torture is "almost universally deplored" (par. 1), they assert that there
are times when it would be morally indecent *not* to use torture
(par. 3).

4   These are assertions that appeal to the pragmatic inclinations of
many people but do little to advance a moral argument. Bagaric and
Clarke conclude the essay by asserting that "no right or interest is
absolute" and that consequences "are the ultimate criteria upon which
the soundness of a decision is gauged" (par. 14). This is an assumption,

however, not an argument. There are plenty of thinkers who argue that consequences are *not* the ultimate criteria for making moral decisions. Simply asserting the opposite is not an adequate substitute for a real argument.

One of the authors' major claims is that using torture in order to extract information needed to avert an imminent tragedy is analogous to self-defense, which they say is "an inviolable right . . . , which of course extends to the defence of another" (par. 3). They refine this analogy by claiming that the so-called "ticking time-bomb" scenario parallels a scenario in which a wrongdoer kidnaps someone (pars. 4–6). Since we would allow a police officer to shoot the kidnapper, they reason, and since killing is obviously worse than torture, then torture should be allowed in "ticking time-bomb" situations.

Even granting Bagaric and Clarke some questionable assumptions — specifically, that killing is always worse than torture, and that it is indeed morally acceptable for the police to shoot someone holding a gun to a hostage's head — their analogy does not work. Asserting that self-defense "of course" extends to "defense of another" is just that — an assertion, not an argument. Similarly, claiming that torturing someone for information is equivalent to the defense of an innocent "other" is a muddier proposition than the authors seem to acknowledge. In the hostage-taking case, killing the wrongdoer with a clean shot stops him from killing the hostage. In the ticking time-bomb case, torture only yields the *possibility* that the wrongdoer will divulge accurate information that *might* enable the police to disarm the bomb.

Further, the authors are unable to produce a single real-life example of the ticking time-bomb situation. While the image of police sharp-shooters poised to take a "clear shot" of the hostage-taker/terrorist is vivid and familiar from television news as well as from innumerable crime programs and films, it poorly represents the situations in which war-on-terror detainees have actually been tortured.

The authors seem to acknowledge the importance of this point by asking, "Will a real-life situation actually occur where the only option is between torturing a wrongdoer or saving an innocent person? Perhaps not." (par. 12). They seem to suggest that such cases *do* exist, however, by immediately afterwards bringing up the case of Douglas Wood, who was taken hostage in Iraq and held for six weeks until he was rescued by U.S. and Iraqi soldiers. In doing so, Bagaric and Clarke attempt at the same time to put a face to the hostage scenario and thereby tap into readers' emotions.

9   However, a news report about the rescue of Wood published in the *Age*, where Bagaric and Clarke's essay was also published, says that the soldiers "effectively 'stumbled across Wood' during a 'routine' raid on a suspected insurgent weapons cache" ("Firefight"). Torture played no role in Wood's rescue. This explains the need for the "minor alteration" (par. 12) that Bagaric and Clarke suggest would be necessary for the case to fulfill the requirements of their scenario. People caught up in the drama of the situation may overlook the detail that Bagaric and Clarke call "minor." But the authors' failure to provide this or indeed any real-world situation to bolster their analogy and the hypothetical scenario they propose is an important, indeed a crucial, detail that undercuts their argument.

10   The authors argue (though, as we have seen, with questionable effectiveness) that there are some extreme instances in which torture is moral, and they want to move from this conclusion to the conclusion that the law should be amended to allow for torture in these situations. There are, however, many situations in which what is moral to do and what is legal to do part ways. For instance, most people would accept that it is morally acceptable to break the law and run a red light to take a critically ill child to the hospital. It does not follow from this, however, that a variety of exceptions for obeying traffic signals should be incorporated into the law. Accordingly, then, Bagaric and Clarke need to do more than show that torture is morally acceptable in some instances — they need to show that these instances are significant enough to justify changes in legislation. The authors fail to offer any convincing evidence that such legal change is necessary.

Works Cited

Bagaric, Mirko, and Julie Clarke. "A Case for Torture." *theage.com.au*.

The Age, 17 May 2005. Web. 1 May 2009.

"Firefight as Wood Rescued." *theage.com.au*. The Age, 16 June 2005.

Web. 2 May 2009.

From Analysis to Synthesis

Synthesizing involves presenting ideas and information gleaned from different sources, and it suggests the ways in which those sources relate to one another. For example, one source may provide information that expands on the information in another source, or it may present arguments that challenge arguments in another reading. When you synthesize material from different sources, you construct a conversation among your sources, a conversation in which you also participate.

Synthesis is a critical step in the process of writing on any topic in which you use multiple sources. In order to create an effective synthesis, you need first to read the sources to see what you want to focus on. This kind of reading will be faster and at least initially more superficial than the kind of close analysis that is required to write an essay analyzing just one or two sources, as illustrated above in Mae's analysis essay, "'A Case for Torture': A Questionable Argument." For an essay based on a multisource synthesis, you read to identify the important arguments offered by the sources and you search for quotes to illustrate these arguments.

Before you can do any of this, of course, you have to find credible sources that speak in interesting ways to the topic on which you are writing. For helpful information on finding and evaluating sources, see Chapters 16 and 17.

A Sample Synthesis

Melissa Mae's Process

After analyzing "A Case for Torture" (see pp. 377–80), Melissa Mae continued to work on the issue of government-sponsored torture. In looking through additional sources that treated the issue, Mae realized that what interested her most was the ways in which various sources addressed the ticking time-bomb scenario, so she decided to focus her synthesis on this scenario.

Mae annotated the sources, highlighting passages where they discuss the scenario. She also tried to identify the topic or argument of each highlighted passage. As she worked with the sources, Mae began to identify several arguments that she thought she might be able to use in her essay. She created a Synthesis chart by collecting quotes and evidence from the sources and by organizing them under headings that each quote or piece of evidence supported. She found that a number of the sources discussed several of the arguments, so there were numerous good quotes to choose from. For other arguments, she could only use one or two possible quotes. (A small portion of her chart appears below.)

After Mae had charted her sources, she reread the chart, thinking about which arguments she should include and what order would make the most sense. Her solution to this challenge, and her way of illuminating the various arguments for her readers, appear in the sample synthesis essay after the chart, on pp. 382–86.

Melissa Mae's Synthesis Chart	
Argument	*Supporting Quotes/Evidence*
The ticking time-bomb (TTB) scenario's frequent discussion may have increased support for torture.	Bellamy describes TTB's ubiquity in discussion and fictional portrayals (141) 1.7 million search results for TTB on Google On *24*: "Each season of *24*, which has been airing . . . But on our show it happens every week" (Mayer) — use whole thing? Television Council Chart "tolerance for torture" (Ip, 40) Henry Shue: "moral reasons for not saying it . . ." (47) — quote all? Žižek quote: "And, in a way, essays like Alter's . . ." (from *London Review of Books*)
The TTB scenario supports the government's practice of torture.	Mayerfeld quote starting "the main justification for . . ." (110) quote from the Bybee memo in Ip (44)
The TTB scenario shows that absolute prohibition on torture is unsustainable.	Bagaric and Clarke use in "A Case for Torture" from Bagaric and Clarke: "Torture is permissible where . . ." Brecher's take on Dershowitz Scarry quote on Dershowitz: ""Alan Dershowitz has asked . . ." (285) Marc Thiessen quote: "The fact is, in real life . . ." (192) Jeff McMahan: "If nothing else, this example exposes . . ." (114)

The Centrality of the Ticking Time-Bomb Scenario
in Arguments Justifying Torture

Melissa Mae

In the post-9/11 world, the ticking time-bomb scenario has   1
played a central role in arguments justifying the use of torture.
As Alex J. Bellamy, professor of peace and conflict studies at the
University of Queensland, has pointed out, the scenario is ubiquitous
(141). A Google search of "ticking bomb scenario" and "ticking time-
bomb scenario" calls up more than 1.7 million results. The scenario
dominates discussion of torture in much mass-media reporting,
commentary, and debate. It is also an important focus of the numerous scholarly books and articles published about torture in the last
decade.

But possibly the most persuasive evocation of the scenario is in   2
the television program *24*. Here's how the program was described in
a *New Yorker* article by investigative reporter Jane Mayer, author of *The
Dark Side: The Inside Story of How the War on Terror Turned Into a War
on American Ideals* (2008), a study of the legal and political debate
over torture inside President George W. Bush's administration:

Each season of *24*, which has been airing on Fox since 2001,
depicts a single, panic-laced day in which Jack Bauer . . . must
unravel and undermine a conspiracy that imperils the nation.
Terrorists are poised to set off nuclear bombs or bioweapons, or
in some other way annihilate entire cities. . . . Frequently, the
dilemma is stark: a resistant suspect can either be accorded due
process — allowing a terrorist plot to proceed — or be tortured in
pursuit of a lead. Bauer invariably chooses coercion. With unnerv-
ing efficiency, suspects are beaten, suffocated, electrocuted,
drugged, assaulted with knives, or more exotically abused; almost
without fail, these suspects divulge critical secrets.

The show's appeal, however, lies less in its violence than in
its giddily literal rendering of a classic thriller trope: the "ticking time bomb" plot. . . . Bob Cochran, who created the show
with Surnow, admitted, "Most terrorism experts will tell you that

the 'ticking time bomb' situation never occurs in real life, or very rarely. But on our show it happens every week." (Mayer)

As the Parents Television Council has demonstrated (see Fig. 1), scenes of torture dominated television in the period following 9/11 and may have intensified the persuasive power of the ticking time-bomb scenario. In fact, John Ip argues that the rise in the public's "tolerance for torture" can be attributed mainly to the ticking bomb scenario (40). In order to take a responsible position on the critical issue of government-supported torture, it is necessary to understand the power — and the real-world applicability — of this well-known scenario.

3   Not only is the ticking bomb scenario ubiquitous, but according to Jamie Mayerfeld the scenario is "the main justification for the use of torture by the U.S. government in the 'War on Terror'" (110). The scenario was often part of official statements, most notably the Bybee memos justifying harsh interrogation methods:

[A] detainee may possess information that could enable the United States to prevent attacks that potentially could equal or surpass

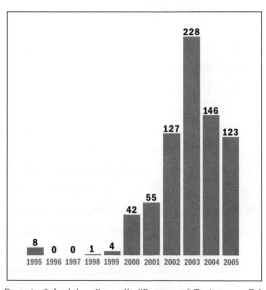

Fig. 1. Parents Television Council, "Scenes of Torture on Primetime Network TV"; rpt. in "Primetime Torture," *Human Rights First* (Human Rights First, 2009; Web; n. pag.).

the September 11 attacks in their magnitude. Clearly, any harm that might occur during an interrogation would pale to insignificance compared to the harm avoided by preventing such an attack, which could take hundreds or thousands of lives. (qtd in Ip 44)

It is relatively easy to find examples of the scenario used by proponents of government-sponsored torture: The article "A Case for Torture" by legal scholars Mirko Bagaric and Julie Clarke is one of many that uses the scenario to argue for the limited use of the otherwise "universally deplored" practice of torture. Bob Brecher, like many other commentators, is especially concerned that the influential Harvard Law professor Alan Dershowitz bases his argument that torture is justified on the scenario. A number of essays have been published refuting Dershowitz's argument — for example, Brecher's chapter titled "The Fantasy of the Ticking Bomb Scenario" in his book *Torture and the Ticking Bomb* and Elaine Scarry's "Five Errors in the Reasoning of Alan Dershowitz." Scarry writes: "Alan Dershowitz has asked us to put aside our commitment to an unwavering prohibition on torture, to enter into an open debate with him, and to step into that debate by passing through the threshold of the ticking bomb case, a case whose framing assumptions are erroneous" (285).

The scenario is used by virtually everyone, however — critics as well as proponents of torture. In a review of a collection of scholarly essays on torture published by Oxford University Press, Corey Robin wrote: "Neo-cons in the White House are not the only ones in thrall to romantic notions of danger and catastrophe. Academics are, too. Every scholarly discussion of torture . . . begins with the ticking time-bomb scenario" (qtd. in Brecher 16-17). What Bob Brecher finds "remarkable . . . is that so many *opponents* of interrogational torture appear not to have given much more thought to the 'facts' of the ticking bomb scenario examples than its supporters" (18).

The primary argument against the ticking bomb scenario is that it is unrealistic, a "fantasy," as Brecher says. Jamie Mayerfeld asserts that "in the long history of counter-terrorist campaigns there has not been one verified report of a genuine ticking bomb torture scenario. There has not been a verified incident that even comes close to the ticking bomb torture scenario" (111). Bush administration officials such as Vice President Dick Cheney and CIA Director George Tenet and supporters like columnist Charles Krauthammer disagree, claiming that "enhanced interrogation techniques" used on Khalid Sheik Mohammed and Abu Zubaydah produced information that forestalled terrorist attacks.

7   However, an August 2009 *Newsweek* article referring to recently released CIA documents makes the point that the documents are vague as to "whether, under the stress and pain of intense interrogation, detainees gave false information that their questioners wanted to hear" and "whether the same information could have been obtained through nonviolent interrogation tactics." Moreover, the article calls into question the claims of immediacy and imminent threat on which justifications of torture are based:

> A former intelligence officer . . . noted that in selling the notion of "enhanced" interrogation techniques to congressional leaders, the Bush administration regularly argued that the main purpose of the techniques was to extract information that could be used to foil imminent terror plots. But the inspector general said his investigation failed to "uncover any evidence that these plots were imminent." (Hosenball)

If torture is used even when there is no ticking bomb — and no credible evidence to suggest there is one — then shouldn't the argument based on the scenario be called into question?

8   David Luban makes the point that if there is no imminent threat — what in the law is referred to as necessity — then torture is revealed to be merely "a fishing expedition" and should not be justifiable under "[t]he limitation to emergency exceptions, implicit in the ticking-bomb story" (1441). Everyone agrees that the scenario dramatizes the necessity of acting quickly and aggressively to prevent disaster. It has been used to open the door for torture under extraordinary circumstances. But if torture is used when we are in a continual state of war but there is no immediate threat, then torture becomes normalized. As Luban argues, "any responsible discussion of torture must address the practice of torture, not the ticking-bomb hypothetical. . . . But somehow, we always manage to forget this and circle back to the ticking bomb. Its rhetorical power has made it indispensable" (1445).

9   The ticking time-bomb scenario as a justification for torture is a rhetorical ploy — Luban calls it "an intellectual fraud" (1452).

The scenario provides a powerful visual image that manipulates our emotions, so vulnerable after the appalling visual images of 9/11. It makes us believe that we are reasonable people, following the law and not acting out of a desire for vengeance. As Luban points out, the ticking bomb scenario converts the torturer from a "cruel" sadist into a "conscientious public servant" like Jack Bauer, the hero of *24* (1436, 1441). In order to take an informed position on issues, like government-sponsored torture, that are literally matters of life and death, we need to be particularly careful in challenging received wisdom and, in this case, in responding viscerally to powerful rhetorical moves.

Works Cited

Bagaric, Mirko, and Julie Clarke. "A Case for Torture." *theage.com.au*. The Age, 17 May 2005. Web. 1 May 2011.

Bellamy, Alex J., "No Pain, No Gain? Torture and Ethics in the War on Terror." *International Affairs* 82.1 (2006): 121-48. Print.

Brecher, Bob. *Torture and the Ticking Bomb*. New York: Wiley, 2007. Print.

Dershowitz, Alan. *Why Terrorism Works*. New York: Yale UP, 2002. Print.

Hosenball, Mark. "Did Waterboarding Actually Work?" *Newsweek*. Newsweek, 24 Aug. 2009. Web. 21 Apr. 2011.

Ip, John. "Two Narratives of Torture." *Northwestern Journal of International Human Rights* 7.1 (2009): 35-77. Print.

Krauthammer, Charles. "The Torture Debate, Continued." *Washington Post*. Washington Post, 15 May 2009. Web. 11 June 2011.

Luban, David. "Liberalism and the Unpleasant Question of Torture." *Virginia Law Review* 91.6 (2005): 1425-61. Web. 20 Apr. 2011.

Mayer, Jane. "Whatever It Takes." *New Yorker*. Condé Nast Digital, 19 Feb. 2007. Web. 20 Apr. 2011.

Mayerfeld, Jamie. "In Defense of the Absolute Prohibition of Torture." *Public Affairs Quarterly* 22.2 (2008): 109-28. Print.

Scarry, Elaine. "Five Errors in the Reasoning of Alan Dershowitz." *Torture: A Collection*. Ed. Sanford Levinson. New York: Oxford UP, 2004. Print.

Analyzing Visuals

We live in a highly visual world. Every day we are barraged with a seemingly endless stream of images from television, magazines, billboards, books, Web pages, newspapers, flyers, storefront signs, and more — all of them competing for our attention, and all of them loaded with information and ideas. Forms of communication that traditionally used only the written word (letters, books, term papers) or the spoken word (telephone conversations, lectures) are today increasingly enhanced with visual components (PowerPoint slides, cell-phone graphics, video, photos, illustrations, graphs, and the like) for greater impact. And most of us would agree that visuals do, indeed, have an impact: A picture, as the saying goes, is worth a thousand words.

In part because of their potentially powerful effect on us, visuals and visual texts* should be approached the way we approach written texts: analytically and critically.

Figure 12.1 Times Square at Dusk, February 9, 2007

---

*In this chapter, we use the word *image* to refer primarily to photographs. We use the word *visual* as a broader designation for visual elements of texts (including images, but also such components as diagrams, charts, and graphs), and *visual text* for documents such as ads, brochures, and the like, in which visuals are strongly featured but which consist of more than a single image.

Whether their purpose is to sell us an idea or a car, to spur us to action or inspire us to dream, visuals invite analysis both of their key components and of their rhetorical context. As we "read" a visual, therefore, we should ask ourselves a series of questions: Who created it? Where was it published? What audience is it addressing? What is it trying to get this audience to think and feel about the subject? How does it attempt to achieve this purpose?

Let's look, for example, at the visual text on this page: a public service announcement (PSA) from the World Wildlife Fund (WWF).

The central image in this PSA is a smiling fisherman holding up a fish. Most of us will immediately recognize his posture and facial expression as those of a man excited about and proud of an impressive catch; the photo's wooden frame makes the image seem like a real photo from a fishing trip, as opposed to an ad agency's creation (which would be easier to ignore). After noting these things, however, we are immediately struck by what is wrong with the picture: the fish is tiny — a far cry from the sort of catch any normal fisherman would be satisfied with — the lake in the background is almost entirely dried up, and the fisherman is covered in bloody sores from severe sun damage.

Figure 12.2 "Fishing," from the WWF's 2007 "Beautiful Day U.S." Series

So what do we make of the disruption of the convention (the vacation photo) on which the PSA image is based? In trying to decide, most of us will look next to the text below the image: "Ignoring global warming won't make it go away." The disjunction between the fisherman's pleased expression and the barren lake and measly catch — not to mention his grotesquely sunburned skin — turns out to be the point of the PSA: Like the fisherman in the picture, the PSA implies, we are all blithely ignoring the impending disaster that global warming represents. The reputable, non-profit WWF's logo and URL, which constitute its "signature," are meant to be an assurance that this threat is real, and not just an idea a profit-seeking ad agency dreamed up to manipulate us.

People continue to argue about how urgent the problem of climate change is and what, if anything, we need to do about it. The WWF suggests that, like the oblivious fisherman, too many of us have adopted a "head-in-the-sand" attitude about the problem. Lest the implied criticism be construed as an outright insult and alienate viewers, the implied connection to the fisherman also flatters us by implying that we are fun-loving and well intentioned. Global warming, in the WWF's view, threatens the bright future we all like to imagine we have ahead of us.

Not everyone will be convinced by this PSA to support the work of the WWF, and some viewers may feel manipulated by the visual image. They may disagree that the problem is as dire as the depiction implicitly claims it is. They may feel that our resources and energy would be better directed toward other problems facing our nation. Nevertheless, most people would agree that with a single cleverly constructed image, a single line of text, and a logo, the PSA delivers its message clearly and forcefully.

Criteria for Analyzing Visuals

The primary purpose of this chapter is to help you analyze visuals and write about them. In your college courses, some of you will be asked to write entire papers in which you analyze one or more visuals (a painting or a photo, for example). Some of you will write papers in which you include analysis of one or more visual texts within the context of a larger written essay (say, by analyzing the brochures and ads authorized by a political candidate, in an argument about her campaign).

Of course, learning to analyze visuals effectively can also help you gain a more complete understanding of any document that *uses* visuals but that is not entirely or predominantly composed of them. Why did the author of a remembered event essay, for example, choose a particular photo of a person mentioned in the text — does it reinforce the written description, add to it, or contradict it in some way? If there is a caption under the photo, how does it affect the way we read it? In a concept explanation, why are illustrations of one process included, but not another? How well do the charts and graphs work with the text to help us understand the author's explanation? Understanding what visuals can do for a text can also help you effectively integrate images, charts, graphs, and other visuals in your own essays, whatever your topic.

The following chart outlines key criteria for analyzing visuals and provides questions for you to ask about documents that include them.

CRITERIA FOR ANALYZING VISUALS

Key Components

Composition

- Of what elements is the visual composed?
- What is the focal point — that is, the place your eyes are drawn to?
- From what perspective do you view the focal point? Are you looking straight ahead at it, down at it, or up at it? If the visual is a photograph, what angle was the image shot from — straight ahead, looking down or up?
- What colors are used? Are there obvious special effects employed? Is there a frame, or are there any additional graphical elements? If so, what do these elements contribute to your "reading" of the visual?

People/Other Main Figures

- If people are depicted, how would you describe their age, gender, subculture, ethnicity, profession, level of attractiveness, and socioeconomic class? How do these factors relate to other elements of the image?
- Who is looking at whom? Do the people represented seem conscious of the viewer's gaze?
- What do the facial expressions and body language tell you about power relationships (equal, subordinate, in charge) and attitudes (self-confident, vulnerable, anxious, subservient, angry, aggressive, sad)?

Scene

- If a recognizable scene is depicted, what is its setting? What is in the background and the foreground?
- What has happened just before the image was "shot"? What will happen in the next scene?
- What, if anything, is happening just outside of the visual frame?

Words

- If text is combined with the visual, what role does the text play? Is it a slogan? A famous quote? Lyrics from a well-known song?
- Does the text help you interpret the visual's overall meaning? What interpretive clues does it provide?
- What is the tone of the written text? Humorous? Elegiac? Ironic?

Tone

- What tone, or mood, does the visual convey? Is it lighthearted, somber, frightening, shocking, joyful? What elements in the visual (color, composition, words, people, setting, etc.) convey this tone?

Context(s)

Rhetorical Context

- **What is its main purpose?** Are we being asked to buy a product? Form an opinion or judgment about something? Support a political party's candidate? Take some other kind of action?

- **Who is its target audience?** Children? Men? Women? Some sub- or super-set of these groups (for example, African American men, "tweens," seniors)?

- **Who is the author? Who sponsored its publication?** What background/associations do the author and the sponsoring publication have? What other works have they produced?

- **Where was it published, and in what form?** Online? On television? In print? In a commercial publication (for example, a sales brochure, billboard, ad) or an informational one (newspaper, magazine)?

- **If the visual is embedded within a document that is primarily written text, how do the written text and the visual relate to each other?** Do they convey the same message, or are they at odds in any way? Does the image seem subordinate to the written text, or is it the other way around?

- *Social Context.* **What is the immediate social and cultural context within which the visual is operating?** If we are being asked to support a certain candidate, for example, how does the visual reinforce or counter what we already know about this candidate? What other social/cultural knowledge does the visual assume its audience already has?

- *Historical Context.* **What historical knowledge does it assume the audience already possesses?** Does the visual refer to other historical images, figures, events, or stories that the audience would recognize? How do these historical references relate to the visual's audience and purpose?

- *Intertextuality.* **How does the visual connect, relate to, or contrast with any other significant texts, visual or otherwise, that you are aware of?** How do such considerations inform your ideas about this particular visual?

A Sample Analysis

In a composition class, students were asked to do a short written analysis of a photograph of their choosing. In looking for ideas online, one student, Paul Taylor, came across the Library of Congress's *Documenting America*, an exhibit of photographs done between 1935 and 1945 for the federal government's Farm Security Administration. The work of African American photographer Gordon Parks struck

Figure 12.3 *Ella Watson*, Gordon Parks (1942)

Paul as particularly interesting, especially his photos of Ella Watson, a poorly paid office cleaner employed by the federal government. (See Figure 12.3.)

After studying the photographs, Paul read what the site had to say about the context from which they emerged:

Gordon Parks was born in Kansas in 1912.... During the Depression a variety of jobs ... took him to various parts of the northern United States. He took up photography during his travels.... In 1942, an opportunity to work for the Farm Security Administration brought the photographer to the nation's capital; Parks later recalled that "discrimination and bigotry were worse there than any place I had yet seen."[1]

The exhibit also quotes Parks's recollection of his first photo session with Watson:

> She began to spill out her life's story. It was a pitiful one. She had struggled alone after her mother had died and her father had been killed by a lynch mob.... Her husband was accidentally shot to death two days before their daughter was born.... My first photograph of [Watson] was unsubtle. I overdid it and posed her, Grant Wood style, before the American flag, a broom in one hand, a mop in the other, staring straight into the camera.[2]

Paul did not understand Parks's reference to "Grant Wood" in his description of the photo, so he did an Internet search using the terms *"Grant Wood" "Gordon Parks" "Ella Watson"*

[1]Martin H. Bush, "A Conversation with Gordon Parks," in *The Photographs of Gordon Parks* (Wichita, Kansas: Wichita State University, 1983), 36.

[2]Gordon Parks, *A Choice of Weapons* (New York: Harper & Row, 1966), 230–31.

and discovered that Parks was referring to a classic painting by Wood called *American Gothic* (Figure 12.4). Reading further about the connection, he discovered that Parks's photo of Watson is itself commonly titled *American Gothic* and discussed as a parody of Grant Wood's painting.

Intrigued by what he had learned so far, Paul decided to delve into Parks's later career. A 2006 obituary of Parks in the *New York Times* reproduced his 1952 photo *Emerging Man*, which Paul decided to analyze for his assignment. First, he did additional research on the photo. Then he made notes on his responses to the photo using the criteria for analysis provided on pp. 390–91.

Art © Figg Art Museum, Successor to the Estate of Nan Wood Graham/ Licensed by VAGA, New York, NY.

Figure 12.4 *American Gothic*, **Grant Wood, American (1930)**

© The Gordon Parks Foundation. Courtesy The Gordon Parks Foundation.

Figure 12.5 *Emerging Man, Harlem*, **Gordon Parks (1952)**

PAUL TAYLOR'S ANALYSIS OF *EMERGING MAN*

Key Components of the Visual

Composition

- **Of what elements is the visual composed?** It's a black-and-white photo showing the top three-quarters of a man's face and his hands (mostly fingers). He appears to be emerging out of the ground — out of a sewer? There's what looks like asphalt in the foreground, and buildings (out of focus) in the far background.

- **What is the focal point — that is, the place your eyes are drawn to?** The focal point is the face of the man staring directly into the camera's lens. There's a shaft of light angled (slightly from the right?) onto the lower-middle part of his face. His eyes appear to glisten slightly. The rest of his face, his hands, and the foreground are in shadow.

- **From what perspective do you view the focal point?** We appear to be looking at him at eye level — weird, since eye level for him is just a few inches from the ground. Was the photographer lying down? The shot is also a close-up — a foot or two from the man's face. Why so close?

- **What colors are used? Are there obvious special effects employed? Is there a frame, or are there any additional graphical elements?** There's no visible frame or any graphic elements. The image is in stark black and white, and there's a "graininess" to it: We can see the texture of the man's skin and the asphalt on the street.

People/Other Main Figures

- **If people are depicted, how would you describe their age, gender, subculture, ethnicity, profession, level of attractiveness, and socioeconomic class?** The man is African American, and probably middle-aged (or at least not obviously very young or very old). We can't see his clothing or any other marker of class, profession, etc. The fact that he seems to be emerging from a sewer implies that he's not hugely rich or prominent, of course — a "man of the people"?

- **Who is looking at whom? Do the people represented seem conscious of the viewer's gaze?** The man seems to be looking directly into the camera, and at the viewer (who's in the position of the photographer). I guess, yes, he seems to look straight at the viewer — perhaps in a challenging or questioning way.

- **What do the facial expressions and body language tell you about power relationships (equal, subordinate, in charge) and attitudes (self-confident, vulnerable, anxious, subservient, angry, aggressive, sad)?** We can only see his face from the nose up, and his fingertips. It looks like one eyebrow is slightly raised, which might mean he's questioning or skeptical. The expression in his eyes is definitely serious. The position of his fingers implies that he's clutching the rim of the manhole — that, and the title, indicate that he's pulling himself up out of the hole. But since we see only the fingers, not the whole hand, does his hold seem tenuous — he's "holding on by his fingertips"? Not sure.

Scene

- **If a recognizable scene is depicted, what is its setting? What is in the background and the foreground?** It looks like an urban setting (asphalt, manhole cover, buildings, and lights in the blurry distant background). Descriptions of the photo note that Parks shot the image in Harlem. Hazy buildings and objects are in the distance. Only the man's face and fingertips are in focus. The sky behind him is light gray, though — is it dawn?

- **What has happened just before the image was "shot"? What will happen in the next scene?** He appears to be coming up and out of the hole in the ground (the sewer).

- **What, if anything, is happening just outside of the visual frame?** It's not clear. There's no activity in the background at all. It's deserted, except for him.

Words

- **If text is combined with the visual, what role does the text play?** There's no text on or near the image. There is the title, though — *Emerging Man.*

- **Does the text help you interpret the visual's overall meaning?** The title is a literal description, but it might also refer to the civil rights movement — the gradual racial and economic integration of African Americans into American society.

- **What is the tone of the written text?** Hard to say. I guess, assuming wordplay is involved, it's sort of witty (merging traffic?)?

Tone

- **What tone, or mood, does the image convey? What elements in the visual (color, composition, words, people, setting, etc.) convey this tone?** The tone is serious, even perhaps a bit spooky. The use of black and white and heavy shadows lend a somewhat ominous feel, though the ray of light on the man's face, the lightness of the sky, and the lights in the background counterbalance this to an extent. The man's expression is somber, though not obviously angry or grief-stricken.

Context(s)

Rhetorical Context

- **What is its main purpose?** Given Parks's interest in politics and social justice, it seems fair to assume that the image of the man emerging from underground — from the darkness into the light? — is a reference to social progress (civil rights movement) and suggests rebirth of a sort. The use of black and white, while certainly not unusual in photographs of the era, emphasizes the division between black and white that is in part the photo's subject.

- **Who is its target audience?** Because it appeared first in *Life*, the target audience was mainstream — a broad cross-section of the magazine-reading U.S. population at mid-twentieth century.

- **Who is the author? Who sponsored its publication?** During this era, Gordon Parks was best known as a photographer whose works documented and commented on social conditions. The fact that this photo was originally published in Life magazine (a mainstream periodical read by white Americans throughout the country) is probably significant.

- **Where was it published, and in what form?** In *Life*, it accompanied an article on Ralph Ellison's novel *Invisible Man*.

- **If the visual is embedded within a document that is primarily written text, how do the written text and the visual relate to each other?** The photo accompanied an article about Ellison's *Invisible Man*, a novel about a man who goes underground to escape racism and conflicts within the early civil rights movement. Now the man is reentering mainstream society?

- *Social Context.* **What is the immediate social and cultural context within which the visual is operating?** The civil rights movement was gaining ground in post-World War II society.

- *Historical Context.* **What historical knowledge does it assume the audience already possesses?** For a viewer in 1952, the image would call to mind the current and past situation of African Americans. Uncertainty about what the future would hold (Would the emergence be successful? What kind of man would eventually emerge?) would be a big part of the viewer's response. Viewers today obviously feel less suspense about what would happen in the immediate (post-1952) future. The "vintage" feel of the photo's style and even the man's hair, along with the use of black and white, probably have a "distancing" effect on the viewer today. At the same time, the subject continues to be relevant — most viewers will likely think about the progress we've made in race relations, and where we're currently headed.

- *Intertextuality.* **How does the visual connect, relate to, or contrast with any other significant texts, visual or otherwise, that you are aware of?** *Invisible Man*, which I've already discussed, was a best-seller and won the National Book Award in 1953.

After writing and reviewing these notes and doing some further research to fill in gaps in his knowledge about Parks, Ellison, and the civil rights movement, Paul drafted his analysis. He submitted this draft to his peer group for comments, and then revised. His final draft follows.

Paul Taylor

Professor Stevens

Writing Seminar I

4 October 2010

The Rising

Gordon Parks's 1952 photograph *Emerging Man* (Fig. 1) is as historically significant a reflection of the civil rights movement as are the speeches of Martin Luther King and Malcolm X, the music of Mahalia Jackson, and the books of Ralph Ellison and James Baldwin. Through striking use of black and white--a reflection of the racial divisions plaguing American cities and towns throughout much of the nineteenth and twentieth centuries--and a symbolically potent central subject--an African American man we see literally "emerging" from a city manhole--Parks's photo evokes the centuries of racial and economic marginalization of African Americans, at the same time as it projects a spirit of determination and optimism regarding the civil rights movement's eventual success.

In choosing the starkest of urban settings and giving the image a gritty feel, Parks alerts the viewer to the gravity of his subject and gives it a sense of immediacy. As with the documentary photographs Parks took of office cleaner Ella Watson for the Farm Security Administration in the 1940s--see Fig. 2 for one example--the carefully chosen setting and the spareness of the treatment ensure the viewer's focus on the social statement

© The Gordon Parks Foundation. Courtesy The Gordon Parks Foundation.

Fig. 1. Gordon Parks, *Emerging Man, Harlem* (1952)

Taylor 2

Fig. 2.   Gordon Parks, *Ella Watson* (1942)

the artist is making (*Documenting*). Whereas the photos of Ella Watson document a particular woman and the actual conditions of her life and work, *Emerging Man* strips away any particulars, including any name for the man, with the result that the photo enters the symbolic or even mythic realm.

The composition of *Emerging Man* makes it impossible for us to focus on anything other than the unnamed subject rising from the manhole--we are, for instance, unable to consider what the weather might be, though we might surmise from the relatively light tone of the sky and the emptiness of the street that it is dawn. Similarly, we are not given any specifics of the setting, which is simply urban and, apart from the central figure, unpopulated. Reducing the elements to their outlines in this way keeps the viewer focused on the grand central theme of the piece: the role of race in mid-twentieth-century America and the future of race relations.

The fact that the man is looking directly at the camera, in a way that's challenging and serious but not hostile, speaks to the racial optimism of the period among a large cross-section of the society, African American and white alike. President Truman's creation of the President's Committee on Civil Rights in 1946 and his 1948 Executive Order for the integration of all armed services were significant steps toward the emergence of the full-blown civil rights movement, providing hope that African Americans would be able, for perhaps the first time in American history, to look directly into the eyes of their white counterparts and fearlessly emphasize their shared humanity (Leuchtenburg). The "emerging man" seems to be daring us to try to stop his rise from the manhole, his hands gripping its sides, his eyes focused intently upon the viewer.

According to several sources, Parks planned and executed the photograph as a photographic counterpart to Ralph Ellison's 1952 *Invisible Man*, a breakthrough novel about race and society that was both a best-seller and a critical success. *Invisible Man* is narrated in the first person by an unnamed African American man who traces his experiences from boyhood. The climax of the novel shows the narrator hunted by policemen controlling a Harlem race riot; escaping down a manhole, the narrator is trapped at first, but eventually decides to live permanently underground, hidden from society ("Ralph Ellison"). The correspondences between the photo and the book are apparent. In fact, according to the catalog accompanying an exhibit of Parks's photos selected by the photographer himself before his death in 2006, Ellison actually collaborated on the staging of the photo (*Bare Witness*).

More than just a photographic counterpart, however, it seems that Parks's *Emerging Man* can be read as a sequel to *Invisible Man*, with the emphasis radically shifted from resignation to optimism. The man who had decided to live underground now decides to emerge, and does so with determination. In this compelling photograph, Parks--himself an "emerging man," considering he was the first African American photographer to be hired full-time by the widely respected mainstream *Life* magazine--created a photograph that celebrated the changing racial landscape in American society.

Works Cited

Bare Witness: Photographs by Gordon Parks. Catalog. Milan: Skira; Stanford,
    CA: Iris & B. Gerald Cantor Center for Visual Arts at Stanford
    University, 2006. Traditional Fine Arts Organization. *Resource Library.*
    Web. 28 Sept. 2010.

Documenting America: Photographers on Assignment. 15 Dec. 1998. *America
    from the Great Depression to World War II: Black-and-White Photographs
    from the FSA-OWI, 1935-1945.* Prints and Photographs Div., Lib. of
    Cong. Web. 27 Sept. 2010.

Leuchtenburg, William E. "The Conversion of Harry Truman." *American Heritage*
    42.7 (1991): 55-68. *America: History & Life.* Web. 28 Sept. 2010.

Parks, Gordon. *Ella Watson.* Aug. 1942. *America from the Great Depression to
    World War II: Black-and-White Photographs from the FSA-OWI, 1935-1945.*
    Prints and Photographs Div., Lib. of Cong. Web. 26 Sept. 2010.

---. *Emerging Man.* 1952. *PhotoMuse.* George Eastman House and ICP, n.d.
    Web. 30 Sept. 2010.

"Ralph Ellison: *Invisible Man.*" *Literature and Its Times: Profiles of 300
    Notable Literary Works and the Historical Events that Influenced Them.*
    Ed. Joyce Moss and George Wilson. Vol. 4. Gale Research, 1997.
    Literature Resource Center. Web. 30 Sept. 2010.

Exercise 12.1

Dorothea Lange's *First-Graders at the Weill Public School* shows children of Japanese descent reciting the Pledge of Allegiance in San Francisco, California, in 1942. Following the steps below, write an essay suggesting what the image means.

1. Do some research on Lange's work. (Like Paul Taylor, you might start at the Library of Congress's online exhibit *Documenting America*, which features Lange, along with Gordon Parks and other photographers.)

2. Analyze the image using the criteria for analysis presented on pp. 390–91.

3. From this preliminary analysis, develop a tentative thesis that says what the image means and how it communicates that meaning.

4. With this thesis in mind, plan your essay, using your analysis of the image to illustrate your thesis. Be aware that as you draft your essay, your thesis will develop and may even change substantially.

■ Dorothea Lange, *First-Graders at the Weill Public School* (1942)

Exercise 12.2

Analyze one of the ads that follow by using the criteria for visual analysis on pp. 390–91. Be sure to consider the role that writing plays in the ad's overall meaning. Write an essay with a thesis that discusses the ad's central meaning and significance.

■ Magazine Ad for Continental Savings Bank (2008)

■ Billboards for Pepsi (2008)

■ Magazine Ad for Novopelle Laser Hair Removal (2008)
(Text reads: "A closet full of low-cut blouses. Countless hours at the gym. A small fortune in pushup bras. And he can't stop staring at my upper lip.")

Exercise 12.3

Find an ad or public service announcement that you find compelling in its use of images. Analyze the ad by using the criteria for visual analysis on pp. 390–91. Be sure to consider the role that writing plays in the ad's overall meaning. Write an essay with a thesis that discusses the ad's central meaning and significance.

13 ●●●● Arguing

This chapter presents the basic strategies for making arguments in writing. In it, we focus on asserting a thesis, backing it up with reasons and support, and counter-arguing — responding to readers' questions and refuting their arguments.

Asserting a Thesis

Central to any argument is the **thesis**. In a sentence or two, a thesis asserts or states the main point of any argument you want to make. It can be assertive only if you make it clear and direct. The thesis statement usually appears at the beginning of an argument essay.

There are three kinds of argument essays in Part One of this book. Each of these essays requires a special kind of assertion and reasoning:

- *Assertion of opinion:* What is your position on a controversial issue? (Chapter 5, "Arguing a Position")

  When overzealous parents and coaches impose adult standards on children's sports, the result can be activities that are neither satisfying nor beneficial to children.
  — JESSICA STATSKY, "Children Need to Play, Not Compete"

- *Assertion of policy:* What is your understanding of a problem, and what do you think should be done to solve it? (Chapter 6, "Proposing a Solution")

  Although this last-minute anxiety about midterm and final exams is only too familiar to most college students, many professors may not realize how such major, infrequent, high-stakes exams work against the best interests of students both psychologically and intellectually. . . . If professors gave additional brief exams at frequent intervals, students would be spurred to study more regularly, learn more, worry less, and perform better.
  — PATRICK O'MALLEY, "More Testing, More Learning"

- *Assertion of evaluation:* What is your judgment of a subject? (Chapter 7, "Justifying an Evaluation")

  Overall, the Web site is well designed, amusing, and extremely helpful.
  — WENDY KIM, "Grading Professors"

As these different thesis statements indicate, the kind of thesis you assert depends on the occasion for which you are writing and the question you are trying to answer for

404

your readers. Whatever the writing situation, to be effective, every thesis must satisfy the same three standards: It must be *arguable, clear,* and *appropriately qualified.*

Chapters 5–7 contain essays that argue for each of these kinds of assertions, along with guidelines for constructing an argument to support such an assertion.

Arguable Assertions

Reasoned argument is called for when informed people disagree over an issue or remain divided over how best to solve a problem, as is so often the case in social and political life. Hence the thesis statements in reasoned arguments make **arguable assertions** — possibilities or probabilities, not certainties.

Therefore, a statement of fact could not be an arguable thesis statement because facts can be verified as true or not true — whether by checking an authoritative reference book, asking an authority, or observing the fact with your own eyes. For example, these statements assert facts:

Jem has a Ph.D. in history.

I am less than five feet tall.

Eucalyptus trees were originally imported into California from Australia.

Each of these assertions can be easily verified. To find out Jem's academic degree, you can ask him, among other things. To determine a person's height, you can use a tape measure. To discover where California got its eucalyptus trees, you can search the library or Internet. There is no point in arguing such statements, unless there is a question about the authority of a particular source or the accuracy of someone's measurement. If a writer asserts something as fact and attempts to support the assertion with authorities or statistics, the resulting essay is not an argument but a report.

Like facts, expressions of personal feelings are not arguable assertions. Whereas facts are unarguable because they can be definitively proved true or false, feelings are unarguable because they are purely subjective.

You can declare, for example, that you detest eight o'clock classes, but you cannot offer an argument to support this assertion. All you can do is explain why you feel as you do. If, however, you were to restate the assertion as "Eight o'clock classes are counterproductive," you could then construct an argument that does not depend solely on your subjective feelings, memories, or preferences. Your argument could be based on reasons and support that apply to others as well as to yourself. For example, you might argue that students' ability to learn is at an especially low ebb immediately after breakfast, and you might provide scientific support for this assertion — in addition, perhaps, to personal experience and reports of interviews with your friends.

Clear and Precise Wording

The way a thesis is worded is as important as its arguability. The wording of a thesis, especially its key terms, must be clear and precise.

Consider the following assertion: "Democracy is a way of life." The meaning of this claim is uncertain, partly because the word *democracy* is abstract and partly because the phrase *way of life* is inexact. Abstract ideas like democracy, freedom, and patriotism are by their very nature hard to grasp, and they become even less clear with overuse. Too often, such words take on connotations that may obscure the meaning you want to emphasize. *Way of life* is fuzzy: What does it mean? Does it refer to daily life, to a general philosophy or attitude toward life, or to something else?

Thus a thesis is vague if its meaning is unclear; it is ambiguous if it has more than one possible meaning. For example, the statement "My English instructor is mad" can be understood in two ways: The teacher is either angry or insane. Obviously, these are two very different assertions. You would not want readers to think you mean one when you actually mean the other.

Whenever you write an argument, you should pay special attention to the way you phrase your thesis and take care to avoid vague and ambiguous language.

Appropriate Qualification

In addition to being arguable and clear, an argument thesis must make **appropriate qualifications** that suit your writing situation. If you are confident that your case is so strong that readers will accept your argument without question, state your thesis emphatically and unconditionally. If, however, you expect readers to challenge your assumptions or conclusions, you must qualify your statement. Qualifying a thesis makes it more likely that readers will take it seriously. Expressions like *probably, very likely, apparently,* and *it seems* all serve to qualify a thesis.

Exercise 13.1

Write an assertion of opinion that states your position on one of the following controversial issues:

- Should English be the official language of the United States and the only language used in local, state, and federal governments' oral and written communications?
- Should teenagers be required to get their parents' permission to obtain birth control information and contraceptives?
- Should high schools or colleges require students to perform community service as a condition for graduation?
- Should marriage between same-sex couples be legal?

Constructing a persuasive argument on any of these issues would obviously require careful deliberation and research. For this exercise, however, all you need to do is construct an arguable, clear, and appropriately qualified thesis.

Exercise 13.2

Find the thesis in one of the argument essays in Chapters 5–7. Then decide whether the thesis meets the three requirements: that it be arguable, clear, and appropriately qualified.

> ## Exercise 13.3
>
> If you have written or are currently working on one of the argument assignments in Chapters 5–7, consider whether your essay thesis is assertive, arguable, and appropriately qualified. If you believe it does not meet these requirements, revise it appropriately.

Giving Reasons and Support

Whether you are arguing a position, proposing a solution, or justifying an evaluation, you need to give **reasons** and **support** for your thesis.

Think of reasons as the main points supporting your thesis. Often they answer the question "Why do you think so?" For example, if you assert among friends that you value a certain movie highly, one of your friends might ask, "Why do you like it so much?" And you might answer, "*Because* it has challenging ideas, unusual camera work, and memorable acting." Similarly, you might oppose restrictions on students' use of offensive language at your college *because* such restrictions would make students reluctant to enter into frank debates, *because* offensive speech is hard to define, and *because* restrictions violate the free-speech clause of the First Amendment. These *because* phrases are your reasons. You may have one or many reasons, depending on your subject and your writing situation.

For your argument to succeed with your readers, you must not only give reasons but also support your reasons. The main kinds of support writers use are examples, statistics, authorities, anecdotes, and textual evidence. Following is a discussion and illustration of each kind of support, along with standards for judging its reliability.

Examples

Examples may be used as support in all types of arguments. For examples to be believable and convincing, they must be representative (typical of all the relevant examples you might have chosen), consistent with the experience of your readers (familiar to them and not extreme), and adequate in number (numerous enough to be convincing and yet not likely to overwhelm readers).

The following illustration comes from a book on illiteracy in America by Jonathan Kozol, a prominent educator and writer.

> Illiterates cannot read the menu in a restaurant.
>
> They cannot read the cost of items on the menu in the window of the restaurant before they enter.
>
> Illiterates cannot read the letters that their children bring home from their teachers. They cannot study school department circulars that tell them of the courses that their children must be taking if they hope to pass the SAT exams. They cannot help with homework. They cannot write a letter to the teacher. They are afraid to visit in the classroom. They do not want to humiliate their child or themselves.
>
> Illiterates cannot read instructions on a bottle of prescription medicine. They cannot find out when a medicine is past the year of safe consumption; nor can they read of allergenic risks, warnings to diabetics, or the potential sedative effect of

certain kinds of nonprescription pills. They cannot observe preventive health care admonitions. They cannot read about "the seven warning signs of cancer" or the indications of blood-sugar fluctuations or the risks of eating certain foods that aggravate the likelihood of cardiac arrest.

— Jonathan Kozol, *Illiterate America*

Kozol collected these examples in his many interviews with people who could neither read nor write. Though all of his readers are literate and have never experienced the frustrations of adult illiterates, Kozol assumes they will accept that the experiences are a familiar part of illiterates' lives. Most readers will believe the experiences to be neither atypical nor extreme.

Exercise 13.4

Identify the examples in paragraphs 9 and 11 in Jessica Statsky's essay "Children Need to Play, Not Compete" and paragraphs 16–18 in Amitai Etzioni's essay "Working at McDonald's" (both in Chapter 5). If you have not read the essays, pause to skim them so that you can evaluate these examples within the context of the entire essay. How well do the examples meet the standards of representativeness, consistency with experience of readers, and adequacy in number? You will not have all the information you need to evaluate the examples — you rarely do unless you are an expert on the subject — but make a judgment based on the information available to you in the headnotes and the essays.

Statistics

In many kinds of arguments about economic, educational, or social issues, **statistics** may be essential. When you use statistics in your own arguments, you will want to ensure that they are up-to-date, relevant, and accurate. In addition, take care to select statistics from reliable sources and to cite them from the sources in which they originally appeared if at all possible. For example, you would want to get medical statistics directly from a reputable and authoritative professional periodical like the *New England Journal of Medicine* rather than secondhand from a supermarket tabloid or an unaffiliated Web site, neither of which can be relied on for accuracy. If you are uncertain about the most authoritative sources, ask a reference librarian or a professor who knows your topic.

The following selection, written by a Harvard University professor, comes from an argument speculating about the decline of civic life in the United States. Civic life includes all of the clubs, organizations, and communal activities people choose to participate in.

The culprit is television.

First, the timing fits. The long civic generation was the last cohort of Americans to grow up without television, for television flashed into American society like lightning in the 1950s. In 1950 barely 10 percent of American homes had television sets, but by 1959, 90 percent did, probably the fastest diffusion of a major technological innovation ever recorded. The reverberations from this lightning bolt continued for decades, as viewing hours grew by 17–20 percent during the 1960s and by an additional 7–8 percent during the 1970s. In the early years, TV watching was concentrated among the less educated sectors of the population, but during the 1970s the viewing time of the more educated sectors of the population began to converge upward. Television viewing increases with age, particularly upon retirement, but each generation since the introduction of television has begun its life cycle at a higher starting point. By 1995 viewing per TV household was more than 50 percent higher than it had been in the 1950s.

Most studies estimate that the average American now watches roughly four hours per day (excluding periods in which television is merely playing in the background). Even a more conservative estimate of three hours means that television absorbs 40 percent of the average American's free time, an increase of about one-third since 1965. Moreover, multiple sets have proliferated: By the late 1980s three-quarters of all U.S. homes had more than one set, and these numbers too are rising steadily, allowing ever more private viewing. . . . This massive change in the way Americans spend their days and nights occurred precisely during the years of generational civic disengagement.

— Robert D. Putnam, "The Strange Disappearance of Civic America"

These statistics come primarily from the U.S. Bureau of the Census, a nationwide count of the number of Americans and a survey, in part, of their buying habits, levels of education, and leisure activities. The Census reports are widely considered to be accurate and trustworthy. They qualify as original sources of statistics.

Chapter 16 provides help finding statistical data in the library.

Exercise 13.5

In Chapter 5, underline the statistics in paragraphs 5 and 6 of Jessica Statsky's essay. If you have not read the essay, pause to skim it so that you can evaluate the writer's use of statistics within the context of the whole essay. How well do the statistics meet the standard of up-to-dateness, relevance, accuracy, and reliance on the original source? Does the writer indicate where the statistics come from? What do the statistics contribute to the argument?

Authorities

To support an argument, writers often cite experts on the subject. Quoting, paraphrasing, or even just referring to a respected **authority** can add to a writer's credibility. Authorities must be selected as carefully as facts and statistics, however. One qualification for authorities is suggested by the way we refer to them: They must be authoritative — that is, trustworthy and reputable. They must also be specially qualified to contribute to the subject you are writing about. For example, a well-known expert on the American presidency might be a perfect choice to support an argument about the achievements of a past president but a poor choice to support an argument on whether adolescents who commit serious crimes should be tried as adults. Finally, qualified authorities must have training at respected institutions or have unique real-world experiences, and they must have a record of research and publications recognized by other authorities.

The following example comes from a *New York Times* article about some parents' and experts' heightened concern over boys' behavior. The author believes that the concern is exaggerated and potentially dangerous. In the full argument, she is particularly concerned about the number of boys who are being given Ritalin, a popular drug for treating attention-deficit hyperactivity disorder (ADHD).

> Today, the world is no longer safe for boys. A boy being a shade too boyish risks finding himself under the scrutiny of parents, teachers, guidance counselors, child therapists — all of them on watch for the early glimmerings of a medical syndrome, a bona fide behavioral disorder. Does the boy disregard authority, make snide comments in class, push other kids around and play hooky? Maybe he has a conduct disorder. Is he fidgety, impulsive, disruptive, easily bored? Perhaps he is suffering from attention-deficit hyperactivity disorder, or ADHD, the disease of the hour and the most frequently diagnosed behavioral disorder of childhood. Does he prefer computer games and goofing off to homework? He might have dyslexia or another learning disorder.
>
> "There is now an attempt to pathologize what was once considered the normal range of behavior of boys," said Melvin Konner of the departments of anthropology and psychiatry at Emory University in Atlanta. "Today, Tom Sawyer and Huckleberry Finn surely would have been diagnosed with both conduct disorder and ADHD." And both, perhaps, would have been put on Ritalin, the drug of choice for treating attention-deficit disorder.
>
> — NATALIE ANGIER, "Intolerance of Boyish Behavior"

In this example, Angier relies on *informal* citation within her essay to introduce Melvin Konner, the authority she quotes, along with a reference to his professional qualifications. Such informal citation is common in newspapers, magazines, and some books intended for general audiences. In other books and in academic contexts, writers use *formal* citation, providing a list of works cited at the end of the essay.

For examples of two formal citation styles often used in college essays, see Chapter 17.

Exercise 13.6

Analyze how authorities are used in paragraphs 4 and 5 of Patrick O'Malley's essay "More Testing, More Learning" in Chapter 6. Begin by underlining the authorities' contributions to these paragraphs, whether through quotation, summary, or paraphrase. On the basis of the evidence you have available, decide to what extent each source is authoritative on the subject: qualified to contribute to the subject, trained appropriately, and recognized widely. How does O'Malley establish each authority's credentials? Then decide what each authority contributes to the argument as a whole. (If you have not read the essay, take time to read or skim it.)

Anecdotes

Anecdotes are brief stories about events or experiences. If they are relevant to the argument, well told, and true to life, they can provide convincing support. To be relevant, an anecdote must strike readers as more than an entertaining diversion; it must seem to make an irreplaceable contribution to an argument. A well-told story is easy to follow, and the people and scenes are described memorably, even vividly. A true-to-life anecdote seems believable, even if the experience is foreign to readers' experiences.

The following anecdote appeared in an argument taking a position on gun control. The writer, an essayist, poet, and environmentalist who is also a rancher in South Dakota, always carries a pistol and believes that other people should have the right to do so.

> I was driving the half-mile to the highway mailbox one day when I saw a vehicle parked about midway down the road. Several men were standing in the ditch, relieving themselves. I have no objection to emergency urination, but I noticed they'd dumped several dozen beer cans in the road. Besides being ugly, cans can slash a cow's feet or stomach.
>
> The men noticed me before they finished and made quite a performance out of zipping their trousers while walking toward me. All four of them gathered around my small foreign car, and one of them demanded what the hell I wanted.
>
> "This is private land. I'd appreciate it if you'd pick up the beer cans."
>
> "What beer cans?" said the belligerent one, putting both hands on the car door and leaning in my window. His face was inches from mine, and the beer fumes were strong. The others laughed. One tried the passenger door, locked; another put his foot on the hood and rocked the car. They circled, lightly thumping the roof, discussing my good fortune in meeting them and the benefits they were likely to bestow upon me. I felt very small and very trapped and they knew it.
>
> "The ones you just threw out," I said politely.
>
> "I don't see no beer cans. Why don't you get out here and show them to me, honey?" said the belligerent one, reaching for the handle inside my door.
>
> "Right over there," I said, still being polite, " — there, and over there." I pointed with the pistol, which I'd slipped under my thigh. Within one minute the cans and the men were back in the car and headed down the road.
>
> I believe this incident illustrates several important principles. The men were trespassing and knew it; their judgment may have been impaired by alcohol. Their response to the polite request of a woman alone was to use their size, numbers, and sex to inspire fear. The pistol was a response in the same language. Politeness didn't work; I couldn't match them in size or number. Out of the car, I'd have been more vulnerable. The pistol just changed the balance of power.
>
> — LINDA M. HASSELSTROM, "Why One Peaceful Woman Carries a Pistol"

Most readers would readily agree that this anecdote is well told: It has many concrete, memorable details; there is action, suspense, climax, resolution, and even dialogue. It is about a believable, possible experience. Finally, the anecdote is clearly relevant to the author's argument about gun control.

See Chapter 2, Remembering an Event, for more information about narrating anecdotes.

Exercise 13.7

Evaluate the way an anecdote is used in paragraph 16 of Amitai Etzioni's essay "Working at McDonald's" in Chapter 5. Consider whether the story is well told and true to life. Decide whether it seems to be relevant to the whole argument. Does the writer make the relevance clear? Does the anecdote support Etzioni's argument?

Textual Evidence

When you argue claims of value (Chapter 7), **textual evidence** will be very important. In your college courses, if you are asked to evaluate a controversial article, you must quote, paraphrase, or summarize passages so that readers can understand why you think the author's argument is or is not credible. If you are analyzing a novel, you must include numerous excerpts to show just how you arrived at your conclusion.

For textual evidence to be considered effective support for an argument, it must be carefully selected to be relevant. You must help readers see the connection between each piece of evidence and the reason it supports. Textual evidence must also be highly selective — that is, chosen from among all the available evidence to provide the support needed without overwhelming the reader or weakening the argument with marginally relevant evidence. Textual evidence usually has more impact if it is balanced between quotation and paraphrase, and it must be smoothly integrated into the sentences of the argument.

The following example comes from a student essay in which the writer argues that the main character (referred to as "the boy") in the short story "Araby" by James Joyce is so self-absorbed that he learns nothing about himself or other people.

> The story opens and closes with images of blindness — a framing device that shows the boy does not change but ends up with the same lack of understanding that he began with. The street is "blind" with an "uninhabited house . . . at the blind end" (par. 1). As he spies on Mangan's sister, from his own house, the boy intentionally limits what he is able to see by lowering the "blind"until it is only an inch from the window sash (par. 4). At the bazaar in the closing scene, the "light was out," and the upper part of the hall was "completely dark" (par. 36). The boy is left "gazing up into the darkness," seeing nothing but an inner torment that burns his eyes (par. 37).
>
> The boy's blindness appears to be caused by his obsession with Mangan's sister. When he tries to read at night, for example, the girl's "image [comes] between [him] and the page," in effect blinding him (par. 12). In fact, he seems blind to everything except this "image" of the "brown-clad figure cast by [his] imagination" (par. 16). The girl's "brown-clad figure" is also associated with the houses on "blind" North Richmond Street, with their "brown imperturbable faces" (par. 1). The houses stare back at the boy, unaffected by his presence and gaze.
>
> — SALLY CRANE, "Gazing into the Darkness"

Notice how the writer quotes selected words and phrases about blindness to support her reasoning that the boy learns nothing because he is blinded. There are twelve smoothly integrated quotations in these two paragraphs, along with a number of paraphrases, all of them relevant. The writer does not assume that the evidence speaks for itself; she comments and interprets throughout.

For more information on paraphrasing, see pp. 340–41 in Chapter 9.

Exercise 13.8

Analyze the use of evidence in paragraphs 4 and 5 of Christine Romano's essay "'Children Need to Play, Not Compete,' by Jessica Statsky: An Evaluation" in Chapter 7. If you have not read this essay, read it now. Identify the quotes and paraphrases Romano uses, and then try to identify the phrases or sentences that comment on or explain this evidence. Consider whether Romano's evidence in these two paragraphs seems relevant to her thesis and reasons, appropriately selective, well balanced between quotes and paraphrases, integrated smoothly into the sentences she creates, and explained helpfully.

Counterarguing

Asserting a thesis and backing it with reasons and support are essential to a successful argument. Thoughtful writers go further, however, by **counterarguing** — anticipating and responding to their readers' objections and questions, their alternative position, or preferred solution to a problem.

To counterargue, writers rely on three basic strategies: acknowledging, accommodating or conceding, and refuting. Writers show they are aware of readers' objections and questions (acknowledge), modify their position to accept readers' concerns they think are legitimate (concede), or explicitly argue that readers' objections may be invalid or that their concerns may be irrelevant (refute). Writers may use one or more of these three strategies in the same essay. Readers find arguments more convincing when writers have anticipated their concerns in these ways.

Acknowledging Readers' Concerns

When you **acknowledge readers' questions or objections**, you show that you are aware of their point of view and that you take it seriously even if you do not agree with it, as in the following example.

> The homeless, it seems, can be roughly divided into two groups: those who have had marginality and homelessness forced upon them and want nothing more than to escape them, and a smaller number who have at least in part chosen marginality, and now accept, or, in a few cases, embrace it.
>
> I understand how dangerous it can be to introduce the idea of choice into a discussion of homelessness. It can all too easily be used for all the wrong reasons by all the wrong people to justify indifference or brutality toward the homeless, or to argue that they are getting only what they deserve.
>
> And I understand, too, how complicated the notion can become: Many of the veterans on the street, or battered women, or abused and runaway children, have chosen this life only as the lesser of evils, and because, in this society, there is often no place else to go.
>
> And finally, I understand how much that happens on the street can combine to create an apparent acceptance of homelessness that is nothing more than the absolute absence of hope.
>
> Nonetheless we must learn to accept that there may indeed be people on the street who have seen so much of our world, or have seen it so clearly, that to live in it becomes impossible.
>
> — PETER MARIN, "Go Ask Alice"

You might think that acknowledging readers' objections in this way — addressing readers directly, listing their possible objections, and discussing each one — would weaken your argument. It might even seem reckless to suggest objections that not all readers would think of. On the contrary, however, most readers respond positively to this strategy because it makes you seem thoughtful and reasonable. By researching your subject and your readers, you will be able to use this strategy confidently in your own argument essays. And you will learn to look for it in arguments you read and use it to make judgments about the writer's credibility.

Accommodating Readers' Concerns

To argue effectively, you must often take special care to **accommodate readers' concerns** by acknowledging their objections, questions, and alternative positions, causes, or solutions. Occasionally, however, you may have to go even further. Instead of merely acknowledging your readers' concerns, you may decide to accept some of them and incorporate them into your own argument. This strategy can be very disarming to readers. It is sometimes referred to as **concession**, for it seems to concede that opposing views have merit. The following example comes from an essay enthusiastically endorsing e-mail.

> To be sure, egalitarianism has its limits. The ease and economy of sending email, especially to multiple recipients, makes us all vulnerable to any bore, loony, or commercial or political salesman who can get our email address. It's still a lot less intrusive than the telephone, since you can read and answer or ignore email at your own convenience. But as normal people's email starts mounting into the hundreds daily, which is bound to happen, filtering mechanisms and conventions of etiquette that are still in their primitive stage will be desperately needed.
>
> Another supposed disadvantage of email is that it discourages face-to-face communication. At Microsoft, where people routinely send email back and forth all day to the person in the next office, this is certainly true. Some people believe this tendency has more to do with the underdeveloped social skills of computer geeks than with Microsoft's role in developing the technology email relies on. I wouldn't presume to comment on that. Whether you think email replacing live conversation is a good or bad thing depends, I guess, on how much of a misanthrope you are. I like it.
>
> — MICHAEL KINSLEY, "Email Culture"

Notice that Kinsley's accommodation or concession is not grudging. He readily concedes that e-mail brings users a lot of unwanted messages and may discourage conversation in the workplace.

Exercise 13.9

How does Patrick O'Malley attempt to accommodate readers in paragraphs 8 and 9 of his Chapter 6 essay arguing for more frequent exams? What seems successful or unsuccessful in his argument? How do his efforts at accommodation make his argument seem more convincing?

Refuting Readers' Objections

Your readers' possible objections and views cannot always be accommodated. Sometimes they must be refuted. When you **refute readers' objections**, you assert that they are wrong and argue against them. Refutation does not have to be delivered arrogantly or dismissively, however. Because differences are inevitable, reasoned argument provides a peaceful and constructive way for informed, well-intentioned people who disagree strongly to air their differences.

In the following example, a social sciences professor refutes one argument for giving college students the opportunity to purchase lecture notes prepared by someone else.

> Now, it may well be argued that universities are already shortchanging their students by stuffing them into huge lecture halls where, unlike at rock concerts or basketball games, the lecturer can't even be seen on a giant screen in real time. If they're already shortchanged with impersonal instruction, what's the harm in offering canned lecture notes?
>
> The amphitheater lecture is indeed, for all but the most engaging professors, a lesser form of instruction, and scarcely to be idealized. Still, Education by Download misses one of the keys to learning. Education is a meeting of minds, a process through which the student educes, draws from within, a response to what the teacher teaches.
>
> The very act of taking notes — not reading someone else's notes, no matter how stellar — is a way of engaging the material, wrestling with it, struggling to comprehend or take issue, but in any case entering into the work. The point is to decide, while you are listening, what matters in the presentation. And while I don't believe that most of life consists of showing up, education does begin with that — with immersing yourself in the activity at hand, listening, thinking, judging, offering active responses. A download is a poor substitute.
>
> — Todd Gitlin, "Disappearing Ink"

As this selection illustrates, writers cannot simply dismiss readers' possible concerns with a wave of their hand. Gitlin states a potential objection fully and fairly but then goes on to refute it by claiming that students need to take their own lecture notes to engage and comprehend the material that is being presented to them.

Effective refutation requires a restrained tone and careful argument. Although you may not accept this particular refutation, you can agree that it is well reasoned and supported. You need not feel attacked personally because the writer disagrees with you.

Exercise 13.10

Evaluate Robert Kuttner's use of refutation in paragraphs 11–12, 14–16, and 20–21 of "Good Jobs for Americans Who Help Americans" (Chapter 6). In each case, how does Kuttner signal or announce the refutation? How does he support the refutation? What is the tone of the refutation, and how effective do you think the tone would be in convincing readers to take the writer's argument seriously?

Logical Fallacies

Fallacies are errors or flaws in reasoning. Although essentially unsound, fallacious arguments seem superficially plausible and often have great persuasive power. Fallacies are not necessarily deliberate efforts to deceive readers. Writers may introduce a fallacy accidentally by not examining their own reasons or underlying assumptions, by failing to establish solid support, or by using unclear or ambiguous words. Here is a summary of the most common logical fallacies (listed alphabetically):

- *Begging the question:* Arguing that a claim is true by repeating the claim in different words (also called *circular reasoning*)

- *Confusing chronology with causality:* Assuming that because one thing preceded another, the former caused the latter (also called *post hoc, ergo propter hoc* — Latin for "after this, therefore because of this")

- *Either-or reasoning:* Assuming that there are only two sides to a question and representing yours as the only correct one

- *Equivocating:* Misleading or hedging with ambiguous word choices

- *Failing to accept the burden of proof:* Asserting a claim without presenting a reasoned argument to support it

- *False analogy:* Assuming that because one thing resembles another, conclusions drawn from one also apply to the other

- *Hasty generalization:* Offering only weak or limited evidence to support a conclusion

- *Overreliance on authority:* Assuming that something is true simply because an expert says so and ignoring evidence to the contrary

- *Oversimplifying:* Giving easy answers to complicated questions, often by appealing to emotions rather than logic

- *Personal attack:* Demeaning the proponents of a claim instead of refuting their argument (also called *ad hominem* — Latin for "against the man" — *attack*)

- *Red herring:* Attempting to misdirect the discussion by raising an essentially unrelated point

- *Slanting:* Selecting or emphasizing the evidence that supports your claim and suppressing or playing down other evidence

- *Slippery slope:* Pretending that one thing inevitably leads to another

- *Sob story:* Manipulating readers' emotions to lead them to draw unjustified conclusions

- *Straw man:* Directing the argument against a claim that nobody actually makes or that everyone agrees is very weak

Designing Documents 14

The way a document is designed — the arrangement of text, visuals, and white space on a page — has a major impact on the readability of the document and may influence the reader's attitude toward it. This chapter introduces basic components of document design, offers guidelines for designing effective documents, and discusses some common formats for documents you may be asked to create in your college courses or in the workplace.

The Impact of Document Design

When we read a well-designed document, part of the meaning we take away from it is attributable to design. When we read a poorly designed document, however, it may be difficult to discern its meaning at all. We can probably all agree that effectively written documents are easy to navigate and that their meanings are accessible to the intended audience. Good design should accordingly make readability easier and make the intended meaning clearer and more vivid.

The ways in which design affects the way we read documents can be illustrated fairly simply. Consider the following familiar phrase, rendered in four different ways:

I   l   o   v   e   y   o   u

I love you

The words in each rendering are the same, but the different uses of fonts, colors, and white space encourage us to read them very differently. The first message is vaguely unsettling (is that a ransom note? a message from a stalker?); the second seems conventionally sweet; the third carries no emotional or context clues, but the spacing makes it irritatingly difficult to read; and the fourth offers no tone or context clues at all (though this in itself might strike us as odd, given the meaning of the words). Thus design does far more than add visual interest: It actually directs how we read and to a certain extent determines the meaning we derive from texts.

The freedom you have in terms of using design elements and visuals in your college writing projects will vary quite a bit, depending on your instructors' preferences and the nature of the projects. As you write, however, you should always remain aware of the impact document design can have on your reader. And anytime you read a document — whether it is a textbook, a blog, or even an ad on the subway — you should stop to think about how that document was designed and how that design affects your reading of it.

Considering Context, Audience, and Purpose

Context, audience, and purpose are the key components to consider in designing any document. For instance, if you are writing an essay for a college course, you can expect that your instructor and/or your classmates will read it carefully. Your design decisions should therefore make sustained reading as easy as possible; fonts that are too small to read easily or print that is too light to see clearly will make the reader's job unnecessarily difficult. Additionally, instructors usually ask students to submit hard-copy work that is double-spaced text with one-inch margins to give the instructor and/or a classmate room to write comments on the page.*

In most college courses, guidelines on design have traditionally followed a "less is more" rule — written assignments were generally expected to be printed on white, 8.5 × 11-inch paper, and the use of colors, extravagant fonts, sheerly decorative visuals, and the like was in most cases discouraged. However, in many college classrooms, what constitutes an acceptable course "paper" or project is in transition; many instructors now allow or in some cases require the creation of multimodal projects — Web sites, video, PowerPoint presentations, playlists, and the like — in place of traditional papers.

Developments like these, driven largely by advances in technology, have obviously required some adjustments to traditional notions of acceptable design for college writing.

---

*It is important to note that MLA, APA, and other style systems have specific rules regarding such things as spacing, margins, and heading formats. Be sure to ask your instructor whether you will be expected to adhere closely to these rules; if so, your choices regarding document design will be limited. For more on MLA and APA styles, see pp. 497–516.

"Less is more" still applies, however, in principle. Good design gives priority to clarity: Whatever the project, you should use design not for its own sake, but only in order to make your points as clearly, effectively, and efficiently as possible.

Of course, the same principle of clarity applies to most *non*academic documents you will write. In writing for nonacademic audiences, however, you cannot necessarily expect all readers to read your writing closely. Some readers may skim through your blog entries looking for interesting points; others might scan a report or memo for information important specifically to them. Design elements such as headings, bullets, and chunking will help these readers find the information of most interest to them.

Frequently, too, your document design decisions will be predetermined by the kind of document you are preparing. Business letters and memos, for example, traditionally follow specific formats. Because your readers will bring certain expectations to these kinds of documents, altering an established format can cause confusion and should therefore be avoided.

To analyze the context in which a document is read or used, ask yourself the following questions:

- ***Where will my document be read?*** *Will the document be read on paper in a well-lighted, quiet room, or in another context — perhaps on a laptop in a noisy, dimly lit coffee shop?*
- ***Do my readers have specific expectations for this kind of document?*** *Am I writing a memo, letter, or report that requires certain design conventions? Does my instructor expect me to follow MLA style, APA style, or another system?*
- ***How will the information be used?*** *Are my readers reading to learn or to be entertained? Do I expect them to skim the document or to read it carefully?*

Elements of Document Design

Readable fonts, informative headings, bulleted or numbered lists, and appropriate use of color, white space, and visuals like photographs, charts, and diagrams all help readers learn from your document.

Font Style and Size

Typography is a design term for the letters and symbols that make up the print on a page or a screen. You are already using important aspects of typography when you use capital letters, italics, boldface, or different sizes of type to signal a new sentence, identify the title of a book, or distinguish a heading from body text.

Word processing programs enable you to use dozens of different fonts, or typefaces; bold and italic versions of these fonts; and a range of font sizes. Fortunately, you can rely on some simple design principles to make good typographic choices for your documents.

Perhaps the most important advice for working with typography is to choose fonts that are easy to read. Some fonts are meant for decorative or otherwise very minimal use, and they are hard to read in extended passages. Font style, font size, and combinations of style and size are features that can add to or detract from readability.

Considering Font Style. For most academic and business writing, you will probably want to choose a traditional font that is easy to read, such as Arial or Times New Roman. This book is set in Minion. Sentences and paragraphs printed in fonts that imitate *calligraphy* (typically called script fonts) or those that mimic *handwriting* are not only difficult to read but also too informal in appearance for most academic and business purposes.

Some Fonts Appropriate for Academic and Business Writing

Arial

Georgia

Tahoma

Times New Roman

Verdana

Considering Font Size. To ensure that your documents can be read easily, you also need to choose an appropriate font size (traditionally measured in units called **points**). For most types of academic writing, a 12-point font is standard for the main (body) text. For Web pages, however, you should consider using a slightly larger font to compensate for the difficulty of reading from a computer monitor. For computer-projected displays, you should use an even larger font size (such as 32-point, and typically no smaller than 18-point) to ensure that the text can be read from a distance.

Combining Font Styles and Sizes. Although computers now make hundreds of font styles and sizes available to writers, you should avoid confusing readers with too many different fonts in one document. Limit the fonts in a document to one or two that complement each other well. A common practice, for instance, is to choose one font for all titles and headings (such as Arial, 14-pt, boldface) and another for the body text (such as Times New Roman, 12-pt), as shown in the example here.

This Is an Example Heading

This is body text. This is body text.
This is body text. This is body text.
This is body text. This is body text.

This Is an Example Heading

This is body text. This is body text.
This is body text. This is body text.
This is body text. This is body text.

Headings and Body Text

Titles and headings are often distinguished from body text by boldface, italics, or font size. Headings are helpful in calling attention to certain parts or sections of a piece of writing and in offering readers visual cues to its overall organization. Always check with your instructor about the conventions for using (or not using) these elements in the particular discipline you are studying.

Distinguishing between Headings and Subheadings. Typically, headings for major sections (level-one headings) must have more visual impact than those subdividing these sections (level-two headings), which should be more prominent than headings within the subdivisions (level-three headings). The typography should reflect this hierarchy of headings. Here is one possible system for distinguishing among three levels of headings:

LEVEL-ONE HEADING
Level-Two Heading
Level-Three Heading

Notice that the level-one and level-two headings are given the greatest prominence by the use of boldface and that they are distinguished from one another by the use of all capital letters for the major heading versus capital and lowercase letters for the subheading. The third-level heading, italicized but not boldfaced, is less prominent than the other two headings but can still be readily distinguished from body text. Whatever system you use to distinguish headings and subheadings, be sure to apply it consistently throughout your document.

For more on selecting appropriate headings and subheadings, see Chapter 10, pp. 366–67.

Positioning Headings Consistently. In addition to keeping track of the font size and style of headings, you need to position headings in the same way throughout a piece of writing. You will want to consider the spacing above and below headings and determine whether the headings should be aligned with the left margin, indented a fixed amount of space, or centered. In this book, headings like the one that begins this paragraph — **Positioning Headings Consistently** — are aligned with the left margin and followed by a period and a fixed amount of space.

Using Type Size to Differentiate Headings from Text. In documents that do not need to observe the MLA or APA styles, which have specific rules about formatting, you may wish to use font size to help make headings visually distinct from the body of the text. If you do so, avoid making the headings too large. To accompany 12-point body text, for instance, a 14-point heading will do. The default settings for heading and body text styles on most word processing and desktop publishing programs are effective, and you may want to use them to autoformat your heading and text styles.

Numbered and Bulleted Lists

Lists are often an effective way to present information in a logical and visually coherent way. Use a **numbered list** (1, 2, 3) to present the steps in a process or to list items that readers will need to refer back to easily (for instance, see the sample e-mail message on p. 436). Use a **bulleted list** (marking each new item with a "bullet" — a dash, circle, or box) to highlight key points when the order of the items is not significant (for instance, see the sample memo on p. 433). Written instructions, such as recipes, are typically formatted using numbered lists, whereas a list of supplies, for example, is more often presented in the form of a bulleted list.

Colors

Color printers, photocopiers, and online technology facilitate the use of color, but color does not necessarily make text easier to read. In most academic print documents, the only color you should use is black. While color is typically used more freely in academic writing produced in other media (for example, Web pages or slideshow presentations), it should still be used in moderation and always with the aim of increasing your readers' understanding of what you have to say. Always consider, too, whether your readers might be color-blind and whether they will have access to a full-color version of the document.

Although the slideshow design in Figure 14.1 is visually interesting and the heading is readable, the bulleted text is very hard to read because there is too little contrast between the text color and the background color.

In Figure 14.2, it is clear that the person who created the pie chart carefully chose the colors to represent the different data. What the person did not consider,

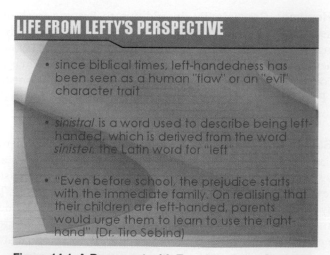

Figure 14.1 A Document with Too Little Color Contrast

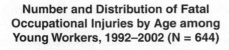

Number and Distribution of Fatal Occupational Injuries by Age among Young Workers, 1992–2002 (N = 644)

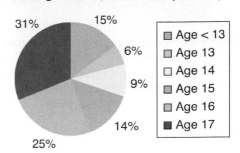

Figure 14.2 A Pie Chart That Requires a Color Printer to Be Understandable

Source: National Institute for Occupational Safety and Health, "Data on Young Worker Injuries and Illnesses in Worker Health" (2004).

however, is how the colors would look when printed out on a black-and-white printer. It is nearly impossible to associate the labels with the slices of the pie and thus to read the chart.

Also consider the meanings associated with different colors. For example, in the United States and other Western cultures, white typically is associated with goodness and purity; in China, however, white represents grief and mourning. Although your use of color in an essay, a Web page, or a slideshow presentation might not carry such deep meaning, bear in mind that most people have emotional or psychological responses to colors and color combinations.

White Space

Another basic element of document design, white space, is the open, or blank, space surrounding the text. White space is usually used between a heading, for instance, and the paragraph that follows the heading. You also use white space when you set the margins on the page, and even when you double-space between lines of text. In all of these cases, the space makes your document easier to read. When used generously, white space facilitates reading by keeping the pages of a document uncluttered and by helping the eye find and follow the text.

Chunking. Chunking, the breaking up of text into smaller units, also facilitates reading. Paragraphing is a form of chunking that divides text into units of closely related information. In most academic essays and reports, text is double-spaced, and paragraphs are distinguished by indenting the first line one-half inch.

In single-spaced text, you may want to make reading easier by adding extra space between paragraphs, rather than indenting the first lines of paragraphs. This format, referred to as **block style**, is often used in memos, letters, and electronic documents. When creating electronic documents, especially Web pages, you might consider chunking your material into separate "pages" or screens, with links connecting the chunks.

Margins. Adequate margins are an important component of general readability. If the margins are too small, your page will seem cluttered. Generally, for academic essays, use one-inch margins on all sides unless your instructor (or the style manual you are following) advises differently. Some instructors ask students to leave large margins to accommodate marginal comments.

Visuals

Tables, graphs, charts, diagrams, photographs, maps, and screen shots add visual interest and are often more effective in conveying information than prose alone. Be certain, however, that each visual has a valid role to play in your work; if the visual is merely a decoration, leave it out or replace it with a visual that is more appropriate.

You can create visuals on a computer, using the drawing tools of a word processing program, the charting tools of a spreadsheet program, or software specifically designed for creating visuals. You can also download visuals from the Internet or photocopy or scan visuals from print materials. If your essay is going to be posted on the Web on a site that is not password-protected and a visual you want to use is from a source that is copyrighted, you should request written permission from the copyright holder (such as the photographer, publisher, or site sponsor). For any visual that you borrow from or create based on data from a source, be sure to cite the source in the caption, your bibliography, or both, according to the guidelines of the documentation system you are using.

Choose Appropriate Visuals and Design Them with Their Final Use in Mind

Select the types of visuals that will best suit your purpose. The following list identifies various types, explains what they are best used for, and provides examples. If you plan to incorporate a visual into a computer-projected display, try to envision the original version as it would appear enlarged on a screen. Similarly, if you intend the visual for use on a Web page, consider how it will appear when displayed on a computer screen.

- *Tables.* A table is used to display numerical or textual data that is organized into columns and rows to make it easy to understand. A table usually includes several items as well as variables for each item. For example, the first column of Table 14.1 includes states; the next two columns show the state population in 2000 and in 2010; and the final two columns show the change in population from 2000 to 2010 in number and percentage.

Table 14.1 Population Change for the Ten Largest U.S. States, 2000–2010

State	Population 2010	Population 2000	Change Number	Change Percentage
California	37,253,956	33,871,648	3,382,308	10.0
Texas	25,145,561	20,851,820	4,293,741	20.6
New York	19,378,102	18,976,457	401,645	2.1
Florida	18,801,310	15,982,378	2,818,932	17.6
Illinois	12,830,632	12,419,293	411,339	3.3
Pennsylvania	12,702,379	12,281,054	421,325	3.4
Ohio	11,536,504	11,353,140	183,364	1.6
Michigan	9,883,640	9,938,444	–54,804	–0.6
Georgia	9,687,653	8,186,453	1,501,200	18.3
North Carolina	9,535,483	8,049,313	1,486,170	18.5

Source: U.S. Census Bureau, Census 2010.

- ▪ *Bar graphs.* A bar graph typically compares numerical differences for one or more items. For example, Figure 14.3 charts how fifth graders' ability to watch what they want on television varies according to their place in sibling order.

- ▪ *Line graphs.* A line graph charts change over time, typically with only one variable represented (unlike in Figure 14.3, where the bar chart data are organized into four variables). For example, Figure 14.4 shows the average age of mothers at first birth between 1970 and 2006.

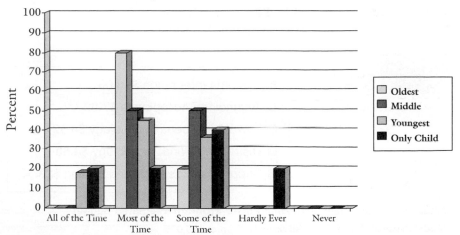

Figure 14.3 Results from Survey on Television Viewing

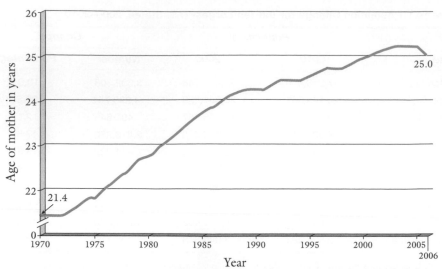

Figure 14.4 Average Age of Mothers at First Birth: United States, 1970–2006

Source: CDC/NCHS, National Vital Statistic System.

- ■ *Pie charts.* A pie chart shows the relative sizes of parts making up a whole. For instance, the whole (100 percent) in the chart shown in Figure 14.5 is the U.S. Department of Energy's 2010 estimated budget for wind power; the parts are specific expenditures, such as systems integration (30 percent) and technology acceptance (13 percent).

- ■ *Flowcharts.* A flowchart shows a process broken down into parts or stages. Flowcharts are particularly helpful for explaining a process or facilitating a decision based on a set of circumstances, as shown, for instance, in Figure 14.6.

Wind Power Activities
$54.37 (figures in millions)

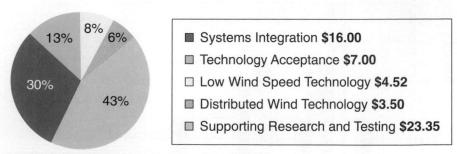

Figure 14.5 Fiscal Year 2010 Wind Power Program Estimated Budget

Note: Figures in millions rounded down to nearest $10,000.

Source: U.S. Department of Energy.

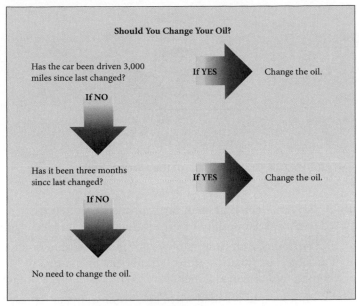

Figure 14.6 Oil-Changing Decision Process

- ***Organization charts.*** An organization chart does what its name suggests — it creates a map of lines of authority within an organization, such as a company. Typically, the most important person — the person to whom most employees report — appears at the top of the chart, as seen in Figure 14.7, where the managing editor, who oversees the entire daily newspaper, appears at the top.

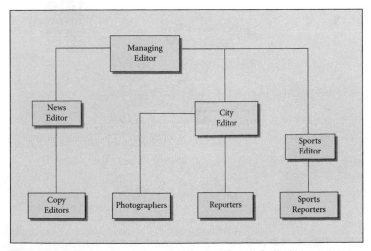

Figure 14.7 The Newsroom of a Typical Small Daily Newspaper

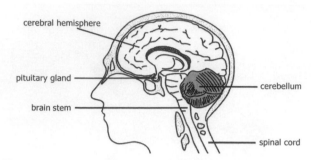

Figure 14.8 A Cross-Section of the Human Brain

- *Diagrams.* A diagram depicts an item or its properties, often using symbols. It is typically used to show relationships or how things function. (See Figure 14.8.)
- *Drawings and cartoons.* A drawing shows a simplified version or an artist's interpretation of an object or situation. Cartoons, like the one in Figure 14.9, are drawings typically used to make an argumentative point, usually in a humorous way.
- *Photographs.* Photographs are used when an author wants to represent a real and specific object, place, or person, often for its emotional impact. For instance, a student selected Figure 14.10, a still from the movie *Emma,* in an essay comparing that film with *Clueless.* Although photographic images are generally assumed to duplicate what the eye sees, a photograph may, in fact, be manipulated in a variety of ways for special effects. Photographs that have been altered should be so identified.

Figure 14.9 A Cartoon That Makes an Argument about Using Native American Names for Sports Teams

Figure 14.10 *Emma,* dir. Douglas McGrath, perf. Gwyneth
Paltrow, Toni Colette, Alan Cumming, and Jeremy
Northam (Miramax, 1996; film)

- *Maps.* Maps are used to show geographical areas, lay out the spatial relationships of objects, or make a historical or political point. Figure 14.11 identifies
  World War II–era War Relocation Authority (WRA) Centers and states that had
  a high Japanese American population during World War II. The map reveals that

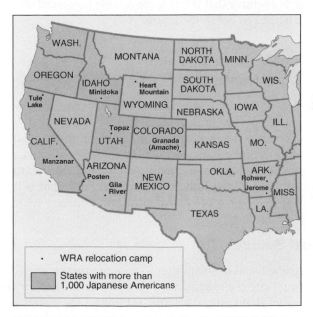

Figure 14.11 War Relocation Authority (WRA) Centers,
1942–1947

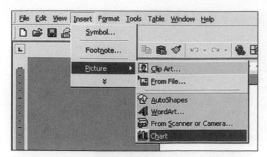

Figure 14.12 Screen Capture to Accompany Written Instructions, "How to Insert a Chart into a Word Processing Document"

though they posed no threat to U.S. security, many Japanese Americans were relocated a great distance from their homes during the war.

- **Screen shots.** A screen shot duplicates the appearance of a specific computer screen or of a window or some other section within it. Screen shots can be used to capture a Web page to include in a print document or to describe steps or instructions for using a piece of software (see Figure 14.12).

Number and Title Your Visuals

Number your visuals in sequential order, and give each one a title. Refer to tables as *Table 1, Table 2,* and so on, and to other types of visuals as *Figure 1, Figure 2,* and so on. (In a long work with chapters or sections, you may also need to include the chapter or section number [*Figure 14.1*], as is done in this chapter of this book.)

Make sure each visual has a title that reflects the subject of the visual (for example, income levels) and its purpose (to compare and illustrate changes in those income levels): *Figure 1. Percentage of U.S. Households in Three Income Ranges, 1990–2000.* Notice that MLA style requires that the title for a table be placed above the table and the title for a figure be placed below the figure.

Label the Parts of Your Visuals and Include Descriptive Captions

To help readers understand a visual, clearly label all of its parts. In a table, for instance, give each column a heading; likewise, label each section of a pie chart with the percentage and the item it represents. You may place the label on the chart itself if it is readable and clear; if that is not practical, place a legend next to the chart.

Some visuals may require a caption that provides a fuller description than the title alone does. Your caption might also include an explanation that is helpful in understanding the visual, as in Figure 14.11.

Cite Your Visual Sources

Finally, if you borrow a visual from another source or create a visual from borrowed information, you must cite the source, following the guidelines for the documentation style you are using (see Figure 14.2 and Table 14.1 for examples). In addition, be sure to include the source in your list of works cited or references at the end of your document.

Integrate the Visuals into the Text

Visuals should facilitate, not disrupt, the reading of the body text. To achieve this goal, you need to first introduce and discuss each visual in your text and then insert each visual in an appropriate location.

Introducing the Visual. Ideally, you should introduce each visual by referring to it in your text immediately *before* the visual appears. An effective textual reference answers the following questions:

- What is the number of the visual?
- Where is it located?
- What kind of information does it contain?
- What important point does it make or support?

Here is an example of an effective introduction for the line graph shown earlier (Figure 14.4):

> Notice the rise in the age of mothers giving birth for the first time, which rose steadily over the period between 1970 and 2005 (see Figure 14.4).

Placing the Visual in an Appropriate Location. MLA style requires and APA style recommends that you place a visual in the body of your text as soon after the discussion as possible, particularly when the reader will need to consult the visual. In APA style, visuals can also be grouped at the end of an essay if they contain supplemental information that may not be of interest to the reader or if the visuals take up multiple pages. (See Figure 14.13 on the next page for a section from a sample student paper with a figure included. Note that the figure is mentioned in the text and placed directly after this introduction, and that it includes a descriptive title with source information.)

Use Common Sense When Creating Visuals on a Computer

If you use a computer program to create visuals, keep this advice in mind:

- *Make the decisions that your computer cannot make for you.* A computer can automatically turn spreadsheet data into a pie chart or bar graph, but only you can decide which visual — or what use of color, if any — is most appropriate for your purpose.
- *Avoid "chart junk."* Many computer programs provide an array of special effects that can be used to alter visuals, including three-dimensional renderings, textured backgrounds, and shadowed text. Such special effects often detract from the intended message of the visual by calling attention to themselves instead. Use them sparingly, and only when they emphasize key information.
- *Use clip art sparingly, if at all.* Clip art consists of icons, symbols, and other simple, typically abstract, copyright free drawings. Because clip art simplifies ideas, it is of limited use in conveying the complex information contained in most academic writing.

Stanford University anchors the reputation and identity of their law school via their Web site (see Fig. 1). The page features strongly contrasting colors—red, black, and light grey—and includes graphics that change each time the page is reloaded: photos of students and professors, in class and on campus, as well as questions whose answers are likely to be of interest to prospective students and other visitors to the site. These rotating graphics are meant to represent the various facets of Stanford Law School.

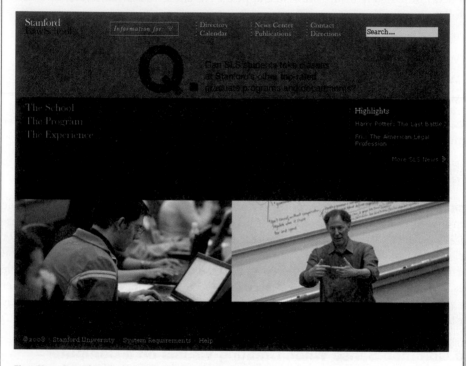

Fig. 1. Home Page of Stanford Law School, captured March 14, 2008.

The question and photos are the most prominent features of the page, but the basic information about the law school (linked from "The School," "The Program," and "The Experience" at left) is easy to locate.

Figure 14.13 Excerpt from Sample Student Paper with Figure

Sample Documents

Earlier in this chapter you saw examples of various types of visuals; in this section you will take a look at various types of documents that you may be asked to prepare. Each sample document is accompanied by a discussion of appropriate design conventions.

As you examine the documents, try also to analyze the way that typography, color, white space, and visuals serve to guide the reader's eye across the page. What design features make the documents easy to read? What features make finding specific information within the documents easy? What features make the document easy to use?

In addition to examining the sample documents with these questions in mind, look at the sample research paper in Chapter 17, pp. 518–25.

Memos

Memos, such as the one shown in Figure 14.14, are documents sent between employees of the same organization (in contrast to business letters, which are sent to people outside the organization). The conventions for writing a memo listed on page 434 are well established and should rarely be altered. In addition, some organizations have specific guidelines for memos (such as the use of letterhead).

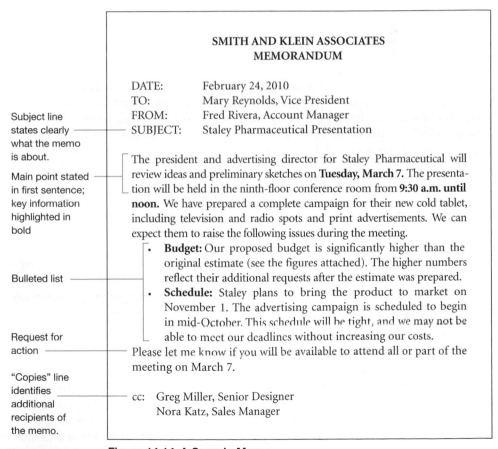

<table>
<tr><td></td><td colspan="2">SMITH AND KLEIN ASSOCIATES
MEMORANDUM</td></tr>
<tr><td></td><td>DATE:</td><td>February 24, 2010</td></tr>
<tr><td></td><td>TO:</td><td>Mary Reynolds, Vice President</td></tr>
<tr><td>Subject line</td><td>FROM:</td><td>Fred Rivera, Account Manager</td></tr>
<tr><td>states clearly
what the memo
is about.</td><td>SUBJECT:</td><td>Staley Pharmaceutical Presentation</td></tr>
</table>

Subject line states clearly what the memo is about.

The president and advertising director for Staley Pharmaceutical will review ideas and preliminary sketches on **Tuesday, March 7.** The presentation will be held in the ninth-floor conference room from **9:30 a.m. until noon.** We have prepared a complete campaign for their new cold tablet, including television and radio spots and print advertisements. We can expect them to raise the following issues during the meeting.

Main point stated in first sentence; key information highlighted in bold

Bulleted list

- **Budget:** Our proposed budget is significantly higher than the original estimate (see the figures attached). The higher numbers reflect their additional requests after the estimate was prepared.
- **Schedule:** Staley plans to bring the product to market on November 1. The advertising campaign is scheduled to begin in mid-October. This schedule will be tight, and we may not be able to meet our deadlines without increasing our costs.

Request for action

Please let me know if you will be available to attend all or part of the meeting on March 7.

"Copies" line identifies additional recipients of the memo.

cc: Greg Miller, Senior Designer
        Nora Katz, Sales Manager

Figure 14.14 A Sample Memo

- *Heading.* A memo should carry the major heading *Memorandum* or *Memo.* If you are using letterhead stationery, position the heading just below the letterhead. The heading may be centered on the page or positioned at the left margin (depending on your organization's guidelines). In either case, the heading should be distinguished in some way from the rest of the body text, such as by a large font size, boldface type, or capital letters.
- *Content headings.* Just below the heading and separated by at least one line of space are the content headings: *Date, To, From,* and *Subject.* Place the content headings at the left margin and in the same size font as the body text.
- *Body text.* The main text of a memo is usually presented in block style: single-spaced with an extra line of space between paragraphs. (Do not indent the first line of paragraphs in block style.) If you need to call attention to specific information, consider presenting it in a numbered or bulleted list, or highlight the information visually by using boldface or extra white space above and below it. In a memo announcing a meeting, for example, you might boldface the date, time, and place of the meeting so the reader can quickly find the information, or you might set off the date, time, and place on separate lines.

Letters

The **business letter** (such as the one shown in Figure 14.15) is the document most often used for correspondence between representatives of one organization and representatives of another, though e-mail messages are increasingly being used in place of business letters. Business letters are written to obtain information about a company's products, to register a complaint, to respond to a complaint, or to introduce other documents (such as a proposal) that accompany the letter. As with memos, the design conventions for letters are long-established, although letters have more variations. Check to see whether there are specific business letter guidelines for your organization.

The heading of a business letter consists of the contact information for both the sender and the recipient of the letter. Block style is the most commonly used format for business letters.

Be sure to state the purpose of your letter in the first few lines and to provide supporting information in the paragraphs that follow. Always maintain a courteous and professional tone throughout a business letter. Include enough information to identify clearly any documents you refer to in the letter.

E-mail

Increasingly, students and instructors rely on electronic mail to exchange information about assignments and schedules as well as to follow up on class discussions (see Figure 14.16 on page 436). **E-mail** messages are usually concise, direct, relatively informal, and limited to a single subject. Effective e-mails include a clear subject line.

In many organizations, e-mail messages are replacing handwritten or typed memos. When you send a memo electronically, make sure the headings automatically provided by the e-mail program convey the same essential information as the content headings

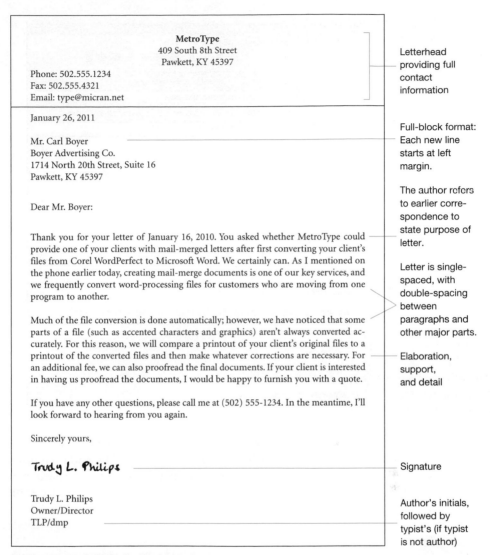

Figure 14.15 A Sample Business Letter

in a traditional memo. If you are part of a large or complex organization, you may want to repeat your name and add such information as your job title, division, and telephone extension in a "signature" at the end of the document.

E-mail is a broader medium of communication than the business memo. Nevertheless, in anything other than quick e-mails to friends, you should maintain a professional tone. Avoid sarcasm and humor, which may not come across as you intend, and be sure to proofread and spell-check your message before sending it. Also, because e-mail messages are accessible to many people other than the person to whom you are writing, always be careful about what you write in an e-mail message.

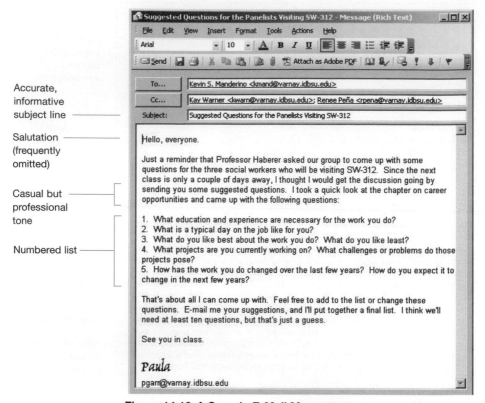

Accurate, informative subject line

Salutation (frequently omitted)

Casual but professional tone

Numbered list

Figure 14.16 A Sample E-Mail Message

While e-mail messages are among the simplest forms of electronic documents, new software programs allow you to attach files, insert hypertext links, and even insert pictures and graphics into your e-mail documents. As a matter of courtesy, check to be sure that the recipient of your e-mail message has the software to read these electronic files before you include them with the message.

Résumés

A **résumé** serves to acquaint a prospective employer with your work experience, education, and accomplishments. All résumés contain such basic information as your name, address, phone number, and e-mail address.

The résumé is a good example of why the context in which a document is read is so important. An employer may receive dozens of résumés for one position. Your résumé may not be read closely in a first screening. Consequently, your résumé should highlight your important qualifications visually so that the reader can quickly find the pertinent information by scanning the page.

The format of résumés varies among disciplines and professions. Some professions require traditional formatting, while others allow for some flexibility in design. Be sure to research your field and the potential employers to see if a particular résumé format is preferred; consider consulting recently published reference books that show examples of good résumés. Also consider whether posting your résumé on a Web site such as Monster .com might be advisable. Always tailor your résumé to the job for which you are applying.

Résumés may also vary in terms of what they emphasize — educational or work experience, for example. If you have little work experience, focus your résumé on your grade-point average, the courses you have taken, the projects you have completed, and the applicable skills and abilities you have acquired in college. (For an example of such a résumé, see Figure 14.17.) If you have extensive, relevant, and continuous work

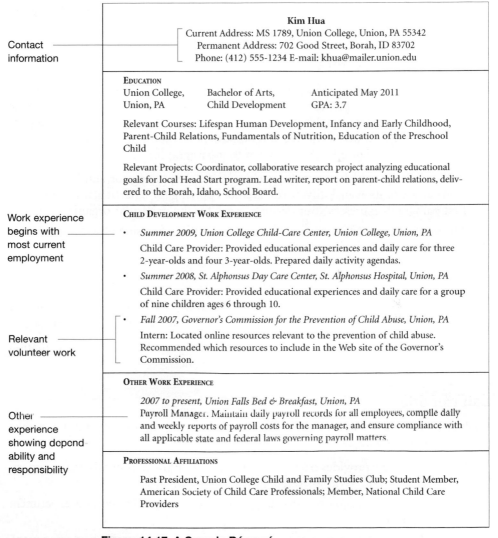

Contact information

Kim Hua
Current Address: MS 1789, Union College, Union, PA 55342
Permanent Address: 702 Good Street, Borah, ID 83702
Phone: (412) 555-1234 E-mail: khua@mailer.union.edu

EDUCATION
Union College,   Bachelor of Arts,   Anticipated May 2011
Union, PA   Child Development   GPA: 3.7

Relevant Courses: Lifespan Human Development, Infancy and Early Childhood, Parent-Child Relations, Fundamentals of Nutrition, Education of the Preschool Child

Relevant Projects: Coordinator, collaborative research project analyzing educational goals for local Head Start program. Lead writer, report on parent-child relations, delivered to the Borah, Idaho, School Board.

Work experience begins with most current employment

CHILD DEVELOPMENT WORK EXPERIENCE
• *Summer 2009, Union College Child-Care Center, Union College, Union, PA*
Child Care Provider: Provided educational experiences and daily care for three 2-year-olds and four 3-year-olds. Prepared daily activity agendas.

• *Summer 2008, St. Alphonsus Day Care Center, St. Alphonsus Hospital, Union, PA*
Child Care Provider: Provided educational experiences and daily care for a group of nine children ages 6 through 10.

Relevant volunteer work

• *Fall 2007, Governor's Commission for the Prevention of Child Abuse, Union, PA*
Intern: Located online resources relevant to the prevention of child abuse. Recommended which resources to include in the Web site of the Governor's Commission.

Other experience showing dependability and responsibility

OTHER WORK EXPERIENCE
2007 to present, Union Falls Bed & Breakfast, Union, PA
Payroll Manager. Maintain daily payroll records for all employees, compile daily and weekly reports of payroll costs for the manager, and ensure compliance with all applicable state and federal laws governing payroll matters.

PROFESSIONAL AFFILIATIONS
Past President, Union College Child and Family Studies Club; Student Member, American Society of Child Care Professionals; Member, National Child Care Providers

Figure 14.17 A Sample Résumé

experience, consider a reverse-chronological résumé, listing the jobs you have held (beginning with the most recent job) and describing the duties, responsibilities, and accomplishments associated with each one. If you have shifted directions during your adult life, consider organizing your résumé in a way that emphasizes the strengths and skills you have acquired and used in different settings — for instance, your experience speaking in front of groups, handling money, or working with specific software programs.

Do not include such personal information as your height, weight, and age. Mention personal interests or hobbies only if they are relevant to the position. Finally, proofread your résumé carefully; it must be error-free. Your résumé is the first impression you make on a potential employer. Do everything you can to make a good first impression.

Job-Application Letters

A **job-application letter** (sometimes called a **cover letter**) is sent with a résumé when you apply for a job. The primary purpose of the job-application letter is to persuade your reader that you are a qualified candidate for employment and to introduce your résumé. For college students and recent graduates, most job-application letters (such as the one shown in Figure 14.18) consist of four paragraphs:

1. The *first paragraph* identifies the position you are applying for and how you became aware of its availability. If you are not applying for a particular position, the first paragraph expresses your desire to work for the particular organization.
2. The *second paragraph* briefly describes your education, focusing on specific achievements, projects, and relevant course work.
3. The *third paragraph* briefly describes your work experience, focusing on relevant responsibilities and accomplishments.

Note that the second and third paragraphs should not merely restate what is in your résumé; rather, they should help persuade your reader that you are qualified for the job.

4. The *fourth paragraph* expresses your willingness to provide additional information and to be interviewed at the employer's convenience.

Lab Reports

A **lab report** serves to summarize the results of an experiment or test, and it generally consists of the following five sections:

1. The *Introduction* provides background information: the hypothesis of the experiment, the question to be answered, how the question arose.
2. The *Methods* section describes how the research was conducted or how the experiment was performed.
3. The *Results* section describes what happened as a result of your research or experiment.

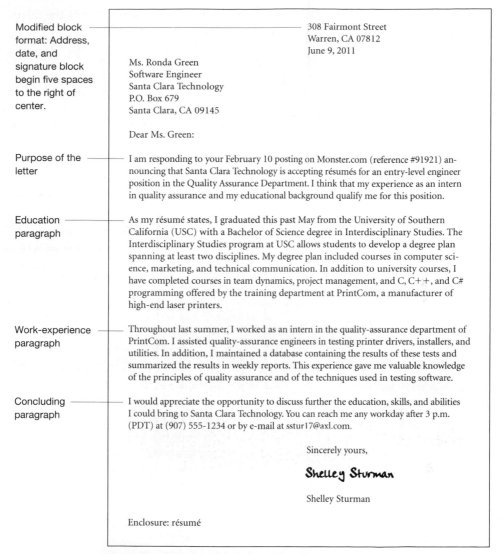

Modified block format: Address, date, and signature block begin five spaces to the right of center.

308 Fairmont Street
Warren, CA 07812
June 9, 2011

Ms. Ronda Green
Software Engineer
Santa Clara Technology
P.O. Box 679
Santa Clara, CA 09145

Dear Ms. Green:

Purpose of the letter

I am responding to your February 10 posting on Monster.com (reference #91921) announcing that Santa Clara Technology is accepting résumés for an entry-level engineer position in the Quality Assurance Department. I think that my experience as an intern in quality assurance and my educational background qualify me for this position.

Education paragraph

As my résumé states, I graduated this past May from the University of Southern California (USC) with a Bachelor of Science degree in Interdisciplinary Studies. The Interdisciplinary Studies program at USC allows students to develop a degree plan spanning at least two disciplines. My degree plan included courses in computer science, marketing, and technical communication. In addition to university courses, I have completed courses in team dynamics, project management, and C, C++, and C# programming offered by the training department at PrintCom, a manufacturer of high-end laser printers.

Work-experience paragraph

Throughout last summer, I worked as an intern in the quality-assurance department of PrintCom. I assisted quality-assurance engineers in testing printer drivers, installers, and utilities. In addition, I maintained a database containing the results of these tests and summarized the results in weekly reports. This experience gave me valuable knowledge of the principles of quality assurance and of the techniques used in testing software.

Concluding paragraph

I would appreciate the opportunity to discuss further the education, skills, and abilities I could bring to Santa Clara Technology. You can reach me any workday after 3 p.m. (PDT) at (907) 555-1234 or by e-mail at sstur17@axl.com.

Sincerely yours,

Shelley Sturman

Shelley Sturman

Enclosure: résumé

Figure 14.18 A Sample Job-Application Letter

4. The *Discussion* section consists of your explanation of and reasoning about your results.

5. The *References* section cites the sources used in conducting the research, performing the experiment, or writing the report.

The content and format of a lab report may vary from discipline to discipline or from course to course. Before writing a lab report, be certain that you understand your instructor's requirements. The sample in Figure 14.19 (see pp. 440–41) shows excerpts from a lab report written by two students in a soils science course. It uses the documentation format advocated by the Council of Science Editors (CSE).

Bulk Density and Total Pore Space

Joe Aquino and Sheila Norris

Soils 101

Lab Section 1

February 22, 2011

Introduction

Soil is an arrangement of solids and voids. The voids, called pore spaces, are important for root growth, water movement, water storage, and gas exchange between the soil and atmosphere. A medium-textured soil good for plant growth will have a pore-space content of about 0.50 (half solids, half pore space). The total pore space is the space between sand, silt, and clay particles (micropore space) plus the space between soil aggregates (macropore space).[1]

> Background information that the reader will need to understand the experiment

[The Introduction continues with a discussion of the formulas used to calculate bulk density, particle density, and porosity.]

Methods

To determine the bulk density[2] and total pore space of two soil samples, we hammered cans into the wall of a soil pit (Hagerstown silt loam). We collected samples from the Ap horizon and a Bt horizon. We then placed a block of wood over the cans so that the hammer did not smash them. After hammering the cans into the soil, we dug the cans, now full of soil, out of the horizons; we trimmed off any excess soil. The samples were dried in an oven at 105°C for two days and weighed. We then determined the volume of the cans by measuring the height and radius, as follows:

> Detailed explanation of the methods used

volume $= 1/4\ r^2 h$

We used the formulas noted in the Introduction to determine bulk density and porosity of the samples. Particle density was assumed to be 2.65 g/cm^3. The textural class of each horizon was determined by feel; that is, we squeezed and kneaded each sample and assigned it to a particular textural class.

Results

We found both soils to have relatively light bulk densities and large porosities, but the Bt horizon had greater porosity than the Ap. Furthermore, we determined that the Ap horizon was a silt loam, whereas the Bt was a clay (see Table 1).

Figure 14.19 A Sample Lab Report   *(continued)*

(continued)

Presents the results of the experiment, with a table showing quantitative data

Table 1 Textural class, bulk density, and porosity of two Hagerstown soil horizons

Textural Class	Ap Silt Loam	Bt Clay
Bulk density (g/cm^3)	1.20	1.08
Porosity	0.55	0.59

[The Results section continues with sample calculations.]

Discussion

Explains what was significant about the results of the research

Both soils had bulk densities and porosities in the range we would have expected from the discussions in the lab manual and textbook. The Ap horizon is a medium-textured soil and is considered a good topsoil for plant growth, so a porosity around 0.50 is consistent with those facts. The Bt horizon is a fine-textured horizon (containing a large amount of clay), and the bulk density is in the predicted range.

[The Discussion section continues with further discussion of the results.]

[The References section begins on a new page.]

References

The references are in the format recommended by the Council of Science Editors (CSE)

1. Brady NC, Weil RR. The nature and properties of soils. 11th ed. New York: Prentice-Hall; 1996. 291 p.

2. Blake GR, Hartge KH. Bulk density. In: Klute A, editor. Methods of soil analysis. Part 1. 2nd ed. Agronomy 1986;9:363-376.

Figure 14.19 A Sample Lab Report

Web Pages

While Web pages offer the potential for expanded use of color and visuals (including animation and video), the general principles of design used for paper documents can be applied to them. Again, you will want to evaluate the context in which the document will be read. Will your reader be reading from a computer screen or printing the document on paper for reading? If the reading takes place on a computer screen, how big is the screen and how good is its resolution? Reading from a computer screen can be more difficult than reading on paper, so you will want to avoid small fonts and confusing backgrounds that distract from the core content.

Web pages and other electronic texts differ from print texts in large part because they can include links to additional text or graphics, to other Web pages, or to short clips of video, animation, or sound. As an author, you must consider that because of these links, readers may navigate your text in a nonlinear fashion, starting almost anywhere they like and branching off whenever a link piques their curiosity. To help readers find their way around, Web authors often provide a navigation scheme, usually in the form of site maps or "index" pages.

HTML (hypertext markup language) is the standard language used for creating Web pages. Software programs called **HTML editors** provide novices with an easy way to create Web pages, and most word processing programs allow a document to be converted into HTML and saved as a Web page.

As you design a Web page, beware of letting unnecessary graphics and multimedia elements distract from your message. Yes, you *can* add a textured background to the screen that will make it look like marble or cloth, but will that background make reading the text easier? Will a sound file improve communication of your main points, or are you adding sound simply because you can? Consider the following guidelines when designing a Web page:

- *Make sure your text is easy to read.* Many Web pages are difficult to read because of textured and brightly colored backgrounds. Keep the background of a Web page light in tone so that your text can be read with ease. Because color type can also be difficult to read, avoid vibrant colors for long blocks of text. Bear in mind that most readers are used to reading dark (typically black) text on a light (typically white) background.

- *Chunk information carefully, and keep your Web pages short.* Because many people have difficulty reading long documents on a computer screen, be sure to chunk your information into concise paragraphs. Also, readers often find it difficult to read a Web page that requires extensive scrolling down the screen. Break up long text blocks into separate Web pages that require no more than one or two screens of scrolling. Use hypertext links to connect the text blocks and to help readers navigate across the pages.

- *Limit the file size of your Web pages.* A Web page that is filled with visuals and sound files can be slow and clunky to load, especially for users with old computers or dial-up connections to the Internet. Limiting your use of visuals and sound files so that your pages load quickly will help ensure that your documents are read.

- *Use hypertext links effectively.* Make sure that all of your links work correctly and that all the pages of your Web site include a link back to your home page so that readers can access it easily. You can make your text easier to read by judiciously limiting the number of links you embed in it. In addition to embedded text links, consider including a list of important links on a separate page for readers' convenience.

- *Use the elements of document design.* Remember what you have learned in this chapter about typography, white space, color, and visuals when you create Web pages. Most principles of good print document design apply to Web page design as well.

PART 3

Doing Research

15

●●●● **Field Research**

In universities, government agencies, and the business world, field research can be as important as library research or experimental research. If you major in education, communication, or one of the social sciences, you will probably be asked to do writing based on your own observations, interviews, and questionnaire results. You will also read large amounts of information based on these methods of learning. You might also use observations or interviews to help you select or gain background for a service-learning project.

Observations and interviews are essential for writing profiles (Chapter 3). In proposing a solution to a problem (Chapter 6), you might want to interview people involved; or if many people are affected, you might find it useful to prepare a questionnaire. In writing to explain an academic concept (Chapter 4), you might want to interview a faculty member who is a specialist on the subject. As you consider how you might use such research most appropriately, ask your instructor whether your institution requires you to obtain approval for your field research.

Observations

This section offers guidelines for planning an observational visit, taking notes on your observations, writing them up, and preparing for follow-up visits. Some kinds of writing are based on observations from single visits — travel writing, social workers' case reports, insurance investigators' accident reports — but most observational writing is based on several visits. An anthropologist or a sociologist studying an unfamiliar group or activity might observe it for months, filling several notebooks with notes. If you are profiling a place (Chapter 3), you almost certainly will want to make more than one observational visit, some of them perhaps combined with interviews.

Planning the Visit

To ensure that your observational visits are productive, you must plan them carefully.

Getting Access. If the place you propose to visit is public, you will probably have easy access to it. If everything you need to see is within view of anyone passing by or using the place, you can make your observations without any special arrangements.

However, most observational visits require special access. Hence, you will need to call ahead or stop by to introduce yourself and to make an appointment, if necessary.

Announcing Your Intentions. State your intentions directly and fully. Say who you are, where you are from, and what you hope to do. You may be surprised at how receptive people can be to a college student on assignment. Not every place you wish to visit will welcome you, however. In addition, private businesses as well as public institutions place a variety of constraints on visitors.

Taking Your Tools. Take notetaking tools such as an iPad, laptop, or a pen and a notebook with a firm back so that you will have a steady writing surface. Some writers dictate their observations, but because transcribing takes a lot of time, we recommend simply writing your notes.

Observing and Taking Notes

Here are some basic guidelines for observing and taking notes.

Observing. Your purposes in observing are twofold: to describe what you observe and to analyze the activity or place, discovering a perspective that enables you to reveal insights into its meaning and significance.

Some activities invite the observer to watch from multiple vantage points, whereas others may limit the observer to a single vantage point. Take advantage of every point of view available to you. Study the scene from a stationary position, and then try to move around it. The more varied your points of view, the more details you are likely to observe.

Try initially to be an innocent observer: Pretend that you have never seen anything like this activity or place before. Then consider your own and your readers' likely preconceptions. Ask yourself which details are surprising and which ones confirm your expectations.

Taking Notes. Perhaps the most important advice about notetaking during an observational visit is to record as many details as possible about the place or activity and to write down your insights (ideas, interpretations, judgments) as they come to mind. You will undoubtedly find your own style of notetaking, but here are a few pointers.

- Take notes in words or phrases.
- Draw diagrams or sketches if they will help you recall details later on. Take photos if you are given permission to do so, but be aware that some people do not want their pictures taken.
- Use abbreviations as much as you like, but use them consistently and clearly.
- Note any impressions, ideas, questions, or personal insights that occur to you.

- If you are expecting to see a certain behavior, try not to let this expectation influence what you actually do see. But note how your expectations are overturned.
- Use quotation marks around any overheard remarks or conversations you record.

Do not worry about covering every aspect of the activity or place. At the same time, however, you want to be sure to include details about the setting, the people, and your reactions.

■ *The Setting.*   Describe the setting: Name or list objects you see there, and record details about them — their color, shape, size, texture, function, relation to similar or dissimilar objects. Although your notes will probably contain mainly visual details, you might also want to record sounds and smells. Be sure to include some notes about the shape, dimensions, and layout of the place as a whole. How big is it? How is it organized?

■ *The People.*   Note the number of people you observe, their activities, their movements and behavior, and their appearance or dress. Record parts of overheard conversations. Indicate whether you see more men than women, more members of one nationality or ethnic group than another, more older than younger people. Most important, note anything surprising, interesting, or unusual about the people and how they interact with one another.

Reflecting on Your Observations

Immediately after your visit (within a few minutes, if possible), find a quiet place to reflect on what you saw, review your notes, and fill in any gaps. Give yourself at least a half-hour to add to your notes and to write a few sentences about your perspective on the place or activity. Ask yourself the following questions:

- *What did I learn?*
- *How did what I observed fit my own or my readers' likely preconceptions of the place or activity? Did it upset any of my preconceptions?*
- *What interests me the most about the activity or place? What are my readers likely to find interesting about it?*
- *What, if anything, seemed contradictory or out of place?*

Writing Up Your Notes

Your instructor may ask you to write up your notes. If so, review your notes, looking for a meaningful pattern. You might find clustering or taking inventory useful for discovering patterns in your notes.

Assume that your readers have never been to the place, and decide on the perspective of the place you want to convey. Choose details that will convey this, and then draft a brief description of the place.

Clustering is described in Chapter 8, p. 317. Inventory-taking is described in Chapter 9, p. 337.

Exercise 15.1

Arrange to meet with a small group (three or four students) for an observational visit somewhere on campus, such as the student center, campus gym, cafeteria, or restaurant. Assign each person in your group a specific task; one person can take notes on the appearance of the people, for example; another can take notes on their activities; another on their conversations; and another on what the place looks and smells like. After twenty to thirty minutes, report to one another on your observations. Discuss any difficulties that arise.

Preparing for Follow-Up Visits

It is important to develop a plan for your follow-up visits: questions to be answered, insights to be tested, types of information you would like to discover. If possible, do some interviewing and reading before a repeat visit so that you will have a greater understanding of the subject. For additional ideas on what to aim for in a follow-up visit, you might want to present your notes from your first visit to your instructor or to your class.

Interviews

Like making observations, interviewing tends to involve four basic steps: (1) planning and setting up the interview, (2) taking notes during the interview, (3) reflecting on the interview, and (4) writing up your notes.

Planning and Setting Up the Interview

The initial steps in interviewing involve choosing an interview subject and then arranging and planning for the interview.

Choosing an Interview Subject. For a profile of an individual, most or all of your interviews would be with that person. If you are writing about some activity in which several people are involved, however, choose subjects representing a variety of perspectives. For instance, you might interview several members of an organization to gain a more complete picture of its mission or activities. You should be flexible because you may be unable to speak with the person you initially targeted and may wind up interviewing someone else — the person's assistant, perhaps. Do not assume that this interview subject will be of little use to you. With the right questions, you might even learn more from the assistant than you would from the person you had originally expected to see.

Arranging an Interview. You may be nervous about calling up a busy person and asking for some of his or her time. Indeed, you may get turned down. But if so, it is possible that you will be referred to someone who will see you, perhaps someone whose job it is to talk to the public.

Do not feel that just because you are a student, you do not have the right to ask for people's time. Most people are delighted to be asked about themselves, particularly if you reach them when they are not feeling harried. Since you are a student on assignment, some people may even feel that they are performing a public service by talking with you.

When introducing yourself to arrange the interview, give a brief description of your project. If you talk too much, you could prejudice or limit the interviewee's response. At the same time, it is a good idea to exhibit some sincere enthusiasm for your project. If you lack enthusiasm, the person may see little reason to talk with you.

Keep in mind that the person you want to interview will be donating valuable time to you. Be certain that you call ahead to arrange a specific time for the interview. Arrive on time. Dress appropriately. Bring all the materials you need. Express your thanks when the interview is over. Finally, try to represent your institution well, whether your interview is for a single course assignment or is part of a larger service-learning project.

Planning for the Interview. The best interview is generally the well-planned interview. Making an observational visit and doing some background reading beforehand can be helpful. In preparation for the interview, you should consider your objectives:

- Do you want details or a general orientation (the "big picture") from this interview?
- Do you want this interview to lead you to interviews with other key people?
- Do you want mainly facts or opinions?
- Do you need to clarify something you have observed or read? If so, what?

The key to good interviewing is flexibility. You may be looking for facts, but your interview subject may not have any to offer. In that case, you should be able to shift gears and go after whatever your subject is in a position to discuss. Be aware that the person you are interviewing represents only one point of view. You may need to speak with several people to get a more complete picture.

Composing Questions. In addition to determining your objectives, you should prepare your questions in advance. Good questions can be the key to a successful interview.

Good questions come in two basic types: open and closed. **Open questions** give the respondent range and flexibility. They also generate anecdotes, personal revelations, and expressions of attitudes. **Closed questions** usually request specific information.

Suppose you are interviewing a small-business owner. You might begin with a specific (closed) question about when the business was established and then follow up with an open-ended question such as, "Could you take a few minutes to tell me something about your early days in the business? I'd be interested to hear how it got started, what your hopes were, and what problems you had to face." Consider asking directly for an anecdote ("What happened when your employees threatened to strike?"), encouraging reflection ("What do you think has helped you most? What has hampered you?"), or soliciting advice ("What advice would you give to someone trying to start a new business today?"). Here are some examples of open and closed questions:

Open Questions

- What do you think about (*name a person or an event*)?
- Describe your reaction when (*name an event*) happened.
- Tell me about a time you were (*name an emotion*).

Closed Questions

- How do you (*name a process*)?
- What does (*name a word or phrase*) mean?
- What does (*name a person, object, or place*) look like?
- How was (*name a product, process, etc.*) developed?

The best questions encourage the subject to talk freely but to the point. If an answer strays too far from the point, you may need to ask a follow-up question to refocus the talk. Another tack you might want to try is to rephrase the subject's answer, to say something like "Let me see if I have this right" or "Am I correct in saying that you feel . . . ?" Often, a person will take the opportunity to amplify the original response by adding just the anecdote or quotable comment you have been looking for.

Avoid questions that place unfair limits on respondents. These include forced-choice questions and leading questions.

Forced-choice questions impose your terms on respondents. If you are interviewing a counselor at a campus rape crisis center and want to know what he or she thinks is the motivation for rape, you could ask this question: "Do you think rape is about control or about rage?" But the counselor might not think that either control or rage satisfactorily explains the motivation for rape. A better way to phrase the question would be as follows: "People often fall into two camps on the issue of rape. Some think it is an expression of control, while others argue that it is an expression of rage. Do you think it is either of these? If not, what is your opinion?" Phrasing the question in this way allows interviewees to react to what others have said but also gives them freedom to set the terms for their response.

Leading questions assume too much. An example of this kind of question is this: "Do you think the number of rapes has increased because women are perceived as competitors in a highly competitive economy?" This question assumes that there is an increase in the occurrence of rape, that women are perceived (apparently by rapists) as economic competitors, and that the state of the economy is somehow related to acts of rape. A better way of asking the question might be to make the assumptions more explicit by dividing the question into its parts: "Has the occurrence of rape increased in recent years? If so, what could have caused this increase? I've heard some people argue that the state of the economy has something to do with rape. Some have suggested that rapists perceive women as competitors for jobs, and that this perception is linked to rape. Do you think there might be any truth to this?"

Bringing Your Tools. As for an observational visit, when you interview someone, you will need notetaking tools such as an iPad or a pen and a notebook with a firm back so you can write in it easily without the benefit of a table or desk. You might find it useful to divide several pages into two columns by drawing a line about one-third of the width of the page from the left margin. Use the left-hand column to note details about the scene, the person, the mood of the interview, and other impressions. Head this column *Details and Impressions.* At the top of the right-hand column, write several questions. You may not use them, but they will jog your memory. This column should be titled *Information.* In it, you will record what you learn from answers to your questions.

Taking Notes during the Interview

In taking notes, your goals are to gather information and to record a few quotations, key words and phrases, and details of the scene, the person, and the mood of the interview. Remember that *how* something is said is as important as *what* is said. Look for material that will give texture to your writing — gesture, verbal inflection, facial expression, body language, physical appearance, dress, hair, or anything that makes the person stand out as an individual. In general, it is probably a good idea to do more listening than notetaking. You may not have much confidence in your memory, but if you pay close attention, you are likely to recall a good deal of the conversation afterward.

Reflecting on the Interview

As soon as you finish the interview, find a quiet place to reflect on it and review your notes. This reflection is essential because so much happens in an interview that you cannot record at the time. Spend at least a half-hour adding to your notes and thinking about what you learned.

At the end of this time, write a few sentences about your main impressions from the interview. Ask yourself these questions:

- *What did I learn?*
- *What seemed contradictory or surprising about the interview?*
- *How did what was said fit my own or my readers' likely expectations about the person, activity, or place?*
- *How can I summarize my impressions?*

Writing Up Your Notes

Your instructor may ask you to write up your interview notes. If so, review them for useful details and ideas. Decide what perspective you want to take on the person you interviewed. Choose details that will contribute to this perspective. Select quotations and paraphrases of information you learned from the person.

You might also review notes from any related observations or from other interviews, especially if you plan to combine these materials in a profile, ethnographic study, or other project.

Questionnaires

Questionnaires let you survey the opinions and knowledge of large numbers of people. Compared to one-on-one interviews, they have the advantages of economy, efficiency, and anonymity. Some questionnaires, such as the ones you filled out when entering college, just collect demographic information: your name, age, sex, hometown, religious preference, intended major. Others, such as the Gallup and Harris polls, collect opinions on a wide range of issues. Before elections, we are bombarded with the results of such polls. Still other kinds of questionnaires, such as those used in academic research, are designed to help answer important questions about personal and societal problems.

This section briefly outlines procedures you can follow to carry out an informal questionnaire survey of people's opinions or knowledge.

Focusing Your Study

A questionnaire survey usually has a limited focus. You might need to interview a few people to find this focus, or you may already have a limited focus in mind. If you are developing a questionnaire as part of a service-learning project, discuss your focus with your supervisor or other staff members.

As an example, let us assume that you go to your campus student health clinic and have to wait over an hour to see a doctor. Sitting in the waiting room with many other students, you decide that this long wait is a problem that would be an ideal topic for an assignment you have been asked to do for your writing class, an essay proposing a solution to a problem (Chapter 6).

You do not have to explore the entire operation of the clinic to study this problem. You are not interested in how nurses and doctors are hired or in how efficient the clinic's system of ordering supplies is, for example. Your primary interests are how long students usually wait for appointments, what times are most convenient for students to schedule appointments, how the clinic accommodates students when demand is high, and whether the long wait discourages many students from getting the treatment they need. With this limited focus, you can collect valuable information using a fairly brief questionnaire. To be certain about your focus, however, you should talk informally with several students to find out whether they also think there is a problem with appointment scheduling at the clinic. You might want to talk with staff members, too, explaining your plans and asking for their views on the problem.

Whatever your interest, be sure to limit the scope of your survey. Try to focus on one or two important questions. With a limited focus, your questionnaire can be brief, and people will be more willing to fill it out. In addition, a survey based on a limited amount of information will be easier to organize and report on.

Writing Questions

The same two basic types of questions used for interviews, closed and open, are also useful in questionnaires. Figure 15.1 illustrates how these types of questions may be employed in the context of a questionnaire about the student health clinic problem. Notice that the questionnaire uses several forms of *closed questions* (in items 1–6): two-way questions, multiple-choice questions, ranking scales, and checklists. You will probably use more than one form of closed question in a questionnaire to collect different kinds of information. The sample questionnaire also uses several *open questions* (items 7–10) that ask for brief written answers. You may want to combine closed and open questions in your questionnaire because both offer advantages: Closed questions will give you definite answers, while open questions can elicit information you may not have anticipated as well as provide lively quotations for your essay explaining what you have learned.

Whatever types of questions you develop, try to phrase them in a fair and unbiased manner so that your results will be reliable and credible. As soon as you have a collection of possible questions, try them out on a few typical respondents. You need to know which questions are unclear, which seem to duplicate others, and which provide the most interesting responses. These tryouts will enable you to assess which questions will give you the information you need. Readers can also help you come up with additional questions.

Designing the Questionnaire

Begin your questionnaire with a brief, clear introduction stating the purpose of your survey and explaining how you intend to use the results. Give advice on answering the questions, and estimate the amount of time needed to complete the questionnaire (see Figure 15.1 for an example). You may opt to give this information orally if you plan to hand the questionnaire to groups of people and have them fill it out immediately. However, even in this case, your respondents will appreciate a written introduction that clarifies what you expect.

Select your most promising questions, and decide how to order them. Any logical order is appropriate. You might want to arrange the questions from least to most complicated or from general to specific. You may find it appropriate to group the questions by subject matter or format. Certain questions may lead to others. You might want to place open questions at the end (see Figure 15.1 for an example).

Design your questionnaire so that it looks attractive and readable. Make it look easy to complete. Do not crowd questions together to save paper. Provide plenty of space for readers to answer questions, especially open questions, and encourage them to use the back of the page if they need more space.

This is a survey about the scheduling of appointments at the campus Student Health Clinic. Your participation will help determine how long students have to wait to use clinic services and how these services might be more conveniently scheduled. The survey should take only 3 to 4 minutes to complete. All responses are confidential. Thank you for your participation.

Two-way question

1. Have you ever made an appointment at the clinic?   (Circle one.)

   Yes   No

2. How frequently have you had to wait more than 10 minutes at the clinic for a scheduled appointment?   (Circle one.)

   Always   Usually   Occasionally   Never

Multiple-choice questions

3. Have you ever had to wait more than 30 minutes at the clinic for a scheduled appointment?   (Circle one.)

   Yes   No   Uncertain

4. From your experience so far with the clinic, how would you rank its system for scheduling appointments?   (Circle one.)

0	1	2	3	4	5
no experience	inadequate	poor	adequate	good	outstanding

Ranking scale

5. Given your present work and class schedule, when are you able to visit the clinic?   (Check all applicable responses.)

   _____ 8–10 a.m.   _____ 1–3 p.m.
   _____ 10 a.m.–Noon   _____ 3–5 p.m.
   _____ 12–1 p.m.

Checklist

6. Given your present work and class schedule, which times during the day (Monday through Friday) would be the most and least convenient for you to schedule appointments at the clinic?   (Rank the four choices from 1 for most convenient time to 4 for least convenient time.)

   _____ Morning (7 a.m.–Noon)   _____ Dinnertime (5–7 p.m.)
   _____ Afternoon (12–5 p.m.)   _____ Evening (7–10 p.m.)

Ranking scale

7. How would you evaluate your most recent appointment at the clinic?

8. Based on your experiences with scheduling at the clinic, what advice would you give to other students about making appointments?

Open questions

9. What do you believe would most improve the scheduling of appointments at the clinic?

10. If you have additional comments about scheduling at the clinic, please write them on the back of this page.

Figure 15.1 Sample Questionnaire: Scheduling at the Student Health Clinic

Testing the Questionnaire

Make a few copies of your first-draft questionnaire, and ask at least three readers to complete it. Time them as they respond, or ask them to keep track of how long they take to complete it. Discuss with them any confusion or problems they experience. Review their responses with them to be certain that each question is eliciting the information you want it to elicit. From what you learn, reconsider your questionnaire, and make any necessary revisions to your questions and design or format.

Administering the Questionnaire

Decide whom you want to fill out your questionnaire and how you can arrange for them to do so. The more respondents you have, the better, but constraints of time and expense will almost certainly limit the number. You can mail or e-mail questionnaires, distribute them to dormitories, or send them to campus or workplace mailboxes, but the return will likely be low. Half the people receiving questionnaires in the mail usually fail to return them. If you do mail the questionnaire, be sure to mention the deadline for returning it. Give directions for its return, and include a stamped, self-addressed envelope, if necessary. Instead of mailing the questionnaire, you might want to arrange to distribute it yourself to groups of people in class or around campus, at dormitory meetings, or at work. Some colleges and universities have restrictions about the use of questionnaires, so you should check your institution's policy before sending one out.

Note that if you want to do a formal questionnaire study, you will need a scientifically representative group of readers (a random or stratified random sample). Even for an informal study, you should try to get a reasonably representative group. For example, to study satisfaction with appointment scheduling at the clinic, you would want to include students who have been to the clinic as well as those who have avoided it. You might even want to include a concentration of seniors rather than first-year students because, after four years, seniors would have made more visits to the clinic. If many students commute, you would want to be sure to have commuters among your respondents. Your essay will be more convincing if you demonstrate that your respondents represent the group whose opinions or knowledge you claim to be studying. As few as twenty-five respondents could be adequate for an informal study.

Writing Up the Results

Once you have the completed questionnaires, how do you write up the results?

Summarizing the Results. Begin by tallying the results from the closed questions. Take an unused questionnaire, and tally the responses next to each choice. Suppose that you have administered the student health clinic questionnaire to twenty-five students. Here is how the tally might look for the checklist in question 5 of Figure 15.1.

5. Given your present work and class schedule, when are you able to visit the clinic? (Check all applicable responses.)

_____ 8–10 a.m. ℕℕ ℕℕ ℕℕ III (*18*)   _____ 1–3 p.m. III (*3*)

_____ 10 a.m.–Noon ℕℕ II (*7*)   _____ 3–5 p.m. ℕℕ IIII (*9*)

_____ 12–1 p.m. ℕℕ ℕℕ III (*13*)

Each tally mark represents one response to that item. The totals add up to more than twenty-five because respondents were asked to check all the times when they could make appointments.

You can give the results from the closed questions as percentages, either within the text of your paper or in one or more tables or graphs. Conventional table formats for the social sciences are illustrated in the *Publication Manual of the American Psychological Association*, 6th edition (Washington, DC: American Psychological Association, 2010). For larger surveys, you can use computer spreadsheet programs to tabulate the results and even generate the tables and graphs.

Next, consider the open questions. Read all respondents' answers to each question separately to see the kinds and variety of responses they gave. Then decide whether you want to code any of the open questions so that you can summarize results from them quantitatively, as you would with closed questions. For example, you might want to classify the types of advice given as responses to question 8 in the clinic questionnaire: "Based on your experiences with scheduling at the clinic, what advice would you give to other students about making appointments?" You could then report the numbers of respondents (of your twenty-five) who gave each type of advice. For an opinion question (for example, "How would you evaluate your most recent appointment at the clinic?"), you might simply code the answers as positive, neutral, or negative and then tally the results accordingly for each kind of response. However, you will probably want to use the responses to most open questions as a source of quotations for your report or essay.

Because readers' interests can be engaged more easily with quotations than with percentages, plan to use open responses in your essay, perhaps weaving them into your discussion like quoted material from published sources.

For strategies for integrating quoted material, see Chapter 17, pp. 490–91.

Organizing the Write-Up. In organizing your results, you might want to consider a plan that is commonly followed in the social sciences.

Reporting Your Survey

Statement of the problem

    Context for your study

    Question or questions you wanted to answer

      Need for your survey
      Brief preview of your survey and plan for your report

Review of other related surveys (if you know of any)

Procedures

      Questionnaire design
      Selection of participants
      Administration of the questionnaire
      Summary of the results

Results: Presentation of what you learned, with limited commentary or interpretation

Summary and discussion

      Brief summary of your results
      Brief discussion of their significance (commenting, interpreting, exploring implications, and possibly comparing with other related surveys)

Library and Internet Research 16

●●●●

Research requires patience, careful planning, hard work, and even luck. The rewards are many, however. Each new research project leads you to unexplored regions of the library or of cyberspace. You may find yourself in a rare-book room reading a manuscript written hundreds of years ago or involved in a lively discussion on the Internet with people hundreds of miles away. One moment you may be surfing the Web, and the next you may be threading a microfilm reader, watching a DVD, or squinting at the fine print in a periodical index.

This chapter is designed to help you learn how to use all of the resources available to you. It gives advice on how to use the library and the Internet, develop efficient search strategies, keep track of your research, locate appropriate sources, and read them productively. Chapter 17 provides guidelines for using and acknowledging these sources in an essay and presents a sample research paper on home schooling.

Orienting Yourself to the Library

To conduct research in most college libraries, you will need to become familiar with a wide variety of resources. Library catalogs, almost all of them now electronic, provide information on books, journals, and other materials (such as DVDs) held by the library. Periodical databases and indexes, used to locate magazine and journal articles, are available in electronic format, in print, or both. The material you find may be in print, in downloadable electronic format, or on microfilm or microfiche.

Taking a Tour

Most college libraries are more complex than typical high school or public libraries, so make a point of getting acquainted with your school's library. Your instructor may arrange a library orientation tour for your composition class. If not, find out whether the library offers tours, and, if so, take one. Otherwise, design your own tour (for suggestions of important resources to look for in your college library, see Table 16.1).

When you visit the library in person, make the most of your time there. Pick up copies of any available pamphlets and guidelines, including a floor map of materials and facilities. See whether your library offers any special workshops or presentations that might help you in your work.

457

Table 16.1 Designing Your Self-Guided Library Tour

Library Resource	What You Can Do with This Resource
Circulation desk	Check out materials, place holds and recalls, pay fees or fines.
Reference desk/room	Obtain help from reference librarians to locate and use library resources. Find reference materials such as encyclopedias, dictionaries, handbooks, atlases, bibliographies, statistics, and periodical indexes and abstracts.
Reserves	Gain access to books and journal articles that are on reserve for specific classes.
Interlibrary loan	Request materials not available on site. *(Note: Many libraries now offer this service online only.)*
Open-access computers	Gain access to the library catalog, electronic periodical indexes, the campus network, and the Internet.
Periodicals	Locate bound and unbound current issues of newspapers, journals, and magazines. *(Note: Many periodicals are now available electronically through the library databases.)*
Government publications	Locate publications from federal, state, and local government agencies.
Multimedia resources	Locate nonprint materials such as videos, CD-ROMs, and audiotapes.
Microforms	Locate materials on microfilm (reels) and microfiche (cards).
Special collections/ Rare-book room	Find rare or highly specialized materials not readily available in most library collections *(in larger libraries only)*.
Archives	Find collections of papers from important individuals and organizations that provide source material for original research *(in larger libraries only)*.
Maps and atlases	Locate maps and atlases (housed in a special location because of their size and format).
Copiers, printers, and scanners	Make copies, print, and/or scan material. *(Note: Be aware that you almost always pay for copies by the page, and some libraries charge for printing or require students to supply their own paper.)*
Reading areas	Read in quiet, comfortable areas.
Study rooms	Study in rooms reserved for individuals or small groups.
Computer labs	Use networked computers for word processing, research, and other functions.

You don't have to visit in person, though, to find out what your college library offers. Most libraries have useful Web sites describing their resources and services, and many offer virtual tours. Many of these sites also offer access to online databases, tutorials for using the library's resources, expert advice on doing research and writing, and more.

Consulting Librarians

Think of college librarians as instructors whose job is to help you understand the library and get your hands on resources you need to complete your research projects. Most librarians have years of experience answering the very questions you are likely to ask. You should not hesitate to approach them with any questions you have about getting started, locating sources, or completing your research project. Remember, however, that they can be most helpful when you can explain your research assignment clearly and ask questions that are as specific as possible. You need not do so face-to-face: Many libraries now offer e-mail, phone, or Internet chat or messaging options to connect library users to a reference librarian.

Getting Started

Let's say you have just been given a writing assignment that requires significant research. You already have a sense of how your college library is organized, and you think you know what you want to write about. If you are like most students, you will still be wondering at this point, "But where do I start?" The sections below provide an answer to that common question.

Knowing Your Research Task

Before you start a research project, learn as much as you can about the assignment. How long should the paper be? How much time do you have to do it? Does your instructor specify how many sources you will need, or which kinds? Ask your instructor to clarify any confusing terms and to define the purpose and scope of the project. Asking a question or two in advance can prevent hours — or even days — of misdirected work.

Finding Out What Your Library Offers

You should try to get to the library or do a thorough search of its resources online as soon as you understand the assignment. If many of your classmates will be working on similar projects, you may be competing with them for a limited number of books and other resources. More important, for your library research to be manageable and productive, you will want to work carefully and systematically, and this takes time. Although specific search strategies may vary to fit the needs of individual research tasks, the general process presented in Figure 16.1 on the next page should help you organize your time. Remember that you will be constantly refining and revising your research strategy as you find out more about your topic.

At this early stage, you need an overview of your topic. If you are researching a concept or an issue in a course you are taking, your textbook and your course materials

Know your research task and your resources.

Find out what your library offers.

Get an overview of your topic.

- Look in encyclopedias and bibliographies.
- Review textbooks and other course materials.
- Explore newspapers, magazines, and Internet sites.
- Consult with your instructor and/or a reference librarian.
- Construct a list of keywords and subject headings.
- Develop a preliminary topic statement.

Keep track of what you learn.

- Keep a working bibliography.
- Take notes.

Search for in-depth information on your topic.

Conduct a preliminary search for sources, using keywords and subject headings.

- Check the online catalog for books.
- Check periodical databases for articles.
- Check Internet sites.

Evaluate and refine your search by asking yourself:

- Is this what I expected to find?
- Am I finding enough?
- Am I finding too much?
- Do I need to modify my keywords?
- Do I need to recheck background sources?
- Do I need to modify my topic statement?

Refine your search based on the answers.

Locate sources.

- Books
- Magazine and journal articles
- Newspaper articles
- Internet sites
- Government and statistical sources
- Other sources appropriate to your topic

Evaluate your sources.

- For information
- For relevance
- For accuracy
- For comprehensiveness
- For bias
- For currency

Continue to evaluate and refine your search strategy based on the research results.

Figure 16.1 Overview of an Information Search Strategy

provide the obvious starting point. Your instructor and/or a reference librarian can advise you about other sources that provide overviews of your topic. If your topic is currently in the news, you will want to consult newspapers, magazines, or Web sites. For all other topics, encyclopedias and bibliographies are often the place to start.

Consulting Encyclopedias

General encyclopedias, such as the *Encyclopaedia Britannica* and the *Columbia Encyclopedia,* provide basic information about many topics. Like many encyclopedias, these works are available online and in print. Wikipedia, too, offers a wealth of information, and it is often the first stop for students who are accustomed to consulting the open Internet first for information. Be aware, though, that Wikipedia is user-generated, rather than traditionally published, and for this reason the quality of information found there can be inconsistent. Many academics do not consider Wikipedia to be a reliable source, so you should ask your instructor for advice on consulting it at this stage. Whichever general encyclopedia you consult, bear in mind that general encyclopedias should be used only for an overview of a topic; on their own, they are not adequate resources for college research.

Specialized encyclopedias cover topics in more depth than general encyclopedias do. In addition to providing an overview of a topic, they often include an explanation of issues related to the topic, definitions of specialized terminology, and selective bibliographies of additional sources.

As starting points, specialized encyclopedias have two distinct advantages: (1) They provide a comprehensive introduction to key terms related to your topic, terms that will help you find related material in catalogs and indexes, and (2) they provide a comprehensive presentation of a subject, enabling you to see many possibilities for focusing your research.

The following list identifies some specialized encyclopedias in the major academic disciplines:

ART	*Dictionary of Art*
BIOLOGY	*Concise Encyclopedia Biology*
CHEMISTRY	*Concise Encyclopedia Chemistry*
COMPUTERS	*Encyclopedia of Computer Science and Technology*
ECONOMICS	*Fortune Encyclopedia of Economics*
EDUCATION	*Encyclopedia of Educational Research*
ENVIRONMENT	*Encyclopedia of the Environment*
FOREIGN RELATIONS	*Encyclopedia of U.S. Foreign Relations*
	Encyclopedia of the Third World
HISTORY	*Encyclopedia USA*
	New Cambridge Modern History
LAW	*Corpus Juris Secundum*
	American Jurisprudence
LITERATURE	*Encyclopedia of World Literature in the Twentieth Century*
	Encyclopedia of Literature and Criticism
MEDICINE	*American Medical Association's Complete Medical Encyclopedia*

MUSIC	*New Grove Dictionary of Music and Musicians*
NURSING	*Miller-Keane Encyclopedia and Dictionary of Medicine, Nursing, and Allied Health*
PHILOSOPHY	*Routledge Encyclopedia of Philosophy*
PSYCHOLOGY	*Encyclopedia of Psychology*
RELIGION	*Encyclopedia of Religion*
SCIENCE	*McGraw-Hill Encyclopedia of Science and Technology*
SOCIAL SCIENCES	*International Encyclopedia of the Social Sciences*
SOCIOLOGY	*Encyclopedia of Sociology*
WOMEN'S STUDIES	*Women's Studies Encyclopedia*

Many of these specialized encyclopedias are available both online and in print. You can locate them in the library by doing a title search in your library's catalog. Find other specialized encyclopedias by doing a keyword search using the name of the discipline, such as *psychology*, and adding the word *encyclopedia* or *dictionary*. As always, it is a good idea to consult with a reference librarian for further suggestions.

Consulting Bibliographies

A **bibliography** is simply a list of publications on a given subject. All researched articles and books include bibliographies to document their sources of information. In addition, separately published, book-length bibliographies exist for many subjects that have attracted significant amounts of writing. These are useful for in-depth research. Some bibliographies are annotated with brief summaries and evaluations of the entries.

Even if you attend a large research university, your library is unlikely to hold every book or journal article that a bibliography might direct you to. If a source looks likely to be useful but your library does not have a copy, ask a reference librarian about the possibility of acquiring it from another library through interlibrary loan.

For more information on annotated bibliographies, see Chapter 18.

Keeping Track of Your Research

As you research your topic, you will want to keep a careful record of all the sources you locate by setting up a working bibliography. You will also want to take notes on your sources in some systematic way.

Keeping a Working Bibliography

A **working bibliography** is a preliminary, ongoing record of books, articles, Web sites, and other sources of information you discover as you research your subject. In addition, you can use your working bibliography to keep track of any encyclopedias and bibliographies you consult, even though these general reference tools are usually not cited in an essay.

Each entry in a working bibliography is called a **bibliographic citation**. The information you record in each bibliographic citation will help you to locate the source in the library and then, if you end up using it in your paper, to *cite* or *document* it in the list of references or works cited you provide at the end of your essay. *Recording this information for each possible source as you identify it, rather than reconstructing it later, will save you hours of work.* In addition to the bibliographic information, note the library location where the source is kept, the name of the database or other reference work where you learned about it, and the date you accessed it, just in case you have to track it down again. (See Figures 16.2 and 16.3 for guidelines on what to record for a book or a print periodical article. For guidelines for Internet sources, see Figure 16.6 on p. 479.)

Chapter 17 presents two common documentation styles — one adopted by the Modern Language Association (MLA) and widely used in the humanities, and the other advocated by the American Psychological Association (APA) and used in the social sciences. Other disciplines have their own preferred styles of documentation. Confirm with your instructor which documentation style is required for your assignment so that you can follow that style for all the sources you put into your working bibliography.

Practiced researchers keep their working bibliography in a computer file, in a notebook, or on index cards. Researchers who record the information in a computer file use either standard software (such as Word or Excel) or specialized software (such as RefWorks, EndNote, Zotero, or the Bedford Bibliographer) designed for creating bibliographies. Others find index cards convenient because they are portable and easy

Author	
Title	
Place of publication	
Publisher	
Date of publication	
Location	
Notes	

Figure 16.2 Information for Working Bibliography — Books

Author of article	
Title of article	
Title of journal	
Volume / issue number	
Date of issue	
Page numbers	
Location	
Notes	

Figure 16.3 Information for Working Bibliography — Periodical Articles

to arrange in the alphabetical order required for the list of works cited or references. Still others find cards too easy to lose and prefer instead to keep everything — working bibliography, notes, and drafts — in a notebook.

Whatever method you use for your working bibliography, your entries need to be accurate and complete. If the call number you record for a book is incomplete or inaccurate, for example, you may not be able to find the book easily on the shelves. If the author's name is misspelled, you may have trouble finding the book in the catalog. If the volume number for a periodical is incorrect, you may not be able to locate the article. If you initially get some bibliographic information from a catalog or an index, check it again for accuracy when you examine the source directly.

Taking Notes

After you have found some useful sources, you will want to begin taking notes.

When you find a useful **electronic source**, print it out and/or download the material to a flash drive or network drive, if possible. It is also a good idea to e-mail it to yourself. Be sure your electronic version includes all the source information required by the documentation system you are using. To take notes on a document you have downloaded, you can either print it out and annotate by hand, copy and paste relevant passages into a separate document, or (depending on the format in which you download it) annotate it electronically.

When you find a useful **print source**, photocopying it can be helpful, because you can make notes directly on the photocopied page and highlight material you may wish to quote, summarize, or paraphrase. Photocopying also allows you to reread and analyze important sources at your leisure. While these advantages make photocopying in many ways an ideal option, it can be costly, so you will want to be selective. If you do choose to photocopy, be sure to copy title pages or other publication information for each source, or otherwise record this information on your copy of the text.

Some libraries now offer the option of scanning documents. As with photocopying, this can be expensive, so you will need to be selective. Once you have scanned a document, however, you can print and annotate it, or, depending on the format in which you have scanned it, annotate it electronically or cut and paste key information into another document. Be sure your scanned version includes all the source information required by the documentation system you are using.

If you can neither photocopy, download, nor scan a source, you will have to record source information, notes, and quotations carefully in a separate document. *If you record notes separately, be sure to include the page numbers where you find information, so that you can go back and reread if necessary.* You will also need to give page numbers when you cite sources within your essay and in your list of works cited.

Be sure *never* to copy an author's phrases and sentences without enclosing them in quotation marks and noting the source, and always double-check all your notes for accuracy. Messy or inaccurate notes can lead to **plagiarism**, the unacknowledged and therefore improper use of another's phrases and sentences or ideas.

Outlining, paraphrasing, and summarizing are discussed in Chapter 9, and quoting is discussed in Chapter 17. For tips on avoiding plagiarism, see Chapter 17, p. 487.

Finding Library Sources

Books and periodical articles are the two types of sources most commonly used for academic research projects. Books housed in college library collections offer several advantages to the student researcher: They provide in-depth coverage of topics, and they tend to be published by reputable presses that guarantee that the material meets standards of accuracy and reliability.

The most up-to-date information on a subject, however, is usually found not in books but in articles published in periodicals. A **periodical** is a publication such as a magazine, newspaper, or scholarly journal that is published on an ongoing basis, at regular intervals (for instance, daily, weekly, monthly, or annually), and with different content in each issue. Examples of periodicals include *Sports Illustrated* (magazine), the *New York Times* (newspaper), *Tulsa Studies in Women's Literature* (scholarly journal), *Kairos* (online journal), and *Slate* (online magazine).

Books can be found in the library's **online catalog**. Articles in periodicals, however, are not listed in the library catalog; to find them, you must use **periodical databases** or **indexes**. Much of the success of your research will depend on your ability to effectively search online library catalogs and periodical databases. The next sections will give you strategies for doing so.

General Search Strategies

Doing Basic Searches

Computerized library catalogs and periodical databases consist of thousands or even millions of records, each representing an item such as a book, an article, or a government publication. Each record is made up of different fields describing the item.

Basic search strategies include author, title, keyword, and subject searches. When you perform an **author search**, the computer looks for a match between the name you type and the names listed in the author field of all the records in the online catalog or other database. When you perform a **title search**, the computer looks for a match in the title field. When performing these searches, most systems will try to match only the exact terms you enter. Therefore, accuracy counts.

Most online catalogs now permit a **keyword search**, which is an effective way to get started in most cases. Keywords are words or phrases that describe your topic. As you read about your subject in an encyclopedia or other reference book, you should keep a list of keywords that may be useful.

As you review the results of a keyword search, look for the titles that seem to match most closely the topics that you are looking for. (It is usually a good sign, for example, if your keyword(s) appear in the title.) If you get too few relevant returns, try different keywords. When you call up the detailed information for titles that seem promising, look for the section labeled "Subject" or "Subject Heading." **Subject headings** are specific words and phrases used in library catalogs and periodical databases to categorize the contents of books and articles. In many catalogs and databases, these subject headings are links that you can click on to get a list of other materials on the same subject. Here is an example of an online catalog listing for a book on home schooling:

For an example of an online catalog reference to a periodical, see p. 475.

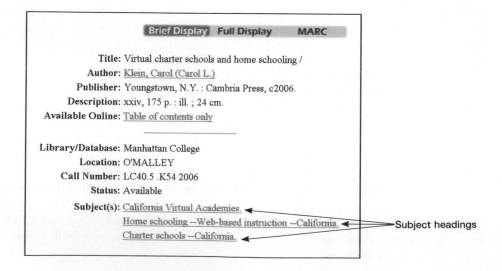

                    Brief Display   **Full Display**   **MARC**

Title: Virtual charter schools and home schooling /
Author: Klein, Carol (Carol L.)
Publisher: Youngstown, N.Y. : Cambria Press, c2006.
Description: xxiv, 175 p. : ill. ; 24 cm.
Available Online: Table of contents only

Library/Database: Manhattan College
Location: O'MALLEY
Call Number: LC40.5 .K54 2006
Status: Available
Subject(s): California Virtual Academies.
                Home schooling --Web-based instruction --California.
                Charter schools --California.

Subject headings

Table 16.2 below describes some search capabilities commonly offered by library catalogs and databases.

Doing Advanced Searches and Using Boolean Operators

The real power of using online catalogs or other databases is demonstrated when you need to look up books or articles using more than one search term. For example, suppose you want information about home schooling in California. Rather than looking through an index listing all the articles on home schooling and picking out those that

Table 16.2 Common Search Capabilities Offered by Library Catalogs and Databases

Type of Search	How the Computer Conducts the Search	Things to Know
Author Search (exact)		
• Individual ("*Guterson, David*") • Organization ("*U.S. Department of Education*")	Looks in the author field for the words entered	• Names are usually, but not always, entered *last name, first name* (for example, "Shakespeare, William"). • Organizations can be considered authors. Enter the name of the organization in natural word order. • An exact-match author search is useful for finding books and articles by a particular author.
Title Search (exact)		
• Book title • Magazine or journal title	Looks in the title field for words in the exact order you enter them	• An exact-match title search is useful for identifying the location of known items, such as when you are looking for a particular journal or book.
Subject Search (exact)		
	Looks in the subject heading or descriptor field for words in the exact order you enter them	• An exact-match subject search is useful when you are sure about the subject heading.
Keyword Search		
	Looks in the title, note, subject, abstract, and text fields for the words entered	• A keyword search is the broadest kind you can use. It is useful during early exploration of a subject.

mention California, you can ask the computer to do the work for you by linking your two keywords. Most online catalogs and databases offer the option of an **advanced search**, sometimes on a separate page from the main search page, that allows you to search for more than one keyword at a time, search for certain keywords while excluding others, or search for an exact phrase. Many systems allow for the use of quotation marks to specify exact phrases (for example, "home schooling"), plus signs for terms that must appear in results (+"home schooling"), or minus signs for terms that should not appear in results (−"adult"). Most systems also allow you to perform advanced searches by using the **Boolean operators** AND, OR, and NOT.

To understand the operation of **Boolean logic** (developed by and named after George Boole, a nineteenth-century mathematician), picture one set of articles about home schooling and another set of articles about California. A third set is formed by articles that are about both home schooling and California. The figures below provide an illustration of how each Boolean operator works.

AND

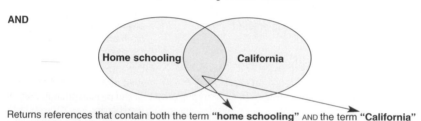

Returns references that contain both the term **"home schooling"** AND the term **"California"**
- Narrows the search
- Combines unrelated terms
- Is the default used by most online catalogs and databases

OR

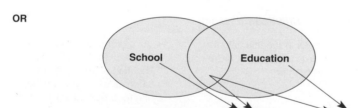

Returns all references that contain either the term **"school"** OR the term **"education"** OR both terms
- Broadens the search **("OR is more")**
- Is useful with synonyms and alternate spellings: ("home schooling" and "homeschooling")

NOT

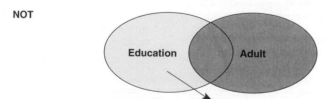

Returns references that include the term **"education"** but NOT the term **"adult"**
- Narrows the search
- Caution: By narrowing your search, you may eliminate relevant material.

Table 16.3 Electronic Search Tips

If You Find Too Many Sources on Your Topic	If You Find Insufficient Information on Your Topic
• Use a subject search instead of a keyword search. • Add additional words to your search. • Use a more precise vocabulary to describe your topic. • Use an advanced search to restrict your findings by date, format, language, or other options.	• Use a keyword instead of a subject. • Eliminate words from your search terms. • Try truncated forms of your keyword. • Use different words to describe your topic. • Check the spelling of each term you type.

Using Truncation

Another useful search strategy employs **truncation**. With this technique, you drop the ending of a word or term and replace it with a symbol, which indicates you want to retrieve records containing any term that begins the same way as your term. Truncation symbols vary with the catalog or database. The question mark (?), asterisk (*), and pound sign (#) are frequently used. Truncation is useful when you want to retrieve both the plural and singular forms of a word or any word for which you are not sure of the ending. For example, in systems using the asterisk, the term "*home school**" would return all the records that have terms such as *home school, home schooling, home schools, home schooled,* or *home schoolers.*

Table 16.3 offers suggestions for expanding or narrowing an electronic search.

Finding Books: Using the Online Library Catalog

Look again at the sample catalog listing for a book on home schooling:

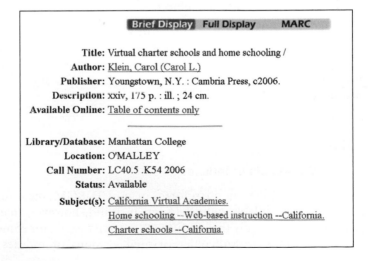

<table>
<tr><td colspan="3" align="center">Brief Display   Full Display   MARC</td></tr>
</table>

Title: Virtual charter schools and home schooling /
Author: Klein, Carol (Carol L.)
Publisher: Youngstown, N.Y. : Cambria Press, c2006.
Description: xxiv, 175 p. : ill. ; 24 cm.
Available Online: Table of contents only

Library/Database: Manhattan College
Location: O'MALLEY
Call Number: LC40.5 .K54 2006
Status: Available

Subject(s): California Virtual Academies.
Home schooling --Web-based instruction --California.
Charter schools --California.

Whether you perform your search by author, title, subject, or keyword, each record you find will provide the following standard information.

1. *Title:* The title appears exactly as it does on the title page of the book, except that only the first word and proper nouns and adjectives are capitalized.

2. *Author:* The author's name usually appears last name first, sometimes followed by birth and (if applicable) death dates. For books with multiple authors, the record includes an author entry under each author's name.

3. *Publication information:* The place of publication, the publisher, and the year of publication are listed. If the book was published simultaneously in the United States and abroad, both places and publishers are indicated.

4. *Physical description:* This section provides information about the book's page length and size. A roman numeral indicates the number of pages devoted to front matter (such as a preface, table of contents, and acknowledgments).

5. *Location:* While a call number explains where a book is shelved in relation to other books, large library systems might be divided across more than one physical location. If that's the case, the name of that location will be listed.

6. *Call number:* Most college libraries use the Library of Congress system, and most public libraries use the Dewey decimal system. Call numbers provide an exact location for every book in the library, and because they are assigned according to subject classifications, they group together books on the same topic. When you go to the stacks to locate the book, therefore, always browse for other useful material on the shelves around it.

7. *Status:* Most catalogs will tell you whether a book is on the shelf, already checked out, lost, and so on. Some will allow you to reserve or hold a book.

8. *Subject headings:* These headings indicate how the book is categorized in terms of subject. Often, these subject headings are active links; clicking on them will bring up a list of other books on the same subject.

If your search for books in your college library turns up little that is useful to you, do not give up. Most college libraries belong to one or more **interlibrary networks** that can be useful to you in your search. Known by different names in different regions, these networks allow you to search in the catalogs of colleges and universities in your area and across the country.

Examples of records in online catalogs are shown on pp. 466 and 475.

Finding Articles

Using Periodical Databases or Indexes

Traditionally available in print, in microform, or on CD-ROM, most major periodical indexes are now available online. (Keep in mind, however, that some of these online databases cover only the last fifteen to twenty years; for some research projects, you may need to consult older printed versions of indexes as well.)

Some of the general databases serve mainly as indexes. Others, however, include **abstracts** or short summaries of articles, and some give you access to the **full text** of articles.

On the following pages you will find a list of some of the most common periodical databases, divided into three categories: general, newspaper, and subject-specific. Your college library will likely subscribe to some but not all of these databases. Note that many online databases listed here are delivered via one of three major online reference database services — EBSCOhost, InfoTrac, and WilsonWeb — which allow you to search multiple databases in a single search. Many libraries also offer access to a separate **federated search engine**, which allows you to search multiple databases across database services.

General guidelines for searching online databases are given on pp. 466–69. Because online databases contain so much information, however, you may want to consult with a librarian to develop an efficient search strategy.

General Databases and Indexes. These indexes are a good place to start your research because they cover a broad range of subjects in popular periodicals and scholarly journals.

Academic OneFile (InfoTrac) provides access to thousands of peer-reviewed journals.

Academic Search Premier (EBSCOhost) provides full text for thousands of academic journals, including many peer-reviewed titles.

CQ Researcher offers an overview, background, and bibliography on newsworthy or controversial topics (e.g., terrorism, global warming, stem-cell research) in public health, social trends, criminal justice, international affairs, education, the environment, technology, and the economy.

General OneFile (InfoTrac) offers full text for thousands of general-interest magazines.

JSTOR offers a high-quality, interdisciplinary archive of over 1,000 academic journals across the humanities, social sciences, and sciences.

MasterFILE (EBSCOhost) provides full text for general-interest, business, consumer health, general science, and multicultural periodicals.

Project Muse offers scholarly journals in the arts and humanities, social sciences, and mathematics; currently the database includes hundreds of journals.

The example from *Academic Search Premier* in Figure 16.4 on the next page is typical of entries found in general periodical databases.

Newspaper Databases and Indexes. Newspapers provide useful information for research topics in such areas as foreign affairs, economics, public opinion, and social trends. Libraries used to photograph newspapers and store them in miniature form on microfilm (reels) or microfiche (cards) that must be placed in viewing machines to be read. Now much of this material is available online. Newspaper indexes such as the *Los*

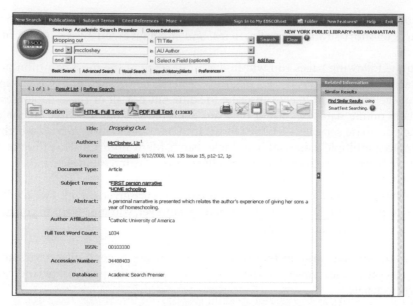

Figure 16.4 *Academic Search Premier* **Database Search Result**

Angeles Times Index, New York Times Index, and *London Times Index,* which are available online as well as in print, can help you locate specific articles on your topic. Many include the full text of articles going back a number of years. Your library may also subscribe to the following:

Alt-PressWatch offers full-text access to selected newspapers, magazines, and journals of the alternative and independent press.

LexisNexis provides full-text access to documents from thousands of news, business, legal, medical, and reference publications, including U.S. and international newspapers, magazines, wire services, newsletters, trade journals, company and industry analyst reports, and broadcast transcripts.

NewsBank provides full-text newspaper articles from the *New York Times, Los Angeles Times, Washington Post, Atlanta Journal-Constitution, Chicago Tribune, Christian Science Monitor,* and many others. *NewsBank* is especially useful for local and regional (United States) papers.

Newspaper Source provides cover-to-cover full text for many national and international newspapers and selective full text for hundreds of regional (U.S.) newspapers, in addition to full-text television and radio news transcripts.

Proquest Newspapers provides full-text access to articles from U.S. national newspapers, international English-language newspapers, and selected regional/state newspapers.

Subject-Specific Databases and Indexes. These databases list or summarize articles from periodicals devoted to specific fields of study. Here is a list of some of the more common subject-specific periodical databases:

America: History and Life indexes a large number of journals from 1910 to the present, covering the history and culture of the United States and Canada, from prehistory to the present.

Business Source Premier (EBSCOhost) provides full text for thousands of marketing, management, MIS, POM, accounting, finance, and economics journals.

ERIC (Educational Resource Information Center) contains links to hundreds of thousands of full-text documents and more than one million records of education-related literature, including coverage of conferences, meetings, government documents, theses, dissertations, reports, audiovisual media, bibliographies, directories, books, and monographs.

Humanities Index offers full text (starting 1995) plus abstracts and bibliographic indexes (starting 1984) of scholarly sources in the humanities.

MEDLINE allows users to search abstracts from thousands of current biomedical journals covering the fields of medicine, nursing, dentistry, veterinary medicine, the health care system, pre-clinical sciences, and more.

MLA (Modern Language Association) International Bibliography indexes thousands of English language and foreign periodicals as well as books, book chapters, and dissertations dating back to the 1920s.

PAIS International indexes articles, books, conference proceedings, government documents, book chapters, and statistical directories in the area of public affairs. Topics include business, government, international relations, banking, environment, health, social sciences, demographics, law and legislation, political science, public administration, finance, agriculture, education, and statistics.

PsycINFO contains millions of citations to and summaries of peer-reviewed articles and other documents in the field of psychology dating as far back as the early 1800s.

Science Full Text Select offers full text, indexing, and abstracts from hundreds of journals in the fields of zoology, biology, earth science, environmental science, genetics, botany, and chemistry.

Social Sciences Full Text covers concepts, trends, opinions, theories, and methods from hundreds of English-language periodicals in the social sciences.

Distinguishing Scholarly Journals and Popular Magazines

Although they are both called periodicals, journals and magazines have important differences.

Journals publish articles written by experts in a particular field of study, frequently professors or researchers in academic institutions. Journals are usually specialized in their subject focus, research oriented, and peer reviewed (that is, extensively reviewed by specialists) prior to publication. They are intended to be read by experts and students conducting research. **Magazines,** in contrast, usually publish articles written to entertain and educate the general public.

Journals contain a great deal of original research. For example, a scientist might publish an article in a medical journal about the results of a new treatment protocol for breast cancer. Articles in magazines report on and summarize original research to inform the general public about new and interesting developments in scientific and other areas of research. In most college courses requiring research, original research published in journals is preferred to the accounts of research and other trends published in magazines. For this reason, it is important to note that many periodical databases will let you limit a search to scholarly journals.

Table 16.4 below summarizes some of the important differences between scholarly journals and popular magazines.

Locating Periodicals in the Library

Let us say that you have identified a promising magazine, journal, or newspaper article in a periodical index or database. If that article is not available in full text electronically, you must go to the library's online catalog or online periodicals list to learn whether the library subscribes to the periodical, whether the issue is available, and, if so, where you can find it. No library can subscribe to every periodical, so as you go through indexes and databases, be sure to identify more articles than you actually need. This will save you from having to repeat your search later.

Although every library arranges its print periodicals differently, recent issues are usually arranged alphabetically by title on open shelves. Older issues may be bound like books or filmed and available in microform.

Table 16.4 How to Distinguish a Scholarly Journal from a Popular Magazine

Scholarly Journal	*Popular Magazine*
• It is usually published once every other month or four times per year.	• It is published frequently, usually once a week or once a month.
• The authors of articles have Ph.D. or academic affiliations after their names.	• The authors of articles are journalists or reporters.
• Many articles have more than one author.	• Most articles have a single author but may quote experts.
• A short summary (abstract) of an article may appear on the first page.	• A headline or engaging description may precede the article.
• Most articles are fairly long, five to twenty pages.	• Most of the articles are fairly short, one to five pages.
• The articles may include charts, tables, figures, and quotations from other scholarly sources.	• The articles have color pictures and sidebar boxes.
• The articles have a bibliography (list of references to other books and articles) at the end.	• The articles do not include a bibliography.

Suppose you want to look up the following article from the *Journal for the Scientific Study of Religion* that you found indexed in *Academic Search Premier:*

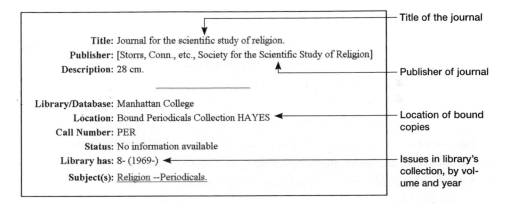

Since the article is not available online, you need to do a bit more digging to find a copy. You start with the library's online catalog or online periodicals list, searching by the title of the journal, and you find the following record:

Title: Journal for the scientific study of religion.	── Title of the journal
Publisher: [Storrs, Conn., etc., Society for the Scientific Study of Religion]	
Description: 28 cm.	── Publisher of journal
Library/Database: Manhattan College	
Location: Bound Periodicals Collection HAYES	── Location of bound copies
Call Number: PER	
Status: No information available	
Library has: 8- (1969-)	── Issues in library's collection, by volume and year
Subject(s): Religion --Periodicals.	

From this record, you would learn that the library does subscribe to the journal and that you could locate the December 2008 issue in the library's periodicals collection. If your library does not subscribe to a journal you are looking for, consult a reference librarian for other ways to access it (interlibrary loan, for example).

Finding Government and Statistical Information

Federal, state, and local governments now make many of their publications and reference services available directly through the Web, though most college libraries still maintain print collections of government publications. Ask a reference librarian for assistance in locating governmental sources and other sources of statistical information in the library or on the Web. The following sources can be useful in finding information on political subjects and national trends:

> ***Congressional Quarterly (CQ.com)*** is a news and analysis service that includes up-to-date summaries of congressional committee actions, congressional votes, and executive branch activities as well as overviews of current policy discussions and other activities of the federal government.

Google U.S. Government Search (www.google.com/unclesam) is a search engine for federal, state, and local government material.

GPO Access, a service of the U.S. Government Printing Office, provides free electronic access to documents produced by the federal government.

Statistical Abstract of the United States is a publication of the Bureau of the Census, providing a variety of social, economic, and political statistics from 1878 to the present, including tables, graphs, charts, and references to additional sources of information.

WorldAlmanac presents information on a variety of subjects drawn from many sources, including a chronology of the year, climatological data, and lists of inventions and awards.

Finding Other Library Sources

Libraries hold vast amounts of useful materials other than books, periodicals, and government documents. Some of the following may be appropriate for your research:

- *Digital collections:* Materials that have been scanned or otherwise saved in digital format and made available online
- *Special collections:* Manuscripts, rare books, and materials of local interest
- *Audio collections:* Records, audiotapes, music CDs, readings, and speeches
- *Video collections:* Slides, filmstrips, videotapes, and DVDs
- *Art collections:* Drawings, paintings, and engravings
- *Computer resources:* Interactive computer programs that combine text, video, and audio resources in history, literature, business, and other disciplines

Determining the Most Promising Sources

As you search for sources in your library's catalog and databases, you will discover many seemingly relevant books and articles. How do you decide which ones to track down? You may have little to go on but author, title, date, and publisher or periodical name, but these details actually provide useful clues. Look again, for example, at the online catalog listing for *Virtual Charter Schools and Home Schooling* (p. 469). Note that the publication date, 2006, is fairly recent. From the subject headings, you can see that the geographic focus of the book is California. Finally, from the title and subject headings, you can see that the book emphasizes online (or virtual) learning.

Now look at Figure 16.5, which shows search results from *ERIC*, an electronic periodical database of education journals, searched through EBSCOhost. The search on the term *home schooling* yielded 689 articles. Looking just at the titles of the article and the journal, you can surmise that the first article is a government publication on home schooling in Pennsylvania between 2006 and 2007; the second expresses a librarian's point of view; and the third and fourth address different technological

Figure 16.5 ERIC Database Search Results

aspects of the issue. With such variety in only the first four articles, you will clearly have to be careful to stay focused. In fact, it might be a good idea at this point to limit your search by adding another search term.

Each entry contains the information that you will need to locate it in a library, and some databases provide links to the full text of articles from selected periodicals. Here is what each piece of information means:

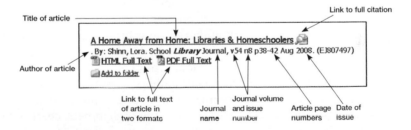

Always consider the following points when deciding whether you should track down a particular source:

- **Relevance to your topic:** Examine the title, subtitle, subject headings, and abstract (if provided) to determine whether the source addresses your topic.

- **Publication date:** How recent is the source? For current controversies, emerging trends, and scientific or technological developments, consult recent material. For historical or biographical topics, start with present-day perspectives but consider exploring older sources that offer authoritative perspectives.

- *Description:* Does the length of the source indicate a brief treatment of the topic or an extended treatment? Does the work include illustrations that may illuminate concepts discussed? Does the source include a bibliography that could lead you to other works or an index that could give you an overview of the text?

From among the sources that look promising, select publications that seem to address different aspects of your topic or to approach it from different perspectives. Avoid selecting sources that are mostly by the same author, from the same publisher, or in the same journal.

For a discussion of periodical indexes, see pp. 470–71.

Using the Web for Research

In this section, we discuss the open Web — the open-access areas of the Internet that exclude proprietary subscription services like the databases available through your library. By now, most of you are familiar with searching the Web. This section introduces you to some tools and strategies that will help you use it more efficiently.

Keep the following concerns and guidelines in mind:

- *Many significant electronic sources require a paid subscription or other fees.* Electronic periodical indexes, full-text article databases, and other valuable electronic resources are often available only by subscription. If your college subscribes to these resources, your tuition grants you access to them. For these reasons (as well as the ones discussed in this section), you should plan to use the resources available via your library's Web site for much of your electronic research.

- *Open-access Web sources may be less reliable than print sources or electronic sources to which your library or campus subscribes.* Because it is relatively easy for anyone to publish on the Web, judging the reliability of online information is a special concern. Depending on your topic, purpose, and audience, the sources you find on the Web may not be as credible or authoritative as print sources or subscription electronic sources, which have usually been screened by publishers, editors, librarians, and authorities on the topic. For some topics, most of what you find on the Web may be written by highly biased or amateur authors, so you will need to balance or supplement these sources with information from print sources. When in doubt about the reliability of an online source for a particular assignment, check with your instructor. (See Evaluating Sources on pp. 482–85 for more specific suggestions.)

- *Web sources may be less stable than print sources or the electronic sources to which your library or campus subscribes.* A Web site that existed last week may no longer be available today, or its content may have changed.

- *Web sources must be documented.* You will need to follow appropriate conventions for quoting, paraphrasing, summarizing, and documenting the online sources you use, just as you do for print sources. Because a Web source can change or disappear quickly, be sure to record the information for the working-bibliography entry when you first find the source. Whenever possible, download and print out the source to preserve it. Make sure your download or printout includes all the items of information required for the entry, or at least all those you can find. (See Figure 16.6 for guidelines on what to record for an Internet source.)

Citing Internet sources using MLA style is discussed in Chapter 17, pp. 497–509; APA style is discussed on pp. 509–16.

Finding the Best Information Online

Search tools like Google and Yahoo! are important resources for searching the Web for information on your topic. To use these tools effectively, you should understand their features, strengths, and limitations.

Search engines like Google are based on keywords. They are simply computer programs that scan the open Web — or that part of the Web that is in the particular search engine's database — looking for the keyword(s) you have entered. Search engines are useful whenever you have a good idea of the appropriate keywords for your topic or if you are not sure under what category the topic falls.

Author(s) of work	
Title of work	
Title of site	
Sponsor of site	
URL (address)	
Date of electronic publication or of latest update	
Date you accessed source	
Publication information for print version of work (if any)	
Notes	

Figure 16.6 Information for Working Bibliography — Internet Sources

Google deserves special mention among search engines for the pace at which it has been evolving. In addition to its general Web search, at the time of this writing Google offers subsearches of images, maps, videos, and many other categories of potentially useful material. Of particular interest to the academic writer are Google Scholar, which searches peer-reviewed articles from forty-five scholarly databases including JSTOR, Project Muse, Wiley, Sage, etc., and Google Book Search, which searches a wide range of general-interest and scholarly books. Both Google Scholar and Google Book Search offer overviews and, in some cases, full text of indexed material.

Subject directories like Yahoo! are based on categories, like the subject headings in a library catalog or periodical index. Beginning with a menu of general subjects, you click on increasingly narrow subjects (for example, going from Science to Biology to Genetics to DNA Mapping), until you reach either a list of specific Web sites or a point where you have to do a keyword search within the narrowest subject you have chosen. Subject directories can help quickly narrow your search to those parts of the Web that are likely to be most productive and thus avoid keyword searches that produce hundreds or thousands of results.

Always click on the link called Help, Hints, or Tips on a search tool's home page to find out more about the recognized commands and advanced-search techniques for that specific search tool. Most search engines allow searches using the Boolean operators discussed on pp. 467–68. (In fact, Google automatically assumes an "AND" between multiple search terms.) Most recognize the use of quotation marks to limit results to pages containing an exact phrase. Many also let you limit a search to specific dates, languages, or other criteria.

As with searches of library catalogs and databases, the success of a Web search depends to a great extent on the keywords you choose. Remember that many different words often describe the same topic. If your topic is "ecology," for example, you may find information under the keywords *ecosystem, environment, pollution,* and *endangered species*, as well as a number of other related keywords, depending on the focus of your research. When you find a source that seems promising, be sure to create a bookmark for the Web page so that you can return to it easily later on.

No matter how precise your keywords are, search engines can be unreliable, and you may not find the best available resources. You might instead begin your search at the Web site of a relevant and respected organization. If you want photos of constellations, for example, go to the NASA Web page. If you want public laws, go to a government Web page like GPO Access. In addition, be sure to supplement your Internet research with other sources from your library, including books, reference works, and articles from appropriate periodicals.

The following open-access sources can also be of use to you in some research projects:

American Memory from the Library of Congress (memory.loc.gov) is a gateway to the Library of Congress's vast digitized collection of American historical and cultural materials, including manuscripts, prints, photographs, posters, maps, sound recordings, motion pictures, books, pamphlets, and sheet music. Comprising more than 9 million items, American Memory is organized into more than 100 thematic collections based on format, subject matter, and other criteria.

Project Gutenberg (gutenberg.org), a pioneer in the development of and distribution of e-books, was founded in 1971 and now offers over 36,000 digitized public-domain texts.

Wikimedia Commons (commons.wikimedia.org/wiki/Main_Page) consists of a collection of over 3.5 million images and other media that are in the public domain.

WorldCat.org is an enormous online network of library content and services that allows you to search for books, DVDs, CDs, audiobooks, research articles, and other content and either download them directly or locate them in a library nearby.

YouTube (youtube.com), a phenomenally popular video-sharing site, offers some resources of interest to academic writers. Be aware that YouTube is an open site that attracts a great deal of material of questionable quality. Also, remember that any YouTube material you do wish to introduce in your projects must be fully cited.

Two other sources of online information are **blogs** and **RSS**. A blog, or Web log, is a Web site, often based on a particular topic, that is maintained by an individual or organization and updated on a regular basis, often many times a day. Blogs may contain postings written by the sponsor(s) of the site; information such as news articles, press releases, and commentary from other sites; and comments posted by readers. Blogs are usually organized chronologically, with the newest post at the top. Because they are not subjected to the same editorial scrutiny as published books or periodical articles and may reflect just one person's opinions and biases, it is a good idea to find several blogs from multiple perspectives about your subject. Some Web sites, such as Blogwise (www.blogwise .com) and Blogger (www.blogger.com), provide directories and search functions to help you find blogs on a particular topic. You can search the content of literally millions of blog posts by using blog search engines such as technorati.com or blogsearch.google.com.

If you are researching a very current topic and need to follow constantly updated news sites and blogs, you can use a program called an **aggregator**, which obtains news automatically from many sources and assembles it through a process called RSS (Really Simple Syndication). Using an aggregator, you can scan the information from a variety of sources by referring to just one Web page or e-mail and then click on links to the news stories to read further. Many aggregators, such as NetNewsWire, NewsGator, and SharpReader, are available as software that you can download to your computer; others are Web sites you can customize to your own preferences, such as Bloglines (www.bloglines.com) and NewsIsFree (www.newsisfree.com). Google Alerts offers Google account holders updates on news, Web pages, blogs, and videos relevant to key terms entered into their Alerts homepage.

Using E-mail and Online Communities for Research

You may find it possible to use your computer to do research in ways other than those already discussed in this chapter. In particular, if you can find out the e-mail address of an expert on your topic, you may want to contact the person and ask whether he or she would agree to a brief online (or telephone) interview. In addition, several kinds of electronic communities available on the Internet may possibly be helpful. Many Web sites consist of or incorporate tools known as **message boards**, in which anyone who registers may post messages to and receive them from other members. Older Internet servers known as news servers also provide access to message boards or variants called **newsgroups**. Another kind of community, **mailing lists**, are groups of people who subscribe to and receive e-mail messages shared among all the members simultaneously. **Chat rooms** allow users to meet together at the same time in a shared message space. Finally, **wikis** — of which Wikipedia is the best known example — offer content of various kinds contributed and modified collaboratively by a community of users. These can be very useful for background information, but be aware that most instructors will not accept information from wikis as sources for papers.

These different kinds of online communities often focus on a specific field of shared interest, and the people who frequent them are sometimes working professionals or academics with expertise in topics that are obscure or difficult to research otherwise. Such experts are often willing to answer both basic and advanced questions and will sometimes consent to an e-mail or telephone interview. Even if they are not authorities in the field, online community members may stimulate your thinking about the topic in new directions or save you a large amount of research time by pointing you to resources that might otherwise have taken you quite a while to uncover. Many communities provide some kind of indexing or search mechanism so that you can look for "threads" (conversation) related to your topic.

As with other sources, however, it is important to evaluate the credibility and reliability of online communities. Also be aware that while most communities welcome guests and newcomers, others may perceive your questions as intrusive or unwanted. What may seem new and exciting to you may be old news for veterans. Finally, remember that some online communities are more active than others; survey the dates of posts and frequency of activity to determine whether a given group is still lively or has gone defunct.

For most topics, you will be able to find a variety of related newsgroups; www .groups.google.com catalogs many of them (and allows you to start your own). For mailing lists, you have to register for a subscription to the list. Remember that unless a digest option (an option that compiles messages into one daily or weekly e-mail) is available, each subscription means you will be receiving a large amount of e-mail, so think about the implications before you sign up.

Evaluating Sources

From the beginning of your library and Internet search, you should evaluate potential sources that you have tracked down to determine which ones you should take the time to examine more closely and then which of these you should use in your essay. Obviously, you must decide which sources provide information relevant to the topic.

But you must also decide how credible or trustworthy the sources are. Just because a book or an essay appears in print or online does not necessarily mean that an author's information or opinions are reliable.

Selecting Relevant Sources

Begin your evaluation of sources by narrowing your working bibliography to the most relevant works. Consider them in terms of scope, date of publication, and viewpoint.

Scope and Approach

To decide how relevant a particular source is to your topic, you need to examine the source in depth. Do not depend on title alone, for it may be misleading. If the source is a book, check its table of contents and index to see how many pages are devoted to the precise subject you are exploring. In most cases, you will want an in-depth, not a superficial, treatment of the subject. Read the preface or introduction to a book or the abstract or opening paragraphs of an article, as well as any biographical information given about the author, to determine the author's basic approach to the subject or special way of looking at it. As you attend to these elements, consider the following questions:

- Does the source provide a general or specialized view? General sources are helpful early in your research, but you will also need the authority or up-to-date coverage of specialized sources. Extremely specialized works, however, may be too technical.
- Is the source long enough to provide adequate detail?
- Is the source written for general readers? Specialists? Advocates? Critics?
- Is the author an expert on the topic? Does the author's way of looking at the topic support or challenge your own views? (The fact that an author's viewpoint challenges your own does not mean that you should reject the author as a source, as you will see from the discussion on viewpoints.)
- Is the information in the source substantiated elsewhere? Does its approach seem to be comparable to, or a significant challenge to, the approaches of other credible sources?

Date of Publication

Although you should always consult the most up-to-date sources available on your subject, older sources often establish the principles, theories, and data on which later work is based and may provide a useful perspective for evaluating it. If older works are considered authoritative, you may want to become familiar with them. To determine which sources are authoritative, note the ones that are cited most often in encyclopedia articles, bibliographies, and recent works on the subject. If your source is on the Web, consider whether it has been regularly updated.

Viewpoint

Your sources should represent multiple viewpoints on the subject. Just as you would not depend on a single author for all of your information, so you do not want to use only authors who belong to the same school of thought. (For suggestions on determining authors' viewpoints, see the following section on Identifying Bias.)

Using sources that represent a variety of different viewpoints is especially important when developing an argument for one of the essay assignments in Chapters 5–7. During the invention work in those chapters, you may want to research what others have said about your subject to see what positions have been staked out and what arguments have been made. You will then be able to define the issue more carefully, collect arguments supporting your position, and anticipate arguments opposing it.

Identifying Bias

One of the most important aspects of evaluating a source is identifying any bias in its treatment of the subject. Although the word *bias* may sound accusatory, most writing is not neutral or objective and does not try or claim to be. Authors come to their subjects with particular viewpoints. In using sources, you must consider carefully how these viewpoints are reflected in the writing and how they affect the way authors present their arguments.

Although the text of the source will give you the most precise indication of the author's viewpoint, you can often get a good idea of it by looking at the preface or introduction or at the sources the author cites. When you examine a reference, you can often determine the general point of view it represents by considering the following elements.

Title

Does the title or subtitle indicate the text's bias? Watch for loaded words or confrontational phrasing.

Author

What is the author's professional title or affiliation? What is the author's perspective? Is the author in favor of something or at odds with it? What has persuaded the author to take this stance? How might the author's professional affiliation affect his or her perspective? What is the author's tone? Information on the author may be available in the book, article, or Web site itself or in biographical sources available in the library. You could also try entering the author's name into a search engine and see what you learn from sites that discuss him or her.

Presentation of Argument

Almost every written work asserts a point of view or makes an argument for something the author considers important. To determine this position and the reason behind it,

For more detail on these argumentative strategies, see Chapter 13.

look for the main point. What evidence does the author provide as support for this point? Is the evidence from authoritative sources? Is the evidence persuasive? Does the author make concessions to or refute opposing arguments?

Publication Information

Is the book published by a commercial publisher, a corporation, a government agency, or an interest group, or is it self-published? Is the Web site sponsored by a business, a professional group, a private organization, an educational institution, a government agency, or an individual? What is the publisher's or sponsor's position on the topic? Is the author funded by or affiliated with the publisher or sponsor? If you cannot determine the sponsor of a Web site, it is very likely not a credible source.

Editorial Slant

What kind of periodical published the article — popular, academic, alternative? If you found the article on a Web site, is the site maintained by a commercial or an academic sponsor? Does the article provide links to other Web resources? For periodicals, knowing some background about the publisher can help to determine bias because all periodicals have their own editorial slants. Where the periodical's name does not indicate its bias, reference sources may help you determine this information. Some of the most common are the following:

Encyclopedia of Associations (called *Associations Unlimited* online) is a directory of nonprofit voluntary membership organizations, such as professional societies, trade associations, labor unions, and cultural and religious organizations.

Gale Directory of Publications and Broadcast Media is a useful source providing descriptive information on newsletters, newspapers, and periodicals. Entries often include an indication of intended audience and political or other bias.

Serials Directory (EBSCOhost) offers up-to-date bibliographic information for popular U.S. and international serials from tens of thousands of publishers.

Ulrich's Periodicals Directory is an international directory of hundreds of thousands of current magazines, journals, annuals, irregular publications, and newspapers, as well as nearly 50,000 publications discontinued since 1979.

17

●●●● **Using Sources**

In your college writing, you will be expected to use and acknowledge secondary sources — books, articles, interviews, Web sites, computer bulletin boards, lectures, and other print and nonprint materials — in addition to your own ideas and insights.

When you do use material from another source, you need to acknowledge the source, usually by citing the author and page or date in your text and including a list of works cited or references at the end of your essay. Failure to acknowledge sources constitutes *plagiarism,* a serious transgression. By citing sources correctly, you give appropriate credit to the originator of the words and ideas you are using, offer your readers the information they need to consult those sources directly, and build your own credibility.

This chapter provides guidelines for using sources effectively and acknowledging them accurately. It includes model citations for both the Modern Language Association (MLA) and the American Psychological Association (APA) documentation styles and presents a sample researched essay that follows the MLA format.

Acknowledging Sources

The only types of information that do not require acknowledgment are common knowledge (John F. Kennedy was assassinated in Dallas), facts widely available in many sources (U.S. presidents used to be inaugurated on March 4 rather than January 20), well-known quotations ("To be or not to be / That is the question"), or material you created or gathered yourself, such as photographs that you took or data from surveys that you conducted. Remember that you need to acknowledge the source of any visual (photograph, table, chart, graph, diagram, drawing, map, screen shot) that you did not create yourself or of any information that you used to create your own visual. (You should also request permission from the source of a visual if your essay is going to be posted online without password protection.) When in doubt about whether you need to acknowledge a source, do so.

The documentation guidelines later in this chapter present two styles for citing sources, MLA and APA. Whichever style you use, the most important thing is that your readers be able to tell where words or ideas that are not your own begin and end. You can accomplish this most readily by taking and transcribing notes carefully, by placing parenthetical source citations correctly, and by separating your words from those

486

of the source with **signal phrases** such as "According to Smith," "Peters claims," and "As Olmos asserts." (When you cite a source for the first time in a signal phrase, you may use the author's full name; after that, use just the last name.)

Avoiding Plagiarism

Writers — students and professionals alike — occasionally fail to acknowledge sources properly. The word **plagiarism**, which derives from the Latin word for "kidnapping," refers to the unacknowledged use of another's words, ideas, or information. Students sometimes mistakenly assume that plagiarizing occurs only when another writer's exact words are used without acknowledgment. In fact, plagiarism also applies to such diverse forms of expression as musical compositions and visual images as well as ideas and statistics. Therefore, keep in mind that you must indicate the source of any borrowed information or ideas you use in your essay, whether you have paraphrased, summarized, or quoted directly from the source or have reproduced it or referred to it in some other way.

Remember especially the need to document electronic sources fully and accurately. Perhaps because it is so easy to access and distribute text and visuals online and to copy material from one electronic document and paste it into another, some students do not realize, or may forget, that information, ideas, and images from electronic sources require acknowledgment in even more detail than those from print sources (and are often easier to detect as plagiarism if they are not acknowledged).

Some people plagiarize simply because they do not know the conventions for using and acknowledging sources. If you are unfamiliar with these conventions, this chapter makes clear how to incorporate sources into your writing and how to acknowledge your use of those sources. Others plagiarize because they keep sloppy notes and thus fail to distinguish between their own and their sources' ideas. If you keep a working bibliography and careful notes, you will not make this serious mistake.

Another reason some people plagiarize is that they feel intimidated by the writing task or the deadline. If you experience this anxiety about your work, speak to your instructor. Do not run the risk of failing a course or being expelled from your college because of plagiarism.

If you are confused about what is and what is not plagiarism, be sure to ask your instructor.

For more on keeping a working bibliography, see Chapter 16, pp. 462–64.

Quoting, Paraphrasing, and Summarizing

Writers use sources by quoting directly, by paraphrasing, and by summarizing. This section provides guidelines for deciding when to use each of these three methods and for doing so effectively. Note that all examples in this section follow MLA style for in-text citations, which is explained in detail on pp. 497–500.

Deciding Whether to Quote, Paraphrase, or Summarize

As a general rule, quote only in these situations: (1) when the wording of the source is particularly memorable or vivid or expresses a point so well that you cannot improve it, (2) when the words of reliable and respected authorities would lend support to your position, (3) when you wish to cite an author whose opinions challenge or vary greatly from those of other experts, or (4) when you are going to discuss the source's choice of words. Paraphrase passages whose details you wish to use but whose language is not particularly striking. Summarize any long passages whose main points you wish to record as support for a point you are making.

Quoting

Quotations should duplicate the source exactly. If the source has an error, copy it and add the notation *sic* (Latin for "thus") in brackets immediately after the error to indicate that it is not your error but your source's:

> According to a recent newspaper article, "Plagirism [sic] is a problem among
> journalists and scholars as well as students" (Berensen 62).

However, you can change quotations for the following purposes, as long as you signal your changes appropriately: (1) to emphasize particular words, (2) to omit irrelevant information, (3) to insert information necessary for clarity, or (4) to make the quotation conform grammatically to your sentence. Note that "(Berensen 62)" represents a proper MLA-style in-text citation. For explanation of the rules for in-text citations, see pp. 497–500.

Using Italics for Emphasis. You may italicize any words in the quotation that you want to emphasize; add a semicolon and the words *emphasis added* (in regular type, not italicized or underlined) to the parenthetical citation.

> In her 2001 exposé of the struggles of the working class, Ehrenreich writes, "The
> wages Winn-Dixie is offering--*$6 and a couple of dimes to start with*--are not enough,
> I decide, to compensate for this indignity" (14; emphasis added).

Using Ellipsis Marks for Omissions. A writer may decide to omit words from a quotation because they are not relevant to the point being made. When you omit words from within a quotation, you must use ellipsis marks — three spaced periods (. . .) — in place of the missing words. When the omission occurs within a sentence, include a space before the first ellipsis mark and after the closing mark.

> Hermione Roddice is described in Lawrence's *Women in Love* as a "woman of the new
> school, full of intellectuality and . . . nerve-worn with consciousness" (17).

When the omission falls at the end of a sentence, place a period *directly after* the final word of the sentence, followed by a space and three spaced ellipsis marks.

But Grimaldi's commentary contends that for Aristotle rhetoric, like dialectic, had "no limited and unique subject matter upon which it must be exercised. . . . Instead, rhetoric as an art transcends all specific disciplines and may be brought into play in them" (6).

A period plus ellipsis marks can indicate the omission of the rest of the sentence as well as whole sentences, paragraphs, or even pages.

When a parenthetical reference follows the ellipsis marks at the end of a sentence, place the three spaced periods after the quotation, and place the sentence period after the final parenthesis:

But Grimaldi's commentary contends that for Aristotle rhetoric, like dialectic, had "no limited and unique subject matter upon which it must be exercised. . . . Instead, rhetoric as an art transcends all specific disciplines . . ." (6).

When you quote only single words or phrases, you do not need to use ellipsis marks because it will be obvious that you have left out some of the original.

More specifically, Wharton's imagery of suffusing brightness transforms Undine before her glass into "some fabled creature whose home was in a beam of light" (21).

For the same reason, you need not use ellipsis marks if you omit the beginning of a quoted sentence unless the rest of the sentence begins with a capitalized word and still appears to be a complete sentence.

Using Brackets for Insertions or Changes. Use brackets around an insertion or a change needed to make a quotation conform grammatically to your sentence, such as a change in the form of a verb or pronoun or in the capitalization of the first word of the quotation. In this example from an essay on James Joyce's short story "Araby," the writer adapts Joyce's phrases "we played till our bodies glowed" and "shook music from the buckled harness" to fit the grammar of her sentences:

In the dark, cold streets during the "short days of winter," the boys must generate their own heat by "play[ing] till [their] bodies glowed." Music is "[shaken] from the buckled harness" as if it were unnatural, and the singers in the market chant nasally of "the troubles in our native land" (30).

You may also use brackets to add or substitute explanatory material in a quotation:

Guterson notes that among Native Americans in Florida, "education was in the home; learning by doing was reinforced by the myths and legends which repeated the basic value system of their [the Seminoles'] way of life" (159).

Some changes that make a quotation conform grammatically to another sentence may be made without any signal to readers: (1) A period at the end of a quotation may be changed to a comma if you are using the quotation within your own sentence, and (2) double quotation marks enclosing a quotation may be changed to single quotation marks when the quotation is enclosed within a longer quotation.

Integrating Quotations

Depending on its length, a quotation may be incorporated into your text by being enclosed in quotation marks or set off from your text in a block without quotation marks. In either case, be sure to integrate the quotation into the language of your essay.

In-Text Quotations

Incorporate brief quotations (no more than four typed lines of prose or three lines of poetry) into your text. You may place the quotation virtually anywhere in your sentence:

At the Beginning

"To live a life is not to cross a field," Sutherland, quoting Pasternak, writes at the beginning of her narrative (11).

In the Middle

Woolf begins and ends by speaking of the need of the woman writer to have "money and a room of her own" (4)--an idea that certainly spoke to Plath's condition.

At the End

In *The Second Sex*, Simone de Beauvoir describes such an experience as one in which the girl "becomes an object, and she sees herself as object" (378).

Divided by Your Own Words

"Science usually prefers the literal to the nonliteral term," Kinneavy writes, "--that is, figures of speech are often out of place in science" (177).

When you quote poetry within your text, use a slash (/) with spaces before and after to signal the end of each line of verse:

Alluding to St. Augustine's distinction between the City of God and the Earthly City, Lowell writes that "much against my will / I left the City of God where it belongs" (4-5).

Block Quotations

In the MLA style, use the block form for prose quotations of five or more typed lines and for poetry quotations of four or more lines. Indent the quotation an inch (ten character spaces) from the left margin, as shown in the following example.

In "A Literary Legacy from Dunbar to Baraka," Margaret Walker says of Paul Lawrence Dunbar's dialect poems:

> He realized that the white world in the United States tolerated his literary genius only because of his "jingles in a broken tongue," and they found the old "darky" tales and speech amusing and within the vein of folklore into

which they wished to classify all Negro life. This troubled Dunbar because he
realized that white America was denigrating him as a writer and as a man. (70)

In the APA style, use block form for quotations of forty words or more. Indent the
block quotation one-half inch (five to seven spaces), keeping your indents consistent
throughout your paper.

In a block quotation, double-space between lines just as you do in your text. *Do
not* enclose the passage within quotation marks. Use a colon to introduce a block
quotation, unless the context calls for another punctuation mark or none at all. When
quoting a single paragraph or part of one in the MLA style, do not indent the first line
of the quotation more than the rest. In quoting two or more paragraphs, indent the
first line of each paragraph an extra quarter inch (three spaces). If you are using the
APA style, the first line of subsequent paragraphs in the block quotation indents an
additional half inch or five to seven spaces from the block quotation indent.

Note that in MLA style the parenthetical page reference follows the period in block
quotations.

Introducing Quotations

Statements that introduce in-text quotations take a range of punctuation marks and
lead-in words. Here are some examples of ways writers typically introduce quotations.

Introducing a Quotation Using a Colon

A colon usually follows an independent clause placed before the quotation.

As George Williams notes, protection of white privilege is critical to patterns of discrimination: "Whenever a number of persons within a society have enjoyed for a considerable
period of time certain opportunities for getting wealth, for exercising power and authority,
and for successfully claiming prestige and social deference, there is a strong tendency for
these people to feel that these benefits are theirs 'by right'" (727).

Introducing a Quotation Using a Comma

A comma usually follows an introduction that incorporates the quotation in its sentence structure.

Similarly, Duncan Turner asserts, "As matters now stand, it is unwise to talk about
communication without some understanding of Burke" (259).

Introducing a Quotation Using that

No punctuation is generally needed with *that*, and no capital letter is used to begin the
quotation.

Noting this failure, Alice Miller asserts **that** "the reason for her despair was not her suffering
but the impossibility of communicating her suffering to another person" (255).

Punctuating within Quotations

Although punctuation within a quotation should reproduce the original, some adaptations may be necessary. Use single quotation marks for quotations within the quotation:

Original from David Guterson's Family Matters *(pages 16–17)*

E. D. Hirsch also recognizes the connection between family and learning, suggesting in his discussion of family background and academic achievement "that the significant part of our children's education has been going on outside rather than inside the schools."

Quoted Version

Guterson claims that E. D. Hirsch "also recognizes the connection between family and learning, suggesting in his discussion of family background and academic achievement 'that the significant part of our children's education has been going on outside rather than inside the schools'" (16-17).

If the quotation ends with a question mark or an exclamation point, retain the original punctuation:

"Did you think I loved you?" Edith later asks Dombey (566).

If a quotation ending with a question mark or an exclamation point concludes your sentence, retain the question mark or exclamation point, and put the parenthetical reference and sentence period outside the quotation marks:

Edith later asks Dombey, "Did you think I loved you?" (566).

Avoiding Grammatical Tangles

When you incorporate quotations into your writing, and especially when you omit words from quotations, you run the risk of creating ungrammatical sentences. Three common errors you should try to avoid are verb incompatibility, ungrammatical omissions, and sentence fragments.

Verb Incompatibility. When this error occurs, the verb form in the introductory statement is grammatically incompatible with the verb form in the quotation. When your quotation has a verb form that does not fit in with your text, it is usually possible to use just part of the quotation, thus avoiding verb incompatibility.

he describes seeing himself

▶ The narrator suggests his bitter disappointment when "~~I saw myself~~

"as a creature driven and derided by vanity" (35).

As this sentence illustrates, use the present tense when you refer to events in a literary work.

Ungrammatical Omission. Sometimes omitting text from a quotation leaves you with an ungrammatical sentence. Two ways of correcting the grammar are (1) adapting the quotation (with brackets) so that its parts fit together grammatically and (2) using only one part of the quotation.

▶ From the moment of the boy's arrival in Araby, the bazaar is presented as a

commercial enterprise: "I could not find any sixpenny entrance and . . .

hand[ed]
~~handing~~ a shilling to a weary-looking man" (34).
 ^

▶ From the moment of the boy's arrival in Araby, the bazaar is presented as a

He
commercial enterprise: "~~I~~ "could not find any sixpenny entrance ," and ~~...~~
 ^   ^
so had to pay a shilling to get in (34).
~~handing a shilling to a weary-looking man" (34).~~
 ^

Sentence Fragment. Sometimes when a quotation is a complete sentence, writers neglect the sentence that introduces the quote — for example, by forgetting to include a verb. Make sure that the quotation is introduced by a complete sentence.

                                        leads
▶ The girl's interest in the bazaar ~~leading~~ the narrator to make what amounts to a
                                         ^
sacred oath: "If I go . . . I will bring you something" (32).

Paraphrasing and Summarizing

In addition to quoting sources, writers have the option of paraphrasing or summarizing what others have written.

Paraphrasing. In a **paraphrase**, the writer restates all the relevant information from a passage, without any additional comments or any suggestion of agreement or disagreement with the source's ideas. A paraphrase is useful for recording details of the passage when the order of the details is important but the source's wording is not. Because all the details of the passage are included, a paraphrase is often about the same length as the original passage. Paraphrasing allows you to avoid quoting too much. Anyway, it is better to paraphrase than to quote ordinary material, where the author's way of expressing things is not worth special attention.

Here is a passage from a book on home schooling and an example of an acceptable paraphrase of it:

Original Source

Bruner and the discovery theorists have also illuminated conditions that apparently pave the way for learning. It is significant that these conditions are unique to each learner, so unique, in fact, that in many cases classrooms can't provide them. Bruner also contends that the more one discovers information in a great variety of circumstances, the more likely one is to develop the inner categories required to organize that information. Yet life at school, which is for the most part generic and predictable, daily keeps many children from the great variety of circumstances they need to learn well.

— David Guterson, *Family Matters: Why Homeschooling Makes Sense*, p. 172

Acceptable Paraphrase

According to Guterson, the "discovery theorists," particularly Bruner, have found that there seem to be certain conditions that help learning to take place. Because each individual requires different conditions, many children are not able to learn in the classroom. According to Bruner, when people can explore information in many different situations, they learn to classify and order what they discover. The general routine of the school day, however, does not provide children with the diverse activities and situations that would allow them to learn these skills (172).

Readers assume that some words in a paraphrase are taken from the source. Indeed, it would be nearly impossible for paraphrasers to avoid using any key terms from the source, and it would be counterproductive to try to do so, because the original and the paraphrase necessarily share the same information and concepts. Notice, though, that of the total of 86 words in the paraphrase, the paraphraser uses only a name (*Bruner*) and a few other key nouns and verbs (*discovery theorists, conditions, children, learn[ing], information, situations*) for which it would be awkward to substitute other words or phrases. If the paraphraser had wanted to use other, more distinctive language from the source — for example, the description of life at school as "generic and predictable" — these adjectives should have been enclosed in quotation marks. In fact, the paraphraser puts quotation marks around only one of the terms from the source: "discovery theorists," a technical term likely to be unfamiliar to readers.

Paraphrasers must, however, avoid borrowing too many words from a source and repeating the sentence structures of a source. Here is an unacceptable paraphrase of the first sentence in the Guterson passage:

Unacceptable Paraphrase: Too Many Borrowed Words and Phrases

Apparently, some conditions, which have been illuminated by Bruner and other discovery theorists, pave the way for people to learn.

If you compare the source's first sentence and the paraphrase of it, you will see that the paraphrase borrows almost all of its key language from the source sentence, including the entire phrase *pave the way for*. Even if you cite the source, this heavy borrowing would be considered plagiarism.

Here is another unacceptable paraphrase of the same sentence:

Unacceptable Paraphrase: Sentence Structure Repeated Too Closely

Bruner and other researchers have also identified circumstances that seem to ease the path to learning.

If you compare the source's first sentence and this paraphrase of it, you will see that the paraphraser has borrowed the phrases and clauses of the source and arranged them in an identical sequence, simply substituting synonyms for most of the key terms: *researchers* for *theorists, identified* for *illuminated, circumstances* for *conditions, seem to* for *apparently,* and *ease the path to* for *pave the way for.* This paraphrase would also be considered plagiarism.

Summarizing. Unlike a paraphrase, a **summary** presents only the main ideas of a source, leaving out examples and details.

Here is one student's summary of five pages from *Family Matters.* You can see at a glance how drastically summaries can condense information, in this case from five pages to five sentences. Depending on the summarizer's purpose, the five pages could be summarized in one sentence, the five sentences here, or two or three dozen sentences.

In looking at different theories of learning that discuss individual-based programs (such as home schooling) versus the public school system, Guterson describes the disagreements among "cognitivist" theorists. One group, the "discovery theorists," believes that individual children learn by creating their own ways of sorting the information they take in from their experiences. Schools should help students develop better ways of organizing new material, not just present them with material that is already categorized, as traditional schools do. "Assimilationist theorists," by contrast, believe that children learn by linking what they don't know to information they already know. These theorists claim that traditional schools help students learn when they present information in ways that allow children to fit the new material into categories they have already developed (171-75).

Summaries like this one are more than a dry list of main ideas from a source. They are instead a coherent, readable new text composed of the source's main ideas. Summaries provide balanced coverage of a source, following the same sequence of ideas and avoiding any hint of agreement or disagreement with them.

Documenting Sources

Although there is no universally accepted system for acknowledging sources, most documentation styles use parenthetical in-text citations keyed to a separate list of works cited or references. The information required in the in-text citations and the order and content of the works cited entries vary across academic disciplines. This section presents the basic features of two styles: the author-page system that is advocated by the Modern Language Association (MLA) and widely used in the humanities (for example, literature and history) and the author-year system that is advocated by the American Psychological Association (APA) and widely used in the social sciences (for example, psychology and economics).

In Part One of this book, you can find examples of student essays that follow the MLA style and the APA style. (See pp. 516–17 for a full list.) For more information about these documentation styles, consult the *MLA Handbook for Writers of Research Papers*, Seventh Edition (2009), or the *Publication Manual of the American Psychological Association*, Sixth Edition (2010).

Check with your instructor about which of these styles you should use or whether you should use some other style. A list of common documentation style manuals is provided in Table 17.1.

Table 17.1 Some Commonly Used Documentation Style Manuals

Subject	Style Manual	Online Source
General	*The Chicago Manual of Style.* 16th ed. 2010.	http://www.chicagomanualofstyle.org
	A Manual for Writers of Research Papers, Theses, and Dissertations. 7th ed. 2007.	http://www.turabian.org
Online sources	*Columbia Guide to Online Style.* 2nd ed. 2006.	http://cup.columbia.edu/ book/ 978-0-231-13210-7/ the-columbia-guide-to-online-style
Biological sciences	*Scientific Style and Format: The CSE Manual for Authors, Editors, and Publishers.* 7th ed. 2006.	http://www.councilscienceeditors.org/ publications/style.cfm
Chemistry	*The ACS Style Guide.* 3rd ed. 2006.	http://www.pubs.acs.org/page/ books/styleguide/index.html
Government documents	*The Complete Guide to Citing Government Documents.* Rev. ed. 1993.	http://exlibris.memphis.edu/resource/ unclesam/citeweb.html
Humanities	*MLA Handbook for Writers of Research Papers.* 7th ed. 2009.	http://www.mla.org
	MLA Style Manual and Guide to Scholarly Publishing. 3rd ed. 2008.	
Psychology/ Social sciences	*Publication Manual of the American Psychological Association.* 6th ed. 2010.	http://www.apastyle.apa.org

The MLA System of Documentation

Citations in Text

A WORK WITH A SINGLE AUTHOR

The MLA author-page system generally requires that in-text citations include the author's last name and the page number of the passage being cited. There is no punctuation between author and page. The parenthetical citation should follow the quoted, paraphrased, or summarized material as closely as possible without disrupting the flow of the sentence.

> Dr. James is described as a "not-too-skeletal Ichabod Crane" (Simon 68).

> One reviewer compares Dr. James to Ichabod Crane (Simon 68).

Note that the parenthetical citation comes before the final period. With block quotations, however, the citation comes after the final period, preceded by a space (see pp. 490–91 for an example). If you mention the author's name in your text, supply just the page reference in parentheses.

> Simon describes Dr. James as a "not-too-skeletal Ichabod Crane" (68).

> Simon compares Dr. James to Ichabod Crane (68).

A WORK WITH MORE THAN ONE AUTHOR

To cite a source by two or three authors, include all the authors' last names; for works with more than three authors, use all the authors' names or just the first author's name followed by *et al.*, meaning "and others," in regular type (not italicized or underlined).

> Dyal, Corning, and Willows identify several types of students, including the "Authority-Rebel" (4).

> The Authority-Rebel "tends to see himself as superior to other students in the class" (Dyal, Corning, and Willows 4).

> The drug AZT has been shown to reduce the risk of transmission from HIV-positive mothers to their infants by as much as two-thirds (Van de Perre et al. 4-5).

TWO OR MORE WORKS BY THE SAME AUTHOR

To cite one of two or more works by the same author, include the author's last name, a comma, a shortened version of the title you are citing, and the page number(s).

> When old paint becomes transparent, it sometimes shows the artist's original plans: "a tree will show through a woman's dress" (Hellman, Pentimento 1).

A WORK WITH AN UNKNOWN AUTHOR

Use a shortened version of the title, beginning with the word by which the title is alphabetized in the works cited list. ("Awash in Garbage" was the title in the following example.)

> An international pollution treaty still to be ratified would prohibit all plastic garbage from being dumped at sea ("Awash" 26).

TWO OR MORE AUTHORS WITH THE SAME LAST NAME CITED IN YOUR ESSAY

In addition to the last name, include each author's first initial in the citation. If the first initials are also the same, spell out the authors' first names.

> Chaplin's *Modern Times* provides a good example of montage used to make an editorial statement (E. Roberts 246).

A CORPORATE OR GOVERNMENT AUTHOR

In a parenthetical citation, give the full name of the author if it is brief or a shortened version if it is long. If you name the author in your text, give the full name even if it is long.

> A tuition increase has been proposed for community and technical colleges to offset budget deficits from Initiative 601 (Washington State Board 4).

> According to the Washington State Board for Community and Technical Colleges, a tuition increase . . . from Initiative 601 (4).

A MULTIVOLUME WORK

When you use two or more volumes of a multivolume work in your paper, include the volume number and the page number(s), separated by a colon and one space, in each citation.

> According to Forster, modernist writers valued experimentation and gradually sought to blur the line between poetry and prose (3: 150).

If you cite only one volume, give the volume number in the works cited (see p. 502) and include only the page number(s) in the parenthetical citation.

A LITERARY WORK

For a novel or other prose work available in various editions, provide the page numbers from the edition used as well as other information that will help readers locate the quotation in a different edition, such as the part or chapter number.

> In *Hard Times,* Tom reveals his utter narcissism by blaming Louisa for his own failure: "'You have regularly given me up. You never cared for me'" (Dickens 262; bk. 3, ch. 9).

For a play in verse, such as a Shakespearean play, indicate the act, scene, and line numbers instead of the page numbers.

> At the beginning, Regan's fawning rhetoric hides her true attitude toward Lear: "I profess / myself an enemy to all other joys . . . / And find that I am alone felicitate / In your dear highness' love" (*King Lear* 1.1.74-75, 77-78).

For a poem, indicate the line numbers and stanzas or sections (if they are numbered), instead of the page numbers. If the source gives only line numbers, use the term *lines* in the first citation and give only the numbers in subsequent citations.

> In "Song of Myself," Whitman finds poetic details in busy urban settings, as when
> he describes "the blab of the pave, tires of carts . . . the driver with his interrogating
> thumb" (8.153-54).

A RELIGIOUS WORK

For the Bible, indicate the book, chapter, and verse instead of the page numbers. Abbreviate books with names of five or more letters in your parenthetical citation, but spell out full names of books in your text.

> She ignored the admonition "Pride goes before destruction, and a haughty spirit before a
> fall" (*New Oxford Annotated Bible,* Prov. 16.18).

A WORK IN AN ANTHOLOGY

Use the name of the author of the work, not the editor of the anthology, but use the page number(s) from the anthology.

> In "Six Days: Some Rememberings," Grace Paley recalls that when she was in jail for pro-
> testing the Vietnam War, her pen and paper were taken away and she felt "a terrible pain
> in the area of my heart--a nausea" (191).

A QUOTATION FROM A SECONDARY SOURCE

Include the secondary source in your list of works cited. In your parenthetical citation, use the abbreviation *qtd. in* (in regular type, not italicized or underlined) to acknowledge that the original was quoted in a secondary source.

> E. M. Forster says "the collapse of all civilization, so realistic for us, sounded in Matthew
> Arnold's ears like a distant and harmonious cataract" (qtd. in Trilling 11).

AN ENTIRE WORK

Include the reference in the text without any page numbers or parentheses.

> In *The Structure of Scientific Revolutions,* Thomas Kuhn discusses how scientists change
> their thinking.

A WORK WITHOUT PAGE NUMBERS

If a work has no page numbers or is only one page long, you may omit the page number. If a work uses paragraph numbers instead, use the abbreviation *par.* (or *pars.,* plural) in regular type, not italicized or underlined, and use a comma after the author's name.

> The average speed on Montana's interstate highways, for example, has risen by only 2 miles
> per hour since the repeal of the federal speed limit, with most drivers topping out at
> 75 (Schmid).

Whitman considered African American speech "a source of a native grand opera" (Ellison, par. 13).

TWO OR MORE WORKS CITED IN THE SAME PARENTHESES

When two or more different sources are used in the same passage of your essay, it may be necessary to cite them in the same parentheses. Separate the citations with a semicolon. Include any specific pages, or omit pages to refer to the whole work.

A few studies have considered differences between oral and written discourse production (Scardamalia, Bereiter, and Goelman; Gould).

MATERIAL FROM THE INTERNET

Give enough information in the citation to enable readers to locate the Internet source in the list of works cited. If the author is not named, give the document title. Include page, section, paragraph, or screen numbers, if available.

In handling livestock, "many people attempt to restrain animals with sheer force instead of using behavioral principles" (Grandin).

List of Works Cited

The list of works cited provides full information for all the sources the writer uses. Entries are alphabetized according to the first author's last name or by the title if the author is unknown. Every source cited in the text must refer to an entry in the list of works cited. Conversely, every entry in the list of works cited must correspond to at least one in-text citation.

In the MLA style, multiple works by the same author (or same group of authors) are alphabetized by title. The author's name is given for the first entry only; in subsequent entries, three hyphens and a period are used.

Kingsolver, Barbara. *High Tide in Tucson: Essays from Now or Never.* New York: HarperCollins, 1995. Print.

---. *Small Wonder.* New York: HarperCollins, 2002. Print.

The information presented in a works-cited entry for a book follows this order: author, title, publication source, year of publication, and medium of publication. The MLA style requires a "hanging indent," which means that the first line of a works cited entry is not indented but subsequent lines of the entry are. The MLA specifies an indent of half an inch or five character spaces.

Note that in the list of works cited, publishers' names are given in shortened form. Compound or hyphenated names are usually limited to the first name only (with "Bedford," for example, used for "Bedford/St. Martin's"). The words "University" and "Press" are shortened to "U" and "P," respectively.

Books

Here is an example of a basic MLA-style entry for a book:

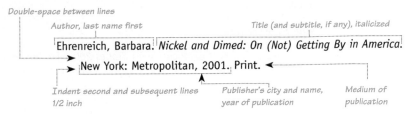

Double-space between lines

Author, last name first

Title (and subtitle, if any), italicized

Ehrenreich, Barbara. *Nickel and Dimed: On (Not) Getting By in America.*
New York: Metropolitan, 2001. Print.

Indent second and subsequent lines
1/2 inch

Publisher's city and name,
year of publication

Medium of
publication

A BOOK BY A SINGLE AUTHOR

Lamb, Sharon. *The Secret Lives of Girls.* New York: Free, 2002. Print.

A BOOK BY AN AGENCY OR A CORPORATION

American Medical Association. *Family Medical Guide.* 4th ed. Hoboken: Wiley, 2004. Print.

A BOOK BY MORE THAN ONE AUTHOR

Saba, Laura, and Julie Gattis. *The McGraw-Hill Homeschooling Companion.* New York: McGraw,
2002. Print.

Wilmut, Ian, Keith Campbell, and Colin Tudge. *The Second Creation: Dolly and the Age of
Biological Control.* New York: Farrar, 2000. Print.

A WORK BY MORE THAN THREE AUTHORS

The MLA lists all the authors' names *or* the name of the first author followed by *et al.*
(in regular type, not italicized or underlined).

Hunt, Lynn, et al. *The Making of the West: Peoples and Cultures.* Boston: Bedford, 2001. Print.

A BOOK BY AN UNKNOWN AUTHOR

Use the title in place of the author.

Rand McNally Commercial Atlas and Marketing Guide. Skokie: Rand, 2003. Print.

A BOOK WITH AN AUTHOR AND AN EDITOR

If you refer to the author's text, begin the entry with the author's name.

Arnold, Matthew. *Culture and Anarchy.* Ed. Samuel Lipman. New Haven: Yale UP, 1994. Print.

If you cite the editor in your paper, begin the entry with the editor's name.

Lipman, Samuel, ed. *Culture and Anarchy.* By Matthew Arnold. New Haven: Yale UP,
1994. Print.

AN EDITED COLLECTION

Waldman, Diane, and Janet Walker, eds. *Feminism and Documentary*. Minneapolis: U of
   Minnesota P, 1999. Print.

A WORK IN AN ANTHOLOGY OR A COLLECTION

Lahiri, Jhumpa. "Nobody's Business." *The Best American Short Stories 2002*. Ed. Sue Miller.
   Boston: Houghton, 2002. 136-72. Print.

TWO OR MORE WORKS FROM THE SAME ANTHOLOGY

To avoid repetition, you may create an entry for the collection and cite the collection's
editor to cross-reference individual works to the entry.

Boyd, Herb, ed. *The Harlem Reader*. New York: Three Rivers, 2003. Print.

Wallace, Michelle. "Memories of a Sixties Girlhood: The Harlem I Love." Boyd 243-50. Print.

ONE VOLUME OF A MULTIVOLUME WORK

If only one volume from a multivolume set is used, indicate the volume number after
the title.

Freud, Sigmund. *The Standard Edition of the Complete Psychological Works of Sigmund Freud*.
   Vol. 8. Trans. and ed. James Strachey. New York: Norton, 2000. Print.

TWO OR MORE VOLUMES OF A MULTIVOLUME WORK

Sandburg, Carl. *Abraham Lincoln*. 6 vols. New York: Scribner's, 1939. Print.

A BOOK THAT IS PART OF A SERIES

After the medium of publication, include the series title in regular type (not italicized
or in quotation marks), followed by the series number and a period. If the word *Series*
is part of the name, include *Ser.* before the number. Common abbreviations may be
used for selected words in the series title.

Zigova, Tanya, et al. *Neural Stem Cells: Methods and Protocols*. Totowa: Humana, 2002. Print.
   Methods in Molecular Biology 198.

A REPUBLISHED BOOK

Provide the original year of publication after the title of the book, followed by publication information for the edition you are using.

Alcott, Louisa May. *An Old-Fashioned Girl*. 1870. New York: Puffin, 1995. Print.

A LATER EDITION OF A BOOK

Rottenberg, Annette T., and Donna Haisty Winchell. *The Structure of Argument*. 6th ed.
   Boston: Bedford, 2009. Print.

A BOOK WITH A TITLE IN ITS TITLE

Do not italicize a title normally italicized when it appears within a book title.

> Hertenstein, Mike. *The Double Vision of* Star Trek: *Half-Humans, Evil Twins, and Science Fiction*. Chicago: Cornerstone, 1998. Print.

> O'Neill, Terry, ed. *Readings on* To Kill a Mockingbird. San Diego: Greenhaven, 2000. Print.

Use quotation marks around a work normally enclosed in quotation marks when it appears within the title of a book.

> Miller, Edwin Haviland. *Walt Whitman's "Song of Myself": A Mosaic of Interpretation*. Iowa City: U of Iowa P, 1989. Print.

A TRANSLATION

If you refer to the work itself, begin the entry with the author's name.

> Tolstoy, Leo. *War and Peace*. Trans. Constance Garnett. New York: Modern, 2002. Print.

If you cite the translator in your text, begin the entry with the translator's name.

> Garnett, Constance, trans. *War and Peace*. By Leo Tolstoy. New York: Modern, 2002. Print.

A DICTIONARY ENTRY OR AN ARTICLE IN A REFERENCE BOOK

"Homeopathy." *Webster's New World College Dictionary*. 4th ed. 1999. Print.

Rowland, Lewis P. "Myasthenia Gravis." *The Encyclopedia Americana*. 2001 ed. Print.

AN INTRODUCTION, PREFACE, FOREWORD, OR AFTERWORD

Graff, Gerald, and James Phelan. Preface. *Adventures of Huckleberry Finn*. By Mark Twain. 2nd ed. New York: Bedford, 2004. iii-vii. Print.

Articles

AN ARTICLE FROM A SCHOLARLY JOURNAL

Here is an example of a basic MLA-style entry for an article in a scholarly journal:

Author, last name first   Article title, in quotation marks

Simon, Robin W. "Revisiting the Relationship among Gender, Marital Status, and Mental Health." *American Journal of Sociology* 107.4 (2002): 1065-96. Print.

Double-space between lines; indent second and subsequent lines 1/2 inch Periodical title, italicized Volume and issue number Date, in parentheses, followed by colon Page numbers Medium of publication

Scholarly journals are typically identified using their volume and issue numbers, separated by a period. If a journal does not use volume numbers, provide the issue number only, following the title of the journal.

> Fee, Margery. "Predators and Gardens." *Canadian Literature* 197 (2008): 6-9. Print.

If the article is not on a continuous sequence of pages, give the first page number followed by a plus sign, as in the following example.

AN ARTICLE FROM A DAILY NEWSPAPER

> Stoll, John D., et al. "U.S. Squeezes Auto Creditors." *Wall Street Journal* 10 Apr. 2009:
> A1+. Print.

Note that magazines and newspapers are identified not by volume and issue number but by date, with the names of most months abbreviated.

AN ARTICLE FROM A WEEKLY OR BIWEEKLY MAGAZINE

> Doig, Will. "America's Real First Family." *Advocate* 17 July 2007: 46-50. Print.

AN ARTICLE FROM A MONTHLY OR BIMONTHLY MAGAZINE

> Shelby, Ashley. "Good Going: Alaska's Glacier Crossroads." *Sierra* Sept.-Oct. 2005:
> 23. Print.

AN EDITORIAL

> "Addiction behind Bars." Editorial. *New York Times* 12 Apr. 2009: A20. Print.

A LETTER TO THE EDITOR

> Orent, Wendy, and Alan Zelicoff. Letter. *New Republic* 18 Nov. 2002: 4-5. Print.

A REVIEW

> Cassidy, John. "Master of Disaster." Rev. of *Globalization and Its Discontents*, by Joseph
> Stiglitz. *New Yorker* 12 July 2002: 82-86. Print.

If the review does not include an author's name, start the entry with the title of the review and alphabetize by that title. If the review is untitled, begin with the words *Rev. of* and alphabetize under the title of the work being reviewed.

AN UNSIGNED ARTICLE

Begin with the article title, alphabetizing the entry according to the first word after any initial *A, An,* or *The.*

> "A Shot of Reality." *U.S. News & World Report* 1 July 2003: 13. Print.

Electronic Sources

Much of the information required in citations of electronic sources takes the same form as in corresponding kinds of print sources. For example, if you are citing an article from an online periodical, put the article title in quotation marks and italicize the name of the periodical. If the source has been previously or simultaneously published in print, include the print publication information if it is available. You also should include information specific to electronic sources, where it is appropriate and available, including the following:

- The version or edition used.
- The publisher or sponsor of the site; if not available, use *N.p.*
- Date of publication; if not available, use *n.d.*
- Medium of publication (*Web*).
- The date you accessed the source.

Electronic content frequently changes or disappears, and because it is not organized in the ways that print books and periodicals are, finding the information needed for documentation is often difficult. If you cannot find some of this information, include what you do find. Always keep your goal in mind: to provide enough information so that your reader could track the source down later.

A DOCUMENT FROM A WEB SITE

Here is an example of a basic MLA-style entry for the most commonly cited kind of electronic source, a specific document from a Web site:

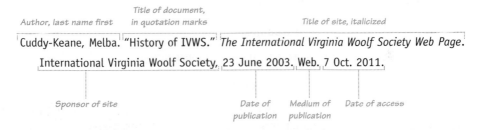

Cuddy-Keane, Melba. "History of IVWS." *The International Virginia Woolf Society Web Page.* International Virginia Woolf Society, 23 June 2003. Web. 7 Oct. 2011.

AN ENTIRE WEB SITE

Gardner, James Alan. *A Seminar on Writing Prose.* N.p., 2001. Web. 12 Feb. 2011.

If the author's name is not known, begin the citation with the title.

The International Virginia Woolf Society Web Page. International Virginia Woolf Society, 31 Aug. 2002. Web. 25 Dec. 2010.

For an untitled personal site, put a description such as *Home page* (in regular type, not italicized), followed by a period, in the position a title would normally be cited.

Chesson, Frederick W. Home page. N.p., 1 Apr. 2003. Web. 5 June 2010.

AN ONLINE SCHOLARLY PROJECT

For a complete project, provide the title, italicized, and the name of the editor, if given. Then give the electronic publication information — the version number (if any), the name of the sponsoring organization, and the date of electronic publication or latest update — followed by the medium and date of access.

> *The Darwin Correspondence Project*. Ed. Duncan Porter. Cambridge U Library, 2 June 2003. Web. 10 Aug. 2011.

A BOOK OR SHORT WORK WITHIN A SCHOLARLY PROJECT

Begin with the author's name and the title (italicized for a book or in quotation marks for an article, essay, poem, or other short work). Follow with the print publication information, if any, and the information about the project.

> Corelli, Marie. *The Treasure of Heaven*. London: Constable, 1906. *Victorian Women Writer's Project*. Ed. Percy Willett. Indiana U, 10 July 1999. Web. 13 Mar. 2011.

> Heims, Marjorie. "The Strange Case of Sarah Jones." *The Free Expression Policy Project*. FEPP, 24 Jan. 2003. Web. 14 Mar. 2011.

MATERIAL FROM AN ONLINE PERIODICAL DATABASE

If you access an article through an online database, after the print publication information, give the name of the database set in italics, the medium of publication, and the date of access.

> Braus, Patricia. "Sex and the Single Spender." *American Demographics* 15.11 (1993): 28-34. *Academic Search Premier*. Web. 25 Oct. 2011.

A NONPERIODICAL PUBLICATION ON A CD-ROM

> *Picasso: The Man, His Works, the Legend*. Danbury: Grolier Interactive, 1996. CD-ROM.

AN ARTICLE FROM AN ONLINE SCHOLARLY JOURNAL

Include the volume number and issue number, if given, after the title of the journal. Also include the number of pages, paragraphs, or other sections, if given, after the date of publication; if none are given, use *n. pag.*

> Cesarini, Paul. "Computers, Technology, and Literacies." *Journal of Literacy and Technology* 4.1 (2004/2005): n. pag. Web. 1 Apr. 2011.

A POSTING TO A DISCUSSION GROUP OR NEWSGROUP

Include the author's name (if you know it), the title or subject line of the posting (in quotation marks), the group name, the sponsor, the posting date, the medium, and the access date.

> Willie, Otis. "In the Heat of the Battle." *soc.history.war.us-revolution*. Google, 27 Sept. 2005. Web. 15 June 2011.

Martin, Francesca Alys. "Wait--Did Somebody Say 'Buffy'?" *Cultstud-L*. U of S Fl, 8 Mar. 2000.
Web. 8 Mar. 2010.

AN E-MAIL MESSAGE

The subject line of the message is enclosed in quotation marks. Identify the persons
who sent and received it and the date it was sent. End with the medium (*E-mail*), neither italicized nor underlined.

Olson, Kate. "Update on State Legislative Grants." Message to the author. 27 Sept. 2011.
E-mail.

COMPUTER SOFTWARE

How Computers Work. Indianapolis: Que, 1998. CD-ROM.

Other Sources

A LECTURE OR PUBLIC ADDRESS

Birnbaum, Jack. "The Domestication of Computers." Conf. of the Usability Professionals
Association. Hyatt Grand Cypress Resort, Orlando. 10 July 2002. Lecture.

A GOVERNMENT DOCUMENT

If the author is known, the author's name may either come first or be placed after the
title, introduced with the word *By*.

United States. Dept. of Health and Human Services. *Trends in Underage Drinking in the United
States, 1991-2007*. By Gabriella Newes-Adeyi et al. Washington: GPO, 2009. Print.

A PAMPHLET

BoatU.S. Foundation for Boating Safety and Clean Water. *Hypothermia and Cold Water
Survival*. Alexandria, VA: BoatU.S. Foundation, 2001. Print.

PUBLISHED PROCEEDINGS OF A CONFERENCE

If the name of the conference is part of the title of the publication, it need not be
repeated. Use the format for a work in an anthology (see p. 502) to cite an individual
presentation.

Duffett, John, ed. *Against the Crime of Silence*: *Proceedings of the International War Crimes
Tribunal*. Nov. 1967, Stockholm. New York: Clarion-Simon, 1970. Print.

A PUBLISHED DOCTORAL DISSERTATION

Cite as you would a book, but add pertinent dissertation information before
publication data.

Botts, Roderic C. *Influences in the Teaching of English, 1917-1935: An Illusion of Progress*. Diss. Northeastern U, 1970. Ann Arbor: UMI, 1971. Print.

Jones, Anna Maria. *Problem Novels/Perverse Readers: Late-Victorian Fiction and the Perilous Pleasures of Identification*. Diss. U of Notre Dame, 2001. Ann Arbor: UMI, 2001. Print.

AN UNPUBLISHED DOCTORAL DISSERTATION

Enclose the title of an unpublished dissertation in quotation marks.

Bullock, Barbara. "Basic Needs Fulfillment among Less Developed Countries: Social Progress over Two Decades of Growth." Diss. Vanderbilt U, 1986. Print.

A LETTER

Use *MS* ("manuscript") if written by hand, and *TS* ("typescript") if produced using technology.

DuHamel, Grace. Letter to the author. 22 Mar. 2008. TS.

A MAP OR CHART

Map of Afghanistan and Surrounding Territory. Map. Burlington: GiziMap, 2001. Print.

A CARTOON OR COMIC STRIP

Provide the title (if given) in quotation marks directly following the artist's name.

Cheney, Tom. Cartoon. *New Yorker*. 10 Oct. 2005: 55. Print.

AN ADVERTISEMENT

Hospital for Special Surgery. Advertisement. *New York Times* 13 Apr. 2009: A7. Print.

A WORK OF ART OR MUSICAL COMPOSITION

De Goya, Francisco. *The Sleep of Reason Produces Monsters*. 1799. Etching with watercolor. Norton Simon Museum, Pasadena.

Beethoven, Ludwig van. *Violin Concerto in D Major, Op. 61*. 1809. New York: Edwin F. Kalmus, n.d. Print.

Gershwin, George. *Porgy and Bess*. 1935. New York: Alfred, 1999. Print.

If a photograph is not part of a collection, identify the subject, the name of the person who photographed it, and when it was photographed.

Washington Square Park, New York. Personal photograph by author. 24 June 2006.

A PERFORMANCE

Proof. By David Auburn. Dir. Daniel Sullivan. Perf. Mary-Louise Parker. Walter Kerr Theatre, New York. 9 Sept. 2001. Performance.

A TELEVISION PROGRAM

"Murder of the Century." *American Experience*. Narr. David Ogden Stiers. Writ. and prod. Carl
Charlson. PBS. WEDU, Tampa, 14 July 2003. Television.

A FILM OR VIDEO RECORDING

Space Station. Prod. and dir. Toni Myers. Narr. Tom Cruise. IMAX, 2002. Film.

Casablanca. Dir. Michael Curtiz. Perf. Humphrey Bogart, Ingrid Bergman, and Paul Henreid.
1942. Warner Home Video, 2003. DVD.

A MUSIC RECORDING

Beethoven, Ludwig van. *Violin Concerto in D Major, Op. 61*. U.S.S.R. State Orchestra. Cond.
Alexander Gauk. Perf. David Oistrakh. Allegro, 1980. Audiocassette.

Springsteen, Bruce. "Dancing in the Dark." *Born in the USA*. Columbia, 1984. CD.

AN INTERVIEW

Ashrawi, Hanan. "Tanks vs. Olive Branches." Interview with Rose Marie Berger. *Sojourners
Magazine* Feb. 2005: 22-26. Print.

Ellis, Trey. Personal interview. 3 Sept. 2008.

The APA System of Documentation

Citations in Text

AUTHOR INDICATED IN PARENTHESES

The APA author-year system calls for the last name of the author and the year of
publication of the original work in the citation. If the cited material is a quotation,
you also need to include the page number(s) of the original. If the cited material
is not a quotation, the page reference is optional. Use commas to separate author,
year, and page in a parenthetical citation. The page number is preceded by *p.* for a
single page or *pp.* for a range. Use an ampersand (&) to join the names of multiple
authors.

> The conditions in the stockyards were so dangerous that workers "fell into the vats; and
> when they were fished out, there was never enough of them left to be worth exhibiting"
> (Sinclair, 2005, p. 134).

> Racial bias does not necessarily diminish through exposure to individuals of other races
> (Jamison & Tyree, 2001).

If you are citing an electronic source without page numbers, give the paragraph number if it is provided, preceded by the abbreviation *para.* If no paragraph number is

given, give the heading of the section and the number of the paragraph within it where the material appears, if possible.

> The subjects were tested for their responses to various stimuli, both positive and negative (Simpson, 2002, para. 4).

AUTHOR INDICATED IN SIGNAL PHRASE

If the author's name is mentioned in your text, cite the year in parentheses directly following the author's name, and place the page reference in parentheses before the final sentence period. Use *and* to join the names of multiple authors.

> Sinclair (2005) wrote that workers sometimes "fell into the vats; and when they were fished out, there was never enough of them left to be worth exhibiting" (p. 134).

> As Jamison and Tyree (2001) have found, racial bias does not diminish merely through exposure to individuals of other races (Conclusion section, para. 2).

SOURCE WITH MORE THAN TWO AUTHORS

To cite works with three to five authors, use all the authors' last names the first time the reference occurs and the last name of the first author followed by *et al.* (in regular type, not italicized or underlined) subsequently. If a source has six or more authors, use only the last name of the first author and *et al.* at first and subsequent references.

First Citation in Text

> Rosenzweig, Breedlove, and Watson (2005) wrote that biological psychology is an interdisciplinary field that includes scientists from "quite different backgrounds" (p. 3).

Subsequent Citations

> Biological psychology is "the field that relates behavior to bodily processes, especially the workings of the brain" (Rosenzweig et al., 2005, p. 3).

TWO OR MORE WORKS BY THE SAME AUTHOR

To cite one of two or more works by the same author or group of authors, use the author's last name plus the year (and the page, if you are citing a quotation). When more than one work being cited was published by an author in the same year, the works are alphabetized by title and then assigned lowercase letters after the date (2005a, 2005b).

> Middle-class unemployed workers are better off than their lower-class counterparts, because "the white collar unemployed are likely to have some assets to invest in their job search" (Ehrenreich, 2005b, p. 16).

UNKNOWN AUTHOR

To cite a work listed only by its title, the APA uses a shortened version of the title.

An international pollution treaty still to be ratified would prohibit all plastic garbage from being dumped at sea ("Awash," 1987).

SECONDARY SOURCE

To quote material taken not from the original source but from a secondary source that quotes the original, give the secondary source in the reference list, and in your essay acknowledge that the original was quoted in a secondary source.

E. M. Forster said "the collapse of all civilization, so realistic for us, sounded in Matthew Arnold's ears like a distant and harmonious cataract" (as cited in Trilling, 1955, p. 11).

List of References

The APA follows this order in the presentation of information for each source listed: author, publication year, title, and publication source; for an article, the page range is given as well. Titles of books, periodicals, and the like should be italicized. For books and articles, capitalize only the first word of the title, proper nouns, and the first word following a colon (if any). Capitalize the titles of magazines and journals as you would normally capitalize them.

When the list of references includes several works by the same author, the APA provides the following rules for arranging these entries in the list:

- Same-name single-author entries precede multiple-author entries:

Zettelmeyer, F. (2000).

Zettelmeyer, F., Morton, F. S., & Silva-Risso, J. (2006).

- Entries with the same first author and a different second author are alphabetized under the first author according to the second author's last name:

Dhar, R., & Nowlis, S. M. (2004).

Dhar, R., & Simonson, I. (2003).

- Entries by the same authors are arranged by year of publication, in chronological order:

Golder, P. N., & Tellis, G. J. (2003).

Golder, P. N., & Tellis, G. J. (2004).

- Entries by the same authors with the same publication year should be arranged alphabetically by title (according to the first word after *A*, *An*, or *The*), and lower-case letters (*a*, *b*, *c*, and so on) are appended to the year in parentheses:

Aaron, P. (1990a). *Basic* . . .

Aaron, P. (1990b). *Elements* . . .

The APA recommends that the first line of each entry be indented one-half inch (or five spaces) in papers intended for publication but notes that student writers may use a hanging indent of five spaces. Ask your instructor which format is preferred. The following examples demonstrate a hanging indent of one-half inch.

Books

A BOOK BY A SINGLE AUTHOR

Ehrenreich, B. (2001). *Nickel and dimed: On (not) getting by in America*. New York, NY: Metropolitan.

A BOOK BY AN AGENCY OR A CORPORATION

American Medical Association. (2004). *Family medical guide*. Hoboken, NJ: Wiley.

A BOOK BY MORE THAN ONE AUTHOR

Saba, L., & Gattis, J. (2002). *The McGraw-Hill homeschooling companion*. New York, NY: McGraw-Hill.

Hunt, L., Po-Chia Hsia, R., Martin, T. R., Rosenwein, B. H., Rosenwein, H., & Smith, B. G. (2001). *The making of the West: Peoples and cultures*. Boston, MA: Bedford/St. Martin's.

If there are more than seven authors, list only the first six, then insert three periods, and add the last author's name.

A BOOK BY AN UNKNOWN AUTHOR

Use the title in place of the author.

Rand McNally commercial atlas and marketing guide. (2003). Skokie, IL: Rand McNally.

When an author is designated as "Anonymous," identify the work as "Anonymous" in the text, and alphabetize it as "Anonymous" in the reference list.

A BOOK WITH AN AUTHOR AND AN EDITOR

Arnold, M. (1994). *Culture and anarchy* (S. Lipman, Ed.). New Haven, CT: Yale University Press. (Original work published 1869)

AN EDITED COLLECTION

Waldman, D., & Walker, J. (Eds.). (1999). *Feminism and documentary*. Minneapolis: University of Minnesota Press.

A WORK IN AN ANTHOLOGY OR A COLLECTION

Fairbairn-Dunlop, P. (1993). Women and agriculture in western Samoa. In J. H. Momsen & V. Kinnaird (Eds.), *Different places, different voices* (pp. 211-226). London, England: Routledge.

A TRANSLATION

Tolstoy, L. (2002). *War and peace* (C. Garnett, Trans.). New York, NY: Modern Library. (Original work published 1869)

AN ARTICLE IN A REFERENCE BOOK

Rowland, R. P. (2001). Myasthenia gravis. In *Encyclopedia Americana* (Vol. 19, p. 683). Danbury, CT: Grolier.

AN INTRODUCTION, PREFACE, FOREWORD, OR AFTERWORD

Graff, G., & Phelan, J. Preface (2004). In M. Twain, *Adventures of Huckleberry Finn* (pp. iii-vii). New York, NY: Bedford/St. Martin's.

Articles

AN ARTICLE FROM A DAILY NEWSPAPER

Peterson, A. (2003, May 20). Finding a cure for old age. *The Wall Street Journal*, pp. D1, D5.

AN ARTICLE FROM A WEEKLY OR BIWEEKLY MAGAZINE

Gross, M. J. (2003, April 29). Family life during war time. *The Advocate*, 42-48.

AN ARTICLE FROM A MONTHLY OR BIMONTHLY MAGAZINE

Shelby, A. (2005, September/October). Good going: Alaska's glacier crossroads. *Sierra, 90*, 23.

AN ARTICLE IN A SCHOLARLY JOURNAL WITH CONTINUOUS ANNUAL PAGINATION

The volume number follows the title of the journal.

Shan, J. Z., Morris, A. G., & Sun, F. (2001). Financial development and economic growth: A chicken and egg problem? *Review of Economics, 9*, 443-454.

AN ARTICLE IN A SCHOLARLY JOURNAL THAT PAGINATES EACH ISSUE SEPARATELY

The issue number appears in parentheses after the volume number.

Tran, D. (2002). Personal income by state, second quarter 2002. *Current Business, 82*(11), 55-73.

AN ANONYMOUS ARTICLE

Communities blowing whistle on street basketball. (2003). *USA Today*, p. 20A.

A REVIEW

Cassidy, J. (2002, July 12). Master of disaster [Review of the book *Globalization and its discontents*]. *The New Yorker*, 82-86.

If the review is untitled, use the bracketed information as the title, retaining the brackets.

Electronic Sources

While the APA guidelines for citing online resources are still something of a work in progress, a rule of thumb is that citation information must allow readers to access and retrieve the information cited. The following guidelines are derived from the *Publication Manual of the American Psychological Association,* Sixth Edition (2010). Regular updates are posted on the APA's Web site (www.apastyle .apa.org/elecref.html).

For most sources accessed on the Internet, you should provide the following information:

- Name of author (if available).
- Date of publication or most recent update (in parentheses; if unavailable, use the abbreviation *n.d.*).
- Title of document.
- Publication information, including volume and issue numbers for periodicals.
- Retrieval information, including information necessary to locate the document. Note that the APA now requires the date of access *only* for content that is likely to be changed or updated.

For more information on using the internet for research see Chapter 16, pp. 478–82.

DOCUMENT FROM A WEB SITE

When you cite an entire Web site, the APA does not require an entry in the list of references. You may instead give the name of the site in your text and its Web address in parentheses. To cite a document that you have accessed through a Web site, follow these formats:

American Cancer Society. (2003). *How to fight teen smoking.* Retrieved from http://www
.cancer.org/docroot/ped/content/ped_10_14_how_to_fight_teen_smoking.asp

Heins, M. (2003, January 24). *The strange case of Sarah Jones.* Retrieved from http://
www.fepproject.org/commentaries/sarahjones.html

ARTICLE FROM A DATABASE

Follow the guidelines for a comparable print source, but conclude with the article's DOI (Digital Object Identifier), if one is assigned. If there is no DOI, conclude with the URL of the journal's home page.

Houston, R. G., & Toma, F. (2003). Home schooling: An alternative school choice. *Southern
Economic Journal, 69*(4), 920-936. Retrieved from http://www.southerneconomic.org

Tharp, R. G. (1989). Psychocultural variables and constants: Effects on teaching and
learning in schools. *American Psychologist, 44*(2), 249-359. doi:10.1037/0003
-066X.44.2.349

AN ARTICLE FROM AN ONLINE PERIODICAL

Include the same information you would for a print article. If the article has a DOI, include it; if not, include the URL for the article or the periodical's home page.

> Jauhar, S. (2003, July 15). A malady that mimics depression. *The New York Times*. Retrieved from http://www.nytimes.com

Retrieval information is always required for periodicals that are published only online.

> Cesarini, P. (2004/2005). Computers, technology, and literacies. *The Journal of Literacy and Technology, 4*(1). Retrieved from http://www.literacyandtechnology.org/v4/cesarini.htm

ONLINE POSTINGS

Include online postings in your list of references only if you can provide data that would allow retrieval of the source. Provide the author's name, the date of the posting, the subject line, and any other identifier in brackets after the title. Include the words "Retrieved from" followed by the URL where the message can be found. Include the name of the list, newsgroup, or blog, if this information is not part of the URL.

> Paikeday, T. (2005, October 10). "Esquivalience" is out [Electronic mailing list message]. Retrieved from http://listserv.linguistlist.org/cgi-bin/wa?A1=ind0510b&L=ads-1#1

> Ditmire, S. (2005, February 10). NJ tea party [Newsgroup message]. Retrieved from http://groups.google.com/group/TeaParty

AN E-MAIL MESSAGE

In the APA style, it is not necessary to list personal correspondence, including e-mail, in your reference list. Simply cite the person's name in your text, and in parentheses give the notation *personal communication* (in regular type, not underlined or italicized) and the date.

COMPUTER SOFTWARE

If an individual has proprietary rights to the software, cite that person's name as you would for a print text. Otherwise, cite as you would an anonymous print text.

> How Computers Work [Software]. (1998). Available from Que: http://www.howcomputerswork.net

Other Sources

A GOVERNMENT DOCUMENT

> U.S. Department of Health and Human Services. (2009). *Trends in underage drinking in the United States, 1991-2007*. Washington, DC: Government Printing Office.

Note: when the author and publisher are the same, use the word *Author* (not italicized) as the name of the publisher.

AN UNPUBLISHED DOCTORAL DISSERTATION

Bullock, B. (1986). *Basic needs fulfillment among less developed countries: Social progress over two decades of growth* (Unpublished doctoral dissertation). Vanderbilt University, Nashville, TN.

A TELEVISION PROGRAM

Charlsen, C. (Writer and producer). (2003, July 14). Murder of the century [Television series episode]. In M. Samels (Executive producer), *American Experience*. Boston, MA: WGBH.

A FILM OR VIDEO RECORDING

Myers, T. (Writer and producer). (2002). *Space station* [Motion picture]. New York, NY: IMAX.

A MUSIC RECORDING

If the recording date differs from the copyright date, the APA requires that it appear in parentheses after the name of the label. If it is necessary to include a number for the recording, use parentheses for the medium; otherwise, use brackets.

Beethoven, L. van. (1806). Violin concerto in D major, op. 61 [Recorded by USSR State Orchestra]. (Cassette Recording No. ACS 8044). New York, NY: Allegro. (1980)

Springsteen, B. (1984). Dancing in the dark. On *Born in the U.S.A.* [CD]. New York, NY: Columbia.

AN INTERVIEW

When using the APA style, do not list personal interviews in your reference list. Simply cite the person's name (last name and initials) in your text, and in parentheses give the notation *personal communication* (in regular type, not italicized or underlined) followed by a comma and the date of the interview. For published interviews, use the appropriate format for an article.

Some Sample Research Papers

As a writer, you will want or need to use sources on many occasions. You may be assigned to write a research paper, complete with formal documentation of outside sources. Several of the writing assignments in this book present opportunities to do library or field research — in other words, to turn to outside sources. Among the readings in Part One, the essays listed here cite and document sources. (The documentation style each essay follows is given in parentheses.)

"Cannibalism: It Still Exists," by Linh Kieu Ngo, Chapter 4, pp. 112–17 (MLA)

"Children Need to Play, Not Compete," by Jessica Statsky, Chapter 5, pp. 165–71 (MLA)

"More Testing, More Learning," by Patrick O'Malley, Chapter 6, pp. 213 – 19 (APA)

"Win-Win Flexibility," by Karen Kornbluh, Chapter 6, pp. 219 – 24 (MLA)

"Grading Professors," by Wendy Kim, Chapter 7, pp. 266 – 72 (MLA)

"'A Case for Torture': A Questionable Argument," by Melissa Mae, Chapter 11, pp. 372 – 74 (MLA)

"The Centrality of the Ticking Time-Bomb Scenario in Arguments Justifying Torture," by Melissa Mae, Chapter 11, pp. 382 – 86 (MLA)

"The Rising," by Paul Taylor, Chapter 12, pp. 397–400 (MLA)

An Annotated Research Paper

On the following pages is a student research paper speculating about the causes of a trend — the increase in home schooling. The author cites statistics, quotes authorities, and paraphrases and summarizes background information and support for her argument. She uses the MLA documentation style.

1"

All lines double-spaced

1"

Cristina Dinh

Professor Cooper

English 100

15 May 2009

Title centered; no underlining, quotes, or italics

Educating Kids at Home

Paragraphs indented one-half inch

Every morning, Mary Jane, who is nine, doesn't have to worry about gulping down her cereal so she can be on time for school. School for Mary Jane is literally right at her doorstep.

1"

In this era of serious concern about the quality of public education, increasing numbers of parents across the United States are choosing to educate their children at home. These parents believe they can do a better

Author named in text; no parenthetical page reference because source not paginated

job teaching their children than their local schools can. *Home schooling*, as this practice is known, has become a national trend over the past thirty years, and, according to education specialist Brian D. Ray, the home-schooled population is growing at a rate of between 5% and 12% per year. A 2008 report by the U.S. Department of Education's Institute of Education Sciences

Abbreviated title used in parenthetical citation because works cited lists two sources by author; no punctuation between title and page number

estimated that, nationwide, the number of home-schooled children rose from 850,000 in 1999 to approximately 1.5 million in 2007 (*1.5 Million* 1). Some home-schooling advocates believe that even these numbers may be low because not all states require formal notification when parents decide to teach their children at home.

What is home schooling, and who are the parents choosing to be home-schoolers? David Guterson, a pioneer in the home-schooling movement, defines home schooling as "the attempt to gain an education

Author named in text; parenthetical page reference falls at end of sentence

outside of institutions" (5). Home-schooled children spend the majority of the conventional school day learning in or near their homes rather than in traditional schools; parents or guardians are the prime educators. Former teacher and home-schooler Rebecca Rupp notes that home-schooling parents vary considerably in what they teach and how they teach, ranging from those who follow a highly traditional curriculum within a structure that

1"

Dinh 2

parallels the typical classroom to those who essentially allow their children
to pursue whatever interests them at their own pace (3). Home-schoolers
commonly combine formal instruction with life skills instruction, learning
fractions, for example, in terms of monetary units or cooking measurements
(Saba and Gattis 89). According to the U.S. Department of Education's
2008 report, while home-schoolers are also a diverse group politically and
philosophically--libertarians, conservatives, Christian fundamentalists--most
say they home school for one of three reasons: they are concerned about the
quality of academic instruction, the general school environment, or the lack
of religious or moral instruction (*1.5 Million* 2).

*— Work by two
authors cited*

  The first group generally believes that children need individual attention
and the opportunity to learn at their own pace to learn well. This group
says that one teacher in a classroom of twenty to thirty children (the
size of typical public-school classes) cannot give this kind of attention.
These parents believe they can give their children greater enrichment and
more specialized instruction than public schools can provide. At home,
parents can work one-on-one with each child and be flexible about time,
allowing their children to pursue their interests at earlier ages. Many of these
parents, like home-schooler Peter Bergson, believe that

> home schooling provides more of an opportunity to continue the
> natural learning process that's in evidence in all children.
> [In school,] you change the learning process from self-directed
> to other-directed, from the child asking questions to the
> teacher asking questions. You shut down areas of potential
> interest. (qtd. in Kohn 22)

*Quotation of
more than four
lines typed as
a block and
indented ten
spaces*

*— Brackets
indicate
alteration of
quotation.*

*Parenthetical
citation of
secondary source
falls after period*

  This trend can be traced back to the 1960s, when many people
began criticizing traditional schools. Various types of "alternative schools"
were created, and some parents began teaching their children at home
(Friedlander 151). Parents like this mention several reasons for their
disappointment with public schools and for their decision to home

Dinh 3

school. A lack of funding, for example, leaves children without new textbooks. In a 2002 survey, 31% of teachers said that their students are using textbooks that are more than ten years old, and 29% said that they do not have enough textbooks for all of their students (National Education Association). Many schools also cannot afford to buy laboratory equipment and other teaching materials. At my own high school, the chemistry teacher told me that most of the lab equipment we used came from a research firm he worked for. In a 2006 Gallup poll, lack of proper financial support ranked first on the list of the problems in public schools (Rose and Gallup).

Corporate author's name cited

Parents also cite overcrowding as a reason for taking their kids out of school. The more students in a classroom, the less learning that goes on, as Cafi Cohen discovered before choosing to home school; after spending several days observing what went on in her child's classroom, she found that administrative duties, including disciplining, took up to 80% of a teacher's time with only 20% of the day devoted to learning (6). Moreover, faced with a large group of children, a teacher ends up gearing lessons to the students in the middle level, so children at both ends miss out. Gifted children and those with learning disabilities particularly suffer in this situation. At home, parents of these children say they can tailor the material and the pace for each child. Studies show that home-schooling methods seem to work well in preparing children academically. Lawrence Rudner, director of the ERIC Clearinghouse on Assessment and Evaluation at the University of Maryland and a researcher on home schooling, found that testing of home-schooled students showed them to be between one and three years ahead of public school students their age (xi). Home-schooled children have also made particularly strong showings in academic competitions; since the late 1990s, 10% of National Spelling Bee participants have been home schooled, as have two National Spelling Bee and two National Geographic Bee winners (Lyman). More and more selective colleges are admitting, and even recruiting, home-schooled applicants (Basham, Merrifield, and Hepburn 15).

Dinh 4

Parents in the second group--those concerned with the general
school environment--claim that their children are more well-rounded
than those in school. Because they don't have to sit in classrooms all day,
home-schooled kids can pursue their own projects, often combining crafts
or technical skills with academic subjects. Home-schoolers participate in
outside activities such as 4-H competitions, field trips with peers in home-
school support groups, science fairs, musical and dramatic productions, church
activities, and Boy Scouts or Girl Scouts (Saba and Gattis 59-62). In fact, they
may even be able to participate to some extent in actual school activities.
A 1999 survey conducted by the U.S. Department of Education's Institute
of Education Sciences found that 28% of public schools allowed home-
schooled students to participate in extracurricular activities alongside enrolled
students, and 20% allowed home-schooled students to attend some classes
(*Homeschooling* 12).

Many home-schooling parents believe that these activities provide
the social opportunities kids need without exposing their children to the
peer pressure they would have to deal with as regular school students. For
example, many kids think that drinking and using drugs are cool. When I was
in high school, my friends would tell me a few drinks wouldn't hurt or affect
driving. If I had listened to them, I wouldn't be alive today. Four of my
friends were killed under the influence of alcohol. Between 1992 and 2008,
the number of high school seniors surveyed who had used any illicit drug in
the last year climbed from 27.1% to 36.6% (Johnston et al. 59).

*Work by more
than three
authors cited*

Another reason many parents decide to home school their kids is
that they are concerned for their children's safety. Samuel L. Blumenfeld
notes that "physical risk" is an important reason many parents remove their
children from public schools as "[m]ore and more children are assaulted,
robbed, and murdered in school" and a "culture of violence, abetted by rap
music, drug trafficking, . . . and racial tension, has engulfed teenagers" (4).
Beginning in the mid-1990s, a string of school shootings--including the

Dinh 5

1999 massacres in Littleton, Colorado, and Conyers, Georgia, and the 2001 massacre in Santee, California--has led to increasing fears that young people are simply not safe at school.

While all of the reasons mentioned so far are important, perhaps the single most significant cause of the growing home-schooling trend is Christian fundamentalist dissatisfaction with "godless" public schools. Sociologist Mitchell L. Stevens, author of one of the first comprehensive studies of home schooling, cites a mailing sent out by Basic Christian Education, a company that markets home-schooling materials, titled "What Really Happens in Public Schools." This publication sums up the fears of fundamentalist home-schoolers about public schools: that they encourage high levels of teenage sexual activity and pregnancies "out of wedlock"; expose children to "violence, crime, lack of discipline, and, of course, drugs of every kind"; present positive portrayals of communism and socialism and negative portrayals of capitalism; and undermine children's Christian beliefs by promoting "New Age philosophies, Yoga, Transcendental Meditation, witchcraft demonstrations, and Eastern religions" (51).

As early as 1988, Luanne Shackelford and Susan White, two Christian home-schooling mothers, were claiming that because schools expose children to "[p]eer pressure, perverts, secular textbooks, values clarification, TV, pornography, rock music, bad movies . . . [h]ome schooling seems to be the best plan to achieve our goal [to raise good Christians]" (160). As another mother more recently put it:

> I don't like the way schools are going. . . . What's wrong with Christianity all of a sudden? You know? This country was founded on Christian, on religious principles. [People] came over here for religious freedom, and now all of a sudden all religious references seem to be stricken out of the public school, and I don't like that at all. (qtd. in Stevens 67)

Although many nonfundamentalist home-schoolers make some of these

Brackets indicate changes in capitalization and addition to quotation for clarification.

Ellipsis marks indicate words left out of quotations.

Quotation cited in a secondary source

Dinh 6

same criticisms, those who cite the lack of "Christian values" in public schools have particular concerns of their own. For example, home-schooling leader Raymond Moore talks of parents who are "'sick and tired of the teaching of evolution in the schools as a cut-and-dried fact,' along with other evidence of so-called secular humanism" (qtd. in Kohn 21), such as textbooks that contain material contradicting Christian beliefs. Moreover, parents worry that schools undermine their children's moral values. In particular, some Christian fundamentalist parents object to sex education in schools, saying that it encourages children to become sexually active early, challenging values taught at home. They see the family as the core and believe that the best place to instill family values is within the family. These Christian home-schooling parents want to provide their children not only with academic knowledge but also with a moral grounding consistent with their religious beliefs.

Single quotation marks indicate a quotation within a quotation.

Citation placed close to quotation, before comma but after quotation marks

Still other home-schooling parents object to a perceived government-mandated value system that they believe attempts to override the values, not necessarily religious in nature, of individual families. For these parents, home schooling is a way of resisting what they see as unwarranted intrusion by the federal government into personal concerns (*Alliance*).

Armed with their convictions, parents such as those who belong to the Christian Home School Legal Defense Association have fought in court and lobbied for legislation that allows them the option of home schooling. In the 1970s, most states had compulsory attendance laws that made it difficult, if not illegal, to keep school-age children home from school. Today, home schooling is permitted in every state, with strict regulation required by only a few (Home School). As a result, Mary Jane is one of hundreds of thousands of American children who can start their school day without leaving the house.

Internet source cited by shortened form of title; author's name and page numbers unavailable

Shortened form of corporate author's name cited

Works Cited entries begin on a new page; entries are in alphabetical order.

Title centered

Entries begin flush with left margin; subsequent lines indent one-half inch. All lines are double-spaced.

Periods separate author, title, publication information, medium, and date of access.

Works Cited

Alliance for the Separation of School and State. Home page. Alliance for the
    Separation of School and State, 26 Feb. 2009. Web. 10 Apr. 2009.

Basham, Patrick, John Merrifield, and Claudia R. Hepburn. *Home Schooling:
    From the Extreme to the Mainstream*. 2nd ed. Vancouver: Fraser
    Institute, 2007. Studies in Education Policy. *Fraser Institute*. Web. 13
    Apr. 2009.

Blumenfeld, Samuel L. *Homeschooling: A Parent's Guide to Teaching Children*.
    Bridgewater: Replica, 1999. Print.

Cohen, Cafi. *And What about College?: How Home-schooling Leads to
    Admissions to the Best Colleges and Universities*. Cambridge: Holt,
    1997. Print.

Friedlander, Tom. "A Decade of Home Schooling." *The Home School Reader*.
    Ed. Mark Hegener and Helen Hegener. Tonasket: Home Education, 1988.
    147-56. Print.

Guterson, David. *Family Matters: Why Homeschooling Makes Sense*. San
    Diego: Harcourt, 1992. Print.

Home School Legal Defense Association. "State Action Map." HSLDA, 2009.
    Web. 5 Apr. 2009.

Johnston, Lloyd D., et al. *Monitoring the Future: National Results on
    Adolescent Drug Use, Overview of Key Findings, 2008*. Bethesda:
    National Institute on Drug Abuse, 2009. Web. 20 Apr. 2009.

Kohn, Alfie. "Home Schooling." *Atlantic Monthly* Apr. 1988: 20-25. Print.

Lyman, Isabel. "Generation Two." *American Enterprise* Oct.-Nov. 2002:
    48-49. *InfoTrac OneFile*. Web. 10 May 2009.

National Education Association. *2002 Instructional Materials Survey*. Sept.
    2002. Association of American Publishers, 2002. Web. 21
    Apr. 2009.

Ray, Brian D. "Research Facts on Home Schooling." *National Home Education
    Research Institute*. NHERI, 2008. Web. 10 Apr. 2009.

Dinh 8

Rose, Lowell C., and Alec M. Gallup. "The 38th Annual PDK/Gallup Poll of
the Public's Attitudes toward the Public Schools." *Phi Delta Kappan*
88.1 (2006): n. pag. *Phi Delta Kappa International*. Web. 1 May 2009.

Rudner, Lawrence. Foreword. Saba and Gattis xi–xiv.

Rupp, Rebecca. *The Complete Home Learning Source Book*. New York: Three
Rivers, 1998. Print.

Saba, Laura, and Julie Gattis. *The McGraw-Hill Home-schooling Companion*.
New York: McGraw, 2002. Print.

Shackelford, Luanne, and Susan White. *A Survivor's Guide to Home Schooling*.
Westchester: Crossway, 1988. Print.

Stevens, Mitchell L. *Kingdom of Children: Culture and Controversy in the
Homeschooling Movement*. Princeton: Princeton UP, 2001. Print.

United States. Dept. of Education. Institute of Education Sciences.
Homeschooling in the United States: 1999. Washington: GPO, 2001.
National Center for Education Statistics. Web. 23 Apr. 2009.

---. *1.5 Million Homeschooled Students in the United States in 2007*.
Washington: GPO, 2008. *National Center for Education Statistics*. Web.
23 Apr. 2009.

⌐*Source with no
pagination is
marked "n. pag."*

——*For multiple
source(s) by the
same author,
replace author's
name with three
hyphens followed
by a period.
(The name of
this government
source has
three separate
components.)*

18 Annotated Bibliographies

In college courses and in your career, you will often need to read multiple sources on a subject. Compiling information on these sources can be helpful for you as you continue to work on a project and for others working on similar projects; in some cases, you may be required to submit this information in the form of an **annotated bibliography** for a grade. For instance, for a research project in a philosophy course, Dominic heads to the library to learn what others have written about the topic "altruism." For each relevant source he finds, he records full source information, writes a brief summary, takes notes on how he might use the source, and copies down useful quotations. Armed with the annotated bibliography he has created, he sits down to write his paper. Thanks to the bibliography, he writes much more efficiently, without having to leaf through stacks of notes and photocopies whenever he needs a reminder of what a source says.

The term annotated bibliography (sometimes also called the *annotated list of works cited*) might sound intimidating, but, as the preceding scenario illustrates, this type of bibliography comes in very handy. The following diagram will help you review its meaning.

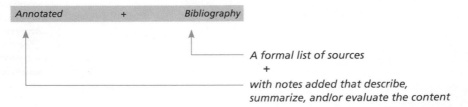

Basic Features

Basic Features

Annotated bibliographies have the following basic features.

● Well-Documented Sources

Regardless of the format you choose for your annotated bibliography, your audience will expect to see clear citations in recognized citation formats like MLA, APA, or *Chicago*. If your readers decide to look up a source, they need to be able to find it easily, so providing them with complete and accurate information in a familiar, readable format is critical.

● An Indication of Content

Your description of sources' content will vary in terms of depth, depending on your purpose and your readers. For some projects, you might merely indicate the topic of a source, while for others you might thoroughly summarize your sources, describing their conclusions or even their methodologies in detail. Comments per source in annotated bibliographies can range in length from a sentence to a paragraph or two.

● A Discussion of Context and Significance

Annotated bibliographies often go beyond summary to tell the reader something important about their central question or topic, and how each source connects to it. You might help the reader understand the significance of studies in your field generally, or you might evaluate their significance with regard to the question you are researching. In an annotated bibliography, you must discuss each source independently.

● An Assertion of One's Place in the Conversation

If you are writing your bibliography as part of a larger document, such as a research or paper proposal, you will want to show how your own work fits into the scholarly or professional conversation. Are you championing an underdog's vision? Are you synthesizing multiple points of view? Or is your idea new?

Purpose and Audience

Instructors who require you to write an annotated bibliography usually have one or both of the following motives:

1. An annotated bibliography is a good first step in a research project, so writing this type of bibliography will help you write a better paper.
2. Professionals in your field need to know how to write an annotated bibliography, so your professor wants you to practice writing one.

When you write for your instructor, you should keep these motives in mind. Of course, some people write annotated bibliographies for their own needs rather than as a requirement. These goals can dramatically shape the annotated bibliography's format, content, and tone.

For instance, like Dominic in the opening example of this chapter, some students and researchers create annotated bibliographies for themselves because doing so is a good way to develop a better understanding of the field and an efficient way to write. These bibliographies are not necessarily intended for anyone else to read. However, a properly constructed annotated bibliography can be very useful beyond its immediate purpose: The author might consult it later while working on other projects and might share it with others who are also working on the topic. In many departments, graduate students preparing for comprehensive exams circulate annotated bibliographies they have created, with users adding entries as new research is published.

Other writers create bibliographies expressly for readers who might be new to a field. After all, an annotated bibliography is easy to skim and thus fairly reader-friendly.

THEY'RE GOOD TO *READ*, TOO

One reason to write annotated bibliographies is to help your readers find more information on your subject. This works both ways: When you need to do research, you can make use of existing bibliographies on your subject. These sources can help you "catch up" on your topic, while also leading you to relevant sources you can consult for more depth. There's another benefit to reading them, too: The more often you read other people's bibliographies, the more comfortable you will be when you need to write them yourself, because as a user you will have a better idea of readers' expectations.

Examples of Annotated Bibliographies

When you write an annotated bibliography, you choose how much to say, and what to say, about each source. Your choices will depend largely on your purpose. Are you simply trying to give the reader an idea of what each source contains? If so, a sentence or two might suffice. But if you are writing an annotated bibliography as part of an effort to analyze the field or persuade the reader, you might want to write a paragraph or so for each source, evaluating it or discussing briefly how it fits into what has been published on the subject. One approach is to ask yourself the following three questions. The type of annotated bibliography you produce will reflect your answers, as illustrated in the discussion that follows.

- What kind of source is this?
- What does the source say?
- How can I use the source?

Most annotated bibliographies have introductions of one or more paragraphs, appearing above the list of sources. These introductions describe for the reader the subject, purpose, and scope of the annotated references. Introductions might also describe how and why the author selected those sources. For instance, an annotated bibliography featuring works about computer animation might have the following introduction:

> Early animations of virtual people in computer games tended to be oblivious to their surroundings, reacting only when hit by moving objects, and then in ways that were not always appropriate--that is, a small object might generate a large effect. In the past few years, however, computer animators have turned their attention to designing virtual people who react appropriately to events around them. The sources below represent the last two years' worth of publications on the subject from the IEEE Xplore database.

Different Types of Annotation

In this section, we provide a range of sample annotations, each based on the following article about the development of an advanced carbon-based fiber. The citations are in APA format.

Source Article (from *Science News*, Aug. 30, 2008)

Carbon Tubes Leave Nano Behind

DAVIDE CASTELVECCHI

1   Take solace, all ye who've grown weary of carbon nanotube promises: The latest tubes are anything but nano.

2   While trying to grow better, longer nanotubes, researchers accidentally discovered a new type of carbon filament that's tens of thousands of times thicker. Christened "colossal carbon tubes," they aren't quite as strong as nanotubes but are 30 times stronger than Kevlar per unit weight, and are potentially easier to turn into applications, suggests a study to appear in *Physical Review Letters*.

3   Though exceptionally strong, nanotubes are hard to weave into larger fibers that could be used in futuristic products, such as ultralight bulletproof vests.

4   Recently at Los Alamos National Laboratory in New Mexico, materials scientist Huisheng Peng and colleagues were trying to grow "forests" of long nanotubes from carbon gas in a vacuum oven. When Peng opened the door, he saw a scene that could be compared to a barbershop floor: Thin, black hairs were scattered everywhere.

5   "At first, I thought they were a lot of carbon nanotubes bonded together," says Peng, who recently moved to Fudan University in Shanghai, China.

6   Tests revealed that the filaments, which were centimeters long and 0.1 millimeter thick, were not clumps of nanotubes, but "colossal" tubes which had the same type of carbon bonds as nanotubes. The atoms were also arranged in the same hexagonal webs resembling chicken wire.

7   Instead of being simple cylindrical structures, the colossal tubes have two concentric layers. The researchers believe that each layer is made of many chicken wire sheets sandwiched together. Walls that are 100 nanometers thick connect the layers and divide the space between the layers into canals that run along the entire length of the tubes — similar to the gaps inside corrugated cardboard.

8   The tubes are easily bent and stretched, and are at least twice as strong as the strongest fibers made from carbon nanotubes to date, the researchers report. The larger tubes are also good electrical conductors.

9   László Forró of the École Polytechnique Fédérale in Lausanne, Switzerland, believes that the authors may have rushed to publication with results that are too preliminary. "At this stage it is only a cookbook," he says. "Basically, they do not know anything about the structure."

10   More research is needed to understand how the tubes form and grow, admits senior author Quanxi Jia of Los Alamos.

1. Descriptive annotation: What kind of source is this?

Descriptive (sometimes called *indicative*) annotations, which are typically very short, simply identify a source's topic. Example:

> Castelvecchi, D. (2008, August 30). Carbon tubes leave nano behind. *Science News, 174*(5), 9-9. Retrieved from http://www.sciencenews.org

> This news article describes the accidental discovery of "colossal carbon tubes"--filaments of carbon much larger than the nanotubes studied in nanotechnology.

2. Summary annotation: What does the source say?

Summary annotations provide information on the source's content — not just the topic, but what the source does with the topic.

> Castelvecchi, D. (2008, August 30). Carbon tubes leave nano behind. *Science News, 174*(5), 9-9. Retrieved from http://www.sciencenews.org

> This news article describes how researchers at the Los Alamos National Laboratory in New Mexico accidentally created what they dub the "colossal carbon tube"--a hair-sized structure made up of carbon atoms. Although the new fiber is not as strong as some earlier carbon structures, groups of such fibers might be easier to weave together for useful applications like bulletproof vests because of their size.

The summary approach is particularly useful if your goal is to explain something without making an argument. For instance, the above annotation might be at home in an essay explaining the role carbon plays in scientific research, as in the following example.

"Carbon: The Miracle Element"

[. . .] So far, we have seen why many astrobiologists expect there to be carbon-based life forms on other planets, and we have seen

The opening sentences recap earlier parts of the paper while providing a transition to the next part.

that our longevity on our own planet might very well depend on how much (or how little) carbon we put into the air. So carbon appears to be the stuff of life and death. But it's rapidly becoming the stuff of stuff, too. If you want to build something that has great strength but little weight--a car, a laptop, a cable elevator to space--you'll find that much of the advanced materials research is focused on carbon.

The highlighted text summarizes and clearly cites the source.

Researchers at Los Alamos National Laboratory, for instance, have come up with a kind of carbon thread that's 30 times stronger than Kevlar, but flexible enough that it might help us build a better bulletproof vest (Castelvecchi, 2008). [. . .]

3. Evaluative annotation: How useful is this source?

If you are writing the annotated bibliography to remind yourself or tell readers what you thought of the sources, you might use an *evaluative* annotation. Sometimes, at an early stage in your research project, an instructor might ask you for an annotated bibliography in which you say how you plan to use each source you found. In this case, the result might look something like this annotation for a criminal justice student's paper on crime-fighting technology:

> Castelvecchi, D. (2008, August 30). Carbon tubes leave nano behind. *Science News, 174*(5), 9-9. Retrieved from http://www.sciencenews.org
>
> This source, which describes a new, flexible lightweight material 30 times stronger than Kevlar and possibly useful for better bulletproof vests, provides evidence of yet another upcoming technology that might be useful to law enforcement. I can focus on the ways in which lighter, stronger bulletproof materials might change SWAT tactics, for instance, enabling them to carry more gear, protect police vehicles, or blend into crowds better.

Notice that this annotation begins by summarizing the source and then goes on to indicate explicitly how it might be useful in the essay the student is researching. One of the benefits of this approach is that it forces you to think about how you might use the sources ahead of time, so that you have a chance to revise or improve your ideas. You do not have to follow what you propose in your evaluative annotation. If you find that your final paper uses the source differently than you had originally planned, that is fine.

For instance, the criminal justice student might later decide that since drug cartels are often better funded than police and have started to appropriate police technology for their own uses, the result of developing those carbon tubes might be a kind of arms race between law enforcement and the criminal class. In that case, her paper might eventually say something like this:

"Prospects for a Cop-Cartel Arms Race"

[. . .] The problem is that drug cartels own companies and can afford scientists, so that any high-tech edge law enforcement obtains against them is likely to be short-lived. Take, for instance, a recent discovery of a carbon thread that might yield a lighter, tougher body armor (Castelvecchi, 2008). If the technology lives up to its promise, it might appear at first glance to be good news for police: It would mean they could wear concealed armor more comfortably under street clothes or uniforms. But if it is that good, it might also mean cartels might start to armor their cars and homes with the stuff, or that crooks might wear concealed body armor to restaurants. If

The opening sentence gives the author's new thesis.

This passage briefly summarizes the source. Note that the goal here is not to dwell on the information, but to move on to a discussion of its ramifications.

This passage explores the possible impacts of the discovery on police

work. As with the anno-
tation, the goal here is to
evaluate. The annotation
on p. 530 reaches differ-
ent conclusions because
it was written earlier. If it
were submitted with the
paper, it would need to
be revised to reflect the
paper's new thesis.

more drawn-out gunfights like 1997's "North Hollywood shootout"
result, civilians might buy body armor, too--and then be more likely
to attempt heroics or get in the way when bullets start flying. None
of this, however, means the police should avoid new technologies--if
they do, they'll simply be left behind. But police do need to be aware
that their jobs might soon get a bit more complicated.

4. A mixed approach

Perhaps the most common kind of annotated bibliography takes a *mixed approach*, combining description, summary, and evaluation. This is particularly true in instances when the annotated bibliography is part of a larger report or is an early step toward creating a larger report: You will want to include an element of description and/or summary so that users have an idea what the sources say, but you will also want to include evaluative comments so that they know what to do with the information, or so that the presentation supports a point you want to make about the field.

Let us assume, for instance, that Rajeev, a political science and environmental engineering double-major, wants to evaluate proposals for "geo-engineering" — ideas for saving the planet from climate change through massive and often expensive engineering projects. Which ideas should receive government funding? Rajeev writes a paper evaluating the options and includes an annotated bibliography that combines summary and evaluation. Below is a sample annotation from this hypothetical bibliography. Notice that in this annotation, the lead sentence answers the first question — What kind of source is this, and who are the readers? — in just a few words before moving on to summary.

Castelvecchi, D. (2008, August 30). Carbon tubes leave nano behind. *Science News, 174*(5), 9-9. Retrieved from http://www.sciencenews.org

This news article for science professionals describes an accidental discovery of "colossal carbon tubes" by Los Alamos National Laboratory researchers. Although the hair-sized tubes are weaker than the nanotubes that have so far dominated carbon fiber research, they remain 30 times stronger than Kevlar and because of their size might be easier to weave together into useful materials. If true, this could be significant: Many geo-engineering plans require cables that can handle a great deal of stress. If colossal tubes are strong enough, they might help us build "space elevators"--cables that reach from the planet's surface into orbit, enabling us to implement space-based solutions to climate change more easily. The tubes even reportedly conduct electricity, which suggests they might be used both to tether floating wind turbines and to conduct power to users on the ground, simultaneously. It is not yet clear from the literature whether colossal tubes can do these jobs, but they might be the best contenders discovered so far.

Because Rajeev's purpose shapes both his annotations and his paper, his paper will also — in all likelihood — balance summary and evaluation, as in the excerpt that follows:

"Die by the Sword, Live by the Sword?"

1 [. . .] But if carbon, industrial progress, and high technology appear to be damning us to a hellish climate, they might also prove to be our salvation. In August 2008, scientists at the Los Alamos National Laboratory in New Mexico announced they had created a new carbon-based thread that is incredibly strong--30 times more so than Kevlar--and versatile enough that it might be easily woven into useful new materials. The stuff is lightweight, flexible, and even conducts electricity (Castelvecchi, 2008).

2 Why is this significant? Because many of the most ambitious plans to fix the problem require materials with these same properties: We're talking about churning out lighter, more fuel-efficient cars; creating blimp-mounted air turbines that send wind power by wire down to ground level; and using a space elevator to "launch" satellites that collect solar power from orbit and beam it to Earth. [. . .]

Rajeev opens with the thesis.

This passage summarizes the content of the source.

This passage begins to evaluate the significance of the discovery mentioned in the source. Note that because the text and the annotation have similar goals — to note the discovery and evaluate its impacts — they have ended up with similar structures, even though they offer slightly different details.

A Map for Writing an Annotated Bibliography

1. Determine Purpose and Audience

- Should your annotations describe, summarize, and/or evaluate the source?
- Is your bibliography for your own purposes, for experts, or for newcomers? Will you need to define terms and provide background information for your readers?

2. Prepare Research Questions Come up with a list of questions that you should try to answer about each source, such as the following:

- How can I tell if the source is credible? (See Chapter 16 for advice on evaluating sources.)
- How can I describe the topic?
- How can I summarize what the source says?
- How can I use it in my paper?
- How does the source relate to other sources I might use?

3. Conduct Research; Take *Good* Notes

- Research your chosen topic. Pay attention to the authors who are frequently cited by others in the field, and find their work — you will want to include it. (For help with research, see Chapter 16.)
- Each time you find a source, create a full citation for it. (See Chapter 17 for help with citation formats.)
- Under each citation, answer the questions you came up with in the previous step.

Always: Reflect and Rethink

Has your research given you reason to rethink your purpose, audience, guiding questions, or even your topic? If so, back up and rethink or redo some steps. It is fine to backtrack as new ideas spring to mind.

4. Prepare Your Entries

- Working from your notes, draft a few sentences or paragraphs on each source, heading each annotation with a full citation.
- Decide on an organizational scheme. Most documents list entries in alphabetical order; but with a long, intensive bibliography, you might want to group your sources by subtopic, with each group listed alphabetically under its own header.
- Revise and edit your entries for space, tone, and content. If an annotation is longer than 150 words, consider tightening it.

5. Consider an Introduction

If you plan for your annotated bibliography to be a stand-alone document, you should consider giving it an introduction that tells readers what it covers, what its purpose is, and how you approached the research.

Acknowledgments

Text Credits

Amanda Coyne. Excerpt from "The Long Good-Bye: Mother's Day in Federal Prison." Copyright © 1997 by Harper's Magazine. All rights reserved. Reproduced from May 1997 issue by special permission.

Annie Dillard. Excerpt from *An American Childhood*. Copyright © 1987 by Annie Dillard. Reprinted with permission of HarperCollins Publishers and Russell & Volkening as agents for the author.

John T. Edge. "I'm Not Leaving Until I Eat This Thing." Originally published in the *Oxford American* (September/October 1999). Copyright © 1999 by John T. Edge. Reprinted with permission of the author.

Trey Ellis. "When the Walls Came Tumbling Down." From *The New York Times*, June 15 © 2008 The New York Times. All rights reserved. Used by permission and protected by the Copyright Laws of the United States. The printing, copying, redistribution, or retransmission of the Material without express written permission is prohibited. www.nytimes.com

Amitai Etzioni. "Working at McDonald's." Copyright © 1986 by Amitai Etzioni. Author of *The Spirit of Community*. Director, George Washington University Center for Communication Policy Studies. Reproduced with the permission of the author.

Amy Goldwasser. "What's the Matter with Kids Today?" This article first appeared in Salon.com, at http://www.salon.com. Reprinted with permission of the author.

Ann Hulbert. "Culture Wars." From *Slate*. Copyright © December 18, 2007, The Slate Group. All rights reserved. Used by permission and protected by the copyright laws of the United States. The printing, copying, redistribution, or retransmission of the Material without express written consent is prohibited.

Jeffrey Kluger. "What Makes Us Moral." From *Time*, December 3, 2007. Copyright © 2007 Time, Inc. Reprinted with permission of TIME Inc. News Group.

Karen Kornbluh. "Win-Win Flexibility." Originally published in *The Atlantic Monthly* (January/February 2003). From *New America Foundation*, June 29, 2005. Copyright 2005. Reprinted with the permission of the author.

Robert Kuttner. "Good Jobs for Americans Who Help Americans." From *The American Prospect*, Volume 19, Number 5: May 08, 2008. www.prospect.org. The American Prospect, 1710 Rhode Island Avenue, NW, 12th Floor, Washington, DC 20036. All rights reserved. Reprinted by permission.

Anastasia Toufexis. "Love: The Right Chemistry." From *Time*, February 15, 1993. Copyright © 1993 Time Inc. Reprinted by permission. *Time* is a registered trademark of Time Inc. All rights reserved.

Art Credits

14 (top left) Huy Lam / Getty Images; (top right) Library of Congress; (bottom) Reza Estakhrian / Getty Images; **16** Rudy Sulgan / Corbis; **23** Phyllis Rose; **29** Paul Provenzano; **30** © Donna Svennevik / American Broadcasting Companies, Inc.; **56** (top left) Bill Aron / PhotoEdit; (top right) David Young-Wolff / PhotoEdit; (bottom) Somos / Veer / Getty Images; **58** Library of Congress; **62** Scott Ryan; **67** Kyle Hood; **68** Shannon Brinkman; **74** Courtesy Amanda Coyne; **106** (top left) David Young-Wolff / PhotoEdit; (top right) Comstock Images / Alamy; (bottom) DigitalGlobe / Getty Images; **108** NationalGeographic.com; **117** Courtesy Anastasia Toufexis; **120** Nigel Holmes; **124** Saez Pascal / SIPA / Newscom; **127, 129, 131** John Ritter; **158** (top left) Jim Wilson / The New York Times / Redux; (top right) Michael Newman / PhotoEdit; (bottom) Todd Heisler / The New York Times / Redux; **160** Courtesy Ad Council; **171** Jessica McConnell (Photographer, University Relations, The George Washington University); **177** Peter Arkle; **206** (top left) Children's Television Workshop / Getty Images; (top right) David Young-Wolff / PhotoEdit (bottom) Blend Images / Alamy; **208** The AICPA; **219** Center for Economic and Policy Research; **227** Carolina Manero; **260** (top left) Photofest; (top right) © Nancy Richmond / The Image Works; (bottom) Photofest; **262** Copyright 2008 by Consumers Union of U.S., Inc. Yonkers, NY 10703-1057, a nonprofit organization. Reprinted with permission from the August 2008 issue of Consumer Reports for educational purposes only. No commercial use or reproduction permitted. www.ConsumerReports.org; **267** "www .ratemyprofessors.com" used with permission by MTV Networks. © 2011 MTV Networks. All Rights Reserved. MTV, all related titles, characters and logos are trademarks owned by MTV Networks, a division of Viacom International Inc.; **273** (bottom) Photofest; **383** Graph courtesy Human Rights First. Source: Parents Television Council; **387** © Bo Zaunders / Corbis; **388** World Wildlife Fund PSA; **392, 398** Library of Congress; **393** (top) Grant Wood, American, 1891–1942, *American Gothic*, 1930, Oil on Beaver Board, 78 x 65.3 cm (30 3/4 x 25 3/4 in.), Friends of American Art Collection, 1930.934, The Art Institute of Chicago. Photography © The Art Institute of Chicago, Art © Figge Art Museum, successor to the Estate of Nan Wood Graham/Licensed by VAGA, New York, NY; (bottom), **397** *Emerging Man, Harlem*, 1952. Photograph by Gordon Parks. Copyright The Gordon Parks Foundation. Courtesy The Gordon Parks Foundation; **401** Library of Congress; **402** (top) Agency: Freight Train, CD: Kevin Brown, AD: Dan LaVigne, Writer: Kevin Brown, Photographer: Dan Bishop (Digital Skylab); (bottom) Richard B. Levine / Newscom; **403** Creative Director: Carlos Cortinas; **428** (bottom) Lalo © 2002 Lalo Alcaraz. Used by permission of Universal Uclick. All rights reserved; **429** (top) Photofest; **430, 436** Microsoft product screen shot reprinted with permission from Microsoft Corporation; **432** Courtesy Stanford Law School; **472, 475, 477** Courtesy EBSCO Publishing.

Subject Index

ABC test, 348–50
above, 365
absolute phrases, 96
abstracts, in periodical databases, 471
accommodating readers' concerns, in counterarguments, 414
accordingly, 363
accuracy of statements, 349
acknowledging readers' concerns, in counterarguments, 413–14
across, 365
actually, 363
ad hominem arguments, 416
adjacent to, 365
adjectives
    adjective clauses, 153–54
    adjective order, 103–4
advanced searches, 467–68
adverbs, conjunctive, 203–4
after, 47
afterward, 364
again and again, 364
agents, sentences that lack, 257–58
aggregators, 481
all in all, 363
all the same, 235, 364
along, 365
alongside, 365
altogether, 363
American Heritage Dictionary of the English Language, 204
analogies, false, 416
analyzing arguments
    annotating a text and creating a chart, 370–71
    criteria for, 368–70
    focus for analysis, 372
    sample analysis: Mae, "'A Case

for Torture': A Questionable Argument," 372–80
and, 53, 363
anecdotes
    in argument essays, 164, 181
    believability of statements and, 349
    in concept explanation essays, 143
    defining the problem in proposals with, 211
    supporting arguments with, 410–11
Angelou, Maya, 8
annotated bibliographies
    basic features, 526–27
    map for writing, 533–34
    purpose and audience, 527–28
    types of annotation, 530–32
annotating, as critical reading strategy, 330–37
announcing the topic, 356–57
antecedents, 360
APA documentation style
    in-text citations, 509–11
    reference list, 511–16
apparently, 406
appositive phrases, combining sentences with, 311
appositives, 147
appropriateness of logical arguments, 348–49
argument essays: overview
    analyzing visuals: drunk-driving PSA, 160, 161
    collaborative activity: practice arguing a position, 162–63
    introduction, 161
    reading and writing, 161–62
    real-world applications, 159

argument essays, reading
    analyzing writing strategies, 175, 180–82
    basic features: counterarguments, 164, 176, 181–82, 190–91, 200; readable plans, 164, 176–77, 182, 200; well-presented issues, 163, 175, 180–81, 189–90, 199; well-supported positions, 164, 175–76, 181, 199
    considering topics for your own essay, 171, 177, 182
    critical reading guide, 199–200
    making connections, 174, 180
    purpose and audience, 165
    readings: Etzioni, "Working at McDonald's," 171–74; Goldwasser, "What's the Matter with Kids Today?," 177–80; Statsky, "Children Need to Play, Not Compete," 165–71 (*see also* "'Children Need to Play, Not Compete,' by Jessica Statsky: An Evaluation"; Romano)
argument essays, writing
    collaborative activity: testing your choice of topic, 189
    considering social dimensions: suppressing dissent, 205–6
    editing and proofreading: commas with coordinating conjunctions, 202–3; ESL problems: subtle differences in meaning, 204; punctuation with conjunctive adverbs, 203–4

invention and research: choosing an issue to write about, 185–87; defining purpose for readers, 192; researching argument, 192; testing your choice, 188–89; thesis statements, 193; ways in: bringing issue and audience into focus, 187–88; ways in: developing argument and counterargument, 189–91; ways in: using the Web to find or explore an issue, 187
overview, 183
planning and drafting: drafting, 196–98; outlining your draft, 195–96; refining your purpose and setting goals, 193–94; working with sources: quoting opposing positions, 198–99
reflecting on writing, 205
revising, 200–202
starting points, 184–85
arguments, analyzing and synthesizing
analyzing: annotating a text and creating a chart, 370–71; criteria for, 368–70; focus for analysis, 372; sample analysis: Mae, "'A Case for Torture': A Questionable Argument," 372–80
synthesizing: from analysis to synthesis, 380; sample synthesis: Mae, "The Centrality of the Ticking Time-Bomb Scenario in Arguments Justifying Torture," 380–86
arguments, mechanics of
asserting a thesis: appropriate qualification, 406–7; arguable assertions, 405; clear and precise writing, 405–6; overview, 404–5
counterarguing: accommodating readers' concerns, 414; acknowledging readers' concerns, 413–14;

refuting readers' objections, 415
giving reasons and support: anecdotes, 410–11; authorities, 409–10; examples, 407–8; statistics, 408–9; textual evidence, 412–13
logical fallacies, 416
Aristotle, 327
articles
finding, 470–75
information for working bibliography, 464
as a result, 363
as it was happening, 364
assertions, arguable, 405
as well as, 363
at first, 364
at last, 364
at that moment, 364
at that time, 364
at the same time, 364
audience
of argument essays, 165
of concept explanation essays, 111–12
for document design, 418–19
of evaluative essays, 265
of profile essays, 62
of proposal essays, 212–13
of remembered-event essays, 19, 44
authority
believability of statements and, 350
citing in position statements, 164, 181
invoking, in logical arguments, 349
overreliance on, 416
supporting arguments with, 409–10
author searches, 466
autobiographical significance, 18, 28–29, 34
away, 365
away from, 365

Bagaric, Mirko, "A Case For Torture," 372–74
balancing criticism and praise, 303

Bambara, Toni Cade, 2
bar graphs, 425
Barry, Dave, 9
because, 363
before, 47
before then, 364
begging the question, 416
behind, 365
beliefs and values, challenges to, 347–48
believability, evaluating, 349–50
below, 365
besides, 363
beyond, 365
bias, identifying, 484
bibliographies
annotated: basic features, 526–27; map for writing, 533–34; purpose and audience, 527–28; types of annotation, 530–32
researching with, 462
working, 462–64
binary thinking, 370
block quotations, 490–91
block style, 424
blogs, 481
books
citing (*see* APA documentation style; MLA documentation style)
finding, 469–70
information for working bibliography, 463
Boolean operators, 467–68
brackets, 489
Brandt, Jean, "Calling Home," 19–23
briefly, 364
bulleted lists, 422
burden of proof, 416
Burke, Edmund, 1
business letters, 434
but, 53, 235, 364

Cable, Brian, "The Last Stop," 62–67
"Calling Home" (Brandt), 19–23
"Cannibalism: It Still Exists" (Ngo), 112–17
captions, 430
cartoons, 428

Cary, Joyce, 10
"Case for Torture, A" (Bagaric and Clarke), 372–74
"'Case for Torture': A Questionable Argument, 'A'" (Mae), 377–80
catalog, library online, 469–70
causes and effects
   identifying, in profile essays, 60
   post hoc, ergo propter hoc fallacy, 416
   reporting, in concept explanation essays, 123, 143
"Centrality of the Ticking Time-Bomb Scenario in Arguments Justifying Torture, The" (Mae), 382–86
certainly, 235, 364
challenges to beliefs and values. *See* beliefs and values, challenges to
charts
   for argument analysis and synthesis, 370–71
   design of, 426–27
   using, to choose a problem to write about, 238–39
chat rooms, 482
"'Children Need to Play, Not Compete,' by Jessica Statsky: An Evaluation" (Romano), 280–85
"Children Need to Play, Not Compete" (Statsky), 165–71
choosing an event to write about, 38–40
chronology, confusing with causality, 416
chunking
   in scratch outlines, 320
   white space and, 423–24
circular reasoning, 416
citing visuals, 430
Clarke, Julie, "A Case for Torture," 372–74
classification
   in concept explanation essays, 123, 143
   in profile essays, 60
clauses, adjective, 153–54

clearly, 363
climax, in pyramid structure, 32
closed questions, 449
close to, 365
clustering, 317
cohesive devices
   collocation, 361–62
   in concept explanation essays, 133–34
   overview, 359
   pronoun reference, 360
   sentence structure repetition, 361
   synonyms, 361
   word repetition, 360
collaborative activities
   argument essays: practice arguing a position, 162–63; testing choice of topic, 189
   concept explanation essays: practice explaining a concept, 109; testing your choice of topic, 141
   evaluative essays: practice evaluating a subject, 263; testing your choice of topic, 295
   profile essays: practice conducting an interview, 59; testing your choice of topic, 88
   proposal essays: practice proposing a solution, 210; testing your choice of topic, 243
   remembered-event essays: practice remembering an event, 17; testing your choice of topic, 42
collocation, 360
colors, in document design, 422–23
commas
   with conjunctive adverbs, 203–4
   with coordinating conjunctions, 202–3
   fused sentences and, 53
   with interrupting phrases, 154–55
   missing, after introductory elements, 52
   with quotation marks, 103

common ground, testing for, 352
comparability of statistics, 349–50
comparison and contrast
   in concept explanation essays, 123, 143
   in profiles, 60
   as sentence strategy, 302–3
comparisons, complete and correct, 310
completeness of facts, 349
concept explanation essays, overview
   collaborative activity: practice explaining a concept, 109
   introduction, 108
   reading and writing, 108–9
   real-world applications, 107
concept explanation essays, reading
   analyzing visuals: flowcharts, 124; "Moral Dilemmas," 135
   analyzing writing strategies, 122–23, 133
   basic features: appropriate explanatory strategies, 110–11, 123, 134, 149–50, 152; focused explanations, 110, 133, 149, 151; readable plans, 110, 122–23, 133–34, 149, 151–52; smooth integration of sources, 111, 123, 134–35, 150, 153
   considering topics for your own essay, 124, 135
   critical reading guide, 149–50
   making connections, 121, 132–33
   purpose and audience, 111–12
   readings
      Kluger, "What Makes Us Moral," 124–32
      Ngo, "Cannibalism: It Still Exists," 112–17
      Toufexis, "Love: The Right Chemistry," 117–21
concept explanation essays, writing
   collaborative activity: testing your choice, 141

considering social dimensions: concept explanations and the nature of knowledge, 156

editing and proofreading: commas with interrupting phrases, 154–55; punctuation with adjective clauses, 153–54

invention and research choosing a concept to write about, 138–40; defining purpose for readers, 143; designing your document, 143; explanatory strategies, 142–43; in-depth research, 142; testing your choice, 141; thesis statements, 144; ways in: focusing the concept, 141; ways in: gaining an overview, 140

overview, 136

planning and drafting: drafting, 146–47; outlining your draft, 145–46; refining your purpose and setting goals, 144–45; working with sources: using descriptive verbs, 148–49

reflecting on writing, 155–56

revising, 150–53

starting points, 137–38

concerns, acknowledging and accommodating, 413–14

conflict, in remembered-event essays, 40

conjunctive adverbs, 203–4

connection with others, writing's influence on, 3

connectives. *See* transitional words and phrases

consequently, 363

consistency and completeness, 350

context for document design, 418–19

contextualizing, 343–44

coordinating conjunctions, 202–3

counterarguments
by essay type: argument essays, 164, 176, 181–82,

190–91, 200; evaluative essays, 264–65, 278, 287–88, 295–96, 306–7; proposal essays, 211–12, 226, 234, 244, 253–54

guidelines for: accommodating readers' concerns, 414; acknowledging readers' concerns, 413–14; refuting readers' objections, 415

identifying, in argument analysis, 369

cover letters, 438

Coyne, Amanda, "The Long Good-Bye: Mother's Day in Federal Prison," 74–79

credentials, identifying with appositives, 147

credibility
judging, as reading strategy, 351–52

persuasiveness of statistics and, 252–53

critical thinking, 11–12

criticism, balancing with praise, 303

cubing, 322–23

cueing strategies
cohesive devices: overview, 359; pronoun reference, 360

collocation, 361–62

by essay type: concept explanation essays, 133–34; proposal essays, 234–35

headings and subheadings: frequency and placement of headings, 367; headings and genres, 366–67; heading systems and levels, 366

orienting statements: forecasting statements, 354–55; thesis statements, 353–54

paragraphing: paragraph cues, 355–56; topic sentence strategies, 356–59

rhetorical questions, 235

sentence structure repetition, 361

synonyms, 361

transitional words and

phrases: logical relationships, 363–64; spatial relationships, 365; temporal relationships, 364

word repetition, 360

databases and indexes, 470–73

day after day, 364

definitions
appositives for, 147

in concept explanation essays, 123, 142

in profile essays, 60

description
dominant impressions and, 33

naming and detailing, 28

in profile essays, 60

descriptive annotations, 530

descriptive verbs, 148–49

designing documents. *See* document design

details
in profile essays, 60, 71–72, 80, 100

in remembered-event essays, 28

diagrams, 428

dialoguing, as invention and inquiry strategy, 323

Didion, Joan, 3

Dillard, Annie, 6, 9, 11
"An American Childhood," 23–27

discovering new ideas, learning strategies for, 8–9

division, 123

documentation. *See* sources, documenting

document design
context, audience, and purpose, 418–19

elements: colors, 422–23; font style and size, 419–20; headings and body text, 421; numbered and bulleted lists, 422; white space, 423–24

impact of, 417–18

reading to design texts that work, 6–7

sample documents: e-mail, 434–36; job-application letters, 438, 439; lab reports, 438–41; letters,

434; memos, 433–34; résumés, 436–38; Web pages, 440–42

visuals: computer considerations, 431–32; integrating into text, 431; numbering, labeling, and citing, 430; types of, 424–30

dominant impressions
    in profile essays, 61
    in remembered-event essays, 33, 41

down, 365

drafting, quick, 328

drafting and revising, learning strategies for, 9–10

dramatizing, 323–25

drawings, 428

Dunne, John Gregory, 12

during, 364

Edge, John T., "I'm Not Leaving Until I Eat This Thing," 67–70

editing and proofreading
    complete and correct comparisons, 310
    past perfect, 53
    punctuation: with adjective clauses, 153–54; commas with coordinating conjunctions, 202–3; commas with interrupting phrases, 154–55; with conjunctive adverbs, 203–4; missing commas after introductory elements, 52
    sentences: combining sentences, 311; fused sentences, 53; missing agents in, 257–58
    word choice: ambiguous use of *this* and *that,* 256–57; subtle differences in meaning, 205

editorial slant, 485

either-or reasoning, 416

electronic sources, taking notes from, 464

Eliot, T. S., 10

ellipsis marks, 488–89

Ellis, Trey, "When the Walls Came Tumbling Down," 29–31

Ellison, Ralph, 9

e-mail
    document design and, 434–36
    in research process, 481–82

Emerging Man (Parks), 393–400

emotional manipulation, 350–51

encyclopedias, 461

equivocating, 416

ESL problems
    adjective order, 103–4
    past perfect, 53
    subtle differences in meaning, 204

Etta Watson (Parks), 392, 398

Etzioni, Amitai, "Working at McDonald's," 171–74

evaluating sources
    identifying bias, 484
    overview, 482–83
    selecting relevant sources, 483–84

evaluative annotations, 531

evaluative essays, overview
    collaborative activity: practice evaluating a subject, 263
    introduction, 262
    reading and writing, 262–63
    real-life applications, 261

evaluative essays, reading
    analyzing visuals: still from *Juno,* 273, 279
    analyzing writing strategies, 276–79, 286–88
    basic features: effective counterarguments, 264–65, 278, 287–88, 306–7; readable plans, 265, 278–79, 288, 308; well-presented subjects, 264, 276–77, 286, 306; well-supported judgments, 264, 277–78, 286–87, 308
    considering topics for your own essay, 280
    critical reading guide, 306
    making connections, 276, 285–86
    purpose and audience, 265
    readings: Hulbert, "*Juno* and the Culture Wars," 273–75; Kim, "Grading Professors," 266–72; Romano,

"'Children Need to Play, Not Compete,' by Jessica Statsky: An Evaluation," 280–85

evaluative essays, writing
    collaborative activity: testing your choice of subject, 295
    considering social dimensions: evaluators' hidden assumptions, 312–13
    editing and proofreading: combining sentences, 311; complete and correct comparisons, 310
    invention and research: choosing a subject to write about, 291–93; defining purpose for readers, 297; making a tentative judgment, 295; researching your argument, 297; testing your choice, 295; thesis statements, 298; ways in: bringing subject and audience into focus, 293–94; ways in: developing your argument and counterargument, 295–96
    overview, 289
    planning and drafting: drafting, 301–3; outlining your draft, 300–301; refining your purpose and setting goals, 298–300; working with sources: using summaries to support evaluative arguments, 304–5
    reflecting on writing, 312
    revising, 307–9
    starting points, 290

even though, 235, 364

eventually, 364

every so often, 364

evidently, 363

examples
    believability of statements and, 349
    defining the problem with, 211
    as explanatory strategy, 134, 143
    in position statements, 164, 181
    in profile essays, 60
    supporting arguments with, 407–8

explanatory strategies, 110–11, 123, 134, 149–50, 152
exposition, in pyramid structure, 32

facing, 365
facts
  believability of, 349
  in position statements, 164, 181
fairness, testing for, 352
fallacies, logical, 416
falling action, in pyramid structure, 32
false analogies, 416
far, 365
Faulkner, William, 6
fears and concerns, identifying, 370
federated search engines, 471
field research
  collecting profile information from, 89–91
  interviews: planning and setting up, 447–50; reflecting, 450; taking notes, 450; writing up notes, 450–51
  observations: observing and taking notes, 445–46; planning the visit, 444–45; preparing for follow-up visits, 447; reflecting on observations, 446; writing up notes, 446–47
  questionnaires: administering the questionnaire, 454; designing the questionnaire, 452–53; focusing your study, 451–52; testing the questionnaire, 454; writing questions, 452; writing up results, 454–56
figurative language, 344–46
finally, 363, 364
first . . . second, 235, 363
flowcharts, 124, 426, 427
focused explanations, 110, 133, 149, 151
font style and size, 419–20
for, 53, 363
for a long time, 364
forced-choice questions, 449
forecasting statements

as cueing strategy, 354–55
thesis statements and, 176–77
for example, 235, 363
formal outlines
  as critical reading strategy, 338–39
  as invention and inquiry strategy, 322
for one thing . . . for another, 363
Forster, E. M., 8
framing of issues, 163, 175, 188.
    See also reframing of issues
frequency and placement of headings, 367
frequently, 364
full-text databases, 471
furthermore, 235, 363
fused sentences, 53

general encyclopedias, 461
generalizations, hasty, 416
genres
  experiences with different genres exercise, 7
  headings and, 366–67
Ghosh, Amitav, 8
Goldwasser, Amy, "What's the Matter with Kids Today?," 177–80
"Good Jobs for Americans Who Help Americans" (Kuttner), 227–32
Google, 479–80
government and statistical information, 475–76
"Grading Professors" (Kim), 266–72
granted, 235, 364
graphs, design of, 425–26
Guides to Writing, using, 10–11

hasty generalizations, 416
headings and subheadings
  as cues, in concept explanation essays, 133
  in document design, 421
  frequency and placement of headings, 367
  genres and, 366–67
  systems and levels, 366
Hemingway, Ernest, 4
hence, 363

heuristics. See invention and inquiry, strategies for
hourly, 364
however, 235, 364
Hulbert, Ann, "Juno and the Culture Wars," 273–75

ideology and ideals, identifying, 370
illustration, as explanatory strategy, 123
images, defined, 387
"I'm Not Leaving Until I Eat This Thing" (Edge), 67–70
in addition, 235, 363
in conclusion, 363
in contrast, 235, 364
infographics, 108
in front of, 365
in other words, 363
in particular, 235, 363
inside, 365
in simpler terms, 363
interlibrary networks, 470
Internet research
  by essay type: argument essays, 187, 192; concept explanation essays, 140, 142; evaluative essays, 292; profile essays, 86; proposal essays, 240, 244
  guidelines for: finding information online, 479–81; overview, 478–79; using e-mail and online communities, 481–82
interrupting phrases, commas with, 154–55
interviews
  guidelines for conducting: planning and setting up, 447–50; reflecting, 450; taking notes, 450; writing up notes, 450–51
  integrating quotations from, 97–98
  practice conducting, 59
in the beginning, 364
in the distance, 365
in the end, 364
in the meantime, 47, 364
in those days, 364
intimacy, 32

invention, as writing strategy, 8
invention and inquiry, strategies
    for
    mapping strategies: clustering,
        317; listing, 317; outlining,
        318–22; overview, 316
    writing strategies: cubing, 322–
        23; dialoguing, 323; dra-
        matizing, 323–25; keeping
        a journal, 325–26; looping,
        326; questioning, 327–28;
        quick drafting, 328
inventory, taking, 337
issues
    identifying, 369
    well-presented, 163, 175,
        180–81, 189–90, 199
italics for emphasis, 488
it is true, 364
it seems, 406

job-application letters, 438, 439
Jobs, Steve, 7
journal, keeping a, 325–26
journal articles. *See* articles
judgments, well-supported, 264,
    277–78, 286–87, 308
"*Juno* and the Culture Wars"
    (Hulbert), 273–75

Kazin, Alfred, 3
Keillor, Garrison, 9
keyword searches
    Internet search engines, 192
    library catalogs and periodical
        databases, 466
Kim, Wendy, "Grading
    Professors," 266–72
King, Martin Luther, Jr., "Letter
    from Birmingham Jail"
    (annotated excerpt),
    330–36
King, Stephen, 5
Kingsolver, Barbara, 3–4
Kingston, Maxine Hong, 3
Kluger, Jeffrey, "What Makes Us
    Moral," 124–32
knowledge, testing for, 351
Kornbluh, Karen, "Win-Win
    Flexibility," 219–24
Kuttner, Robert, "Good Jobs for
    Americans Who Help
    Americans," 227–32

lab reports, 438–41
Lange, Dorothea, "Migrant
    Mother," 58
last, 363
"Last Stop, The" (Cable), 62–67
later, 364
leading questions, 449
learning, writing's influence on, 2
learning to write
    overview, 4–5
    by reading: reading to design
        texts that work, 6–7; read-
        ing to understand how
        texts work, 5–6; reading
        to write texts that work, 6
    strategies: for discovering new
        ideas, 8–9; for drafting
        and revising, 9–10; for
        getting started, 8; for
        organizing ideas, 9; over-
        view, 7
L'Engle, Madeleine, 8
"Letter from Birmingham Jail"
    (King; annotated ex-
    cerpt), 330–36
letters, 434. *See also* job-
    application letters
levels of headings, 366
library and Internet research
    determining the most promis-
        ing sources, 476–78
    evaluating sources: identifying
        bias, 484; overview, 482–
        83; selecting relevant
        sources, 483–84
    finding library sources:
        articles, 470–75; books,
        469–70; general search
        strategies, 466–69; gov-
        ernment and statistical in-
        formation, 475–76; other
        library sources, 476; over-
        view, 465
    getting started: bibliographies,
        462; encyclopedias, 461;
        finding out what the
        library offers, 459–60;
        knowing research task, 459
    Internet research: finding
        information online,
        479–81; overview, 478–79;
        using e-mail and online
        communities, 481–82

keeping track of
    research: taking notes,
        464; working bibliogra-
        phies, 462–64
orienting yourself to the
    library: librarians, 459;
    tours, 457–58
line graphs, 425, 426
lists
    as invention and inquiry
        strategy, 317
    numbered and bulleted,
        422
literacy, 4–5
literacy narratives, 1
logic
    Boolean, 467–68
    evaluating with ABC test,
        348–50
logical comparisons, 310
logical fallacies, 416
"Long Good-Bye: Mother's Day
    in Federal Prison"
    (Coyne), 74–79
looping, 326
"Love: The Right Chemistry"
    (Toufexis), 117–21

Mae, Melissa
    "'A Case for Torture': A
        Questionable Argument,"
        377–80
    "The Centrality of the Ticking
        Time-Bomb Scenario in
        Arguments Justifying
        Torture," 382–86
mailing lists, 482
"Mapping Memory" (*National
    Geographic* online),
    108
mapping strategies
    clustering, 317
    listing, 317
    outlining, 318–22
    overview, 316
maps, 429–30
margins, 424
Mead, Margaret, 4
meaning, subtle differences in,
    204
meanwhile, 364
memorabilia, 42–43
memos, 433–34

message boards, 482
metaphors
    reading strategies and, 344
    reflection exercise, 12
"Migrant Mother" (Lange), 58
minute by minute, 364
MLA documentation style
    in-text citations, 497–500
    works cited list, 500–509
"Moral Dilemmas," 127, 129,
        131, 135
moreover, 235, 363
"More Testing, More Learning"
        (O'Malley), 213–19
motivating factors for arguments,
        369–70

namely, 363
naming, 28
narration
    in concept explanation essays,
        123, 143
    in profile essays, 60, 101
naturally, 364
near, 365
needs and interests, identifying,
        370
neither, 235, 364
nevertheless, 235, 364
newsgroups, 482
next, 363, 364
next to, 365
Ngo, LinhKieu, "Cannibalism: It
        Still Exists," 112–17
nonetheless, 235, 364
nor, 53, 364
notes, taking
    for field observations, 445–46
    for interviews, 450
    in research process, 464
now, 364
now and then, 364
numbered lists, 422
numbering visuals, 430

objections, refuting, 415
observations
    observing and taking notes,
        445–46
    planning the visit, 444–45
    preparing for follow-up visits,
        447

reflecting on observations, 446
    writing up notes, 446–47
occasionally, 364
of course, 235, 363, 364
often, 364
Oliver, Mary, 6
O'Malley, Patrick, "More Testing,
        More Learning," 213–19
online catalog. *See* catalog, library
        online
online communities, 481–82
on the contrary, 364
on the other hand, 364
opening sentences
    argument essays, 196
    concept explanation essays,
        146
    evaluative essays, 302
    proposal essays, 249
    remembered-event essays,
        46–47
open questions, 449
opposition, patterns of, 346–47
or, 53
organizational plans, narrative vs.
        topical, 60
organization charts, 427
organizing ideas, learning strate-
        gies for, 9
orienting statements
    forecasting statements, 354–55
    thesis statements, 353–54
Osgood, Lawrence, 12
outlining
    as critical reading strategy:
        formal outlines, 338–39;
        overview, 337–38, 340;
        scratch outlines, 339
    drafts: argument essays, 195–
        96; concept explanation
        essays, 145–46; evaluative
        essays, 300–301; profile
        essays, 95; proposal es-
        says, 248; remembered-
        event essays, 45–46
    as invention and inquiry strat-
        egy: formal outlines, 322;
        scratch outlines, 318–20;
        topic and sentence out-
        lines, 320–21
pyramid structure, 32–33
outside, 365

overreliance on authority, 416
oversimplifying, 416
Ozick, Cynthia, 12

paradoxes, 133
paragraphing
    paragraph cues, 355–56
    topic sentence strategies, 356–59
parallelism
    in comparisons, 310
    in grammatical structure of
        headings, 366
paraphrasing
    as critical reading strategy,
        340–41
    integrating sources by, 493–95
    in profile essays, 60
    in remembered-event essays,
        48–49
Parks, Gordon, *Etta Watson* and
        Emerging Man, 391–400
participant observer, writer's role
        as, 61, 102
past perfect, 53
patterns of opposition. *See* oppo-
        sition, patterns of
people, describing, 28, 33, 41
periodical articles. *See* articles
periodicals, defined, 465
periods, 103
personal attacks, 416
personal development, writing's
        influence on, 2–3
photographs, document design
        and, 428, 429
pie charts, 426
Pike, Kenneth, 327
pivotal or revealing moments, 40
places, describing, 28, 41
plagiarism
    note-taking process and, 465
    overview, 487
    quoting appropriately to avoid,
        198–99
popular magazines vs. scholarly
        journals, 473–74
Porter, Katherine Anne, 6
portraits, visual, 58
positioning the topic sentence,
        358–59
positions
    identifying, 369

well-supported, 164, 175–76, 181, 199
post hoc, ergo propter hoc, 416
precision of statistical methods, 350
prepositional phrases, 27
present perspective, 34, 43–44
print sources, taking notes from, 465
priorities and agendas, identifying, 370
probably, 406
problems, well-defined, 211, 225, 233, 253
profile essays, overview
    collaborative activity: practice conducting an interview, 59
    introduction, 58
    reading and writing, 58–59
    real-world applications, 57–58
profile essays, reading
    analyzing visuals: photograph of a pig, 68, 73–74
    basic features: clear organizational plan, 60, 72, 80; detailed information, 60, 71–72, 80; perspective on subject, 61, 73, 81; role for the writer, 61, 72–73, 80–81
    considering social dimensions: entertainment vs. showing whole picture, 105
    considering topics for your own essay, 74, 81
    critical reading guide, 98–99
    making connections, 71, 79
    purpose and audience, 61–62
    readings
        "I'm Not Leaving Until I Eat This Thing" (Edge), 67–70
        "The Last Stop" (Cable), 62–67
        "The Long Good-Bye: Mother's Day in Federal Prison" (Coyne), 74–79
profile essays, writing
    collaborative activity: testing your choice, 88
    editing and proofreading: adjective order, 103–4;

punctuation of quotations, 102–3
    invention and research: choosing a subject, 84–86; collecting information from field research, 89–91; considering your thesis, 92–93; designing your document, 93; exploring preconceptions, 87; finalizing choice, 86–87; reflecting on purpose and perspective, 92; tentative schedule, 88–89; testing your choice, 88
    overview, 82
    planning and drafting: drafting, 95–96; outlining your draft, 95; refining your purpose and setting goals, 93–94; working with sources: integrating quotations from interviews, 97–98
    reflecting on writing, 104–5
    revising, 99–102
    starting points, 83–84
pronoun reference, 360
proofreading. *See* editing and proofreading
proposal essays, overview
    collaborative activity: practice proposing a solution, 210
    introduction, 209
    reading and writing, 209 10
    real-world applications, 207
    visuals: ad for feedthepig.org, 208, 209
proposal essays, reading
    analyzing writing strategies, 224–26, 233–34
    basic features: counterarguments, 211–12, 226, 234, 253–54; readable plans, 212, 226, 234–35, 254; well-argued solutions, 211, 225–26, 233–34, 253; well-defined problems, 211, 225, 233, 253
    considering topics for your own essay, 226, 235
    critical reading guide, 253–54
    making connections, 224, 232–33

purpose and audience, 212–13
    readings: Kornbluh, "Win-Win Flexibility," 219–24; Kuttner, "Good Jobs for Americans Who Help Americans," 227–32; O'Malley, "More Testing, More Learning," 213–19
proposal essays, writing
    collaborative activity: testing your choice, 243
    considering social dimensions: frustrations of effecting real change, 259
    invention and research: choosing a problem to write about, 238–40; defining purpose for readers, 245; researching proposals, 245; testing your choice, 243; thesis statements, 245–46; ways in: bringing problem and audience into focus, 240–42; ways in: counter-arguing alternative solutions, 244; ways in: exploring tentative solutions, 242–43
    overview, 236
    planning and drafting: drafting, 249; editing and proofreading: ambiguous use of *this* and *that*, 256–57; editing and proofreading: sentences that lack an agent, 257–58; outlining your draft, 248; refining your purpose and setting goals, 246–47; revising, 254–56; sentence strategy: rhetorical questions, 249–51; working with sources: establishing a problem's existence and seriousness, 251–53
    reflecting on writing, 258
    starting points, 237
punctuation
    brackets, 489
    commas: with conjunctive adverbs, 203–4; with

coordinating conjunctions, 202–3; with interrupting phrases, 154–55; missing commas after introductory elements, 52; with quotation marks, 103
ellipsis marks, 488–89
periods, 103
quotation marks, 103
in specific situations: adjective clauses, 153–54; conjunctive adverbs, 203–4; quotations, 102–3, 198–99, 488–89, 492
purpose
of argument essays, 165
of concept explanation essays, 111, 143
for document design, 418–19
of evaluative essays, 265
of profile essays, 61–62
of proposal essays, 212
of remembered-event essays, 18, 44
pyramid structure, 32–33, 45–46

qualifying thesis statements, 406–7
questioning, invention and inquiry strategy, 327–28
questionnaires
administering the questionnaire, 454
designing the questionnaire, 452–53
focusing your study, 451–52
testing the questionnaire, 454
writing questions, 452
writing up results, 454–56
questions
begging the question, 416
rhetorical, 235, 249–51
writing: for interviews, 448–49; for questionnaires, 452
quick drafting, 328
Quindlen, Anna, 10
quotations
integrating, 97–98, 490–91
introducing, 491
punctuation of, 102–3, 488–89, 492

quoting
avoiding grammatical tangles, 492–93
to avoid plagiarism, 198–99
opposing positions, 198–99
in profile essays, 60
in remembered-event essays, 48–49

reading
to design texts that work, 6–7
to understand how texts work, 5–6
to write texts that work, 6
reading strategies
annotating, 330–37
challenges to beliefs and values, 347–48
contextualizing, 343–44
evaluating logic, 348–50
figurative language, 344–46
judging writer's credibility, 351–52
outlining: formal outlines, 338–39; overview, 337–38, 340; scratch outlines, 339
paraphrasing, 340–41
patterns of opposition, 346–47
recognizing emotional manipulation, 350–51
summarizing, 341–42
synthesizing, 342–43
taking inventory, 337
reasons and support for arguments
anecdotes, 410–11
authorities, 409–10
examples, 407–8
statistics, 408–9
textual evidence, 412–13
red herring fallacy, 416
reflection exercises
becoming literate, 4–5
experiences with different genres, 7
last writing project, 11
literacy experience through metaphor and simile, 12
literacy story, 1
writing that mattered, 4
reframing of issues, 175, 180–81

refuting readers' objections, in counterarguments, 415
remembered-event essays, overview
collaborative activity: practicing remembering an event, 17
introduction, 16
reading and writing, 16–17
real-world applications, 15
remembered-event essays, reading
analyzing visuals, 34–35
basic features: autobiographical significance, 18, 28–29, 34; vivid description of people and places, 18, 28, 33; well-told stories, 18, 27, 32–33
considering social dimensions: autobiography and self-discovery, 54–55
considering topics for your own essay, 35
critical reading guide, 49–50
purpose and audience, 18–19
readings: "An American Childhood" (Dillard), 23–27; "Calling Home" (Brandt), 19–23; "When the Walls Came Tumbling Down" (Ellis), 29–31
remembered-event essays, writing
editing and proofreading: fused sentences, 53; missing commas after introductory elements, 52; past perfect, 53
invention and research: choosing an event to write about, 38–40; considering your thesis, 44; constructing a well-told story, 40–41; creating a dominant impression, 41; defining purpose and audience, 44; exploring memorabilia, 42–43; reflecting on autobiographical significance, 43–44; testing your choice, 42

overview, 36
planning and drafting: drafting, 46–48; outlining drafts, 45–46; refining purpose and setting goals, 45; working with sources: quoting, paraphrasing, and summarizing, 48–49
reflecting on writing, 54
revising, 50–52
starting points, 37–38
remembered feelings and thoughts, 34, 43
repetition, 133, 134, 360
research. See field research; library and Internet research
resolution, in pyramid structure, 32
résumés, 436–38
revealing or pivotal moments, 40
rhetorical questions, 235, 249–51
rhetorical situation, 276–77
rising action, in pyramid structure, 32
roles for writer
in profiles: as spectator or participant observer, 80–81
Romano, Christine, "'Children Need to Play, Not Compete,' by Jessica Statsky: An Evaluation," 280–85
RSS (Really Simple Syndication), 481

scenarios, 211
scholarly journals vs. popular magazines, 473–74
scratch outlines
as critical reading strategy, 339
as invention and inquiry strategy, 318–20
screen shots, 430
search engines
federated, 471
Internet, 479–80
search strategies
general, 466–69
Internet, 479–81
library catalogs, 469–70
periodical databases, 470–75

self-discovery, 54–55
semicolons, 53
sentence outlines
as invention and inquiry strategy, 320–21
sentences
opening: argument essays, 196; concept explanation essays, 146; evaluative essays, 302; proposal essays, 249
strategies for: absolute phrases, 96; appositives, 147; balancing criticism and praise, 303; comparing and contrasting subjects, 302–3; concession followed by refutation, 196–98; rhetorical questions, 249–51; time transitions and verb tenses, 47–48; topic sentences, 356–59
structure of: combining, 311; fused, 53; lack of agent in, 257–58; repetition, 360
shaping a story, 40
showing
in profile essays, 60
in remembered-event essays, 28
sideways, 365
signal phrases, 487
similarly, 363
similes
reading strategies and, 344
reflection exercise, 12
simultaneously, 47, 364
since, 363, 364
sketching a story, 40
slanting, 416
slippery slope fallacy, 416
so, 53, 363
sob stories, 416
social dimensions, considering
autobiography and self-discovery, 54–55
concept explanations and the nature of knowledge, 156
entertainment vs. showing whole picture, 105

evaluators' hidden assumptions, 312–13
frustrations of effecting real change, 259
suppressing dissent, 205–6
solutions, well-argued, 211, 225–26, 233–34, 253
sources, documenting
APA style: in-text citations, 509–11; reference list, 511–16
MLA style: in-text citations, 497–500; works cited list, 500–509
overview, 495–96
sources, integrating
deciding whether to quote, paraphrase, or summarize, 488
descriptive verbs, 148–49
paraphrasing, 493–95
quoting: avoiding grammatical tangles, 492–93; integrating quotations, 97–98, 490–91; introducing quotations, 491; punctuation around quotations, 488–89; punctuation within quotations, 492; quoting opposing positions, 198–99
in specific essay types: concept explanation essays, 111, 123, 134–35, 150, 153; remembered-event essays, 48–49
summarizing, 495
See also sources, documenting; sources, working with
sources, working with
acknowledging sources, 486–87
annotated research paper, 517–25
establishing a problem's existence and seriousness, 251–53
plagiarism: note-taking process and, 465; overview, 487; quoting appropriately to avoid, 198–99
sample research papers, 516–17
See also sources, documenting; sources, integrating

spatial transitions, 365
speaker tags, 97–98, 103
specialized encyclopedias, 461–62
specifically, 235, 363
specific narrative actions, 27
spectator, writer's role as, 61, 102
spelling checkers, 153, 202, 256
Stafford, William, 8
statistics
    believability of, 349–50
    defining the problem in pro-
        posals with, 211
    establishing a problem's exis-
        tence and seriousness
        with, 251–53
    in position statements of argu-
        ment essays, 164, 181
    supporting arguments with,
        408–9
Statsky, Jessica, "Children Need
    to Play, Not Compete,"
    165–71. *See also*
    "'Children Need to Play,
    Not Compete,' by Jessica
    Statsky: An Evaluation"
    (Romano)
still, 235, 364
strategies, writing
    for discovering new ideas, 8–9
    for drafting and revising, 9–10
    for getting started, 8
    for organizing ideas, 9
    overview, 7
straw man arguments, 416
subheadings. *See* headings and
    subheadings
subject directories, Internet,
    480
subject headings, 466
subjects, well-presented, 264,
    276–77, 286, 306
subordinate clauses, 53
subsequently, 364
success in college and work, writ-
    ing's influence on, 3–4
summarizing
    as critical reading strategy,
        341–42
    integrating sources by, 495
    in profile essays, 60
    in remembered-event essays,
        48–49

supporting evaluative argu-
    ments by, 304–5
summary annotations, 530
support for arguments. *See* rea-
    sons and support for
    arguments
Suri, Manil, 10
symbolism, 344
synonyms, 133, 134, 360
synthesizing
    of arguments: from analysis to
        synthesis, 380; sample
        synthesis: Mae, "The
        Centrality of the Ticking
        Time-Bomb Scenario in
        Arguments Justifying
        Torture," 380–86
    as critical reading strategy,
        342–43

tables, design of, 424–25
tagmemics, 327–28
telling, 28
temporal transitions. *See* time
    transitions
testimony, 211
textual evidence, 412–13
that, 256–57
that is, 235, 363
then, 363, 364
there, 365
therefore, 363
thesis statements
    as cueing strategy, 353–54
    by essay type: argument
        essays, 193; concept expla-
        nation essays, 122, 133,
        144; evaluative essays,
        298; profile essays, 92–93;
        proposal essays, 245–46;
        remembered-event
        essays, 44
    guidelines for asserting a
        thesis: appropriate quali-
        fication, 406–7; arguable
        assertions, 405; clear and
        precise writing, 405–6;
        overview, 404–5
thinking, writing's influence on,
    1–2
thinking critically. *See* critical
    thinking

this, 256–57
thus, 363
time transitions
    as cueing strategy, 364
    establishing action sequences
        with, 47–48
title searches, 466
to be sure, 235, 364
topical organizational plan, 60, 101
topic outlines, 320–21
topic sentences, 133, 356–59
to put it differently, 363
to sum up, 363
to the right/left, 365
Toufexis, Anastasia, "Love:
    The Right Chemistry,"
    117–21
tours, library, 457–58
toward, 365
transitional words and phrases
    as cueing strategy, 133, 363–64
    revising, 101
    topic sentences and, 357–58
    types of: logical relationships,
        363–64; spatial relation-
        ships, 365; temporal rela-
        tionships, 364
truncation, 469
trustworthiness of sources
    believability of statements
        and, 349
    believability of statistics
        and, 350
typography, 419–20

up, 365

values, identifying, 370
Van Allen, James, 2
verbal phrases, combining sen-
    tences with, 311
verbs, descriptive, 148–49
verb tenses
    establishing action sequences
        with, 47–48
    past perfect, 53
    time transitions and verb
        tenses, 47–48
very likely, 406
visuals
    in concept explanation essays,
        108, 143

criteria, 389–91
defined, 387
in document design: computer considerations, 431–32; integrating into text, 431; numbering, labeling, and citing, 430; types of, 424–30
examples: ad for feedthepig.org, 208, 209; "Dr. William Ellis," 30; drunk driving PSA, 160, 161; flowcharts, 124; "Mapping Memory" (*National Geographic* online), 108; "Migrant Mother" (Lange), 58; "Moral Dilemmas," 127, 129, 131, 135; Parks, *Etta Watson* and *Emerging Man,* 391–400; photograph of a pig, 73–74; still from *Juno,* 273, 279; World Wildlife Fund PSA, 388–89
overview, 387–89

visual texts, defined, 387
vivid descriptions, 18

Web pages, design of, 440–42
well-told stories
    pyramid structure, 32–33
    in remembered-event essays, 18
    specific narrative actions and prepositional phrases, 27
"What Makes Us Moral" (Kluger), 124–32
"What's the Matter with Kids Today?" (Goldwasser), 177–80
when, 47–48, 364
"When the Walls Came Tumbling Down" (Ellis), 29–31
while, 364
white space, 423–24
wikis, 482
Williams, Sherley Anne, 3
"Win-Win Flexibility" (Kornbluh), 219–24
word repetition, 360

"Working at McDonald's" (Etzioni), 171–74
working bibliographies, 462–64
writing
    importance of: for connection with others, 3; for learning, 2; for personal development, 2–3; for success in college and work, 3–4; for thinking, 1–2
    learning: overview, 4–5; by reading, 5–7; writing strategies, 7–10
writing strategies for invention and inquiry
    cubing, 322–23
    dialoguing, 323
    dramatizing, 323–25
    keeping a journal, 325–26
    looping, 326
    questioning, 327–28
    quick drafting, 328
writing that mattered exercise, 4

yet, 53, 364
Yourcenar, Marguerite, 12

Sitting around waiting for inspiration is for amateurs.
TOM ROBBINS

Write in the kitchen, lock yourself up in the bathroom.
Write on the bus or the welfare line, on the job or during meals.
GLORIA ANZALDÚA

**Don't tear up the page and start over again when you write a
bad line—try to write your way out of it. Make mistakes and plunge
on. . . . Writing is a means of discovery, always.**
GARRISON KEILLOR

I have rewritten—often several times—every word
I have ever published. My pencils outlast their erasers.
VLADIMIR NABOKOV

Inspiration usually comes during work, rather than before it.
MADELINE L'ENGLE

I've always thought best when I wrote.
TONI MORRISON

Writing is a political instrument.
JAMES BALDWIN

I write to find out what I'm thinking. I write to find out who I am.
I write to understand things.
JULIA ALVAREZ

Writing is the act of saying *I*, of imposing yourself upon other
people, of saying *listen to me, see it my way, change your mind*.
JOAN DIDION

The beautiful part of writing is that you don't have
to get it right the first time—unlike, say, brain surgery.
ROBERT CORMIER

Writing and rewriting are a constant search for what one is saying.
JOHN UPDIKE